T0178250

LEADERSHIP, MANAGEMENT AND COMMAND:
RETHINKING D-DAY

Also by Keith Grint and published by Palgrave Macmillan

Leadership (0–333–96387–3)

LEADERSHIP, MANAGEMENT and COMMAND

RETHINKING D-DAY

KEITH GRINT

palgrave
macmillan

Softcover reprint of the hardcover 1st edition 2008 978-0-230-54317-1

First published 2008 by
PALGRAVE MACMILLAN
Houndmills, Basingstoke, Hampshire RG21 6XS and
175 Fifth Avenue, New York, N.Y. 10010
Companies and representatives throughout the world

PALGRAVE MACMILLAN is the global academic imprint of the Palgrave
Macmillan division of St. Martin's Press, LLC and of Palgrave Macmillan Ltd.
Macmillan® is a registered trademark in the United States, United Kingdom
and other countries. Palgrave is a registered trademark in the European
Union and other countries.

ISBN 978-1-349-36064-2   ISBN 978-0-230-59050-2 (eBook)
DOI 10.1057/9780230590502

10	9	8	7	6	5	4	3	2	1
17	16	15	14	13	12	11	10	09	08

Transferred to Digital Printing 2011

Contents

List of Figures, Maps and Photos

Figures

Maps

Photos

Acknowledgements

This book has been in the making for over eight years. It began life as the final chapter to one of my previous books, *The Arts of Leadership*, but, like Topsy, it just grew. It has sat on various floors and computers half finished for about five of these years and only recently have I managed to find the time and motivation to finish it – thanks to Stephen Rutt for providing the last piece of the jigsaw. Many people have helped me in this marathon journey. Institutionally I would like to thank the ESRC, Templeton College and the Saïd Business School at Oxford University, Lancaster University, and Cranfield University at the Defence Academy of the UK. Individually I would like to thank Mike Harper for many conversations about D-Day and his old unit; Hal Nelson for showing me round Normandy the first time; whoever the German train guard was that arrested me in 1971 in Germany for not having the appropriate papers and whose stories of his capture on D-Day by the British passed the small hours of the night away waiting for the next train; Sapper Anderson for his marvellous conversations, memories and letters about D-Day+2 when he arrived there; Connie Woolgar for alerting me to the role of the German-speaking British Commandos on D-Day; David Benest and Peter Gray at the Defence Academy for trying to put me straight on the military road to D-Day; Tara Moran for helping select the cover and keeping me organized; the many recipients of my various witterings over the years; Katy for providing the music via Past Perfect; Richie for advice on small arms; and finally Sandra, Beki, Simon and Kris for putting up with yet another holiday built around a book – sorry guys and gals!

I would like to thank HMSO for permission to reproduce the maps.

Part One

Leadership, Management and Command at D-Day

1 Problems, Understanding and Decision-Making

Introduction: contingency and determinism

> In spite of the enemy's intentions to defeat us on the beaches, we found no surprises awaiting us in Normandy. Our measures designed to overcome the defences proved successful. Although not all our D-Day objectives had been achieved – in particular, the situation at Omaha beach was far from secure – and in all the beach-head areas there were pockets of enemy resistance, and a very considerable amount of mopping up remained to be done, we had gained a foothold on the Continent of Europe.[1]

Thus did Montgomery describe D-Day. But success in Normandy was by no means foreordained. Brooke's war diary for 5 June 1944 reads:

> I am very uneasy about the whole operation. At best it will fall so very very far short of the expectation of the bulk of the people, namely all those who know nothing of its difficulties. At worst it may well be the most ghastly disaster of the whole war. I wish to God it was safely over.[2]

Brooke later accepted that a defeat would have been likely if strong counter-attacks had been launched at mid-day on the Allied beach-heads – as Rommel had intended – but they were not. Partly this was because the Allied control over the air and over the immediate hinterland inhibited this – but, since the weather was so poor, for much of the time Allied flying sorties were very restricted. It was also the case that the Germans redeployed their own reinforcement *away* from Omaha just at the time when the situation was critical for the Americans: the Germans had assumed the situation was no longer critical for them because the invaders appeared to be defeated. There is an argument for assuming that the overwhelming number of soldiers and machines on the Allied side would – at some point – have necessarily overwhelmed the defenders but this deterministic approach ignores the fact that the defenders moved half their ammunition back to 'places of safety' just before the invasion and could not get access to it once the onslaught had begun.

In effect, I want to suggest that the temptation to explain the success as an inevitable consequence of superior Allied strategy and matériel should be resisted in the same way that we should avoid explaining German defeat simply through their inferior strategy and matériel. We often attribute success and failure of organizations, armies and countries to the role of individual leaders, often in terms of their brilliant or flawed strategy, but the precise connection between strategy and result is often very unclear. That is to say that whether a strategy will be successful or not is seldom predictable and usually uncertain. Thus if the strategy works, we will assume it's the consequence of individual genius; if it fails, it's because of stupidity. Yet there are many reasons for organizational success and failure and to retrospectively attribute success or failure to the role of individual leaders is a step too far: from correlation to causation – we know the result and retrospectively we assume (without robust evidence) that certain actions determined it. We know, for instance, that the invasion succeeded, but it was not just because the Allies fooled the Germans into thinking Normandy was a ruse and it was not just because Hitler refused to release the Panzer reserves until it was too late to push the Allies back into the sea. Both of these are true but they don't account for success and failure. For this we would need to be able to evaluate the effect of every decision, action and consequence before and during the event, but this is never possible – we simply do not have the resources to do this. What we can do is avoid the deterministic approaches that imply inevitable consequences flow from single decisions or actions and try to understand not just the enormous complexity of the situation, but the enormous contingency therein. In other words, we need to bring the subjunctive mood back into the narrative that retains the doubt or uncertainty of an action and is often used in conjunction with 'if': if Hitler had ordered, rather than because Hitler ordered … . The implication of this is not only that we can never be certain that another outcome was impossible but that the explanation for the outcome must remain tentative. For example, despite Hitler's refusal to release the Panzer divisions until late in the afternoon of D-Day it would have been possible for subordinates to order their movements under the conditions appertaining at the time. That this did not happen, therefore, is not just a consequence of Hitler's erroneous and erratic strategic leadership but of many other people's theoretically contingent compliance. In short, it need not have happened thus. Hence, when we are trying to understand events on the day we should always bear these contingencies and uncertainties in mind: consequences are seldom determined by single decisions of formal leaders – even if it produces a much tidier version of history and places all the responsibility onto specific individuals.

Yet a contingent approach is not the equivalent of micro-determinism – that is where a small chance factor determines what happens next to the point where a war is lost or won because of some equivalent of chaos or complexity theory where, in Gleick's famous account, a butterfly over Peking causes a storm over New York three weeks later.[3] Intriguingly the seepage of some complexity approaches sometimes seems to have generated an apparently novel concentration on chance factors – that subsequently determine what happens next, thus managing to smuggle determinism back in through the back door of naïve complexity. For example, Durschmied suggests that the military halt by the German army at Dunkirk operated as a 'Hinge Factor', that would have altered – nay determined – the course of the war.[4] Tsouras has a few more variables to change but the consequence is equally determined by these small changes: Germany defeats the Allies in 1944.[5] Even Ambrose suggests that if the weather on 6 June 1944 had not improved enough for the Allied landings to have occurred then all kinds of *inevitable* effects would have occurred: 'There would have been no air cover and no paratroop support as the air-drops would have been scattered to hell and gone ... . No supporting bombardment from the two- and four-engined bombers ... . Eisenhower would have had no choice but to order the follow-up landings cancelled ... . The Allied fleet would have pulled back to England in disarray ... Eisenhower would have certainly lost his job ... . A climax would have come in the late summer of 1945, with atomic bombs exploding over German cities'.[6]

Thus to summarise, the contingent or subjunctivist approach I am suggesting here, like complexity theory, implies that managing dynamic conditions requires us to abandon mechanical strategic planning and work flexibly with the chaos that emerges. However, some versions of this suggest that we can now act like Greek gods looking down from Mount Olympus on the poor mortals whose fates are altered by the smallest change in initial conditions that, in turn, set off chains of consequences that somehow escape that very same dynamic complexity. Rather than Gleick's butterfly, we now have Ambrose's storm causing a mushroom cloud over Berlin a year later.

What is intriguing about this scenario is the precision with which the future rolls out: the weather changes and everything else changes. But the 'everything else' is not affected by any other altered variables because these variables are held in place by the determinism of the observer. Thus the 'chaos' of small things – any small change in the initial conditions may have a significant impact – degenerates into the determinism of one thing. But this can only occur because once one variable has been altered all the rest must remain in place.

For example, to claim that a worsening in the weather would have left the Allies exposed to air attack assumes both that the *Luftwaffe* could fly in conditions that the Allied air forces could not, and that the *Luftwaffe* existed in sufficient numbers close enough to the beaches to inflict significant damage on the Allies: but neither of these claims holds true. Indeed, German fighter aircraft losses were running at over 2,000 a month just prior to D-Day – twice the number of Allied losses in aircraft at this time and twice the rate at which new German fighter pilots could be trained.[7] In effect, in the first five months of 1944 the pilot turnover in the *Luftwaffe* was 99 per cent.[8] Between January 1944 and D-Day the *Luftwaffe* lost 6,259 planes in combat and roughly half that number in non-combat accidents.[9] From an average force of 2,283, the deaths in that six months amounted to 2,262. In the first two days of the invasion 200 fighters were moved from Germany to France, but the pilots had been trained for air defence not ground attack so within two weeks the Germans had lost another 594 aircraft.[10] On D-Day itself the *Luftwaffe* – which had promised to have 1,000 fighters in the air for the invasion – had only 319 operational aircraft within flying distance of Normandy: 88 bombers, 172 fighters and 59 reconnaissance aircraft to attack the invasion beaches.[11]

Similarly, to claim that the air bombardment would have been cancelled implies that it made much difference – but we know this not to be the case, and its failure was one critical factor in the problems on Omaha. For instance, at 0000 hours 6 June, 1,333 heavy bombers began attacking the coastal defences, and as the light progressed so the shift to the medium and light bombers of the USAAF occurred. The final bombing plan was agreed so late that only ten major batteries were targeted by the heavy bombers, each receiving 500 tons of bombs on the evening of 5 June.[12] Even this agreement was wrung from General Spaatz, commander of the US Strategic Air Forces in Europe, with deep foreboding because heavy bombers simply did not have the capability of hitting such small targets from the great heights they operated from. Spaatz, ever-concerned to minimize 'friendly fire' casualties, insisted that the first waves of landing craft delay their approach to give the bombers a chance to do their work accurately but the ground commanders insisted on the original timings. Thus the American bombers were instructed to delay their drops until certain that no Allied troops would be hit – and as a consequence almost no troops of either side were hit where that delay was compounded by the low cloud cover over Omaha Beach.[13]

All told, over 5,000 Allied bombers and nearly 5,500 Allied fighters were in the air on D-Day; none was shot down by the *Luftwaffe* though 113 were shot down by anti-aircraft fire. If the light was good the bombing was due to stop five minutes before the first landing; if the light was bad it was extended to ten minutes. Neither the sea nor the air bombardment was as thoroughly planned as they should have been. First because the air forces were reluctant to commit themselves until very late in the planning timetable and second because the responsibility for deciding *what* was necessary lay with the army but the responsibility for *how* that was executed remained with the navy and the airforce. The result was a generally weak and poorly executed plan. For instance, at Omaha Beach, each B-17 Flying Fortress was to drop its sixteen 500lb bombs from 20,000 feet, a height that made accuracy through cloud cover virtually impossible. They were followed by B-24 Liberators due to fly at 500 feet and drop 1,285 tons of bombs to destroy and bewilder the defenders while leaving plenty of craters and debris to protect the attacking troops. In the event the B-26 Marauders that attacked Utah proved much more effective than the B-24 attacks upon Omaha, Gold, Juno and Sword and in general the air attacks were disappointing.[14] Particularly ineffective were the attacks upon 13 critical defensive positions on Omaha for the poor visibility dissuaded the pilots from dropping their bombs until they were well past their own troops – in fact 3 miles inland.

Likewise, Ambrose's suggestion that the paratroop drops would have been massively dispersed is precisely what happened anyway. Some soldiers from the US 82nd Airborne Division were dropped in the wrong zone completely, landing amongst troops from the 101st Airborne Division and vice versa. Indeed it has been claimed that 75 per cent of the 13,000 American paratroopers landed so far from their targets that they played no effective part in any of the planned attacks.[15] Ridgeway's scattered troops from the 82nd were unable to mount any major attack upon German positions but ironically the very same distribution led the Germans to assume a much heavier airborne attack than had actually occurred, not just because the 82nd seemed to be everywhere but because they cut every telephone line they found, making it very difficult for the Germans to verify the position and density of the paratroopers.

The experience of the other American Airborne Division, the 101st, was very similar. The 101st was due to land in four concentrated groups but instead they were spread over 300 square miles of Normandy with 35 'sticks' (plane-load) outside their designated drop zones, and some people 20 miles from their drop zone.[16] This was partly because only 38 of the 120 pathfinders were themselves put down on target.[17] Once again the Germans were unable to take advantage of the situation because the scattered troops, the use of dummy paratroopers, and the effective cutting of many telephone lines by the French Resistance, left them unable to assess the picture with any accuracy. The confusion was only to be expected for even by the end of D-Day only 1,100 of the 6,600 soldiers of the 101st had assembled.

In short, whatever the significance of the weather, it did not determine future events any more than it ensured the defeat of the Germans and the victory of the Allies: there is, therefore, no invariant line between Gleick's butterfly and Ambrose's mushroom cloud.

Casualties, cogs and contingencies

To say that the weather did not determine subsequent events is not to suggest that it was irrelevant; indeed, it may well have played some (inde-terminate) role in reducing Allied casualties by encouraging the Germans to relax their guard. But despite the casualties remaining radically lower than many experts feared they were still significant. The Allied planners for D-Day calculated that on D-Day itself the initial assault divisions would suffer 15 per cent casualties, with the actual first wave Regimental Combat Teams (RCTs) suffering 25 per cent. Some 70 per cent of these would, they assumed, be wounded, 30 per cent would be dead, missing or Prisoners of War (POWs). The follow-up divisions would, they assumed, suffer 8 per cent casualties overall, with the combat regiments taking 15 per cent (Hall, 1994: 138). Casualty figures are notoriously unreliable: there are no official German figures for D-Day itself, and of the three main Allied forces only Canada collected data from individual soldiers. Overall Allied casualties seem to be somewhere between 8,443 (4.3 per cent) and 10,865 (5.5 per cent) depending on whose figures are accepted. Roughly one-third of these were deaths.[18] Whatever the number it was still far smaller than the 29,500 the planners had assumed. Churchill had feared 70,000, and the generally expected number had been half this at around 35,000. In fact the Supreme Headquarters Allied Expeditionary Force (SHAEF) secret prediction had been the most accu-rate at 10,000 dead.[19] Ambrose estimates that perhaps 10 per cent is a more accurate account.[20]

One particular reason for the casualties and tardiness of progress on the ground was that the Allied superiority in matériel and numbers was rendered of marginal significance against an enemy that was well dug-in, well armed and prepared to stay put. Ironically, then, it was in some respects a rerun of the First World War – most of the advantages lay with the defender and it might seem that only the ability to win a bloody battle of attrition ensured a victory for the invaders – though events on Omaha suggested otherwise. Furthermore, for all the information made available for the assault on the beaches – and this aspect was markedly successful in general – it was in sharp contrast to the very problematic information available about the defences and deployment of defenders behind the beaches. And even when the Allies correctly identified their enemies they almost always underestimated the skill and tenacity with which these enemies held their ground or counter-attacked when their ground was lost. For all that Montgomery was the great planner, the plan really only covered the beaches; after that there was neither a coherent plan nor were local commanders empowered to use their initiative because the great planner, allegedly, already had an infallible plan; if only the Germans had allowed it to unfold.

For Field Marshal Slim the issue was closely related to the metaphorical clock:

> A Clock is like an army ... . There's a main spring, that's the Army Commander, who makes it all go; then there are other springs, driving the wheels round, those are his generals. The wheels are officers and men. Some are big wheels, very important; they are the chief staff officers and the colonel sahibs. Other wheels are little ones that do not look at all important. They are like you. Yet stop one of these little wheels and see what happens to the rest of the clock![21]

The value of small cogs is also represented in Carell, quoting the official Canadian account of the war:

> The allied operations were better co-ordinated at the supreme command level than were the German; but one cannot say that of events on the battle field. There the German soldiers and their troop commanders were the better practitioners. The German front-line soldier was brave, determined and skilful. At times he was fanatical, occasionally brutal, but he was always and everywhere a formidable fighter, even under such difficult conditions as in Normandy. Seen from the point of view of the men and the fighting front, one cannot say that we won the Battle of Normandy through tactical superiority.[22]

The implication of the latter quote suggests that the Allied superiority lay in strategic not tactical terms; success came through the superior planning of the senior leadership and the superior production of senior management, but even if this was true it was almost negated by the better fighting abilities of the defenders. Although the strategy ultimately worked it was not successful because of some inherent logic within the plan itself but because those on the ground made it work after they discovered – and paid for – the strategic errors that the Allied senior leadership made.

The poverty of Allied tanks in particular is a case in point. Out of water the Shermans were no match for German tanks and in water the DDs could only survive in swells of less than three foot without being flooded:

these were errors of management that need not have occurred. That they did, and that unprotected infantry had to assault heavily defended beaches with little more than rifles, then begs the question of how success was snatched from the jaws of defeat, for defeat was surely likely. On D-Day it was often the tactical actions of Allied junior officers, NCOs and ordinary soldiers that snatched victory from the jaws of defeat where their leaders' strategic plan was failing.

In contrast, the strategic failures of the German leadership were not rescued by the more junior leaders – even though many such officers knew what needed to be done and could have acted differently. In short, the poor bloody infantry of the Allied side made up for the errors and limits of their senior commanders; the poor bloody infantry on the German side were generally able but usually unwilling to do the same for their leaders.

There are already many narrative accounts of D-Day and this book is not designed to replicate these. Carlo D'Este's[23] account is one of the best and he suggests, in contrast to Neillands,[24] that the over-cautious nature of the Allied commanders (Montgomery and Bradley but not Patton) unnecessarily extended the fighting, while Max Hastings' approach is to highlight the way the superior combat skills of the German army were gradually worn away by the Allies' superior matériel.[25] My intention here is to offer an alternative understanding of the battle, or rather elements of it which I will use to illustrate the issues.[26] My argument is that the success and failures of D-Day, on both sides, cannot be explained by comparing the competing strategies of each side because this implies a level of determinism that is unsustainable either theoretically or empirically. Instead I suggest that we might provide a more robust but still tentative account of the battle through the overarching nature of the relationship between leaders and followers. In short, the way a very large number of individuals on both sides took and enacted decisions on the day amidst the fog of war. This bottom-up approach is still not a deterministic approach because so many of the decisions and actions could have been otherwise and so many that must have occurred were not recorded. Thus we can only ever reconstruct a partial account and explanation of what happened and why it happened.

To help make sense of these decisions and actions I will suggest that our understanding of the invasion can be facilitated by a typology of problems: Wicked Problems, Tame Problems and Critical Problems. In order, I take these as cases where Leadership, Management and Command occur and I suggest that the way the combatants approached these problems, and the way they had learned to address them, holds the key to improving our understanding of how the invasion was won and lost. Let us briefly divert into the theory to set the background to the book.

Tame, Wicked and Critical Problems[27]

Much of the writing in the field of leadership research is grounded in a typology that distinguishes between Leadership and Management as different forms of authority – that is legitimate power in Weber's conception – with leadership tending to embody longer time periods, a more strategic perspective, and a requirement to resolve novel problems.[28] Another way to put this is that the division is rooted partly in the context: management is the equivalent of *déjà vu* (seen this before), whereas leadership is the equivalent of *vu jàdé* (never seen this before).[29] If this is valid then the manager is simply required to engage the requisite process to resolve the problem like the last time it emerged. In contrast, the leader is required to reduce the anxiety of his or her followers who face the unknown by facilitating the construction of an innovative response to the novel problem, rather than rolling out a known process to a previously experienced problem.

Management and Leadership, as two forms of authority rooted in the distinction between certainty and uncertainty, can also be related to Rittell and Webber's typology of *Tame* and *Wicked* Problems.[30] A *Tame Problem* may be complicated but is resolvable through unilinear acts because there is a point where the problem is resolved and it is likely to have occurred before. In other words, there is only a limited degree of uncertainty and thus it is associated with Management. The manager's role, therefore, is to provide the appropriate *processes* to solve the problem. Examples would include: timetabling the railways, building a nuclear plant, training the army, planned heart surgery, a wage negotiation, enacting a tried and trusted policy for eliminating global terrorism, or in our case planning the naval bombardment of coastal fortifications.

A *Wicked Problem* is more complex, rather than just complicated, it is often intractable, there is no unilinear solution, moreover, there is no 'stopping' point, it is novel, any apparent 'solution' often generates other 'problems', and there is no 'right' or 'wrong' answer, but there are better or worse alternatives. In other words, there is a huge degree of uncertainty involved and thus it is associated with *Leadership*. The leader's role with a Wicked Problem is to ask the right *questions* rather than provide the right *answers* because the answers may not be self-evident and will require a collaborative process to make any kind of progress. Examples would include: developing a transport strategy, or an energy strategy, or a defence strategy, or a national health system or an industrial relations strategy; and, in our case, developing a strategy for a successful invasion of France. Wicked Problems are not necessarily rooted in longer time frames than Tame Problems because oftentimes an issue that appears to be Tame can be turned into a Wicked Problem by delaying the decision. For example, President Kennedy's actions during the Cuban Missile Crisis were often based on asking *questions* of his civilian assistants that required some time for reflection – despite the pressure from his military advisers to provide instant *answers*. Had Kennedy responded to the American Hawks we would have seen a third set of problems that fall outside the Leadership/Management dichotomy. This third set of problems I will refer to as *Critical*.

A *Critical Problem*, e.g. a 'crisis', is presented as self-evident in nature, as encapsulating very little time for decision-making and action, and it is often associated with authoritarianism – *Command*.[31] Here there is virtually no uncertainty about what needs to be done – at least in the behaviour of the Commander, whose role is to take the required decisive action – that is to provide the *answer* to the problem, not to engage processes (management) or ask questions (leadership). Of course, it may be that the Commander remains privately uncertain about whether the action is appropriate or the presentation of the situation as a crisis is persuasive, but that uncertainty will probably not be apparent to the followers of the Commander. Examples would include the immediate response to: a major train crash, a leak of radioactivity from a nuclear plant, a military attack, a heart attack, an industrial strike, the loss of employment or a loved one, or a terrorist attack such as 9/11 or the 7 July bombings in London.

That such 'situations' are constituted by the participants rather than simply being self-evident is best illustrated by considering the way a situation of ill-defined threat only becomes a crisis when that threat is defined as such. For example, financial losses – even rapid and radical losses – do not constitute a 'crisis' until the shareholders decide to sell in large numbers, and even then the notion of a crisis does not emerge objectively from the activity of selling but at the point at which a 'crisis' is pronounced by someone significant and becomes accepted as such by significant others. In another intriguing example the British government under James Callaghan was apparently in free-fall in 1979 after Callaghan returned from an economic conference in the West Indies as strikes in the British public services mounted. Asked how he was going to solve 'the mounting chaos' by journalists at the airport Callaghan responded, 'I don't think other people in the world would share the view [that] there is mounting chaos'. But the headlines in the *Sun* newspaper the following day suggested he had said 'Crisis – What Crisis?'. In this case the formal political leader was unable to counter 'the critical situation', as constituted by the news media, and Labour lost the subsequent general election.[32] Similarly, it would be difficult to state objectively at what point the Battle of Britain became a crisis and when it ceased to be one because that definition rested upon the persuasive rhetoric of various parties involved. As Overy suggests,

> Many of those 'decisive strategic results' became clear only with the end of the war and the process of transforming the Battle into myth. The contemporary evidence suggests that neither side at the time invested the air conflict with the weight of historical significance that it has borne in the sixty years since it was fought.[33]

The links between Command and the military are clear, and may well explain why discussion of non-military leadership has tended to avoid the issue of command or explain it as authoritarian leadership that may be appropriate for the military but not in the civilian world.[34] These three forms of authority – that is legitimate power – Command, Management and Leadership are, in turn, another way of suggesting that the role of those responsible for decision-making is to find the appropriate Answer, Process and Question to address the problem respectively.

This is not meant as a discrete typology but a heuristic device to enable us to understand why those charged with decision-making sometimes appear to act in ways that others find incomprehensible. Thus I am not suggesting that the correct decision-making process lies in the correct analysis of the situation – that, again, would be to generate a deterministic approach – but I am suggesting that decision-makers tend to legitimize their actions on the basis of a persuasive account of the situation. In short, the social construction of the problem legitimizes the deployment of a particular form of authority. Moreover, it is often the case that the same individual or group with authority will switch between the Command, Management and Leadership roles as they perceive – and constitute – the problem as Critical, Tame or Wicked, or even as a single problem that itself shifts across these boundaries. Indeed, this movement – often perceived as 'inconsistency' by the decision-maker's opponents – is crucial to success as the situation, or at least our perception of it, changes.

Nor am I suggesting that different forms of problem construction restrict those in authority to their 'appropriate' form of power. In other words, Commanders, for example, having defined the problem as Critical, do not only have access to coercion but coercion is legitimated by the constituting of the problem as Critical in a way that Managers would find more difficult and Leaders would find almost impossible. In turn, Commanders who follow up on their constitution of the problem as Critical by asking followers questions and seeking collaborative progress (attributes of Leadership) are less likely to be perceived as successful Commanders than those who provide apparent solutions and demand obedience.

That persuasive account of the problem partly rests in the decision-maker's access to – and preference for – particular forms of power, and herein lies the irony of 'leadership': it remains the most difficult of approaches and one that many decision-makers will try to avoid at all costs because it implies (1) that the leader does not have the answer (2) that the leader's role is to make the followers face up to their responsibilities (often an unpopular task)[35] (3) that the 'answer' to the problem is going to take a long time to construct and that it will only ever be 'more appropriate' rather than 'the best', and (4) that it will require constant effort to maintain. It is far easier, then, to opt either for a Management solution – engaging a tried and trusted process – or a Command solution – enforcing the answer upon followers – some of whom may prefer to be shown 'the answer' anyway.

The notion of 'enforcement' suggests that we need to consider how different approaches to, and forms of, power fit with this typology of authority, and amongst the most useful for our purposes are Etzioni's[36] typology of compliance, and Nye's distinction between Hard and Soft Power. Nye has suggested that we should distinguish between power as 'soft' and 'hard'. 'Soft', in this context, does not imply weak or fragile but rather the degree of influence derived from legitimacy and the positive attraction of values.[37] 'Hard' implies traditional concepts of power such as coercion, physical strength, or domination achieved through asymmetric resources rather than ideas. Thus the military tend to operate through 'hard' power while political authorities tend to operate through ideological attraction – 'soft power'. Of course, these are not discrete categories – the military has to 'win hearts and minds' and this can only be through 'soft power' while politicians may need to authorize coercion – hard power. Indeed, as Nye recognizes, 'The Cold War was won with a strategy of containment that used soft power along with hard power'.[38]

If we return to some of the early modern theorists on power, like Dahl, Schattschneider, and Bachrach and Baratz, all summarized in Lukes'[39] 'Three Dimensions of Power', then we can see how the very denial of Soft Power is – in itself and ironically – an example of Soft Power – where certain aspects of the debate are deemed irrelevant and thus subordinated by those in power. In other words, and to adopt Nye's terminology again, to deny that any other option exists (e.g. soft power) is itself an ideological claim – e.g. soft power, and not simply a claim to the truth. While Soft Power seems appropriate to Leadership with its requirement for persuasion, debate and ideological attraction, Hard Power clearly fits better with Command, but Management sits awkwardly between the two rooted in both or neither, because coercion is perceived as inappropriate within a free labour contract, while ideological attraction can hardly explain why all employees continue to turn up for work.

The limits of using an analysis based on Hard and Soft Power might also be transcended by considering Etzioni's alternative typology.[40] Etzioni distinguished between Coercive, Calculative and Normative Compliance. Coercive or physical power was related to total institutions, such as prisons or armies; Calculative Compliance was related to 'rational' institutions, such as companies; and Normative Compliance was related to institutions or organizations based on shared values, such as clubs and professional societies. This compliance typology fits well with the typology of problems: Critical Problems are often associated with Coercive Compliance; Tame Problems are associated with Calculative Compliance and Wicked Problems are associated with Normative Compliance.

Again, none of this is to suggest that we can divide the world up objectively into particular kinds of problems and their associated appropriate authority forms, but that the very legitimacy of the authority forms is dependent upon a successful rendition of a phenomenon as a particular kind of problem. In other words, while contingency theory suggests precisely this (rational) connection between (objective) context (problem) and (objective) leadership style (authority form), I am suggesting here that what counts as legitimate authority depends upon a persuasive rendition of the context and a persuasive display of the appropriate authority style. In other words, success is rooted in persuading followers that the problematic situation is either one of a Critical, Tame or Wicked nature and that therefore the appropriate authority form is Command, Management or Leadership in which the role of the decision-maker is to provide the answer, or organize the process or ask the question, respectively.

This typology can be plotted along the relationship between two axes as shown in Figure 1.1 one with the vertical axis representing increasing uncertainty about the solution to the problem – in the behaviour of those in authority – and the horizontal axis representing the increasing need for collaboration in resolving the problem. Again, it should be recalled that the uncertainty measure used here is not an objective element of the situation but the way the situation is constituted by those in authority. Of course, that authority and problem may be disputed by others but the model assumes that successful constitution of a problem as Wicked, Tame or Critical provides the framework for particular forms of authority. The model also represents the most likely variant of authority model, but note again, that while, for example, Commanders may use the resources more commonly adopted by Leaders, or Managers, the most prevalent is likely to be that of coercion.

What might also be evident from this figure is that the more decision-makers constitute the problem as Wicked and interpret their power as essentially Soft or Normative, the more difficult their task becomes, especially with cultures that associate leadership with the effective and efficient resolution of problems. In other words, a democratic contender seeking election on the basis of approaching the problem of global terrorism as a Wicked Problem – that requires long term and collaborative leadership processes with no easy solutions, and where everyone must participate and share the responsibility – might consider this a very problematic approach because they may be less likely to be elected. Hence the Irony of Leadership: it is often avoided where it might seem most necessary.

Where no one can be certain about what needs to be done to resolve a Wicked Problem then the more likely decision-makers are to seek a

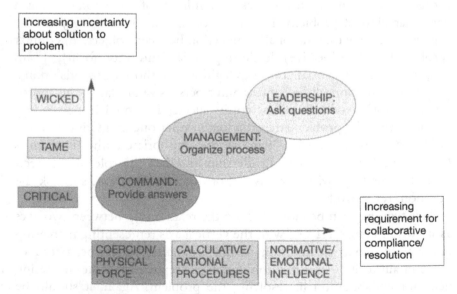

Figure 1.1 Typology of problems, power and authority

collective response. For example, a road traffic accident is usually deemed to need rapid and categorical authority – Command – by those perceived to have the requisite knowledge and authority to resolve the problems: usually the police, the fire service and the ambulance service. Those who are uncertain about what to do in a road traffic accident should – and usually do –make way for those that seem to know what they're doing, especially if they are in an appropriate uniform. We will, therefore, normally allow ourselves to be commanded by such professionals in a crisis. However, when the problem is not an emergency but, for instance, the poor phasing of an urban traffic light system, we are less likely to comply with a flashing blue light than with a traffic management expert – at least as long as the procedures work.

Even more difficult is rethinking a traffic strategy that balances the needs of the environment with those of rural dwellers, those without private transport, and those whose houses would be demolished if private roads or public railways were to be built. In effect, as the level of uncertainty increases so does our preference for involvement in the decision-making process. The implication of this is that political leaders might well seek to construct political scenarios that either increased or decreased assumptions about uncertainty in order to ensure sufficient political support. For example, it might not be in the interests of political leaders to equivocate about the threat posed by terrorism but to imply that the threat was obvious and urgent such that any necessary measure was taken – including pre-emptive strikes and internment without trial.

The shift from Command through Management to Leadership also relates to the degree of subtlety necessary for success. For instance, a sergeant with a gun standing over a squad of soldiers facing an attack does not need to be very subtle about his or her Command to stand and fight. Similarly, a police officer coming upon a train crash need not spend a lot of time, effort or rhetorical skill in persuading on-lookers to move away; she or he may simply Command them to move. However, for that same police officer to operate as a Manager in a police training academy requires a much more sophisticated array of skills and behaviours in order to train police cadets in the art of policing; and many of these techniques and processes are already well known, tried and tested. But to develop a new policing strategy for Iraq might mean more than Commanding civilians and more than simply training up Iraqi cadets through Management processes; instead it might require a whole new framework for constituting a post-Baathist society and that may necessitate sophisticated Leadership.

In what follows I take this model of problem-solving and apply it to aspects of D-Day to try to understand why some aspects seemed to fail while others were more successful. In Part 2, I consider the role of Leadership at the level of strategy on both sides of the conflict and examine the difficulties both sides had and the role of subordinates in inhibiting or allowing their superordinates to make decisions that increased or reduced the risk of failure. Of course, I am not suggesting that either strategy was 'accurate' – that is predestined to succeed or doomed to failure – rather I want to note how often success and failure are fleetingly and tantalizingly available to both sides and even in hindsight it is not possible to predict what happened.

Part 3 considers the role of Management at the Operational level, in this case the focus lies on the mobilization of the various countries involved, the management of logistics and the role of technology.

Part 4 looks at Command and Critical Problems, particularly the role of commanders in both the airborne and amphibious assaults.

Part 5 provides a retrospective view on the invasion and our understanding of it.

Part Two

Leadership and Wicked Problems

> This operation is not being planned with any alternatives. This operation
> is planned as a victory, and that's the way it's going to be.[1]

Introduction

In this part of the book I will use the theory of Wicked Problems to try
and explain the strategic decisions employed by all sides in the lead up to
D-Day. As suggested in Chapter 1, Wicked Problems are designated as
the responsibility of leadership, defined as a decision-making category
where the novelty or recalcitrance of the problem implies that the decision-maker cannot know what to do, and where he or she needs to know
what process to deploy to engage the necessary collaborative effort to
make some progress with the problem. Oftentimes Wicked Problems do
not have a solution – such as crime, for example, which will always be
with us: we may limit or encourage the extent of crime but we will never
be able to rid ourselves of crime. Other forms of Wicked Problem – such
as global warming – do offer the possibility of action that effectively
tames the worst excesses of the problem, without necessarily 'solving' it.
Still others – such as developing a strategy to invade France or resist that
invasion – will come to some form of conclusion, but it's unlikely in the
extreme that the strategy will roll out as planned. If the latter did happen,
if everything worked perfectly to plan, it is more likely that the problem
was Tame, and therefore open to a scientific solution rather than a political agreement – as Wicked Problems tend to be settled by. Of course, the
failure of a strategy may generate a Critical Problem, a crisis that requires
the role of a Commander but these will be covered in Part 3.

To remind ourselves let us reconsider the nature of Wicked Problems. They tend to comprise the following attributes:

1. They are often novel and complex
2. They often have no stopping rule – thus no definition of success
3. They may be intransigent problems that we have to learn to live with
4. They are often embedded in other problems – their 'solution' often generates another 'problem'
5. They have no right or wrong solutions, but better or worse developments
6. Each stakeholder may have a different approach and understanding
7. Understanding the problem is developed through the construction of the solution
8. Securing the 'right' answer is not as important as securing collective consent
9. They are problems for Leadership not Management
10. Collaborative not Authoritarian processes are more appropriate for Wicked Problems.

This part of the book looks at the various strategies constructed and adopted by various parties and one aspect of this that suggests the whole arena might be framed by a Wicked Problem approach is to consider why strategies do not fit naturally under the Tame Problem approach. This is best illustrated by reference to the game called 'Scissor, Paper, Stone' that embodies a fundamental dilemma for strategic leadership. In the game the winner of each round cannot be predicted because it depends on the relationship between the two 'hands': a hand that mimics a 'stone' beats a hand that mimics 'scissors' because the stone crushes the scissors, but loses to 'paper' because the paper wraps around the stone; scissors beats paper because it cuts paper. Where the same hand is used a 'draw' is declared. The simplicity of this game should not allow us to escape its critical lesson for strategic leadership: it is relative in both space and time. The same hand used consecutively may not win because the second time your opponent may have changed his or her hand.[2] If your strategy to beat your competition is rooted in, say, driving down prices – and they do the same – you may have a price war that benefits neither side. But if your opposition moves to a strategy grounded in a niche quality market then you may both prosper. If you devise a military strategy that seeks to knock out your enemy by bringing their main force to battle, your success will depend upon them not disengaging and adopting guerrilla tactics. In effect you cannot construct a 'winning' strategy in isolation because its utility is dependent on the strategy deployed by your opposition. There is, therefore, no objectively correct strategy for a particular situation – and hence it usually falls outside the Tame Problem approach – because the situation is likely to be in permanent flux as both sides adopt and adapt to what they perceive the opposition to be doing. Naturally, where leaders are impaled by their own hubris they may assume that a strategic plan is fated to succeed by dint of their superior intelligence or genius or luck – as Hitler often seemed to assume after 1941. Indeed, one of the Wicked issues that unhinged Operation Barbarossa, the German invasion of the USSR in 1941, was that the strategy had no stopping point – was the invasion to secure land? – if it was where was the stopping point? Was the invasion to secure a Soviet surrender? – if it was what would happen if Stalin refused to comply? As we shall see, then, developing a successful strategy – both against your enemy and with your allies – depends upon recognition that success is not foreordained. In short, if the problems facing both sides are known and quantifiable, and they have been faced before so that a body of experience has been accumulated, then the problems are probably Tame Problems. If that is so then they are open to a scientific, or at least a rational, analysis and they fall within the remit of Management. If the problems are critical and there is no time for debate let alone dissent, then the Commander takes precedence. But how, precisely, the Allies were ever going to return to France and how the Germans were going to defend against that invasion, was not something that either side could work out by reference to the past or to science. The two sides of the strategy problem, then, might appear Wicked in nature, that is, where problems have no clear 'rational' solution and instead they require some form of collaboration. Thus Wicked Problems exclude coercion – they are intransigent and irredeemably political in that many voices demand to be heard but no voice holds 'the answer' because there may not be a single 'correct' answer.

On the other hand, if some of those involved perceive the problem as Tame, that is, open to scientific and rational solution based on prior successful efforts, then the 'correct' solution is indeed the one that needs to be sought. In this case, for example, the prior 'invasions' at Dieppe, in Italy and in the Pacific might provide all the necessary data for the Allies to compute the solution. On the German side, the equivalent prior experiences of resisting invasions or raids in Europe might have persuaded them that the coming invasion could indeed be planned by recourse to existing expertise. However, on the German side there were two contradictory sets of experts with some seeking to halt the invasion on the beaches (such as Rommel) and some wanting to concentrate on the subsequent inland counter-attack using the armoured reserves (such as von Schweppenburg, and von Rundstedt). This mirrors a Tame Problem approach – both sides claimed they had the answer to the problem, they just disagreed on the answer. For the Germans a Wicked Problem approach would have been to admit the difficulty of the decision and to facilitate a more collaborative approach to secure some political agreement, but Hitler's default response to such issues was the precise opposite of this and to use (as he saw it) Darwinian competition to allow the strong to prevail over the weak. Worse, since Hitler only really trusted himself for such complex decisions his decision to demand personal control over the deployment of the Panzer reserves effectively reduced a Wicked Problem to a Tame one that only he could solve. Tame problems, as was suggested in Chapter 1, are resolved by science and expertise not by political collaboration and compromise; unfortunately for the Germans Hitler confused a Wicked Problem with a Tame Problem. This did not mean defeat was an inevitable consequence of this decision – there were, as we shall see, plenty of opportunities for the Germans to rescue victory from the jaws of defeat, and plenty of opportunities on the Allied side to rescue defeat from the jaws of victory. But this is to get ahead of ourselves: let us begin by considering how the Allies responded to the strategic questions of the day: where to invade, when to invade and how to invade?

2 Western Allied Strategy: the Boxer and the Karateka

2.1 Introduction

Strategy is fundamentally the concern of the senior leadership in war-time for both political and military leaders. This was the land of those with an obsessional focus on long-distant goals, and the first strategic decision the Western Allied leaders had to make was whether to concentrate on Germany or Japan. Despite the greater fear and animosity amongst the American population for the threat from Japan, it was apparent to most – though not all – the political and military leadership that Germany posed the greater threat. Moreover, the USA was the only significant Allied power in the Pacific, especially after Britain's ignominious expulsion from Singapore, and therefore the USA assumed that the post-war situation in the Pacific would be relatively simple to control. In effect, political leadership for all the Allies was as much concerned with the post-war settlement as it was with finding a way to win the war.

The second strategic decision was where and how to take the war to Germany: the USA was intent on a direct assault through France and eastwards to Berlin; the UK regarded this as problematic and preferred to weaken Germany first through a series of smaller assaults, coupled with an emphasis on strategic bombing, to the point where a very much weakened opponent could then be knocked out with a frontal assault if necessary. This was not just related to Churchill's concerns about British manpower for he also had ambitions beyond the war, and they principally involved ensuring that Western Europe came under British influence after the war. However, the longer the war continued and the more delayed the invasion of Europe became the more important became the American influence – but also the more likely that the USSR would get to Berlin first.

This division in strategy replicates two different martial arts: boxing and karate. While boxers sometimes knock their opponents out in the first round this is an unusual occurrence and the more traditional strategy is to wear the opponent down through attrition by delivering a series of body and head blows to the point where either a points victory is assured or the opponent is weakened to the point of collapse. Karate, on the other hand, is premised on a first knockout blow because there maybe no time for a second or subsequent attack. Of course, sport karate has minimized this in the same way that boxing has altered bare-knuckle fighting, but in essence the karateka – a practitioner of karate – should be intent on stopping an opponent with a first and decisive blow. In this respect the American strategy mirrors karate and the British strategy embodies boxing; neither is guaranteed success and neither requires greater bravery than the other – but they are different. In the end the American karateka failed to deliver the knockout blow in Normandy and the fight turned into a bloody attrition more resemblant of a 15-round heavyweight boxing match than a karate tournament; neither Allied leader managed to ensure the execution of their preferred strategy. And a primary reason for this was that no one on the Allied side had told the Germans what they were supposed to do to facilitate the roll out of the plan.

General George Patton certainly embodied the essence of the karateka and he had always hoped to be in command of the drive from Normandy to Berlin but his temperament was, according to Roosevelt and Marshall, profoundly unsuited to the delicate task of keeping the feuding family of Allies together. The Quebec conference in August 1943 agreed that an American would become the supreme commander to lead SHAEF (Supreme Headquarters of the Allied Expeditionary Forces), yet Churchill had already told Brooke that the job was his. But when it became clear that the American input to Overlord exceeded that of the British, Churchill had to submit to an American commander. Henry Stimson – Roosevelt's Secretary for War – also suggested that the British should not lead the campaign because their preference was for 'pinprick warfare' which wouldn't work and because 'their hearts are not in it' for the necessary head-on assault.[3]

Roosevelt's preference for the supreme commander was General Marshall but since Marshall was already US Army Chief of Staff this would have involved a demotion. Moreover, the American senior commanders – Admiral King, Admiral Leahy and General Pershing – had all warned Roosevelt that only Marshall was strong enough to deal with the British over strategy. Roosevelt then settled on General Eisenhower (the only other American officer that would have been acceptable to Churchill) who, at the time, was in command of the Italian campaign. Many Americans, though, regarded Eisenhower as too keen to compromise with the British – some even referred to him as the 'best commander the British have'.[4] But Roosevelt was certain that such a tactful approach was essential if the Anglo-American relationship was to remain firm.[5] As General Bradley recognized, 'compromise is essential to amity in an Allied struggle'.[6] Moreover, although Eisenhower's previous career had primarily involved administrative positions (he had served as a desk-bound major for 20 years) he had by 1943 overseen three successful joint Allied amphibious landings and his diplomatic and political skills were regarded by many as an essential ingredient to holding the feuding Allies together.

The compromise that cemented the Americans to the British involved the latter supplying all the deputy commanders but the cement rapidly dissolved onto a quagmire of political infighting and lobbying. Churchill immediately began to lobby for Alexander (then in Italy) rather than Montgomery as land commander but when Marshall insisted on taking Air Chief Marshal Tedder from Italy as his air controller Churchill baulked at losing both Commanding Officers (COs) from the Italian theatre. With Brooke also lobbying against Alexander (whom he regarded as inadequately strategic in orientation) and for Montgomery, it soon became clear to Churchill that Montgomery would have to be given command of the ground forces. Eisenhower, who preferred Alexander, regarded Montgomery as arrogant, inflexible and abrasive, while Montgomery considered Eisenhower an amateur at war. As Montgomery quipped, 'Ike doesn't know the difference between Christmas and Easter'.[7] Eisenhower, who did know the difference between an intemperate comment and a constructive criticism, was duly appointed in December 1943 and drew upon his recent past to plan the immediate future. He made it quite clear that two leadership qualities in particular were crucial for Allied success: co-operation and morale:

> Our Mediterranean experience had reaffirmed the truth that unity, co-ordination and co-operation are the keys to successful operations. War is waged in three elements but there is no separate land, air or naval wars … . Not only would I need commanders who understood this truth but I must have those who appreciated the importance of morale and had demonstrated a capacity to develop and maintain it. Morale is the greatest single factor in successful war … . It breeds most readily upon success; but under good leaders it will be maintained among troops even during extended periods of adversity. A human understanding and a natural ability to mingle with all men on a basis of equality are more important than any degree of technical skill.[8]

Eisenhower took many of his staff from the Mediterranean campaign with him, including Tedder as his second in command and Bedell Smith as his Chief of Staff. Ramsay, who had organized the Dunkirk evacuation, was again appointed to direct naval forces for 'Operation Neptune' (transporting 1 million troops and their supplies in six days). Air control was the responsibility of Air-Marshal Trafford. Eisenhower recommended to Marshall that Bradley (the only senior commander he really trusted) be appointed to command the US forces in the field for Overlord, that is the US 1st Army, and he was duly appointed on 23 December 1943. Bradley, no fan of Montgomery's idiosyncratic personal style, was nevertheless clear that Montgomery brought two things to Overlord that would be critical to its success.

First, Monty's incomparable talent for the 'set' battle – the meticulous planned offensive that he had created after he witnessed the chaos and bloodshed of the First World War as a divisional commander – made him invaluable in the Overlord assault. For the Channel crossing was patterned to a rigid plan; nothing was left to chance or improvisation in command. 'Until we gained a bridgehead we were to put our trust in The Plan'.[9]

Second, Montgomery was one of the very few British commanders who had actually been successful against the Germans, a rare quality at this time and something which propelled him to hero-status in the eyes of the British.[10] Bradley recognized Eisenhower's diplomatic skills in maintaining the alliance, but these were not the kind of qualities necessary to encourage troops in battle. In contrast,

> Psychologically the choice of Montgomery as British commander for the Overlord assault came as a stimulant to us all. For the thin, bony, ascetic face that stared from an unmilitary turtleneck sweater had, in little over a year, become a symbol of victory in the eyes of the Allied world. Nothing becomes a general more than success in battle, and Montgomery wore success with such chipper faith in the arms of Britain that he was cherished by a British people wearied of various setbacks ... Even Eisenhower with all his engaging ease could never stir American troops to the rapture with which Monty was welcomed by his.[11]

Later, Eisenhower was to tire of Montgomery's idiosyncrasies and proclaimed that 'Monty is a good man to serve under; a difficult man to serve with; and an impossible man to serve over'. Eisenhower was probably right about Montgomery's insubordination. As Montgomery's brother in law, General Hobart, insisted, 'the secret of success in the Army is to be sufficiently insubordinate'.[12] Montgomery was, as one British historian suggested, 'enslaved by logistics', though an American historian was rather less generous, calling him 'the most overrated general in the war'.[13]

Indeed, one of the reasons Montgomery survived so long in command of the British was that his Chief of Staff, de Guingand, was able to prevent some of his master's errors or at least mitigate their significance. This was probably just as well, for as Alan Brooke suggested in his diary a year before D-Day,

Montgomery ... requires a lot of educating to make him see the whole situation and the war as a whole outside the 8th Army orbit. A difficult mixture to handle, brilliant commander in action and trainer of men, but liable to commit untold errors due to lack of tact, lack of appreciation for other people's outlook. It is most distressing that the Americans do not like him. ... He wants guiding and watching continually.[14]

Manny Shinwell, Secretary of State for War between 1947 and 1950, was equally split on Montgomery's merits, for he was, 'as a fighting general ... supreme ... but as a politician – quite infantile'.[15]

Certainly, Montgomery was besotted by planning – always the mark of a decision-maker whose default was to assume all problems were either Tame or tameable – and much less concerned with exploiting initial success through the use of initiative by subordinates. As one of his Brigadiers pointed out, when he wanted to know what would happen next in a battle he would look it up in the exercise![16]

2.2 Where first?

British planning for the return to France began on the night of 22 June 1940, a mere two weeks after Dunkirk, within hours of the Franco-German armistice being signed and 18 months before the Arcadia conference. However it was not until the latter, on 20 December 1941, two weeks after Pearl Harbour, that Churchill met Roosevelt in Washington to set up the Combined Chiefs of Staff, a joint Anglo-American command structure that would liaise with the Soviet Union about the strategy for the war effort. That strategy was to attack Germany first, since Germany was regarded as the strongest opponent – much to Admiral King's disdain, who, as Commander-in-Chief of the US Navy, preferred to attack Japan first in the Pacific.[17] The 'Germany First' strategy was not a new idea because a 'Europe First' strategy was already in existence in the 1930s US war plans.[18] However, in 1942 the US had 460,000 troops in the Pacific and only 380,000 in Europe and North Africa combined, and the Japanese remained the most hated enemy throughout the war as far as most American citizens were concerned.[19]

The comparative significance of the Japanese and the German enemies should not simply be seen in the military short term – there was also a long term political agenda to consider at the same time. The US felt relatively secure in the Pacific as the only significant Allied power that would inherit the post-war situation. But the European dimension was much more complex. Assuming the Allies won, the US still faced competition from its erstwhile allies, Britain and the Soviet Union, and it was considered vital to America's political interests to ensure that it ended the European war in a dominant position vis-à-vis the British imperial interests in the Mediterranean, and the Soviet imperial interests in Eastern Europe and the Balkans. As Roosevelt said just prior to the Cairo conference, 'there would definitely be a race for Berlin. We have to put the United States' divisions into Berlin as soon as possible'.[20] That meant both prioritizing the German war and dissuading the American populace from perceiving the Japanese as the major threat or considering that the war against Germany was assured of victory.

The US asserted that a single frontal assault to eliminate the main German forces (the karateka option) was greatly preferable to the British predisposition for a series of smaller attacks on the periphery of the Third Reich (the boxer's option), which, the British argued, would minimize casualties for the final assault. For his part, Churchill persisted in his attempt to secure indirect ground attacks on Germany – through Italy or the Balkans in particular – or continuing the policy of massive air bombing on Germany itself. His justification often involved the notion of 'grinding down' the enemy but avoiding a head-on clash wherever possible. Partly this related to a concern for the limited numbers of British troops available as the war progressed but, like the Americans, Churchill had one eye on the post-war settlement. And that suggested that Britain could dominate post-war Europe if, and only if, the Soviet Union could be held in place by a dominant Western alliance. In other words, Churchill was more concerned about Eastern Europe than Western Europe and that meant driving a wedge along North Africa and up through Italy or the Balkans to reach Berlin from the south, not the west.[21]

To the Americans, Churchill's strategy resembled what Admiral Nimitz called (referring to his arch-rival in the Pacific, General MacArthur) a 'hit-'em-where-they-ain't' strategy.[22] In contrast, the American preference for a head-on clash with the *Wehrmacht* was best summed up by Eisenhower in a letter to his son Elliott: 'the way to kill the most Germans with the least loss of American soldiers is to slam them with everything we've got'. 'Where the British saw calculated attrition, suggests Overy, 'American soldiers saw action that was piecemeal and indecisive'.[23] The US view prevailed, not because it was a more rational choice but because politically the US had become the dominant war partner of the British by this time and, as in all Wicked Problems, collaboration is more important than rational analysis and the search for the scientific solution.

It is obvious now that neither the strategic vision of Roosevelt nor that of Churchill was realized: the Soviet Union entered Berlin alone in April 1945 but 12 months earlier the Americans began to doubt British resolve to take the war to the heart of Germany via a mainland assault from Britain. At the same time the British began to worry that the Americans were more intent on destroying Japan before Germany. As Lt General Morgan, the British officer responsible for much of the detailed planning of D-Day between April and December 1943 wondered: 'Were we really only taking part in a gigantic plan or hoax?'[24] He had good reason to worry: in November 1943, only six months before the original date for D-Day in May 1944, no US senior commander had received a directive concerning the operation, and a month later there was still no Supreme Commander appointed. The indecision reflected the political negotiations rather than military difficulties, though all sides tried to pretend otherwise. Indeed, it is a common manifestation of a Wicked Problem that few are prepared to admit that there really is not a scientific answer to the problem, and fewer ready to admit that the most important thing was to facilitate collaboration by appointing a wise and politically astute Supreme Commander rather than seeking out the military commander with the greatest array of military successes.

That is not to say that the problem of strategy did not have self-evident technical – or tame – aspects or prerequisites. As the British General, Alan Brooke, had insisted at Quebec in August 1943 the three preconditions that were necessary before the invasion of Europe could occur were: (1) reducing the strength of the *Luftwaffe* (2) preventing the *Wehrmacht* from bringing reserves to the landing area, and (3) solving the problem of re-supply. However, with a not so subtle trick of the hand Brooke then concluded that the only answer was the obvious one – attack through Italy. Admiral King – never a great supporter of the Germany First plan – had heard enough and proceeded to deny all of Brooke's points. Non-plussed by the British tactics, Marshall hinted that if the British did not fall into line [with a direct invasion of France first] 'the entire (Allied) strategic concept would have to be revised'.[25] That meant only one thing: the US would shift their priorities to the Pacific. As Brooke later commented on Marshall's performance: 'the only real argument he produced was a threat'.[26] Threat or argument it was enough, Churchill had lost in his attempt to control post-war Western Europe and Brooke had lost what he assumed was an assured position as Allied commander for the invasion of Europe. None of this, note, was rooted in rational analysis of a Tame problem but rather it was the unenthusiastic but resigned collaboration of the junior partner at the table.

However, the following day, when rumours of an Italian collapse spread through the delegates, the Americans were persuaded that an immediate invasion of Italy was critical to take advantage of the crisis. Recall that a crisis is both self-evident to those affected by it and effectively inhibits the development of debate or dissent. Nevertheless, it was only agreed by the Americans providing the British agreed to Overlord taking place on 1 May 1944. The Combined Chiefs of Staff duly accepted Morgan's initial strategy and authorized him to begin the detailed planning.[27]

Yet even Churchill's support for Overlord was never really apparent until very late. As late as 26 May 1944 – just ten days before the intended invasion date of 5 June, Churchill told Eisenhower that he was – at last – 'hardening to this enterprise'. It was, according to Eisenhower, a 'painful discovery' that Churchill had not believed in the plan until that point.[28] Churchill subsequently insisted that he actually meant that he was, by then, convinced that the operation should go ahead even if the conditions were not perfect.[29] Note that the implications of Churchill's conditions requirements were both a manifestation of a search for certainty common to those seeking to tame Wicked Problems and simultaneously an impossible demand.

What about Roosevelt? In early 1944 three forces operated to cajole Roosevelt to take action. First, the Presidential election was due on 7 November and Roosevelt had to persuade the voters that his 'Germany-First-and-don't-start-winding-down-the-war-effort-yet' programme was supportable (he won the election with the lowest of his four Presidential victories on 52.8 per cent of the vote). Second, the Soviet Army, which had defeated the Germans at Stalingrad in February 1943, and crossed the Dnieper River in October that year, had relieved the siege of Leningrad in early January 1944 and had begun the long advance against Germany, entering Poland and Romania by 2 April. Third, the assault on the Japanese was still proving extremely costly by US standards: the 72 hour battle for Tarawa in November 1943 for example, cost 3,319 US casualties, while only 146 of the 4,700 Japanese troops and Korean labourers (including 129 Korean labourers) had surrendered. At this rate the war to subdue the Japanese was going to prove immensely costly, the Soviets were going to enter Berlin first, and he was going to have trouble persuading the American voters that Germany remained the most important problem. This was especially important when he could not remove the prickly and pro-Pacific focus of General MacArthur, given the latter's powerful Republican and media friends back home.[30]

One response to all three problems was to pursue the amphibious assault on Normandy irrespective of the cost. Indeed, one could argue, paradoxically, that the last thing Roosevelt wanted was an unopposed landing because that would confirm to the American voters that (a) the European war was almost over, and (b) the tougher enemy – and therefore the most resources – ought to be funnelled to the war against the Japanese in the Pacific.

That popular American optimism may have been rooted in a direct comparison of the resources arraigned against Germany by the Allies. Simply in terms of population figures the main Allies (including the dominions and colonies of the British Empire)[31] grossly outnumbered the main Axis by around three to one. And if we compare the natural resources, the Allies had almost twice the coal reserves of Germany, twice the oil, twice the iron ore, triple the crude steel, and twice the aluminium.[32] But the real differences were in manufacturing capacity rather than raw materials. For example, in 1938 the US had 29 per cent of the world's manufacturing output – Germany had just 13 per cent. By the end of the war the disparity was even greater with the US accounting for half the world's output, and it was this capacity that facilitated not just D-Day and the campaign in Europe, but the Soviet campaigns too (the US, for example, provided the USSR with 665,000 vehicles).[33] This imbalance did not guarantee victory for the Allies – if such a calculation was possible it would have proved to be a classic Tame Problem – but the conventional assumption seems to have been that, providing no colossal errors were made, the Germans could not win in the long term. Eisenhower, however, was less sanguine about the utility of relying simply on a massive advantage in war matériel: 'I believe we can lick the Hun only by being ahead of him in ideas as well as in material resources'.[34] Given the potential role of new weapons, such as jet aircraft, rockets and atomic bombs it should have been clear that having more tanks and lorries was no guarantee of success.

2.3 When?

The second problem was: when should the invasion occur? As early as 1941 the British made clear to the US that any invasion of France would be – to quote Montgomery inverting Churchill – 'the beginning of the end' not the 'end of the beginning' – as Montgomery thought the Americans assumed.[35] As Copp suggests, the entire British strategy was framed around avoiding a head-on clash between British and German troops and reducing the German resistance by whatever other means were available.[36] The consequence was not just Montgomery's careful shepherding of British troops but the overall construction of an Allied strategy that was always slightly deficient in the number of troops available, especially the numbers of infantry soldiers; it was 'the ninety division gamble'.[37]

By the end of 1943 the political and military leadership of the Allies had indeed achieved some success – as measured by the results. They had made three relatively successful amphibious landings: in North Africa in November 1942, Sicily in July 1943 – where the US designed amphibious vehicle or DUKW[38] and the British designed LSTs (Landing Ship Tank – or Long Slow Target as their occupants called them) were deployed – and at Salerno in September 1943. But unlike the Dieppe raid, the three invasions were against unfortified coastlines. Moreover, the Sicilian invasion provided clear warnings of what might happen in Normandy. First, the US 82nd paratroopers were scattered in the high winds right across the island and many of the second wave were dropped at the same time as a *Luftwaffe* attack and consequently shot by US forces by mistake. Second, many of the British 1st Airborne's gliders were lost in the sea as they were cast off too early by their tow planes. Several DUKWs also proved themselves unseaworthy in any kind of swell – as much because the seasick soldiers' vomit blocked up the bilge pumps as because of any inherent design problem in the vehicle itself that subsequently proved invaluable in the absence of port facilities for unloading.[39]

The gradual realization that the troop numbers were insufficient for a full scale European invasion led to a radical reduction in the relatively rigorous selection policies of the American forces in 1942. For example, the dental requirements were reduced from having *all* your own teeth to having *enough* – natural or artificial – to survive on army rations.[40] Even the Rangers' Colonel Rudder ignored the requirement for having your own teeth after a relatively toothless Private William Petty appealed against his rejection: 'Hell, Sir', he is alleged to have remonstrated to Rudder, 'I don't want to bite 'em, I want to fight 'em'.[41] But for the British the luxury of dental sufficiency never entered into the equation; by the middle of August 1944 – just two months after D-Day – Montgomery informed Alan Brooke that 'My infantry divisions are now so low in effective rifle strength they can no longer – repeat, no longer – fight effectively in major operations'.[42] Furthermore, he knew very well that the Second Army in France was the last he could send – as far as he knew there simply were not enough replacements left.[43]

The US had been keen to go in 1943, especially since the Soviet position had looked very weak during 1942, and Stalin (who had sent Ivan Maisky, the Soviet Ambassador to plead for British help the day after 186 German divisions involved in Barbarossa began the invasion in 1941) may have been forced out of the war if there was any delay in opening a second front. Within a month Stalin requested 25–30 British divisions either to land in France and draw off German reinforcements or to fight with the Red Army on the eastern front.[44] Churchill, however, wanted to delay as long as possible, primarily because it would take time to assemble the necessary troops and their associated war materials, but also because he still hoped that the German war machine would be ground down by – and in turn undermine – the Soviet war machine. Indeed, Stalin suspected that the Western Allies would not enter Europe against Germany unless they thought the Red Army would reach Berlin before them.[45] For Churchill, as for Stalin and Roosevelt, the post-war era was as important as the war itself and would facilitate Churchill's secret agenda first to dominate Europe and, if necessary, to continue the war – but this time against the Soviet Union using some reassembled German forces.[46] In the end the delay until 1944 was more a consequence of the time required for preparation and planning than anything else.

2.4 Testing the strategy: taming or compounding the problem?

A crucial aspect that differentiates Tame from Wicked Problems is the utility of practice. Problems become tamed through successful experience – and they remain Wicked if such practice fails to resolve the problem. On the other hand, with Wicked Problems it is often the case that the problem itself is not always apparent until the search for a solution clarifies exactly what that problem is. Thus practising the invasion – through rehearsals and through related but isolated assaults against German positions – provided the essential test of the category of problem faced. Preparation for the return could not simply be a paper exercise because there were so many unknown factors that needed to be tested in practice. That practice began with a landing by a small party of British commandos near Boulogne on 23 June 1940, the day after France signed an armistice with Germany and Hitler boasted that the British had been 'driven from the continent forever'.[47] There were supposed to be 200 commandos involved but there were only enough boats for 12 and the force took with them 20 Thompson sub-machine guns (Tommy guns) – that was half the number currently in existence in Britain. Somehow the vast armada of boats that had saved 339,000 British and French troops at Dunkirk, and a huge quantity of small arms, had mysteriously disappeared.[48] The contrast between the mass evacuation and the first return raid was completed when, on the latter's return, one group of commandos landed at the wrong port and was promptly arrested by the British Military Police for desertion.

Three other significant tests were executed, in the Lofoten Islands, at Saint-Nazaire, and at Dieppe. The first was in March 1941 when 1,000 British Commandos landed on the Norwegian Lofoten Islands. The raid was of marginal value to the immediate war effort, merely destroying 9,000 tons of enemy shipping, but more importantly it encouraged the Germans to maintain 300,000 troops in Norway when they could have been redeployed to help staunch the invasion in France.[49] In October 1941 Churchill decided to formalize the raiding organization and appointed Lord Louis Mountbatten to head the Combined Operations Command with a remit to 'start the preparations for our great counter-invasion of Europe. Unless we can land overwhelming forces and beat the Nazi in battle in France, Hitler will never be defeated'.[50]

The second test occurred on the evening of 28 March 1942, when 630 Commandos and sailors drove an old American Lend-Lease destroyer, the *Campbeltown*, into the gate of the dry-dock at Saint-Nazaire, the only dry-dock large enough to take the German battleship the *Tirpitz*. The subsequent explosion put the dry-dock out of action, preventing the *Tirpitz* from using its facilities, and killed several hundred Germans. But despite this relative success, and despite the large numbers of casualties sustained by the British, the raid had one very problematic consequence: it suggested – wrongly – that surprise was all that was needed to launch a successful attack upon a well defended port.[51]

In January 1942, just after the Arcadia conference, the Allies met in Washington D.C. to co-ordinate the strategy under the Combined Chiefs of Staff. Perhaps co-ordination is too strong a word and 'glue' is more accurate because the Combined Chiefs of Staff had very different ideas. As we have seen, Churchill was still keen to attack Germany through what he called its 'soft underbelly' – somewhere in the Mediterranean- and to delay any attack across the Channel until the following year. The USA, deeply concerned at the apparent collapse of Soviet forces under ferocious German attack (and the potential redeployment west of some of the 3 million German soldiers there), preferred to organize an immediate cross-Channel invasion to draw German troops away from the East.[52] The US Army staff, in particular, was certain that the USSR would be defeated by the summer of 1942 and that would enable Hitler to exploit Russian economic resources by the summer of 1943. Thus July 1943 was set as the latest date for an Allied invasion of France.[53] In the end they agreed to a small scale landing in the late summer of 1942, 'Operation Sledgehammer' which was to seize Cherbourg with 12 divisions (ten British) and break out during the spring of 1943 with American support (Operation Roundup).

However, while the planning for that went ahead, a request was made to Combined Operations for a third test. This was the inaugural raid by the Anglo-American planners – the Combined Commanders – to institute an attack upon one of a list of ports supplied, 'to persuade the enemy to react as if he were faced with actual invasion'.[54] Dieppe was chosen and the Canadian Army in Britain, then numbering 150,000 and deployed primarily on anti-invasion duties, was chosen to lead the way. The choice of Canadians had more to do with political than military requirements for the Canadian Prime Minister, William MacKenzie, had complained to Churchill on a visit in September 1941 that recruitment was tailing off because of the perceived irrelevance of the as-yet undeployed Canadian forces in Britain. The Canadian 2nd Division stationed at Horsham in Surrey, for example, had been there since December 1939 and had not seen active service in the 22 months since then. 'I don't know', implored MacKenzie, 'how long I can go on leading my country while our troops remain inactive'.[55] Throughout July 1942 the Canadians' routine of training suddenly changed as they were shipped off to Freshwater on the Isle of Wight to prepare for the Dieppe raid.

The attempt to seize and hold Dieppe in August 1942, to evaluate the strategy, tactics and technologies for such an invasion, was a disaster. The 11 mile assault front was considered difficult but not impregnable by Combined Operations, after all, the defending troops comprised either very old, very young or very Polish men. And against the flower of the Canadian Army and the British Commandos what could such a ragtag army hope to achieve? In the event this was a lesson that the Allied leadership failed to learn: planning the raid on the basis of assumed expertise and superiority over the enemy – that is on a Tame basis – is viable providing you have successfully achieved an equivalent operation before and the operation is a replication of the original. If that is not the case then the problem is likely to manifest itself as Wicked, that is where decentralized collaboration not centralized expertise is the most likely key to success. In this case the difficulty lay in not recognizing that the quality of defenders was a problem.

The raid was to last for nine hours only, involving five hours ashore and four hours for the withdrawal. Some 10,000 troops and 100 Churchill tanks were to be involved in this operation, originally code named 'Operation Rutter', and six separate beaches were to be attacked. On the extreme flanks the British commandos were to destroy coastal batteries, leaving six Canadian infantry divisions and one regiment of tanks to assault the beaches around Dieppe itself. They were to move through the town, capture the port intact, and destroy the German airfield at St Aubin and the radar station at Pourville, before returning to the port to embark for home.

Unlike the last mass amphibious raid, in Gallipoli in 1915, nothing could go wrong because the 199 page attack plan, partly written by Montgomery but under Mountbatten's overall leadership, guaranteed success – or so the planners argued. In fact the planners were so confident that they demanded that no Canadian unit commander use his initiative since this itself might undermine the guarantee of success. In fact, Major-General J.H. Roberts, the Canadian CO, was quite optimistic about the whole affair, for 'The plan is good, the men are keen and they know what to do'.[56]

If ever there was an attempt to tame an essentially Wicked Problem this was it. In the end the effect of this was that the results were both disastrous and, in this case, directly attributable to the strategic leaders. The British Commandos, fortunately, refused to accede to the plan and won the right to use whatever tactics they thought best at the time. That plan was probably akin to another of Montgomery's used in 1944 – Operation Market Garden at Arnhem – that prompted the Polish General Sosabowski to ask after seeing the plan, 'But what about the Germans?'[57] Major Brian McCool of the Royal Regiment of Canada, captured and interrogated by the Germans at Dieppe, was equally uncertain. His interrogator said to him, 'Look, McCool, it was too big for a raid and too small for an invasion. What is it?' To which McCool replied, 'If you can tell *me* the answer, I would be very grateful'.[58]

There was no overall commander since the naval and army commanders had equal status. There was no aerial bombardment, not just because Leigh-Mallory was reluctant to provide any bombers but because Major-General Roberts, CO of the Canadian 2nd Division, preferred to use the element of surprise than the element of explosives.[59] There were no airborne troops because the weather forecast was unfavourable. And, despite Mountbatten's insistence that a naval bombardment be provided, Admiral Pound, then the 1st Sea Lord, refused to risk any battleships in such dangerous waters.

So on 19 August 1942, against a very inauspicious background in which the Allied leaders vied with each other for insanity badges, 6,000 Canadian infantry and tankers, 1,100 British Commandos and 50 US Rangers crossed the channel in 237 vessels to execute Operation Jubilee, as it was now called. No. 4 Commando was led by Lt Colonel the Lord Lovat, whose corduroy trousers and grey pullover marked him out as a confirmed eccentric. Eccentric or not, at the cost of around 16 dead and 40 wounded, his 252 commandos scaled the 400 foot cliffs at Varengvillea and eliminated 108 of the 112 German defenders, blowing up the six 150mm gun battery and re-embarking on time with the four remaining German prisoners. Lovat was deeply unimpressed with the planners and considered the raid 'a disaster ... the changed plan [was] nothing short of suicidal'.[60]

The element of suicide was most clearly visible among the Canadian infantry assaults in the centre. The fire of the defenders' guns decimated the first waves of the Royal Regiment of Canada, and naval officers with drawn pistols forced the second waves out of the landing craft to certain death. The troops had nowhere to hide – they could not climb the 12-foot sea wall and there was no cover. At 0800, after almost two and a half hours of butchery, the Canadians who were still alive began surrendering, though the final fighting ceased at 1630. Of the 650 Royals who landed, 614 (95 per cent) were either dead or wounded or captured. Back at the beach the commanders on the ships were unable to see the beach itself because of their own smokescreen and unable to contact the Royals ashore for three hours because most of the radios had been lost or destroyed.

Just to make matters worse, confused signals about success then led to the further landings of the Fusiliers Mont Royal and the Royal Marine Commandos. The former group landed just in time to be captured. The latter group landed last in thick smoke, and when Col. J.P. Philips, their commanding officer, saw the catastrophe that had preceded them he ordered those craft still at sea (carrying 1,000 troops) to return to the ships. At last a withdrawal was ordered for 1100. The retreat was chaotic, so overloaded were the boats that some Canadian troops shot their German prisoners to lighten the load. By 1220 the last evacuees were taken on board and just over an hour later the sorry convoy headed back to Newhaven on the English south coast.

Though the raid was an unmitigated disaster, the *Daily Mirror*'s headline ran: 'Big Hun Losses in 9-hr Dieppe Battle'; the first casualty of war had already fallen. When the debriefings finished the results were catastrophic: 5,100 troops landed and 3,648 failed to return. The 2nd Canadian Division no longer existed: 907 were dead, 568 wounded, and 1,946 were prisoners. Of the 100 Churchill tanks that embarked only 27 reached the beach and none could negotiate across the shingle let alone burst through the defences of the sea wall. The Commandos lost 247 dead, wounded and prisoners. The Royal Navy lost one destroyer, 33 landing craft and 550 sailors. The RAF lost 106 planes and 153 aircrew. The *Luftwaffe* lost 48 aircraft and 162 aircrew. In total, only 591 German casualties were inflicted with 297 of these dead. It was, as the Vichy government informed their German overlords, a great victory.[61] The British Army's unofficial newspapers told a different but ambiguous story. According to *Parade* on 29 August 1942, 'It may be some time before the complete story of the Commando raid on Dieppe is told, some time before the full details of the plan and the immediate and remote objectives are made known. The losses on the side of the Allies will soon be declared but it is the German fashion to pretend they are perpetually inflicting tremendous losses on the Allies at the cost of quite negligible casualties to themselves'. In this instance the German propaganda, not the British, was more accurate.

Mountbatten subsequently claimed that every Allied casualty at Dieppe saved ten on D-Day because of the learning and improvements that were made as a consequence, but a large element of rationalization seemed to emerge in the justifications for the raid. Almost everything had gone wrong but little of this was completely unforeseeable and not every lesson seemed to have been learned by the D-Day planners. Communications between the landing parties and the off-shore force were virtually non-existent, the plywood landing craft obviously offered no protection against German guns, and there seems to have been no prior experimentation with tank movement on sandy beaches or against concrete anti-tank obstacles.[62] Less obvious, perhaps, the balance of force between defender and attacker had to be radically reconsidered because the advantages secured by the defenders against attackers moving over open beaches were overwhelming. This was irrespective of the quality of the defending troops because the Dieppe defenders were not a first rate German unit – an issue the D-Day planners quickly forgot. More problematic still, somehow a mechanism had to be constructed for discharging heavy equipment and supplies in very large numbers at great speed to provide support for the initial groups. Finally, a weapon to shatter the beach defences immediately prior to the assault was required.

It could be argued, then, that the leadership could still count Dieppe as a success – because the results have to be gauged against D-Day rather than just Dieppe. However, even if the losses at Dieppe may have reduced the casualties on D-Day they may simultaneously have increased casualties in the subsequent battle for Normandy. After Dieppe, the focus of attention switched from concentrating on the battle with German forces *after* the landings (on the prior assumption that the landing would be relatively easy), to concentrating on the landing itself (on the assumption that the landing was the most difficult task) and after this was achieved the weight of forces would ensure the defeat of the Germans.

Field-Marshal Karl von Rundstedt, the supreme German Commander in France, Belgium and Holland (*Oberbefehlshaber* West [OB West]), drew a different conclusion from Hitler about the significance of Dieppe: 'It would be an error', he noted in his battle report, 'to believe that the enemy will mount his next operation in the same manner ... . Next time he will do things differently'. Indeed, this should have been relatively obvious given the German High Command's assessment of the raid, for it was an 'amateur undertaking ... carried out in opposition to all good military sense'.[63]

Von Rundstedt was right: the Dieppe fiasco had persuaded the Allies that a head-on assault against a port was too dangerous and thus something different was necessary – in this case, a beach area was essential – but it had to be close to a port or ports to ensure eventual re-supply. The area also had to be within fighter-cover distance of Britain – which restricted the possibilities to a beach area along the French, Belgian or Dutch coast within around 150 miles. Finally, the area had to be easily isolated from counter-attack and reinforcements. That meant using some form of natural barrier to inhibit German troop and armour movement and using air attacks to disrupt road and rail transport networks.

So extensive were the defences at the Pas de Calais that even the most aggressive American commanders regarded an invasion here as impossible, or at least extremely costly in human and material losses. Moreover, the Allies were certain that the Germans would move some of their Normandy divisions north to support an invasion in Calais but they would be reluctant to move any of the divisions guarding Calais in the opposite direction.[64] Anyway, the Pas de Calais contained high cliffs, narrow beaches and few beach exits, making an assault even more precarious. Additionally, the port facilities of Calais, and the adjacent facilities of Boulogne, were regarded as inadequate in themselves to support an army all the way to Berlin. For that, the Allies would also have to assault and take Antwerp or Le Havre, themselves very heavily defended. And if there were doubters left, it soon became apparent that the small ports in southeast England – besides Dover itself – simply could not accommodate the number of landing craft and naval vessels envisaged for a Calais based invasion.[65] Ironically, despite all this, the German High Command still believed that Calais would be the prime target, if for no other reason than that it was the direct route to the Rhine, the Ruhr and Berlin. Moreover, although the landing would be very difficult and the German 15th Army defending the area was very strong, many Germans knew that in the words of General Blumentritt, the land behind the 15th Army 'was practically free from troops capable of fighting'.[66]

Since port facilities would be necessary to re-supply an invasion two other alternatives were Le Havre, or the Cotentin peninsular and Cherbourg; certainly there were few other ports worth considering. As an 1811 edition of *The New Seaman's Guide and Coaster's Companion* suggested, 'The bay formed by Cape de Caux and Cape Barfleur is about 7 leagues deep: on the south and west part of it are several small harbours, of which description is unnecessary' (quoted in Maher, 1996:

113). But Le Havre and Cherbourg were very heavily defended and airfields would be difficult to build in the *bocage* countryside, where a patchwork landscape of high and virtually impenetrable hedges bordered sunken roads along small fields. The small fields had allegedly resulted from the dispersal of property between several sons over many generations and the stability of the system, linked to natural erosion over several centuries, had created hedgerows that were up to eight feet high and ten feet thick. Moreover, the Cotentin peninsular would allow the Germans to cut off the invasion at the base and hold the Allies indefinitely. Another alternative invasion route would have been north of Calais through Flanders, but the area was subject to flooding and had already proved itself a killing ground in the First World War.

Eventually the Allies reversed positions: the British wanted to attack the main German army defending the Calais region and the territory north of the Seine but the Americans preferred the flanking attack through Normandy; again the US domination of strategy and the provision of matériel prevailed. But before Normandy there was still a lot of learning to do. The failure of Dieppe, in association with the power of the German U-boat menace[67] and the lack of available landing craft, enabled Churchill to persuade the Americans that a landing on French colonial territories in North Africa was a preferable option to an immediate landing on the French mainland and thus was born 'Operation Torch'.

Brigadier-General Dwight D. Eisenhower was chosen to direct the Torch landings just as Rommel, commander of the *Afrikakorps* was recalled to Germany and appointed commander of Army Group B, with responsibility for defending the Normandy coast against Allied invasion. Eisenhower assembled a team of four subordinates to oversee Torch: Clark, an American, as second-in-command, and three British deputies: Tedder to control air operations, Ramsay for sea operations and Alexander for land forces. The landings were made successfully in January 1943 at Algiers, Casablanca and Oran with minimum resistance from the Vichy French forces.

One consequence of the British concern to avoid a head-on clash with Germany, and to weaken German forces elsewhere before attempting a landing in France, was that the Americans still doubted whether the British were serious about Overlord and organized a meeting with Churchill, Stalin and Roosevelt in Teheran in November 1943, ostensibly to discuss the Far East and the Mediterranean campaigns that Churchill favoured. However, on 26 November 1943, shortly after arriving in Teheran, Roosevelt was whisked away from the US Embassy and transported to the Soviet Embassy after a 'security scare' that allegedly involved a threat to assassinate Roosevelt. This also gave Stalin the chance to discuss the Balkans with Roosevelt and it provided the President with the excuse for his preliminary meeting with Stalin to thrash out the importance of Overlord – and all without Churchill's presence. As Brooke said later, on hearing of the meeting: 'This conference is over before it even begins'.[68] When Churchill heard of the meeting he first tried to see Roosevelt – who told him he had another meeting to go to; this was true, but Churchill did not know it was another meeting with Stalin. When Churchill then secured a meeting with Stalin he explained his concern that Overlord might cause thousands of unnecessary casualties, he had talked of 'the beaches of Normandy choked with the flower of American and British youth',[69] and said he still preferred wearing down the Germans through smaller scale attacks upon the periphery of the German empire, in Greece, the Balkans, Italy and North Africa. Stalin was unmoved; indeed, he explained, the Soviet Union had already suffered 4 million casualties and, as one Russian put it, on being told that the US had already suffered 200,000 battle casualties in the war, 'We lose that many each day before lunch'.[70] This may have been a wild exaggeration though if the German claims about Soviet casualties are accurate then the 12,593,000 dead and wounded between the outbreak of war in June 1941 and the collapse of the German eastern defences in February 1945 equate to almost 9,000 for every one of the 1,400 days of the war until that point. Put another way, the Western Allies' casualties on D-Day (around 8,600) amounted to less than the average daily loss for the Soviet forces throughout the war. Relatedly, when the Soviet offensive began on 20 June 1944 the Germans lost approximately 300,000 troops in just 12 days, a daily rate of 25,000 casualties – almost three times the D-Day rate for the Western Allies.[71]

To the Soviets and sometimes the Americans, British prevarication looked uncomfortably close to a strategy of allowing the Germans and the Soviets to exhaust themselves against each other so that the British could mop up at the end and reassert control over the Mediterranean and the Balkans.[72] Hence, Stalin continued, if Overlord did not take place in May 1944, then the Soviet Union would have little option but to 'do business with Hitler'.[73]

Churchill appeared to have been outmanoeuvred, for Stalin dismissed Churchill's concerns and his counter-proposal for a further Mediterranean invasion, and insisted that the main operation for the Anglo-American forces in 1944 must be Overlord and that he would plan a simultaneous invasion by Soviet forces from the east. The date was agreed at 1 May 1944, as was the proposal that the Supreme Commander be American.[74] Originally it had been assumed that General Marshall would lead Overlord – indeed he had even packed to go to London before Roosevelt told him to stay – but straight after Teheran Roosevelt informed Eisenhower of the decision to send him instead. But before the Allies landed in France, they had first to land in Italy.

On 9 September 1943 Allied troops landed at Salerno, partly because the desire for surprise prevented any pre-assault naval or air bombardment, to be 'welcomed' ashore by two, and soon afterwards six, German divisions. A relatively small amphibious operation cost 15,000 Allied troops and the outlook for Overlord looked grim – though one lesson allegedly taken on board was the critical role of the pre-assault. The 'allegedly' is important because the US beaches only received a 40-minute bombardment on D-Day and that was retrospectively acknowledged as inadequate by Rear-Admiral Hall.[75] That the Utah attack was so successful can be put down, in part, to the more accurate bombing of this beach and to the fact that this area had the weakest section of defences: only 15 per cent of the fortifications here had been bomb-proofed by 6 June.[76]

Churchill had yet one more card to play, for he still feared that Normandy would simply produce a catastrophe that would outscale anything like Salerno. As he mentioned to his doctor on the way to the Cairo meeting with Roosevelt just before Teheran, he was 'more and more certain that an invasion of [Northern] France as planned must fail'.[77] Churchill's fears and Montgomery's concern for minimizing casualties were self-evidently problematic to the Americans, keen as they were to square up to the German army as soon and as violently as possible. 'The shadow of Passchendaele and Dunkerque' suggested Stimson, Roosevelt's Secretary for War, 'still hang too heavily over the imagination of these leaders [Churchill and Montgomery]'.[78]

Yet Churchill was not quite finished with the Mediterranean and in December 1943 he persuaded the Combined Chiefs of Staff to hurl 'a raging wildcat' onto the beaches at Anzio (60 miles north of the German lines in Italy and 30 miles south of Rome – which was the target) 'to rip the bowels out of the Boches'.[79] This two division attack would, according to Churchill, force the Germans to make a strategic retreat far to the north – though Eisenhower suggested instead that the Germans would – as indeed they did – stay put rather than withdraw. Thus, although the Allies planned an advance through Italy premised upon a German strategic withdrawal to a line roughly from Genoa to Venice, again nobody informed the Germans of their part in the plan and they fought a bloody holding battle – much as they were to do in Normandy.[80]

Unfortunately no-one on the Allied side seemed to have learned from the Anzio landings, or indeed the invasion of Italy as a whole, that the

Wehrmacht simply did not operate on the same form of military rationality that pervaded the Allied side: when the going got tough the Germans did not retreat, they simply got tougher. Partly as a consequence, Major-General Lucas' assault on Anzio, which started so well (13 dead, 97 wounded and 44 missing from a 40,000 strong force) failed to maintain momentum after eight German divisions surrounded the landing site ('the world's largest self-sustaining prisoner-of-war compound' was how the Germans saw it). The 'wild cat' became, again in Churchill's word: 'a stranded whale'. Churchill had presumed the Germans would run from the wild cat when in fact they did the opposite: Churchill's 'scissors' had simply been stopped by the German 'stone'.[81] The omens for Normandy did not look good but Anzio should have proved to be a necessary stage in the taming of Normandy, that is, by bringing the realization that the German defenders would probably not retreat to shorten their defensive lines but would stay put and slug it out until one side or other was defeated.

2.5 Taming (some of) the problem through planning

Having undertaken a significant degree of practice, much of which ended up as a bloody run rather than a dry run, the next set of nested problems within this Wicked box involved the detailed planning for the invasion, that is effectively an attempt to tame the problem, or at least tame those parts that could be tamed. This raises an important issue about problems because they seldom come neatly packaged in a box with a label saying 'Tame' or 'Wicked' or 'Critical' and more often to arrive as much outside as inside a box and with no labels or confusing labelling. Thus, to accept that the strategic issues were Wicked does not mean that no answer will be forthcoming, but rather that some elements of the problem can be tamed while others will become Critical and still others will always remain obscure and beyond any simple taming procedure.

Lt General Morgan was appointed as Chief of Staff to the Supreme Allied Commander (COSSAC) to plan the full scale invasion of France – 'Operation Overlord' – but his introduction to the problem could hardly have been more Wicked. General Alan Brooke handed Morgan the conclusions of the Combined Commanders which suggested that an invasion with at least ten divisions was necessary but that only enough transport for five would be ready by the due deadline. As Alan Brooke is reported to have said to Morgan: 'Well, there it is. It won't work. I know it won't work, but you will bloody well have to make it work'.[82] This was little different from Brooke's own experience of taking over from

Edmund Ironside on 20 July 1940 as Commander in Chief Home Forces: Ironside had left before Brooke arrived and merely left a note saying 'good luck!' and noting that the Rolls Royce was for his use.[83]

Morgan had been a task force commander in the 1942 invasion of North Africa and had already finished the initial planning for the invasion of Sicily. Operation Overlord (the invasion of France) was not a goal in and of itself but the means to the goal, and that goal was the defeat of Germany in Germany. Thus Morgan had to work backwards from establishing what would be needed to achieve the defeat of Hitler to arrive at the requirements to establish a successful lodgement on the French coast.

Planning Overlord was Tame in the sense that there was a science to it and routine processes already existed, but it was hardly a routine operation: it required plans to move a city the equivalent of Birmingham in the UK across the channel, under enemy fire, and keep it moving until it got to Berlin.[84] Morgan and his team began planning Overlord on the opposite basis to that employed by the Germans who were planning to resist the invasion: to the Allies a port was the last place to begin an invasion. Primarily this derived from the post-Dieppe realization that the level of bombardment necessary to induce the defenders to surrender would all but eliminate the port facilities that were the very reason for the attack. In the event all the ports were defended by first class troops who were ordered not to surrender under any conditions and, as the post-D-Day invasion was to prove, the vast majority of major ports remained in German hands long after the surrounding territory had fallen to the Allies.

Morgan's approach had been premised on the available shipping and he concluded that only three divisions could be carried by sea to assault a 25-mile stretch of the Normandy coast, supported by two airborne divisions. But when Montgomery – and Eisenhower, though Montgomery claimed the changes were his – scrutinized the plan at the end of 1943 it was clear to them that only by increasing the amphibious divisions to five, and the airborne divisions to three, to assault a 59-mile stretch of coast, could the assault have any chance of succeeding. Only such a large scale assault would, it was argued, prevent the Germans from establishing the kind of effective concentration of fire against the over-narrow beach-head that Salerno had witnessed – when 15,000 Allied troops became casualties.[85] Thus two further landing areas were added, one area to the west – Utah Beach on the Cotentin peninsula – and one to the east– Sword Beach up to the Orne River.

A conference in January 1944 confirmed the postponement of the invasion back from May to June 1944.[86] The delay allowed two issues to be resolved: first, the building or requisitioning from other areas of additional shipping: 47 Landing Ship Tank (LSTs), 144 Landing Craft Tank (LCTs), 72 Landing Craft Infantry (Large) (LCI(L)s), 5 cruisers and 24 destroyers. The extra warships were primarily US in origin but it had taken all Bradley's persuasive skills to secure them from the US Navy. As late as April 1944 the US Navy could only spare two battleships, four cruisers and 12 destroyers. This force was eventually increased by a further two battleships (ex-World War 1) and 14 destroyers.[87] Given the significance of the latter in opening up Omaha Beach this was probably a critical addition.

The second issue was the extra time for bombing: a further month to facilitate the bombing of transportation centres in France would prevent, or at least delay, the build up of German reserves.[88] By late 1943 the core of the invasion force was in the UK: there were 1.5 million US troops, 1.75 million British troops, 150,000 from the Commonwealth and 40,000 from occupied Europe.[89] The construction of the enhanced plan began in December 1943 at Norfolk House, St James's Square, London, and the first draft of the plan was issued on 1 February 1944 and the following month SHAEF – now numbering 6,000 soldiers and 750 officers – moved to Bushey Park in Middlesex.[90] Since many of the planners had already been through the experience of planning three previous amphibious assaults, and since the planning had gone on almost continuously for several years, the complexity of the operation did not provide an insurmountable problem to G-3, the battle planning section of the General Staff at SHAEF. 'The long time available for administrative planning', Admiral Ramsay commented, 'coupled with the fact that the resources of the United Kingdom were available to ANCXF (Allied Naval Commander-in-Chief, Expeditionary Force) enabled most of these problems to be solved, but this exceptionally favourable situation is unlikely to be repeated in another theatre'.[91] Nevertheless, 12-hour days and seven-day weeks became the norm for senior officers involved in the planning – and thus the taming of the problem.[92]

Merely securing information about the French coastline proved to be a complex operation in itself and one that illustrates the way Wicked Problems can in part be tamed. In this case the Wicked Problem was that no one individual or organization had the information about the French coastline necessary to plan the invasion. So the issue was: how to secure collaboration of the many people necessary whose collective access to knowledge could tame this aspect of the problem? The solution was innovative: in March 1942 Commander Rodney Slessor, Royal Navy Volunteer Reserve (RNVR), delivered a radio broadcast in which he explained that a successful commando raid on a radar station near Le Havre had been accomplished using thousands of holiday photos and postcards to map out the area. In preparation for the future invasion of Europe he then asked everyone – everywhere – to send in postcards and photographs of the entire French coast to facilitate planning. Thirty-six hours later 30,000 items had been delivered and within two years 10 million items were duly handed in. Some 150,000 were then reconstructed into maps of the French coastline by cartographers at Oxford University working for the Inter-Service Topographical Unit.[93] Even assuming that some people sent multiple photos and postcards it is apparent that planning D-Day took the individual acts of thousands of people.

On the other hand the military could and did have enough resources of their own to tame the problem of contemporary photographic data. Reconnaissance flights over the coastal waters secured updated data by the day, and between 1 April and 5 June 1944 the Allied Expeditionary Air Force (AEAF) made 3,215 photographic sorties. Most of these were at medium or low level because the weather conditions were often too poor for high altitude photography and because oblique photographs were essential to reproduce the view from sea level for the assault troops.[94] In the two weeks prior to D-Day alone, a single RAF photographic section made 12,000 prints of the Normandy coast.[95] On the eve of the invasion 40,000 copies of the French coastline were printed off for the assault troops – a production process that used up 730 miles of photographic paper and 10 tons of chemicals every other day. Despite the detail, though, the photographs often failed to establish that many of the beach fortifications were constructed to provide enfilading fire onto the beaches with their seaward side almost invulnerable to all but the largest shells.[96] This remains a puzzle because many of the training beaches had – and in parts of Devon still have – replica defences built to mirror this enfilading fire. Indeed, Devon contains many topographical aspects that mirror those in France, including the high hedges and narrow roads known as the *bocage* in Normandy. Thus some aspects of the subsequent invasion that manifested themselves as Wicked, especially to the American troops inland of Omaha Beach, were only Wicked because so little notice had been taken of their equivalent on the American training areas in the West Country of England.

Where the Allies were much more successful was in inhibiting the movement of German troops in Normandy up to and just after D-Day. The Allies became aware that the Germans were using secondary roads to replenish their coastal forces rather than main roads but British maps could not always distinguish main from secondary roads. Brigadier Belchem, Montgomery's Chief of Staff, solved the problem by simply buying a Michelin map that marked all main roads in red and the secondary roads in yellow – as indeed they still do. The planners then established which sections of these roads were the most difficult to back-up or circumvent and these became primary fighter-bomber targets just before, during and immediately after D-Day. As expected this caused enormous problems of supply and reinforcement for the Germans.[97]

The overall plan for the Allied armies' landings for the first day divided the task between the US Western Task Force and the British/Canadian Eastern Task Force. This division reflected the initial establishment of the units in Britain and perhaps more significantly the source of the post-invasion forces and the source of the breakout: that would occur in the west using American troops and most would come directly from the USA, hence it made sense to deploy the American troops on the western side.[98] On the other hand, since the shortest route to Berlin was from the east it might have been just as useful to deploy American units to the eastern beaches.[99]

The American first line ground assault forces were encamped in south-west England, with the 1st Division (Omaha) around Weymouth and Blandford, the 4th Division (Utah) around Torquay and Dartmouth. The follow-up forces were in Cornwall (29th Division), Bristol (9th Division), and in south Wales (2nd Division and 90th Division). The Anglo-Canadian first line ground assault forces were encamped around Southampton (British 50th Division, Gold), Portsmouth (Canadian 3rd Division, Juno), and Shoreham (British 3rd Division, Sword). The follow-up forces were in East Anglia (British 49th Division {Polar Bears}).

For the initial assault eight 'overweight' brigades or Regimental Combat Teams (RCTs) were deployed, three American, three British and two Canadian, as follows:

Utah Area – 4th US Division:
Initial assaults by:
   1st Battalion 8th Infantry on Tare Green
   2nd Battalion, 8th Infantry on Uncle Red
   Rangers to capture St Marcouf Islands

Omaha Area – 1st US Division (including elements of the 29th Division):
Initial assaults by:
   116th Regimental Combat Team (29th Div) (RCT – the equivalent of
     a British brigade) on Dog Green, White and Red
   16th RCT (1st Div) on Easy Red and Fox Green
     Three Ranger companies at Pointe du Hoc on Charlie

82nd and 101st US Airborne Division:
To land behind Utah and prevent German reinforcements linking to coastal troops

Gold Area – 50th (Northumberland) Division:
Initial assaults by:
    231st Infantry Brigade on Jig Green
    69th Infantry Brigade on King Green and Red
    47 Commando to take Port en Bessin with 231st Infantry Brigade

Juno Area – 3rd Canadian Division:
Initial assaults by:
    7th Canadian Infantry Brigade on Mike Green and Red and Nan Green
    8th Canadian Infantry Brigade on Nan White and Red
       48 Commando to clear east area with 8th Canadian Infantry
         Brigade

Sword Area – 3rd British Division:
Initial assaults by:
    8th Infantry Brigade on Queen White and Red
    41 Commando to clear west area with 8th Infantry Brigade
    4 Commando to clear Ouistreham

6th (British) Airborne Division (x 5th Parachute Brigade):
To land east of Caen across the River Orne to secure eastern flank

The overall plan also envisioned a three phase assault:

Phase 1: The softening of beach defences with pre-H-Hour air and naval
    bombardment
Phase 2: Beach assault to create lanes through the defences to allow
    vehicle exits
Phase 3: Landing of reserve battalions[100]

Detailed plans operated from the top down in vertical sequence: first
army, then corps, division, regiment, battalion, company, platoon and
squad, but it was decided early on that each subordinate level must
resolve its own problems in its own way. At each horizontal level planning was a tortuous political negotiation: Who controlled the bombers?
Should they land on Utah given the flooding behind? Should they
attempt airborne drops to seal off the bridgehead and facilitate the movement off the beach? Who should take the decision where to land for each
individual landing craft and so on?

Of particular import were the 'Beach masters', designated in control
of their own beach area and tasked with simply making the beach work,
to generate some order out of the chaos that would otherwise descend
on the sand and gravel of Normandy. To that end – and in one of the few

cases of heterarchy (a flexible hierarchy where control shifts with the situation) on the Allied side – they were able to overrule officers that would otherwise outrank them in matters concerned with beach movements.

The precise temporal aspect of planning for D-Day involved detailed deployments, broken down into minutes, for the first 4 hours of the assault from 0630 for Utah and Omaha, 0725 on Gold, 0735 on Juno and 0725 for Sword (the different times related to the tidal movements). Over 350,000 men and women were involved in the meticulous planning and preparation for D-Day alone and between January and June 1944, 9 million tons of supplies and 800,000 soldiers had been shipped across the Atlantic to Britain for the first wave assault. Such an operation clearly required detailed planning: Admiral Ramsay's five-inch thick planning document for Operation Neptune (the actual assault on D-Day, as opposed to the overall plan – Overlord) contained 700 pages of instruction with a subsequently issued preface explaining which sections were relevant to whom. There were over 31 pages that simply listed the 1,400 American units. There were also 280,000 charts of the invasion area distributed and 65,000 operational booklets.[101]

2.6 Normandy: the Allied decision

Normandy is opposite Southampton – the largest British passenger port with its unique double tides – and Portsmouth – the leading naval base – and this area of Hampshire was to become 'the largest naval and military base the world had yet seen'.[102] Two thirds of the Anglo-Canadian troops embarked through Southampton for D-Day and by the end of the war 3.5 million troops had passed through it.[103] The invasion target area was between the ports of Le Havre and Cherbourg which would eventually provide the facilities for the drive on Berlin but, in the meantime, the Allies would solve the initial absence of a port in Normandy – surely a Wicked Problem at the time for the planners – by taking one or two with them in the shape of artificial harbours.

The Calvados coast from the River Orne to the River Vire also offered another advantage: a wide, relatively flat (except between the River Vire and Arromanches) and sandy coastline sheltered from the worst Atlantic gales by the Cotentin peninsular. Normandy was still within air cover, it could be isolated from the rest of the country relatively easily, and it provided relatively good beaches and close ports. Since the reinforcement time was critical for both sides Normandy was proposed and at the Trident Conference in May 1943 US and British planners formally agreed to land on the French coast in May 1944.

Morgan's original plan had called for a three-divisional assault under a combined task-force HQ, but Montgomery's enlargement of the assault to five divisions also embodied the separation of responsibilities so that the two American divisions would be virtually self-contained, as would the three Anglo-Canadian divisions. The plan was to land 11 divisions ashore on D-Day itself, three airborne divisions, six infantry divisions in the initial assault and two reserve divisions in the immediate follow-up. There would then be two more the following day, 21 divisions by D+12, 26 divisions by D+20, 31 by D+35 and 39 by D+90.[104]

Using the Normandy beaches offered a shallow gradient that would enable troops and vehicles to land directly onto the shoreline, and a large tide that would expose the beach obstructions at low tide and facilitate their dismantling by gunfire, bombing and engineers. However, the low-tide line on the Calvados coastline meant up to 500 yards of exposed beach for the troops to cross, so the decision was taken to run in at the midpoint between high and low tide so that most of the obstacles would be visible but the distance to the high-tide line would be shortened.[105] Taking all this into consideration meant a run in between three and four hours before high water and 40 minutes after 'nautical twilight'. However, when extensive underwater obstacles were laid the US demanded a change to allow the troops to clear them at low tide, though Juno Beach was protected by a rocky reef that could only be crossed at the half-way point between low and high tide. Given the associated requirement for a simultaneous assault (which was impossible given the different times of the tides across the landing zones) the compromise times were set between 0639 for the Western Task Force and 0745 for Juno Beach.[106]

At one point a night-time assault was considered to protect the troops but the overwhelming superiority of air and naval forces (and the need to provide accurate bombardment and bombing) persuaded most – though not all – commanders that a daylight attack was preferable. This decision was taken before the Normandy beaches became heavily mined and defended but when the defences were strengthened it was decided, on 1 May, that the landings would occur three to four hours before high tide so that most of the defences would be exposed. Even then there were two subsequent attempts to switch to a night assault.[107]

Finally, Normandy provided a relatively easy area to isolate, assuming the crossings over the Seine could be destroyed by bombing, and presupposing that the bridges over the smaller rivers could be held against attack. Normandy also provided moderately close proximity to a port (Le Havre, Cherbourg and the Brittany ports) without having to land at the port itself. Furthermore, since the Pas de Calais was the assumed invasion spot this was also the best defended, it terms of quantity and quality of fortifications and troops. Normandy, on the other hand, was much less well defended in terms of concrete and artillery and the troops there were deemed by the Germans to be of a lower fighting ability.

The invasion also needed three minimal natural conditions:

1. a surface wind of not more than Force 3 (8–12 mph) on-shore and Force 4 (13–18 mph) off-shore to protect the landing craft from flooding;
2. visibility of not less than 3 miles to facilitate the naval bombardment;
3. a cloud base of at least 2,500 feet to facilitate the air transport, at least 1,000 feet for fighter cover, 4,500 feet over the target for medium bombers and 11,000 feet over the target for heavy bombers.[108]

The chances of all of these occurring together were put anywhere between 60 to 1 at worst to 12 to 1 at best for the whole of May and June but the precise conjunction of moon and tides limited the actual invasion to just three days in June, between the 5th and the 7th and that was estimated to be a 50 to 1 possibility.[109] Given the odds against such an occurrence one might have thought that the planners would have reconsidered the possibility of the plans not taming the problem of the initial assault; that is, of not landing the amphibious tanks or not engaging the bombers in close level support for the ground troops. But for whatever reasons this seems not to have happened. Hence when, as we shall see at Omaha Beach, neither the amphibious tanks nor the bombers played a significant role in the initial assault the troops were exposed to withering fire from the defenders.

SHAEF began the detailed planning of the invasion in early 1944 but the original D-Day of 1 May was postponed to June because of the scarcity of landing craft and 5 June was not chosen until 8 May 1944. This was exacerbated by the decision to expand the initial invasion from three to five divisions and to extend the landing zones west of the River Vire to enable Cherbourg to be captured more quickly – hopefully by D-Day+40.[110] The expansion of the intended assault from 25 miles to 50 miles also required a reorganization of the air assaults, for the troops landing on Utah would need support inland to prevent the flooded interior – and the consequent narrow exit points – from inhibiting their progress. Thus one US airborne division, originally marked to drop over Caen, was switched to land behind Utah Beach.[111] On the other hand it enabled a closer co-ordination between Overlord and the Soviet Summer Offensive.[112]

With five invasion beaches now planned (from west to east: Utah, Omaha, Gold, Juno and Sword), the initial overall strategy was to secure the flanks through airborne troops and move sufficiently far inland to prevent the expected armoured counter-attack pushing the troops straight back into the sea. If the Calvados coastline was isolated by the pre-invasion bombing of the road and rail network, sufficient numbers of troops, artillery and armour could be poured in to facilitate a rapid assault upon Cherbourg thus in turn facilitating the liberation of France by the winter of 1944. Precisely how this occurred was, and is, the subject of much dispute. The British and Canadian troops failed to take Caen early on as German armour raced to defend it, and the delay undermined the initial momentum of the invasion, a delay which was eventually ended by an American breakout, Operation Cobra, in the West under Bradley who assumed command of the 12th Army Group on 1 August with Patton in command of the Third (US) Army and Hodges leading the First (US) Army.

Omar Bradley, the son of poor farming stock, had been commissioned in 1915 and enjoyed considerable support from Marshall and Eisenhower throughout his career. Given his modest background – in contrast to Patton's – Bradley was known as the 'GIs' General' and regarded as a deliberative and methodical leader, again in complete contrast to Patton but much closer to Montgomery's style. After Operation Cobra, Montgomery claimed that he always intended to peg the German forces at Caen to allow the Americans to swing round unhindered; but there has been an immense amount of controversy over this claim by Montgomery – or 'God Almonty' as the Canadians referred to him.[113] What is clear is that von Rundstedt, and the rest of the German High Command, were uncertain whether Normandy was the real invasion or just a large scale deception. Either way, it was preferable to keep the main German defences against the Anglo-Canadian forces at Caen because if it was a ruse they could be transferred faster from Caen than from the American beach-head further west. If it was not a ruse then the Caen defensive line blocked the direct route to Paris and Berlin. Moreover, since transportation was so difficult in Northern France, it was actually easier to move the German reinforcements around Paris and south of Normandy, the short distance to Caen rather than the longer distance to the Cherbourg region.[114] Bradley subsequently argued in defence of Montgomery that although 'in the minds of most people success in battle was measured in terms of mileage gained; the public would find it difficult to understand that the greater the hornets' nest was stirred up by Monty, the less he would advance'. Note here the contrast between the US metaphor for war – American football – where progress is measured in yards gained – and the British metaphor for war – cricket, where whichever side accumulates the highest total score is the eventual winner. More importantly, this then raises a problem for leadership because whether the eventual success of Bradley's breakout was a result of Montgomery's strategy or Bradley's skill depends upon which source one believes. But a greater problem is establishing whether the breakout was ever a result of any decision by a senior leader since there were so many variables and so many individual and collective actions that determined which way the course of the battle would go.

Part of the dispute hinges around the use of 'phase lines' by Montgomery in the April presentation of the final plan to the political and military leaders. Montgomery had marked in phase lines to suggest where he thought the Allies should have reached by certain days, finishing with them reaching the Seine on D-Day plus 90. Bradley thought they implied a level of rigidity which he disapproved of and he demanded that the lines be removed from the American forces. Montgomery also suggested, after the campaign, that it was obvious that the Germans would have to funnel their reinforcements through Caen and therefore it was the primary job of the Anglo-Canadian forces to stop them linking up with their colleagues further west who would be the primary target for the US forces (Montgomery, 1995: 106/8). D'Este (1983) claims that Montgomery's 'hinge' was indeed the original plan, as noted on 7 April, but it was intended to be unleashed at Falaise not Caen and Montgomery changed the plan retrospectively to maintain the myth of his invincibility. Indeed, as Gray concludes, given Montgomery's claims about Caen 'being taken by speed and aggression on D-Day itself ... there was no question of using the city as "a hinge" or maintaining a defensive posture on the flank'.[115]

Either way, since the weather in early June over the Channel was so poor the Germans decided that the invasion would not occur in the immediate future; the Allies could not have organized the weather – that indeed was an insoluble Wicked Problem – but they could, and did, take advantage of the uncertainty it offered.

2.7 The weather

Several issues were important to the competing strategies for control over Normandy but few were so indeterminate as the weather. Given the chances against the right wind, tides, light and cloud cover, the Allies' strategy hung precariously on the fickleness of the weather, even in summer. In fact, the significance of the weather – especially cloud cover that would prevent Allied aircraft from attacking the assumed Panzer counter-attacks – had persuaded Eisenhower to monitor the reliability of his weather experts for months beforehand, and twice a week in May Eisenhower tested the forecasts of his advisers. But the critical problem was that accuracy beyond 48 hours was difficult, yet at least that length of time was necessary to get the assault troops and the first reinforcements across the Channel.[116] What made the decision to go even more difficult was that the huge assembly of soldiers and machinery had to begin embarkation procedures several days before D-Day itself, when it was not self-evident that the invasion would occur within the next few days. Clearly the weather was a Wicked Problem, but it is important to consider two other related aspects of the weather. First the Germans misread the weather and allowed themselves to be misled by it. Second, Eisenhower's decision allowed the weather to lead them secretly across the English Channel.

On Sunday 28 May Captain James Stagg, the chief meteorologist of the RAF and the SHAEF Meteorological Unit ('Six feet two of Stagg, and six feet one of gloom' Admiral Creasy called him) forecast that 'mainly quiet wind conditions would continue during the coming week … . (Risk of a gale seemed rather small)'. When he was asked 'What will the weather be on D-Day in the Channel and over the French coast?' he replied; 'To answer that question would make me a guesser, not a meteorologist'.[117] By Wednesday 31 May he advised that prospects were not favourable for weather after Sunday 4 June. By Friday 2 June the 'present relatively quiet weather may end about Tuesday' (6 – D-Day), and 'no improvement – risk of Force 5 winds now forecast for Monday' was the summary of Saturday 3 June and D-Day was subsequently postponed for 24 hours.[118] So poor were the forecast conditions that it was commonly assumed to be the worst weather in June for 50 years.[119]

Nonetheless, loading for the groups furthest away, such as the 29th Division in Falmouth and Fowey, began on 31 May and for the next few days the south of England crawled with transports, troops, fear and adrenaline soaked anticipation. Eisenhower spoke of this time as the point at which 'the whole mighty host was tense as a coiled spring'[120] and twice a day he held a weather meetings at 2130 and 0400 using information relayed by the four Allied warships stationed in the Atlantic and by the six RAF Mosquito aircraft of No. 1409 (Meteorological Reconnaissance) Flight.[121] The reports were analysed at three different ground stations in the UK: the British Meteorological Office at Dunstable, the Admiralty in London and the US Army Air Force centre at Widewing, Teddington. From 1 June until 5 June the Widewing experts – using a method of comparison with prior weather maps – were as optimistic as the Meteorological Office, helped by a Norwegian,

Sverre Petterssen, and using wind and temperature observations from high altitude provide by the RAF, were pessimistic; the Admiralty usually favoured the centre line. Stagg, seconded from the Meteorological Office, leant heavily towards the Dunstable analysis.[122]

On the German side the weather information was sparse at best: the stations on Jan Mayen Island, Spitzbergen and on the Lofoten Islands had been destroyed, all the German ship stations had been sunk, and the U-boat fleet was unable to operate freely.[123] But on 2 June a storm lashed the Channel and it must have seemed self-evident to both sides that no invasion could take place. Certainly the German Chief Meteorologist, Colonel Professor Walter Stöbe forecast rain, cloud and high wind.[124] To Rommel, well aware that 5 to 7 June was a likely period for the invasion, the poor forecast all but eliminated the chance of an invasion. He assumed a good five clear days would be necessary – as they had been for all their previous amphibious landings, in North Africa, Sicily and Italy. Unfortunately for the Germans, unpredictability was almost the only predictable thing about the weather in the Channel and unpredictability has always been a primary ally of successful military leaders.[125]

By Saturday 3 June the forecasts from two of the ships in the Atlantic were completely contradictory but despite the calm weather in London, Stagg advised a postponement and this was confirmed by the 0415 meeting on the morning of 4 June: the wind was west, 3–4, backing south-west and increasing to force 5. Since some of the convoys had already set sail they were recalled. Section 'U2A' of the Utah convoy (each force had around 12 separate convoys divided into three or four sections) had left Salcombe at 1653 the previous day and had accumulated 138 ships in the course of its journey, including 128 LCTs. Four hours after the recall message had been sent it was 25 miles south of the Isle of Wight – just 38 miles from Normandy – before it was successfully intercepted.[126] Had this force continued and been spotted it is very likely that a catastrophe would have awaited the main invasion force. By the time this section eventually reached Omaha Beach some of the officers had been on the bridge for 70 hours without sleep – yet only seven of the 128 LCTs failed to make the final assault.[127]

The predicted 'storm' clearly did not reach some parts of the Normandy coast. Private Franz Gockel, a machine gunner overlooking Omaha Beach at the Colleville 'draw' or exit, reported on the evening of the 4th that 'nothing moved on the calm surface of the water'.[128] But by 5 June the wind off the eastern Normandy coast was between Force 4 and 5, the rain lashed down and German mine-layers had been forced back into harbour.[129] As far as the Germans were concerned there was no prospect of an invasion.

At 1745 on Sunday 4 June Stagg announced a 'substantial change ... It is now likely that there will be a fair interval starting about mid-day today and lasting till about dawn on Tuesday ... cloud amounts will probably be substantially smaller than given in the forecast this morning; winds will also moderate temporarily on Monday night and at first on Tuesday; weather on subsequent days will continue unsettled and disturbed'. At 2100 hours on the same evening Stagg announced 'some rapid and unexpected developments ... an interval of fair conditions which ... should last at least until dawn on Tuesday ... winds will be mainly Force 4 on the English Channel coasts and Force 3–4 on French Channel coasts'.[130]

What followed neatly encapsulates the collaborative process required for Wicked Problems, for still no technical or objective answer existed. Despite the cheering that followed Stagg's report, Leigh-Mallory advised a second postponement to help air-cover and bombing, but he was told by Eisenhower to stop being pessimistic. Montgomery advised him to go – though the predicted 36-hour window might have left only the first waves on the beaches and thus it would have been relatively easy for the Germans to push them back into the sea. But a further postponement would have meant delaying the invasion for several weeks – in fact until 17 or 18 June – just before the great storm lashed the Normandy coast on 19 June destroying the Mulberry harbour in the US sector. To have gone then would have been disastrous and to have delayed once more could have had a devastating effect upon Allied morale and may have allowed the Germans to realize the true intentions of the Allies. As it was, the landings took place in winds approaching Force 5 or even 6 in some places – though the exercises had been limited to Force 4 conditions.[131] Ironically, then, the indeterminacy of the weather led the Germans to conclude that an assault was impossible and led the Allies to believe that it was feasible. The weather, as it turned out, was better than the Germans expected and worse than the Allied hoped for and as a consequence the assault secured a remarkable ally. As Eisenhower said: 'Some soldier said the weather is always neutral. Nothing could be more untrue'. The weather was no friend of the Allied soldiers during the crossing but the very discomfort they suffered provided them with a degree of protection from the German defences that no prior bombing campaign could hope to match. At 2145 (4 June) Eisenhower, already suffering the immense strain of a supreme commander that, he argued, 'no-one could understand',[132] asked for his commanders' opinions as the rain poured down amidst the wild winds outside. Leigh-Mallory was still reluctant, while Montgomery remained keen but Ramsay reminded Eisenhower that either way a decision had to be made in 30 minutes or

the Navy would need another 48 hours notice. Eisenhower then summarized his decision: 'Well, I'm positive that we must give the order; the
only question is whether we should meet again in the morning. Well I
don't like it but there it is. Well boys there it is, I don't see how we can
possibly do anything else'.[133]

When Bradley, aboard the *Augusta*, was informed that the invasion
was on he was very worried about the weather prospects:

> That evening as I fell into bed worrying about the weather, I was quite uneasy on
> three counts:
>
> 1. Unless the wind and surf abated, they might swamp our DD tanks in their
>   unsheltered run to Omaha Beach. We had bargained on the shock effect of
>   those tanks. It would hurt us badly to lose them.
> 2. If the overcast were to prevent spotter aircraft from directing naval gunfire, we
>   might lose the effectiveness of our principal weapon in the initial assault.[134]
>   With but slight superiority in ground forces, we had banked heavily on this fire
>   support to help break through the water's edge defences. Fear of losing the
>   naval gunfire worried me more than the likelihood of a washout in heavy-
>   bomber missions.
> 3. The Channel could be distressingly cruel to GI stomachs. A heavy surf might
>   defeat our troops with sea-sickness before they landed.[135]

A further early morning weather meeting was planned for 0400 but by
2300 every vessel in the assorted fleets had been given the green light
and by midnight the convoys were moving. Eisenhower went back to his
trailer to sleep but was awoken at 0330 by the buffeting of the wind. The
planned 0400 meeting to consider recalling or confirming the invasion
began at 0415 – just as the rain and wind died away. Eisenhower listened
to his commanders once more and despite the fears of the air force leaders he was more concerned that a postponement would undermine both
morale and the secrecy they had worked so hard to maintain. Moreover,
he was also certain that the German defences would grow stronger with
each day and fearful that the German secret weapons might be able to
inflict terrible damage on the crowded British harbours.[136] Finally – and
after a full eight minutes of silence according to Air Vice Marshall Robb
– he announced: 'OK Let's go'.[137] He then went back to his trailer and
wrote out a press release for the possible failure of the landings:

> Our landings in the Cherbourg-Havre area have failed to gain a satisfactory
> foothold and I have withdrawn the troops. My decision to attack at this time and
> place was based upon the best information available. The troops, the air and the
> Navy did all that bravery and devotion to duty could do. If any blame or fault
> attaches to the attempt it is mine alone.[138]

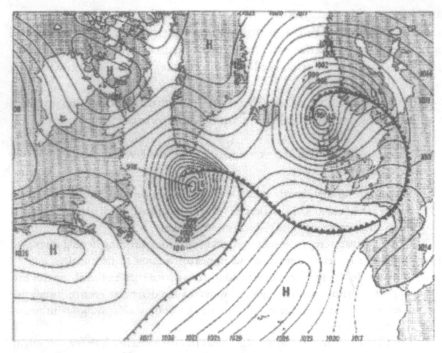

Source: www.metservice.co.nz/learning/weather_d_day.asp

Figure 2.1   Weather forecast for 5 June 1944

At about 0530 on D-Day an Allied plane reported conditions over Normandy to be 'shocking' with 'low cloud and heavy rain'.[139]

The poor weather might convince the Germans that an invasion was unlikely and it would help to impede the inevitable German response if they could be persuaded that Calais was the real target – an issue of strategic misleading that we will come to later. But another route was to remove the infrastructure that would allow the movement in the first place, in other words, to use aerial bombing to protect the landing beaches from both the armoured divisions and, equally important, the *Luftwaffe*.

3 Allied Air Strategy

3.1 Introduction

This chapter begins with an analysis of the American bombing strategy that focused upon oil production and then proceeds to evaluate the role of Operation Pointblank – the attempt to destroy the *Luftwaffe* before D-Day. In this, the strategy of the Allies was to fight and win a war of attrition – the boxer's approach – and it was remarkably successful if very expensive in Allied air crew. We then consider the effectiveness of the Transportation Plan design to disrupt the French rail and road system and how aerial and naval bombardments were supposed to destroy German coastal defences. The latter task was much less successful and can be attributed, in part, to the tardy nature of the political decision-making by strategic leaders and to the inability of commanders to recognize the limits of aerial bombing against fortified gun emplacements. Finally, the campaign to provide aerial cover for the invasion itself is reviewed. Once again it is often difficult to trace 'effects' back to individual strategic decisions made by leaders and, more than anything else, success can be traced back to the individual and collective decisions of thousands of pilots and air crew to do what they considered best at the time and in the space that they found themselves inhabiting.

3.2 The Oil Plan, Operation Pointblank and the destruction of the *Luftwaffe*

It may be recalled that one of the preconditions for a successful landing in France was domination of the skies and the prevention or interruption of German reinforcements to the battlefield. As ever, what at first appeared to be a relatively tame strategic requirement soon embroiled large numbers of Allied political and military leaders in all kinds of feuds about personal domination over resources and strategy. For the most part the Allied air leaders were unimpressed with the ground plans for D-Day, believing it an unnecessary and distracting sideshow from their priority – which was to bomb Germany into submission. This was not just a dispute about saving lives because the air commanders were already overseeing an air strategy that was decimating their own aircrews, it was also about the domination of the air forces over the armies, and in the American case of building a political case for the separation of the air force from the army. Nevertheless, air commanders were not the chiefs of staff nor were they able to dominate their political leaders so, in the end, they were forced to divert resources to support the invasion of Normandy; this was just as well because without the interdiction of German reinforcements and without the almost total air domination on D-Day by the Allies, it is very unlikely that the ground strategy would have worked.

In January 1944 Tedder and Solly Zuckerman – a British scientist who had observed the effects of bombing in the Mediterranean and concluded that bridges could not be successfully attacked from the air – drew up plans for a 90-day bombing campaign to destroy the French railway system and then to destroy the coastal defences. But the Allied air forces commanders were, at best, reluctant supporters of the Air-Strategy – the so called Transportation Plan – to support D-Day. Fortuitously, the leaders of both air forces were also very concerned that if the *Luftwaffe* was not ground into the dust in early 1944 then the development of the ME-262 jet fighter would render all their efforts futile. In that respect the leaders of both air forces were at one with Eisenhower.

Nevertheless, if D-Day seemed vital to Stalin, Roosevelt and Churchill it did not to General Carl Spaatz, leader of the US Eighth Air Force. Spaatz mirrored his airmen in his frequently unshaven and unkempt appearance and occasionally flew bombing missions with them as a nose-gunner. He also had his own strategy for winning the war: daylight precision bombing of the German industrial machine, especially its oil refining potential – the Oil Plan. Indeed, he claimed he could end the war in 30 days if he was given the resources to destroy German oil production and thus bring German industry and the *Luftwaffe* to a halt.[1] At a meeting on 25 March, however, Spaatz admitted that his plan would have no instant effect upon Germany and would therefore be of marginal value to the invasion. Eisenhower therefore supported Tedder's plan for interruption the transport system and, since it was Tedder's plan and not Leigh-Mallory's (whom Spaatz detested), Spaatz agreed.[2]

In fact, by D-Day German armaments manufacture was a third higher than the previous year and by July 1944 it had peaked at 45 per cent higher. In 1940 Germany had built 10,826 planes and by 1944 this had soared to 39,807. June 1944 also marked the peak production of tanks and U-boats. But oil production, especially the synthetic oil made from combining coal with hydrogen, was desperately short. By July 1944 only 53,000 tons was produced, just over a quarter of the May consumption total of 195,000 tons.[3] By 11 August 1944 the *Luftwaffe* was so short of oil that it prohibited all flights except those undertaken by fighter aircraft against Allied bombers.[4] Even these aircraft preserved what fuel they had by not starting their engines until positioned on the runway for takeoff – having been towed from the hangars by cows.[5]

By February 1944 the first leg of the Overlord aerial strategy, the Transportation Plan, had begun when Allied air forces were retargeted to destroy the German fighter industry, and although fighter production actually *increased* it was probably slowed by the bombing. That had been part of Spaatz's strategy since January 1944 when he had realized that simply attacking aircraft manufacturing plants was not going to destroy the *Luftwaffe*. This also explains his support for electronic technology that would facilitate daylight bombing under poor weather conditions: if he could continue to bomb German industrial targets in poor weather that would force the *Luftwaffe* up to defend them and hence increase the potential casualties the increasingly inexperienced pilots would suffer from risky landings and takeoffs. More significantly, the raids forced the *Luftwaffe* into the air to attack the bombers where they, in turn, were attacked by the Allied fighter protection. This classic war of attrition fits the Tame Problem criteria of known processes and prior expertise for it was the superior numbers, technology and experience of the Western Allies that prevailed over their under-resourced and ill-experienced German opponents.

Much of the technical superiority derived from the new American P-51 D Mustang fighter, quicker than, and as manoeuvrable as, the Spitfire but with a much greater range, at 2,300 miles, allowing it to cover the deepest Allied bomber raids into the heart of Germany.[6] The Allied bomber escorts, especially the more robust P-47 Thunderbolts, also began pro-actively seeking out German fighters either in the air or on the ground, rather than just reacting to their attacks. The results were devastating for the *Luftwaffe*: on just 14 missions between 8 March and 30 May, on average 56 German fighters were shot down. The declining quality of the *Luftwaffe* pilots is clear both from the asymmetric casualties and from the numbers brought down by individual American pilots: three pilots claimed four 'kills' and seven claimed three 'kills'. On 6 August Major George Preddy, the leading Mustang pilot, shot down six Me 109s.[7]

In fact, the number of hours flown by trainee *Luftwaffe* pilots before engaging in combat was about 170, only marginally more than half the 310 hours spent by US pilots in training. The consequences to the *Luftwaffe* were an ever-increasing attrition rate due to accidents and combat. In November 1943 an Allied report suggested that the *Luftwaffe* comprised 4,854 aircraft in total, with 1,968 on the western front, 1,771 on the eastern front, and 1,115 on the southern front. That suggested a huge loss over the year given that at least 25,000 German aircraft had been produced in that year. In contrast, the Western Allies had 8,351 aircraft available by May 1944.[8] In January 1944 the Germans lost 1,311 aircraft; by February the monthly loss was running at 2,121 and this included the deaths of 434 almost irreplaceable pilots (18 per cent). The so called 'Big Week', between 20 and 25 February 1944 resulted in the loss of almost 2,500 Allied air crew as 240 US bombers and 33 fighters were shot down but the attacks on German aircraft manufacturers broke the back of the *Luftwaffe*. This was not in terms of destroying the capacity to build aircraft, because the original 27 major factories had already been redistributed into 729 smaller construction units, and in 1944 alone the Germans managed to build 40,500 aircraft. But they could not replace the aircrew lost in defending the factories.[9] By the spring of 1944 the new 108-gallon drop tank fitted to the P-51b Mustang provided fighter cover all the way to Berlin and average Allied bomber loss rates fell from 20–25 per cent to just 6 per cent.[10] By March a further 2,115 *Luftwaffe* planes were destroyed, including 511 pilots killed (22 per cent).[11] The German pilot loss was 20 per cent in April, and 25 per cent in May.

This strategy ensured that German fighter aircraft losses were running at over 2,000 a month just prior to D-Day – twice the number of Allied losses in aircraft at this time and twice the rate at which new German fighter pilots could be trained.[12] In effect, in the first five months of 1944 the pilot turnover in the *Luftwaffe* was 99 per cent.[13] Between January 1944 and D-Day the *Luftwaffe* lost 6,259 planes in combat and roughly half that number in non-combat accidents.[14] From an average force of 2,283, the deaths in that six months amounted to 2,262. In the first two days of the invasion 200 fighters were moved from Germany to France, but the pilots had been trained for air defence not ground attack and within two weeks the Germans had lost another 594 aircraft.[15] In fact, the *Luftwaffe* was probably never short of planes – Cooper, for example, came across an airfield near Frankfurt in 1945 with roads running into some local woods wherein lay over 2,000 planes, including many Me109s, FW190s and Ju88s. The *Luftwaffe* ran out of pilots, ground crew and fuel but not planes.[16] Hence, the complaints of the German ground troops when they appeared to have been deserted by the *Luftwaffe* in their greatest hour of need should have been tempered by the realization that almost all the pilots that had protected them as they celebrated the beginning of the year were already dead. Adolf Galland, commander of the *Luftwaffe*'s fighter forces certainly argued that by

1944 the loss of pilots was far more important than the loss of planes, indeed Germany's greatest plane production occurred in September 1944 – but by this time Allied air attacks on oil plants and the Soviet assault on Romania had reduced German oil production to less than one third of its rate produced in June.[17] Moreover, so great was the demand for troops to defend Germany from Allied air attack that 900,000 were involved in the air defence system alone (search light, anti-aircraft batteries and radar facilities).[18]

As the Allied air crews shot the *Luftwaffe* out of the sky in the day time, Air Chief Marshal Sir Arthur Harris's RAF Bomber Command maintained its nightly assaults upon German *areas*, especially industrial cities, even proclaiming that if *his* plan was fully implemented a German surrender by April 1944 was 'inevitable'[19] while 'to divert Bomber Command from its true function would lead directly to disaster'.[20] Harris's appearance and style was the opposite of Spaatz's [to the extent that Harris never even visited his bomber stations] but his methods appeared, at least to him, to be equally effective: between November 1943 and March 1944 only 50 per cent of planned German aircraft production occurred.[21] The debate over the utility of strategic bombing of German industry need not delay us here; suffice to say that although German military output trebled between 1941 and 1944 – in line with the escalation of the bombing – Overy is surely right in his conclusion that the effect of bombing on the German economy was not to prevent a sustained increase in output, but to put a strict ceiling on that expansion.[22]

From 11 May for three weeks all known *Luftwaffe* maintenance and repair units within 150 miles of Caen were attacked incessantly. These included 40 operational airfields and 59 other aircraft repair facilities.[23] But the cost was high: in April and May 1944 the Allies had lost 12,000 aircrew and 2,000 planes to German fighters and anti-aircraft fire.[24]

Operation Pointblank – the destruction of the *Luftwaffe* – was profligate with the lives of Allied air crew whose average survival rate was down to 15 missions in 1943, with 25 per cent of aircraft struck by anti-aircraft fire on their first mission.[25] But the rewards were also high: by D-Day the *Luftwaffe* – which had promised to have 1,000 fighters in the air for the invasion – had only 319 operational aircraft within flying distance of Normandy: 88 bombers, 172 fighters and 59 reconnaissance aircraft to attack the invasion beaches.[26] Indeed, 124 of the fighters in the 26th Fighter Wing were moved *back* from the coast on the afternoon of 4 June, presumably in accordance with the German strategy of preserving aircraft from Allied air attack so that they could return once the invasion began.[27] Colonel Priller, commander of the 26th Fighter Wing, protested vehemently to his group commander about the move: 'This is crazy! If we're expecting an invasion the squadrons should be moved up not back! And what happens if the attack comes during the transfer? My supplies can't reach the new bases until tomorrow or maybe the day after. You're all crazy!'[28]

The Allies had 11,500 aircraft available on D-Day, including 3,800 fighters, and they hit Normandy exactly at the time that Priller forecast, but by then Priller's fighter wing had shrunk from 124 planes to just 2.[29] Early on the morning of D-Day Priller received a phone call from 2nd Fighter Corps HQ informing him that 'some sort of invasion is taking place. I suggest you put your wing on alert'. Priller was less than pleased: 'Who in hell am I supposed to alert? I'm alert. Wodarczyk is alert! But you fatheads *know* I only have two damned planes!'[30] Even if there had been more planes available to Priller it is not clear whether there would have been enough fuel available for anything like a constant assault upon the beaches because just the day before D-Day a message had demanded that only pre-authorized flights could take place, due to the 'renewed interference with (the) production of aircraft fuel by Allied action'.[31]

Thus the *Luftwaffe* was noticeable by its absence and by 1000 hours although German aircraft had been seen between 35 and 50 miles south off Le Havre none had ventured near the beaches and the Allies had only lost one plane, missing after being hit by ground-fire. As Lt General Dihm, Special Assistant to Rommel suggested after the war:

> Except for this air supremacy, it would have been possible, in my opinion, to prevent a successful invasion during the first days after the initial assault. These were the most critical days for the Allies. Later, the constant and increasing reinforcement of the Allies could be less and less equalized by the arrival of German reinforcements, hindered by the destruction of important traffic routes.[32]

In fact, the *Luftwaffe* had made several attempts to attack the beaches but seldom penetrated the defensive cover provided by the Allied air forces. For example, the 3rd Airforce (covering France, Belgium and the Netherlands) group of Ground Attack Aircraft had two squadrons of Focke-Wulf FW 190s and was responsible for virtually all the ground attack missions over the Normandy beaches of D-Day. Five were shot down as they moved forward from Saint Quentin to their forward base at Laval on the morning of 6 June. In the afternoon, 13 aircraft set out to attack the British on Sword Beach but all bar two planes were driven off by fighter cover. The two that made it had no time to assess whether they had inflicted any damage with their bombs. The following day 24 FW 190s again headed for Sword and this time none managed to get through. In the meantime two FW 190s were shot down by Mustangs and four were destroyed in an attack upon Laval airfield. On D-Day+2 three attacks were launched against the beaches and none got through, though one FW 190 was shot down. D-Day+3 saw six FW 190s and two ME 109s destroyed for no palpable gain and the 3rd Group was stood down to await reinforcements since they had run out of aircraft.[33]

The German fighter cover was provided primarily by the 168 Me 109s and FW 190s of the 1st Group of the II Fighter Corps (*Jagdkorps*) from Le Mans airfield (200 more planes arrived on D-Day+2 and a further 100 on D-Day+3). These planes had virtually no radar assistance by D-Day and by D-Day+3 all the planes were fitted with a 550lb bomb for attacks on the ships off the coast – but none of the pilots had any experience in ground attack operations and no ship was hit in either the attacks of 8 or 9 June. On 10 June the airfield at Le Mans was bombed by the RAF and half the planes were destroyed on the ground, the rest had to move to Alençon. In the following week the 1st Group of the 2nd *Jagdkorps* claimed to have shot down 12 Allied planes for the loss of nine of their own pilots (25 per cent of their D-Day strength).[34]

In the event the Germans claimed to have made 319 sorties on D-Day though Allied figures put the number much lower with only 36 over the Anglo-Canadian beaches, and of these seven were shot down, while the US 9th Air Force shot five more down. When four Ju-88s did appear briefly over Omaha at dusk on D-Day one was immediately shot down by anti-aircraft fire from the ships and the other three fled the scene. Off Gold Beach LCF2 (Landing Craft Flak) shot down a German fighter on D-Day[35] while beach balloons on the US beaches brought down one fighter and the 474th AAA shot down a P 51 with 'friendly fire' on D-Day+1 off the American beaches. So good was the information from Ultra by this time that warnings of three *Luftwaffe* raids were received by the beach commanders before the planes appeared – one raid arriving four hours after information was received that it had been ordered.[36] Despite this, the HQ ship for co-ordinating fighter-cover against incoming *Luftwaffe* attacks, HMS Bulolo, was itself bombed on 7 June in an attack which killed three officers – although the FW 190 that made the attack was itself shot down by anti-aircraft fire from other ships.[37] Only one other German attack caused any significant damage when a single FW109 destroyed over 100,000 gallons of fuel and 400 tons of ammunition stored on Sword Beach on D-Day+1. On the Allied side 14,000 sorties were flown and 127 aircraft shot down.[38]

The results of the destruction of the *Luftwaffe* were evident not just on D-Day but for several weeks afterwards. When the breakout through St Lô was being organized the US army had 4,400 vehicles in an area of about one square mile. This was contrary to all traditional tactics which demanded the dispersal of vehicles to minimize air attacks – but since the chances of these were so small the armour and transport simply used the area as a gigantic overnight tank and vehicle parking lot.[39]

In contrast, so effective was the Allied air force that, providing the weather was suitable and communications operational, an Allied air attack could be called within minutes. For example, Cooper recalls during an early phase of the St Lô breakout suddenly finding his unit, armed only with a 57mm anti-tank gun facing a Panther tank.[40] The unit commander immediately called for an air strike which his air force liaison officer organized. Within 45 seconds two P 51 Mustang fighter-bombers arrived and destroyed the tank.

Nevertheless, the Allied fighter bombers which did so much damage to the *Wehrmacht* were themselves very vulnerable to ground fire and often at a considerable disadvantage when attacked by their lighter-loaded *Luftwaffe* opponents. Some 248 American pilots were lost in the month after D-Day, including 30 out of 70 P 47 pilots from one formation. Of the 280 RAF Typhoons lost between June and September 1944 only 25 were known to have been shot down by German fighters; the rest are presumed to have been hit by ground fire.[41]

3.3 The Transport Plan

Getting the bomber chiefs to agree amongst themselves about strategy – a Wicked Problem – was hard enough but getting them to switch from attacking the *Luftwaffe* to attacking the French transport system was far more difficult. Initially, since neither the American nor the British bomber groups were under Eisenhower's formal command at SHAEF, he could do little to persuade them to change, and he wrote to Marshall that he was tired 'of trying to arrange the blankets smoothly over several prima donnas in the same bed'.[42] Nor was he helped by Churchill or the British Cabinet who refused to countenance the handover of RAF bomber command to SHAEF. Thus on the one hand the Oil Plan was condemned (primarily by the British) because of the difficulties of reaching the targets, many of which were in the heavily defended Ruhr or Berlin areas. The Transportation Plan, on the other hand, was condemned (primarily by the Americans) because the French and Belgian railways were not being used to their full capacity by the Germans anyway, hence the elimination of some elements would merely remove excess capacity.[43] And because the French railway system was so dense, even successful bombing would have difficulty in completing the interdiction. As one Allied intelligence report insisted: 'Hitler had three times the rail capacity needed for military traffic, four times the required numbers of cars, eight times the required locomotives, and ten times the required servicing facilities'.[44]

Eisenhower, exasperated by the actions of his so-called allies, threatened to resign his 'command' saying: 'I will tell the Prime Minister to get someone else to run this damn war. I'll quit!'[45] Subsequently, both air commanders acceded to his demands – though they replaced the word 'command' with 'supervision' in an effort to limit Eisenhower's control which effectively ensured that they would accept Eisenhower's requirements but not release their planes to his air commander, Leigh-Mallory. On 22 March Eisenhower told Churchill that he wasn't threatening to resign this time, he was actually going home. Only on 14 April, six weeks after Leigh-Mallory had planned to take control over the strategic bombers, and only seven weeks before D-Day, an agreement emerged, and the word 'direction' magically appeared to replace the word 'supervision' on the final agreement. But the compromise ensured that the air interdiction of Normandy by heavy bombers remained in the hands of Spaatz and Harris. Spaatz also threatened to resign if he was not allowed to continue attacking German oil installations.[46]

Even then Churchill refused to agree to the bombing if it meant killing large numbers of innocent French civilians – which the British government estimated at between 80,000 and 160,000. He also remained unmoved by Eisenhower's pleas, demanding instead an alternative plan that would limit the French casualties to around 100 per target (having revised the total possible casualties of the original plan down to between 10,000 and 15,000). Churchill even wrote to Roosevelt suggesting that the plan be ditched because of the 'slaughter' (a word used four times) of French civilians that would result.[47]

Roosevelt's reply on 11 May was uncompromising. 'However regrettable the attendant loss of civilian lives is, I am not prepared to impose from this distance any restriction on military action by the responsible commanders that in their opinion might militate against the success of 'Overlord' or cause additional loss of life to our Allied forces of invasion'.[48] Even General Koenig, commander of the French forces in Britain, accepted that the inevitable French casualties would be the price the French would have to pay to escape their bondage, and with that Churchill finally acceded.[49]

The strategic bombing leaders, then, were not simply engaged in a turf war over control of their own resources, or simply in a competition to win the war single-handed. Spaatz, and particularly Harris, insisted that the kinds of targets Zuckerman required to be hit in the Transportation Plan were simply beyond the capabilities of strategic bombers. What particularly riled Spaatz was Leigh-Mallory's insistence that the defeat of the *Luftwaffe* was not a *prerequisite* for Overlord because it would occur *during* Overlord. In other words, Leigh-Mallory assumed that dog-fights over the beaches would be the place where the *Luftwaffe* was destroyed. Spaatz was adamant that this would be too late and too dangerous – though he admitted that many battles over Normandy were expected.

Spaatz was also convinced that since there were fewer oil targets than railway targets, and since they both required the same tonnage of bombs for destruction, it made more sense to go for oil than for transportation. Moreover, since only a fraction of the traffic on the railways was military, even the destruction of most of it would not necessarily hinder military transportation. But at the final meeting on 25 March Eisenhower sided with the Transportation Plan over the Oil Plan and Spaatz and Harris were forced to come into line.

To assuage those who remained doubtful about the viability of precision bombing of rail centres, and those who remained concerned about the effect of civilian casualties, the Chief of the Air Staff, Air Chief Marshal Tedder, proposed a test raid on Trappes, west of Paris, which took place on the evening of 6 March. The rail centre was inoperative for a month afterwards but the raid on Le Mans on 7 March resulted in 31 French civilian deaths and the sudden appearance of anti-British graffiti. Despite this, a further 78 rail centres were bombed between then and D-Day with 51 rendered out of action, 25 regarded as severely damaged but requiring a further raid, and four considered to be still fully operational requiring an immediate second attack. The most significant losses occurred in an attack upon the rail centre at Lille by over 500 aircraft in which 456 French civilians died, at Noisy-le-Sec (north-east Paris) where 464 deaths were recorded, and at Ghent where 428 Belgians were killed. Subsequent attacks used 'Master Bombers' who marked the target and who sometimes aborted raids if the marking flares were inaccurate. Most of the raids managed to keep civilian deaths down to between 100 and 150 and some were extremely accurate. For instance, the attack upon Chambly (north of Paris) on the evening of 1 May by 120 aircraft resulted in 500 bombs hitting the target and only five reported civilian deaths.[50] Where railway centres were situated in heavily populated areas (for instance at Le Bourget) areas adjacent to the centres were sometimes targeted instead. But to ensure that no indication of the invasion area was given away by the pattern of bombing every target within the invasion zone was matched by two attacks outside the zone.[51]

By then the Transportation Plan was beginning to take effect. In May 1944 von Rundstedt was informed that only 32 out of every 100 German military trains was getting through the disrupted French railway system, though only four of the 80 targets in France had not been hit.[52] Equally important, on 8 May the German military supreme command – *Oberkommando der Wehrmacht* (OKW) – approved the withdrawal of 10,000 members of the Todt Organization from construction duties on the Atlantic Wall to repair duties on the French railways. A further 18,000 were withdrawn just before D-Day.[53]

However, at this point Spaatz suggested that, contrary to Zuckerman's analysis of the Mediterranean attacks, it was possible to destroy bridges from the air, albeit with tactical fighter-bombers not strategic heavy bombers. Such an approach would also minimize civilian casualties while achieving the same unhinging of German transportation that the original Transportation Plan sought. On 7 May, just less than a month before D-Day, Spaatz plans were tried out on the Seine Bridge at Vernon with great success. Thereafter bridge attacks became an essential component of, rather than a replacement for, the Transportation Plan.[54]

Most of this activity was undertaken by the Allied Expeditionary Air Force (formed to co-ordinate the 'immediate and direct support of the land battle'),[55] either in the form of the 2nd Tactical Air Force (TAF) or the Air Defence of Great Britain (ADGB). The TAF was an offensive-oriented body, designed to concentrate on cross-Channel actions. The ADGB's primary task was defensive, protecting the airfields, bomber bases and shipping of the Allies.[56]

Fighter-bomber attacks against trains and locomotives in France and Belgium, as opposed to medium and heavy bomber attacks upon railway lines and centres, were inaugurated on 21 May 1944. On this single day 504 Thunderbolts, 233 Spitfires and Typhoons and ten Tempests of the AEAF claimed 67 locomotives destroyed and 91 damaged. The 8th Air Force Fighter Command sent 131 Lightnings, 135 Thunderbolts and 287 Mustangs and claimed 95 locomotives destroyed and 134 damaged.[57] In these two weeks before D-Day the 'Chattanooga Choo-Choo' missions of the 9th Tactical Air Command's fighter-bombers under Major-General Quesada wrought havoc: the first mission on 21 May 1944 involved 617 fighters, 27 of which did not return. But the damage caused to the Germans was considerable: 225 locomotives were attacked and 91 destroyed, 83 aircraft were destroyed on the ground and 20 shot down in the air. By D-Day they had destroyed 475 locomotives and cut railway lines in 150 places.[58]

Sealing off the invasion area from the south and east was also regarded as critical for two different reasons. First, it would prevent the build up of reserves and reinforcements. Second, it would cut off the existing German troops within Normandy and enable the Allies to destroy a significant proportion of them. Initially attacks on bridges were deemed difficult because experience in Italy had demonstrated that at least 600 tons of bombs were needed to destroy any bridge using medium or heavy bombers. However, Leigh-Mallory's fighter-bombers of the AEAF had demonstrated in experimental attacks that a bridge could be destroyed using around 100 sorties and 100–200 tons of bombs. To avoid arousing suspicion the bridges over the Loire sealing off Normandy from the south were not attacked until after D-Day but from 21 April bridges in France and Belgium received particular attention.[59]

The overall results of the shift from the Oil Plan to the Transportation Plan were significant. By D-Day 76,000 tons of bombs had landed on French railway targets alone, destroying 12 rail bridges and 12 road bridges across the Seine (though not, inexplicably, barge traffic along the Seine), reducing the rail traffic west of Paris by almost two-thirds, though only about 10 per cent of the rolling stock had been eliminated.[60] In fact, until the Transportation Plan was implemented, the French Resistance were much more effective at destroying trains (808 between January and March 1944) than any strategic bombing from the air,[61] though much of the most effective destruction was wrought by the fighter-bombers under Leigh-Mallory's overall control.[62]

By mid-May 1944 rail traffic between France and Germany had fallen by 50 per cent; rail traffic inside France was reduced to 20 per cent and between March and June 1944 1,500 French locomotives were destroyed.[63] Perhaps a good example of the significance of the bombing campaign can be gauged from the actions of the 9th SS Panzer and 10th SS Panzer, forming the II SS Panzer Corps, which was intended to form the spearhead of an armoured counter-attack against the Allies. Since the tracks of German tanks wore out five times quicker than the Allies' equivalent, they were always transported by rail where possible, and on 12 June they left the Polish-Russian border to head west. They travelled across Poland and Germany to reach France in four days – but it took another ten to get across France.[64] Although German tank production remained high, and could have replaced the losses suffered in Normandy, it was simply impossible to transport the tanks there.[65] Thus by the middle of June only 15 per cent of German daily expenditure of fuel and munitions was arriving at the front and by the end of June only just over one third of munitions that had been sent had actually arrived.[66]

3.4 Coastal defences

Attacks upon the coastal batteries began on 10 April, and by D-Day all 49 of the known installations in the assault area had been bombed, as well as twice that number outside the area, as far north as Ostend. Leigh-Mallory was not optimistic that bombing would destroy the already completed batteries – since they had been designed to withstand precisely the kind of attacks he planned – but luckily those close to Cherbourg were the last to be completed and many were damaged or destroyed before they were completed. By D-Day 8,765 sorties had dropped 23,049 tons of bombs and fired 495 60-pound rockets. Of the 40 batteries allocated to the AEAF, 38 were attacked and 23 received direct hits on one or more emplacements. The largest guns were at Le Grand Clos, near Le Havre, which was designed to house three 15-inch (380mm) guns with a range of 55 kilometres – that is capable of firing on all the Anglo-Canadian beaches. Fortunately only one gun had been installed by D-Day.[67] In fact, Bomber Command was well aware of the difficulties of destroying casemated gun positions. The 12,000lb 'Tallboy' Deep Penetration (DP) bombs, capable of penetrating to great depths before exploding, were just becoming available but they were in short supply and very expensive, thus the decision was made to use conventional high explosive bombs to 'discourage' the German defenders, even if the guns could not be destroyed. Subsequent interrogation of German gunners by the RAF suggested that conventional bombs could never have penetrated the strongest casemated gun positions.[68]

Precisely what guns were in position in which battery remains a perennial controversy. For example, according to Dunphie and Johnson, the St Marcouf battery housed three 210mm guns with a range of 27km in 13 feet of reinforced concrete, one 150mm gun, six anti-aircraft guns and four 20mm guns, all operated by 287 soldiers, 7 NCOs and 3 officers.[69] Holt and Holt, on the other hand, suggest there were two 155mm, six 75mm guns, three 21mm and three 20mm guns.[70] Whatever the weaponry involved, the battery sank one destroyer and damaged several other warships before being bombarded from the sea. Nevertheless, the garrison held out until 12 June. The adjoining battery at d'Azeville was captured on 9 June by Private Riley, 22nd US Infantry Division, whose flame thrower assault ignited ammunition inside the building, forcing 169 Germans to surrender.

Besides the gun batteries there were also 92 radar stations operating along the coast and between 10 May and 5 June Typhoons carried out 604 low-level sorties and fired over 4,500 rockets, while Spitfires and 'Bomphoons' (bomb-carrying Typhoons) had launched 759 attacks.[71] By 3 June the 12 primary radar sites of the 39 within the invasion area were extensively damaged, as were the two navigation sites at Sortosville and Lanmeur. On D-Day only 18 of the 92 radar sites operated normally and none of these were within the invasion zone.[72]

At 0000 hours, 6 June, 1,333 heavy bombers began attacking the coastal defences, and as the light progressed so the shift to the medium and light bombers of the USAAF occurred. The final bombing plan was agreed so late that only ten major batteries were targeted by the heavy bombers, each receiving 500 tons of bombs on the evening of 5 June.[73] Even this agreement was wrung from Spaatz with deep foreboding because heavy bombers simply did not have the capability of hitting such small targets from the great heights they operated from. Spaatz, ever-concerned to minimize 'friendly fire' casualties, insisted that the first waves of landing craft delay their approach to give the bombers a chance to do their work accurately but the ground commanders insisted on the original timings. Thus the American bombers were instructed to delay their drops until certain that no Allied troops would be hit – and as a consequence almost no troops of either side were hit where that delay was compounded by the low cloud cover over Omaha Beach.[74]

All told, over 5,000 bombers and nearly 5,500 fighters were in the air on D-Day; none was shot down by the *Luftwaffe* though 113 were shot down by anti-aircraft fire. If the light was good the bombing was due to stop five minutes before the first landing; if the light was bad it was extended to ten minutes. Neither the sea nor the air bombardment was as thoroughly planned as they should have been. First because the air forces were reluctant to commit themselves until very late in the planning timetable and second because the responsibility for deciding *what* was necessary lay with the army but the responsibility for *how* that was executed remained with the navy and the air force. The result was a generally weak and poorly executed plan. For instance, at Omaha Beach, the B-17 Flying Fortresses were to drop their sixteen 500lb bombs from 20,000 feet, a height that made accuracy through cloud cover virtually impossible. In theory this was less an attempt to destroy the concrete bunkers than to kill and bewilder the defenders.[75] They were followed by B-24 Liberators due to fly at 500 feet and drop 1,285 tons, many of them small 100lb bombs over the beaches to leave plenty of craters and debris to protect the attacking troops. In the event the B-26 Marauders that attacked Utah proved much more effective than the B-24 attacks upon Omaha, Gold, Juno and Sword and in general the air attacks were disappointing.[76] Particularly ineffective were the attacks upon 13 critical defensive positions on Omaha for the poor visibility dissuaded the pilots from dropping their bombs until they were well past their own troops – in fact 3 miles inland.

The naval bombardment that took up when the bombers had left was itself a complex plan of operations. The targets, the timings and the number of rounds fired were all established in advance, and once the landings commenced the bombardment would move inland and then provide fire support for the assault troops. Thus it was designed to achieve three aims. First, to neutralize whatever inland batteries the bombers failed to destroy. It was always assumed that the heavy concrete emplacements would protect the defenders from all but a direct hit but it was also assumed that a shocked gun-crew and a disrupted ammunition supply would provide the attackers with enough time to get ashore relatively unscathed. Second, the ships would concentrate their fire on the beach strong-points. Third, just before the landings themselves, the ships, including the destroyers and particularly the rocket ships, would provide 'drenching fire' to deter any defender from firing upon the attackers. The destroyers were allocated to specific beach areas and given relative freedom to fire upon whatever targets of opportunity arose.

Rather different approaches to beach-firing were adopted by the American and British forces. The US tended to provide what might be called a short 'thin' drenching by air and sea over the whole of Utah and Omaha Beach, whereas the British opted for a long 'thick' drenching at specific strong-points, leaving some areas virtually untouched. Rear-Admiral Vian subsequently accepted that the problems at Omaha were partly a consequence of the failure of thin drenching fire.[77]

Rather more effective seems to have been the bombardment from the warships that opened up after the bombers had left to silence whatever was left of the German strong-points, which unhappily for the approaching troops on Omaha was just about everything. Inland, for example, at Longues-sur-Mer, four 155mm cannon strongly encased in concrete had withstood the 1,500 tons of pre-invasion bombing and began shelling the Allied battleships at 0557 without success, though the first salvo straddled the HMS Bulolo – the flag ship of the Commander of Assault Force off Gold Beach, Commodore Douglas-Pennant.

Within 23 minutes HMS Ajax silenced the battery from 11 kilometres off-shore – about the same distance that the British troops reached in the other direction by the end of D-Day. Later that morning the battery resumed shelling and was finally silenced by HMS Argonaut, and then captured by C Company, 1st Battalion The Hampshire Regiment. Subsequent inspection revealed that 150 six-inch and 29 five-and-a-half-inch shells had fallen around the target area, two of the four guns had received direct hits and the casement of a third had been hit.[78]

The accuracy and distance of the naval fire (targets 17 miles inland were hit) was primarily assured through the activities of the 104 spotter aircraft and 39 Forward Observer Bombardment parties (naval personnel with radio communication for shore to ship). Indeed Rommel subsequently accepted that 'our operations in Normandy (were) tremendously

Photo 3.1 Gun emplacement at Longues Battery

Photo 3.2 Observation post at Longues Battery

Photo 3.3 Longues Battery from the west

hampered ... by the superiority of the enemy air force (and) the effect of the heavy naval guns'.[79] By 0930 all the major German batteries had been hit, though there was some sporadic fire throughout the day. Most of the damage to the landings from large artillery was achieved through mobile guns hidden in woods that proved difficult to track down.[80]

3.5 Air cover

The provision of air cover was anything but a simple deployment of the massive superiority achieved by D-Day. To secure that meant, amongst other things, integrating the USAAF and RAF administration where required, re-equipping 110 RAF squadrons with modern aircraft and ensuring the total staff involved (232,000 British and 181,000 Americans) were trained and in the right place do their jobs.

It was assumed that many enemy airfields would be damaged in capture or sabotaged so planning replacement landing strips began in December 1942 with photographic reconnaissance for the five levels of airfield required:

- Emergency Landing Strips (ELS) – minimum length 1,800 feet.
- Refuelling and Rearming Strips (RRS) – minimum length 3,600 feet with provision for rearming and refuelling.
- Advanced Landing Ground (ALG) – an upgraded RRS to provide temporary accommodation to alternate squadrons.

- Airfield – an upgraded ALG with permanent squadrons.
- All Weather Airfield – an airfield with hardened surface (these included any captured enemy airfields that were either undamaged or where the damage was minimal). The hardened surface was either Square Mesh Track (SMT) – rather like large scale chicken wire) or Pierced Steel Plank (PSP).

By early 1943, as a consequence of lessons learned in the desert war, a system for establishing tactical fighter squadrons as close to the front as possible was developed and tested in England in March 1943 and perfected within a year.[81] It was assumed that three ELSs would be required on D-Day itself, four RRSs by D+4, ten ALGs by D+8, 18 airfields by D+14, and 93 by D+90. Eighteen American and six British airfield construction units were formed to build them and though no ELS was built on D-Day there were three available by D+1 and by D+90 89 of the 93 planned airfields were built.[82] All the early strips near the coast were built parallel to each other to minimize collisions on takeoff and landing because they were often only a mile or two apart.

It was also always assumed by the Allies, despite the intense air war of attrition to grind down the *Luftwaffe* in the run-up to D-Day, that at least a week of intense air attacks upon the invasion forces was inevitable. Hence the 40 airfields within a 130-mile radius of the Norman coast line were attacked along with the usual bombing attacks from 10 May. As a result between 1 April and 5 June over 2,650 German aircraft were destroyed.

In the end the Allied air cover plan for D-Day itself, as opposed to the Transportation Plan, was not finally agreed until just 36 hours before the invasion.[83] That meant that many of the ships were actually at sea before an agreed plan for air cover was in place.[84] The air cover element of Overlord was designed 'to attain and maintain an air situation which would assure freedom of action for our Forces without effective interference by enemy air forces and to render air support to our Land and Naval Forces in the achievement of this objective'.[85]

The plan called for several phases. First, the interdiction of enemy naval and air assets in the Channel region. Second, the destruction of targets associated with the invasion (fortresses, naval facilities, radar installations and all forms of communication and transport) – still with an overwhelming emphasis on the Pas de Calais. Third, the move to defend the invasion proper, with 54 squadrons covering the beaches, 15 squadrons protecting the fleet, 33 fighter squadrons on bomber escort duties, 36 bomber squadrons providing land support to the land battle, and seven fighter squadrons providing fire-control.[86] The 2nd Tactical Air

Force also provided 11 rocket-firing Typhoon squadrons and seven Bombphoon squadrons to attack beach defences 20 minutes before the troops landed and to destroy any close target that came to hand. They were first called on for help at 0734 to attack the HQ of the German 84th Corps near St Lô but no major request for concerted action came until almost 1500 when the movement of armour towards Caen and Bayeux was reported. In fact two major problems for the Typhoons were their limited ability to communicate directly with the beach commanders initially, as well as their limited range and time over the target. The latter problem was more easily addressed than the former and a rapid switch was made to reduce the payload of the aircraft and increase the number of drop fuel tanks. On D-Day+7 reports came in from Port en Bessin that Allied troops were being bombed by Typhoons but it was subsequently determined that the Typhoon pilots were merely shedding their empty fuel tanks.[87]

In theory, the former problem should have been resolved by truck mounted radar and radio equipment operated from the beaches to direct fighter cover but much of it was destroyed, especially on Omaha where half the air-ground liaison parties were unable to operate. The fragile communication link from beach liaison group to Fire Direction Tenders (FDT) to beach HQ ships to Portsmouth and then to Uxbridge simply could not operate in the conditions that prevailed. Indeed, at one time a request from a general on board the USS Augusta took 30 minutes to reach Uxbridge. By 1315 on D-Day General Quesada delegated responsibility for his 1,500 US planes over the beaches from himself down to the two colonels operating on HQ ships directly off Omaha and Utah and it was this switch that allowed the 358th Fighter Group to intercept and destroy 80 per cent of the German 6th Parachute Regiment under von der Heydte at Isigny on its way to the beach between Utah and Omaha.[88] Here was an unusual illustration of a formal leader ceding control and having a significant and traceable effect.

Four squadrons of Lightnings (about 16 aircraft per squadron) were allocated to cover the shipping lanes during daylight and six Mosquito squadrons took over for night protection. Given the propensity for German air attack at dawn and dusk 12 US, and 12 British, fighter squadrons operated at these times over the whole area. In daylight nine fighter squadrons were allotted to cover the beach and assault areas: six Spitfire squadrons for low cover and three Thunderbolt squadrons for high cover. Two Spitfire squadrons covered the British-Canadian beaches while a third covered the American beaches. Two further Spitfire squadrons patrolled the eastern and western flanks and the three Thunderbolt squadrons were strung out across the entire invasion area and up to ten miles inland. All the aircraft were controlled from the Combined Control Centre at Uxbridge and thence through three Fighter Direction Tenders operated just off the Normandy coast.[89]

The naval gunfire spotting aircraft (two squadrons of Spitfires and six squadrons of [RAF] Mustangs plus the Fleet Air Arm's own Seafire aircraft) were in direct contact with their allocated ships.[90] For example, HMS Glasgow, the British cruiser firing on St Laurent behind Easy Green Beach on Omaha, was in regular contact with its spotter plane, a Mustang flown by Flt Lt Weighill. But not everything went so well: an RAF Mustang exploded in mid-air off Sword Beach at Lion-sur-Mer, probably hit by one of the naval shells it was supposed to be tracking.[91] Overall, 394 spotting sorties were mounted on D-Day itself and between 6 and 19 June 1,318 spotting sorties were flown at the cost of five aircraft.[92]

We can surmise from this review that although it looked as though Allied domination was inevitable, given the *Luftwaffe* losses in the previous months, in reality the political disputes between the Allied commanders could quite easily have forced Eisenhower to resign or left the invasion without adequate protection or possibly made an invasion unnecessary. In hindsight air superiority played a major role in ensuring a successful invasion but hindsight is blind to the precarious nature of the unfolding of events. If, for example, the German Panzer reinforcements had been allowed to reach the beaches within 24 hours of D-Day it is not at all self-evident that the Allies would have been able to resist them. But depriving the German tanks of spatial freedom facilitated the Allies taking advantage of time to build up their reinforcements instead. So weak was the German reaction to the bombing campaign on the night of 5 June that only 54 German aircraft took off and 53 of these stayed outside the invasion area. Only 1 per cent of British aircraft that took part in the night campaign failed to return. Indeed, while fears of heavy bomber losses in the first two days after D-Day were rife, the numbers available to the RAF's Bomber Command on 5 June were 1,795, by 7 June the total strength was down by just one.[93]

3.6 Conclusion

This chapter considered the varying degrees of success with which the Allies' air strategy facilitated the invasion on D-Day. At the heart of the issue lay significant political disputes between the various leaders about the best strategy and so deep were the divisions that some vital aspects were inadequately executed. Thus, for example, although the plan to destroy the *Luftwaffe* was carried out effectively, guaranteeing almost total air superiority on D-Day, the bombing of coastal defences was inadequate at best and almost fatal on Omaha Beach. Even when the military leaders were bent into submission by their political overlords, there was still significant dispute within the political leadership, especially over the number of French casualties that could be inflicted by bombing raids on the French transport system. But where the Allied political and military leadership engaged in vigorous debates and disputes, some of which were decidedly counter-productive, as we are about to see, the domination of decision-making by Hitler and the German military leadership, against the suggestions of their subordinates, effectively undermined the ability of the *Wehrmacht* and what was left of the *Luftwaffe* to attack the invaders with any degree of success. But if the hard power of the air forces played a significant role in isolating the landing area and destroying the *Luftwaffe* what role did the soft power of disinformation play in securing a respite for the soldiers clinging desperately to a thin crust of the Normandy coastline?

4 Planning to Mislead

> Great part of the information obtained in War is contradictory, a still greater part is false, and by far the greatest part is of a doubtful character .... . This difficulty of seeing things correctly ... is one of the greatest sources of friction in War.[1]

4.1 Introduction

In theory Overlord could well have failed: despite the planning expertise available to the Western Allies the invasion remained untameable: it remained a Wicked Problem simply because it was not possible to predict whether the German response would be scissor, paper or stone. The Germans had more troops and armour in the area than the Allies would be able to land for several weeks. The German defences would have – and indeed had – several hours' notification that the invasion was on its way and had known that an invasion was imminent for long enough to move submarines, E-boats and aircraft near enough to cause havoc with the armada. Even a successful initial landing could well have been repulsed within 48 hours by the movement of Panzer and infantry forces close to the beaches or within a week by the movement of German reinforcements from the 15th Army encamped around Calais. That the Allies succeeded was the result of both luck and skill on their part, particularly involving relatively junior officers and troops, and ineptitude on the part of the German High Command who were not rescued by their senior officers. This chapter considers the role that information and misinformation played in leading the defenders astray. In short, leadership was critical not just in successfully leading the Allies to and across the beaches of Normandy but also in *mis*leading the defenders away from those same beaches. However, the successful 'leadership' that made the most difference was not that deployed by Churchill or Eisenhower but by an array of leaders doing small things on the ground; and if Hitler's role in bungling the German response was important, he was not alone because it was a collective failure of leadership that encouraged the German forces to be deceived. And that collective failure implies that there were several opportunities to turn events around, but few were taken.

Five aspects of intelligence gathering and distribution were critical to the success of Overlord:

- Operation Fortitude
- the double agents
- Ultra
- the French Resistance, and
- the German responses.

4.2 Operation Fortitude: a bodyguard of lies

Of the problems facing the planners the most Wicked was how to prevent the Germans from moving reinforcements to Normandy from elsewhere in north-west Europe, especially northern France. The Germans had long regarded the region directly opposite Dover, the Pas de Calais, as the most obvious site for an invasion because it offered the shortest sea route and provided the optimum air cover for the Allies. Thus the *Wehrmacht* stationed the bulk of its forces in and around this area and left a much weaker force defending Normandy. They remained committed to this false assumption, and refused to redeploy elements of the 15th Army south to Normandy for weeks after the landings, thereby denuding the resources of the hard pressed 7th Army and allowing the Allies to secure a local advantage in troops and matériel. As we shall see, the Germans were well aware of this possibility but chose to tame their side of the problem by deferring to superordinate – so called – experts rather than securing collaborative efforts from lower down the military hierarchy – though it was here that the warning voices were loudest and the evidence most apparent.

Falsehoods have always been common practice in war. For example, on 16 September 1940, when the invasion of Britain was a very real threat, the Germans mounted Operation *Herbstreise* (Autumn Journey) which was a fake invasion of the north-east coast of Britain between Edinburgh and Scarborough to deflect attention away from the real invasion zone and to release German naval vessels into the North Sea.[2] And in early 1942 the Germans mounted Operation *Kreml* to fool the Soviets into thinking that an attack would soon be launched against Moscow, rather than Stalingrad where it actually occurred. Early in 1944 a body identified as Major William Martin of the British Royal Marines was washed up on a Spanish beach carrying documents suggesting an impending invasion of the Balkans: after the Germans had buttressed their defences in that region the Allies promptly invaded Sicily.[3]

At about the same time the Allies began to plan an equivalent operation to ensure that German forces would not be concentrated at the intended invasion site in France; this was 'Operation Fortitude' and upon its successful communication to the Germans hinged the entire invasion programme. As the Chief of Staff to the Supreme Allied Commander (COSSAC) admitted: 'If the enemy obtains as much as 48 hours' warning of the location of the assault area, the chances of success are small, and any longer warning spells certain defeat'.[4]

Planning Fortitude did not commence until the initial Overlord plan was complete in July 1943, but it was accepted that such a huge accumulation of matériel could not be kept from the eyes of the enemy. Thus the original deception – Plan JAEL – to persuade the Germans that their defeat could be brought about solely by bombing – was dropped. Plan COCKADE suggested that moves against Boulogne, Brittany and Norway were intended but the Germans remained unpersuaded by these.

However, the Allies did not want to alert the Germans to the fact that an assault on Normandy was actually in preparation so the amount of information leaked had to be carefully controlled. Even if Normandy was not the main landing there was nothing to be gained from alerting the Germans to its imminent arrival. Indeed, it was also decided that too much mention or concentration on the Pas de Calais might persuade the Germans that something else was afoot, so blatant might be the leaks, thus any mention of landing sites was decreasingly used as D-Day approached. After all, if the double agents were to be believed after D-Day by the Germans it would be necessary for them to have *some* information that did not automatically point to the Pas de Calais.

Operation Fortitude was initiated by Roger Hesketh. Fortitude North was the pre-Normandy deception, suggesting that Norway was the target of a feint with the seven divisions of the British 4th Army stationed in Scotland and Eastern England, while the Pas de Calais was the real target. The plan allegedly involved using two divisions in a northern landing with Soviet assistance and a single divisional attack upon the airfields at Stavanger. Within three months six divisions would be landed and Sweden would be 'persuaded' to allow Allied aircraft to use its airfields to facilitate the invasion of Denmark. Although the Fortitude North plan was the less successful of the two deceptions nevertheless the Germans had moved a large number of U-boats to southern Norway for D-Day.[5] Ironically no German forces were sent north during the apparent invasion of Normandy to defeat the illusory British 4th Army because German observation of Scotland was very limited. Indeed, two divisions were entirely fictitious (US 55th Infantry Division and British 58th Infantry Division), in addition to three imaginary US Ranger Battalions and none of the real 4th Army Divisions was ever dedicated to the largely imaginary unit. Most of the 'work' of the army was undertaken by 20 British officers and a few wireless operatives ensconced in Edinburgh Castle. In late spring 1944 radio traffic simulated the arrival of three bomber squadrons, in addition to eight real and eight dummy Spitfires. In fact, the German radio operators covering this area were all listening to the manoeuvres of the Red Army further east so no apparent troop movements were noted but this handful of soldiers tied down 12 or 13 German divisions in Norway (about 200,000 soldiers) during the invasion of France. This was distributed leadership in action – a far cry from images of heroic leaders battling alone against impossible odds – but far more effective. The pretence was maintained until 30 September 1944, by which time no significant reserves were left in Norway anyway.[6]

Although the Allies regarded the Pas de Calais as an impossible invasion site, given the defences constructed there, this did not mean that it could not be used and Fortitude South suggested, initially, that the Pas de Calais was the primary target and no forces would be landed in Normandy. Of course, once the invasion of Normandy had occurred the ruse would rapidly be uncovered but as D-Day approached it occurred to General de Guingand that a second phase could be added, in which the deception would be extended to persuade the Germans that the main landing would still occur at the Pas de Calais, thus holding the German 15th Army in that region for as long as possible. Hopefully, the pretence over the 'main' invasion could be maintained for at least two weeks after the Normandy invasion to allow sufficient reinforcements to land before the Germans had moved troops south.

Fortitude South rested on the 'ghost army' of the First US Army Group (FUSAG), nominally under Patton's command, and theoretically landing a larger force of troops along the Pas de Calais than actually landed in Normandy. In fact, the code word for Fortitude was 'Bodyguard' after Churchill's suggestion that: 'In wartime truth is so precious that she should always be attended by a bodyguard of lies'.[7] It is clear that upon this deception rested the success of the landings for no amount of leadership would have been able to guarantee a successful landing against forewarned and prepared German opposition.

It might seem strange, then, that Patton – the army commander most feared by the Germans – was first, not involved in D-Day and second, responsible for maintaining a critical hoax to mislead the Germans. The removal of Patton from the D-Day landings had derived from several reprimands from Eisenhower, the most serious for slapping a soldier in

Sicily. But the public humiliation of Patton played perfectly into the requirements of Fortitude South – because the Germans could not believe that the Americans would remove their most feared opponent from leading the expected invasion. Thus, when Patton's name became connected to FUSAG – and the invasion of Calais – they were assured that FUSAG was the force to fear not any feint led by somebody else and landing somewhere else.

Patton's habit of embarrassing his political and military superiors continued throughout 1944. On 25 April he was due to open a 'Ladies' Welcome Club' at the Ruskin Rooms in Knutsford, Cheshire. Known to Eisenhower as 'Chief Foot-in-the-Mouth', Patton was warned against saying anything controversial.[8] He finished his speech – which he was assured would not be reported anyway – by saying, 'It is the evident destiny of the British and Americans [long pause] and of course the Russians, to rule the [post-war] world'. The next day the papers were full of his final sentence, but they excluded 'and of course the Russians'. Naturally all those not British or American on the Allied side were alarmed at the thoughts, but none more so than the Russians – and none so embarrassed as Eisenhower. Breuer speculates that Patton's presence in England as part of the FUSAG deception may have been missed by the Germans and some intelligence elements on the Allied side may have framed Patton simply to ensure that the controversy would be noticed in Germany – and thus increase the assumptions about a Pas de Calais invasion led by Patton.[9]

It was certainly the case that German maps as of 31 December 1943 did not show the whereabouts or even existence of Patton's First US Army Group, even though they did suggest that 55 divisions were present in the country (when there were only 38). Indeed, the Germans consistently overestimated the strength of the Western Allies – even when they used aerial reconnaissance rather than the false information fed to them by 'turned' agents. For example, on 25 April 1944 they estimated that sufficient shipping was in place to carry twice the number of divisions that was actually available.[10] But whatever the truth, the Germans assumed Patton's real role was as commander of the 'real' invasion force that would land at the Pas de Calais, probably just after a diversionary attack further south to draw away the Panzer forces.[11]

Even the German military leadership was used to deceive itself. In May 1944 General Cramer from the German *Afrikakorps* was repatriated to Germany from Britain under a prisoner exchange scheme organized through the Red Cross. Cramer was transported south through the country but false road signs, incorrectly identified army units, and carefully constructed 'overheard' conversations, confirmed to him that the

Photo 4.1 Ruskin Rooms, Knutsford, Cheshire

attack would be at the Pas de Calais and that 70–80 divisions would be involved – precisely what the German High Command suspected and precisely wrong.[12] All this was supported by 'helpful' photographs published in the *National Geographic* showing soldiers with fictional shoulder badges.[13]

The persuasive utility of the ruse can be gleaned not only from the action – or rather inaction – of the German forces outside Normandy in June 1944, but in the planning that explained this. In May 1944 a German map (captured later in Italy) marked the British order of battle almost exactly as Fortitude South predicted. The ruse was supplemented by the information provided by the double agents Garbo and Brutus that we shall consider shortly.

The attempt to confuse the Germans even involved some British units being issued with coupons to draw tropical clothing. This, it appears, was just to persuade any German informants in Britain that many of the landing craft on the move prior to D-Day were heading to the Far East or to the Mediterranean rather than to France.[14]

The first plan for Fortitude was delivered on 4 September 1943 and, after seven revisions, it went before the British Chiefs of Staff on 20 November 1943. Once the Teheran Conference had agreed the overall strategy the final plan was accepted on Christmas Day 1943. 'Bodyguard' was the codename for the overall strategic deception and Fortitude was one element of this, albeit the main element, and was accepted on 26 February 1944.

The alleged assault on the Pas de Calais was planned to occur in July. Thus the German troops in Norway would be delayed there until it was too late to intervene in Normandy (it was calculated that the journey would take at least three weeks) and the 15th Army would have to remain in northern France irrespective of what happened in Normandy on the assumption that when the assault in Normandy occurred it would be seen as a ruse.

To persuade the Germans that the main assault would occur at the Pas de Calais radio traffic was conducted to stimulate the activities of the divisions allegedly involved. In February 1944 the British No. 5 Wireless Group the War Office (Signals 9) was formed. All signals were recorded in advance and a device was developed to multiply the number of signals six-fold. Thus a single truck could represent the signals traffic of an entire division. The following month the US 3103 Signals Service Battalion arrived and used mobile communications units to simulate traffic. Between the two groups the radio traffic for nine divisions was generated, and three naval signals units representing radio signals between and within the naval assault units. In fact only 256 dummy landing craft were deployed in support of Fortitude South, in addition to a few dummy aircraft. The rest of the deception comprised the false information – and that included explaining why so few landing craft were ready for the 'real' assault. Usually that involved suggesting that industrial relations disputes in America would put back the invasion date yet again and that the invasion would probably be delayed until after the expected Soviet offensive in late summer 1944.[15]

As we have seen, Wicked Problems, and the leadership required to address them, necessarily involve a large dose of humility on the part of decision-makers and an admission that they may not know the answer to such problems. Yet despite the literal fog of war the arrogance of the German intelligence system also played a major role in its own downfall. For example, a report from the double agent Brutus dated 23 April 1944 claimed to have established the location of the (imaginary) 7th English Army Corps in Dundee. This was actually the first time that anyone had mentioned such a unit but the *Abwehr* intimated that it was useful to *confirm* their position.[16] Indeed, 'according to "Johnny" Jebsen, a double agent, Admiral Canaris [head of the *Abwehr*], 'did not care if all the agents in Britain were fakes as long as he could go to Field Marshall Keitel, the head of the German high command, and report that he had 12 agents in Britain, each of them writing a letter once a week'.[17]

The major Allied effort concentrated upon the build up of imaginary forces in the south-east of England. Much of this took the form of inflatable tanks and vehicles, stockpiled amongst plywood fighter aircraft on illusory airfields scattered around the south-east, in addition to canvas landing craft tied up in the ports of Kent. There was even a fake oil dock, occupying three square miles of Dover, which German reconnaissance aircraft were 'allowed' to photograph by the apparently negligent RAF.[18] The same level of 'negligence' was not permitted for German aircraft attempting to fly further west to where the 'real' build up of the invasion forces continued throughout early 1944. Here, cooking was only allowed from smokeless stoves and white towels were replaced by khaki ones.[19] Yet even when the *Luftwaffe* managed to fly over the bulging harbours of central-southern and south-western England they still failed to take the action that could have devastated the armada of landing craft.

In contrast, the Allied strategic bombing of Germany was regularly involving raids of between 500 and 1,000 heavy bombers. In all, only 129 sorties were flown by the *Luftwaffe* in the six weeks up to D-Day, and the level of intelligence-gathering from these was poor.[20] Indeed, Rommel's report for the week ending 21 May simply stated: 'There are *no* results of air reconnaissance of the island for the entire period'.[21] The Allies, on the other hand, flew 4,340 sorties just against German U-boats in the same period.[22] The disparity is partly explained by the Allied air attacks on mainland Germany which in the previous months had persuaded Hitler to withdraw many of his fighter squadrons to defend the Reich. But it was also the case that many of the airfields in France had been badly damaged by more recent Allied bombing raids rendering them inoperable. In fact, General Galland, commanding officer of the German fighter forces, claimed that even if all the available fighter aircraft had been scrambled against the invasion they would still have been outnumbered by 20 to 1.[23] About 600 Luftwaffe aircraft were in France on D-Day but less than half of them were in flying distance of Normandy. By the end of D-Day+7 there were 1,000 available aircraft.[24]

It was clearly impossible to conceal Exercise Fabius – the four-divisional dress rehearsal assault on the south coast of England in the first week of May – but even this embodied an element of deception. In particular the wireless traffic was organized so that it would mirror the same traffic on D-Day itself, thus, hopefully, persuading the Germans that Overlord was simply the second dress rehearsal. Even Churchill was involved in this deception after Eisenhower had persuaded him to insert a sentence about the likelihood of 'many dress rehearsals' in his speech to the nation on 27 March 1944.[25]

In the run-up to D-Day 49 airfields within 150 miles of Caen were attacked but only four were within the Normandy area while 11 were close to the Pas de Calais. Similarly, 19 rail junctions around Calais were bombed while none were hit in Normandy nearer than Rouen. Even the presence of so many fighter aircraft around Southampton was masked by a 66-squadron attack on Calais on 29 May in which the aircraft first flew to bases in Kent, Surrey and Sussex before taking off for the attack.[26]

So secret was Overlord that Stalin only knew the month and general area for the invasion, de Gaulle (whose offices in Algiers had been penetrated by a German spy) knew even less, and Eisenhower solved the tricky political problem of not telling de Gaulle by showing him maps marked 'Top Secret' which had been so altered that even Eisenhower could not recognize them. Knowing de Gaulle's vanity, Eisenhower gambled that de Gaulle would not ask for clarification as to where in France the maps referred to; he was right.[27]

But keeping the secret proved to be an enormous problem. Normally privileged diplomatic communications were banned on 17 April 1944 (excluding the USA and the USSR), though this did not stop two American officers from revealing classified information about D-Day at two separate parties; both men were returned to the US in disgrace. Nor did it prevent an envelope full of Overlord information falling open in a Chicago post office where a US soldier, Sergeant T.P. Kane, had mistakenly sent it to his sister. Kane remained under surveillance by the FBI for the rest of the war.[28] In England, Theodore R. Nuttmann, a Second Lieutenant of the US Adjutant General's department, was court martialled for disclosing classified (BIGOT) information to Lieutenant Robert A Wahlquist, but this was one of a very small number of leaks. The American forces were not alone in their poor security: Brigadier Lionel Harris, the CO of Overlord Communications, left the complete plan for Operation Neptune in the back of a taxi. Fortunately it was handed in to Scotland Yard by the driver.[29] And, of course, although the names and locations on the maps were changed to reveal only the code-names there were many French soldiers in the Allied forces, some of whom came from Normandy. Hence members of the French Commando unit in No. 10 Commando immediately recognized Ouistreham and the Caen Canal.[30,31] Bizarrely, there was also a full scale alert when the *Daily Telegraph* crossword in May and June 1944 contained five words in its answers that seemed incredibly coincidental: 'Overlord', 'Utah', 'Mulberry', 'Neptune' and 'Omaha'.[32] The compiler, Leonard Dawe, a 54 year old physics teacher at Strand School, Effingham, was interviewed by MI5 but no action was taken against him, or his brother-in-law who worked in the Admiralty – Eisenhower was aghast: 'This breach of security is so serious it practically gives me the shakes'.[33]

Nor was the cartoonist in the *John Bull* reprimanded for correctly guessing – and illustrating – the Normandy beaches as the probable target in their 'Old Bill' cartoon of 27 May 1944.[34] Ironically, in 1943 Major F.O. Miksche, a Czech, had published a book, *Paratroops*, which had already suggested not just that Normandy was a good invasion spot but that paratroop drops – in precisely the spot where the 82nd and 101st Airborne were due to land – would be the best way of occupying critical points.[35] But although the Germans – and particularly Kurt Student, founder of the German airborne forces – were aware of the book they assumed, wrongly, that it was just part of the deception plan to turn attention away from the Pas de Calais. In fact Fortitude was itself just one deception plan, albeit the fulcrum, around which Overlord's success depended.

4.3 Beyond Fortitude

A whole series of similar but smaller scale deceptions were deployed to keep various other German armies out of Normandy including wireless operators in the embarkation ports who maintained radio-traffic on D-1 when most of the ships were already at sea.[36] Beyond this: 'Operation

Glimmer' involved six motor launches simulating an assault at the Pas de Calais, each of which towed two 29-foot balloons, one in the air and one on a raft. Each balloon carried a nine-foot reflector that simulated the movements of a 10,000-ton troop transport ship.[37]

Elsewhere, 'Operation Ironside' sought to keep the German First Army stationary in Bordeaux where an invasion was expected. 'Operation Taxable' moved towards the Cap d'Antifer – and the 13 small ships persuaded the coastal defences to open fire on the 'invasion' force, no doubt certain that a large force was approaching because Leonard Cheshire led 16 Lancasters of the 617 Dambuster Squadron to drop bundles of 'window' every 12 seconds to simulate an approaching force 14 miles wide.[38] This was no easy task since the aircraft had to maintain precise distances between each other and had to manoeuvre at exactly the same time and speed every seven minutes to create the illusion of a seaborne convoy through a field of fluttering aluminium foil 16 miles long and 14 miles wide.[39] 'Operation Vendetta' did the same for the German 19th Army in Marseilles; 'Operation Diadem' kept the Germany army in Italy in its place; 'Operation Zeppelin' threatened an invasion of the Balkans; and finally, 'Operation Big Drum' feinted towards Cape Barfleur.[40]

In the skies above Normandy many of those *Luftwaffe* pilots that did get into the air were misdirected away from the invasion by German-speaking British radio transmissions on the *Luftwaffe* frequencies. When German ground controllers noticed the mispronounced words they immediately began alerting their pilots but to little avail. At one point a German operator swore into the microphone and was immediately followed by a British operator telling the *Luftwaffe* pilots that it was the British operator that was swearing. The response from the German operator was equally swift: 'It is not the Englishman who is swearing it is me!'[41] Further confusion was supplied by electronic jamming missions flown over eastern France and these were so successful that no single glider tow plane or parachute carrier was attacked by a German fighter.[42]

Another elaborate plan was 'Operation Titanic', executed by soldiers of the British SAS.[43] The overall plan was to drop dummy parachutists, record-players carrying recordings of soldiers' conversations, and pintail bombs which released a Very light on landing thus drawing attention to the drop, illuminating the 'paratroopers' in the air and giving the appearance of an Allied force already on the ground. Each dummy exploded on landing to simulate airborne landings away from the actual drop zones.[44] Titanic 1 simulated the dropping of an entire airborne division north of the Seine with 500 dummy parachutists and three parties of three SAS soldiers between Doudeville and Fauville-en-Caux. Titanic 2 dropped 50 dummies around Bois de Villers. Titanic 3 dropped 50 dummies to the south-west of Caen to draw German troops away from the British 6th Airborne attack to the north-east of the city. Finally, Titanic 4 dropped 200 dummies and two parties of three SAS troops near Isigny to draw the Germans south, away from the landings by the US 101st Airborne. The SAS involved were told to attack only lone despatch riders and to allow them to escape – thereby confirming that the drop was real. They were also provided with empty weapons containers that were to be scattered across the area to simulate a large body of troops.[45]

All the landings caused consternation amongst the defenders, and some for the SAS. Lt Poole, the mission commander for Titanic 4, tripped on exiting from the plane, somersaulted and knocked himself out. The other officer, Lt Fowles, dropped wide with the 'real' heavy equipment container, and this left the four remaining soldiers with just 20 Lewes bombs to attract the attention of the mass of German defenders. Perhaps fortunately, only a single bicycle patrol passed. All six were later reunited and subsequently captured on 10 July. Despite this the operation was successful. For instance, 2,000 soldiers of the 915th Grenadiers, the reserve Regiment of Lt General Kraiss's 352nd Infantry Division, spent the night searching the woods south-east of Isigny for the airborne landing of the six SAS members of Titanic 4 instead of moving towards the beaches.[46] But dummies, firecrackers and aluminium foil would not have worked unless the Germans already believed what these devices suggested, and to that end, little was more important that the misleading activities of 'turned' German agents.

4.4 The double agents

Before the war, Hitler had always assumed that the British would comply with German demands and not until 1939 was a large deployment (27 individuals) of *Abwehr* spies sent into Britain, by plane or sea. But they were largely unsuccessful: in 1940, when Operation Sea Lion, the invasion of Britain, was being planned, Colonel Blumentritt, on von Rundstedt's staff, was well aware of the problematic nature of German intelligence:

> No one knew whether there were any coast defences or field fortifications on the English coast, or where they were if they existed. It was not known which beaches were mined. No one could say exactly what forces the British had available for defence ... Our maps were inaccurate ... . Naval charts were little better.[47]

Here, captured perfectly, is the essence of a Wicked Problem – no-one knew. However, British Counter-Intelligence had every intention of keeping it that way. There seems to have been little improvement in intelligence over time, though there was a marked increase in information. This was primarily due to the success that British Counter-Intelligence had in detecting, turning or executing German spies but in almost every case the initial failing was one of detail not of strategy. Some were caught almost immediately: two were caught when they were eating German sausage on a beach after being landed by submarine; one asked for a pint of cider at 0900, not knowing that the pubs did not open until 1000. One used a ration coupon to pay for a restaurant meal, and one paid £10 and six shillings for a rail ticket when the clerk had asked for 'ten and six' – ten shillings and sixpence.[48] All 40 turned agents in Britain were members of the *Abwehr*, the German Military Counter-Intelligence Service, and the British Counter-Intelligence Twenty Committee (XX: double-cross) met weekly to decide what information should be fed to the Germans through each controlled agent's Case Officer.[49] Colonel Thomas Robertson ran the Twenty Committee, ably supported by a double agent of a different kind, Anthony Blunt, who was exposed as a Soviet agent in 1979.[50]

At the beginning of 1944, 15 such agents still existed in Britain, seven of whom had wireless transmitters.[51] Lily Sergueiev, a Russian woman, recruited by the *Abwehr* to watch the West Country ports – since this was self-evidently where any invasion of Normandy or Brittany would be launched – had a particularly important role to play for the Twenty Committee, for if *no* reports emanated from her area it would seem far too coincidental and arouse German suspicion. Thus Sergueiev sent messages that did indeed speak of troop movements, but in such a confusing way and in such a minimal format in invisible ink on envelopes to Spain, that the *Abwehr* dismissed her accounts.[52]

German agents in Eire were more forthcoming, so much so that in February 1944 the US insisted that the Irish government close down the German and Japanese embassies in Dublin to stop the leakage of Allied classified information; if this did not happen 'serious consequences could result'. Whatever these words meant – and the US threatened to send troops stationed in Britain to storm the embassies and arrest all the Germans and Japanese found therein – de Valera, the Irish prime minister, put the Irish army on full alert, but the crisis eventually died away.[53] Nonetheless, civilian travel between Ireland and Britain was suspended on 9 February 1944.[54]

The turned agents were managed by the London Controlling Section (LCS) which co-ordinated the deception efforts and operated under

COSSAC and the Supreme Headquarters of the Allied Expeditionary Force (SHAEF). LCS dealt with what was called Special Means – that is, the controlled leakage of information, as opposed to physical deception and almost the entire plan was conducted through three turned agents, Schmidt, Garbo and Brutus. In 1944, 208 references in the German military logs to the (false) landings were made, 86 from Garbo and 91 from Brutus.[55]

Brutus (real name: Roman Garby-Czerniawski) was a Polish officer who had escaped to France after the German invasion of Poland where he worked for the Allies until his arrest in November 1941. In the spring of 1942 Brutus persuaded the Germans that he would work for them as a double agent and he was sent to Britain in July – where he immediately contacted his former British controllers and began working for the Allies again – not as a 'double' agent but as a 'triple' agent. Brutus was given a 'job' with FUSAG helping to recruit Poles for when the First Army over-ran parts of Germany where Polish help would be useful.[56]

But by far the most influential double agent was Garbo. Juan Pujol, as he was really called, was a liberal Spaniard who had allegedly fought for Franco in the Spanish Civil War, but then apparently spied for the Germans after British MI6 officers rejected his offers of help. Garbo, however, always maintained that his quest was the downfall of anti-liberal forces, and Russell[57] claims that Garbo operated as a freelance spy, always working *against* the German interest but not *always* employed by the British. By the end of the war Garbo had received £20,000 from the *Abwehr* in exchange for 400 letters and 2,000 wireless messages.[58]

In 1941 he provided information to Germany that was, according to the British, 'superbly inaccurate' – probably because he fooled his German controllers and was not in Britain at the time, instead working in Portugal from an Ordnance Survey map, a 'Blue Guide to Britain' and a Portuguese book on the British fleet. So poor was his knowledge of Britain that he insisted that there were men to be bought in Glasgow for 'a litre of wine'. Nevertheless the Germans trusted him and his German controller, Karl Erich Kühlenthal, wrote to him in glowing terms: 'Your activity and that of your informants gave us a perfect idea of what is taking place over there. These reports have ... an incalculable value'. So influential did Garbo become that he was allegedly 'turned' by Cyril Mills as early as February 1942 when he was brought to Britain, having fooled the Germans into planning an assault upon a convoy from Liverpool to Malta that did not exist.

A ring of imaginary sub-agents whom he employed on behalf of German intelligence enabled Garbo to deny responsibility if the information proved false, and then to employ a different sub-agent as a replacement. And since all the activities of his sub-agents were highly dangerous Garbo – obviously – could not reveal their real names to the Germans. Hence they could never establish whether these sub-agents were real or fake. However, when Garbo failed to warn the Germans that Operation Torch was underway with an invasion force from Liverpool bound for North Africa, the *Abwehr* were obviously uneasy about their 'master spy'. Garbo responded by announcing that his sub-agent in Liverpool had been ill – and then died – thus no reports had filtered up to him to pass on.[59]

A critical problem for Garbo was how to persuade the Germans that he was a reliable agent when he did not tell them that the landings were imminent and heading for Normandy not the Pas de Calais. If the original deception plan (which limited Fortitude to persuading the Germans that the Pas de Calais was the only target) had been pursued this would not have been a problem since Garbo would have achieved all that he set out to achieve. However, since the extended plan now called for delaying tactics to be in place to prevent immediate German reinforcements, Garbo faced another problem. In the end the solution – with Eisenhower's explicit permission – was to copy a report by a fictional waiter in Otterbourne, Hampshire, of massive Canadian troop movements, complete with vomit bags. The landings were obviously imminent but equally obviously neither Wilhelm Leisner, the *Abwehr* chief in Lisbon, nor Karl Erich Kulenthal, in the German Embassy in Madrid was awake at 0300 on the morning of D-Day. When the message eventually got through at 0608 Garbo could claim that he sent the first warning hours earlier but now it was too late to matter. Just to add a further dose of realism, Garbo then complained bitterly to his German contacts about the ineptitude of Madrid and threatened to resign; he was persuaded not to by his German handler.[60]

Having covered his back, two of Garbo's other messages were to prove of inestimable value to the Allies. The first followed the speeches by the Allied leaders on D-Day itself. To ensure that no-one compromised the Fortitude deception, all the leaders were warned to use phrases like 'the first in a series of landings' to maintain the illusion that the Pas de Calais was next in line. However, de Gaulle spoke of Normandy as 'the supreme battle' and the *Abwehr* immediately contacted Garbo for clarification and to examine the possibility that everything *but* Normandy was just a feint. Garbo concocted an official memorandum, which had purportedly been issued on the eve of D-Day warning all leaders to talk as though there *was* only one landing because the others were so imminent. De Gaulle, explained Garbo, was the only Allied leader not to be sucked into the success of the day and he was the only one disciplined enough to remember not to mention the other landings. The double bluff worked.[61] Perhaps it was just as well, because Churchill ordered Desmond Morton, Churchill's personal intelligence adviser, to have de Gaulle deported to Algiers, if necessary in chains. He subsequently rescinded the order later that day.[62]

The second message was to be Garbo's initial assessment of the landings – which was to be delayed for 48 hours so that he could establish a 'realistic' assessment of the situation. Nevertheless, by that time (8 June) some preliminary movements from northern France to Normandy had been authorized. However, on 9 June at 1335 a message from London to a Resistance group in Brussels suggested that a second invasion force was already at sea and heading for Belgium. German Intelligence suggested that the British knew the Brussels group was controlled by the Germans but OKW overruled this possibility and took the message at face value. In fact the message was probably misinterpreted for no such message was sent from London and it was regarded as insignificant anyway by Berlin. Less than five hours later, at 1810, a message from a German agent in Stockholm suggested that an assault upon Calais was imminent. But perhaps more critical was Garbo's message despatched on 8 June and received by teleprinter at OKW at 2230 on 9 June 1944. It was seen by Krummacher, Jodl and Hitler and stated:

> After personal consultation on 8th June in London with my agents Jonny, Dick and Dorick, whose reports were sent today, I am of the opinion, in view of the strong troop concentrations in South-East and Eastern England which are not taking part in the present operations, that these operations are a diversionary manoeuvre designed to draw off enemy reserves in order then to make a decisive attack in another place. In view of the continued air attacks on the concentration area mentioned, which is a strategically favourable position for this, it may very probably take place in the Pas de Calais area, particularly since in such an attack the proximity of the air bases [would] facilitate the operation by providing continued strong air support.[63]

A further message confirmed Garbo's suspicions:

> I never like to give my opinion unless I have strong reasons to justify my assurances, thus the fact that these concentrations which are in the east and south-east of the island are now inactive means that they must be held in reserve to be employed in other large scale operations. The constant aerial bombardments, which the area of the Pas de Calais has suffered, and the strategic disposition of these forces give reasons to suspect an attack in that region of France ... I learnt yesterday that there were seventy-five divisions in this country before the present assault commenced. Supposing they were to use a maximum of twenty to twenty-five divisions, they would be left with some fifty divisions with which to attempt a

second blow ... . The whole of the present attack is set as a trap for the enemy to make us move all our reserves in a hurried strategical disposition which we would later regret.[64]

In short, it was self-evidently an attempt to draw German forces away from the real target, which was the Pas de Calais. By the morning of 10 June the information had persuaded the German High Command to stop and reverse the movement south from Bruges – towards Normandy – first of the 1st SS Panzer Division which was already on its way. Then, after a phone call from Keitel to von Rundstedt, a 'State of Alarm' was issued for the 15th Army in northern France and Belgium and the initial movements of three further divisions (116th Panzer Division, 85th Infantry Division and the 16th German Airforce Division) towards Normandy were halted and they were diverted towards Calais. And, as a further direct consequence, seven new German divisions were sent immediately to the Pas de Calais instead of to Normandy. Indeed, in the first few days when the Germans struggled to hold back the flood of Allied matériel with diminishing resources, three Panzer and two infantry divisions stood idly by within 100 miles of Caen but on the wrong side of the Seine and unable to move because of the fear of a further attack near the Pas de Calais.[65] The 1st SS division did not leave for Normandy until D-Day+11 and by that time the landing was secure. As Eisenhower remarked in his report to the Combined Chiefs of Staff:

> I cannot over-emphasise the decisive value of this most successful threat [to invade the Pas de Calais], which paid enormous dividends, both at the time of the assault and during the operations of the two succeeding months. The German 15th Army, which, if committed to battle in June or July, might possibly have defeated us by sheer weight of numbers, remained inoperative throughout the critical period of the campaign, and only when the breakthrough had been achieved were its infantry divisions brought west of the Seine – too late to have any effect upon the course of victory.[66]

On 29 July Garbo was awarded the Iron Cross by a grateful Hitler, and subsequently with an MBE by the British! He was the only individual to be decorated by both sides.[67] Garbo is a perfect example of the leadership of individuals from outside formal hierarchies and his effect is also a classic case for the role of 'small things', because this one individual seems to have stymied the movement of thousands of German reinforcements.

At face value this successful conclusion of a Wicked Problem by the Allies seems to undermine the collaborative efforts that conventionally comprise the necessary approach, however, on closer examination it should be clear that success also rested upon the secrecy of millions of British civilians and Allied soldiers, rather than just one or two double agents. By January 1944 virtually the whole of southern England had been transformed into a giant training and transit camp for the 2 million troops of the invading armies. Large sections of the southern English coastline, especially those areas that resembled the Normandy coast, were requisitioned by the military authorities for assault training and, as the time for the landing approached, the port and final transit camp areas were sealed off with barbed wire and armed guards to ensure no civilians got in and no military personnel got out – at least in theory. No prior warning was given to the troops about the sealing and many were disconsolate at the 'captivity'. As Gunner Ernest Brewer wrote to his mother on 28 May 1944: 'It seems a rotten trick not to tell us beforehand so that we could let you know that it might be our last time at home ... . We are, so far as I can understand, kept here for security reasons, though I myself can't see what we would give away. We don't know anything'.[68] Ironically, this was the day when the date of the invasion was released to those with a 'need to know' and from then until D-Day not only were the troops sealed in their various camps, but so were their letters. Even when mistakes were made rapid recoveries were possible. For example, all the tugs were issued with maps of the Seine bay area rather earlier than intended and, to cover the problem, a subsequent issue provided detailed maps of Boulogne marked 'Immediate. Top Secret'.[69] But some lapses did occur. Soldiers of the British 3rd Division, locked up inside West Ham's football ground in London were less concerned about their sudden incarceration than the equally sudden disappearance of the beer and cigarette ration. They took it upon themselves to cut the wire surrounding them and spent a night in the East End where at least two landlords accepted their French invasion money. They were subsequently – and peacefully – returned to 'barracks' by the local police.[70]

Even as the Allied troops boarded their landing craft most did not know their destinations. They had been trained to identify their target areas using the detailed maps and photographic panoramas taken by reconnaissance planes and made into books, but the place names for the villages were likely to be 'Brazil', 'Cairo' and 'Dresden' as anything else, so that any overheard radio communications would be of little use to the Germans. Only those privileged by membership of BIGOT security clearance were aware of the real targets, though this information was passed down to army, corps, divisional and regimental commanders as D-Day moved closer. On 25 May all ships' captains were ordered to open their sealed orders at precisely 2330. Three days later the date for D-Day – then fixed for 5 June – was announced to them and H-Hours for the five beaches were revealed. Simultaneously, all naval personnel were sealed in their landing craft or ships and all troops sealed in their camps and no contact was allowed between service personnel and civilians.[71]

To ensure that the cloak of secrecy that hung over Overlord did not extend to obscuring the identity of Allied vehicles they were all painted with a white star on both sides and the top.[72] Similarly, all Allied aircraft involved in D-Day were painted with three white strips around the wings and fuselage.[73] This involved virtually all the white paint in the country (100,000 gallons or 1,500 tons) and took 48 hours and 20,000 paint-brushes to achieve. Security was so tight that even on the second mission of D-Day the crew of a Halifax bomber was still not informed that D-Day was officially on, they were merely told: 'If you have to jettison any bombs please don't do it in the Channel as there will probably be a few extra ships around!'[74] Sam Stone, a member of 'Sweet 17 Gee', a bomber in the 337th Bomb Squadron, 96th Bomb Group, wrote that he was awakened at 0200 on 6 June for a briefing and, since he never knew the target in advance, was unprepared for what happened next – a major at the door checked everyone's name off but no-one knew why. Then the cover over the map was withdrawn to reveal Normandy and another offi-cer climbed onto the stage and said, 'Anyone who divulges any of the information given at this briefing will be shot'.[75]

Even the problem of media correspondents suddenly disappearing on the eve of D-Day was forestalled: on 24 May (the day after the provi-sional date for D-Day had been set for 5 June) 60 correspondents boarded the landing craft and remained there for 24 hours.[76] On the eve of the intended D-Day, 5 June, Bradley briefed the three accredited jour-nalists aboard Kirk's flagship, the USS Augusta, about the plans and corrected himself when he unwittingly said that they were going to 'swim 64 tanks ashore' – even at this late stage DD tanks were still top secret.[77]

But not everything went to plan. On the night of 4 June Lt Colonel Hellmuth Meyer in the HQ building of the German 15th Army was handed a message that his troops had just picked up from the interna-tional press: 'Urgent Press Associated NYK Flash Eisenhower's HQ Announces Allied Landings in France'. Meyer knew this could not be true because he had received no information from German sources about a landing and because he was still awaiting the second part of the coded message for the French Resistance giving them 48 hours notice. In fact, Joan Ellis, a teletype operator had simply been practising to improve her speed and by error the message had been sent rather than removed. The message was deleted by Irene Henshall but[78] at 1640 the newsflash reached the US east coast and thousands of people poured onto the streets to celebrate with one minute's silence though the news did not leak out in Britain.[79] But if keeping hold of the truth was difficult enough, discovering what the enemy was up to seemed impossible; that is, until Ultra.

4.5 Ultra

The early advantage in code-breaking had been with the German navy's *Beobachtungs-Dienst* because they had cracked the Royal Navy's Administrative Code and the Navy Cypher and were reading up to half the Royal Naval signal traffic by April 1940 – though never the signals of Flag Officers or the Commanders-in-Chief. Only in 1944 was German ability significantly denuded.[80] Much of the Allied advantage in information and communication was supplied by 'Ultra', the Allied code name for the system to reveal the secrets of the German Enigma encoding machine, capable of 200 million transpositions for any single key. The first Enigma machine had been built in 1923 by Arthur Scherbius and developed by the Cipher Machine Corporation of Berlin. The encoding produced a message so complex that a replicant machine, working on the identical coding system (one of 3×10^{18}), was necessary to decode it. Fortunately for the Allies, a box containing an Enigma machine addressed to a German firm in Poland was intercepted at the Polish customs and its contents photographed in 1929. From then on it was a rush to keep up with the frequent changes made to the German machines with first the Polish, then the French and British, and finally the American intelligence agencies all becoming involved in cracking the codes. They were helped by a German called Hans-Thilo Schmid who sold an instruction manual and updated information to the French authorities in 1931 and the entire body of experts was ensconced at Bletchley Park, England in 1940 to maintain Allied knowledge of changing codes and technical enhancements to the Enigma machines.

So complex was the code that it was assumed that only lax discipline on the part of a handful of German operators and the capture of a code would enable the Allies to crack it.[81] The latter occurred when David Balme, a Royal Navy sublieutenant, went down into the hull of the German submarine U-110 after it was attacked off Greenland in May 1941. The U-boat's captain, Fritz Lemp, had rigged the usual scuttling charges to destroy the boat and its encoding machine and documents but the charges failed to ignite. All the materials were rescued from the submarine by Balme and his crew and immediately returned to Britain. The submarine, meanwhile, was reported as having been sunk so that the Germans would not be aware of the find. Once deciphered the materials enabled the Allies to predict the movements of the submarine wolfpacks and reduce the monthly sinkings from 200,000 tons to 50,000 tons. A change in codes brought the monthly sinkings back up to 627,000 in March 1943 but the new code was cracked by May and after that point the battle for the Atlantic was all but won.[82]

Some 10,000 people worked at Bletchley in pursuit of German intelligence and weekly decodings suggested that the Germans never guessed that the invasion would not be at Calais. Of course, this also meant that the Allies had to 'allow' certain failures to occur by not warning their own forces of German intentions to ensure that the Germans would not realize the extent of the information leakage – including, for example, the invasion of Crete.[83] Furthermore, since there were ten times as many air raids over the Calais region as the Normandy region, there was little to indicate otherwise.[84] Even when mistakes were made they seemed to favour the Allies: in May 1944 a member of a beach survey party was captured – but he had been operating in the Somme area, thus giving credence to an invasion other than in Normandy.[85]

Nevertheless, by D-Day Ultra had secured information on the identity of over half of the German garrisons in Normandy and all the armoured divisions, but the whereabouts of many infantry units remained uncertain. For example, the 352nd Infantry Division was mentioned once on 22 January but it was not known that the unit had moved to the Cotentin in March and on to Omaha Beach just before the landings.[86] The main problem for the Allies was that most of the Ultra intercepts were limited to those originating with the *Luftwaffe* because most German army signals in France were transmitted by landlines that were obviously impervious to Allied intervention.

On D-Day+2 an Ultra intercept suggested that the 17th SS *Panzergrenadier* Division would move to Normandy via a tunnel at Saumur, south-east of Angers, and on the evening of 8 June Leonard Cheshire's 617 Squadron of Lancaster bombers duly dropped several 'Tallboy' 14,000lb bombs on it.[87] It was not reopened until 1948, though the delay to the 17th SS seems to have been minimal.

Three days after D-Day an Ultra intercept mentioned the location of the Panzer Group West. This group had been made operational at 1600 on D-Day and made responsible for the invasion area by OB West on the morning of 7 June. But it could do little until 9 June because its journey from Paris to Normandy was hindered by air attacks in which 75 per cent of its radios were destroyed. The same day, its location was discovered in the chateau at Le Caine, a hamlet south-east of Villers-Bocage. To have attacked it immediately would have roused German suspicions so a meandering Allied aircraft wandered over the site on 9 June until it had been spotted from the ground. The next day, 10 June, the building was attacked by 61 Mitchells and 40 Typhoons. In under an hour the primary command and control centre of the *Wehrmacht* in Normandy was destroyed. Eighteen Germans were killed in the attack, including the Chief of Staff of the Panzer Group West, Major General Dawans, and the control of the Panzers moved from Panzer Group West to the First Panzer Corps. So great was the confusion that Rommel was inhibited from co-ordinating an armoured counter-attack to split the Allied landings.[88] In fact Hinsley, one of the Bletchley officers at the heart of the Ultra project, has always denied that it won the war but accepted that it shortened it and it also provided the Allied commanders with the confidence to go ahead with D-Day.[89] It might also be added that Ultra was the consequence of many people's actions, and not all of them heroic and many of them almost invisible examples of distributed leadership so common to addressing Wicked Problems. A similar conclusion can be drawn about the final element in the Allied information arsenal: the French Resistance.

4.6 The Resistance

In February 1943 the Vichy government passed a forced-labour law, requiring all French men of mobilizable age to work for the Germans. Many men refused and some, especially in the unoccupied area of southern France, took to the countryside and formed the French Forces of the Interior (FFI) better known as the *Maquis*, a Corsican term meaning 'scrubby undergrowth'. This army of resisters eventually became an Army of Resistance and fought both the Germans and the 40,000 members of the French collaborationist police force, the *Milice*. Between the Germans and the *Milice*, 25,000 French people were executed, and 150,000 killed in action. In the weeks after liberation about 11,000 French collaborators were summarily executed, 39,000 jailed and 40,000 had their civil rights revoked. Many of those executed had supported the Germans but many of those that benefited from the occupation went unpunished. As one Parisian saying went, 'a collaborator went free if he built the Atlantic Wall but went to jail if he had written that it was a good idea'.[90]

By no means, then, were all the French happy to see the Allies. Some were pro-German, some anti-British or Anti-American or simply distressed by what the Allies were doing to 'liberate' them. Over 390,000 buildings were destroyed or damaged in Normandy alone.[91] Maher, for example, recalls how the little harbour of St Vaast-la-Hougue on the

Cotentin peninsular was cleared of mines by US forces without any help from the local Norman population whatsoever – even the many French fishermen who stood to gain from the operation and also stood just watching.[92] Others seemed certain that the Germans would win and thus to help the Allies in the short term was to court danger in the long term. For example, Sapper Anderson was told by one Norman farmer that the Germans would soon come and push the Allies 'back into the sea'.[93] In Brest, in contrast, the local Breton population were far more helpful. But many French civilians, and many Normans, were active in the far more dangerous activities of the French Resistance, the *Maquis*. Over 2,700 members of the Norman French Resistance are known to have died over-all and around 3,000 were involved in action for Overlord: eight bridges and 100 German vehicles were destroyed, and many rail and telephone lines were cut in Normandy alone.[94]

Keeping the Germans misinformed was just one part of the Allied communications strategy, a second element was securing information from the French Resistance and informing them about targets and dates for the invasion. While Rommel waited in May 1944 in almost complete ignorance of Allied intentions, Eisenhower received 700 radio reports and 3,000 written despatched from the French Resistance.[95] The network of spies organized by MI6 was particularly valuable in providing information of the German defences to the Allies. Gilbert Renault, who had worked for Eagle Star Insurance in France before the war, fled with de Gaulle and returned via Spain to set up a network of Allied spies to cover the coast of Normandy and Brittany. By the autumn of 1941 Renault had 100 agents working for him in Normandy alone and managed to develop a further 14 networks or Centuries. *Centurie-Caen*, led by Marcel Girard, a cement sales representative, involved 1,500 agents in 1944.

While several famous individuals joined the Resistance, such as Marcel Marceau whose father had been executed by the Germans, and Jacques Cousteau, the inventor of the aqualung, most of the activities were undertaken by people who were, and often remain, unknown. Some, however, achieved enduring positions in history. Amongst these was René Duchez.

René Duchez, who worked with *Centurie-Caen*, was a 40 year old house painter living in Caen but was originally from Lorraine – the site of the First World War German occupation. On 8 May 1942 Duchez's smatter of German had enabled him to be hired to decorate the local offices of the Todt Organization on the Avenue Bagatelle in Caen. The CO, Bauleiter Hugo Schnedderer, was organizing the building of the coastal defences and had left the 12 duplicate sets of blueprints marked

Sonderzeichungen-Streng Geheim (Special Blueprint – Top Secret) on his desk while he explained what painting was required. When Schnedderer left the room momentarily Duchez placed one set of blueprints – which were clearly important even though he was unable to understand their contents – behind a mirror in the room and then left. Three days later, when he returned to start painting he discovered that Schnedderer had been replaced by a new CO, Adalbert Keller, who saw no need for the redecoration and refused Duchez access. However, when Duchez suggested he would do the work for nothing Keller allowed him to start. After two days' work, on 13 May, Duchez managed to steal the blueprint, measuring 10 feet by 2 feet, hidden in a paint tin to the *Centurie-Caen* HQ, the *Café des Touristes* in Caen. Still unaware that the blueprint was for the Normandy section of the Atlantic Wall from Le Havre to Cherbourg, Duchez passed the map to Maurice Himbert, a motorcycle repairer with official permission to visit Paris to purchase spare parts. As Himbert rode to Paris, Renault travelled there to pick up the blueprint, but one of Renault's agents was arrested, tortured and revealed Renault's identity and destination. As the Gestapo searched Paris for Renault he escaped with his family through Port Aven in Brittany on a lobster boat which rendezvoused with a British trawler and landed Renault and family safely in England. On 20 June 1942 the blueprint was handed over, still in its biscuit tin container, to the military authorities and its significance finally assessed. As Colonel John Austin, an ex-Oxford University don from Christchurch College and head of the Intelligence Section then concerned with the Atlantic Wall, explained, 'It scored a very great hit. It turned attention sharply to this weakly defended sector – showing that many earlier estimates of the strength had been alarmist ... and that a good deal of photographic interpretation had been in error'.[96] *Centurie-Caen* were not informed of the significance of their find, for fear of alerting the Germans should one of their agents be arrested and reveal the information, and the Todt Organization never officially reported the loss of one of the blueprints to the *Wehrmacht*.

Thus the Allies had two years to work out how best to overcome the critical first line defences of the Germans.[97] The following year a trip around Normandy by Hiroshi Oshima, the Japanese Ambassador to Germany, resulted in a further long and detailed description of the defences which was sent in code to Tokyo by radio but broken by the American Purple Cipher.[98]

Centurie-Caen continued their observation and mapping activities along the coast, with Robert Thomas co-ordinating the completion of 4,000 maps by the coastal agents, each responsible for a 13-mile stretch. Some, like Olgvie Vauclin, noted developments on her knitting pattern as she rode the coastal bus, others like Duchez, alternated his daytime painting job with a voluntary night job, patrolling the streets of Ouistreham, allegedly watching for air attacks but actually marking out the street defences for Lord Lovat's commandos. Léon Dumis, who ran a garage at Ifs, just south of Caen, used his part time job checking milk production on the surrounding farms to mark out the 40 anti-aircraft positions surrounding Caen. However, tragedy struck on 16 November 1943 when the Gestapo raided the *Centurie-Caen* arresting many agents, though Thomas and Duchez managed to go into hiding until D-Day.[99] That also restricted the ability of the resistance to monitor changes and may well explain the lack of information about the Merderet River flooding and the movement of the 352nd Division up to the beaches.

Alerting the 85,000–100,000 members of the French Resistance (though Allied intelligence assumed that only 10 per cent of these were armed) to the imminent invasion involved the BBC who transmitted various lines of poetry and prose to 350 Resistance cells. The first warned them that the invasion was close and the second told them to execute their allotted tasks.[100] André Heintz, for example, heard his first line: '*L'heure du combat viendra*' on 31 May and the signal to go, '*Les dés sont sur le tapis*',[101] on 5 June at 2115.

Over 1,200 targets were listed for Resistance attention: railway attacks were covered by *Plan Vert*, bridges and roads were dealt with by *Plan Tortue* (tortoise), electricity supplies came under *Plan Bleu*, and *Plan Violet* concerned the communications systems. And to co-ordinate the attacks, as well as provide arms and ammunition, were 5,000 Allied agents and soldiers.[102] Between 2115 and 2215 on 5 June, 325 messages were transmitted initiating attacks on 571 French railway stations and switches, 30 main rail lines, as well as innumerable smaller rail lines, telephone and telegraph lines and bridges.[103] In June 1944 the main railway line between Paris and Toulouse was cut 800 times by members of the Resistance and on D-Day itself 950 railway lines were attacked.[104] The rail lines between Cherbourg, St Lô and Paris were dynamited by the Cherbourg team, led by Yves Gresselin, a Cherbourg grocer. In Caen station, the stationmaster himself, Albert Augé, led a team in smashing steam injectors on locomotives and water pumps in the yards. At Isigny, 40 members of the Resistance in eight teams of five people, led by André Farine, a café owner, cut the telephone lines between Cherbourg and Isigny in eight places.[105]

In some cases the Resistance had no time to inform the Allies of significant changes to German troop deployments. On the afternoon of 5 June Jean Marion, the Resistance sector chief around Grandchamp, noticed a troop movement that was to prove disastrous to the American airborne landings: a 2,500-troop, 25-gun anti-aircraft artillery unit, Flak Assault Regiment No. 1. This began digging in on the precise flight path of the 82nd and 101st paratroopers – a flight path that had been altered to minimize the risk from exactly this kind of defence system. Marion also noticed that the guns destined for Pointe du Hoc were still two miles from their destination. Marion sent the information to Léonard Gille, the Resistance's deputy military intelligence chief in Normandy by courier but Gille was already on a train to Paris and that train was later delayed by the aerial bombardment; the news did not reach London in time to alter any plans.[106] Yet Marion had also informed London that a single artillery piece had been situated on the sea wall at Grandchamp, between Omaha and Utah beaches and a destroyer duly manoeuvred opposite the town and destroyed the gun.[107]

Both the Resistance and the Germans took the invasion as a declaration of unrestricted war. All 92 male prisoners (there were many female members of the Resistance) suspected of being in the Resistance in Caen jail were shot by the Gestapo, though only 40 had any links to the organization.[108] Some elements of the Resistance subsequently returned to the information-gathering it had concentrated on up until the time of the invasion. For others, the bloody reprisals simply hardened them to their new primary task: unhinging the German communication systems wherever possible. For example, the 1st SS Division was unable to complete its tank-driver instruction in Belgium because of the activities of the Belgian resistance, the so-called 'White Army'.[109]

In particular areas the Resistance was remarkably successful and important. For instance, the 2nd SS Panzer Division (*Das Reich*) was stationed at Montauban near Toulouse in April 1944, having moved there in January 1944 after two years on the eastern front. But between March and D-Day over 100 soldiers had been kidnapped or killed by the local Resistance so it was not a rest camp by any means. As an elite unit it comprised 20,000 troops, 99 Tiger and Panther tanks, 75 *Jagdpanzers* (self-propelled assault guns), and 64 assorted other tanks.[110] The tanks were fitted with steel tracks that wore out on roads and, since they were 400 miles away from Normandy, they were ordered to be transported to the battlefield by railcar – normally a three-day journey.[111] Members of the French Resistance managed to siphon the axle oil from the rail cars and replace it with abrasive powder parachuted in by the SOE (Special Operations Executive).[112] The result was that when D-Day occurred and *Das Reich* was called to Normandy by Rommel, their three-day rail journey became a 17-day road journey.

When they began to move, on 7 June, the *Maquis* laid the SOE's cyclonite mines (that looked like cow pats) and even up-turned soup dishes on the road: the former blew off tracks while the latter required the whole column to stop while the 'mine' was inspected. At Souillac, 28 *Maquis* volunteers held up the column for 40 hours and just before the column reached Tulle, 45 miles south-east of Limoges, the local population attacked the German garrison and proclaimed themselves liberated. When *Das Reich* reached Tulle on 9 June the German commanding officer, Brigadier General Lammerding, claimed that 40 of the German garrison had surrendered and then been murdered. As a reprisal he ordered 99 of the inhabitants, men, women and boys, to be hanged from the balconies of houses lining the main street – while he watched the spectacle sipping coffee from the Café Tivoli.[113] Later that day two officers of the division's *Panzergrenadier* Regiment '*Der Führer*', were kidnapped and one was shot at Oradour-sur-Glane. The other escaped and then led SS-*Sturmbannführer* Diekmann and a company of troops to the village. There, the 642 inhabitants were rounded up and the 245 women and 207 children were locked in the local church that was promptly set on fire. The 190 men were separated into smaller buildings and shot. Diekmann was subsequently killed in action.[114]

Das Reich was then constantly harassed by the Resistance on the ground and Allied aircraft from the air all the way to the invasion zone, giving the Allied beach-head a crucial two-week window for reinforcements to arrive.[115] But a month later, just two months after arriving in Normandy, the 20,000 troops and 238 assorted tanks of *Das Reich* had been reduced to just 450 men and 15 tanks, a casualty rate of 98 per cent in troops and 94 per cent in tanks.[116] But the experiences of *Das Reich* were relatively unusual at this point in the war – so what happened to the rest of the *Wehrmacht* and just how taken in were the German High Command?

4.7 The German response

The general success of Fortitude can be gleaned from the movement of troops and armour in the 15th Army sector defending the Calais region, as shown in Figure 4.1.

But ironically, given the tardy and erroneous response of the Germans to the run-up to the invasion, they were actually aware of its imminent arrival, duly announced in code by the BBC, because their secret service, the *SD*, had already broken the code and informed General Canaris of its importance. The SD had already infiltrated the Resistance several months earlier and was duly awaiting one particular line from the BBC. On 1 June Sergeant Walter Reichling, of Colonel Meyer's 15th Army

Divisions	4 April	28 May
Static Coastal Divisions	26	25
Infantry and Parachute Divisions	14	16
Armoured and Mechanized Divisions	5	10
Reserve Divisions	10	7
Total	**55**	**58**

Source: Lewin, 1998: 186

Figure 4.1 Divisions of the 15th Army sector, Calais region

Communications Reconnaissance Post, heard it, the first line of a poem by Paul Verlaine (*Les sanglots longs, Des violins, De l'automne*,[117]) which routine interrogation of two members of the French Resistance by *Oberstleutnant* Oscar Reile, at the Parisian HQ of the *Abwehr* on 14 October 1943 had already suggested would be broadcast on the first, second, 15th or 16th day of the month in which the invasion would occur, while the second line would be broadcast 48 hours before the invasion itself.[118] On 5 June Reile read Reichling's report and duly alerted his chiefs.

In fact, the Germans had assumed the poem would signal a general call to arms for the entire Resistance though it was actually a specific command to a particular group to cut a railway line – code-named the 'Ventriloquist circuit'.[119] That line, '*Blessent mon coeur, D'une langueur, Monotone*'[120] was broadcast 15 times between 1200 and 1430 on 3 June by the BBC and Reile alerted the 23 contacts on his list, including Jodl at Hitler's HQ, von Rundstedt's HQ, and Rommel's HQ. General Salmuth, CO of the German 15th Army also received a copy of the warning and, despite his initial scepticism, the 15th German Army duly went on alert – but only after his Chief of Staff, Pemsel, rang him at 0135 to announce airborne landings. At 0200, after Cherbourg radar had reported large scale ship movements towards Normandy, Pemsel again rang Salmuth to insist that the landings 'constitute the first phase of a larger enemy action'. But Salmuth still resisted, demanding that 'for the time being this is not to be considered as a large operation'.[121] Nevertheless Salmuth put his 15th Army on alert and informed von Rundstedt's and Rommel's headquarters. The message read:

Teletype No. 2117/26 urgent to 67th, 81st, 82nd, 89th Corps; Military Governor Belgium and Northern France. Army Group B; 16th Flak Division; Admiral Channel Coast; *Luftwaffe* Belgium and Northern France. Message of BBC, 2115, 5 June has been decoded. According to our available records it means 'Expect invasion within 48 hours, starting 0000, June 6'.[122]

But the 7th Army, covering the Normandy coast, did not go on alert. General Jodl, Chief of Operations at OKW assumed von Rundstedt had given the order and Ryan suggests von Rundstedt assumed Rommel had given it.[123] Carell, though, claims that the 7th Army was specifically ordered by von Rundstedt *not* to go on alert.[124] This seems unlikely given that he guessed the seaborne landings would occur at daybreak on the Normandy beaches and that he immediately ordered the 12th SS HJ and *Panzer Lehr* to move towards Caen. However, Rommel's Chief of Staff, Lt General Speidel (who had been hosting an anti-Hitler party in Rommel's absence on the evening of 5 June) was alerted to the second part of the poem, and its implications, at 2200. Speidel advised the intelligence officer who had telephoned with the information (*Oberst* Staubwasser) to ring von Rundstedt at OB West for advice. That advice was allegedly that the 7th Army should not go on alert – though there is no written evidence to confirm this.

But if the evidence and advice of subordinates in the security service were disregarded, supplementary evidence from German radar should have provided confirmation one way or the other. The huge Allied armada that had begun sailing well before 6 June was picked up and traced right across the Channel by the US Radar station at Start Point in Devon. So what happened to the German radar? In theory German radar covered the entire coastline from Norway to Spain and there were 92 radar stations operating along the French west coast alone – a station or substation every ten miles. These sites were located by the Allies using a triangulation of bearings measured from three mobile ground direction-finding radars (Ping Pongs) sited on the south coast of England, supplemented by aerial photography. Forty-two sites (involving 106 installations) were designated as primary targets and by D-Day-3, 14 entire sites had been destroyed in the 2,000 sorties targeted at them. At that point the 12 remaining critical sites (involving 39 installations) were targeted. In all 1,668 sorties were made against radar sites by the AEAF alone, primarily flying low level attacks in Typhoons firing 60lb rockets[125] and Spitfires dropping 500lb bombs. Only 18 sites survived the air and naval attacks of the previous month unscathed and no radar was operating between Le Havre and Barfleur – the destination of the invasion.[126] However, the radar at Cherbourg was operational (though the HQ of the German Signals Intelligence at Urville-Hague just west of Cherbourg had been flattened on 3 June) and on 5 June it showed a large formation of ships assembling just before Allied jamming put it out of action. The naval commander, *Konteradmiral* Hennecke, was not persuaded of the accuracy of the information, especially given the weather forecast and the cancellation of a German convoy to Brest because of the expected storm. Since the Germans knew that the next possible invasion period was the middle of June the vast majority concurred with von Rundstedt's assessment: 'There is no indication that the invasion is imminent'.[127]

The huge Allied fleet was spotted at 0145 and Naval Group HQ in Paris informed at 0150 and despite concerns that it could only be seagulls, so many were the targets, the coastal alarm was raised and the 22nd Panzer Regiment of the 21st Panzer Division went on immediate alert.[128] At 0309 German E-boats were ordered to make a visual confirmation – primarily because the normal surface patrol vessels had been ordered to remain in harbour because of the bad weather – and the *Landwirt* group of 36 submarines were put on immediate alert. By the time the E-boats reported back the invasion was on.[129]

But had the German land-based lookouts been doing their jobs a little better they would have known something was going on the previous day because at 1957 on 5 June the British 14th Minesweeping Flotilla was in sight of the Normandy coast and could pick out individual houses ashore. Yet, despite the risk, no alert was given.[130] Even when the warships anchored off the Normandy coast in sight of the German gunners there was no immediate attempt to engage them because many defenders were unsure whether they were German or enemy ships. At Port en Bessin, for example, the German coastal artillery fired recognition flares and did not commence firing until no appropriate signal was received back.[131]

At 0130 a clerk at von Rundstedt's HQ was alerted to take down any reports coming in but he suggests that the reports of landings along the Normandy coast were all regarded as feints, as yet more 'Dieppes'. After all, he suggested: 'The situation map of England showed only a few units along the S.W. shore, but heavy concentrations in the S.E'.[132]

The 7th Army eventually went on alert at 0140 after the 716th Infantry Battalion had responded to the airborne landings. Yet the 7th Army's Chief of Staff, Major-General Pemsel quickly decided that the airborne landings consisted of dummies and baled-out air crews. At 0255 von Rundstedt decided that this was not a ruse – even though just six hours earlier he had suggested that an attack was not imminent – and told General Zimmerman, his operations officer, to telephone Hitler.[133] By 0350 Pemsel had also changed his mind to suggest to General Blumentritt that 'the width of the sector under attack shows that this is no operation of purely local significance'. It was also at that time that Pemsel apparently remembered a report that had arrived that afternoon from an agent in Casablanca, informing him that the invasion would take place in Normandy on 6 June.[134]

At 0430 Pemsel informed Speidel that his artillery was shelling enemy warships but Speidel refused to inform Rommel, suggesting that 'the invasion' as Pemsel had called it, was merely some 'localized encounters'.[135] Nevertheless von Rundstedt ordered the movement of the 12th SS and *Panzer Lehr* up to the coast – an order that would require Hitler's confirmation. That confirmation process required the initial agreement of Jodl, Hitler's Chief of Operations, but Jodl was allowed to continue sleeping until 0630 and even then refused to wake Hitler. When Jodl awoke he immediately cancelled von Rundstedt's order for the 12th SS and *Panzer Lehr* to move north. A little earlier, at 0615 Pemsel reported that the naval bombardment had begun but still Speidel did nothing. Not until 0730 did Speidel eventually agree that the invasion was on and he subsequently informed Rommel – that was at least 30 minutes after Goebbels had announced the invasion on German radio! Two hours later, at 0930 on 6 June, Rommel was back at his HQ at La Roche-Guyon and at the same time John Snagg, the BBC radio presenter, announced an Allied landing 'on the northern coast of France' in Communiqué No. 1 (originally written on 22 May 1944).[136] Precisely where in northern France the landings had occurred was still unclear to both the Germans and the average Allied citizen. Two days later, a map in the *Daily Telegraph*, based on German information, revealed paratroopers dropping on the Channel Islands and directly around Cherbourg.[137] But wherever the landings were the problem for the defenders was that, in Napoleon's words, lost land can always be regained, lost time cannot. Treating the invasion as a Wicked Problem – where decisions should be delayed while a consensus was sought – instead of a Critical Problem – where decisiveness was the key – effectively undermined what chance the defenders had for repulsing the invasion.

The poor weather and the overriding assumption that Calais was the target, associated with a recent spate of false alarms, had undermined German faith in their own intelligence system. Anyway, as one of Rundstedt's intelligence officers responded, when Sergeant Reichling intercepted the second line from Verlaine's poem and warned his superiors, 'would the Allies be so crass as to announce the invasion on the BBC!?'[138] In fact von Rundstedt and his Chief of Staff Blumentritt were surprised when nothing happened immediately and were preparing to call off the alert at 0200 when first news of paratroop landings began. When that came in von Rundstedt was uncertain whether it was the main landing or not, but on one thing he was clear: with three recognized airborne divisions in Normandy there had to be seaborne landings to support them because the Allies would not leave their airborne troops isolated and therefore open to imminent destruction.

What had proved crucial in the success of Fortitude was not *persuading* the Germans that the Pas de Calais was the vital target and everything else diversionary but *confirming* that the Germans were right to believe this. Even the *Oberkommando des Heeres* (OKH) Intelligence Report for 6 June 1944 appeared to confirm to the Germans that all they faced was a large ruse and not *the* invasion.

> The enemy landing on the Normandy coast represents a large-scale undertaking; but the forces already engaged represent a small part of the total available. Of the approximately sixty divisions at present in the south of England, it is likely that at most ten to twelve divisions are at present taking part, including airborne troops ... . Within the framework of his group of forces Montgomery still has over twenty divisions available ... . The entire group of forces which makes up the American First Army group [FUSAG], comprising about twenty-five divisions north and south of the Thames, has not yet been employed. The same applies to the ten or twelve active divisions held ready in the Midlands and Scotland. The conclusion is, therefore, that the enemy command plans a further large-scale undertaking in the Channel area, which may well be directed against a coastal sector in the central Channel area.[139]

The next day the Germans knew precisely what the Allies, or at least the Americans, intended because the entire American invasion plan for Omaha was washed up. As Ziegelmann recalled,

> I have never been so impressed as in that hour when I held in my hands the operation order of the American V Corps. I thought that with this captured order, the German 7th Army and Army Group B would reach a decision – the decision. I learned later that this captured order lay around for days at 7th Army headquarters and only reached the high command much later. Even then it did not get the attention it deserved ... As a young general staff officer, my impression was that the high command 'looked but did not leap'.[140]

Despite this, a report on 8 June suggested that because no elements of FUSAG were engaged in Normandy there was all the more reason to assume a further attack was imminent. That no FUSAG units were involved because there was no FUSAG was not to have been considered as an explanation for their absence – at least by the higher commanders, though at a junior level it was already obvious that the Normandy landings were not a ruse but the real thing. As Major Wiegman reported from the Caen area on D-Day, 'The British 3rd and Canadian 3rd Divisions had been identified by about noon. We know that the 50th London and 7th Armoured Divisions are also there. All that's missing is the 51st Highlanders and the 1st Armoured Division and we'll have

Montgomery's entire 8th Army from Africa at our throats! If this isn't
the invasion what are they going to come with?'[141]

Five days later another German intelligence report argued that no
evidence equalled certainty. 'To sum up, despite the absence of any
concrete information about the enemy's actual intentions it can only be
said that there is no serious evidence against the early employment of the
American Army Group [FUSAG] and that our own measures must therefore take this possibility into account'.[142] Indeed, as the weeks wore on
it became less and less important for the Allies to provide the Germans
with false information as to the precise target of the illusory FUSAG,
simply keeping German reinforcements out of Normandy for as long as
possible was all that was necessary.

By 13 June of the nine German divisions that the Allies had expected
to reinforce Normandy (six from the 15th Army; two from south-west
France, and one from the Mediterranean) only two had moved (2nd
Panzer Division from Amiens and 17th *Panzergrenadier* Division from
south of the Loire). The 2nd Panzer was ordered to move on 9 June but
the blown bridges across the Seine meant that the division had to travel
through Paris. It took three days for the first troops to arrive to support
Panzer Lehr but a further six days for the first tanks to arrive. By then it
was too late to co-ordinate an armoured counter-attack to push the Allies
back into the sea.[143]

Within a month an extra three infantry divisions had arrived – though
the numbers of troops was probably reduced given the casualties inflicted
– and an extra six Panzer divisions. But ironically, most of the reinforcements had been sent to support the 15th Army not the 7th Army. It was
at Calais that the Germans still expected the next assault to occur and
they were certain that Calais would be the graveyard of the main Allied
assault and, at last they were able to explain – and take advantage of – the
fact that all the veteran units were in Normandy. At a conference in Berlin
on 3 July Jodl made it clear that, since most of the experienced Allied
troops were in Normandy, Patton obviously had to rely on untested
troops, and 'in the face of strong German defences, we have every confidence of defeating them'.[144] On 10 July, almost five weeks after D-Day,
Rommel's HQ sent a despatch to von Rundstedt still warning of the
likely second invasion:

> The enemy has at present 35 divisions in the landing area. In Great Britain 60 are
> standing to, 50 of which may at any moment be transferred to the continent ...
> We shall have to reckon with large scale landings of the 1st US Army Group in the
> North for strategic co-operation with Montgomery's Army Group in a thrust on
> Paris.[145]

The Allies, keen to continue the confusion now had to begin to find reasons for explaining the appearance in Normandy of the few divisions from FUSAG that were real. A rationale was concocted which spoke of Montgomery's demands for reinforcements in Normandy and of political rows between Bradley and Patton that had led to Patton being demoted from Army group leader to simply 3rd Army commander. Lt General McNair had been appointed as the new commander for FUSAG to carry out the delayed Calais invasion.

By the middle of July, although the Germans still believed that 30 divisions existed in Britain, they were no longer certain that Calais was the target nor that the attack was the stronger of the two. However, the change was interpreted as a consequence of the attrition rate inflicted on the Allies in Normandy and thus when Jodl assumed that the threat to Calais was finally over, in the middle of July, it was because of German success not German ignorance. Even on 27 July a German Intelligence report insisted that although Patton's FUSAG was 'gradually losing its potential strength for large scale operations ... it will be held ready to attack a sector of the Channel coast when such a sector has definitely been laid bare'.[146] Not until Operation Cobra and the American breakthrough at St Lô at the end of July did elements of the 15th army in the north begin large scale movements south, and by then it was too late.

On 5 August a broadcast from Berlin finally announced: 'Large scale landing operations by the Allies need no longer be reckoned with ... The intentions of the Allies are now quite clear, and that is an advantage to the Germans'.[147] After this ten divisions left for Normandy. On 31 August Garbo announced to his apparent German controllers that the plan to attack the Pas de Calais had definitely been cancelled. On 21 October Brutus announced to the Germans that FUSAG had been disbanded. As Hesketh concludes: 'When all is said, one is left with a sense of astonishment that men is such responsible positions as were those who controlled the destinies of Germany during the late war, could have been so fatally misled on such slender evidence'.[148] This is the crucial point for analysing the role of German strategic leadership on D-Day: despite all the evidence put before them, despite the subordinates' counter-claims that Normandy was the target, and despite the captured plans, the German leaders chose to ignore it all. Had they chosen to approach the problem as if it was Wicked, that is, where they did not have the answers but those around them might have, things might have turned out radically different. But to admit to not knowing was a step too far: better to be decisive and wrong than indecisive and right.

4.8 Conclusion

The intent of the Allies to land a very large invasion force somewhere was already well known to the German High Command and was expected at any time from January 1944 on, but probably in the spring or June/July. Even taking into account the poor information gleaned by the *Luftwaffe* in May and June an array of simple errors by the senior German commanders left the Normandy coast bereft of adequate time and leadership.

First, early on 5 June a large armada of ships was spotted milling around the Portsmouth area and was picked up by the Cherbourg radar just before it was hit by Allied fighter-bombers. That information was available but its significance denied by the senior naval commander. Had it been followed up the German defenders would have had almost 24 hours to prepare.

Second, at 1957 on 5 June the first elements of that flotilla, a British mine-sweeper flotilla, was close enough to the Normandy coast for the British lookouts to see individual houses. Incredibly, no German lookout spotted them and that can only suggest inadequate deployment of troops on the ground by German local commanders.

Third, at 2115 on 5 June the BBC broadcast the verse that the German security services knew meant an invasion was imminent, and certainly due within 48 hours. That information was ridiculed by senior commanders on the grounds that the BBC was hardly likely to announce the invasion in advance.

Fourth, at 0145 on 6 June the fleet was spotted but, despite its direction, the 'wrong' army went onto full alert and the 'right' army was told not to go on full alert.

Fifth, within six hours of the landings it was certainly clear to many junior commanders in the field – given the identities of their attackers – that Normandy was the main invasion site.

But on each and every one of these issues the hubris of the senior German commanders, and their consequent refusal to listen to their subordinates, effectively undermined the German opportunity to do what could so readily – if not easily – have been achieved: they could have thrown the invaders back into the sea. Thus it was not simply that the Allies' intelligence system was superior to the Germans, nor was it that the Germans were betrayed by double agents, nor that the French Resistance effectively uncoupled the German defences from the inside. All of these issues were important but none of them were fatal to the Germans. What was fatal was the poverty of their senior leadership. The soldiers and junior leaders of the *Wehrmacht* were in most cases at least the equal of, and usually more effective than, their Allied counterparts and their actions on the ground – the 'small things' – should have been enough for the big thing – the defence of Normandy – to have been successfully achieved. But the philosophy of German combat – decentralized execution – that had served them so well in the past, was destroyed by the combined actions of several German military commanders, particularly but not only Hitler. The Allied leaders did not so much win the battle for the beaches on 6 June, rather the German leaders lost it on 5 June; they had treated the impending invasion as a Tame Problem that they – and only they – knew how to solve, rather than a Wicked Problem that would require the effective collaboration of many people. But what, precisely, was the German strategy for resisting the invasion?

5 German Strategy: Hard Shell, Soft Shell

5.1 Introduction

While the Allied strategy was built upon isolating the invasion battlefield and persuading the Germans that the real invasion would occur at the Pas de Calais, the German strategy was to hold the invasion up long enough to push the invaders back into the sea. Ironically this inverted both sides' general approach: the prior German successes had been rooted in rapid forward movement of armoured divisions in Blitzkrieg fashion, or, alternatively, in prolonged and skilful fighting retreats on the eastern front; the Allies' successes, such as there were any early in the war, had been by maintaining strong defensive positions. In this sense the Germans, replicating the distinction between exogenous and endogenous skeletons, switched from their traditional 'soft shell' approach to a 'hard shell' approach and the Allies did the reverse. The soft shell approach embodies flexibility at the cost of sustaining reparable damage. In effect, like animals, the surface tissue is easily damaged but repairs easily too. However the 'hard shell'/exogenous skeleton form is much tougher to 'crack' in the first instance because surface damage is easily resisted. However, once the surface is shattered then the integrity of the entire body disintegrates as the shell/skeleton ruptures.

In this chapter we focus on the hard shell German defensive strategy embodied by the Atlantic Wall and once again highlight the extent to which the strategy was a consequence of Leadership decisions, rather than being determined by the situation or a matter of chance. Those decisions were often confused and contradictory, partly because the command structure was so bureaucratic and dysfunctional and partly because the two leading figures charged with defending France, Rommel and von Rundstedt, could not agree upon the most appropriate defensive strategy. The end result was to reproduce the fatal weakness of a Wicked approach – not so much as a delayed decision to weigh up all the options but two contradictory decisions. Thus Hitler placed Rommel's Army Group B, with specific responsibility for defending the northern coast line of

France and the Netherlands, under the overall command of von Runstedt – Commander in Chief West. The strategic Panzer reserves available, Panzer Group West, were in turn under the command of von Schweppenburg who was subordinate to von Rundstedt. Rommel, fearful of the overwhelming power of the Allied air forces, proposed a 'hard shell' system rooted in strongly defended coastal positions and supported by tanks positioned very close to the beaches. Von Schweppenburg, supported by von Rundstedt, preferred the traditional 'soft shell' strategy, allowing the invaders to land but then deploying the tank reserves in large numbers to destroy the Allies as they moved inland. This was actually very close to Brooke's own strategy for the defence of Britain in 1940, as he wrote, 'To my mind our defence should be of a far more mobile and offensive nature. I visualized a light defence along the beaches, to hamper and delay landings to the maximum, and in the rear highly mobile forces trained to immediate aggressive action intended to concentrate and attack any landings before they had time to become too well established'.[1]

Hitler, by this time convinced that only he would be able to distinguish between the expected Allied feint and the real invasion, reserved to himself control over critical tank reserves thus denuding both Rommel and von Rundstedt of the forces necessary for either of their alternative strategies. The resulting 'fatal compromise' was more akin to a tactical farce than a strategic force and it provided the Allies with sufficient time and space to secure a lodgement in Normandy that proved impossible to remove. Moreover, the 'fatal compromise' that ensued limited the possibilities of successfully resisting the invasion because now the forces at the coast were still too weak to resist the invaders whilst the greater dispersal of concentrated armour further inland limited the scope for an effective counter-attack. As a result, the normally mobile defensive units in Normandy became static units so that the lower quality of the troops could be compensated for by providing better defensive protection and by encouraging them to develop in-depth knowledge of the local terrain. And although the Allies were extremely mobile in their ability to land when and where they wanted to, the advantage of mobility would rapidly ebb towards the German defenders as soon as a landing had been made. Moreover, since there would only be five Allied divisions landing on the beaches in the first wave on D-Day – and because the German forces had 50 infantry and ten armoured divisions in France to defeat them – the ultimate victory would go to the side who won the race for reinforcements rather than simply the race for the beach. Indeed, the Allies only had forty-two other divisions to commit to the early stages of the battle for France, so the prospects for victory were not high. Fortunately for the

Allies, as we have already seen, the Germans believed the number was between 75 and 89 in total (thanks to Operation Fortitude). Thus the five division landing in Normandy was even more obviously just a ruse to conceal the much larger landing – of possibly 20 divisions initially – that would come at the Pas-de-Calais later. Indeed, the Germans assessed the shipping accumulating in southern British harbours to be capable of transporting 20 divisions in the first assault wave – four times the number actually involved.[2] Montgomery certainly assumed that the Allies would face five divisions in Normandy on D-Day itself, and that within five days a further seven would arrive; he also assumed that five of the 12 divisions would be armoured. By then he assumed he would have 13 divisions ashore, excluding the airborne divisions, and within 20 days there would be between 23 and 24 divisions ashore.[3]

5.2 The Atlantic Wall

With the failure of the German invasion of Britain and the switch to the east, it became obvious that eventually the Western Allies would attempt an invasion, but the two problems for the Germans were where that would be and when? The 3,500 mile coast from Spain to Norway was all a potential target for the Allies and Hitler implied that the entire length of coastline would form an impregnable 'Atlantic Wall', but in practice the possibilities were much narrower. Nevertheless, in December 1941 Hitler ordered 'the construction of a new West Wall to assure protection of the Arctic, North Sea and Atlantic coasts ... against any landing operation of very considerable strength with the employment of the smallest number of static forces'. It was to be 2,400 miles long, with 15,000 strong points and 300,000 troops. It was designed to be 'impregnable against every enemy'.[4] That impregnability was already apparent in 1941 when the Calais defences were shown to include 16–inch naval guns encased within 23 feet of concrete.

German knowledge about the Allies' strategy – and therefore their own counter-strategy – was premised upon two assumptions, only one of which was accurate: the Allies would have to invade within fighter cover distance from England. That limited the attack to an area from the Netherlands down to the Cotentin peninsular and in this assumption the Germans were right. The second assumption was that any sustained invasion would need the facilities of a major port – here the Germans were wrong. Thus although the whole coastline was deemed to be part of the Atlantic Wall it was assumed that any Allied attack that was not focused upon a port would be a diversionary movement designed to draw

German armour and reinforcements away from the 'real' target. Even though von Rundstedt's own maps showed the potential threat from Normandy and even when a 'war-game' in February 1944 revealed how vulnerable Germany was to a Normandy landing, the High Command chose to ignore it. In May Hitler 1944 himself suggested that Normandy could be the spot but, for once, and fatally, he allowed himself to be dissuaded from strengthening the defences there by Rommel and von Rundstedt.[5]

Much of the explanation behind the preoccupation with defending the ports can be located in the failed Dieppe raid in August 1942. It was heralded by the British as an important learning experience – a euphemism for a poorly planned and executed disaster. Nonetheless, to the Allies Dieppe proved a port could not be taken by force and that an alternative must be found. But perhaps more importantly its effect on the Germans was to confirm their assumptions rather than challenge them: since the German leadership could not countenance an alternative to an assault upon a port, it confirmed that all ports needed to be the focus of the defences.

The most important port was also the one covering the quickest route across the channel, that is from Dover to the Pas-de-Calais, as the French called it, and since the time at sea was also the time of maximum vulnerability to air attack, the quickest and safest route across was there. After all, the British could fly to Calais in just 20 minutes. This line of attack was also the shortest way through Belgium to Berlin and for a long period the British planners favoured this route. For exactly the same reasons the Germans fortified it from early 1942. It was also logical, therefore, for Hitler to situate his 'terror' or 'vengeance' weapons,[6] the V-1 and V-2 rockets, in this area since this also minimized their flight time and would encourage the Allies to attack a position that Hitler considered impregnable. In fact, had the Germans concentrated on the V-1 and launched them in hundreds against the coast of southern England in May 1944, or the coast of Normandy in June 1944, it may well have proved disastrous for the Allies.[7]

Hitler's personal preference for the hard shell strategy became manifest in his *Führer-weisung* (Führer Directive) No. 40, issued on 23 March 1942. In this he admitted that 'even enemy landings with limited objectives can interfere seriously with our own plans if they result in the enemy gaining any kind of foothold on the coast ... Enemy forces that have landed must be destroyed or thrown back into the sea by immediate counterattack'.[8] Hence, between 1942 and June 1944, with a rapid acceleration in the last six months, 250,000 labourers, 90 per cent of whom were conscripted foreign labourers – little more than slaves –

worked on the wall's defences, often with only day off per month and on 12 hour shifts, 7 days a week. Some 700 designs for gun emplacements, living quarters, observation towers and so on were drawn up by the German planners and each strong point was built by selecting a specific number of the available designs, and many embodied disguises to dissuade enemy fire.[9] Not all the guns positions were built by non-German labour, primarily because Rommel recognized that there was simply too much work to do in too little time, for example, the positions of the infantry Division's guns north of Caen were built by German soldiers.[10]

In the summer of 1943 Hitler issued Führer Directive No. 51 that asserted that the western theatre was now the critical place to defend Germany and that the enemy would not be allowed to maintain a foothold on the coast.

> The danger in the East remains, but a greater danger now appears in the West: an Anglo-Saxon landing! In the East, the vast extent of the territory makes it possible for us to lose ground, even on a large scale, without a fatal blow being dealt to the nervous system of Germany. It is very different in the West! Should the enemy succeed in breaching our defences here on a wide front, the immediate consequences would be unpredictable. Everything indicates that the enemy will launch an offensive against the Western front of Europe, at the latest in the spring, perhaps even earlier ... . Should the enemy, by assembling all his forces, succeed in landing, he must be met with a counter-attack delivered with all our weight ... . The *Luftwaffe* and *Kriegsmarine* must go into action against the heavy attacks which we must expect by air and sea with all the forces at their disposal, regardless of the cost.[11]

Von Rundstedt's reply to Hitler, which took several months to write, suggested that the defence of the west was an impossible task given the existing state of the available resources and that without a strategic reserve nothing could be guaranteed. Nevertheless, Hitler promised the resources and insisted that all the necessary bombers and fighters would be switched from the east to the west as soon as the invasion started – but even he should have known that this was an impossible task unless greater production of aircraft and training of aircrew was initiated immediately. Yet there were only 60 divisions allocated to the defence of the west, while 322 remained elsewhere – if 'the greatest danger' was indeed in the west, it is difficult to understand why more divisions were not switched from east to west.[12]

In fact, the Atlantic Wall only existed in sections but it was formidable where it did exist and took around 17 million cubic yards of concrete and 1.5 million tons of iron to build it.[13] The 15,000 strongpoints were composed of a network of related elements: reinforced heavy gun emplacements (some with 13 feet of reinforced concrete) already zeroed in on the beaches, machine guns with their sights fixed onto arcs of fire across the beaches, minefields, barbed wire, anti-tank and anti-landing craft obstacles, underground living quarters, communication tunnels and radar stations. These all existed in places where the Germans assumed a landing was possible. The supporting beach artillery was generally one of four kinds:

- *Heavy coastal defence anti-ship batteries* composed of about four 122–155 mm guns in reinforced concrete housings up to two metres thick and directed by forward observation positions
- *Casemated (armoured compartment) field guns and howitzer batteries* of about four 105–155 mm guns in reinforced concrete housings up to two metres thick firing directly onto the beach. The guns were usually wheeled and could be brought out of the casemate for all-round firing.
- *Open field gun and howitzer batteries* of about four 105–155 mm guns without a direct field of fire onto the beach and therefore directed by forward observation posts
- *Beach defence strongpoints* (*Widerstandnest*, {WN}) built around beach exists or draws and comprising either:
  ○ concrete (2 metre thick) 75–88mm gun emplacements, or
  ○ concrete (2 metre thick) 50mm anti-tank gun shelters, and an inter-connected trench system linking underground living quarters and pill boxes with machine guns and mortar positions
  ○ open 50mm and 75mm mortar positions
  On average such a strongpoint would house around 30 troops with ten machine guns, an artillery piece and an additional 50mm gun.[14]

For example, the 352nd Division defending Omaha had twelve 105mm and twelve 150mm artillery pieces. In addition, the beach could be fired on by 60 smaller artillery pieces and had eight major bunkhouses containing 75 or 88 mm guns, 35 smaller emplacements, 18 anti-tank guns and six removed tank turrets. WN 60 also had automatic flame-throwers and, overall, at least 85 machine guns were sighted onto the beach. Behind the bluffs were mortar and rocket pits, all pre-sighted onto the beach. The heavier artillery behind the beach was directed by forward artillery observers in WN 60, 62, 71, 73 and 74.[15]

But the Atlantic Wall was composed of more than just a physical sea wall with concrete gun emplacements in places; it was also a defensive system in depth. The German army in the First World War had developed 'Defence in Depth' tactics in which, rather than provide a thickly populated and defended front line – a hard shell – they installed an array of between four and seven increasingly well defended lines – sometimes as much as ten miles deep. This soft shell made the possibilities of a clear 'breakthrough' increasingly difficult and costly.[16] In Normandy, although less than a quarter of the materials devoted to the Pas de Calais region were used to build up the defences, similar German tactics were adapted to the local conditions: the 'thin' German front line would allow the Allies past them and only when they had reached the second or third line would the ambush from the first line begin. As Reynolds[17] concludes, 'this type of innovative thinking made great demands on the German troops, particularly in terms of personal discipline, but it had a devastating effect on the Allies'. The defence in depth approach also ensured that whenever the Allies came up against any German opposition it was never clear to the attackers whether it was the first elements of a deep soft shell or simply a few isolated defenders; whatever it was, the Allies tended to halt and call up an artillery barrage or ground-attack aircraft to clear the defenders rather than to push directly through them. As Badsey[18] suggests, 'Defending the hedgerows and farmhouses gave the Germans a massive advantage in close-quarters fighting, and as casualties rose so did the temptation to rely on firepower: "never send a man where you can send a bomb or a bullet" became the motto of many'.

While von Rundstedt was responsible for overall military control in Normandy, on 31 December 1943 Rommel was appointed Inspector General of Defences in the West, thus adding a third element of confusion to the one that saw von Rundstedt and Hitler in competition for control. Rommel submitted a highly critical report after his initial inspection of the wall and suggested that 'The focus of the enemy landing operation will probably be directed against the 15th *Armee* sector, largely because it is from this sector that much of our long range attacks (the V-1) on England and central London will be launched'.[19] Rommel was also convinced that the invaders had to be destroyed on the beachhead if they were to be beaten and certain about the nature of the problem. 'I have only one real enemy now', he told his aide Captain Lang, 'and that is time'.[20] Given the refusal of Hitler to allocate all the available Panzer units to him, Rommel felt he had little choice but to concentrate on strengthening the static defences and he immediately instigated several improvements to the Atlantic Wall. These included: mining of the beaches, flooding of the surrounding areas, improving coastal fortifications, especially concrete bunkers or 'resistance nests', constructing beach obstacles to impede armoured landings, and constructing field obstacles of tall poles to prevent glider landings ('Rommel's asparagus' as it became known). But two months later, in March 1944, Rommel's report on the defences remained pessimistic: 'Our defence line, thin as it is at present, will suffer severely from the enemy bombing and artillery bombardment and it seems very doubtful whether, after this battering, it will be capable of beating off the enemy, whose forces will be approaching over a wide front, in hundreds of armoured assault craft and landing craft and under cover of darkness or fog'.[21]

Rommel's original plan called for 50 million poles and 1,000 metre-deep minefields around the entire coastline using 20 million mines, sometimes with 10 mines per metre[22] and although by D-Day only 4 million mines were in situ, along with 500,000 anti-invasion obstacles, Rommel had already suggested that by the middle of May he was 'more confident than ever before'. Indeed, in April he had admitted that he was satisfied with the beach defences along the coast at the Pas de Calais – but he not happy with those in Normandy. Nonetheless, the erection of beach defences forced the Allies to reconsider the assault. Ironically, given Rommel's assumptions about the problems he would face with a night time or fog bound assault, he also forced the Allies to switch from a night to a dawn attack to minimize the casualties caused by the new defences. The defences also persuaded Montgomery to move the timing of the landing from high tide – which would minimize the run across the sand to the defenders – to a midway point between high and low tide. This would allow the landing craft to see the otherwise submerged defences while limiting the length of the run across the beaches. Furthermore, there would now need to be large numbers of combat engineers who could disarm the defences before the main assault was carried out and the whole invasion would be led – rather than followed – by armoured assault vehicles.[23]

The depth defensive scheme in Normandy involved three lines and extended up to six miles inland from the beach. The first line was the beach itself complete with its obstacles, mines, anti-tank ditches and beach defenders. The second was the network of strong-points up to six miles inland, sited to over look – and hold-up- any infantry breaking through the first line of beach defences. This network was incomplete by D-Day – despite Rommel's attempt to spur on the work by giving out prizes of harmonicas and accordions to any unit completing its tasks ahead of schedule. For example, none existed behind Omaha while the invaders at Sword Beach had to get past Hillman, two miles inland of la Brêche d'Hermanville. But the speed with which the defences were built still astonished the Allies: in just four days over 2,000 yards of beach was laced with a double row of tetrahydra and hedgehogs and by 11 May over 517,000 beach obstacles were in place.[24] Anything breaking beyond these strong-points would then be met by the mobile reserves, the third line of defence. However, Rommel's primary focus lay on the beach itself. As he insisted: 'The high water line must be the main fighting line'.[25] But there were weaknesses, both in the gaps in defences and in the vulnerability of the defences; it was, as one German General called it: 'a thin, in many places fragile, piece of cord with a few small knots'.[26]

Even those knots could be fragile: the very strength of the defences also operated against the defenders since they assumed that many areas could be successfully held by second rate troops (and 25 per cent of the German army was over 34 by 1944), leaving most of the elite to stave off the Red Army in the east. In fact, 20 German battalions were transferred from the west to the east on Hitler's direct orders and he had promised von Rundstedt that 60 'Eastern Volunteer' battalions would replace them. As Zimmerman was later to argue, these were mostly 'former Russian prisoners of war, ill-trained and ill-equipped. What earthly use could such troops be against the enemy's weight or technical skill? What reason was there to believe that these 'volunteers' would even pretend to fight against their Western allies? It was all quite insane'.[27] As early as the spring of 1943 von Rundstedt had already concluded that the situation was impossible and he visited Hitler to demand increased resources but Hitler treated him to a two-hour monologue on the eastern front and von Rundstedt left empty handed. Worse, many of the engineers and the construction workers in *Organization Todt* that were destined to build the coastal defences were transported north to the V-weapons sites without his knowledge.

The inadequate German defences in Normandy were not simply the result of a false assumption about the Pas de Calais being the target but also because the *Kriegsmarine* (German navy) had assured everyone that the fortress at Cherbourg would be able to defend the eastern Normandy beaches with ease while the western beaches were simply too difficult to use as an invasion platform. Equally critical, Hitler was convinced that; 'by far the most important thing for the enemy will be to gain a port for landings on the largest possible scale. This alone gives a wholly special importance to the west coast ports and orders have therefore been issued designating them fortresses ...'[28] In fact Vice Admiral Krancke had already warned Hitler that 'The few available destroyers, torpedo and speed boats can only harass an enemy landing, but they cannot effectively impede it'.[29] Nevertheless *Grossadmiral* Dönitz ordered every available U-boat to attack the invader's shipping on D-Day, and 17 left Brest under cover of darkness but on the surface – as ordered. Four of these were put out of action within hours by Allied aircraft.[30]

However, since at least March 1944 Hitler had demanded that no tactical retreat was to be contemplated when the expected invasion eventually occurred and Rommel's Atlantic Wall, part of the fortress Europe mentality, merely buttressed this approach. The result was that the effort to break through the initial defences of the hard shell was much more difficult than assumed, for the Allies believed that the Germans would act as von Rundstedt suggested and reproduce their traditional soft shell approach – make a tactical retreat and take advantage of their Panzer groups to break up the Allied movements inland. But such was the cost involved to the defenders in pursuit of Fortress Europe, that the 'defence in depth' strategy was uncoupled from the tactical retreat, hence once the German defence shell cracked, the defenders were unable to retreat and regroup thus – eventually – allowing rapid penetration inland. In effect, what was a Wicked Problem: how to deal with the invasion, had been reduced to a Tame Problem by Hitler's intervention and refusal to back either one or the other strategies of resistance properly. The gaps between the fortresses provided self-evident points of vulnerability – as even von Rundstedt acknowledged: 'The strength of our defences is absurdly overrated. The "Atlantic Wall" was an illusion; conjured up by propaganda – to deceive the German people as well as the Allies ... . It was a nonsense to describe it as a 'wall', Hitler himself never came to visit it, and see what it really was'.[31] Rommel privately referred to the Atlantic Wall as 'a figment of Hitler's *Wolkenkuckucksheim* (cloud-cuckoo land).[32] For example, most of the communication systems from the defences back to headquarters were telephone landlines not radio links – and thus very vulnerable to enemy bombardment from the air or sea. Most of the equipment was composed of captured weapons for which there was often a lack of ammunition and little in the way of fire-direction equipment – critical for engaging ships at sea or precise points on beaches.[33] In fact, Goebbels, the German Minister of Propaganda, turned the wall from an admission of the limits and weakness of Germany, into a symbol of defiance, calling it the boundary line of '*Festung Europa*' – Fortress Europe. It was 'a fortress', admitted Franklin D Roosevelt, 'but a fortress without a roof'.[34] But why was Rommel, the arch Panzer general, not given complete control over all the resources available to defend Normandy? The answer to that question explains why German failure on D-Day was not a consequence of inadequate technology but inadequate strategy and bureaucratic incompetence.

5.3 The German command structure and the fatal compromise

The German army was theoretically strong enough to deal effectively with any Allied threat from the west – after all, it had 1,873,000 troops there but the defence was only viable if it could move a sufficient concentration of forces to the invasion area faster than the Allies could. By June 1944 von Rundstedt had 58 divisions, including 10 Panzer divisions, as set out below:

15th Army:
1st SS Panzer Division: Belgium
2nd Panzer Division: Amiens
116th Panzer Division: Pontoise

7th Army:
21st Panzer Division: south of Caen
12th SS Panzer Division: Dreux
Panzer Lehr Division: south of Chartres

1st Army
17th SS Panzer Grenadiers: north-west of Poitiers
11th Panzer Division: east of Bordeaux

19th Army:
2nd SS Panzer Division: Toulouse
9th Panzer Division: Avignon[35]

Allied planners assumed that by D-Day+7 all three of the 7th Army's Panzer divisions north of the Seine would have arrived in Normandy (116th Panzer on D-Day+1, 2nd Panzer and 1st SS Panzer, plus 2nd SS Panzer and 11th Panzer Division by D+7). It was also assumed that three infantry divisions (84th, 85th and 331st) would supplement the armour by the end of the first week.[36]

Forty-six of the 58 divisions were deployed to defend the entire French coastline but only 36 divisions were under Rommel's control and the vast majority were still in northern France, Belgium and Holland.[37] Moreover, he actually had fewer tanks than had been used to invade France four years earlier.[38] In Normandy itself there were just 20 divisions and 14 of these were static divisions.[39] These were what the Germans called *bodenständige* or 'ground-holding' divisions, which, in the absence of any motorized transport and the presence of many middle-aged troops (average age 36) – was probably accurate.[40] The total only amounted to one division for every 120 miles which, given the shrunken state of the average German division by then, meant that each soldier had to guard around 19 yards of coast.[41] Thus, however much concrete and wire and however many guns defended the coast, the co-ordination of the defences lay in the rather more fragile hands of humans, and therein lay a fatal weakness for the Germans.

Hitler had appointed himself Commander in Chief of the armed forces in the office of the *Oberkommando der Wehrmacht* (OKW) but in December 1941, as a consequence of the stalled invasion of the Soviet Union, Hitler appointed himself as head of the army too as *Oberkommando des Heeres* (OKH). The division of responsibilities was set such that OKH fought the war in the east, OKW fought the war in the west. There was, then, no military equivalent of Eisenhower's Supreme Commander. And though Eisenhower set out the strategy but seldom interfered at a tactical level in the decisions of his commanders, he ultimately controlled them by remaining in control of the allocation of resources between different armies and army groups. Von Rundstedt's view on this is nicely captured by his comment, 'You see the guard posted outside? If I want to post him on the other side of the house, I must first ask permission of Berchtesgaden'.[42]

Army Group B contained two armies, the 7th and the 15th. The 7th Army was responsible for the area west of the River Orne (basically Normandy and Brittany), while the 15th guarded from there to the Dutch border with the 88th Corps protecting the Dutch coast. Von Rundstedt had no formal authority over the *Luftwaffe* (OKL) or the navy (OKM). Not that this really mattered since it was widely believed on the German side that the *Luftwaffe* would be outnumbered 50 to 1 and the naval forces were virtually non-existent.[43] The confusion over responsibility also prevailed within von Rundstedt's own forces in Army Group B, which were commanded by Rommel but under von Rundstedt's general responsibility. General Geyr von Schweppenburg's Panzer Group West, stationed near Paris, was under the formal control of von Rundstedt not Rommel, though even here Hitler took overall responsibility for it and it did not become operational until 1600 on D-Day. Thus the chain of command set Hitler, von Rundstedt, Rommel and von Schweppenburg all with conflicting responsibilities.

In March 1944 Rommel managed to secure control over three of the armoured divisions within Panzer Group West but the other three, including Sepp Dietrich's 1st SS Panzer Corps, remained with Hitler's personal control as OKW commander. To complicate matters further, all the Parachute and Air Landing Divisions in the area, including all the 88mm guns used for anti-aircraft and anti-tank artillery, were controlled by the *Luftwaffe's Luftflotte* 3, led by Hugo Sperrle under Goering. In May 1944 Rommel tried to persuade Goering to move the 88mm guns of the 3rd Flak Corps closer to the beaches but – fortunately for the Allies – he failed.[44] The division, nay the confusion, of command reached absurd levels in some areas, for example, control over the coastal batteries remained in the hands of the German navy but only as long as the invading troops remained at sea, once they had landed responsibility passed to the *Wehrmacht*.

Yet the division of responsibilities was not the only issue – what mattered was how the forces were to be deployed, and here there was a sharp difference of opinion between those favouring a hard shell response, such as Rommel, and those favouring a soft shell approach, such as von Rundstedt. As we shall see, the *bocage* areas that so bedevilled the American advance through Normandy, also made German armoured counter-attacks problematic. Indeed, Copp (2006) argues that the mechanical nature of German responses to lost ground – an immediate counter-attack – demonstrates how little German tactical thought developed in Normandy because it was always predictable and usually met by an Allied artillery barrage. However, the philosophy of an immediate counter-attack at least allowed relatively low-level commanders to organize such a response without reference to superior commanders – as Major Hans von Luck did during Operation Goodwood (Melvin, 2006: 26).

In fact the countryside was ideal for defence but not for attack by either side – and even if the German armour could be concentrated there was no significant *Luftwaffe* presence to defend it from Allied air attack. Yet the close support of armoured divisions to support the defenders wherever the Allies landed was vital, for Rommel assumed that however strong his defensive wall was it could only *delay* but not *prevent* an Allied landing. However, this delay would allow the concentration of armoured divisions to defeat the invasion not inland as von Rundstedt insisted, but on the beaches, for Rommel assumed that Allied air superiority would render the mobilization of armour from positions beyond the reach of the Allied warships impossible. For Rommel, 'the enemy's weakest moment is when he lands. The men are uncertain, possibly seasick. The terrain is unfamiliar. Sufficient heavy weapons are not yet available. I must defeat them at that moment ... The invasion will be decided on the beach and in the first twenty-four hours'.[45] Thus Rommel became obsessed with strengthening the coastal defences, even at the expense of training to repel an invasion and even if it meant – as it did – taking almost all tank crews out of their tanks to pour cement into bunkers, with the exception of the 21st Panzers who insisted on offensive training not defensive building.[46] As far as Bayerlain, commander of *Panzer Lehr*,[47] was concerned he was at one with Rommel for:

> There is a real danger that when the invasion does come we will be caught in the wrong place ... . Rommel insists the Bay of Seine is the most likely spot for a landing. I am sure he will be proved correct ... . I fear if they [the Allies] are allowed to build up sufficient strength in matériel and manpower they will overwhelm us. They are capable in time of fielding a huge army on the continent. As to the British, I know them from experience. We are in for a tough fight. Even though I have no great fears over their tank arm.[48]

For their part, the British had already assumed that Rommel's strategy would be rooted in a hard shell style. Montgomery accepted his Chief Intelligence Officer's (Brigadier Williams) assessment that Rommel would try to hold the Allies on the beachhead for 'he is too impulsive for the set-piece battle'[49] and more importantly, because 'his intention is to deny any penetration: Overlord is to be defeated on the beaches'. If that failed Rommel would try to 'rope us off' in the Bocage.[50] Unfortunately, Montgomery does not seem to have considered what the latter remark entailed. Nevertheless he was convinced that Rommel had neither enough good quality soldiers to hold up the invasion on the beach, nor did Hitler allow him enough tanks to support his strategy, nor did the *Luftwaffe* or navy appear in any significant numbers.

Rommel had spoken to Bayerlein on 12 May 1944 about the problem, suggesting that the issue was not about impulsiveness but resources:

> You have no idea how difficult it is to convince these people (at OKW). At one time they looked on mobile warfare as something to keep clear of at all costs, but now that our freedom of manoeuvre in the West is gone, they're all crazy after it. Whereas, in fact, it's obvious that if the enemy once gets his foot in, he'll put every anti-tank gun and tank he can into the bridgehead and let us beat our heads against it, as he did at Medenine. To break through such a front you have to attack slowly and methodically, under cover of massed artillery, but we, of course, thanks to the Allied air forces, will have nothing there in time. The day of the dashing cut-and-thrust tank attack of the early war years is past and gone.[51]

The 21st Division's Lt General Feuchtinger was another adherent to Rommel's cause, concerned that his unit had lost too many good soldiers in Africa and Russia. But he was also concerned, ironically, that the patchwork of farms and villages in Normandy prevented his unit from 'realistic' tank training. Thus he had been unable to practice large scale manoeuvres, even though such tactics were extremely unlikely in the region. Nevertheless, he too was certain that 'the invasion must be defeated on the beaches'.[52]

However, in favour of the soft shell approach was von Rundstedt, with the support of von Schweppenburg (Commander of Panzer Group West), and Guderian (Inspector General of Panzers). Von Schweppenburg was convinced that although Rommel had suffered from the effects of Allied air domination in North Africa, he had learned the wrong lesson.[53] Normandy was not the North African desert and the Bocage provided opportunities for armoured movement that simply did not exist amidst rolling sand dunes. Von Schweppenburg, von Rundstedt and Guderian collectively demanded that the armoured divisions be pooled in a central area further away from the coast – where the Allied battle ships could not destroy them. Such a deployment would then facilitate a significant counter attack inland, where German tank superiority would deliver a knockout counter punch to the Allies. After all, the concentration not the dispersal of force is how German victories in the past had been achieved.[54] This was certainly what Churchill assumed would happen because he had expressed astonishment in 1940 when France fell, for the French had no mobile armoured reserves. As he remarked at the time: 'No one can defend with certainty so wide a front: but when the enemy has committed himself to a major thrust which breaks the line, one can always have, one *must* always have, a mass of divisions which marches up in vehement counterattack at the moment when the first fury of the offensive has spent its force'.[55]

Von Rundstedt and Geyr von Schweppenburg were also concerned about Allied airdrops just behind the coast which could jeopardize any armour placed there in line with Rommel's plans, especially by cutting off fuel supplies. In this instance Rommel's argument was very clear: 'To my mind, as long as we hold the coast, an enemy airborne landing of an operational nature must, sooner or later, finish up in the destruction of the troops who have landed ... . I have disagreed very violently with General Geyr over this question and will only be able to execute my ideas if he is put under Army Group command early enough'.[56]

Rommel eventually sought Hitler's permission to use *Panzer Lehr* and 12th Panzer as mobile reserves close to the coast but Hitler, as ever, avoided a decision and, wary of Rommel's increasing pessimism, compromised by splitting the seven available Panzer divisions into two groups. The largest group of four, the 1st SS Panzer Corps, including *Panzer Lehr*, the 1st SS Panzer Division, the 17th SS *Panzergrenadier* and the 12th SS Panzer, was stationed near Paris as a mobile reserve led by General Sepp Dietrich but under Hitler's personal command. Indeed, it could not be activated without his personal order so convinced was he that part of the invasion would involve a feint in one direction to draw his reserves away from the main site, and that only he would recognize the difference between a feint and a real assault. Anyway, when he did deploy them 'Their part is to get killed behind the fortifications. So they've no need to be mobile'.[57]

As D-Day approached Rommel drove to Paris on 3 June to buy his wife some shoes for her birthday (on 6 June), remarking that the poor weather meant that the invasion would not occur while it held (though he had previously warned his troops not to assume precisely this). Even the Anti-Aircraft crews around Paris were stood down, so poor was the weather. Ironically, Rommel had also been away, in Rome, when the Alamein offensive started and this time was intending to go on from Paris to see Hitler at Berchtesgaden to ask for two more Panzer divisions to be moved to Normandy. Like many senior commanders, Rommel assumed that the Allied invasion would coincide with, or start a little later than, the expected Soviet summer offensive. And since the Soviet attack could not begin until the late Polish spring it was widely accepted that late June would be the earliest date for D-Day.[58] In the event D-Day predated the Soviet Offensive by a couple of weeks and, once again, the German forces assembled their strongest defences in the 'wrong' place, fooled by a Soviet campaign of disinformation equivalent to Allies' Operation Fortitude.[59]

Dollman, Commander of the 7th Army also thought the invasion would be delayed a while yet, especially given the weather forecast from the Cap de la Hague on the Cotentin peninsular which had warned of 'Rough sea, poor visibility, forces 5 to 6 wind, rain likely to get heavier'. Major General Falley, Commander of the German 91st Air Landing Division near St, Mère-Eglise was equally convinced. As he told his Chief of Operations on 5 June: Nothing's going to happen in this lousy weather'.[60] Within 24 hours Falley was ambushed and shot dead by American paratroopers.

But an invasion might come in Normandy, hence Dollman ordered his commanders to attend a *Kriegsspiel* (war game) in Rennes at 1000 on 6 June – based on the possible invasion of Normandy! General Marcks disagreed and asserted he knew the British very well. 'They will go to church on Sunday, they will land here in Normandy on Monday'.[61] Only the 24-hour delay surprised him. Yet Marcks also left for southern Germany and did not return until the afternoon of D-Day. At about the same time – now 1600 – Hitler finally gave permission for the two armoured divisions in Normandy (*Panzer Lehr* and 12th SS *Hitlerjugend* under Fritz Witt) to move towards the coast – by which time the Allies had consolidated their slender foothold and the improving weather allowed them to unleash waves of fighter bombers upon the German armoured columns.[62]

5.4 Conclusion

Rommel's hard shell and von Rundstedt's soft shell strategy were probably both adequate to some extent: near the coast the tanks were vulnerable to shipping attack and away from the coast they were vulnerable to
air attack; either way they were vulnerable because the Luftwaffe had
ceded control of the sky to the Allies. Only poor weather and/or night
movements could hope to succeed – and ironically the weather was poor
early on D-Day and there was enough warning to move the armour into
position under cover of darkness before the landings occurred, but the
strategic ineptitude of the Hitler and the military High Command effectively undermined this window of opportunity. After all, Major-General
Doolittle, CO of the American 8th Air Force, worked from research
suggesting that poor weather would hinder or prevent flying for as many
as 240 days a year (66 per cent).[63] Similarly, on 19 February 1944,
Eisenhower admitted in a letter to Marshall that the Italian evidence
worried him. 'For the past five days there has been good weather in Italy
and our reports show an average of 1,000 sorties per day. Yet with only
two main roads and a railway on which to concentrate, our reports show
a steady stream of enemy traffic by night'.[64] In short with much poorer
weather and a much denser network of roads in France, even a monop-
oly of the air would not bring the German logistics system to a halt. Thus
it was always going to be a possibility that irrespective of the strength of
the relative air forces, the German armour might be able to move
towards the beaches under cover of cloud or darkness. Eisenhower relied
critically upon one thing to ensure success on the beaches, even at the
expense of the airborne attacks:

> If we were not depending so definitely upon the bombardment effect of our
> bombers to help us tactically and strategically, there would be available a greatly
> increased force to support and maintain airborne operations, but present plans call
> for an all-out effort on the part of both day and night bombers for a very consid-
> erable period both preceding and following D-Day.[65]

In fact the cloud base was too low in the early part of D-Day to facilitate fighter-bomber activity thus providing von Rundstedt's option of
moving the reserves with some hope, especially if Hitler had released the
armoured units of the 7th Army to help. And Rommel's original counter-
invasion plan would have deployed the 12th SS and *Panzer Lehr* almost
exactly where the line marking the Allied objectives for D-Day would
have been.[66] And since the sea bombardment proved insufficient to
destroy the beach fortifications Rommel's plan could also have worked

but only if he had sufficient forces to hold the Allies on the beach for long enough to get a sufficient number of his tanks to the beachhead to push the invaders back into the sea. Ironically, then, D-Day morning provided precisely what the Germans needed – but the decision of various leaders, coupled with the inept command and control system, prevented any large scale movement until it was too late.

Since the tanks of 21st Panzer Division did indeed almost reach the coast between Sword and Juno on the afternoon of D-Day – only being stopped by anti-tank guns not aircraft – it is clear that Rommel's aerial pessimism was misplaced. Indeed, even without the *Luftwaffe* the Germans stemmed the advance into Normandy after D-Day for two months. Ironically, it was Rommel who placed an embargo on the movement of the 21st Panzer Division without his personal order – and von Schweppenburg who had ordered it to move towards the coast. Indeed, von Schweppenburg claimed that on 17 July just before being wounded by a passing Spitfire, Rommel had admitted to one of his officers 'It would perhaps have been better after all to have held the Panzer divisions back'.[67] It was also alleged that Rommel had confided to one of his aides on 7 June that the war was lost: 'It is better to end this at once and live as a British dominion than be ruined by continuing this hopeless war'.[68] However, the fatal compromise induced by Hitler and never adequately challenged by his commanders, coupled with his indecision, ensured that the necessary strength to remain at the coast was missing.

Nevertheless, it is important to remember that Hitler's indecisive actions on D-Day did not derive from any fear of invasion on his part, quite the opposite, he positively welcomed it, since, he argued, it would provide him with the opportunity to defeat the Anglo-American forces with such vigour that neither Roosevelt nor Churchill would survive. As he reported to his generals on 18 March 1944:

> Once defeated, the enemy will never try to invade again. Quite apart from their heavy losses they would need months to organize a fresh attempt. And an invasion failure would also deliver a crushing blow to British and American morale ... We shall then transfer (our divisions in the west) to the eastern front to revolutionize the situation there ... so the whole outcome of the war depends on each man fighting in the west and that mean the fate of the Reich itself.[69]

After being informed of the invasion Hitler went to a reception for the new Hungarian Prime Minister in Salzburg.[70] On hearing of the invasion Hitler proclaimed: 'The news couldn't be better. As long as they were in Britain we couldn't get at them. Now we have them where we can destroy them'.[71] His confidence seems to have been supported by a large proportion of the German population for an SD report at the time

suggested (for the last time) that the majority thought that the chance
for victory was now within German hands, especially in the absence of
any expected revolt by the 7 million foreign workers.[72] In fact, the
absence of widespread support either within the army or the civilian
population for the July bombers' assassination attempt on Hitler
suggests that few believed Hitler was dragging the country to its doom
at this time. After all, food supplies remained stable – thanks to the
wholesale transfer of supplies from occupied countries, particularly the
Netherlands, – and working hours remained stable at 60 hours per week.
Only when this was increased to a standard 72-hour week in the latter
part of the war did absenteeism increase markedly, and it wasn't until
Cherbourg fell at the end of June that civilian morale began its slow
descent. As an SD report concluded: 'The enthusiasm of the first days
after the beginning of the invasion and the retribution [against the
Allies] suffers a rapid slackening off everywhere. The initial great happiness and hope that the military situation would decisively change and
that it would 'again go forward with us' has given way to very sober and
sceptical reflections'.[73]

It would be tempting to conclude that the result of this strategic blundering by the German leadership led directly to their defeat in Normandy
and that at least here we have good examples of strategic leaders causing
strategic effects. But even this is difficult to maintain. The poor weather
on the morning of D-Day effectively inhibited not just Allied bombing
of the beaches but Allied destruction of German armoured movements
towards the beach area. It would then, have been possible to move the
Panzer divisions and they would have provided a significant threat to the
precarious Allied landings. That such movements were made by subordinate commanders, and then countermanded by various superordinate
leaders, including Hitler, does not necessarily relieve the subordinates of
responsibility – they could still have overridden their superordinate's
orders, as traditional German military philosophy implied and as subsequently happened when the retreat to Germany was ordered against
Hitler's wishes. The problem for the Germans, then, was not simply that
Hitler interfered, or the strategy was confused, but that the flexibility of
response, so painstakingly embedded into the German military for over a
century, was destroyed by the decisions and actions of many German
leaders. Finally, what about the ground strategy of the Allies?

6 Allied Ground Strategy

6.1 Introduction

All Allied ground troops in the 21st Army Group were under Montgomery's direct command with the American 1st Army under Bradley and the Anglo-Canadians under Lt General Dempsey's British 2nd Army. On the eastern side Crocker commanded the 1st Corps composed of the British at Sword (British 3rd Division) and the Canadian 3rd Division at Juno, while Bucknall (later to be fired by Montgomery) led the British 30th Corps on to Gold (British 50th Division). This was a 25 mile sector of relatively flat land (except between Port en Bessin and Arromanches on Gold), defended by the German 716th Infantry Division in the east and the German 352nd Infantry Division in the west.

6.2 Anglo-Canadian beaches

Sword Beach, the most easterly of the beaches, from St-Aubin-sur-Mer to Ouistreham, was defended by what were thought to be the 150mm guns of the Merville battery (they were actually 75mm guns), just east of Ouistreham which was the target of Otway's 6th Airborne Division. The beach was attacked by the British 3rd Infantry Division supported by the French Commandos and the British 1st Commando Brigade under Lord Lovat. The latter's role was to clear Ouistreham and link up with the British 6th Airborne Division at the Orne bridgehead and by 1300 the link up had been achieved (two minutes behind schedule).[1] The 3rd Infantry Division was to capture Caen while number 41 and 48 Commandos were to establish a common link between Juno and Sword.

Juno Beach extended from La Rivière at the line linking the Juno and Gold beaches in the West to St-Aubin-sur-Mer at the line linking Juno to Sword in the east. The aim of the Canadians was to reach the Caen-Bayeux road and to link up with the British beaches on either side. Gold Beach itself lay between Asnelles and La Rivière and it encompassed Arromanches which was to be taken by No. 47 Royal Marine Commando and used as a base for the British Mulberry harbour.

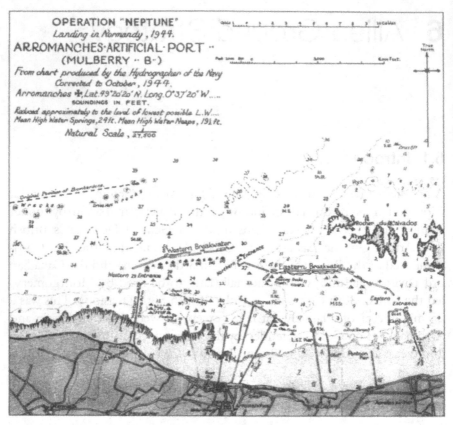

Map 6.1 Arromanches Artificial Port (Mulberry B)

Like the other two Anglo-Canadian beaches, Juno and Sword, Gold Beach comprised small holiday hamlets and seaside towns, not at all like the empty bluffs at Omaha or the bare expanses of beach at Utah. It stretched from Port-en-Bessin to La Rivière and the main assault was to be undertaken by the 5th Battalion the East Yorkshire Regiment on King Red, the 6th Green Howards on King Green, the 1st Battalion the Dorset Regiment on Jig Red and the 1st Battalion the Hampshire Regiment on Jig Green.

The initial role of the Anglo-Canadians was to move south and east of Caen and to hold off German reinforcements until the Americans had completed their initial task and to press south themselves beyond Caen. The task of the 35,000 Americans was to cut off and hold the Cotentin Peninsular and to capture Cherbourg in 15 days. They were to land the US 5th Corps under Gerow on Omaha and the US 7th Corps under Lawton Collins on Omaha, though the Omaha debacle prompted Bradley to alter the timing of the Cherbourg assault so that initially the

7th Corps moved south to support the 5th Corps, rather than the other way round.[2] The American beaches (Utah and Omaha) were hit first because of the tidal difference between the western and the eastern beaches, and because the units involved in the most westerly beach were situated in the most westerly part of the UK they had been at sea the longest – for as many as 60 hours in some cases.

6.3 American beaches

Bradley had taken command of all US ground forces in October 1943 and by D-Day he had over 700,000 troops in 11 divisions. But only four of these had combat experience. On Omaha, the 1st Division had taken part in the amphibious landings in North Africa and Sicily but the 29th Division had not. The Big Red One, as the 1st Division was known, comprised three Regimental Combat Teams (RCTs) and, as far as Bradley was concerned, this division was critical to any successful assault – despite the grievances of the troops that they had already undertaken their share of combat by D-Day. In Bradley's post action report: 'Had a less experienced division that the 1st stumbled into this crack resistance, it might easily have been thrown back into the channel. Unjust as it was, my choice of the 1st to spearhead the invasion probably saved us at Omaha Beach and a catastrophe on the landings'.[3] This may have been the case – but it implies that the 29th Division was the weaker of the two elements – and there is little evidence that this was the case. The day's objectives were to move roughly five miles inland to link up with the British to the east, the Pointe du Hoc Rangers in the west and the airborne troops inland.

The first phase of the assault on Omaha planned for 34,142 troops and 3,306 vehicles to be landed, rapidly followed by the second wave of 25,115 troops and 4,429 vehicles. On D+1 and D+2 a further 17,500 and 2,300 vehicles would land and by D+15 another 32,000 troops and 9,446 vehicles would provide a total paper strength of almost 110,000 soldiers and nearly 20,000 vehicles. Primary responsibility for Omaha on D-Day rested with the 1st Division's 16th RCT and the 29th Division's 116th RCT, the latter under the temporary control of the former.

Between Omaha and Utah beaches lay a spur of land called Pointe du Hoc – or Pointe du Hoe as it was initially known after a typographical error on the Allied maps.[4] At 0251 hours, 11 miles off the coast – the minimum distance that would keep the fleet safe from the 155mm guns that were allegedly in place at the Pointe du Hoc – the large ships began anchoring. The Pointe du Hoc was the priority target for the US 1st

Army and it was known that at least two of the six guns had already been casemated and would therefore prove difficult to destroy from the air or sea. In fact the guns were not 155mm and even if they were it was disputable that the US forces should have disembarked so far out to sea – some three miles further out than the British and Canadian forces of the Eastern Task Force. The extra distance put a huge strain on the troops buffeted by the rough seas and, as Admiral Ramsay subsequently pointed out, 'although one can fully sympathise with the decisions of the US Forces ... it is considered that immunity from coastal batteries should not be given undue weight in the selection of the lowering positions, especially when adequate naval counter battery fire is available'.[5] In the event the post-assault naval counter-battery fire was regarded by the Germans as formidable whilst their own attacks upon the major ships were negligible. On 20 June Admiral Kranke admitted his weakness in the face of these ships for 'It is generally accepted that the intended offensive by the German army has no chance of success unless the exceedingly effective shelling by enemy naval guns of our own land units can be prevented'.[6]

The aim at Omaha was to stake out and protect an area six miles deep inland and 18 miles along the coast from the western base of the Vire estuary at Isigny where the Utah beach-head could be protected, by linking up with the 101st Airborne at Carentan, to the east to link up with the British forces on Gold Beach, almost opposite Bayeux at Port-en-Bessin (where the PLUTO fuel line was to emerge).

The plan for the first four hours of the assault on Omaha Beach on the Dog sector is reproduced in Figure 6.1, and, if nothing else, the plan is a manifestation of the incredibly detailed planning that occurred in the run-up to D-Day. Each beach was divided into sectors on the existing phonetic alphabetical system, and each sector was divided into two or more elements, usually two (red [left/port] and green [right/starboard]) but occasionally into three, with white as an optional central area for large areas.

The order of assault involved the discharging of troops into their LCAs (Landing Craft Assault) from the various assortments of larger ships out at sea (beyond the range of the defending artillery and outside the known minefields) and then the subsequent line up in waves. First to go in should have been the LCS(M), the Landing Craft Support (Medium) which carried artillery spotters to direct the naval gunfire and rockets onto the beach targets and also anti-aircraft guns to deter the expected *Luftwaffe* assault. Second came the DD tanks to provide protective fire for the third line of LCTs (Landing Craft Tank) which carried the specialist armour that would, in turn, cover the landing of the

	Easy Green	Dog Red	Dog White	Dog Green
H-5			16 DD Tks Co. C 743 Tk Bn	16 DD Tks Co. B 743 Tk Bn
H-Hour	4 LCTs (8)Co A 743 Tk Bn	4 LCTs (8)Co A 743 Tk Bn		
H+01	6 LCVPs (200) Co E 116th.	6 LCVPs (200) Co F 116th.	6 LCVPs (200) Co G 116th.	6 LCVPs (200) Co A 116th.
H+03	3 LCMs 146th Eng.	3 LCMs 146th Eng. + Ctl boat	3 LCMs 146th Eng.	3 LCMs 146, 2 LCAs Co. C 24 Rng
H+30	5 LCVPs Co H 116th. HQ	8 LCVPs HQ Co H&F aa Bt	5 LCVPs HQ G, H aa Btry	8 LCVPs HQ Co A&B aa Bt
H+40	1 LCM 112th Eng Bn	1 LCM 149 Eng Beach Bn 4 LCVPs	1 LCVP 149 Eng Beach Bn 1 LCM 121 Eng Bn	4 LCAs HQ 1 Bn, 6 LCVPs Co D 116th 1 LCM 121 Eng.
H+50	7 LCVPs Co L 116th.	7 LCVPs Co I 116th.	7 LCVPs Co K 116th.	7 LCVPs Co C 116 1cm 121 En Bn
H+57		8 LCVPs HQ Co 3 Bn Co M 116th.		4 LCVPs Co B 81 Wpns Bn
H+60	1 LCT 121 Eng Bn	4 LCTs 121 Eng Bn 1 LCVP	1 LCVP HQ Co 116th	3 LCTs 121 Eng bn 5 LCAs Cos A&B 5th Rangers
H+65				7 LCAs 5th Ranger Bn
H+70	1 LCI 149 Eng Beach Bn	1 LCI 112 Eng Bn	1 LCI Alt HQ Co 116th	8 LCAs 5th Rangers Bn 2 LCTs 1 LCM 121 Eng Bn
H+90			5 LCTs 58 FA Bn Armd	
H+100			1 LCI 6th Eng Sp Brig	
H+110	13 DUKWs 111 FA Bn	7 DUKWs AT plats 2, 3 Bns		10 DUKWs AT plat 1 Bn
H+120	3 LCTs 467 aaaw Bn, AT Co 116	5 LCTs 467 AAAW, AT Co, 149 Eng Beach Bn	2 LCTs 467 AAAW Bn	2 LCTs 467 AAAW Bn
H+150		3 LCTs DD Tk, 12 DUKWs 461 Amphib Truck Co	1 LCI HQ Co 104 Med Bn	
H+180	2 LCTs		3 LCTs, 3 LCMs Navy salvage	5 LCTs
H+225	18 DUKWs 461 Amphib	1 LCT	2 LCTs	

Figure 6.1 Invasion Plan H Hour Plus, Omaha Beach, 116th RCT

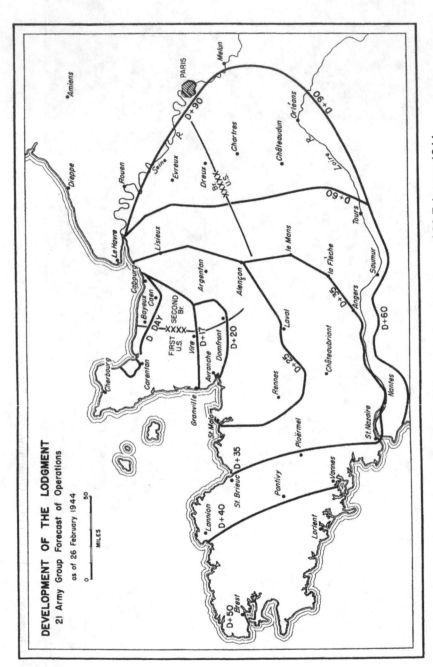

Map 6.2 Development of the lodgment: 21st Army Group forecast of operations as of 26 February 1944

assault infantry whose task was to clear the lanes for the main body of troops.[7] These would land in five waves precisely twenty-seven minutes after the underwater demolition engineers and combat engineers had landed with the first assault wave.[8] Since the chances of any particular ship being sunk or disabled were considered quite high, the larger specialized teams were not all placed in one boat but distributed over several, and each team carried spare capacity in troops and equipment to compensate for assumed losses. Once ashore these groups had to reassemble themselves and that, of course, required each boat to land in more or less the right spot.

So good was the preparation and deployment on the day that, with the exception of the Ranger assault upon the Pointe du Hoc (which was 35 minutes late), every beach was attacked within 15 minutes of the planned time. But timing was only one problem, and less critical than the intent of the defenders to keep the invaders out. For example, Omaha Beach, a four mile stretch of gently curving sand and shingle, is the only plausible landing site for 40 kilometres between the River Douve and Arromanches, with soft sand and a low water mark some 300 to 400 meters from the high water mark – which was then a one to three metre high shingle bank that extended in parts to over 100 metres in depth.[9] A sea wall ran behind the shingle bank and behind the wall there was a grassy plain from 150 to 300 metres deep running up to a steep 30 to 50 metre bluff or cliff from where the entire beach area could be seen. A cross sectional representation of Omaha reproduced below reveals the problems facing the attackers.

First, only four exits or draws existed off the beach, leading to the towns of Vierville-sur-Mer, Les Moulins, Saint-Laurent and Coleville

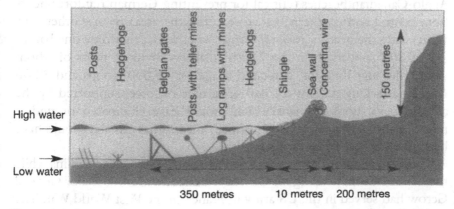

Figure 6.2 Omaha Beach, cross section

Photo 6.1 Bluffs opposite Dog White, Omaha Beach

allowing a great concentration of defensive fire at these points. In particular, each exit had a pair of *Wiederstandsnest* (Resistance Nests) which
provided deeply protected cover for the defenders. Second, the bluffs or
cliffs rising 30 metres behind the beach provided perfect defensive cover
and thus a very difficult approach for the attackers.

Third, the line of shingle, often two or three metres high would prove
virtually impossible for the attacking vehicles to traverse. Fourth, a sea
wall offered the defenders (and the attackers if they could reach it)
further cover. Fifth, the area of marshy land between the wall and the
bluffs left an open 'killing field' for the defenders to cover at their leisure
and the attackers to cross at their peril.

What made the beach a *necessary* target was the impossibility of bridg-
ing the gap between Utah (critical for capturing Cherbourg) and the
Anglo-Canadian beaches (critical for preventing German reinforcements
from central and northern France reaching the area) by any other way.
What made the beach a *plausible* target was the fact that only one battalion of 800 soldiers from the 716th Infantry Division, most of whom
were Poles and Russians, defended it against 40,000 troops and 3,500
vehicles attacking it. This colossal imbalance of force, supported by the
air and naval bombardment which should have eliminated or undermined many of the defenders, essentially meant that Omaha should have
been like Utah, a Tame Problem.

The US 7th Corps troops destined for Utah were under Collins while
the US 5th Corps heading for Omaha were led by Gerow. Major General
Gerow had served in the US army in France in the First World War. The
detailed strategy for Utah Beach involved the American 4th Infantry

landing on the beach and linking up with the 82nd Airborne ten miles inland at Ste.-Mère-Eglise, while the 101st Airborne took Carentan. Utah was critical because from it the Allies would be able to advance on Cherbourg – and without Cherbourg the attack upon Germany itself could not be entertained because the supply problem would simply be too great. Utah had none of the bluffs behind it which made Omaha such a difficult target but it was crossed by two rivers, the Merderet which ran north-south, and the Douve which ran east-west. The rivers met at Carentan and generated an area of marsh land that had been recently flooded by the Germans, leaving just seven exit routes which could be defended relatively easily by well entrenched troops. A concrete sea wall divided the beach from the hinterland but the movement of sand over time had reduced its height from eight to four feet in many places. Behind this lay sand dunes, some 10 to 20 feet high, interspersed with seven German strong-points, of which four overlooked the designated landing beaches, Uncle Red and Tare Green. The attacking force, primarily the 4th Division, was to be led by 57 year old Brigadier General Theodore Roosevelt, eldest son of the former President and cousin of the contemporary president.[10] Again, the planners assumed the landing would be relatively simple but the counter-attacking Panzers would be a much closer-run thing.

6.4 Planning for casualties

But not everyone was going to be alive long enough to worry about the Panzers. The planning for casualties assumed that overall, including all operations and the battle for Normandy as well as D-Day itself, at least 10 per cent and possibly 25 per cent of those involved could expect to be killed or wounded – though many of the ordinary soldiers seemed unaware of the casualty figures expected by the top brass.[11] Cossack certainly planned for 10 per cent of the landing craft to be lost and a further 20 per cent to be damaged.[12] Churchill thought that 11 or 12 per cent (about 20,000) from the initial assault units was probable.[13] Lt Hammerton of the British 22nd Dragoons' Flail tanks supporting the Canadians on Juno was expecting two thirds of his 'Crabs' to be put out of action on the beach.[14] Reg Edwards, skipper on LCT 2436 with the 106th LCT Flotilla was told to expect 70 per cent casualties.[15] Some were only too aware of the dangers: Private John Gale of the 1st South Lancashire Regiment was told that, in all probability, all the first wave would be 'wiped out'. No. 4 Commando was told to expect casualties as 'high as 84 per cent'.[16] Leigh-Mallory thought that barely 30 per cent of the American Airborne Divisions would survive unscathed.[17]

One casualty that was neither expected nor acceptable was that of Churchill himself who, on 30 May 1944, a week before the invasion, casually informed Eisenhower that he wanted to go along to watch the invasion from HMS Belfast. When Eisenhower protested against his idea Churchill informed Eisenhower that, since Ike was not responsible for the naval crews he would sign up as a member of the crew of HMS Belfast and go anyway. Eisenhower drew on his greatest networking powers and persuaded King George VI (who had also wanted to go) to threaten to go too if Churchill insisted. Churchill was adamant that the King could be prevented by the Cabinet from joining but nobody could prevent him. In the event, Churchill had already boarded a train taking him to Portsmouth to embark on HMS Belfast when he received a final telephone message from the King that eventually dissuaded him. Had he not turned back the King had given Admiral Ramsay orders to physically prevent him from embarking.[18] The last thing either Admiral Ramsay or any other Allied military commander wanted was Churchill disturbing the months of planning and training that had gone into the operation but it is a symbol of the political intrigue and negotiation that prevailed over the whole operation. It is also worth pondering just how powerful Churchill was – when he couldn't even secure his own transport for the big day!

6.5 Planning for the enemy

One particular concern was the intervention of the German navy. It was estimated at the time that the *Kriegsmarine* would have in the region up to five destroyers, 130 submarines (of which 40 would be immediately available), 11 torpedo boats, 60 E-boats, 60 R-boats, 30 M-class minesweepers and 60 miscellaneous craft. In all about 350 German naval vessels would threaten the invasion – but against them would sail almost 7,000 Allied ships. From April 1944 onwards there had been a significant increase in activity by the *Kriegsmarine* and one Canadian destroyer had been sunk, taking with it its German attacker.[19]

On 20 May the first German submarine was spotted in the western Channel and Allied forces covering the area were boosted to seal off the intended invasion area. But the main fear was mine-laying which dramatically increased from May 1944, though it remained of marginal significance because most of the mine laying was undertaken by aircraft and Allied air superiority simply deterred most German sorties.[20]

The disparity in aircraft was just as great. The Allies estimated that a total of 590 German aircraft would be operationally available in the area

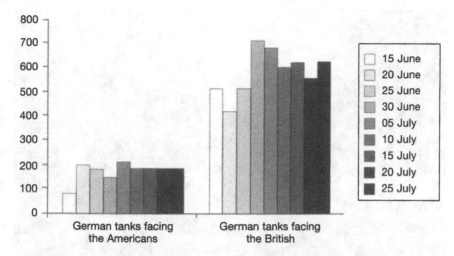

Figure 6.3 Comparison of German tanks facing US and UK forces, 15 June – 25 July 1944

(320 long-range bombers, ten reconnaissance aircraft, 65 fighter-bombers, 75 twin-engined fighters, and 120 single-engined fighters) – though according to German sources only 319 of these were within range on the day.[21] Only in land forces did the Allies lack overwhelming numerical superiority but even here the Allies landed about 50 per cent more troops than the Germans had available to defend the whole of Normandy.

Despite all this evidence concerning the German approach to strategy, especially their reaction at Anzio, from the very beginning of planning Overlord it was assumed that the German defenders would withdraw from the Normandy coast, after their initial attempt to prevent the invasion, to the Seine to give themselves air cover from northeastern France and Belgium. Thus the planners made little effort to construct contingency plans for Hitler's demand that no ground was to be surrendered and no-one was to retreat. As a result the possibility that the countryside just inland would be significant was discounted: the beach was the planners' target, the tank battles to come could be left to the field commanders.

The problem was that the *bocage*[22] countryside of Normandy, especially towards the Cotentin peninsular, was ideally suited to defensive action, since it comprised thick high hedgerows surrounding small fields which could easily conceal tanks, anti-tank artillery and snipers and offered the attackers little alternative but to fight furiously for every yard of ground.

Photo 6.2 Typical road in the *bocage*, near Balleroy

Particularly potent was the German *Panzerfaust*, a short range and hand held anti-tank weapon, the equivalent of the American bazooka or British PIAT but much more formidable.[23] The Panzerfaust 60 could penetrate 200–250mm of armour while the *Panzerfaust* 100 had similar penetrative capabilities but a longer range of up to 150 metres.[24] The only way to avoid such deadly ambushes was to go *through* the hedgerow but when Shermans tried to go straight through the hedges they invariably reared up, lost all momentum and exposed their unarmoured underbellies to enemy fire, so explosives were used to blast holes in the hedges. That, of course, alerted the defenders to where the next assault would come and enabled them to concentrate their fire upon it.[25] So here was another Wicked Problem: it had not been faced before, there were no experts to solve it because those experts that planned the campaign had not assumed that the hedges would provide any kind of problem because the Germans would already have retreated inland. Many Allied casualties fell foul to the German method of defending each field and only a recourse to the tried and tested method of explosives seemed to offer any chance of progress.

One way of taming certain aspects of Wicked Problems is to stand the conventional solution on its head: to assume that progress is more likely to be made by engaging those at the sharp end of the organization rather than those engaged at the refined upper levels of the hierarchy. In other words: to look down not up for the answer.[26] In this case the answer came from Sergeant Curtis C. Culin Junior who improvised a set of tank 'teeth' out of scrap German coastal obstacles that, fixed to a Sherman tank (the renamed 'Rhino') could uproot the hedgerow and allow the tanks and attached infantry to fight cross-country rather than along the country lanes. Culin had cleared hedgerows with a similar device fixed to a bulldozer back home on the family farm and though bulldozers could pierce hedgerows without the 'Rhino' there were few of these available. Importantly for us, this also highlights the nature of problems: for Culin it was a Tame Problem – he had done this before and knew how to fabricate the solution; but for others it was either a Wicked Problem – because they did not know how to resolve it, or it was a crisis because they were suffering the effects of the planners not having a solution already constructed.

When the Rhino was demonstrated to the US top brass, including Patton, on 22 July, the US 3rd Armoured Division immediately demanded 57 Rhino attachments – for the following day's operation. Each Rhino took an estimated 40 hours to complete but even with a 48 hour delay to the operation and no sleep the engineers still only managed to complete under half the required number. Nevertheless, the Rhinos were a great success and significantly reduced the problem of the *bocage*. As Cooper concludes, 'Previously, it had taken twelve days to penetrate eight miles. Including the operation around Villiers-Fossard, our (US 3rd Armoured Division) total tank losses had been 87. In the first phase of operation Cobra, from the morning of 26 through 28 July, the division moved forward 17 miles to Coutances with a loss of only two tanks'.[27] It was just this kind of improvisation that impressed – and unnerved – Rommel: 'What was astonishing was the speed with which the Americans adapted themselves to modern warfare. In this they were assisted by their extraordinary sense for the practical and material and by their complete lack of regard for tradition and worthless theories'.[28]

It seems incredible to think that all the planning had omitted to consider this problem in advance and that it had to rely upon a junior 'leader' to solve it. In fact, a SHAEF planning document had noted the difficulty likely in moving through the *bocage*, but it underestimated the advantages it provided to the defending side and merely suggested that 'The tactics to be employed in fighting through *bocage* country should be given considerable study by formations to be employed therein ...[29] Unfortunately this was not done. Ironically, the areas where the American forces were stationed just prior to the invasion, that is, south-west England, has many areas where very similar high hedged landscape occurs. Instead, almost everything focused upon the initial assault – and its attendant difficulties.

When the final briefings for senior commanders were made in April and May 1944 at St Paul's School in Hammersmith, London, the leaders appeared to exude confidence that their strategies would deliver the expected results. US Rear-Admiral Deyo was one participant sitting behind Churchill and King George as Eisenhower took the stage in front of a 30 foot scale model of the Normandy beaches: 'It had been said that his (Eisenhower's) smile was worth 20 divisions. That day it was worth more. He spoke for ten minutes. Before the warmth of his quiet confidence the mists of doubt dissolved. When he had finished the tension had gone. Not often has one man been called upon to accept so great a burden of responsibility. But here was one at peace with his soul'. Then Montgomery painted in the details and finished with a reminder of the importance of the soldier's attitude: 'They must see red. We must get them completely on their toes, having absolute faith in the plan; and imbued with infectious optimism and offensive eagerness. Nothing must stop them. Nothing. If we send them into battle in this way – then we shall succeed.[30]

That success depended, in Montgomery's mind, on a very quick move inland:

> Having seized the initiative by our initial landing, we must ensure that we keep it. The best way to interfere with enemy concentrations and counter-measures will be to push forward fairly powerful armoured force thrusts on the afternoon of D-Day ... I am prepared to accept almost any risk in order to carry out these tactics. I would risk even the total loss of the armoured brigade groups – which in any event is not really possible.[31]

6.6 Conclusion

Allied strategy was a relatively straightforward affair, in theory. Once Germany was prioritized over Japan the only two areas that were really viable as landing areas were either Calais or Normandy. The issue was then which one to choose and how to secure a successful lodgement. The latter was the most difficult issue – an archetypal Wicked Problem – because it required a complex amalgam of unrelated issues to be held in place for long enough to get the troops onto the beaches and ready to face the expected Panzer counter-attack. But the chances of securing propitious weather, surprise, every Allied unit landing at the right place and time according to the plan, and of the German response being exactly as predicted must have been astronomically unlikely. Given that, for the Allied military leaders, D-Day could never have been a 'walk-over' and was always likely to degenerate from a Tame Problem into a Wicked Problem at best and a Critical Problem at worst.

But for the political leaders D-Day was just one part of a much wider jigsaw that encompassed political in-fights within the Western Allies and between them and the Soviets. At stake was not only the liberation of France and the destruction of Nazi Germany but the reconstruction of post-war spheres of influence. In the end despite all the efforts of Churchill Britain did not finish the war dominating Europe but retreating from its Empire and beginning the long decline under US predominance. But Roosevelt failed to keep the Soviets out of Berlin. Of course both leaders secured their most pressing overall strategic objective: the defeat of Nazi Germany. But it is not self-evident that this success can be laid at their feet because there were so many other people involved in the result, including the Germans. That is not to say that strategic Leadership is irrelevant but it is to suggest that we retain a jaundiced view of claims that Churchill or Roosevelt won the war or that without them both the Allies would have lost; it simply is not possible to prove these claims, even if they do make the deployment of the Allied strategy simpler to explain as causally determined by strategic Leadership.

As to the value of adopting the Problems perspective, it should be clear that, although problems do not emerge neatly packaged as Tame, Wicked or Critical, there is some utility in using the typology to try and understand why the Western Allied strategic planners did what they did. The planners seem to have begun by assuming that Dieppe was a Tame Problem but after it turned into a Critical Problem they then over-learned the lesson and focused so much on the initial assault that they overlooked the problems involved in moving off the beaches and through the *bocage*. For the US forces in particular that movement became a Wicked Problem that was only removed when a sergeant who had experienced the issue back home knew how to fabricate a solution. And while lessons from Anzio were there for all to see it seemed that the planners went back to their default assumption that the Germans in Normandy would, unlike those in Italy, retreat to the Seine when pushed, rather than stand and fight. Again, assumptions that smacked of a Tame approach but which actually failed to learn from experience. On the wider front it is worth recalling just how few decisions seem to have been made on strongly rational grounds and just how many were political decisions and compromises that emerged from the need to collaborate.

Part Three

Managing Tame Problems

Introduction

Part Three of the book swings away from the strategic, long term issues often associated with Wicked Problems and concentrates on those areas where Management might prevail: Tame Problems. These, you may recall, are problems that have been faced before and there is normally an effective, rational process for resolving the problems. This, in contrast to Leadership, is the world of science, of objectivity and of systems; in short, this is the land where certainty should prevail. To examine whether this is the case we shall consider several aspects of the D-Day operation, in particular the recruitment and training of troops, the construction of logistics and the development of technologies.

7 Mobilizing the Anglo-Canadians, the Commonwealth, and the Volunteers

7.1 Introduction

The most puzzling thing about the British Army is how it managed to survive the Second World War at all, despite its successes in 1918. At the beginning of the Second World War it remained grossly under-funded thanks to years of government parsimony; it was not organized for continental European offensive action but for Imperial defence; it was led by an officer corps that retained its preference for the amateur gentleman over the professional; and its tactical doctrines, such as they existed, were still rooted in the disciplined hierarchy of the parade ground rather than the flexible heterarchy of a mobile battlefield. The weaknesses of the British Army did not prevail through all the units however, and the elite groups tended to organize themselves along rather more flexible lines. Moreover, over time the British government and the British Army learned quickly that you could not fight a modern war without huge financial and material resources and that equitation training had little in common with the desperate fighting in Normandy, where casualty rates often replicated the horrors of the First World War. Nevertheless, the British Army persisted in its habit of retaining the highest ratio of officers to soldiers in any major army of the time. In short, the British Army seldom trusted its own soldiers to lead themselves and that proved to be their greatest weakness: once the Germans realized the inability of most of the British soldiers to act without direction from above they could effectively immobilize any unit just by killing the officers and NCOs. Nevertheless, the process of mobilization was at least Tame: the British had been there before.

7.2 Leadership and mobilization in Britain: tardy but total

It is often said that, with the exception of the American War of Independence, the British have never lost a major war. That is probably true, but it is also true that the British have never won a major war on their own either. They have always had to rely on alliances and European armies, usually paid for by British finance. The reason is primarily to be understood through an acknowledgement of the British establishment's paranoia about a standing army, such as that which ruled England under Cromwell's republican Commonwealth in the 17th century. British governments all of political persuasions had long accepted that a standing army was a political threat and hence unacceptable. It was also considered to be economically ruinous.[1] That historical tradition pervaded right through to the twentieth century and hence any changes in modern warfare were always subjected to attack by the other *three* arms of defence: the Royal Air Force, the Royal Navy and a strong economy. The consequent combination of financial rectitude by the government and political weakness of the British army ensured that the army was always last in the line for funding. In turn, that pushed the army into adopting a defensive strategy.[2]

Since the standing army was always under-resourced, it could not really envisage being able to wage war on the continent of Europe. And without a continental commitment there had been no necessity for any of the planning or training that should have accompanied it. This cultural defensiveness, supported by the tradition of *defending* the Empire rather than *attacking* the continent, ensured that the Cardwell regimental system of joint battalions (one at home and one in the Empire – often India, where 60,000 British troops were stationed in the 1930s) dissipated whatever strength the British Army ever had.[3] On the other hand, the British Territorials or reserve organization, first created in 1908, ensured – unlike their US equivalent, the National Guard units – that part-time soldiers were linked to, rather than divorced from, their professional equivalent. Thus many British regiments during the Second World War comprised battalions of Regulars and Territorials, though as the war progressed the division between them evaporated.[4] Sometimes battalions of the same regiment served together but often they were separated.

For the two years after Dunkirk only four British divisions were engaged in war with the Germans, hence experience and learning by troops and their leaders was minimal. It was not really until the battle for Crete in May 1941 that any significant casualties were inflicted by the

British on the Germans. Then, almost 4,000 German paratroopers were killed and 2,000 injured, and despite fewer Allied casualties (3,479 British, New Zealand and Australian troops), the island fell.[5] Crete was the last time the German army deployed large numbers of paratroopers from the air but it also marked a familiar pattern of superior German tactics and morale.

Not that the British *military* was defensively minded or reluctant to embrace new technology or new ideas in general. On the contrary, the Royal Navy still existed to seek out and destroy enemy ships and the Royal Air Force had acquired considerable political and financial support for its offensive bomber doctrine. But that offensive spirit did not prevail in the army and it still did not envisage fighting a war on continental Europe, despite all the evidence that this was probably inevitable given Hitler's ascent. Thus the 'Ten-Year Rule', passed every year from 1919 to 1933, forbade any preparation for landing an army in Europe, and government approval from Prime Minister Chamberlain for such an expedition did not arrive until March 1939, by when it was far too late to expect the Royal Navy and Royal Air Force alone to ensure peace prevailed.

The British government need not have been caught so unaware because from 1925 onwards the General Staff of the British Army had warned its political controllers that a European presence was the only way to guarantee *British* not just *French* security. After all, ran the argument, if the Germans occupied Belgium they would have just 40 miles of hostile air space to navigate their way to London while the RAF would have three times as far to go to German territory. The consequence of the failure to consider the strategic necessity of a European presence was that virtually no preparation work was carried out by the time the BEF were sent to France in 1939. Indeed, only three divisions were ready and in a prequel to the Dunkirk evacuation by civilian ships, the soldiers had to be transported by 14,000 impressed civilian vehicles because the army had virtually no transport of its own.[6] In 1914, in contrast, the BEF had managed to send five divisions.

A parallel case can also be made by comparing the expenditure deployed towards social services and the military in 1913 and 1933. In 1913, 30 per cent of government expenditure went to the social services and 30 per cent to the military; by 1933 the corresponding figures were 47 per cent and 11 per cent. Just after the First World War the government had spent £766 million on defence, by 1932 the figure had sunk to £102 million.[7] This inadequacy manifested itself most clearly on the ground in terms of the parsimony that paralysed the army: between 1935 and 1938, when every other European country was mobilizing for war, the British army's budget was never more than one third of the percentage rate allocated to Germany's army. Still, as long as Hitler was persuaded by the logic of the British Minister for the co-ordination of defence, Inksip, that sound finance was as important as military divisions, Britain would no doubt remain unscathed. And as the Chancellor of the Exchequer reminded the House of the Commons:

> It is not part of my job ... to put before the House of Commons proposals for the expenditure of public money. The function of the Chancellor of the Exchequer ... is to resist all demands for expenditure ... and, when he can no longer resist, to limit the concession to the barest point of acceptance.[8]

With Management of this calibre it is a miracle that the British managed to defend themselves at all.

Chamberlain was no more constructive: as a master of double talk when it came to providing resources for the British Army, he declared, first, that the RAF was the real deterrent and only if that failed would the army be needed – hence there was no point in wasting resources on it. Second, that spending on the Army was politically unpopular, *ergo*, if the government spent too much on the army, the electoral consequences would herald a new government that would spend even less. Thus, it was in the Army's interests to have almost no resources!

The results of this philosophy were clear for all to see. First, the Army's claim for £145 million to modernize in the face of Hitler's election and likely aggression was trimmed to £20 million. Second, only £12 million was to be spent on the BEF – primarily because no continental role for the army could be envisaged by Chamberlain, or by his Secretary of State for War, Hore-Belisha, or by the latter's personal adviser at the War Office, Liddell Hart – architect of mechanized warfare but arch opponent of a continental deployment.[9] Such parsimony even included the Regimental Debts Act of 1893 – only challenged in November 1942 by James Hollins in the House of Commons – that required the first charge against the estate of any service personnel to be the provision of funds for their own coffin.[10]

But the problem was not simply that the government refused to provide the resources for the development of a suitably offensive strategy – the identity of influential army leaders actively stymied all such intent. For example, in 1937 each of the 38 students at the army's cavalry school received £526 in support, while the 550 tank school students received, on average, just £84. Even when trained tank officers existed, the establishment was reluctant to give them commands. For instance, the control of the Experimental Mechanised Force in 1927 (established only because

Liddell Hart had publicly asked why it did not exist) went to Colonel Collins, an *infantry* officer. Ten years later the command of the Mobile Division was steered away from Hobart, Broad and Pile, all senior officers with tank experience.

Nonetheless, the army's leadership had only themselves to blame in the inter-war period for the serious lack of funding because it so seldom complained about the miserly budgets it was allocated. The army went out of its way to ask for little, even when the Cabinet had questioned whether they could provide for national defence on such limited budgets. The Foreign Office in particular warned that the Army and the Air Force were underestimating the strength of their German adversaries but to no avail. When Air Marshall Ellington claimed that the *Luftwaffe* would not reach parity with the RAF until 1945 the temptation to lower their collective guard was all too clear – as was the danger of assuming the *Luftwaffe* was a Tame Problem. Yet the RAF did not even begin assessing the potential damage it could inflict on Germany through strategic bombing until 1937 (though it had maintained since 1919 that strategic bombing would serve as *the* offensive weapon in such a war). That same year, when Hitler's army marched into Austria, the cabinet, egged on by the RAF, decided that there was a problem – but it was of air attack. The correct response, therefore, was to enhance the searchlight and anti-aircraft capabilities of the country, even though this led the cabinet to *cut* the army's budget by 50 per cent for two years to pay for the lights and guns. In 1938, after the Munich crisis, Chamberlain went on the record to calm frayed nerves: there would be no conscription because 'we are not now contemplating the equipment of an army on a continental scale'.[11] The nerves he calmed most were not those of the frightened British but of the frightener of the British: Adolf Hitler. Not until 22 February 1939 did the British cabinet finally support the sending of nine divisions to France. Three weeks later the Germans entered Prague and a fortnight after this, on 29 March, and without consulting the army's chief of staff, Hore-Belisha announced the doubling of the Territorial Army, followed shortly by conscription and an unequivocal support for Poland's national integrity.

By the outbreak of war, on 3 September 1939, the British Army numbered just over 1 million. Three days later the National Service (Armed Forces) Act was passed, making all fit men between 18 and 41 liable for military service. The upper age limit was extended in 1941 to 51 years of age for men, and women were also included – though no man over 45 was called up. By 1940 just over 4 million men had registered and the following year the number reached 6.3 million. By D-Day one third (just under 5 million) of all the eligible men were serving in the forces, including 3 million in the army. That army comprised 47 divisions: 11 armoured, 34 infantry and 2 airborne. Only 11 divisions (2 armoured and 9 infantry) were not called into action – a point I shall return to later. In addition there was a massive force of British Commonwealth troops, numbering a further 5 million, half of whom were Indians.[12]

Despite the tardiness of British mobilization, the history of total war had at least provided Britain with the necessary management processes for engaging the population once the threat was recognized and Britain's political leadership managed to achieve astonishing levels of civilian and military engagement during the war; in short, the labour resource problem was suitably tamed. By 1941 Britain spent over half its GNP on the war effort (as did New Zealand after 1942 and Canada after 1943) and the British remained the most mobilized of all the warring nations. In 1941 as many as 94 per cent of eligible males between the ages of 14 and 64 were mobilized and by D-Day, of a working population of 22 million, just under 5 million were in the armed services, and almost 4 million were making military equipment. The number of women working outside the home increased dramatically by 42 per cent from pre-war levels to just over 7 million, of whom half a million were in the armed services, 300,000 in the civil service and 200,000 in the Women's Land Army. Partly as a consequence of the latter, land under cultivation increased by 40 per cent during the war. But productivity remained low and production actually peaked in early 1943. Only 60 per cent of its munitions needs were manufactured in Britain, the rest coming mainly from the US ($19 billion) and Canada ($3.7 billion).[13]

Conscription into the armed forces was initiated on 26 May 1939 through the Military Training Act, and the National Service Act passed on 1 September 1939 introduced universal compulsory service. It might seem that the political and military leadership of the country achieved miracles: by October four infantry divisions were in France led by General Gort and seven months later another eight infantry divisions had arrived. However, the assumption that any coming conflict would be relatively Tame was quickly undermined when the only armoured division – or rather half armoured division – arrived in May 1940, and was disembarking on 21 May, just in time to leave almost all its armour at Dunkirk. This was a catastrophe and, as we shall see, had significant ramifications for the rearming of the armoured divisions.

After Dunkirk, conscription proceeded apace, and between June and August 1940, a quarter of a million British civilians were called up. This was just the beginning, for by the end of the war there were 11 armoured divisions, 35 infantry divisions, 2 airborne divisions and 9

'County' divisions for beach defence. In addition to the Indian, Australian, New Zealand, South African and Canadian national divisions, there were also five colonial divisions. The political leadership's extraordinary fear of air attack was visibly present in the huge force deployed into anti-aircraft units – the equivalent of 12 divisions. The RAF employed around 1 million people in total, while the army engaged 2.7 million.[14]

British Army strength did not peak at 2.9 million until victory over Germany in June 1945 with a gradual displacement of infantry units (60 per cent of the total just after Dunkirk) by armoured and especially artillery units. By the end of the war the artillery was the largest arm with 22 per cent of all personnel. By D-Day the British and Canadian armies were expected to provide 16 divisions between them – but there was, apparently, precious little left and it was estimated that by the end of 1944 there would be a shortfall of up to 35,000 troops. The shortfall problem was twofold.

First, it was not equally distributed throughout the army but almost wholly located where most of the casualties always occurred: in the rifle companies of the infantry divisions. By late July 1944 not only were the Anglo-Canadians having problems compensating for the expected casualties, and not only were they now realizing just where almost all those casualties were being taken, but they now conceded that casualty rates in the Normandy *Bocage* were far higher than had been predicted. Thus while the first ten days in Normandy had proved to be relatively light in casualties, thereafter the figures were relatively heavy and increasing all the time. By the end of June 1944 the Anglo-Canadians of the 21st Army Group had suffered 24,698 casualties but the US casualty rate was 50 per cent higher at 34,034 (the Germans had taken 80,783), and by the middle of July 37,563 casualties. By the end of July it was clear that the infantry had taken 70 per cent of the casualties but only 15 per cent of the replacements were infantry soldiers. In August Montgomery was forced to disband the 59th Division (the most junior) and redistribute its members to fill the depleted ranks of the rest of the army, and by November the 50th Division followed suit. Fortunately, British casualties peaked in September 1944 and thereafter the system became relatively stable.

The second problem was the overall availability of troops. Montgomery was careful to avoid unnecessary British casualties, not simply because he had witnessed the needless slaughter in the First World War at first hand, but because, after five years of war, Britain was running out of troops.[15] This was partly because the nature of war had changed, so that the RAF and the air defences, and the support services, swallowed huge numbers. However, while the British Army in Normandy was short of 35,000 troops there were 115,000 troops and officers still in Britain, either in uncommitted units or in training centres and so on. While some of these were undoubtedly necessary for the defence of the country, the rest of them were inexplicably missing from the calculations that seemed to show how desperately short of soldiers Britain was in 1944 and 1945. D'Este implies that Churchill could not have been unaware of these troops and that he may have had a hand in keeping them back – just in case Normandy failed or for some other unarticulated purpose – perhaps expecting further conflict with the Soviet Union.[16] Thus the Americans could have recruited more troops but chose not to, and the British did recruit more troops than were officially available but chose not to deploy them. In essence, then, the British had successfully tamed the problem of recruitment but how did the British soldiers approach the war?

7.3 The British approach to war: squaddies, officers, and the Full Monty

The average British soldier seemed to see military service as very much a temporary interlude before resuming civilian life. According to the Army's own morale reports, 'the majority of soldiers … were not interested in a "new Britain", nor the stirring speeches that political leaders made but were simply concerned that they should return to a decent house and secure employment in the post-war world'.[17] Indeed, it seemed that the average British soldier was only interested in three things: 'football, beer and crumpet'.[18] That said, the vast majority of the civilian population remained supporters of the coalition government – at least after the nadir of 1942 when a further string of defeats appeared inevitable.[19]

By D-Day British army morale was said to be at its peak. A letter from Captain Alistair Bannerman, a British platoon commander, to his wife summed it up: 'To soldiers … Churchill's radio rhetoric sounds a bit embarrassing. They have no great faith in the new world; they have no belief in any great liberating mission. They know it's going to be a charnel house. All they want is to put an end to it all, and get back to Civvy Street, to their homes, their private lives, their wives and loved ones'. In this they were little different from their American colleagues: Private Branham in the US 116th Regiment thought along precisely the same lines: 'We wanted to go. This sounds crazy, but we had come this far, we'd been sitting in England so long, we wanted to get this thing over with and get the hell home'.[20] A more general reluctance by the British troops to identify themselves with any allegedly glorious military past or heroic future was also apparent and this is understandable. While the British army had been at war since 1939 (though few of the D-Day troops were veterans of any prior campaigns), their record of achievement was not impressive. Defeat at Dunkirk had been turned into a national icon of heroic resistance by Churchill and the British media, but many of the soldiers involved saw it in rather less positive terms. Montgomery was scathing in his analysis of the BEF in September 1939: 'the British Army was totally unfit to fight a first class war on the continent of Europe ... The field army had an inadequate signals system, no administrative backing, and no organization for high command; all these had to be improvised on mobilization'.[21] Churchill was scarcely less vituperative, particularly in light of the 1918 victory: 'If mortal catastrophe should overtake the British nation, historians a thousand years hence will never understand how it was that a victorious nation suffered themselves to cast away all that they had gained by measureless sacrifice'.[22] And there was little heroic about the inglorious defeats in Singapore and Tobruk against ostensibly 'inferior' Japanese and German forces.

Yet since 1942 British fortunes had improved considerably, and many of those soldiers involved in elite units in particular appeared keen to get on with the job after all the effort of training. On the Motor Launches that would lead the mine laying operations there was a decision to be made about who should go to Normandy and who should take part in the 'mock' attack on Calais. In the end the junior officers tossed a coin and the 'losers' went to Calais.[23] 'If an officer had said to me, "You cannot go," commented Private W.E. Elvin, a member of the 7th battalion destined to support Howard's troops, on the eve of D-Day, 'I would have cried my eyes out, and so would many of my mates. We were all green, having never been in action before, but we all wanted to have a go'.[24] The 'but' in the previous sentence might justifiably be replaced with 'therefore' because most of the subsequent research suggests that the use of green troops was essential to the success of the invasion; had seasoned troops been used they may not have been so willing to step off the landing craft into what was a 'clear and present danger'. This is an intriguing issue for the assumption that experience 'tames' the fears of troops. For example, Eric Codling with the 8th Battalion, the Middlesex Regiment, known as the 'Diehards', recalled how 'Our lack of experience allowed us to take great risks, like standing up to watch the nearby truck being mortared, or taking great pains to dig the mortars in and then sleeping *on top* of the ground!'[25] Certainly Montgomery used his veteran 50th (Northumbrian) Division, 7th Armoured Division (Desert Rats) and the 51st (Highland) Division to bolster the untested rest – but neither of the latter two divisions worked well in Normandy. As General Roberts surmised: 'I think there can be no doubt whatsoever that Monty's principle of including experienced formations and units in the invasion force was unsound; much better results would have been achieved if fresh formations, available in England, had been used in their place'.[26]

Sometimes a change in leadership appeared to resolve a morale problem amongst a veteran unit. For instance, the CO of the 51st Division, Bullen-Smith, was dismissed in Normandy by Montgomery in the middle of July 1944. At that time Montgomery even considered sending the entire division back to England for retraining. Bullen-Smith was replaced by Rennie who managed to bring the division back up to scratch, though Rennie was subsequently killed in 1945, the only British divisional officer to die in the 1944–5 European campaign. Even the 50th Division which performed adequately in Normandy (it lost 6,630 casualties in the entire Normandy campaign – the second highest of any British division {3rd Division suffered the most}) had suffered from pre-invasion problems: in its New Forest encampment just prior to D-Day over 1,000 soldiers had gone AWOL (absent without leave).[27]

For his part Hitler was unimpressed by the British or the Americans. Even the Americans regarded the British as preferring to exhibit parade ground discipline over martial qualities, and of displaying an arrogance towards their American colleagues that was rooted in class snobbery but never professional superiority. The feelings were often mutual: the British did indeed consider the Americans as crass, as unprofessional and as over-reliant upon the matériel of war. To the British, the American GIs were generously rewarded – though this also reflected the greater differentials between soldiers and officers in the British Army. The standard pay of a US soldier was twice that of the British equivalent, and at the level of private with three years' service an American earned £200 per year compared to the British private's £55. An Ordinary Seaman in the British navy earned even less at £33.[28] Equally significant, a British lieutenant-colonel earned 14 times the pay of a British private; the equivalent American lieutenant-colonel earned just 4.5 times the pay of an American private.[29] In effect, A British lieutenant-colonel – normally the most senior 'combat' officer (actually leading troops in the field) – received 86 per cent of the US equivalent. A British private received just 28 per cent of the US equivalent. It was not, then, that all US soldiers and officers were overpaid but rather than all British 'other ranks' were grossly under-paid. The real problem lay in the British class distinctions as much as the Anglo-American national distinctions. Nevertheless, to the average British squaddie, the Americans really were: 'Over-paid, over-fed, over-sexed and over-here'.[30] The GI response was that the British were: 'Under-paid, under-sized, under-sexed and under-Eisenhower'.

The sexual competition to British men from male American troops, and indeed, the general relaxation of moral codes of conduct, proved to be a constant source of concern in the private letters of the male British troops (as read by their censoring officers). One consequence was an eight fold increase in the divorce rate, partly linked to another consequence: over one third of all births in England were illegitimate during the war.[31] As *Reveille* (24 May 1942) pleaded with British service women: 'Do be discreet. Even if you paint the town red with Harry on your last 48–hour leave, don't write and tell Dick about it'. But the fears of many British service men – that the Americans would 'make off' with 'their' women – were not totally unfounded: 70,000 British women went to the US after the war as brides of American servicemen.[32]

A related issue was the social distance between the officers and soldiers, especially those in the infantry regiments – the most likely to become casualties. While the senior officers were in all probability the products of public school, the riflemen came from the opposite end of the social spectrum. Because the ranks of the RAF, the signals, the tankers, the artillery and any other specialized branch of the military always had first choice of the new recruits, what was left over joined the infantry. Brigadier Bidwell remembered being told by a fellow officer about the problems of controlling such people: 'Look, all that I can do with my men, the sort of men I have, is to persuade them to get out of their holes in the ground, march up to the objective, dig a hole there, and get into it'.[33] Under such circumstances, he insisted, fraternizing with them or assuming they would be able to use their initiative was simply a recipe for disaster. Discipline, rather than 'battle training' then, was the only thing that could guarantee success. The same hierarchical system occurred in the American army but it was, paradoxically, an inversion of the approach that drove the *Wehrmacht*, and a great irony that the democratic nations should generate such a hierarchical army while the authoritarian nation generated a more heterarchical army.

Above all, the British Army relied on control and preparation because that was what it deemed essential to victory. This was not novel; indeed, part of the Tame approach is to rely upon precedent that appears to have worked before: in 1926 a training manual had emphasized that anything which lessened control was counter-productive. And victory relied upon traditions that had won the last war: the tank would operate primarily as cavalry or in support of infantry held up by enemy infantry. Thus all the lessons of the mobility and independence of movement achieved by tanks in the First World War and carefully thought through by Fuller and Liddell Hart were ignored by the British – but not the German army. Anyway, since surly members of the Empire, not German Panzer armies, were the envisaged enemy, what possible role could armoured warfare have? Surely, ran the orthodox arguments of the inter-war period, the real issue was one of morale and that morale could only be achieved through discipline induced on the parade ground and inspections, not through irrelevances like combat training or technologies that lessened the importance of the bayonet charge. This 'mechanization mania', suggested an article in the *Army Quarterly*, 'was adverse to efficiency and to the creation of leaders'.[34]

The army officer corps in all this had changed little, it was still a life of privilege based on inherited wealth and rank and it was irredeemably the cultivated amateur that dominated the mess. Indeed, it had to be because the pay was considered more of an honorarium than a salary; it was an institution that gentlemen attended (on a part-time basis) while they waited to inherit their estates. Thus 'training' was entirely unnecessary because an officer's life was merely an extension of the public school that most officers had already attended. Riding was the only really essential skill for a British army officer, not because it improved the ability of the cavalry but because it symbolized all that a gentleman needed to lead soldiers. The abject irrelevance of all that was not encapsulated by equine matters was most starkly revealed in the January 1939 edition of the *Cavalry Journal*. As the editorial stated, 'It is rather difficult to find very much to write about in this editorial'.[35] Anyway, the most important issue was the development of 'character' not some theoretical understanding of the science of war, because British character – apparently – could always be relied upon to improve a pragmatic resolution of any problem – in sharp contrast to the rule bound operations of the German officer corps; in fact the opposite was the case.[36]

Not every branch of the British forces was quite so engrossed in the minutiae of status. RAF officers, for example, were more concerned about enhancing their flying skills and increasing their professional expertise, though it still allocated medals in the early part of the war on the basis of rank not valour. But the cultivated 'slovenliness' of the pilots was altogether too much for the army and associated with what the army regarded as a distinctly unsavoury attitude towards discipline and drill. It was self-evident to the army that the RAF had confused ideas about the role of the military. As one army officer suggested, the state of the uniform was crucial, and one would never find army officers with their top-button undone – the iconic mark of an RAF pilot.[37]

One could perhaps forgive the undone top jacket button of the 'fighter boy', but not the slovenliness so widespread on some RAF stations … . While the Army officer would do all he could to smarten his up by the lining of lapels, creasing of trousers and sleeves, and so on, many RAF officers (and of course, the habit quickly spread to the men) seemed deliberately to set out to be as untidy as possible.[38]

Note, however, that Montgomery was as notorious as Patton for not wearing standard uniform. While Patton wore ivory handled pistols and a mirror helmet, Montgomery usually wore corduroy trousers, a turtleneck sweater, a sheepskin jacket and a beret with two badges on it.

And while the British strenuously avoided anything so controversial as politics and religion over dinner, the army officers mess went one better, prohibiting any discussion about military matters and concentrating on what was important: gentlemanly pursuits, sports, character development and 'good form'. As one hospitalized officer recalled hearing his Colonel exclaim when he spied two military books by the bedside: 'What the devil are you reading those for?' He would certainly not have been reading them to enhance his decision-making capabilities because subordinate officers had virtually none to enhance.[39] Hugh Dowding recalled the great contrast between the theory of freedom of thought – which allegedly distinguished the British from the rest of the world – and the practice that inhibited all unconventional ideas. 'As for expressing an opinion which differed from the general point of view', one officer remembered, 'that would be unheard of … . It would be considered very bad manners not to agree with the senior officer'.[40] Göring had come to the same conclusions when on an exchange visit with a British regiment before the First World War where officers were banned from 'talking shop' in the mess, were mesmerized by parade bashing, bored rigid by field craft training, and were certain that war was won by bravery not tactics or Management.[41]

One might be forgiven at this point for wondering whether the British did indeed assume training to be a Tame Problem since it seemed to have so little to do with the 'science' of war, but for the British, experience had seemed to point towards 'character' as being the critical divider between military success and failure, and that character most certainly excluded any requirement that subordinates might have something to offer their superordinates when it came to understanding war. In the First World War British military leadership expanded such a philosophy of 'destructive consent' to the point where seasoned commanders in the field failed to question their superordinate commanders, even when the latter was perceived to be wrong. For example, Haig demanded changes in Rawlinson's original plan for the Somme offensive and Rawlinson accepted the changes, even though the latter knew they were unwarranted and rash in the extreme.[42] Eventually the British Army's 'Training in the Army' pamphlet recognized this for, as it put it, actual combat is the best way to learn how to fight 'everything else is make believe'.[43] In fact, Eisenhower suggested to Marshall in May 1944 that combat commanders – that is any officer in the field of battle – should be given a green stripe around the shoulder loop of their uniform to distinguish them from non-combat officers.[44]

The important question here is whether such an amateur, class-bound, hierarchical and authoritarian culture provided an appropriate environment for the kind of war that was about to be unleashed by the German military? According to the British Army's assumptions, that war would be fought out from static positions where absolute obedience to an omnipotent central authority – Command – was critical. Furthermore, loyalty was to be directed at the regiment not the army, and where the morale of the troops – formed by hours on the parade ground and led by amateur gentlemen – was more important than weapons or training or tactics. Since this approach seemed to have tamed the Germans in 1918 what could go wrong? What the Germans intended, unfortunately, was a war of unprecedented movement where decentralized control was critical to ensure the full exploitation of local opportunities by low level leaders, and where combat-trained troops were provided with the best professional officer corps, small arms and tanks of any army. One could be forgiven for assuming that the whole of the British army officer culture between the wars was a direct product of a German conspiracy to enervate British military capabilities.[45]

In fact, at the beginning of 1944 many of the 'old-school' officers in the British army were replaced by the new influx of younger men, and training took on a new vigour and rigour. This was the original 'full Monty' as it was called, partly because Montgomery was known to prefer youth and brains to mere longevity in a job.[46] And Monty himself had as little admiration for many of his subordinate officers as Naval command did for those elderly officers manning the Plymouth base and responsible for convoy protection through the Channel. As Montgomery wrote to Brooke:

> Half our corps and divisional commanders are totally unfit for their appointments. If I were to sack them, I could find no better! They lack character, drive and power of leadership. The reason for this state of affairs is to be found in the losses we sustained in the last war of all our best officers who should now be our senior officers.[47]

Nevertheless, 25 per cent of the officers still had a private school background while almost all the rest were ex-grammar schoolboys. Even this

marked a radical change, though, because four years earlier, at the beginning of the war, almost 85 per cent of existing officers were from private
schools.[48]

In marked contrast to the way the class-bound amateur officers of the
pre-1940 British Army operated, those officers of the elite 'professionals',
such as the Commandos, that were promoted through the ranks often
undertook a very different trajectory with their subordinates. When Peter
Masters had lost every single officer from his Commando unit after a few
weeks in Normandy, a replacement was sent for. It turned out to be a
previous member of his own No. 3 Troop, No. 10 Commando who had
been withdrawn for OCTU (Officer Cadet Training Unit). When Lt
James Griffith (aka Kurt Glaser) arrived, rather than attempting to 'pull
rank' on his previous colleagues – who were now much more experienced
in combat than he was – he embodied the opposite tactic. He admitted
to them all that he knew less than them, he appealed to them to help him
catch up, and he volunteered to go with every possible patrol and operation to gain as much experience as possible. According to Masters, 'in no
time [Griffith] gained the respect of both subordinate and superior'.[49]

But whatever most British soldiers thought about their officers they
tended to assume that the role of officers was critical – positively or nega-
tively. By far the greatest criticism was reserved for the senior staff offices
whose lives were assumed to be – and probably were – a great deal more
comfortable and safer than either the ordinary soldiers themselves or
their first and perhaps second line officers in the field. Stanley
Whitehouse recounted a typical example of the kind of positive Leadership by his platoon lieutenant that encouraged soldiers to take risks
themselves. As part of No. 6 Beach Group in the 1st Buckinghamshire
Battalion, his unit's task was to organize and defend a fuel and ammunition dump just off Sword Beach. When a German plane bombed the
dump many of the shells – which were encased in individual cardboard
cylinders – began burning and Whitehouse's junior officer, Lieutenant
Soulsby, demanded that Whitehouse and his colleagues strip off the cardboard to save the shells. At first nobody moved but then 'Lieutenant
Soulsby set an example by ripping open the packaging and carrying the
shells to safety. There was no way out; we had no alternative but to
help'.[50]

In fact Allied officers – British and American – were prime targets for
German snipers throughout the European campaign because, as a German
report recognized: the other ranks, especially, but not only the British,
were so dependent on their officers – and their NCOs were so 'rarely in the
big picture – that if the officer became a casualty, they were unable to act
in accordance with the main plan ... The conclusion is: as far as possible *go*

for the enemy officers.[51] The selection of leaders for killing seems to have
been standard policy from the very first minute on D-Day. For example,
the official history of the 29th Division's landing on Omaha suggests that
'within 7 to 10 minutes after the ramps had dropped, Company A had
become inert, leaderless and almost incapable of action. The Company was
almost entirely bereft of officers ... . Every sergeant was either killed or
wounded. It seemed to the others that enemy snipers had spotted their
leaders and directed their fire so as to exterminate them'.[52]

Brigadier Hargest, the commander of New Zealand's 5th Infantry
Brigade who was captured in Libya, was of the same opinion – British
officers were easily recognizable, especially by their shiny map folders,
and without officers British troops were often unable to move forward or
take the initiative on their own:

> The English soldier ... demands leadership by officers. I notice that, as soon as
> men lose their officers, they lose heart. Today, the 16th, I met several Bren gun
> sections coming back and in reply to my enquiries 'Why?', they said the fire was
> heavy and they got out of touch ... It did not occur to them to go on ... . This is
> not suggesting that they lack courage, they don't.[53]

The consequence of the German policy to eliminate the officers first
led many British officers to begin 'making themselves as inconspicuous as
possible, removing epaulettes and discarding binoculars, clipboards and
other tell-tale signs of authority and carrying rifles instead of revolvers'.[54]
References to ranks were also removed by the adoption of codenames.
For example, the leader of any formation – of any size – was referred to
as SUNRAY and the second in command was SUNRAY MINOR.[55]
Saluting, calling officers 'sir', and so on, all fell by the wayside in many
US units at the front too, as officers learned that survival was preferable
to status.[56] American army combat officers often removed collar insignia
and the stripes on the front of their helmet – which had proved so useful
to enemy snipers – but they retained a vertical white stripe down the *back*
of their helmets to aid identification for their own troops without drawing the attention of enemy snipers. However, some officers even covered
the back stripe with mud when it became clear that German snipers were
often left behind departing German troops to harass the Americans from
the rear.[57] Likewise, Allied tank troop commanders initially led from the
lead tank, often with their heads out of the turret. But the ability of the
Germans to destroy the lead tank – and with it the co-ordination of the
troop – quickly led to all tankers operating with the hatch closed and
with the commanders travelling in the second or third tank with every
other tank taking it in turns to travel at the front, on 'point' duty.[58]

Replacement officers for those killed, wounded or promoted were by no means assured of a respectful welcome and simply had to *earn* the respect of their subordinates by their actions rather than assume it through their badge of rank. Lt Geoffrey Picot with the 1st Hampshire Regiment was certainly concerned that the death of ten company and platoon commanders in Normandy left the regiment bereft of accepted leaders. 'It is surprising that the battalion continued to fight so well, although I doubt whether it ever again performed so superbly as it had done on D-Day'.[59]

The importance of maintaining and reinforcing divisions between officers and soldiers – intended to ensure that the latter only did what the former told them to do – was remarkably successful and remarkably counter-productive. Initially British Army officers were recruited and trained locally in small groups but the policy altered in 1941 when the emphasis on physical training and technical efficiency was seen to generate a very heterogeneous group without any common doctrine. Thereafter, Officer Cadet Training Units (OCTU) were established which trained young officers for between 17 weeks for the infantry to 30 weeks for the Royal Engineers. From 1942 the School of Infantry was formed to develop common training programmes for platoon commanders (28 days), company commanders (21 days) and commanding officers (COs) {of battalions} (21 days). By the end of the war the average age of COs of infantry battalions had dropped from 40 to 30.[60] But even the influx of 'grammar school boys' did not, in and of itself, necessarily generate a greater respect for their officers on the part of the ordinary soldiers.

For related reasons most infantry soldiers seem to have preferred to be led by someone with a battlefield commission – that is someone who had enlisted as an ordinary soldier and been promoted after combat experience – though many of these were regarded with suspicion for 'changing sides'. Yet they were, according to Richard Kirkman, a tanker in the 2nd Armoured Division, 'more efficient and practical than those from military college and officers' training school'.[61] However, Montgomery all but abandoned field commissions in Europe soon after D-Day because 'it encourages fraternization with enlisted men'. Clearly, talking to subordinates – as opposed to ordering them to do something – was regarded as a heinous crime; after all, if the Germans did that it must have been inefficient! Fortunately for the Royal Marine Commandos, formally under Royal Navy control and therefore beyond Montgomery's paranoia, field commissions were still available.[62]

This is important because it underlines an important issue: the problem for Allied soldiers was not that they resented the idea of a military system or formal Leadership (for most recognized its functional requirement), but many resented the way the disciplinary system seemed more intent on humiliating them than on organizing a combat unit. The Anglo-American commands followed conventional military doctrine in assuming that the only way to create and maintain a mass army was through mass coercion, to the point where individuals did not think for themselves but reacted instantly and positively to whatever command they were given. For different reason both the UK and the USA adopted very similar training methods. In the US the military establishment deemed the problem to be the endemic individualism of US culture, but for the British the problem was configured as one relating to the 'collective individualism' which became manifest in British trade unions, a utilitarian adherence to self-protective collective resistance. The solution to both problems was the same: the Anglo-American armies would administer 'intensive shock treatment'. That would render the individual helpless before the institutional power of the military, and this would then allow the latter to rebuild the former in its own image. As Henry Giles quickly realized on joining the US Army, 'The first thing the army teaches you is if you've got any brains it's best to keep it to yourself'.[63] This shock treatment would force the individual to recognize that the group was critical not the individual, and that the group's role was not to protect its own interests but to advance the interests of the body politic and its substitute authority, the army.

The result was a British 'bullshit' and American 'Chickenshit' system that saw soldiers digging 6 foot graves for a carelessly dropped cigarette, cleaning toilets with toothbrushes and endlessly perfecting marching techniques on the parade square. Little seemed to have changed since the 1926 British infantry-training manual which had just two topics: (1), 153 pages on various aspects of drill; (2), 64 pages on 'ceremonial'.[64] Luckily for the Germans there was little or nothing that resembled combat training, but then that would all be taken care of by the orders that would be given by the officers. They, in turn, having been thoroughly versed in regimental tradition, would be 'naturally' capable of doing whatever was necessary to maintain that most important winning formula: morale. The 1924 British cavalry training manual was little better: of the 377 pages, 212 pages (56 per cent) were devoted to equitation, 96 pages (25 per cent) were devoted to drill and ceremonial, and only 36 pages (9 per cent) to weapons and field operations. The contrast with the Royal Air Force, where professional and technical expertise was far more significant and disciplinary perfection of limited relevance, could hardly be more complete.[65] It was not a national cultural hang-up but a social class hang-up. So if the taming of the British working class began on the parade ground how were the skills of combat to be instilled?

7.4 Training the British Army

The British began recruiting 200,000 officers as soon as conscription was inaugurated. In 1939 the British Army operated on the ratio of one officer to every 15 soldiers and this ratio was decreased through the war so that by 1945 one in every 14 members of the army was an officer – a higher proportion than either the German or US armies. In 1939 aspiring officers were usually required to spend some time as regular soldiers from where, with the recommendation of the unit commander, they attended one of the 35 Officer Cadet Training Units for further training of about four months, depending on their specialism. By the end of 1942, following the German precedent, War Office Selection Boards were established to improve the selection procedures. For those officers going beyond junior positions, and uninterested in regimental attractions, the Staff Colleges at Camberley, Haifa (Middle East) and Quetta (India) provided 6 month courses for batches of between 60 and 200 officers.[66]

For non-officer recruits to the British Army six weeks basic training was provided, comprising drill, physical fitness, weapons handling, map reading and tactics. The time was used to assess recruits through the ubiquitous Tests of Elementary Training (TOET), and recruits were allocated to various units on the basis of their performance, their preferences and the service's requirements. Additional 'special-to-Arm' training for different units of the army then began at the destination unit.

The shortest Arms training (ten weeks) went to the infantry, composed, as was the US infantry, of those who had the lowest skills and IQ test scores, plus those who had volunteered. The Royal Signals who received 30 weeks training was the longest of all. Royal Engineers, or 'sappers' had 17 extra weeks of tuition, while those sent to the armoured divisions received 24 weeks extra training, partly because thirty-five different Armoured Fighting Vehicles (AFV) were in service during the war, and partly because the intention was to ensure that each soldier could operate as a crew member of any armoured vehicle in an emergency. Even bicycles had to be trained with. Corporal Bill Bowdidge, 2nd Battalion Royal Warwickshire Regiment, recalled how the adoption of the vehicle called for new methods of drill and formation riding: 'The company would fall in the usual way with the front wheels of our bicycles pointing to the right at an angle of 15 degrees, the officers in front of their platoons holding their bicycles in the same way and the company commander, with his bicycle, facing the company.[67]

After Arms training, each soldier would spend around 6 weeks with a reserve division before moving to a 'holding unit' where the soldier would await a vacancy in a field division.[68] From then on, the majority of troops trained day in, day out, for D-Day – then many months away. But such a long training period inevitably generated a high degree of boredom in the Allied armies. In April 1944, Private Morton Eustis of the US Army was desperate to get into action before the war ended: 'I don't credit the Army with being sufficiently far-sighted to make their training so boring that men are really anxious to go into combat just to get away from it, but this is what actually happens'.[69]

Once the basic and Arms training was completed, almost all the training for D-Day was concentrated on getting to the invasion area, either by practising parachute or glider drops or sea-borne assaults, and then executing particular attacks upon specific fortifications. This taming of the assault problem was perfectly logical but this often meant that training for post D-Day came second best. For example, Dominick Graham, a gunnery officer with the West Somerset Yeomanry, never practised in conjunction with an armoured division, nor did he know of any infantry-armour joint exercises.[70] This was especially critical in Normandy where the Bocage, the dense patchwork of sunken fields bounded by thick hedges, could only be taken in close-knit armoured-infantry support because tanks were too vulnerable without infantry and the infantry simply could not make any progress without tanks. This was particularly problematic in the British army where the regimental traditions inhibited some of the co-operative developments that the Americans, especially Patton, managed to construct.

In principle, the intention was that all personnel would know precisely what their task was. This was not to be an invasion where the individual simply had to get ashore and do what they thought was right, because everyone would have a particular role to play and a particular place to be; in effect, it was an invasion planned and trained for along clear principles associated with managing a Tame Problem. Private J. L. Wagar, a rifleman in C Company, the Queen's Own Rifles of Canada, recalled the value of this training:

> We climbed down the nets to get on board. At this point I don't remember anyone saying anything. Each man's job had been set and memorized days before, and there was really nothing to say. We knew the width of beach we had to cross, the mines we had to avoid, the bunkers, the gun positions, the wall we had to get over or through, the streets and the buildings of the town we had to take, the minefields, the possible enemy strength, the perimeter we had to establish for the next wave to go forward.[71]

This did not mean that the pre-1941 command and control approach survived the Dunkirk debacle because the German blitzkrieg had manifestly exposed the weakness of such an over-controlled approach. Instead, the new Battle Drill developed after Dunkirk had asserted that change was afoot and that while the strategy would remain in the hands of the senior officers, the tactics could be developed by whoever was responsible on the ground. In effect, as the opening address suggested: 'We give you the theme, you provide the orchestration'.[72]

In practice, the drill laid down what a section should do in particular circumstances and this was first practised on the parade ground and then in the field. Once some degree of finesse had been achieved at section level the platoon then practised a larger drill until all potential situations had been covered. This was the theory that became formulated into Standard Operating Procedures (SOPs) that then became the new ortho- doxy, and often proved just as inflexible, for to tame a problem in this way assumed that the consequence of the action was entirely predictable. Sydney Jary, on the other hand, a young officer with Somerset Light Infantry in Normandy, was adamant that the real education in war only came in combat itself:

> We had learned in a hard school how to skirmish, infiltrate and edge our way forward. The right or left flanking platoon attack so beloved of the Battle School staff would rarely succeed in the Normandy *bocage*. I remember being locked into the timetables of meticulously planned large battles. These inevitably left the junior infantry commander no scope for exploitation. If you found a gap in the enemy defence, adherence to the artillery programme, which could rarely be altered, effectively stopped any personal initiative.[73]

The exercises which drilled the SOPs also undermined any thought of going outside the boundaries of tradition because the umpires only awarded high scores to those units and individuals who acted 'appropri- ately', that is, who secured 'enemy' guns or achieved clear cut territorial advantages – and held on to them. But when the real fighting began in Normandy it was difficult to unlearn the traditional measures of success, even if the fluidity of the battlefield made the measures virtually irrele- vant. In short, when the taming plan established objectives then only the achievement of those objectives counted – that other objectives were preferable, but not planned and only emerged in the battle, were learn- ing points that it took the Allies a long time to appreciate.[74]

The persistence of authoritarian command and control systems was not all pervasive in the British Army, however, and many of the self-styled 'elite' units operated along radically different lines, often having more in common with the SOPs of the *Wehrmacht* than the traditional infantry units of the British Army. Amongst these were the Commandos.

7.5 Training the Commandos

The Commandos[75] were amphibious troops specially trained to spear-head the invasion and act as raiders but the first amphibious training was undertaken by the Inter-Service Training and Development Centre (ISTDC), established in 1938. A British Landing Craft Mechanized (LCM) existed in 1926 and by September 1939 the ISTDC had already established the standard format for the Landing Craft Assault (LCA) for carrying 35 soldiers and four crew members; subsequently updated, the LCM could carry a single tank.

Five companies of Commandos – or Independent Units as they were first called – spent two months training in Scotland before being sent to Norway in 1940. It was in the Norwegian campaign that the first LCTs (Landing Craft Tank) and LSTs (Landing Ship Tank) were used – though the successful German invasion of Norway was achieved without specialized amphibious craft.[76] But the continuing inter-service rivalry between the army and the navy persuaded Churchill that a completely independent unit needed to be constructed and so Combined Operations acquired the status of the fourth service, alongside the Royal Navy, Royal Air Force, and the army.

The remit of Combined Operations under Lord Louis Mountbatten was to co-ordinate raids on the continent and test invasion methods. From July 1940 Combined Operations became established at Inverary, Scotland and this remained the main training centre for amphibious operations until 1943, though much work on landing craft was carried out at Hayling Island near Portsmouth. In fact, the Royal Marines were somewhat tardy and only organized the first of their nine Royal Marine Commando units (Nos 40–48) in February 1942. The Royal Navy formed 'Beachhead Commandos' to take control of the beaches during amphibious landings. At this point a Commando Depot was opened at Achnacarry to standardize the rapidly diverging training of the various units.[77]

The first Royal Navy or Beachhead Commando operation was during Operation Ironclad, the capture of Diego Suarez in Madagascar in May 1942. They were trained at Ardentinny and adopted the motto *Imprimo Exculto* (First in last out). They were used at Dieppe, North Africa, Italy, and the Balkans, but the largest single operation was Normandy. There, nine parties of around 75 members, known by letters (F,J,L,P,Q,R.S,T and the Canadian W), operated as beach control units and were present until mid-July.[78]

In contrast to the rest of the services, and indeed the initial recruits to Combined Operations, the initial ten independent companies of (army)

Commandos were all volunteers, and Commando officers were permitted to select their own troops. By March 1941 there were 12 battalions of (army) Commandos, each with between 250 and 500 soldiers. No. 10 Inter-Allied Commando was composed of two troops of Free French forces, one of Dutch, one Norwegian, one Polish, one Belgian, one Yugoslav, and one (No. 3 Troop) of German-speaking anti-Nazis, mainly Jews from Germany and what had been Austro-Hungarian Empire, though there was one Irish and one British member.[79] Many of the Jewish émigrés in No. 3 Troop had been in England for several years but had been interned or, when allowed to join the British Army, had been restricted to the Pioneer Corps that was used for labouring duties, clearing mines, building roads and ammunition dumps and so on. Those who managed to secure entry to No. 3 Troop changed their identities and Anglicized their names to protect their work and themselves. For example, Peter Arany became Peter Masters and Max Lewinsky, destined to die on D-Day, became Max Laddy.[80]

Commando units were normally composed of five Troops of about 60 Commandos plus a heavy weapons troop armed with mortars and medium machine guns. Because the Commandos were only intended to act as raiders, they were lightly armed but they carried a high proportion of automatic weapons, were very mobile, and highly trained in combat skills. Their general role was to lead amphibious landings and hold on until relieved by conventional infantry. As with the German elite groups, discipline in the Commandos was seldom as coercive as in the army. Indeed, when Alan Angus volunteered for No. 4 Commando, he was informed that there would be 'no unnecessary fatigue duties, and there would be no punishments – other than RTU, or return to unit'.[81]

Training seemed to depend on which Commando unit one was with, but fitness played a particular role in them all. The voluntary status of the elite units became a significant factor in their heavy casualties – to the extent that 'volunteers not to go' was often an easier way of selecting people for missions – but was also a means for rewarding some of them.[82] Peter Masters began his Commando training with No. 3 Troop, 10 Commando, in March 1943 at Aberdovey in Wales. In their initial training they took part in one 'speed march' over roads and one 'assault march' across the countryside every week, both in FSMO (Full Service Marching Order: full uniform and weapons). As Masters was told when he arrived:

> They run us within an inch of our lives. There's no falling out unless you faint. There's no punishment for any infraction, but if you can't hack it, or you don't fit in for any reason whatsoever, you get An RTU. ... *It's the worst thing that can happen to you.* But the beginning is the toughest.[83]

Note again the disciplinary system used here for elite units – the only punishment is the worst one imaginable – being sent back to a non-elite unit. Intriguingly then, having broken with the conventional disciplinary system – the Tame approach used by the rest of the army – these elite units then developed their own processes for training elite troops.

Once No. 10 Commando had been formed, on 31 May 1943, training just got tougher: on three consecutive days No. 3 Troop marched 26 miles, 19 miles, and 23 miles – and after each march several individuals went to the local dance to demonstrate their incredible fitness to their instructors.[84] Each Commando unit trained independently but daily marches of ten miles carrying a 90lb load were not unusual.[85]

Realism was also induced by dropping the Commandos near RAF stations and requiring them to infiltrate the camps through live mine-fields and then report back. On such exercises the RAF guards were not informed that the Commandos were present and were quite likely to shoot first and ask later. When Tommy Farr (real name Thomas Freitag), managed not just to gain access to RAF Towyn, but to steal a WAAF's (Women's Auxiliary Air Force) uniform hat, he was ordered to return it – again unseen! Similarly, when training for an attack upon German V1 installations, Commandos of No. 3 Troop were parachuted into Sussex without informing the Home guard or local army units of their where-abouts or mission.[86] In fact, so tough was the training that a 70 per cent casualty rate was expected – not in *combat* but in *training*. However, much of the time of this specialist unit was spent in learning about the German military organizations, their command systems, their weapons and even their slang, so that when the invasion occurred No. 3 Troop (some of whom had already served in the *Wehrmacht*) would be able to interrogate prisoners and operate behind enemy lines on reconnaissance patrols.

When D-Day loomed No. 3 Troop was divided into eight teams of five Commandos and each was attached to one of the eight Commando Battalions involved either in No. 1 or No. 4 Special Services (SS) Brigades. In line with their general remit, it was assumed by many that the Commandos would spearhead the invasion and then be withdrawn for further special duties. After all, their official orders suggested that they would 'stay for a week or two at most, then return to Britain while regular Army troops replace you'. Not everyone was persuaded. As one old Africa veteran from No. 6 Commando – to which Masters was attached – told him, 'Don't you fuckin' believe it. What general is going to let go a couple of elite Commando brigades in the middle of a fuckin' invasion? Two weeks – not bloody likely. More like two months, if you're lucky'.[87]

7.6 Mobilization in Canada, the Commonwealth, and of the volunteers

Like all the Commandos, all of those serving in the Canadian and Commonwealth units on D-Day were volunteers. Historically, the peace-time Canadian army was small, comprising only three permanent regiments – including the Royal Regiment of Canada from Toronto that literally bled to death on 19 August 1942 at Dieppe (95 per cent casualties including 227 dead).[88] Nevertheless, from a call up of almost 500,000 soldiers the Canadians sent around 125,000 overseas. But the inter-war Canadians had mirrored their larger southern cousins in the US by adopting a policy of relative isolationism. Concerned that the internal Anglo-French hostilities might boil over if war was declared, Prime Minister Mackenzie King had promised not to conscript any Canadian for overseas military service and refused to engage in any joint training with the British until 1939. The Militia Act also prevented conscripts from serving for more than a year. However, with the outbreak of war on 1 September 1939 King asked Chamberlain how Canada could assist Britain, and by 10 September had itself declared war on Germany and agreed to send one division of volunteers overseas. When France fell, Canada became Britain's most significant ally, though that ally still remained reluctant to engage in strategic planning for the war.

Six weeks after the Japanese struck at Pearl Harbour on 7 December 1941, King organized a referendum to seek support for conscripting soldiers for overseas duty, but while 80 per cent of the English speaking Canadians supported him, 73 per cent of the French speaking Canadians did not. Ultimately, French-Canadians comprised 10 per cent of the Canadian army with 50,000 troops by January 1941. But ethnic diversity was far more complex than any simple Anglo-French distinction, for amongst the Allied armies the Canadian Army was second only to the US forces in its composition of French, English, Scots, Irish, Poles, Ukrainians, Finns, Swedes and many others besides. Moreover, the conflicting opinions did not rest wholly between the English and French speakers: there was also conflict between French Canadians who did volunteer and the Free French Commandos training in Britain. On one occasion a fight broke out in Eastbourne in which fists, knives and even mortars were used.[89] Only in November 1944, when casualty rates proved unsustainable, was conscription for overseas service finally introduced. Even then not every volunteer was taken – one 76 year old who had blackened his grey hair with boot polish was rejected.[90]

In all, 11,000 Canadian soldiers died in the European war, though actually more Canadian fliers (17,000) were killed. The 1st Canadian Army was never a wholly Canadian outfit because it needed further infantry and artillery from Britain to be operational. On the other hand, such was the dearth of British officers in the British Army that over 600 Canadians volunteered under the Canloan scheme as officers to help lead British infantry divisions. On average each British division took 40 Canloan officers.[91] Some British officers served with the American forces: for example, David Niven, then a Lieutenant Colonel, went ashore on Omaha Beach with the American 1st Division.[92]

The 1st Canadian Division saw action in Sicily, and the 2nd Division was destroyed at Dieppe. The 3rd Canadian Division, which landed on D-Day on Juno Beach, arrived in Britain in the autumn of 1941, just before the Canadian 5th Armoured Division. But the Dieppe disaster effectively prevented the 3rd and 5th Divisions operating together on D-Day, as had been planned, because the 5th were sent to Italy to avoid repeating Dieppe at Normandy and destroying the Canadian forces on one day.[93] Thus the Canadians who comprised the 3rd Canadian Infantry Division landing on Juno Beach on D-Day were all volunteers.

In the air almost 54,000 Canadians also served abroad, either in the Royal Canadian Air Force or the RAF. Canadian pilots and air-crew were involved in all branches of the air forces, attacking German destroyers and U-boats and contributing 19 per cent of the 1,200 sorties carried out by the RAF's Bomber Command on 5–6 June. On the night of 12 June a raid against the Arras railway marshalling yard led to the loss of six Canadian piloted planes, including that carrying Charles Mynarski who won the Victoria Cross.[94] The Royal Canadian Navy also provided around a third of its entire strength in support of the D-Day landings (9,780 people, and 126 ships, including minesweepers, destroyers and 44 landing craft) (in 1939 it only employed 1,500 people).[95]

The diverse ethnic origins within the Canadian forces mirrored the ethnic diversity of those on the Allied side who fought to regain freedom for their countries, or in support of countries identified as strongly related. For example, in the RAF there were 14 squadrons of Polish pilots, 5 squadrons of French pilots, 4 squadrons of Czechs,[96] 4 squadrons of Norwegians, 3 squadrons of Dutch and 2 squadrons of Belgians.[97] The Poles (who had signed an agreement with the Soviet Union for the repatriation {to Britain}of POWs captured during the Soviet invasion of Poland in 1940) also provided the 1st Polish Armoured Division which was deployed in August 1944 as part of the Canadian 1st Army, as well as five warships on D-Day itself. There were also 800 Danes involved, mainly on board the ships.

Beyond occupied Europe there were thousands of Commonwealth

troops from all over the British Empire in the five designated overseas commands: the Middle East, East Africa, Persia and Iraq, India and Malaya. The Australians and Indians were mainly deployed against the Japanese, while the Canadians, New Zealanders and South Africans were deployed in Europe.[98] The Australian 9th Division had fought in Italy and was destined for Normandy until it was withdrawn – much to General Guingand's dismay – to fight the Japanese. Nevertheless there were 11,000 Australians in air and ground crews involved in the airdrops of the British 6th Airborne, and some flew six of the 16 Lancasters in Leonard Cheshire's 617 Dambuster Squadron, dropping bundles of 'window' to simulate an attack upon Calais, and also bombing the Pointe du Hoc gun emplacements. In all, there were ten Royal Australian Air Force squadrons in the UK and the rest worked within the RAF. Some 1,100 Australians also served as naval crews on D-Day.[99] The New Zealanders had one division in Italy, one in the Pacific, and 35,000 assorted personnel in Britain, mainly in the RAF (two JU88s were shot down over Omaha Beach by New Zealand pilots flying RAF Spitfires) or with the Royal New Zealand Air Force or the Royal Navy. Many of the landing craft on D-Day were also piloted by New Zealand naval crews.[100]

7.7 Conclusion

The paradox at the heart of the British forces is that they achieved so much from such a poor beginning. They inherited a cultural system besotted with the pretensions of class and the gifted amateur neither of which proved of much utility in Normandy. They also inherited an impoverished material base, partly as a consequence of the poverty of political and military Leadership in the inter-war period. Despite this, the British had already developed a mobilization system and training procedures that generated an army which after 1941 began to master its enemy, helped considerably by their Commonwealth and other colleagues. Indeed, where that army mirrored the training and organization followed by the *Wehrmacht* it proved remarkably successful. But the basic problems of Leadership remained at the heart of the British Army in particular: the most qualified individuals seldom entered the infantry and it was that reliance on the officer corps for decision-making and direction that effectively undermined the development of initiative by the ordinary infantry soldiers. This self-fulfilling prophecy effectively provided the German army, itself based on a much more flexible and decentralized system, with a clear strategy for immobilizing the Western Allies: kill their officers and NCOs. In short, so critical was formal Leadership on the battlefield to the Allies that it brought them close to failure on several occasions. As we shall see, Hitler's own predilections for authoritarian control undermined the advantages embodied by the German army and allowed the combatants to fight on more equal terms, but it was a close run thing.

8 Mobilizing the Americans: Technology and the Iceberg

8.1 Introduction

The USA became renowned during the war as the Arsenal of Democracy in the profusion of material supplies of all kinds but it began the war as the least prepared of all major combatant nations. What role did the management of Tame Problems play in reducing the US to a state of military inertia in the first instance and then turning it around to the point where it seemed that the number of troops, tanks, trucks and assorted technologies of war stationed in the south of England in early 1944 might actually sink the entire country?[1]

That dependence on technology rather than human flesh to win the war (reflecting Henry Ford's approach to car production problems in Detroit) was both a deliberate choice and has significant ramifications for the selection and training of those who entered the armed forces in the war and, as ever, the cultural predilections of the political and military leadership resulted in a particular kind of military philosophy. Like the British, but for different reasons, the US chose an 'iceberg' approach to combat – a very small proportion of the entire population were to serve at the front supported by a very large proportion engaged in production and in support functions. And those at the very sharp end – in the rifle companies – were overwhelmingly the least educated, the least skilled, the least trusted to take their own decisions, and the most likely to become casualties.

In contrast, the German army reversed the priority both in terms of the proportions engaged in combat and in terms of the quality priorities: where the Allies armies selected the best qualified *out* of the infantry combat units, the German army tended to select them *into* combat units. The response of the American military leaders to the perceived quality of their recruits tended to be one where resort to rigid command and control systems was automatic. For these combat soldiers the recent past had often been associated with unemployment and the experience of suddenly finding 'work' in the army was quickly tempered by the realization that their lives were likely to be the only ones that were expendable. This seldom generated a politically motivated desire to rid Europe of Nazism but it did encourage two important explanations for the eventual motivation of the GIs: to get the job done and go home as fast as possible, and to protect those individuals in their particular 'band of brothers'. That catapulted the local combat Leadership to a critical point for it was the sergeants and the captains that kept these bands going and we shall examine this in the final part of the book. But it also important to note the crucial role of the national leadership, not just Roosevelt and Marshall, but also the Secretary at the War Department, Robert Patterson, in constructing the strategy. In effect Leadership was most significant at the top of the hierarchy where the construction of the strategy occurred and Command was most important for the execution of tactics at the bottom of the hierarchy. In between lay the role of Management in mobilizing the resources.

A further issue to consider is, once again, the role of experience, or in the American case the lack of it, on D-Day. This had two consequences and both were important for the tactical level: first, few combat officers or sergeants had accumulated the experience to improve their command skills but, second, those troops that had experienced amphibious landings in North Africa and Italy were, if anything, more fearful than their 'greenhorn' colleagues. As a result, the novice troops performed relatively well in their baptism of fire but the novice leaders were often less successful – assuming they survived the landing, for the Germans quickly recognized just how vulnerable Allied troops were to the loss of their formal leaders and concentrated their fire upon them. As a result there was often not enough time under combat conditions for the officers and sergeants to learn how to lead.

8.2 Mobilization: the 10 per cent rule

Churchill recognized very early on in the war that for a successful assault upon Germany the material strength of the USA was necessary – but America was even worse prepared than Britain was. In 1939, when war broke out, the US was what Forty describes as 'a third rate military power'.[2] It had 174,000 troops in only 9 divisions[3] of which only three existed beyond good intentions and paper. Historically, like the British Army, the American Army had been limited to minimal significance for political reasons. But while the British establishment had feared the power of a standing army ever since Cromwell's republic, in the US, any armed group was considered a threat to every citizen. Thus in 1894 when an attempt had been made to increase the size of the army the bill had been easily defeated by the 'deep seated assumption that 30,000 men, enlisted from citizens of the Republic, would be a menace to 70,000,000 of their fellow citizens'.[4] Supporting the army were 200,000 troopers of the National Guard whose training involved one evening a week and a fortnight's field exercise a year, using rifles even more outdated than the 1903 Springfield rifles used by the regulars. Beyond these were the 100,000 members of the Organized Reserves, primarily graduates of the Reserve Officers Training Corps. Beyond these there was nothing.

President Franklin D. Roosevelt declared a limited national emergency on 8 September 1939 and authorised the expansion of the regular army to 227,000, and by May 1940 the first Corps strength manoeuvres took place. The Selective Service and Training Act of 1940 introduced the basic conscription requirements into the US – the first US peacetime draft – and by 16 October 1940 16.4 million men between 21 and 35 were listed. Initially, they were on the draft list for one year's service (extended to 18 months in August 1941).

Each of the 6,500 local draft boards was authorized to defer call-ups to all those deemed to fall outside the primary catchment area. These deferrals comprised older men, men under 20 (though 18 and 19 year olds could volunteer), those with disabilities, and those working in 'critical occupations'. The results for a unit like the 29th Division was that older guardsmen and those with critical civilian jobs were retired and the division was formally mobilized on 3 February 1941 for a 12-month period of duty (extended in July 1941 through the Services Extension Act by a further six months). By the time the division was operative, over half of the previous members had been retired.[5]

Besides the 100,000 army reserve officers that had been trained to some degree there were 242,000 in the National Guard, of whom 14,500 were officers and these were called up for one year on 17 August 1940. The existing numbers of officers were supplemented by those selected for Officer Candidate Schools from 1941 after six months in the ranks.[6]

By January 1941 the US could muster 75,000 combat troops ready for action but this increased rapidly so that as July arrived so did the maximum total permitted by the legislation at that time: 1.4 million in 36 divisions. The attack on Pearl Harbour on 7 December 1941, in which the US suffered 3,581 casualties and lost 18 warships, boosted the calls for a greater and quicker expansion of the armed forces. Indeed, it was not until Pearl Harbour that the US population fully threw its weight behind calls to gear up for war. That it eventually did, owed much to the Under Secretary at the War Department, Robert Patterson.[7]

In 1941 Roosevelt asked Major Wedemeyer to work with his father-in-law, Lt General Embick, on a Victory Plan. Assuming it would take until 1943 to get organized, assuming that the Germans would then have 400 infantry divisions and had already defeated the Soviet Union, and assuming the conventional military superiority of two to one, the Victory Plan called for 800 Allied divisions: 32 million soldiers. The plan envisaged America's allies providing 100 divisions, leaving the US to find 700 divisions or 28 million soldiers from a total male population of 67.5 million. The plan also noted that no more than 10 per cent of the male population should actually be called up. In short the plan was impossible to achieve – unless the 316 divisions that looked achievable could substitute the shortfall by the use of technology, specifically air power, mobility and firepower.[8] Here, was the solution to the problem: victory would be achieved by Taming the Problem through the application of what the US did best: the science of Management.

The overriding philosophy of the US government, then, was the so-called '10 per cent rule'. The 90 per cent would provide what only the US could provide – the matériel of war in such quantities that the Axis powers could not win. The US gambled in 1943 that 90 divisions would suffice to win the war: that is, a smaller number of constantly replenished divisions rather than, as with the German Army, a large number of constantly diminishing divisions. Even the figure of 10.8 million in uniform, almost achieved by the end of 1943, only represented 8.5 per cent of the American population, at a time when both the British and Germans had over 13 per cent recruited.[9] By January 1942 the US had mobilized 1.6 million men and by December 1943 this number increased to 7 million, peaking at 8,300,000 with a further 4,000,000 in the Army Air Corps (an increase of 12,000 per cent) and the US Navy.[10]

As with all rational procedures intended to tame a problem an enormous heap of bureaucratic and perfidious impediments to the recruitment process developed over time. Initially, parents had to provide six copies of the consent form for volunteers under 20 years old. University students in many fields of study were given two-year deferments to complete their studies. More importantly, the number of 'critical occupations' leaped to 3,000. By late 1942 the decentralized system was proving inadequate and the War Manpower Commission (WMC) was set up to co-ordinate recruitment. At this time the average age of a soldier in a combat division was 25, and 50 per cent of the recruits at a recruitment centre visited by Morgenthau, the Treasury Secretary, turned out to be over 35. This was probably unsurprising given that 50,000 'dairymen' were categorized as within a 'critical occupation' – as was any other worker linked to agriculture, forestry or mining. By 1944 the average age was 26 (22 in the Marine Corps) and some new infantry divisions had an average age of 28 with ten percent older than 35. But this was not because the US had run out of young men; it was because many of these young men were exempt. For instance, 400,000 under 26–year olds were in exempt occupations, 600,000 were farmers – and therefore also exempt, 400,000 were aged between 18 and 21.[11] Altogether, over 5 million eligible men (18–37) were exempted by dint of their occupation rather than any disability. A further 3 million men were exempted by dint of their status as IV-Fs: 'physically, mentally or morally unfit for service'.[12]

By 1945 there were 100,000 women serving in the US Women's Army Corps including 6,000 officers. Some 17,000 of these served overseas in many areas but primarily in administration and never in actual combat, though 38 were killed in training or driving.[13] There were also 44,000 women nurses in the US army, though these were always stretched to cope with the increasing numbers of casualties after D-Day. Indeed, of 132 million American citizens, the US military only drew 16.3 million into service and of these probably no more than 800,000 (5 per cent of those in the services but just 0.6 per cent of the total population) were involved in actual combat. Here, surely, was a manifestation of how the US had managed to tame the problem: 99.4 per cent of the US population involved in the greatest war it had ever fought (beyond the American Civil War) were never engaged in combat.[14] Here too we can see the reason why the Management of the war was as, if not more, important than the Leadership or Command of the war – almost no-one needed to be commanded to 'engage the enemy'. As we shall see, the German approach tended to reverse this approach, concentrating on the development of effective combat units, often at the expense of the management of resources.

By the end of 1942 almost all the Allied ground troops that were to see combat in the war (not the 200 divisions envisaged but 89 divisions nevertheless) had been mobilized, though only three entered combat before 1944.[15] Indeed, even in late February 1945 the Western Allies could only mount 70 Divisions against 73, albeit depleted, German divisions holding the western line.[16] So tight was the Western Allies' supply of troops that US divisions in particular were permanently committed to battle and almost never pulled out of the line as a complete unit. US divisions managed to rotate one of their three regiments out of the line but they were always stationed in reserve just behind the combat zone and not rested in the same way that even the *Wehrmacht* managed for almost all of the war.[17] But by December 1944 the American army was haemorrhaging men faster than it could replace them and 55,000 air force personnel were assigned to combat duties with the army.[18]

8.3 On officers and soldiers

The reliance on such a small proportion of the population to carry the burden of actual conflict, combined with the selection policies that placed all those not assigned to a 'skilled trade' into the infantry, led the US to replicate an approach to training riflemen that would not have looked amiss under Wellington. It was designed to destroy the resistance of the individual in order to rebuild that person in the image of the military establishment, but, as often as not, it bred work-avoidance routines that made Sergeant Bilko's antics look dull by comparison. As Linderman's review of subordinate resistance and insubordination concludes, 'Soldiers thought these reasonable responses to unreasonable orders'.[19] None of this would have been news to Patterson at the US War Department. Already, in 1941, he had written that four things were causing morale problems in the army: (1) the lack of a sense of urgency; (2) dissatisfaction with officers; (3) a lack of meaningful work; (4) the lack of opportunities for promotion. General Marshall also knew the problem rested with the leaders because, in his words, 'Soldiers will tolerate almost anything in an officer, except unfairness or ignorance'.[20]

Like the UK, the US had proportionately twice as many officers as Germany (7 per cent and 3 per cent respectively) and the Airborne in particular was very heavily populated by officers, with a ratio of officers to ordinary soldiers of almost one to five.[21] But the relationship between officers and ordinary GIs seems to have been worse among the American than the German army.[22] American Officer training took place in Officer Candidate Schools and lasted between three and four months and 75 per cent of US officers came directly from civilian life with less than 5 per cent from any form of previous military background. The primary criterion for officer selection in both the USA and in the UK was education and, by and large, the closer a unit was to the front line – and particularly where officers were directly involved in combat – the better the relationships between officers and soldiers. As one GI suggested, 'regardless of the situation, men turn to the officer for Leadership, and if he doesn't give it to them then they look to the strongest personality who steps forward and becomes a leader'.[23]

Eisenhower was certainly adamant that a heavy burden would fall on the young officers who comprised the leaders in the field of all the Allied nations. As he said to a passing out parade of British officers graduating from Sandhurst:

You young men have this war to win. It is small unit leadership that is going to win the ground battle and that battle must be won before that enemy of ours is finally crushed. It is up to you men to give your units – whether it is a tank crew, platoon or becomes a company – leadership, every hour of the day, every day of the week. You must know every single one of your men. It is not enough that you are the best soldier in that unit, that you are the strongest, the toughest, the most durable and the best equipped technically. You must be their leader, their father, their mentor, even if you are half their age. You must understand their problems. You must keep them out of trouble; you must be the one to go to their rescue. That cultivation of human understanding between you and your men is the one art that you must yet master and you must master it quickly.[24]

However, relations between the ordinary troops and senior officers – whom they would seldom even know let alone see – were rarely good. In one survey of US troops, although 19 per cent of officers thought that 'leadership and discipline' were critical in determining the action of soldiers, only 1 per cent of the soldiers shared this assumption.[25] Nevertheless, contemporary surveys suggested that around two-thirds of the infantry thought that most or all of their officers were good. 'Good' in this context usually meant being willing to share any risk that an officer asked of the soldiers, not using rank to avoid danger and discomfort, not patronizing soldiers, successfully accomplishing a mission at least cost and explaining the reasoning behind all missions. Moreover, 'good' officers recognized that they were often as green as their soldiers and were therefore willing to ask the advice of anyone who had more experience than they did. William Ruf of the 6th Infantry recalled the terms spoken by his immediate officer, 'Sergeant, you let me know when I'm ready for the job'.[26] Indeed, Jason Byrd, a combat engineer with the 1st Infantry Division, remembers one officer who was quite different from the rest:

> He wasn't like the OCS (Officer Cadet School) officers we had. He would get us together. He said, 'Now men they told me we've got to go out and secure this area. I want to ask your ... opinion of how many men I should take ... and if I could have a volunteer to go with me'. I volunteered right off the bat. He was dead honest. He was a man who you knew was a good leader because he asked your opinion.[27]

But the training provided many officers with little that they would find really important once in combat. Lieutenant Leinbaugh was appalled as he experienced combat for the first time: 'You know nothing when you enter combat'.[28]

Some of the knowledge that was useful, like distinguishing between different sounds of incoming shells and assessing the likely impact point, would have been difficult for any army to provide. However, the dispute about the utility of 'bullshit' paled into insignificance when combined with the gross inequities that made the bullshit seem all the more insane to the average soldier. Not only did few soldiers ever see their superior officers from Brigade or Divisional headquarters, institutional systems existed to ensure this was the norm. For example, when the US 100th Division embarked for Europe in the US the enlisted soldiers outnumbered their officers 17:1 but the officers took over half the ship's accommodation and issued orders that enlisted men were not allowed in 'officers' areas'. Quite where this space went to was unclear, particularly to junior officers like Dick Shreffler who travelled to Britain on board the *Queen Elizabeth* and found himself sharing a stateroom designed for two people with 15 other officers. Yet, when Shreffler reached Glasgow, he was himself upbraided and threatened with a court martial by a junior officer for 'fraternizing' with a non-officer: they had gone to a concert together.[29]

On ship and on land American soldiers were not allowed alcoholic spirits though officers were – and officer monopolization of visiting women was notoriously despised by the GIs.[30] Even visiting the toilet in Europe involved an institutional divide that would not have looked out of place in the South African Apartheid system, or the equivalent in the southern US. American officers used private stalls and used holes cut in boards, the ordinary soldiers straddled slit-trenches in the open. In some units it was a court martial offence for an enlisted soldier to use an offi-cers' toilet. The British Army was little different, to the extent that the latrines in the pre-D-Day 'sausage' enclosures were noted by many occu-pants because they were – unusually – unrelated to status.[31]

When Corporal Rev Ehrgott landed in southern France in December 1944 he was astonished when he was ordered to lay out the bedroll of his Lieutenant; he refused – a response that Ehrgott felt his sergeant secretly approved. Bill Mauldin (whose cartoons Patton declared were designed to 'incite mutiny' and who was only prevented from subjecting Mauldin to a stream of abuse by Eisenhower who stepped between them)[32] captured this issue most clearly: 'It is a citizen army and it has in its enlisted ranks many men who in civil life were not accustomed to being directed to the back door and the servants' quarters. To take orders, yes; but to take indignities, no'.[33] But it was not just indignities that troubled the GIs, it was sometimes their very survival. Irwin Shaw's Captain Colclough must surely represent the archetype of this leadership affront to the GIs:

> When this battle is over [Captain Colclough told them] I expect to be promoted
> to Major. And you men are going to get that promotion for me ... . [this]
> Company is going to kill more Krauts than any other Company in the Division
> and I'm going to make Major by this July fourth, and if that means we're going
> to have more casualties than anybody else, all I can say is: see the Chaplain.[34]

Since Captain Colclough could not have been promoted had he died he clearly did not envisage himself as being amongst the casualties that he so carelessly accepted – and it was this 'duty of care' or rather its absence, that so clearly distinguished between what the ordinary troops regarded as good and bad officers. Given the irrelevance of any democratic impulse here, let alone any fragment of equity, it was hardly surprising that so few soldiers seemed to be motivated by higher notions of democracy versus fascism, equality versus inequality – these were simply absent ideas. Indeed, as Lindeman puts it, the term 'democratic army' was actually an oxymoron.[35] Worse, it soon became clear to anyone fighting in the Allied armies that their enemy fought extremely tenaciously for an ideal that most Americans and British troops considered radically worse than their own ideals – but they still fought well. And had they known it, the Germans usually fought in a far more participative command structure than did the Americans or the British.

But there were plenty of ways for ordinary GIs to resist any perceived injustice from the leadership of the officer class. These ranged from the harmless to the lethal. In the former category came reconstructing the requirement for all soldiers to salute their officers in a tame parody of discipline. Usually this was executed as a unit: everyone would salute simultaneously. But when a despised officer was spotted the soldiers began to disperse, marching just far enough apart so that the passing officer had to salute almost continuously as a platoon passed by in single file. In the lethal category came the routines in which unpopular officers on their irregular visits to the front line were exposed to enemy fire. For example, Kurt Gabel, a US paratrooper recalled how one lieutenant had reprimanded them for not seeking 'action'. At this slight some of the paratroopers insisted on accompanying the officer into the open, knowing precisely how long it would take for the nearby German artillery to site them and launch a barrage. At a signal all six paratroopers scattered for safety leaving the lieutenant as the sole remaining target for two 88 shells, though he was only shocked rather than killed by the explosions.[36]

For many junior officers who actually led their soldiers into battle, the maintenance of a strict status apartheid soon proved to be suicidal. Not just because their own survival depended so much on their unit operating cohesively, but also because the Germans soon recognized the institutional dependence the Allied system created on officers: without officers, Allied units often ground to a halt. In battle conditions, strict discipline often relaxed and this sometimes exposed the difference between officers actually accompanying their troops and those simply ordering others to go forward. For instance, Corporal Ehrgott recalled a Sergeant Pope facing off a full colonel (a staff officer without direct combat responsibilities) who demanded to know why the sergeant's unit had not gone forward as ordered at 2000 hours. 'What's the big fucking rush? Where the fuck you think you're at, Louisiana on manoeuvres? This ain't manoeuvres, this is real shit, and I'm going out there not you'.[37]

The post-war Senate Special Committee to Investigate the National Defense Program (chaired first by Truman and then by Mead) was also scathing about the armed services' officer corps. It was clear, according to the committee, that no management system existed for rewarding 'the alert, the intelligent, and the farsighted' nor indeed, for punishing 'the careless, the stupid and wasteful'.[38] Yet ironically precisely the same condemnation could be made of the armed forces in general, because it was already carelessly, stupidly and wastefully misallocating the 10 per cent of the population composed of African-Americans.

8.4 Racism and recruitment

The intelligence testing system that processed the civilians into various units of the armed services was as fallible as any educational or other intellectual test: it suggested that a quarter of all those tested were illiterate while half the whites and 90 per cent of the African-Americans had a mental age below 13 years. Since the tests involved questions such as, 'Scrooge was a character in which of the following: *Vanity Fair, A Christmas Carol, Romola* or *Henry IV*?', and 'What is the term for spatial perspective in renaissance art?' we can rest assured that scientific and cultural objectivity was never a strong point in them. But the practical consequences were to keep most African-American soldiers out of direct combat units until late in the war. Later there were two African-American infantry divisions (92nd and 93rd), an African-American tank battalion (761st). There was also a squadron of African-American fighter pilots (the 99th Fighter Squadron – the Black Eagles) who trained at a training centre in Tuskagee, Alabama. This squadron, together with three other African-American squadrons flew Mustang P-51s in the 332nd Fighter Group in Italy. By the end of the war the 332nd had shot down 108 enemy aircraft.[39] But these pilots were engaged on two fronts: 'We fought two wars', recalled one, 'one with the enemy and the other back home in the United States of America – Hitler and Jim Crow'.[40]

In 1940, although African-Americans made up over 10 per cent of the total population, there were only 4,000 African-American troops in the US armed services, including just 12 African-American officers in the army. By 1945 over 1 million African-American men and women were enrolled. The relative absence of black troops early on, especially combat troops, was not a result of simple tardiness. On 13 September 1940 Roosevelt had denied that African-American men would only serve in labour battalions and insisted that they would enter all arms of the services, including the combat arms. But the Secretary of War, Stimson, was adamant that

> Leadership is not embedded in the Negro race yet and to try to make commissioned officers to lead men into battle – coloured men – is only to work disaster to both. Coloured troops do very well under white officers but every time we try to lift them a little bit beyond where they can go, disaster and confusion follows ... I hope for Heaven's sake they won't mix the white and coloured troops together in the same units for then we shall certainly have trouble.[41]

That hope proved to be fulfilled and – to the profound disappointment of the African-American community – Roosevelt agreed that racially homogeneous units would prevail, and General McNair, for one was relieved for 'The introduction of Negroes throughout our fighting units would tend to leave a commander with no outstanding units'.[42] However, Judge Hastie, then the African-American Dean of Law at Howard University was appointed as a 'civilian aide' to the Secretary of War in October 1940, and when Benjamin Davis, an African-American colonel in the army, was promoted to the rank of Brigadier General, some of the African-American hostility to the government dissipated.[43] But this did not stop some of the more offensive elements of the segregation continuing. For example, medical care for troops was strictly divided on racial grounds so that no African-American doctor or nurse would tend a white soldier, no white medic could tend a black soldier.

Patterson, the Secretary of State for the US War Department, on the other hand had pressed for an African-American armoured force, but General Marshall insisted that the black population did not have the requisite skills to operate the technology properly. Thus, it was concluded, 'It is definitely not to the best interests of national defense to increase the number of Negro units in the Armoured Force, nor to augment any Negro units therein'.[44] However, when A. Philip Randolph threatened a massive march on Washington to proclaim black grievances in July of 1941 the government blinked. On 25 June it insisted that all future government contracts would have to employ a non-discrimination clause. Further unrest followed fights between African-American troops from the 94th Engineering Battalion and white civilians and police in Gurdon, Arkansas in August 1941. But despite intense pressure the government refused to desegregate the army, arguing that it simply reflected society as a whole and therefore could not change radically in isolation. In January 1942 Patterson accepted a proposal to organize an 'experimental' desegregated infantry division with black and white volunteers but nothing came of it.[45]

By 1944 even George Marshall had recognized the problem of directing the best recruits away from the infantry and of keeping African-American soldiers out of combat and he reversed the policies. Thus on D-Day there were African-American units of combat engineers clearing the beaches for the 4th Infantry Division on Utah and at least one unit of tank destroyers. But how did the US authorities allocate the white recruits into the various arms of the US forces?

8.5 Recruitment and selection

In 1940 the total US Army strength stood at a mere 170,000. By 1943 the US army (including the Army Air Force) had grown to 7.2 million and was, at that time, probably the best equipped of any in the world. Most of those who served in the US Navy, the Marines and the elite units such as the Rangers[46] and the Airborne were volunteers but the majority in the Army were conscripts. And since conscripts are usually more difficult to lead than volunteers, the toughest leadership positions were not foisted on those officers who had the greatest Leadership skill or potential, but those who had not got, or could not get, into the Marines, the Rangers, the Navy, or the air force. This uncoupling of the Leadership link between level of difficulty and level of skill was to bedevil the army as its initial leadership became casualties of the war. Patterson, for one, was certain that here the General Staff had been 'asleep at the switch'.[47] When the end of the war looked certain, in early 1944, Marshall began closing down the aviation cadet schools and the specialized training programmes and, as a result, the quality of recruits entering the army began to rise. Thus the army divisions brought on stream towards the end of the war tended to be more effective than those used at the beginning. Or, as O'Neill puts it: 'A peculiarity of the American Army was that the longer the war lasted, the better it became'.[48] The same could not be said of either the British or the German armies, both of which had exhausted their reserves by 1945.

The US Army was certainly one of the fittest. The basic requirements were to be at least 5 foot tall, at least 105lbs in weight, at least 32 natural teeth, correctable vision, no flat feet, hernias or venereal disease.[49] That list led to the rejection of one third of the draftees, though on average a US soldier was 5' 8" and weighed 144lbs. Not all the examinations were careful: Howard Melvin of the 82nd Airborne recounts how his special medical examination to join the paratroopers (he was inexplicably

rejected 24 hours earlier as unfit by the army) involved jumping successfully off the medical examiner's desk![50]

Yet, the recruit who ended up in the typical US infantry battalion
performed less well, physically and intellectually, in the selection tests
than the equivalent individual serving behind the front line or in the air.
Indeed, the lower the socio-economic background the more likely an
individual was to end up carrying a rifle. Of course, some people managed
to evade the draft, initially by having missing teeth or a criminal record
or – in Frank Sinatra's case – a perforated eardrum.[51] This may have
reflected the universal assumption that the war would not be a replica of
the First World War but a war of rapid movement and sophisticated technologies: that is, one where quick brains and powerful machines
displaced slow brains and weak machines. As Wilson put it: anyone 'who
met the army's minimal IQ requirements could learn how to load and
fire a rifle' and the factory model adopted by the US army treated
recruits as 'raw material to be transformed into finished products'.[52]
Thus two forms of problem taming were at work in the US forces: first
to win a war of technology required Management rather than
Leadership; second, even the infantry could be turned into killing
machines through effective management processes.

In fact, even basic training involved a considerable amount of work
beyond firing a rifle. Most GIs had to know how to operate up to a
dozen weapons, how to use camouflage, detect and defuse mines, how
to mount guard and patrol, read maps, recognize vehicles and aircraft,
understand military discipline, deal with prisoners, execute basic first aid
and hygiene, survive in atrocious conditions, and operate as a team.[53]
The hygiene lesson may have been overplayed: Lt Cooper, with the 3rd
Armoured Division wore the same shirt, trousers and long underwear for
51 days in Normandy.[54] But the more important lesson – learned by the
Germans but not by the British (except general Slim) or Americans, was
that the infantry required the best not the worst soldiers because the war
was no longer fought in mass formations where obedience was the most
important criteria for success.[55]

For the elite groups in the US Army, such as the Rangers, or suicide
squads as some called them, training was – and skill levels were – equivalent to those of the British Commandos. Two battalions of Rangers
were available in June 1944, the 2nd and the 5th. Both had been initiated 12 months earlier and were trained very much like the British
Commandos for small-scale amphibious and raiding operations. Colonel
James Rudder was in command of both battalions, united as the
Provisional Ranger Group. Sigurd Sundby had been allotted to a clerk's
job because of poor eyesight in one eye but after he memorized the eye

tests he was allowed to volunteer for the Rangers, which he did along with 500 other soldiers. Only 17 of the 500 were chosen.[56] Their training began with speed marches of seven miles a day, leading to regular 25-mile 'jaunts' and 50-mile 'hikes'. The training was, according to Robert L. Sales, who trained as a Ranger in Scotland with Lord Lovat's No. 4 Commando, 'the toughest battle school in the world. The discipline was unbelievable and we were on British rations up there ... if you don't think you'd ever starve to death you should try that!'[57] Sales would probably have already experienced such an approach in his initial training with Rudder in the US. Rudder was famous not just for holding 'gripe sessions' where anyone could openly complain to him about anything or anyone, but also for threatening to fight every single soldier in his battalion after a poor parade. He also pulled his troops out of a First Class Diner on a Pullman train and made them run back to camp, banishing them all to the local woods for 24 hours without any food to make them live off squirrels and nuts.

Not all Ranger recruitment and training was quite so severe. When Colonel Reeder wanted Lt Mills, one of his Rangers, to procure some extra weapons for his unit, the lieutenant reminded Reeder that the Division Commander's map-reading exam took place that night. Reeder promptly decided to examine the lieutenant's skills himself: 'What's the declination of the compass in Nome, Alaska?' was the first question – to which Mills replied: 'Sir, I don't know'. Reeder then asked the second question: 'Well, what is the exact distance in inches from San Francisco to Brisbane, Australia?' Mills offered a similarly negative reply. So Reeder asked the final question: 'Can you tell me the exact location of Hitler's headquarters?' 'No sir' replied Mills. 'Well', said Reeder, you missed three questions. I know you know the rest. I am awarding you a grade of 97 per cent. Now go get those guns!' Ironically it was Lt Mills who subsequently recognized from Reeder's map that he and the Colonel had been landed two miles south of their intended position on Utah Beach on D-Day.

But the Rangers volunteered for their positions, unlike most combat soldiers who were placed into rifle units because they were deemed to be the most expendable by the Army General Classification Test (AGCT). The AGCT consisted of 150 multiple choice questions with 130 being the necessary minimum to achieve a grade one (officer minimum was 115). It was well known that the higher the result the more likely the candidate was to end up in the air force – the preferred option for most – and the bottom two categories (class IV ['slightly below average to barely functional'] and class V ['mentally deficient']) made up most of the infantry divisions in the first years of the war. In the event the US Army

Air Force received only 20 per cent of its replacements from classes IV and V while the infantry received 44 per cent of its replacements from these two groups.[58] Initially the US Air Force restricted flyers to those who were 21 or over and had pursued two years of college training, but it soon reduced the age limit to 18 and accepted that Sergeant-Pilots, with just a high school education, could fly in an emergency.[59] Indeed, here was a case where formal Leadership qualities in fighter-pilots may have been counter-productive. As Cooper recalls, 'these young men were full of piss and vinegar and had enough hot-rod instincts to make excellent pilots. Men beyond their mid-twenties were supposedly no longer foolhardy enough to make good fighter pilots'.[60]

8.6 Regulars and the National Guard

Such was the scale of the expansion of US army that divisional training was to be completed within 44 weeks from scratch: 17 weeks basic training and establishing the new organization, 13 weeks for unit training; and 14 weeks for tactical training.[61] Basic training included a 25 mile road march in full equipment but the precise format depended on the division. The 351st Division, for instance, marched 62 miles in full gear in 29 hours. Training generally took 44 hours over six days in every week and every day started at 0610 and finished at 2145.[62]

As the war progressed the division between the regular US units and the National Guard units also blurred but at the beginning the regulars had little faith that the guards would ever be fit enough for combat. A *Life* magazine article in August 1941 described the 27th Division, a National Guard unit from New York as on the brink of mass desertion and further newspaper investigations showed similar problems amongst many equivalent units, even claiming that the non-commissioned officers of the 29th Division had been 'recruited from the sewers of Baltimore'. General McNair proposed the immediate demobilization of the entire National Guard organization to General Marshall and a purge of the National Guards' officer corps followed. But the real problem had been the absence of purpose: the self-evident lack of an enemy to fight against.

With the attack on Pearl Harbour in December 1941 all that apparently changed. But the first real tests for the American army were the battles of Sidi-Bou-Zid and Kasserine Pass in early 1943.[63] They were unmitigated disasters: 6,000 US casualties were blamed on the poor deployment of troops (in self-contained and isolated battalions), poor equipment and poor leadership. In the words of one GI: 'Never were so few commanded by so many from so far away!'[64] The defeats soured relationships between the British and Americans but they also stimulated the Americans to reconsider their whole approach, just as Dieppe had done for the British and Canadians.

From 26 January 1942, many of the US troops (and by 1945, 4 million people were in the Allied forces) spent at least some time in Britain, and huge numbers of buildings and facilities were required. For example, the 185,000 personnel of the US 8th Air Force alone required 163 new airfields and the American forces as a whole occupied 100,000 buildings in 1,100 locations across the country.[65] When US troops arrived in Britain many of the local people were shocked by what they saw as the bizarre segregation policies of the US army. They were even more startled when black and white Americans began shooting each other, in what Betty Mackay, a London evacuee living in Dorset, thought resembled a Wild West gunfight in the streets of Portland's Reforne district in early 1944.[66]

The US War Department (1942) had issued all US service personnel going to Britain with a leaflet explaining some of the quirks of the British but focusing far more on the similarities between the nations. After all, the pamphlet suggested, 'in their major ways of life the British and American people are much alike. They speak the same language. They both believe in representative government, in freedom of worship, in freedom of speech'. But it went on to remind the Americans that though the British were different in some respects, they were still Allies. Thus the 'British [are] reserved, not unfriendly ... . They are tough' but they were not 'braggarts' and disliked Americans who were always 'showing off'. In the end, the pamphlet went on, you could get used to the weather, and although they may seem 'old fashioned' they were not enamoured of their Union Jack flag, they were 'flexible and sensitive', very courteous, very law-abiding, and – eventually – could make 'the best friends in the world'. Indeed, the British even had women giving orders to men![67]

Finally, the Americans were warned to stay out of arguments, avoid criticizing the King, graciously accept that the British could not make coffee, but they had put up with more than most Americans would ever face. All in all the GIs were encouraged to 'be friendly', to 'play fair', not to eat too much, not to say 'I look like a bum' in public, or say 'bloody' – in mixed company – 'it's one of their worst swear words', and not to avoid standing to attention when the British national anthem is playing in the cinemas – 'even if it means missing the last bus'.

The western end of Omaha was the target of the 29th Division, a National Guard unit. The 29th Division's General Reckford was also replaced, by Major General Gerow (a graduate of the Virginia Military Institute not West Point) in February 1942. Gerow was himself then replaced in July 1943 by Major General Gerhardt – who was a West Pointer and, like Patton insisted on wearing shiny cavalry boots. Despite his reputation as a disciplinarian Gerhardt's first order gave the 29th Division – used to training seven days a week – three days leave. As far as Gerhardt (or 'Uncle Charlie' as the 29th Division troops called him after this) was concerned, battles were won at the battalion level and if his battalion commanders were not up to it, then he wanted them out. What followed was a ruthless application of management assessment and that was particularly likely if the officer in question was a National Guard officer: all three Regimental COs in the 29th Division were regular officers and when they were replaced in Normandy they were replaced by regular officers. In an intriguing interrogation of the role of his leaders Gerhardt asked all the junior officers about their senior officers and then put his three regimental commanders on 'trial' in front of their immediate subordinates, asking them questions about military technique, weaponry and drill that every soldier should know – including regulations concerning the wearing of helmet chin straps. He even insisted that his own driver clean his jeep as often as it needed cleaning – sometimes five times a day.

In the summer of 1943 Gerhardt's new second in command arrived – General Norman Cota – ex 1st Division and ex Combined Operations Headquarters (Bolkoski, 1999: 15–53, 99). The result of the Gerhardt/Cota combination on the 29th Division was a focus on training that, to some of the trainees at least, must have seemed fanatical: some companies lost 50 per cent of their personnel in the process as it got tougher and tougher.[68] Gerhardt insisted that the 29th Division stop restricting the firing of live weapons to supervised sessions on the firing range and he encouraged his soldiers to carry arms and fire at whatever they liked if they were out on the Cornish moors. Other novel forms of training were less popular: swimming in frozen streams was one but this was just a preparation for the amphibious assaults the division practised from September 1943 on the north Devon coast between Braunton and Barnstaple. At Bideford Bay the Americans built a replica German strong point with concrete walls six foot thick along the beach. Since the site was too small for practising divisional assaults, the three regiments, 116th, 175th and 115th were rotated through the beach on three week courses in late 1943, with the 116th taking a refresher course in early 1944. Many of the assaults upon strong points required the building of mock-up gun emplacements in Britain and systematic drills to counteract the nervousness that would clearly occur during the real attack. But the main Amphibious Assault Training Centre was on the south Devon coast.

8.7 Amphibious assault training

Experience derived through constant practice is a hall mark of a Tame Problem approach and it was clearly visible at the main Assault Training Centre at Woolacombe near Slapton Sands (originally used by Montgomery's 9th Brigade in 1938), where the entire beach area was dedicated to replicating the typical defences to be found in Normandy.[69] 'We enacted this scenario', remembered Colonel Van Fleet, Commander of the 8th Infantry Regiment of the 4th Division, 'countless hundreds of times from 1941 through 1943, often with live ammunition'.[70] So detailed were some of the replicas that when Sergeant Plumb of the Royal Winnipeg Rifles hit Juno Beach near Bernières-sur-Mer he realized that 'it was identical to the beach we had been training on in Inverness, Scotland, right down to the exact locations of pillboxes.[71]

As D-Day approached, the exercises grew larger and more integrated while the level of realism increased each time, including the use of live ammunition. On 3 January 1944 Exercise Duck 1 occurred, a landing the 29th Division at Slapton, followed by Duck II in February where Rhino pontoons were used for the first time. Operation Fox in March saw the US 5th Corps practising with DUKWs for the first time and Operation Beaver witnessed the first combined air drop and beach assault. Next, teams were trained in wire cutting and demolition, followed by company exercise and battalion assaults. Weekly exercise throughout the first third of 1944 were developed in April and May to dress rehearsals, including embarkation, sailing, disembarkation and assaults, all covered by aerial and naval bombardment of the beaches. D-Day itself was the twelfth time that the entire assault had been executed from the beginning.[72] Between 3 and 6 May Exercise Fabius 1 was the US V Corps last chance to practise the Omaha landing and simultaneously the British XXX Corps landed on Hayling Island in its final simulation for Gold Beach in Fabius 2 while the Juno-bound Canadians landed at Selsey Bill in Fabius 3 and those heading for Sword landed at Littlehampton in Fabius 4. Fabius 5 was a full-scale embarkation exercise.[73]

The sea landings were extremely detailed with each individual allocated a task and under strict instructions that no-one was to stop to help the wounded or bury the dead unless they were medics or grave registration crews. One member of the 29th Infantry Division recalled later:

> Loading and unloading landing craft, exiting, peeling off, quickly moving forward, crawling under barbed wire with live machine gun fire just inches overhead and live explosions, strategically placed, detonated all around. We were schooled in the use of explosives: satchel charges and bangalore torpedoes were

excellent for blowing holes in barbed wire and neutralizing fortified bunkers ... Poison-gas drills, first aid, airplane and tank identification, use and detection of booby traps and more gave us the confidence that we were ready. I believe our division was as competent to fight as any green outfit in history.[74]

In short, the temptation to regard the invasion as a problem that could be effectively tamed by constant practice must have been strong, but the real issue was whether the problem could be tamed like this, or whether significant elements of the problem would always remain Wicked – thus requiring a different approach where collaborative effort and decentralized decision-making would be required. For example, although Operation Fabius was deemed a success initially because everything was rolling out as planned, it was halted on the third day (4 May) after the wind rose to force 6 and threatened to damage the landing craft. Ironically, this was the same wind speed that many troops landed in on D-Day itself.[75] Thus the very element of the problem that could never be tamed – the weather – was effectively removed from practice.

What the American assault troops of the US V Corps did not know at this time, and what those in the VII Corps had not expected, was the other element of the plan that could not be tamed through practice: the German intervention in Exercise Tiger.

8.8 Exercise Tiger

Exercise Tiger (24–28 April) was the first and last full scale exercise for the US VII Corps heading for Utah and it was watched by the top brass: Eisenhower, Montgomery, Tedder, Ramsay and Bradley – all in separate landing craft to limit any possible danger from enemy attack. In April 1944 25,000 troops, primarily from the US 4th Infantry and the 101st and (its originating division) the 82nd American Airborne divisions, linked up to 'invade' Slapton Sands in Devon.

The operation was a total failure and did not bode well for D-Day: the Typhoon aircraft destined to rocket the beach failed to arrive on time, persuading Admiral Moon to delay the 'invasion' by one hour to allow them to arrive. Unfortunately they remained absent but this then cut the naval gunfire practice to a minimum. Worse, the DD tanks, though they managed to stay afloat, landed where their commanders felt like rather than where they were supposed to, and the troops simply ignored the designated 'minefields' and walked straight through them. Eisenhower's naval aide, Captain H.C. Butcher, was appalled at what he saw: 'The young American officers seemed to regard the war as one grand manoeuvre in which they are having a happy time. Many seem as green as the growing corn'.[76] Eisenhower was already worried even before this episode because he had seen the significance that combat experience had for developing leadership skills amongst his officer corps and had been distraught that he could not use all of the troops with prior battle experience for the Normandy invasion.[77]

With three days to land and evacuate the troops and their 2,750 vehicles, the exercise became really 'live' when German 'E' boats[78] infiltrated the manoeuvres of a convoy of nine LSTs, slipping past the single escort, HMS *Azalea*. The LSTs had a very shallow draft and were, allegedly, immune from submarine torpedoes which travelled under their hulls, but they were not immune to the shallower travelling E-Boat torpedoes. In an area known locally as Dead Man's Bay, the E-boats sank two LSTs and damaged three others, apparently killing 749 and wounding 300 others.[79] The following day, as the rescue ships arrived in the area, the water was covered in bodies, most of whom had died of hypothermia (many had removed their outer clothes and boots), though some drowned because they had not been instructed on how to wear and inflate their lifejackets (many wore them around their waists rather than under their arm pits) and had either been knocked unconscious in the jump from the ship and drowned or simply been unable to operate the life jacket and drowned.[80] Julien Perkin on HMS *Obedient* recalled that: 'the sight was appalling. There were hundreds of bodies of American servicemen in full battle gear, floating in the sea. Many had their limbs and even their heads blown off … Of all those we took on board there were only nine survivors'.[81]

The participants were forbidden to mention the tragedy to any civilian and threatened with court martial if they did.[82] But perhaps the most disturbing element of Operation Tiger was not the tragedy out at sea, or even accidental killing of troops by either the LCRs (Landing Craft Rocket) or naval ships whose rockets and shells fell either short or late onto 'invading' troops (resulting in around 50 casualties to 'friendly fire'). Rather it was the apparently deliberate killing of the 'invaders' by the 'defenders'. Between 400 and 500 American troops were dug into the cliffs and sand at Slapton and ordered to use live ammunition and fire over the heads of the invaders to simulate real battle conditions. The attackers were not all informed that live ammunition would be used (Small, 1999: 14). In fact, as many as 150 attacking troops were killed by the 'defenders' when the latter fired *into* rather than *over* the troops disembarking from the landing craft. Attempts by both American and British observers to stop the 'mistake' were firmly rejected by the local ground commanders who claimed they were under orders to 'keep firing', though there was a radio communications breakdown because the same single mistyped letter that had prevented the E-boat attacks being reported also caused the timing of the live firing and the attack to run over.[83] The possibility that the killing was planned seems very unlikely: 'real' invasions under fire had already occurred so it was already apparent what 'green' troops would probably do. Even if more information on this issue was necessary, the sight of American troops killing their fellow Americans – so that the commanders could see what would happen – was unlikely to do anything except persuade most Americans that this was a war that they should not be involved in and could not survive. The defenders would have known that they were firing live ammunition into their own troops and it seems likely that the responses of the local ground commanders leaves one to conjecture that the event was both a mistake and an act of gross stupidity and or a crass lack of concern for the lives of ordinary soldiers. And these 'ordinary' soldiers were about to face one of the most effective armies of modern times.

8.9 Gun-fodder and gunmen

According to Hastings, that US 'infantry rifle companies would be called upon to fight Hitler's *Wehrmacht*, "the most professionally skilful army of modern times" with men who were, in all too many cases, the least impressive material America had summoned to the colours'.[84] Despite this, General Marshall was unconcerned with the quality of the troops, at least officially. 'We will have no trouble', he suggested, 'if the men themselves understand what they are doing and the reasons why they are doing it'.[85]

The reality of this claim runs directly counter to the assumption that the American civilian population should also understand what was going on. For example, not until September 1943 were photographs of dead Americans released for publication, initially of bodies on Buna Beach in New Guinea. This was not to protect the population from the sight of death, since photos of dead Germans, dead Japanese and dead black Americans lynched at home in the southern states were commonplace. But the sight of dead GIs was considered too shocking until this time.[86] Indeed, it may be that the government became convinced that a dose of reality was necessary to shake the population out of its apparent complacency.

Yet, paradoxically, the troops who made up the rifle companies knew that they were regarded as simultaneously the scum of the army and its primary asset.[87] As one such GI recalled his lieutenant saying during training: 'You ain't nothing but gun fodder, but you are essential and nobody can take your place'.[88] In the US Airborne the prevalence of death was channelled into marching songs like 'Blood upon the risers' that revelled in death and made light of the gore:

> There was blood upon the risers, there were brains upon the chute
> Intestines were a dangling from this paratrooper's boots
> They picked him up, still in his chute and poured him from his boots,
> He ain't gonna jump no more
> Gory, gory, what a helluva way to die
> Gory, gory, what a helluva way to die
> Gory, gory, what a helluva way to die
> He ain't gonna jump no more.[89]

But the issue that really aggravated the ordinary combat soldier was not the distinction between the army and the paratroopers or the army and the air force, but between combat troops and those in the safety of the rear areas. In fact, only a small proportion of the huge number of army personnel ended up carrying a rifle in Europe or the Pacific. Yet the curious consequence of this was also an inordinate pride in the exclusivity of the combat solider: they would take the brunt of the casualties and they would suffer the worst imaginable conditions – and complain vociferously about both – but the very reasons that the service troops avoided combat were the ones that became embedded in the identity of the combat troops: they were the hard men of the army and were proud of it. Moreover, life on the front line removed all the messy compromises that so sullied normal life. Only there did real comradeship appear to flourish, though when the war was over that comradeship sometimes disappeared as quickly as it had come. 'We yearned for the association with men of great differences', wrote Orval Faubus after the war, 'yet so devoid of prejudice and so imbued with loyalty that we could go out together and fight and die, for each other and for the common cause of freedom. We longed for the spirit of men of combat – a spirit motivated by bravery, honour, compassion and sacrifice, with the absence of pettiness, envy, jealousy and falsehood.[90]

This was especially significant within the US culture of individualism rooted in the 'code of the West' where the heroic icons were not chivalrous knights or monarchs or romantic groups nor disciplined masses but the lone individual intent on preserving 'life, liberty and the pursuit of happiness'.[91] Transposed from the 19th century (Wild) West to the 20th century American Army, the reconstructed icon of a 'real soldier' was, as one wounded veteran put it: 'a guy – he'll drink and swear – but he relies on himself; a guy that can take care of himself'.[92] As a consequence, any officers who put their own lives and careers ahead of their soldiers were unlikely to receive much co-operation from ordinary combat troops. Unfortunately, and despite all the evidence concerning the importance of group loyalty and cohesion to soldiers' morale, the US army was swayed by contending concerns for group casualties into undermining that morale through its own replacement policy: the Repple Depple.

8.10 Greenhorns, veterans and the Repple Depple

The German army had learned and embodied the value of group cohesion for many years: its army units (*Feldheer*) operated in tandem with a replacement unit (*Feldersatzbataillon*) from its local recruitment area. The *Feldheer* managed all the combat troops on the active front, the *Feldersatzbataillon* organized training, replacements and administration. Those recuperating from wounds and so on would rest at the *Feldersatzbataillon* before returning to the *Feldheer*. New, replacement and convalescing troops from the field unit were trained and grouped together (Lucas, 1998: 12). This usually meant a much stronger identification between the replacements and the host unit than occurred in the American system, but it also inhibited the tactical flexibility of the German field commanders. Moreover, the dearth of German replacements towards the end of war often meant that reserve units were not fed into their 'parent' combat unit but deployed directly as a group elsewhere. For example, although the German 352nd Infantry Division had a *Feldersatzbataillon* training in Hanover, it was never used to fill the gaps in the 352nd in Normandy but deployed as an independent unit: there were no replacements for the 352nd in Normandy; it was simply deployed until it was destroyed. Ironically, it was also difficult to use the *Feldersatzbataillon* of any adjoining unit – even if it was available – because the troops were usually only committed to replacing those casualties from their own *Feldheer* unit.[93]

Simply being amongst fellow veterans did not always equate with high morale. As we have already seen with the seasoned British troops on D-Day, being a veteran did not make the landing necessarily easier. Ray Lambert with the 16th RCT certainly did not think it did:

> I had been with the 16th in North Africa in 1942 and in Sicily in 1943. Nothing I had seen in all those battles would compare with what we encountered at 'Easy Red' on June 6, 1944. I was sick from the time I was loaded into the Higgins boat from the LCI as was everyone else. There were so many men throwing up all over the boat and each other that we could hardly stand. The boat to our left got hit and burst into flames ... . The boat on our right blew up and most of the troops

on board were killed. We were under intense fire from machine guns, rifles, mortars and artillery and all from both flanks as well as from dead ahead. Our heavy gun support from the battle ships was halted because they could not tell how far our troops had advanced ... . We could hear the machine gun shells hitting the ramp and side of our boat. We knew when we lowered the ramp we would walk into a death trap, but there was no other way.[94]

Members of the 1st Division insisted that the US Army had become 'the 1st Division and eight million replacements'.[95] It was the oldest division in the US Army, it had been on active service since 1917, and it was one of the few units that had already seen combat, in North Africa, Sicily and Salerno, and few of the troops relished the prospect of a third amphibious landing but, as Bradley noted: Although I disliked subjecting the 1st to still another landing, I felt that as a commander, I had no other choice ... I felt compelled to employ the best troops I had, to minimize the risk and hoist the odds in our favour in any way that I could'.

That responsibility was probably made a little easier by the US replacement policy ('Repple-Depple': Replacement Depots) which had generally been to distribute recruits between units so that no locality would suffer the high level of casualties that occurred in the First World War (as indeed the 'Pals battalions' in the British army did – hence the British split their regimental battalions up to ensure that at least half would survive irrespective of the other). The system, in theory, also ensured not just that the replacements were provided as fast as possible but that the replacements embodied the same degree and form of skill as the casualty – Military Occupational Speciality (MOS), as it was called. Not surprisingly, the most frequent MOS number was MOS 745 – a rifleman. And when units like the 29th Division were constantly in the line (44 days from D-Day) the requirements for replacements were very high and soldiers and officers were often killed before those they were commanded by, or commanded, even knew their names.[96]

Unusually, on Omaha Beach, some elements of the US 29th Division were drawn primarily from local communities and these suffered as a consequence: Company A of the 116th RCT lost 22 men from Bedford a village of 3,000 people, including three sets of brothers.[97] Sergeant John Slaughter, a member of Company D remembered seeing two of the brothers going in:

Raymond and Bedford Holback were killed. Raymond was wounded and lay on the beach. Then when the tide came in he was washed out to sea and drowned. They never found his body ... . On the Saturday (10 June) their family got a telegram that Bedford was killed and then on Sunday they got another one saying Raymond was too.[98]

But the consequence of the general policy of regional dispersion was that little spatial loyalty existed and the identity of any soldier with any unit, except perhaps the elite units, became precarious. However, providing the replacements lasted long enough they would soon become part of the 'brotherhood' simply because so many of their comrades were also replacements.

Such 'Greenhorns' typically made very common mistakes on entry to combat: bunching together, making too much noise, shooting too early, not seeking cover properly and freezing under fire.[99] As one Desert Rat from the British Eighth Army said: 'An old soldier is a cautious soldier, that is why he is an old soldier'.[100] In fact, few Americans had experienced combat before D-Day (the exceptions were the 1st Infantry Division and the 82nd Airborne) but this almost universal naïveté probably helped as much as it hindered, for, as many troops were later to recall – if they had known what it was going to be like they would never have gone. Private Carl Weast, 5th Rangers, certainly agreed that the use of green troops was probably the right decision 'because an experienced infantryman is a terrified infantryman, and they wanted guys like me who were more amazed than they were frozen with fear, because the longer you fight a war the more you figure your number's coming up tomorrow, and it really gets to be God-awful'.[101] Another such green soldier was John Pulliam, a glider soldier with the 82nd Airborne who responded to his company commander's call that 'somebody better shoot' the German approaching them in Normandy. 'Believe it or not I didn't hesitate a bit. They told me to quit shooting, you've got him. You think it would really bother you. It didn't. You're psyched up'.[102]

That flood of adrenalin could often compensate for the nervousness of the greenhorns. Lieutenant Eikner of the 2nd Ranger Battalion, for instance, suggested that D-Day was positively welcomed: 'when we went into battle after all this training there was no shaking of the knees or weeping or praying; we knew what we were getting into; we knew everyone of us had volunteered for extra hazardous duty; we went into battle confident; of course we were tense under fire, but we were intent on getting the job done. We were actually looking forward to accomplishing our mission'.[103]

Strangely, many were warned of what was likely to happen – and a 30 per cent casualty rate was commonly expected – but it did not necessarily deter them. Many were supremely confident like Private Lindley Higgins, especially having seen the materiel which supported them compared to the shortages which he knew the Germans faced: 'We really thought we had only to stop off the beach and all the krauts would put up their hands'.[104]

A Public Relations Colonel had even told the 116th that he expected
100 per cent casualties in the first 24 hours, while another suggested
two-thirds would not return, and 30 per cent was the proportion
suggested to Harry Parley of the 116th.[105] This might appear to have
made the task of the leaders significantly more difficult but soldiers
generally rationalized the likelihood of personal injury in the manner akin
to Charles East of the 29th Division (Omaha Beach) who, when told by
his commanding officer on the eve of D-Day that nine out of ten men
would become casualties, 'looked at the man to his left, then at the man
to his right, and thought to himself, You poor bastards'.[106] The utility of
belief in fate, so common in the First World War[107] was also pervasive in
the Second.[108] Yet a belief in fatalism also acted as a shield against fear,
because if there was nothing you could do to avoid your fate, that also
meant that until that appointment was reached you could not die. For
example, Joseph O'Connell, a soldier with the US 4th Infantry on Utah
Beach was on one of the few landing craft to take heavy casualties and
reached the beach as the lone survivor, but: to reach the safety of a farm-
house meant crossing an area under machine gun fire: 'I lie in the grass
pondering whether to take the chance. Yes-no-yes-no. My brain keeps
whirling ... I must go on, for I'll be killed only when my time comes'.[109]

Some individuals seemed destined to survive no matter what
happened. Edgar A. Schroeder, a glider-borne soldier suggested as much
for:

> This was the day I became a firm believer that if it ain't your time, you ain't going
> to get it, no matter what. One of our officers took a round through the side of his
> helmet, it went up and over between the liner and the outer steel helmet clipping
> his ear on the opposite side. This same guy threw a grenade that hit a tree and
> bounced in his lap – a dud.[110]

Some soldiers seemed to have coped with the fear by accepting – in
traditional Samurai fashion – that they were already dead and thus 'living'
on borrowed time. Indeed, since they were already dead, they had nothing to lose and therefore nothing to fear. 'Death doesn't worry you any
more' recalled Private Wingfield as he listened to a talk by his corporal,
'We have little hope of survival. We accept that and spin it out as best we
can. We don't have any distractions like comfort ... . We're as good as
dead. A slit trench, after all, is the nearest thing to a grave we'll be in
while we're alive'.[111] Nevertheless, few actually courted death by exposing themselves to enemy fire or not digging fox-holes so that fatalism
became as much a ritual to ward off fate as one of accepting it.[112]
Moreover, as time elapsed, the boundaries of the individuals making up

a unit melted and refroze them into a collective where everything was shared including the most important thing of all to a soldier: mail from home.[113] In the words of Sergeant Marsden in the US Army:

> You just share your life with the men in the barracks. This has been going on for twelve weeks. Twelve weeks ago if someone had even suggested that I drink out of the same cup that someone else had taken a drink from I would most likely have retched, but that was twelve weeks ago. Now, five of us drink out of the same canteen. We share a bottle of Coke, taking turns guzzling, eat a box of ice cream with the same spoon. We even wear each other's drawers and socks and shirts.[114]

But consequently and coterminously, anyone outside the small circle of brotherhood was just one of the 'others', not one of your 'own'. Hence those entering veteran platoons as replacements would not always receive the kind of care that Bradley hoped they would receive. Sergeant James Jones with the US Rangers recalled receiving eight replacements at Anzio on one day, and the following day all eight were dead – but no veteran had died. As he explained: 'We weren't going to send our own guys out on point [lead position] in a damn fool situation like that … . We were sewed up tight. And we'd been together through Africa, and Sicily, and Salerno … How are we going to send our own guys into that?'[115] So did the ideological battle between Nazism and Democracy play any part in the minds of US soldiers?

8.11 Ideology, normality and death

In early 1942 the US forces began compulsory lectures twice a week for 13 weeks to explain why the US was at war, what the enemy was like and what was expected of the troops.[116] But they had only marginal impact and we can be more certain that the average US soldier was probably *not* driven by ideological commitment than that the German soldier probably *was*. If anything, the US went out of its way to *avoid* generating an anti-fascist ideology because it so clearly contradicted the cultural mores of the typical soldier; for these people the heroic US cinema icons of the day were not John Wayne (too many children to be conscripted). The best example was Humphrey Bogart, whose sardonic, disinterested and even cynical machismo embodied none of the emotion or attitudes thought necessary to construct a passionately anti-Nazi ideology – but would nevertheless provide the necessary effort to do what had to be done.

The GIs may, of course, have been driven by hatred of what the

German *Wehrmacht* was doing to their buddies (and there is little evidence that such GIs in Europe distinguished much between the Nazis and the Germans; even if the US Government tried to maintain a distinction), but few seemed to adopt this attitude: less than 10 per cent admitted that they would 'really like' to kill a German (the numbers rose to 50 per cent when the Japanese replaced the Germans in the question). However, almost 90 per cent thought that killing Germans was a necessary but unpleasant task and 65 per cent thought that after the war only the leaders should be punished (though 25 per cent thought that 'the whole German nation should be "wiped out"'.[117] This was particularly the case with troops who had been involved in liberating the death camps. Donald Lembeke was one such soldier deeply affected by his experiences:

> Shooting is too good for them. They should be starved, beaten and then shot the same way as they had been treating these other people. Maybe I shouldn't have written this but the people over there (in the U.S.) know so little about what goes on over here. They still think the Germans are civilized. They aren't even human.[118]

But by the time these camps were liberated the war was almost over. Most American soldiers thought that most German soldiers were professional, well trained, well armed, and well led. Indeed, the army magazine *Army Talks* suggested that Fritz Müller, the German equivalent of GI Joe, was not 'a goose stepping mechanical automaton ... . He has been in the army longer than you; he is by nature an eager beaver and extremely anxious to be a good soldier; his officers have carefully instilled in him a spirit of independent action'.[119]

One member of the 29th Infantry Division in Normandy was quite clear that ideological concerns about fascism were the last thing on most front line soldiers' minds: 'Ask any dogface on the line. You're fighting for your own skin on the line. When I enlisted I was patriotic as hell. There's no patriots on the line. A boy up there sixty days in the line is in danger every minute. He ain't fighting for patriotism'.[120]

And this may explain why Patton appears to have been popular with his troops – he did not seek to justify the war with political analysis nor explain why it was their duty to halt Hitler.[121] Instead, Patton located his troops back in their own cultural origins and told them what they probably regarded as the truth: the best way to survive was to win the war and that meant killing as many of the enemy as quickly as they could. But Patton usually demonstrated a passion for killing that went well beyond any notion of professional soldiering. 'We won't just shoot the sons 'a' bitches', he informed his troops, 'we're going to cut out their living guts and use them to grease the treads of our tanks'.[122]

To most American combat soldiers, then, the war was not a crusade against Nazi Germany it was an unpleasant 'job' that had to be done; in this vein it manifested the problem as one that could be pragmatically managed, rather than one that needed ideological Leadership. The US Army pamphlet, 'Army Talks' devoted just one page to the ideological crusade against the Nazis and the CO of the 2nd battalion the 116th Infantry (29th Division) was clear that what most of his soldiers and fellow officers were fighting for 'was not ideals but rather an overwhelming desire to kill Germans, to avoid being killed oneself, and to achieve the terrain objectives we had trained so hard and long to reach'.[123] Even those elite troops who were more ideologically involved than their ordinary infantry colleagues were frequently motivated to return the situation to the status quo ante rather than create some new 'utopia' or more likely 'dystopia'. As one Commando with the Inter-Allied No. 10 Commando suggested: 'We may not have known what we were fighting for but we sure as hell knew what we were fighting against'.

That the task was a 'job' both rationalized the killing and retained some form of link with their pre-war normality – though again for ¼ of the employable population the previous decade had seen unemployment as the nearest thing to a job. Hence, however unpalatable the 'job' of soldiering was, it was at least a job of some form and it provided both financial resources and the source of pride for many that had previously lost everything. In the words of Henry Giles, an American soldier since 1939, 'Nobody knows what the army meant to me – security and pride and something fine and good … . (For) the first time in my life I was *somebody*.[124]

The notion of a job also enabled those not in combat roles to feel that they too were helping the war effort. 'Drivers, supply clerks, cooks, mechanics', wrote Captain Earl Nelson in 1944, 'are all winning the war simply by doing their job'.[125] That many took pride in their achievements can be related to the extent to which those *not* involved in combat have often sought to 'reinterpret' their past so that they could present themselves to the world as legitimate 'veterans'. But few Allied soldiers had been through what most German soldiers went through.

8.12 Conclusion

This chapter explained why an iceberg approach was taken and what that meant for those on the ground in Normandy. It then considered the problems the American army generated for itself through its promotion of a status-based hierarchy that mirrored their British allies. This fed directly into the overtly elitist and discriminatory allocation policy that saw the regular army despising the National Guard, African-American troops shunted into service roles and the least educated white troops corralled into the rifle companies. In turn this policy was rationalized by recourse to the technical nature of the war machine the US was building: this was a war of technology that could be managed to victory, rather than led to victory; though, as I shall suggest in later chapters, that technology was itself soaked in social and cultural mores and was never the 'objective' choice of scientific analysis. Yet, despite – and in some ways because of – the exclusionary and elitist nature of the army, those soldiers who did end up metaphorically at the bottom and literally swimming in blood, constructed self-images that inverted their status from the lowest to the toughest. And this machismo was embodied not just in their resistance towards soldiers of all ranks that were not at the sharp end, but also in their clothing and, more importantly, in their small group solidarity as 'bands of brothers'. So while the problem of winning the war did indeed contain a large element of Management, successful Command on the ground was also necessary and almost always related to this boundary-constructing phenomenon: leaders, both combat officers and sergeants, had to gain access to, or at least respect from, this social group in order to lead it anywhere. Unfortunately, the top leadership failed to capitalize on this through their management of the replacement policy – itself an attempt to appease public opinion on significant regional casualties. As a result that critical social support weakened over time and the proportion of traumatized soldiers crept ever-higher. This may also reflect the general attitude of most American soldiers to the war: in marked contrast to their more ideologically motivated German enemies, most GIs interpreted their status more as employees of Uncle Sam rather than disciples of Adolf Hitler. In the next section I consider how the latter developed.

9 Mobilizing the Germans: the *Wehrmacht* and the SS

9.1 Introduction

German mobilization had started in 1935 and the system operated along strict age categories. The 100,000 members of the *Mannheer*, the post-Versailles Treaty army that the Germans had managed to preserve, formed the nucleus of the army with many individuals assuming the positions of officers or NCOs in the new German army. In fact the *Mannheer* was restricted to 4,000 officers – but had it had 18,000 SNCOs and 30,000 JNCOs so that with 50 per cent of the soldiers recognized as having some formal leadership role it was effectively leaderful. After the invasion of France in 1940, Hitler had even managed to demobilize several categories of older troops (partly to employ them in munitions factories for the future wars) but the categories – and the criteria for avoiding military service – became progressively tightened as the war in the east foundered and the war in the west began again. Only German nationals were permitted to join the army, at least until 1942 forced a change of policy when it began recruiting non-Russians from the USSR, though the *Waffen* SS had recruited foreign volunteers from 1940.[1]

However, German economic organization for war was never as efficient as its military organization: it could turn out the most effective combat troops of any nation but fighting a long war required more than the Command of crises and the Leadership of Wicked Problems, it required the Management of Tame Problems, but the latter either eluded them or were never regarded as important. For instance, when Operation Barbarossa was launched in 1941 the *Wehrmacht* only took a few weeks extra supplies with them – assuming that the Soviets could be destroyed in just ten weeks of fighting. Priorities were either not set or often changed in line with Hitler's increasing penchant for intervention and direction as the war progressed. In other words, Command took increasing precedence over both Leadership and Management. Indeed, in the Polish campaign, he intervened only once when he ordered an air attack on Warsaw on 15 September (subsequently rescinded on von

Rundstedt's request)[2] Hitler had also wanted to invade the Soviet Union in the summer of 1940 originally but had been dissuaded by Keitel and Jodl. Beyond the logistical problems, the strategy was confused, with three competing aims: destroy the Russian armies, seize the industrial regions, and cut off the Baltic. Guderian was particularly concerned: 'Three army groups, each of approximately the same strength, were to attack diverging objectives; no single clear operational objective seemed to be envisaged'.[3]

Yet for the most part the German economy, supported by its conquests, survived well during the war. Indeed, food supplies remained stable – thanks to the wholesale transfer of supplies from occupied countries, particularly the Netherlands, and working hours remained stable at 60 hours per week. Only when this was increased to a standard 72 hour week in the latter part of the war did absenteeism increase markedly and even then night shifts were rare. (The average British working week was 48.6 (51.2 for men).[4] The total civilian workforce stood at 29 million Germans (14.2 million men and 14.8 million women) and 7.1 foreign workers (slaves, POWs and so on). By September 1944 over one third of the workforce was non-German, but many other sources of labour were unused. For example, 3.5 million (of 5.7 million) Soviet POWs died in their camps. By D-Day the German prisons held 190,500 prisoners and the *Wehrmacht* had called up 12.4 million men and 3.3 million of these had become casualties. An additional source of loss was the quarter of a million Germans who were arrested in the first half of 1944, 2,607 of whom were executed.[5] Hence while the combat efficiency of the German troops was usually higher than their enemies, the strategic leadership and economic management was often palpably worse.

9.2 The *Wehrmacht*, the SS and the *Ost* battalions

The adoption of a static defensive strategy was in itself a novelty for the German army. German strategy had long focused on offensive armoured warfare deeply rooted in speed and, as a consequence, decentralized decision making to take advantage of local conditions, threats and opportunities. Despite the assertion that this form of *Blitzkrieg* was a direct consequence of German economic realities (especially the inability to fight a prolonged war through inadequate Management), there is little evidence that economic 'realties' conditioned the strategy. The strategy was a cultural choice, not a determined consequence of economics.[6] The corollary of the over-reliance on formal leaders on the part of the Allied armies was its opposite in the German army: they had proportionately fewer officers than either the American or British army and this necessarily put more emphasis on NCO leadership.[7] For example, the US 29th Infantry Division had 14,281 members, of whom 747 were officers (5.2 per cent). Of the 13,027 members of the German 352nd Infantry Division, only 405 were officers (3.1 per cent). In general the British Army was even more top heavy and operated with officers making up 6.6 per cent of the total at the beginning of the war, climbing to as many as 7.7 per cent of its total numbers by 1945.[8] One of the reasons for the extra American officers was the provision of formal reserves – or 'executives', should any of the original officers be killed or incapacitated. On the German side *all* troops were expected to pick up the responsibilities of leaders wherever necessary and it was not deemed essential to have a 'second team' waiting in the wings all the time.[9] In other words, the German army had effectively *deeper* Leadership than either of the main Allies: there were fewer formal chiefs but paradoxically more people willing and able to become 'acting' chiefs as and when required or to prevent their superiors from making mistakes. Once again this reflects the difference emphasis placed on the Management of problems – the US approach – or the Leadership of problems – the German approach.

But the irony is that while the Germany army was much better equipped to replace dead and injured leaders in the field, their lines of authority at senior level were so deeply bureaucratic that the *Wehrmacht's* top hierarchy remained implacably inflexible. To immobilize the American, and especially the British, army one only needed to kill or injure the junior officers, but to immobilize the German army one only needed to keep the senior leaders *alive*. This was not only with regard to the chaos at the planning and production centres of the Reich induced by the Nazi 'system' but also in specific military decisions made by Hitler. Four of these were critical. First, his ill-defined war objectives in the Soviet Union that ensured that none was achieved. Second, his order to Paulus at Stalingrad not to surrender that doomed the 250,000 Germans who died plus 84,000 of the 90,000 who surrendered. Third, the Mortain counter-attack in early August 1944 which played straight into the Allies' hands and led directly to the slaughter at Falaise. And finally, the Ardennes offensive in December 1944 that squandered whatever reserves the *Wehrmacht* had left. In each case Hitler's subordinate Generals either failed to voice their concerns or allowed Hitler to bully them into submission with catastrophic results for the Germans. Nor was it always the case that refusal to accept Hitler's demands led to death or even dismissal: Kesselring frequently refused to accede to Hitler's whim but remained in command, at least until injured in an air attack on October 1944 in Italy. He had recovered sufficiently to resume control in February and then replaced the – once again dismissed – von Rundstedt after the bridge at Remagen fell into American hands. Guderian also frequently rejected Hitler's demands and was dismissed in 1941 for organizing a retreat, then reinstated in 1943, only to be ordered to take six weeks' leave on 28 March 1945. Had he taken it and returned he would have been back just in time to celebrate VE Day. Lastly, Manstein did what Paulus should have done: he refused to obey Hitler's order not to withdraw when he led the escape from the Cherkassy salient and saved 20,000 troops in the process, though he was subsequently dismissed.[10]

The result of this polarity in the German command system was that German troops in the field almost always proved more than a match for most of the Allied units facing them. As one SS officer recalled: 'I felt when we were in the field that in a fair fight with all things equal we would always win, not because of superior bravery but through better methods which I assure you were always – ALWAYS – designed to preserve lives, or at least to win a battle with fewer casualties'.[11] And since SS casualties, as a proportion of SS troops (25 per cent {253,000 of 1 million} were remarkably similar to those suffered by regular *Wehrmacht* units (24 per cent {2.9 million killed from 12 million called up}), we can assume that the stories of SS suicide actions were little different from any other *Wehrmacht* unit overall.[12] But that deep strength in the field was fatally undone by the catastrophic weaknesses at the top.

The 40 divisions [900,000 troops] of the *Waffen* SS [literally 'Weapons Protection Squad'], were the particular enemy that most Allied soldiers feared most and wanted to eliminate quickest, though almost all the units of the *Wehrmacht* were extremely efficient. In contrast, many German troops were sceptical of the fighting qualities of their American and British enemies and Colonel Trevor Dupuy, an American, suggested in 1977 that 'On a man for man basis, the German ground soldier consistently inflicted casualties at about a 50 per cent higher rate than they incurred from the opposing British and American troops UNDER ALL CIRCUMSTANCES.[13] This was true when they were attacking and when they were defending, when they had a local numerical superiority and when, as was usually the case, they were outnumbered, when they had air superiority, and when they did not, when they won and when they lost'.[14] Church suggests that Dupuy's data is skewed – both the British and German samples are very small and unrepresentative[15] but Hastings concurs with Dupuy, calling the German army:

> ... the finest fighting army of the war, one of the greatest the world has ever seen. This is a simple truth that some soldiers and writers have been reluctant to acknowledge, partly for reasons of national pride, partly because it is a painful

concession when the *Wehrmacht* and SS were fighting for one of the most obnoxious regimes of all times. The quality of the German weapons – above all tanks – was of immense importance. Their tactics were masterly: stubborn defence; concentrated local firepower from mortars and machine guns; quick counter-attacks to cover lost ground. Units often fought on even when cut off, which was not a mark of fanaticism, but of sound tactical discipline, when such resistance in the rear did much to reduce the momentum of Allied advances, as in GOOD-WOOD. German attacks were markedly less skilful, even clumsy ... Their junior leadership was much superior to that of the Americans, perhaps also to that of the British.[16]

However, Hastings also admits that the situations were different: the Germans were fighting for the survival of their country whereas the Allies were undertaken an unpleasant but necessary task; the Germans did not have an apparently unending supply of troops or supplies which ensured that sooner or later victory would be achieved and therefore there was little need for heroics. And, most significantly, from 1943 the Germans were primarily fighting a defensive war where most of the advantages lay with the defenders – though clearly this had proved irrelevant for the French army in 1940 or the Soviet forces in 1941. Ambrose insists, however, that when the Germans went on the offensive against the Allies, at Bastogne and through the Ardennes in the winter of 1944, the American troops in particular proved more than a match for the German elite soldiers.[17] This is probably accurate, though by that time most of the elite German soldiers had already died, either in Russia or in Normandy.

It is worth considering the historical context for this: in the First World War the Central Powers inflicted at the very least 10 per cent more casualties upon the Allies than vice versa and when the comparison is made between German and Allied troops the disproportionate success of the former increases. For example, Dupuy suggests that German troops were 20 per cent more effective than either the British or the American troops.[18] The implication is that even before the SS and the Nazi ideology took hold, the German troops were more effective than the Allied troops – and had already demonstrated this in the previous war.

Whatever the truth of the situational conditions may have been there is little doubt that, unlike the rest of the *Wehrmacht*, the SS were simultaneously feared and loathed by most Allied troops. The SS were under the *Wehrmacht* for operational matters but were not under the latter's disciplinary system, being responsible directly and only to Hitler. That differentiation manifested itself in many ways, not least in the appearance of the SS. The 12th SS Panzer Division *Hitlerjugend* (*HJ*) that fought so effectively in Normandy were allowed to wear their hair much longer than any other division – a symbol of their youth but also an emblem to differentiate them from all others. Not all the officers were diehard Nazis though. Captain Hans Dischke, for example, had fought in Russia for two years before joining the 12th SS HJ, was uninterested in the 'Nazi nonsense on the political level at the officers' school ... so when I joined the 12th SS I had no thoughts whatsoever of trying to indoctrinate the lads ... We did, however, have a very strong belief in our own country, and since we were engaged in a war we saw it as our duty to win if possible. Certainly, we would rather die than let the Bolsheviks take over Germany'.[19]

Originally entry to the SS *Liebstandarte* (Bodyguard) unit had been very strict: at least 1.8 metres tall, good health, no criminal record, joined the Nazi Party before 30 January 1933, no filled teeth, 'well proportioned body' and proof of ancestry back to 1800 for soldiers and 1750 for officers.[20] The black uniformed *Leibstandarte Adolf Hitler* (*LAH*), led by Sepp Dietrich, was involved in the 'night of the long knives' in 1934 and, by 1943 had become the 1st SS Panzer Division *Leibstandarte*. Dietrich, whom von Rundstedt referred to as 'decent but stupid' appears to have been no strategist or military theoretician, but he was immensely popular with his 'boys' as he called all his troops, and a formidable combat commander. He was also very visible in the front line, something which most Allied senior commanders were not.[21]

The *Leibstandarte* had also already lost 53 per cent (5,281 of 9,994) in the first five months of fighting on the Russian front but had gained a reputation as ferocious soldiers – though von Rundstedt was unimpressed by its initial performance in Poland.[22] When they were reformed they were sent to recapture Kharkov in the spring of 1943, and once again suffered enormous casualties – 4,540 (44 per cent of the total). Once more the LAH was rebuilt and half of the division was thrown into the defence of the Reich at the battle of Kursk in July 1943 where 2,753 casualties were taken. Then, following the retreat from Russia over the winter of 1943/44 the LAH was almost annihilated: by March 1944 there were just 1,229 members left. It was this rump that provided the core for the LAH that fought in Normandy after the division had re-equipped in Belgium.[23]

Their approach to war could not have been more different from that of the typical Allied soldier. As one SS captain put it, perfectly capturing the antithesis of the Allied approach to managing the war:

It was those defensive battles in Russia which I shall always remember for the sheer beauty of the fighting, rather than the victorious advances ... . After a time we reached a point where we were not concerned for ourselves or even for Germany, but lived entirely for the next clash, the next engagement with the enemy. There was a tremendous sense of 'being', an exhilarating feeling that every nerve in the body was alive to fight.[24]

By March 1944 this division was reduced to three tanks, four armoured assault guns, 41 officers and 1,188 NCOs and soldiers. Thus when it arrived in Normandy to attack the Allies in June 1944 half of the division had been with it for less than a month. Despite this enormous turnover in personnel it remained a feared – and despised – enemy.[25] When Sepp Dietrich, who led the defence of Caen in Normandy, died in 1966, his funeral was attended by 7,000 former *Waffen*-SS soldiers.[26]

The 12th SS Panzer Division *Hitlerjugend* (*HJ*) was raised virtually from scratch in June 1943 and for most of the Normandy campaign (after Major-General Fritz Witt was killed by an artillery or naval shell on 14 June) it was led by Kurt Meyer, Nazi Germany's youngest General at thirty-four. The 12th SS was the first *Waffen* SS unit in action in Normandy and it was very effective and very large: over 20,500 people were within its ranks, so popular had been its recruitment campaign. As a consequence over 2,000 soldiers were transferred to the depleted *Leibstandarte* to make up its numbers.[27]

The 12th SS was supposed to be composed of youths born in the first half of 1926, which meant that the *Hitlerjugend* division was not full of fanatical *children*, since two thirds were 18 during the Normandy campaign and the rest slightly older.[28] By comparison, the average age of the American soldiers in Europe at this time was 26. Nevertheless, children were engaged in other units as soldiers towards the end of the war. But, as Reynolds makes clear, 'What made the *HJ* division different was that it was *based* on eighteen year olds'.[29] This age-based commonality also undermined any regional allegiances that the members may have had in precisely the same way that the Zulu impis were organized. Equally important, the training provided was different from that given to the rest of the German forces – and markedly in contrast with the norm for the Allied forces. Physical fitness, character training and weapons training were the three critical activities and the three critical prohibitions were alcohol, tobacco and women. This spartan regime – and the similarities between the *HJ* regime and the Spartan regime are noticeable[30] – was not, however, buttressed by the authoritarian obsession with discipline, 'square-bashing' and respect for authority so beloved of martinets in all conventional armies. Parade bashing may have proved of great utility either in practical terms for the practising of close-order battle tactics used up until the American Civil War, or even for the indoctrination of blind obedience that every conventional army allegedly operated on, but, as Meyer recounts, the *Hitlerjugend* was no ordinary army unit and its model of Leadership was quite different from the conventional units of the Allied armies:

> There was no dominant superior relationship, recognizing only orders and uncon-ditional obedience. The relationship between officers, NCOs and other ranks was that between older experienced and younger comrades ... The boys were educated to a sense of responsibility, a sense of community, a willingness to make sacrifices, decisiveness, self-control, camaraderie, and perception ... . During their training square bashing was frowned upon ... Everything focused on training for battle and this took place under the most realistic conditions possible.[31]

Captain Hans Dischke of the 12th SS HJ disclaimed any interest in serving Hitler, though he was keen to fight for Germany, and his assump-tion was that the combat skills of the division were developed through training, not indoctrination:

> Then there was the question of military training, which was all that mattered to us officers: how to teach these boys to survive in battle ... . Our special kind of SS *esprit de corps* was a fact, and as far as we were concerned instilled by mutual confi-dence and real comradeship which produced absolute trust between officers and men to a degree unknown in the German army ... . Of course it is impossible to say to what degree they were fighting for 'Führer and fatherland' and the Nazi way, but I do believe that in the main they had been instilled and inspired by our teachings of comradeship and absolute trust.[32]

Even conventional *Wehrmacht* units minimized distinctions between enlisted men and officers – unlike the American and British armies in particular. In the *Wehrmacht* everyone was *encouraged* to salute everyone else, irrespective of rank – in sharp contrast to the Anglo-American forces where soldiers were *required* to salute officers. Indeed, while the term 'soldiers' covered everyone in the *Wehrmacht*, there was no term for everyone in either the American or British armies, there was just 'soldiers' and 'officers'. Could it ever be imagined that British or American officers ever involved themselves in something that German officers regularly did – despite the obviously and radically subversive consequences for military discipline – singing 'Happy Birthday' to their 'common' soldiers? Since both the British and American officers were formally warned against frat-ernizing with their own soldiers we can rest assured that such a thing was unlikely.[33]

Training for SS troops was tough, and all officers were expected to serve for two years in the ranks before becoming officers, but the enor-mous casualty rate incurred by most SS (and indeed most *Wehrmacht*)

units led to a rapid turnover in staff and a consequently very young officer corps. In fact, so rapid had been the construction of the HJ that when
it went into battle just after D-Day in Normandy over half of its soldiers
had been members of the division for less than one month and most had
been in possession of their weapons for less than this time.[34] In effect,
the HJ was no battle hardened or even trained unit – but it was ideologically committed and it was extraordinarily effective.

A considerable part of the explanation of that effectiveness in the *Waffen*
SS then, lay not just in the devotion to Hitler but also in the devotion to
each other and the limited role of formal Leadership. In effect, followers
wanted to follow their leaders rather than being coerced into following –
ironically, a typically Wicked response to a problem rather than a Tame
response. Soldiers were not expected to address their officers as 'sir' but
by their formal rank and comradeship was institutionalized both in the
tradition of calling each other 'Kamerad' off duty, and in the culture of
mutual trust, such that no locks were allowed on private lockers – and
anyone caught stealing could expect very severe punishment. For example, when two members of the elite *Leibstandarte* SS were caught stealing both were shot and their entire company subsequently trampled on
their graves.[35] But where did this approach to formal Leadership come
from?

9.3 The paradox of hierarchy

Training for non-SS troops comprised 16 weeks of elementary training
and three more weeks of combat training but the whole thrust of that
training was to reinforce the importance of using initiative. As the
Truppenführung (Troop Leadership) manual insisted: 'Orders should be
binding only in so far as circumstances can be foreseen' (quoted in
Balkoski, 1999: 68).

The original German, or rather Prussian, army of Frederick the Great
(1740–86) (Hitler's hero) had been rooted in a social system not unlike
the British: 'amateur' aristocratic officer corps, coupled to a primarily
mercenary force of soldiers kept in line by brutal discipline. But after the
defeats at Jena and Auerstadt in 1806 the Prussian army was reconstructed under the guidance of Scharnhorst (1755–1813) and von
Gneisenau (Chief of Staff of the Prussian Army 1813–15). Some 800
officers were dismissed, conscription as a duty to the state was invoked
and a General Staff was introduced to concentrate, among other things,
on strategy and tactics.[36] Von Gneisenau had introduced a critical
change when the term 'intention' displaced the term 'direct order',

thereby institutionalizing the freedom of movement and decision making, but simply changing the words was not enough – the *action* of subordinates had to be facilitated and supported from above, and that became the task of von Moltke (the elder), chief of the Prussian and the German general Staff 1858–88. Aware of the utility of the railways to move troops six times faster than they could march, von Moltke quickly recognized the implications of this for a more mobile and faster form of warfare. That, in turn, had implications for battlefield planning and control for, 'No plan of operations can look with any certainty beyond the first meeting with the major forces of the enemy ... . All consecutive acts of war, are, therefore, not executions of a premeditated plan, but spontaneous actions, directed by military tact'.[37] Or, in his rather more pithy phrase: 'in the case of tactical victory, strategy submits'.[38]

Thus the German army had long practised what the Allied armies generally found inconceivable, indeed, directly contrary to military common sense: individual initiative rather than deference to formal Leadership. In 1887 the German field regulations were explicitly supportive of this policy: 'This regulation intentionally leaves freedom of action in the field, which will develop initiative in officers of all ranks. This initiative is absolutely necessary, and must not, under any circumstances, be limited by more precise orders'.[39]

In the First World War the Germans had evolved an organizational technique that embodied this combat philosophy, rooted as it was in the knowledge that no battle plan lasted beyond the opening shots. Initiative was therefore encouraged, military education and learning was promoted at all levels, and weak officers were removed – all in strong contrast to the philosophy and practice of Allied armies. The British emphasis on discipline and control, compared to the German emphasis on initiative, is a further contrast between the Management and/or Command approach of the former and the Leadership approach of the latter. On the other hand, the subordination of Management to Leadership by the German approach to war also undermined their ability to fight prolonged wars or support strategic assaults that did not achieve rapid results. In other words, where the Allied armies resembled rhinos – slow to start, lots of armour, inflexible, and difficult to stop once they got going – the German armies were closer to large cats – very rapid, flexible and ferocious in attack but with a tendency to run of steam.

Paradoxically, the background of the German army was not dissimilar to the British: they were both deeply rooted in the aristocratic land owning classes. Yet while the British army persisted in regenerating an aristocratic culture within the cavalry and infantry officer corps, their Prussian counterparts adopted radically different practices and ideologies that, in some ways, inverted the conventions of the aristocracy: the hier-archy and authoritarianism so prevalent in Britain was displaced by a far more egalitarian and individualist orientation. As Kier argues, it was not a case of mechanically relating the class origins of officers to their profes-sional culture because the class backgrounds of the British and the German army were similar but their professional cultures markedly dissimilar.[40] Indeed, the German navy was less aristocratic in origin but more aristocratic in culture than the German army, and even when the British army became less dominated by the aristocracy, it still maintained its aristocratic culture. US army culture was, if anything, closer to the British than the German traditions.

This shift in policy from the traditional *Befehlstaktik* (an uncompro-mising order) to the new *Auftragstaktik* (mission command) also embodied the essence of the division between the German and the Western Allied armies for, ironically, it was the liberal democracies that most clearly relied on *Befehlstaktik* not *Auftragstaktik*. As Lucas suggests, the *Befehlstaktik* principle was clearly present when the US forces landed at Anzio in February 1944, under orders to land and prepare for defence.[41] They did precisely as ordered, even though the German defenders were caught unawares, leaving an opportunity for the exploita-tion of a local contingency that most German commanders would have found impossible to resist had they been the invading force. As Churchill concluded, the Allies had intended to throw a 'wildcat' into the belly of the enemy but instead they had discharged a 'beached whale'.[42] Such defensively minded 'inactivity' was not a consequence of anything other than a culturally conditioned response to what appeared normality. With disarming candour John Hogan, from the US Army's 9th Amphibian Force, captured this perfectly: 'If you haven't got stripes, you aren't doing anything ... Every day I see the problem mounting and more and more maladjustment building up'.[43]

Hargest, an acute analyst of the Allied armies, was also clear about the difference between the German and the Allied armies. It was certainly not lack of courage that distinguished them because the casualty rate of those that led the Allied troops – their field officers – was alarmingly high. But that was the point; if the Allied officers did not lead from the front and expose themselves to enemy fire little could be achieved. 'On the German side, on the other hand, since they were fighting in some-what different circumstances to ourselves and as you say had more reason to fight desperately, they were capable of carrying out their tasks without the continued presence of immediate leadership'.[44] Moreover, the train-ing system adopted by the German army – in sharp contrast to that of the British and American armies – required junior officer cadets to train as private soldiers first, then they were taught platoon, company and battalion tactics so that all young officers could take over senior positions in the field as and when they occurred.[45]

On the eve of the Second World War, and after Hitler – the arch authoritarian whose *Führerprinzip* embodied the *Befehlstaktik* principle – had already spent three years in control, the official army manual repeated the approach that von Moltke had enunciated many years before: 'A favourable situation will never be exploited if commanders wait for orders. The highest commander and the youngest soldier must always be conscious of the fact that omission and inactivity are worse than resorting to the wrong expedient'.[46] The inability of the British to understand the value of this is summed up by a remark made by Sir John Dill in 1935 on visiting the battlefield of Tannenburg; 'How', he asked his host, 'had the Germans achieved such success despite the notorious disobedience of the junior offices?'[47]

Subordinate initiative became apparent at many different levels in the German army: subordinate officers replaced their dead or injured superordinates as quickly as they were themselves replaced by their own NCOs, who, in turn, were often substituted for by privates. And it also enabled local commanders to organized 'battle groups' (*Kampfgruppen*) to respond to local emergencies – as indeed occurred behind Omaha Beach on D-Day. But the opposite tradition that the German military theorists had spent so long to overcome – overt and total control from the top – was reintroduced by Hitler and was critical to the undoing of German defences. As Geyr von Schweppenburg admitted after the war:

> By 1944 Hitler had seriously undermined both the spirit and the principles of the German command system. In the old army, teaching on the subject of command depended upon a cold and sober assessment of every situation, and relied upon the competence of every subordinate to carry out his task in whatever manner seemed best to him. This was replaced by 'intuition' from Berchtesgaden, and by a strict control of every smallest detail from the top. Contrary opinions were not entertained.[48]

But simply decentralizing decision-making beyond formal leaders, or 'empowering' subordinates, could not occur if the subordinates were inadequate to the task, and to avoid that required considerable training. Thus, although the Treaty of Versailles had limited the German army to 100,000 troops, without sophisticated weaponry and without a General Staff, this did not prevent Hans von Seekt, the Commander in Chief of the Army from 1920 to 1926, from developing this group as an officer and NCO corps in waiting – the *Mannheer*. Officers were sent to universities and technical schools and ordinary soldiers were taught to replace their immediate superior whenever necessary. Moreover, officers were rotated between field and staff positions to prevent them from losing touch with operational matters and to deter the creation of a staff culture that divided the officer corps.[49] Hence, when Hitler came to power in 1933 and expanded the army from its existing 7 divisions to 51 divisions by 1939, the cadre of commanders at all levels already existed, it did not have to be taught from scratch as did the British and American equivalent.[50] In all, the Germans raised over 700 divisions during the Second World War.

Paradoxically, then, while the German ideology in its Nazi guise rendered the world beyond ethnic Germans as one full of subordinate races and sub-human species in a vertical hierarchy, the inward focus rendered all Germans as virtually equal. But the official Anglo-American ideologies of liberal democratic capitalism that outwardly espoused tolerance, legal and political equality, human rights and individual freedom, simultaneously generated an inward military focus that polarized the world between the officers and the rest, a polarization at its worst that counter-posed the privileged gentlemen to the coarse cannon-fodder. The general result of this was the fostering of a quite different relationship between officers, NCOs and troops.[51] Whilst the complaints by the Allied troops about their officers (other than those directly in the front line) are common place, Reynolds suggests that: 'it is noteworthy that when talking to German veterans, one rarely encounters the constant criticisms of officers one hears from Allied soldiers'.[52] This should not be that surprising, after all, one of the primary reasons for the strict discipline so pervasive amongst armies is to coerce unwilling or disinterested individuals into risking their lives. For the SS and the HJ units the problem of motivation scarcely seems to have existed; they were, after all, personally devoted to Hitler and often capable of acts of extreme violence.[53]

9.4 Ideology and motivation

However such fanatical devotion to duty, while it spawned frighteningly efficient military units, also created the weak link that undermined the German military on D-Day: the defenders were capable of pushing the Allies back into the sea, but the surrender of initiative by their senior commanders in deference to Hitler's personal control over decision-making effectively immobilized them. After D-Day, General Quesada remarked: 'One's imagination boggled at what the German army might have done to us without Hitler working so effectively for our side'.[54]

There is certainly some truth in this, but what Queseda missed was the irony of the German military performance: it was partly *because* of their personal devotion to, and identification with, Hitler that the elite and SS units fought with such tenacity; thus their strength was simultaneously their weakness. Only if Hitler had been less irrational would their power have been adequately exploited by the Germans but it was only because of their emotional – i.e. non-rational – allegiance to him that their power existed.

As the war turned increasingly against Germany, reports on the morale of the German forces, while not suggesting anything like a collapse, began hinting as early as December 1943 that a decay had set in. The impression of many troops was that surrendering to the Allies was considerably preferable to many of the other alternatives (fighting to the death or surrendering to the Red Army) – hardly the kind of fanaticism that was visibly present on the eastern front where between November 1942 and October 1943 1.7 million casualties had been incurred and which Hitler assumed would consume the Allies in France.[55] Certainly the SS remained loyal to the Führer and appeared to have fought to the bitter end – some even leaping on Allied tanks with explosives attached to their bodies, blowing themselves and the tank up to stop the advance. It was these troops that incurred the wrath of the Allied troops whenever they met up, but many Allied soldiers had little hatred for 'ordinary' *Wehrmacht* soldiers – at least until their close colleagues had been killed or maimed in action against them.

Förster suggests that the motivational commitment that did prevail amongst most *Wehrmacht* soldiers stemmed initially from the complete militarization of German society from 1933, manifest in Blomberg's increasing ties with the Nazi state and his acceptance in 1935 that the educational goal of the *Wehrmacht* was 'not only the thoroughly trained soldier and master of his weapon, but also the man who is aware of his race and of his general duties towards the state'.[56] As for the officers, their role was to become both the political and the tactical leaders of their troops, unlike the Soviet system where political commissars were distinct from the military leader (though both countries adopted the other's system as the fortunes of war were reversed from 1943). Thus although much effort went into the construction of political indoctrination amongst the *Wehrmacht*, the greatest reliance was placed upon the active role played by the local commanders. In other words, the motivational thrust came primarily from the military not the Nazis. The effects of this ideological campaign, of course, are much harder to establish, and perhaps we can get no closer to the 'average' *Wehrmacht* soldier than to suggest, following Schulte that 'there was no 'clear dichotomy between fanatics fighting a religious war, or ideology-free and perhaps bored and apathetic soldiers; but a continuum'.[57]

Even after capture many German soldiers remained fervent admirers of Hitler and Nazism. In the POW Camp Grant, in Illinois, for example, 42 prisoners believed to be less than sympathetic towards Nazism were locked in a building by other prisoners who attempted to burn them all to death. At Camp Tonkawa in Oklahoma, one prisoner was beaten to death by his comrades after 200 of them had accused him of being a traitor and voted to murder him.[58]

For the average German soldier the future was much bleaker: either the Red Army would wreak revenge on the German population for the crimes of the *Wehrmacht* and the SS in the Soviet Union, or the Allies would control Germany but on unconditional terms that could well see the effective end of Germany as a state. The average German soldier was more likely to survive if the Allies took control but he may not live out his life peacefully with his family and he may not have even returned to what was left of Germany at all.[59]

Some Germans clearly believed that the Allied soldiers would show no more mercy than their Soviet counterparts when taking German prisoners, even civilians. For example, Cooper recounts how a German woman at Darmstadt worked at his officers' Mess immediately after the war. She had been married to an officer in the German army and was the daughter of the director of the Merck Chemical Works, a position only held by Nazi members or supporters. As the war closed in on Darmstadt her husband had been killed in Russia and her father and mother persuaded her that the Americans were barbarians and would certainly torture her and her daughters before they were killed. Thus she agreed that all five should commit suicide by taking cyanide tablets. Her parents had swallowed their tablets and the woman had made her daughters take theirs with some sweets and checked they were dead before taking her own. However, she had regurgitated her tablet in a coma and was subsequently revived by the very troops she believed would murder her.[60]

9.5 Identifying the 'Germans' on D-Day

Not all the troops in German uniforms in France were German and not many of the Germans were first class soldiers. The Allied planners had assumed that the presence of such soldiers would ensure a *relatively* easy assault. The real problem would come later, when the SS and Panzer units arrived over the first week. The planners were wrong on both counts. First, although some non-ethnic Germans proved unreliable, many did not, and a large proportion of the ethnic German troops were not 'old and sick men' but veterans of the eastern front who proved more than a match for their green opponents. Second, the position and speed of deployment of first rate infantry, SS and Panzer units ensured that the 'lightening breakout' from the bridgehead turned into a prolonged season of storms.

Since few Germans assumed Normandy would be the invasion area it was generally regarded as a 'rest and recuperation' area for units on leave from the eastern front (where a 3.3 million German army had suffered 3 million losses between June 1941 and December 1943) or a zone where second rate troops could be left in control freeing up the better units for defending the Pas-de-Calais or in Russia.[61] By the end of 1941 Hitler even began conscripting Russian prisoners-of-war into labour battalions to fight the Red Army. However, they proved so unreliable that they were transferred to the west at the rate of two *Ost* (East) battalions for every one (native) German battalion.

The proportion of 'Russians' – that is non-ethnic Germans – in the west has always been disputed. Goldstein et al claim that by D-Day one sixth of the German infantry in the west was non-German.[62] Von Schweppenburg put the total proportion of 'Russians' at one third of the entire 7th Army, though only 17 per cent of the infantry battalions were actually formed from such troops, though there were several *volks-deutsche* units made up of ethnic Germans from outside the 1939 Reich.[63] Of the Ost battalions that Masters came across behind Sword Beach almost all were infantry soldiers commanded by ethnic Germans, and all the artillery and mortar units were composed wholly of ethnic Germans.[64] The irony was that the ethnic diversity of the American troops at Utah was probably greater than that of the defenders – but the *identity* of the attackers was probably more solidaristic than the defenders.

Nonetheless, so great was the ethnic diversity that eight different pay-books were necessary and the Nazi obsession with racial purity became miraculously stretched to include *Volksdeutsche* ('Racial Germans'), non-Aryan *Freiwillige* (volunteers) and *Hilfswillige* (auxiliaries). The 987th Regiment of the 276th Division had 34 different Soviet languages. Lieutenant-General Karl-Wilhelm Von Schlieben, commander of the Cherbourg garrison, justified its surrender on 26 June 1944 partly by reference to the quality of his troops: 'You can't expect Russians and Poles to fight for Germany against Americans in France'.[65] But this did not mean the defenders would buckle under pressure because fighting for some of these people had been a way of life for generations. Moreover, the Ost battalions had been informed that anyone retreating would be shot by his German NCO, while anyone captured by the Allies would be shot as a traitor.[66]

Not that this necessarily implied that the Ost battalions would prove to be poorer soldiers than their German colleagues. Members of the British 6th Airborne came across Russians fighting under German officers near Le Plein and had trouble subduing them – though the Russians subsequently told their captives that they had been told that any Russians captured by the Allies would be shot as traitors.[67] The US Airborne troops also had trouble dislodging a battalion of Georgians (795th Georgian Infantry Battalion, from the 709th Infantry Division) from Turqueville near St Mère-Eglise, though they eventually surrendered on 7 June.[68]

There clearly were some defenders desperately keen to surrender, but not many. On Queen Red, Lance Corporal Flint witnessed five German soldiers climbing out of their defensive trenches when he arrived with the first AVRE but they were immediately shot dead by SS troops behind them.[69] General Cota's group ascending the bluffs at Les Moulins at Dog Green, saw a group of five German prisoners being escorted back down to the landing craft by a single GI when they came under fire from the German-held bluffs. Lt Shea, Cota's aide, saw what happened:

> Their captor drove towards the protecting cover of the seawall, while two of the remaining three sank to their knees ... they seem to be pleading with the operator of the machine gun, situated on the bluffs to the east, not to shoot them. The next burst caught the first kneeling German full in the chest, and as he crumpled the remaining two took to the cover of the seawall with their captor.[70]

The Normandy coast itself was defended by the 711th and the 716th Division. Most of the defences where the Allies were to land were held by the 716th but there were relatively similar in structure and composition. The 711th Division to the west was formed in April 1941 to defend northern France as a static division and comprised older men born between 1901 and 1913 – i.e., 31–43 years old. In the spring of 1944 it moved to Deauville, on the coast 25 miles east of Caen and by D-Day had between 11,000 and 13,000 troops in two infantry regiments and a battalion of artillery. By this time 20 per cent of the division were veterans from the eastern front who had suffered frostbite injuries. One battalion of the 731st Regiment was composed of Russian troops. In total the 711th had 20 anti-tank guns, 60 pieces of field artillery and one squadron of captured French Renault 35 tanks.[71]

The unit facing the 116th Infantry on Omaha Beach was supposed to be the 716th Division, a static division with only 40 per cent native

German composition and the rest a heterogeneous group of Russians, Poles, Tartars, Armenians, Cossacks, Mongolians, Georgians, Yugoslavs, Koreans and even some Indians from the anti-British 'Indian Legion'. The rest were 'old Germans'.[72] However, the 716th Division, originally formed in Bielefeld on 2 May 1941, while it had initially been composed of older men, by D-Day comprised many younger soldiers who had been wounded on the Russian front and the average age was probably closer to late twenties and early thirties rather than late forties.[73] By then it had two infantry regiments of three battalions each (726th and 736th), as well as the 1716th Artillery Regiment. It also had two battalions of 1,000 Ost troops, the 439th and 642nd East Battalions, which were attached as a fourth battalion to the 726th and 736th Regiments. The division also had 36 howitzers and one anti-tank squadron in its artillery regiment, most of which was destroyed in the initial Allied bombardment just before D-Day.[74]

However, unknown to the invading Americans, the 716th were not the only division at Omaha, because the 352nd Division, a first rate assault division was also there. A pigeon carrying information about the change of defenders some weeks before the invasion never reached the Allies, and another was killed by Günter Witte of the 1,262nd Army Coastal Artillery Regiment just two days before D-Day.[75] Bradley was eventually told of the switch – but not until 5 June, *after* the invasion force had left England and Bradley was on board Admiral Kirk's flagship the USS Augusta. Radio silence was maintained throughout this period thus preventing the news from being relayed to the troops approaching Omaha Beach.[76] Facing the nine Canadian battalions on the four mile Juno Beach, on the other hand, was one battalion of the 716th Division, composed of the 736th Infantry Regiment – about 400 Germans of *bodenständige* status, a mixture of very young and rather old German troopers, some of whom were partially disabled veterans of the eastern front, plus an array of Russians and Poles.[77]

The troops facing the British were primarily elements of the 716th Division who were mixed in with both the 352nd Infantry Division and the 21st Panzer Division on D-Day, and an additional 1,000 Ost troops, the 441st Ost Battalion were deployed near La Rivière. It was this unit which collapsed early on D-Day allowing the British to press on towards Bayeux, persuading Marcks to deploy two battalions of the Battle Group Meyer (2nd Battalion of the 915th Infantry Regiment and Fusilier Battalion of the 352nd Infantry Division) as reserves to compensate.

There were some Polish soldiers defending Easy Red sector on Omaha. Early on in the invasion Lieutenant John Spaulding's platoon of E Company 16th Infantry regiment[78] had been completely isolated from the rest of the first assault wave by the strong current (there were soldiers from E Company 116th to the east of them who should have been to the west). But they had managed to get across the beach and climb the bluff relatively unscathed by around 0800. When they rushed a pillbox 16 Poles surrendered and claimed that they had voted to surrender earlier but had been forced to fight on by the German NCOs. Spaulding's platoon went on to take the first German prisoners on the day and ended the day dug in near Coleville where they were surrounded by Germans. Five members of the platoon, including Spaulding were subsequently awarded DSCs.[79]

But far from being a poor group of old men, the 716th grenadiers used tactics perfected in Russia – allowing the British and Canadian troops to pass before opening fire from the flanks and rear, thus greatly delaying the Allies' progress inland – especially towards Caen.[80] They were also intent on inflicting maximum damage on their adversaries before any thoughts of capitulation were entertained. In the process the 716th Infantry Division was virtually destroyed.[81] For example, the North Shore Regiment with the Canadian 3rd Division on Juno, only took one pill box with the help of a Royal Marine Centaur after the pill box had expended 75 rounds from its artillery piece.[82]

In fact, besides the 716th Limited Employment (LE) Coastal Defence Division, the infantry units deployed on the coast itself were two of the 352nd division's three regiments: the 726th Grenadier Regiment and the 916th Grenadier Regiment. Both the 716th and the 352nd were part of General Marcks' 84th Corps.[83] The 716th had been in Normandy since March 1942 under Major-General Richter, and had been reinforced by units from the 77th and 243rd Divisions in early 1944. The Allies regarded it as a weak unit comprising only 7,771 soldiers, of whom about half were Slavs or Poles; that was an error.[84] The 352nd had been activated on 5 November, just two days after Hitler's Directive No. 51 that strengthened the western defences. The division was raised from around Hanover in northern Germany from the remnants of the 321st Infantry Division which had been decimated in Ukraine in the summer of 1943. Using the cadre of remaining 321st soldiers and the new Hanoverian recruits (some young men [18–19}some rather older {30–35}, the 352nd arrived in St Lô on 5 December 1943 where it was supposed to be trained and ready for combat by 15 May 1944. Its construction was so rapid that its chief staff officer, Lt Colonel Ziegelmann wondered whether 'it was only of importance to the high command to announce as soon as possible that another division had been reformed and was at its disposal'.[85] Some units were ready for action sooner than others. For example, Major Pluskat's unit, the I/352 Battalion of the divisional artillery regiment, had been in position since March 1944 when it was moved from the division's location at St Lô by Rommel to take over a 30-mile coastal stretch between the Vire estuary and Arromanches.[86] That stretch of coast had already been declared unbreachable by Admiral Krancke, the naval commander in the west, with the possible exception of the area that was to mark Omaha Beach – though the steep bluffs and poor access for vehicles made it an unlikely spot for an invasion force.[87]

The 352nd were commanded by Major General Kraiss from his HQ in Molay-Littrey, nine miles south of the centre of Omaha Beach. Kraiss, at 54 years old, had fought as CO of the 168th Infantry Division and then the 355th Infantry Division in the Soviet Union for over two years and was thus thoroughly experienced. And his new command, the 352nd Infantry Division, had been equipped with a new anti-tank battalion containing 12 *Sturmgeschutz* (assault guns or tank destroyers) which were often better armoured and gunned than conventional tanks, as well as 14 conventional anti-tank guns and 12 anti-aircraft guns. Just after D-Day the 352nd was reinforced by a *Luftwaffe* regiment of anti-aircraft guns: 60 20mm and 48 88mm guns.[88]

Fortunately for the Allies, although Kraisse allocated one of each of his three 352nd Division regiments to the west (Pointe du Hoc to the estuary), central (Pointe du Hoc to St Honorine) and eastern (St Honorine to Arromanches) sectors, he was more concerned with protecting the western sector towards the Vire estuary than the central or eastern sector, so certain was he that if an invasion came to Normandy it would aim to isolate the Contention peninsular so that Cherbourg could be taken as soon as possible. Yet that coastline was the one area where an amphibious landing was virtually impossible and the Cotentin already had three divisions to defend it.

Thus facing the Americans at Omaha was not a single regiment of the 716th (the second was behind Gold Beach and the third held in reserve at Bayeux), a regiment of static troops whose ages, fitness and identity allegedly rendered them poor opposition), but this plus the two infantry battalions and one artillery battalion of the 916th Regiment of the 352nd Division.[89] It could have been much worse. Kraisse had just 20 per cent of his available troops facing the Allied invaders and his reserves were a full 12 miles behind the coast – a point that even Rommel criticized when he visited Kraisse in May 1944. Moreover, occupying the beach defences themselves were, indeed, troops from one battalion of the 726th Regiment of the 716th Division. At Omaha there was a battalion of the 916th Regiment of the 352nd Infantry Division but they had been deployed back from the beach by Kraisse and were not committed to the coast until the first waves were already landing. Over one third of

Kraisse's troops, including over 2,000 soldiers from both battalions of his 915th Regiment, 352nd Division, and 700 from his 352nd *Füsilierbataillon* in the *Kampfgruppe Meyer*, had moved west towards the Vire estuary at 0310 to prevent what Kraisse assumed to be a parachute drop in numbers trying to separate him from his neighbouring 709th Infantry Division (who had been patrolling with blanks as the Americans landed). In fact the paratroopers were members of the US 101st Airborne who had dropped well outside their designated zones. At 0550 Kraisse realized he had erred and halted the *Kampfgruppe*. They were immobilized for two hours and only at 0735 was a single battalion detached and sent to Omaha, where it was expected to arrive at 0930 – it did not get there until early afternoon, and by then it was too late. In short, when the first waves landed – and were decimated – they were destroyed by one battalion of the 716th Division, the 'poor' troops that the US High Command had talked so disparagingly of for months. Had Kraisse, the leader on the ground at Omaha, not deployed his reserves so far behind the front line, and deployed them erroneously, the situation may have proved much worse on Omaha.[90]

9.6 Conclusion

The alleged fanaticism of the *Waffen* SS and the utility of their identification as elite soldiers dedicated to Hitler is hardly novel but it remains of critical importance to explaining the difficulty the Allies had in driving the German army out of Normandy. The *Waffen* SS and the HJ units were ethnically probably identical to the average *Wehrmacht* soldier but the former groups almost always fought longer, harder and with less compassion than the latter and this may relate both to their loyalty to Hitler and their radical embodiment of heterarchy rather than hierarchy as a primarily Leadership principle. However, the SS played little active role on D-Day itself, except in being unable to mobilize properly or engage the invaders. Their role was crucial in two other ways. First, their rapid deployment prevented the Allies from either securing Caen or breaking out of the bridgehead. Second, their reputation, in stark contrast to that of the 716th Division, persuaded the Allied planners that the *real* fight would not be on the beaches but in the subsequent counter-attack by the infantry and tanks of the SS and Panzer divisions.

And that *real* fight was not necessarily abhorrent to all beyond the bounds of the *Waffen* SS, for many soldiers positively enjoyed their experience of war, either in terms of its spectacle, its excitement or simply the adrenaline buzz of actual danger and combat. For the rest, and probably the majority, the decision to stay and fight was bound up with notions of solidarity and comradeship with close compatriots, of duty, of honour, of the avoidance of shame, or of revenge. For a minority the clear and present danger of being shot by your own side was probably sufficient to hold them in place. However, the reason to stay and fight appeared to get progressively less appealing as the war progressed. Most soldiers soon understood that survival was not coincident with skill but with luck and at that point a rational calculation of odds unnerved all but the strongest. It may seem paradoxical then, that almost all the concerns for shell-shock or simply combat fatigue derived from the Allied side in Normandy when the Germans had already been at war since 1939. In reality, of course, the Germans fighting in Normandy in 1944 were often as green as their opponents. Just taking the members of the LAH as an example, the original division which had invaded Poland, had lost 53 per cent in Operation Barbarossa, 44 per cent at Kharkov in the spring of 1943, and 27 per cent at Kursk in the summer of 1943. In effect, almost no members of the 'veteran' *LAH* that fought in Poland were still with it in Normandy. But such was the strength of its identity that it again performed outstandingly in Normandy, and had to be completely rebuilt after its few remnants escaped through the Falaise gap.

Nevertheless, the identity of the 'ordinary' soldiers defending the beaches does seem relevant. The units defending Omaha Beach were neither first rate infantry nor wholly German, but many had already served on the eastern front and were again to put up stubborn resistance. If anything, the ethnic diversity of the American forces was considerably greater than the Ost battalions, though their identity was probably a lot more cohesive. In effect, it was the self-identity of the defenders not their ethnic origin which seemed to matter.

For most of the Allied troops the war was little more than a job rather than a political crusade; something to be done as quickly as possible, and although the elite units in the US and British armed forces were volunteers – as were all the Canadian combat troops at this time – few appeared to have had the political desire to risk their lives to rid the world of fascism. More seemed to enlist to defend their country rather than attack another, because of love for their own rather than hatred of the other, and because it appeared at the time to be an exciting prospect. Once 'blooded', and this was usually literally, such troops wanted only to get through the war and to get home but this 'semi-detached' approach to the war should not be interpreted as implying a generalized risk-avoidance. On the contrary the 'poor bloody infantry' of the USA constructed a carefully honed image of apparent carelessness that grew directly from the independent and rugged individualism of the frontier and the inner city. The British were more constrained by the military spit and polish traditions of the empire but they too remained dedicated to their cultural traditions of collective solidarity and emotional reticence. And on all sides of the Allied line, the worse the conditions became for the poor bloody infantry the grittier became their identity and the less reliant they became on formal leaders.

The *Wehrmacht* might have been the most professional army of the war, and the SS and HJ units were certainly the most fanatical, and the least constrained by conventional morality, but their collective fanaticism did not overawe the Allied troops who were also driven to succeed, not by a desire to turn the world upside down but simply to turn it the right way up again and go home. For the average Allied soldier on D-Day, the war was probably going to be won at some point in the future so there was a strong reason not to risk one's life unnecessarily. Furthermore, getting ashore alive was probably all that most had trained for and thought about for months now, and having achieved that there seems to have been a limited desire to take the war straight to Berlin. Certainly, after the war Dempsey accepted that they had not set their sights sufficiently high – surviving the landing was all most of them could think about.[91] But this inability to exploit the immediate advantages of a surprise invasion had already cost the Allies dearly on the three previous amphibious assaults: Sicily, Anzio and Salerno. If Montgomery did not imply such speedy movement with his term 'cracking about' deep behind enemy lines, then what did he mean? Ironically, all that Montgomery stood for contradicted such a devolvement of initiative to subordinate commanders, for Montgomery was the arch planner, not the arch anarchist.

Private Shroeder saw some of the earliest enemy prisoners on Omaha Beach, ironically taken by Captain Dawson now transformed from immobilized pessimist to mobile optimist and moving up the bluff. The prisoners 'were really roughed up. Their hair was full of cement, dirt, everything. They didn't look so tough. So we started up the bluff carrying our stuff with us, and others started following us.[92] Stanley Whitehouse, on Sword Beach, contributed to the gradual demythologizing of the 'Master Race' of defenders by de-helmeting prisoners. As he recalled 'Remove his helmet and the mighty *Wehrmacht* warrior looks far less terrifying'.[93] Indeed, one of the most common reports on D-Day was that the captured German soldiers were, after all, not much like 'supermen'.[94] But this was precisely the point – the defenders, German and non-German – were not supermen, they were just ordinary people but they were to prove incredibly difficult to prise out of Normandy. That difficulty lay as much in the inadequacy of the Allied training and command systems as in anything else.

10 Managing Logistics: 'Bag, vomit, one.'

10.1 Introduction

D-Day was the largest-ever amphibious operation. It involved 175,000 Allied troops and 50,000 vehicles, all of which were landed either by air, using 11,000 planes, or by sea, using 6,833 ships, and all within 24 hours.[1] The battle for Normandy, which D-Day initiated, lasted until the end of August 1944 and was the largest single battle ever undertaken by the Western Allies against Germany. The Allied forces involved 40 divisions: 23 American in Bradley's 25th US Army Group, and 17 in Montgomery's 21st Army Group (13 British, 3 Canadian and 1 Polish). On 15 September the Allied armies were joined from the south of France by Denver's US 6th Army Group of 25 divisions (12 French and 13 American). At their height, the American Army Groups totalled 72 Divisions while the Anglo-Canadians, plus Poles, totalled 21 Divisions.[2] By comparison, the battles in the North African desert between Montgomery's Eighth Army and Rommel's *Afrika Korps* seldom involved more than 11 divisions.

D-Day was the most complex military operation ever undertaken but it was not the largest. The battles along the eastern front involved more soldiers (Barbarossa involved 140 divisions {3 million troops}, 7,100 artillery pieces and 3,300 tanks on the German side alone {Williamson, 1999: 52}), but fewer planes and, obviously, no ships. When the Soviet Army launched its summer offensive in 1944 to coincide with Overlord, it had amassed 2.5 million soldiers, 5,200 tanks and 5,300 aircraft, though of course not all of them were deployed in the first 24 hours.[3] However, the military significance of the German losses in Normandy was greater than those at the battle of Stalingrad. In all, only 30,000 German troops and 120 tanks escaped across the river Seine from the encircling Allied forces at the end of the battle for Normandy.[4]

Overall, in the spring of 1944, the German Army – in all theatres of war, had 314 divisions, including 47 armoured divisions. Additionally, it had 66 divisions from its Axis allies. Over half of the total (215 divisions

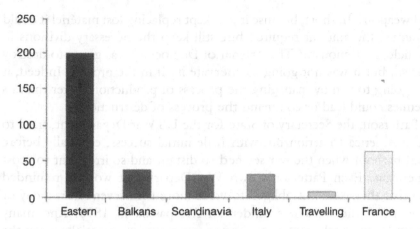

Figure 10.1 Distribution of German Divisions, 1944

– 57 per cent) was stationed on the eastern front. With a further 36 divisions in the Balkans, 27 in Scandinavia, 25 in Italy and 8 travelling between fronts, there were only 61 divisions (16 per cent) available to defend France, including ten armoured, and six SS, divisions.[5]

But even this relatively small number of divisions was, in theory, able to defeat the Allied landing – if the Germans knew where the Allies were going to land and if the apparent Allied advantage in technology could be neutralized. In short, the success of Overlord was anything but inevitable and, assuredly, D-Day was, according to Churchill, 'the most difficult and complicated operation ever to take place'.[6] Such an operation could not possibly have been planned and executed without Management at all levels and in all aspects of the organizations involved. So how did the Allies tame the problem and provide such a huge logistical infrastructure?

10.2 The Arsenal of Democracy: the perils of the assembly line and the farm

The American use of a fixed number of divisions with continuous service for the members, in contrast to the German preference for a proliferation of new divisions, though deleterious to those serving in the divisions at the front, nevertheless limited the requirements for matériel. For example, by 1944 the US Army had constructed 190,000 vehicles and 6,000 artillery pieces for its 89 divisions. Had it equipped 200 separate divisions they would have needed to provide three times the number of vehicles and weapons. In short, because it just kept replacing lost matériel it could minimize the amount required but still keep the necessary divisions in the field continuously.[7] The Arsenal of Democracy was going to destroy Nazism but it was not going to enervate itself in the process. Indeed, it was going to win by managing the process of production better than its enemies could lead or command the process of destruction.

Patterson, the Secretary of State for the US War Department, tried to rouse America to action but with little initial success, especially before Pearl harbour when the war seemed so distant and so irrelevant to most Americans. Even Patterson's own War Department workers reminded him that they were not obliged to work more than seven hours a day or to work at the weekends, under an Act passed in 1895. And many employers were reluctant to engage in war contracts, especially when the prices were held down and their opponents and competitors threw the spectre of 'war profiteering' at them.[8] In truth, few Americans at home suffered economically as a result of the war. Indeed, one poll suggested that 70 per cent admitted that they had not had to make any 'real sacrifices'. Between 1941 and 1945 average hourly wages rose from 66 cents to $1.02 while prices (many of which were frozen in 1942 by the Office of Price Administration) only rose 23 per cent, and per capita consumer purchases ended the war between 10 to 15 per cent higher than they were in 1939. In contrast, British consumption per capita consumption finished the war 16 per cent below pre-war levels.[9]

That initial managerial inertia also prevailed in the development of weapons: in 1940 the US heavy weapons programme did not exist and there were no anti-tank guns or even tanks to speak of. Worse, when Patterson asked General Hap Arnold how many aircraft the US could realistically muster against an aggressor, Arnold's reply was 'only 300'.[10] The original solution to the lack of equipment was to order in bulk at a 'cost-plus-fixed-fee' but even this failed to generate much interest. During November and December 1940 – when the US military capability in the air amounted to just 96 bombers and 193 fighters – Douglas and Lockheed produced just six extra military aircraft – in addition to the 20 commercial aircraft that seemed to have priority. Patterson promptly ordered the National Defense Advisory Commission (NDAC) to look into the matter. They did and declared that civil aviation should have priority; after all, who was going to attack the US by air?[11] Nevertheless, by the end of the war 300,000 military aircraft had been built.[12]

The American government then acquired an array of influential economic levers through which the problem of war production was to be tamed: first, in 1940, the right to provide operating capital to those engaged in war contracts; second, the power to force contractors to prioritize war work; third, via the 1942 General Maximum Price Regulation and the 1943 Revenue Bill, the power to impose a price ceiling on companies whose war business exceeded $500,000; and fourth, the right to renegotiate prices if 'excessive' profits had been achieved.[13]

All this was supported by a budget for the army of $6 billion, approved by Congress on 30 June 1940, and buttressed by an agreement that the 40-hour week was the norm and that all the traditional safeguards of labour would be maintained by the National Labor Relations Board (NLRB). The initial implication – that the government would withhold contracts from anti-union companies like Ford – was refuted, but the Selective Service Act of 1940 enhanced the government's power to requisition any property deemed essential to the war effort.

But just as industrial production under the guidance of the War Production Board was gearing up to mass produce everything the armed forces wanted, the lessons of the German *Blitzkrieg* slowly sank in: most of the matériel on the order books was inadequate. The dilemma was whether to press ahead with the production of existing weapons in the hope that the quantitative superiority of the 'Arsenal of Democracy' would suffocate the enemy, or whether to go back to the drawing board. This would produce a qualitative superiority but it would take time, and thereby reduce the quantitative advantage of the greatest production system in the world.

A contingent analysis of this general quantitative approach would be to suggest that it was the right one, especially in the light of the subsequent Allied victory. However, as I shall demonstrate below, the specific choice of weapon or transport system or logistical approach was often one that remained contested by experts and was ultimately resolved through all kinds of cultural measures: political networking, risk avoidance, the dead hand of tradition and so on.

To some working people, though, the war seemed too good an opportunity to forgo an advantageous position, especially after the disastrous years of the depression. In all, something like 20 million people moved to find employment in the US during the war.[14] By early 1941 industrial disputes were already beginning to restrict war production and a National Defense Mediation Board (NDMB) was established to try and resolve the burgeoning number of disputes. Even this failed to stop the American Federation of Labor (AFL) from calling a strike at Boeing's Seattle plant making the Flying Fortresses in an inter-union dispute with the Congress of Industrial Organizations (CIO) in April 1941. By May, Major Doolittle claimed that 'strike fever' was everywhere and suggested that communist agitators were the root cause (Germany had not invaded the Soviet Union at this time). In the spring of 1941 a strike in an aviation plant at Inglewood, California against the advice of the NDMB, and the strikers' own union leaders, led Roosevelt to send in the army and 2,500 troops with fixed bayonets evicted the strikers. Within three days the plant was handed back to the owners and work resumed. In August 1942 a Boston company manufacturing artillery shells refused to accept a trade union agreement brokered by the War Labor Board (WLB), as the final arbiter of industrial disputes. Eventually the government took over the plant, bringing in a contractor to run it on their behalf.[15]

Even with formal industrial disputes under control, informal problems remained. For example, in the week after Christmas 1942, over a quarter of Boeing's workforce failed to turn up for work. At this time, when average British absences were running at 30 minutes per person per year, US absenteeism was operating at 7 per cent, several times higher than normal.[16] But industrial disputes remained to plague the war effort throughout 1943, especially in the aircraft, copper and coal industries. John L Lewis (President of the United Mineworkers), was a particular target of the government's and military's wrath. As one marine suggested, 'He wouldn't be alive if he was beside me. I don't mean the Japs would kill him. I would'.[17] By the end of that year 13 million days had been lost, and just 80,000 of the planned 131,000 aircraft were built, though most other production plans had been achieved. By comparison, 1,832 days were lost in Britain in 1943, increasing to 3,696 in 1944.[18] Then, over Christmas 1943, the US railroad workers went on strike prompting Roosevelt, at last, to consider a bill for National Service that would extend government control from the military to civilian personnel. After much debate and compromise, a bill was finally debated – and rejected – on 3 April 1945, just a month before the end of the war in Europe.[19] In that last year of the war 3 million workers were involved in 4,600 strikes.[20]

In fact the American Arsenal of Democracy was very slow in getting a head of steam up: in 1941, when half of Britain's and Germany's gross national product was devoted to the war effort, the US only managed to devote 16 per cent to the same end. Patterson began ramping up the effort level by insisting that war production facilities were employed continuously throughout the week, and he began employing his staff to make spot checks on manufacturing plants at night and at the weekends to ensure compliance.[21]

Even that seemed to run up against the problem of priorities in the US war economy. For example, aluminium was regarded by many as the key material since it provided the critical element in aircraft construction and, reflecting a philosophy still common today, since many hoped

American air power would win the war against Germany. But even as Patterson ordered restrictions on the use of aluminium the army's own quartermaster ordered 100,000 aluminium syrup pitchers – because they were 3.8 cents cheaper that the glass alternatives. Despite the restrictions, in late 1941 about 35 per cent of US aluminium was still being used in non-aircraft production, compared to just 8 per cent in Britain.[22]

Copper, a crucial element in munitions, was also in short supply, especially in 1942 when steel was substituted in large calibre munitions. At this point the shortage of 8,000 copper miners was equivalent to an annual loss of 120,000 tons of copper – or 8 billion rounds of .30 calibre ammunition. Nonetheless, American industry was still using copper to manufacture soda siphons, fridges, electric fans, lamps, and so on. A partial resolution to the general labour shortage was for 4,000 copper miners recently recruited to the military to be furloughed back into the mines in 1942 – a resolution of the problem that Patterson thought inherently wrong when many miners were still employed in gold mines. But by October 1942 most of the gold and silver mines were closed. Then in the summer of 1942 another 4,500 soldiers were furloughed back to the copper mines.[23] But this still did not resolve the copper shortage because in the spring of 1943 many of the furloughed copper miners were directed to work on farms instead. Indeed, a serious attempt was made by agricultural interest to furlough 375,000 troops – 10 per cent of the enlisted ground troops – back to the farms. With 3 million men on farms already safe from military conscription, the number avoiding the draft was rapidly undermining the war effort. This was partly the reason for the rapid expansion in the number of women – the mythical Rosie the Riveter amongst them – employed in US industry: in 1940, 25 per cent of the American labour force was female; by 1944, this had increased to 36 per cent.[24]

Even sugar became rationed – though with the US Army drinking 10 million bottles of Coca-Cola this was understandable. Perhaps the most ironic act of the government was in response to the navy's requirement for rope: 50,000 acres of *Cannabis sativa* were grown.[25] Rubber was also in short supply after the Japanese captured 90 per cent of the world's natural rubber supplies and speed restrictions were introduced to increase the life of existing tyres. In addition, 200,000 acres were set aside to grow guayale, a rubber substitute, though only 1,500 tons of rubber was ever produced.[26] A national scheme to collect 10 million tons of 'scrap' rubber items (aided by a threat to remove the petrol ration that had been introduced in December 1942) netted, amongst other things, two rubber bones courtesy of Roosevelt's dog and 6 million spare tyres.[27] In fact these gestures by political figureheads seem important. For instance, the petrol ration operated as follows:

'A' category car: (non-essential) 4 gallons per week (subsequently 3). A prohibition on 'pleasure driving' was adopted but dropped after it was found to be unenforceable.

'B' category: (essential) 4 gallons + additional allowance (travelling sales reps etc.)

'C' category: unlimited amount (doctors, ministers, postal deliverers etc.)

'T' category: (truckers) unlimited

'X' category: unlimited – members of Congress and VIPs

As the applications flooded in it soon became apparent that large numbers of self-elected VIPs were exploiting the system: 12 per cent of Washington's population applied for an X category. But that number dropped dramatically when Eleanor Roosevelt very publicly applied for an 'A' category.

Almost inevitably, the result of ramping up the war economy was a tremendous pressure on all forms of resource – and there were plenty of resources required: the supplies inventory for D-Day added up to 700,000 separate items.[28] At the specific level the problems could be Critical, for example, the new bazookas (hand-held anti-tank weapons) were only issued to the troops on the Torch landings in North Africa as they boarded the invasion ships. Later on, the British Guards Division did not receive their Sherman tanks until they were actually in the 'sausage' concentration areas, and therefore had little time to practice either the handling, firing or communications systems. Worse, as Graham recalled, 'I heard nothing before D-Day about its [Sherman tank] weaknesses when facing the Mark V Panther and the Mark VI Tiger. Its relatively soft armour, its tendency to burn and the penetrative deficiency of its 75mm gun were not discussed.[29]

Generally, the rise of the American army was mirrored by the rise of American industry. In 1939 the US produced 800 military aircraft against a background of 20 per cent unemployment and a factory output down 50 per cent on its potential maximum. By the end of 1943 not only was unemployment negligible but 10 million new jobs had been found and filled and aircraft production was running at 8,000 per month,[30] and, in all, the US produced around 3 million vehicles.[31] At last, the Allied supply problems were being resolved and the Arsenal of Democracy was truly turning the management screw against Germany and Japan. But conterminously the Allied planners were wondering precisely how they were going to get all the matériel across the Atlantic, then across Britain, and only finally across the Channel.

10.3 Stockpiling the Arsenal of Democracy

The organizational requirements for D-Day and the subsequent invasion of Normandy (or 'Liberation' as de Gaulle insisted) were immense and primarily organized by G-4 section at SHAEF. The Normandy beachhead would be the conduit for the 3 million soldiers who would bear the brunt of the fight against Germany. That meant generating all the supplies and equipment necessary to sustain them for the campaign and all the shipping necessary to transport them across the channel and on to Berlin. The plan called for eight divisions to be ashore in the initial assault on D-Day against the four German divisions assumed to be present. By the second day there would be 13 Allied divisions facing an assumed seven German divisions and by D-Day+ 12 there would be 21 divisions ashore.[32] A crucial but still Tame Problem in the main for the Allies, therefore, was the depth and breadth of the support facilities, either in terms of combat support units or simply the logistics system underpinning the invasion.

Britain's logistical infrastructure was hardly designed to cope with such demands. As one US officer responsible for logistics remarked at the time, the task looked impossible, after all, Britain was 'so cramped and small, the railroad equipment so tiny, the roads so small and crooked, and methods so entirely different'.[33] With the average age of the Liverpool dockers at 52, with some trade union restrictions requiring some Belfast dockers to unload ships as slowly as possible, with railway tunnels too small to take tanks on flatbed wagons, and with British civilian imports delaying US military imports in the docks, it began to look as though the invasion would choke itself before it even began.

As the winter of 1942 approached, Operation Bolero – the build up of the US forces in the UK – had still only landed under 35,000 troops, and the numbers hardly increased over that winter as most GIs were diverted to the invasion of North Africa. However, thereafter the numbers mushroomed so that by April 1944 the monthly peak of 216,000 had been reached. By this time 1.5 million US troops, accompanied by 5 million tons of supplies, 8,000 aeroplanes, 1,000 train engines and 20,000 railway wagons had arrived. All these troops were quartered either in the 400,000 prefabricated buildings, or the 280,000 tents, or the 110,000 British buildings occupied by the American forces. The total cost of Operation Bolero was estimated at $644 million just for the new construction. Some of that cost was swallowed in the 170 miles of extra railway track laid down to transport the incoming material, some was used to build almost 75 million square feet of storage space for the 50,000 vehicles and almost half a million tons of ammunition. Some was used to purchase 124,000 hospital beds and a large – but unspecified – number of coffins.[34]

By June 1944 the Allies had 3.5 million soldiers (of whom 1.75 million were British and 1.5 American), 16 million tons of supplies, 13,000 aircraft excluding 3,500 gliders, 4,200 tanks and 3,500 artillery pieces ready for the invasion – including 54,000 cooks – and the whole ensemble prompted Eisenhower to claim that only the enormous number of barrage balloons kept Britain from sinking.[35]

Attempting to deploy, service and supply so many troops required the facilities of huge numbers of ships but German U-boats were still sinking more tonnage than the Allies could build every month, and the American Pacific forces attacking Japan had priority over their European forces attacking Germany for landing craft. The overall ship-ping problem was partially resolved through the construction of 2,500 'Liberty Ships' – 7,000–10,000 ton prefabricated cargo vessels welded together from three prefabricated sections using 'unskilled' labour in just ten days. So fast was the production that, at last, the Allies were building ships faster than the U-boats could sink them. But problems of various kinds continued right up to the last minute: in April 1944, for example, all the landing craft were modified to take the new radio equipment and have their doors redesigned.[36] By that time so dense was the shipping that the Commander in Chief Portsmouth suggested that:

> It is a commonplace expression to say that an anchorage is 'full of ships', but in the case of the East and West Solent with an available area of approximately 22 square miles in which to anchor ships, it was literally true. On 18th May, the Admiralty offered the C.-in-C. Portsmouth, the services of HMS Tyne, but it was only possible to accept her because HMS Warspite was not being sent to Portsmouth till D-Day, which gave one berth in hand.[37]

The stockpiling of the assault troops themselves just prior to the inva-sion, together with their immediate supplies and equipment, took place through the so called 'sausage machine'. This took its name from the 17 sausage shaped assembly areas marked on the maps to locate the initial assault in specific areas prior to embarkation. The US 1st Division, for example, was put on final alert to move on 23 March and actually began relocating south on 7 May. By 26 May they were in the final marshalling yards at the ports and the final embarkation onto the ships was

completed, on 3 June. Only at this point were the junior officers and
NCOs notified of the targets. Ordinary troops generally remained igno-
rant until they were on board and sealed in. That sealing was also associated with the sudden arrival of food stuffs that many, especially the
British and Canadians, had not tasted for months. 'It was', as Norman
Phillips recalled, 'as if we were being fattened like Christmas turkeys'.[38]
And with training now finished, the 'holiday' spirit prevailed: the troops
were entertained by films or entertained themselves with sports,
gambling, reading and writing. Indeed, for many troops waiting in their
boats and ships to cross the Channel, fanatical gambling seemed to
develop into a new religion.[39]

The amount of supplies necessary to maintain the Allied troops in
Normandy were enormous. On the American beaches alone the plan
assumed almost 200,000 tons of matériel would need to be landed by
D+14 days. In the event only 134,000 tons were landed. Some 5,200
tons were supposed to land on D-Day itself on Omaha and Utah but
neither beach unloaded anything other than the first day's fighting
troops and their immediate equipment, with Omaha unable to land more
than a seventh of its requirements by D+3 days.[40]

Each division was allocated 1,600 tons of supplies per day, and this was
calculated – in the European Theatre of Operations (ETO) – down to
the individual soldier whose requirements included 7.7lb of rations (of
which 0.426lb was of clothing and equipment), 7.812lb of construction
materials and 3.64lb of ammunition.[41] And just to ensure that the
bureaucratic requirements were fully complied with and understood,
each sea-borne soldier was issued with a seasickness bag marked on the
lists as: 'Bag, vomit, one'.[42] To ensure that such lost fluids could be
replaced in the first three days of the invasion, the planners loaded
300,000 gallons of fresh water.[43]

The initial requirements for an individual US paratrooper to carry into
Normandy were also very demanding, and included the following:

1. 45 calibre pistol and ammunition belt with 30 rounds of ammunition
2. 30 calibre folding stock rifle with 100 rounds of ammunition
3. small switch blade knife
4. 10-inch knife
5. canteen with two pints of water
6. combat first aid kit containing two shots of morphine, sulphur drugs and
   bandages
7. Mk IV anti-tank mine (weighing 10lbs which was a last minute addition)
8. equipment bag with raincoat, blanket, toothbrush, toilet paper and six meals
   of emergency K rations
9. combination shovel and pick

10. escape kit with a magnetized brass button that could act as compass when balanced on the head of a needle, hacksaw blade, map of France and 200 French Francs[44]
11. identification (dog) tags
12. metal 'cricket' for identification (the British troops carried a 'duck' whistle)[45]
13. five grenades: two fragmentation, one phosphorus, one smoke and one Gammon (2lb anti-tank grenade)
14. emergency rations kit: 4 pieces of chewing gum, 2 stock cubes, 2 Nescafé instant coffees, 2 coffee creamers, 2 sugar cubes, 4 Hershey bars, 1 pack of Charms candy, a pack of pipe tobacco, 1 pack of water purification tablets[46]
15. four blocks of TNT

It was little wonder that many individuals could hardly stand up with an extra 60–100lbs in weight. Some individuals were even more over-weight: Sergeant Louis Truax of the 1st Battalion, 506th PIR, increased his weight from 130lbs to 250lbs,[47] while Frank Brumbaugh, a pathfinder paratrooper with the 82nd Airborne weighed 137lbs normally but jumped weighing 315lbs. So great was the weight that most paratroopers had to be assisted into their planes by two helpers.[48] In theory, the ground assault troops carried a maximum of 44lbs of equipment, in order not to bog them down in the water and to allow them to move inland quickly. But in practice most carried much more than this, primarily made up of extra ammunition or weapons of one form or another. It was a mistake because many soldiers dropped their weapons and ammunition if they were unloaded into deep water and because many soldiers that were wounded on the beaches were too weak to lift their extra weight and subsequently drowned as the tide came in.

Again, let me reiterate the point that the decision to provide a specific item to the troops, and the decision to load as much as possible onto them, was not automatic, rooted in contingent logic that analysed the best option available in the situation. Many had called for the lightening of the initial assault troops' load – and even the Germans were surprised at how much material the invaders had to cope with. Indeed the principle of using light assault troops in the initial assault had been part of the German infantry traditions since the latter stages of the First World War – but the cultural predilections of the Allied commanders transcended such concerns: since the 'shock and awe' of the Allied aerial and naval bombardment would – in theory – debilitate the defenders the problem was not getting to or off the beaches but defending the beaches from the expected German Panzer counter-attacks.

10.4 Embarkation

But the logistics were by no means simple. So dense was the road traffic in Hampshire in the run up to D-Day that many of the roads were designated one-way to facilitate military planning. On Southern Railways, which served the primary loading area, over a thousand trains a week were reserved for military use as D-Day approached.[49] At Dunbridge station, near Romsey, 15 miles of sidings were built just to store matériel for the American Army, increasing Dunbridge's monthly throughput of freight wagons from 182 in 1938 to 5,246 in July 1944.[50]

The large scale embarkation of troops themselves onto the flotilla of landing craft was first simulated in July 1943 when Southampton managed to get 11,000 troops on board on each one of its four high tides; by D-Day this had been increased to a daily total of 54,000 troops and 7,000 vehicles, while Portsmouth managed 29,000 troops. But to do this another 23 slipways or 'hards' had to be built in and around the Solent and a similar number elsewhere.[51] Additional support for loading and landing heavy vehicles onto the sand was developed through the construction of 'chocolate concrete' or beach hardening mats'. These were concrete slabs that were laid onto the beach directly and held in place by iron hooks. The remains of one such mat is shown in Photo 10.1.

These kinds of problems were evidently Tame – in the sense that there was a science of planning and construction to solve most of them – but

Photo 10.1 Beach-hardening mat, Lepe, Hampshire

there were some particular headaches that veered towards the Wicked end. For instance, the immense amount of fuel that would be needed and the early assumptions about the danger of air attack, jeopardized the conventional use of oil tankers. The solution was the PLUTO project (Pipe Line Under The Ocean). A three inch pipeline – codenamed Hamel[52] – was unravelled from a huge floating drum called Tweedledum, and the initial construction involved a 12-mile pipeline being pulled by HMS *Conundrum* and a tug from Poole Bay to a pumping station on Shanklin, the Isle of Wight, in March 1944 to test its feasibility.[53] This armoured pipeline supplied 600 tons of fuel per day through Port en Bessin and was subsequently supplemented by four pipelines from the Shell-Mex/BP storage depot at Hamble, through Lepe to the Isle of Wight, and on to Cherbourg.[54] Eventually these were supplemented by 17 lines between Dungeness and Calais that supplied 2,500 tons of fuel per day.[55] Such vast quantities were certainly needed: during July the AEAF used almost 1 million gallons of fuel a day.[56] Later, fuel could be unloaded as far away as Liverpool and pumped directly to Cherbourg but initially the mine fields and the destruction of Cherbourg harbour prevented the direct pumping of fuel until 18 September, and by 20 September Ostend was opened for direct unloading of fuel by tanker. However, in all, 112 million gallons of fuel were piped through PLUTO.[57]

The heaviest user was probably the 3rd US Armoured Division. Its 4,200 vehicles driven by 17,000 soldiers swallowed 300,000 gallons each time it prepared for combat and that meant re-supplying the entire Allied army required a rolling refuelling procedure. In effect, endless lines of trucks with 200 five-gallon cans struggled between the pipelines and the front lines.[58] But for all the technical ingenuity involved in supplying liquid fuel, the really Wicked Problem lay in unloading the millions of tons of vehicles, ammunition, food, guns and supplies in Normandy. If, as the Dieppe raid suggested, and as turned out to be the case, Cherbourg was going to be rendered inoperable for several months, how on earth were the Allies going to maintain the logistics chain?

10.5 The Mulberries

Morgan had calculated that it would take at least two weeks to capture Cherbourg after landing in Normandy and that a further two to three months would be required to repair the facilities. With storms in the channel a common occurrence, and with good weather for more than four days at a time an unlikely event, the Wicked Problem was how could the troops and supplies be supplied and reinforced across open beaches? The answer was to take one or two ports with them – an idea that was greeted with hoots of laughter when it was first broached by Mountbatten in the spring of 1942.[59] These were the artificial 'Mulberry Harbours'.

The problem of building artificial harbours tall enough to accommodate ships, and cope with the 24 foot tides off Normandy, was resolved by developing floating harbours from the original ideas of Lt Commander Robert Lochner and Commodore Hughes-Hallett (leader of the successful St Nazaire raid). Churchill also claimed to have proposed the idea first in 1917 for an amphibious landing in Flanders.[60] In fact, the idea of a floating caisson, or 'floating dock', which could be lowered to suit the size of a ship was already in circulation in 1811, when plans for a 'Wrought Iron Caisson' weighing 350 tons, 220 foot long, 64 feet wide and 30 foot deep, were made available in the British *Naval Chronicle*.[61] The plans even involved constructing the dock in smaller sections and transporting them abroad. So much for original thought.

What did appear to be original, though, was Churchill's addition to a note concerning the 'piers' by the Chief of Combined Operations, dated 30 May 1942:

> They *must* float up and down with the tide. The anchor problem must be mastered. The ships must have a side-flap cut in them, and a drawbridge long enough to overreach the moorings of the piers. Let me have the best solution worked out. Don't argue the matter. The difficulties will argue for themselves.[62]

In fact, the idea of anchoring these floating harbours to the sea was drawn from the experience of the dredger *Lucayan* which had survived a hurricane in the Bahamas by using three 89 foot 'legs', called 'spuds' to anchor the vessel to the sea floor.[63]

Initially the War Office took charge of the product but the decision to build two complete artificial harbours was not made until September 1943. That was after Professor John Bernal, one of Mountbatten's scientific advisers, and Lt David Grant of the Royal Navy, used a Mae West lifebelt, some paper boats and a bath tub on board the Queen Mary liner bound for the Quebec conference, to demonstrate the viability of an artificial harbour.[64] The conference approved the idea but work did not commence until December 1943. With less than seven months to complete the task (on the initial assumption that 1 May was D-Day) the building began before the designs were completed.

As the design work progressed the complexity increased. The system was designed to unload 12,000 tons of stores and 1,250 vehicles through the two harbours and their piers for the 90 days they were designed to last.[65] This was no more than one third of the total amount required for the post-assault operations – partly because by the time the assault force was raised from three to five divisions it was too late to increase the size or number of artificial harbours. There was then an additional requirement to ensure that small craft would be able to compensate for the unplanned extra supplies by ferrying stores directly from the supply ships to the beach and not via the piers.[66]

Rear Admiral Tennant had remained dubious about the ability of the harbours to withstand any significant wind and the necessity of small craft travelling back and forth across them led him to suggest that the harbours be constructed inside an artificial breakwater or Gooseberry of 60 scuppered ships.[67] When Admiral Tennant and Captain Hickling first suggested their requirement for 60 ships to sink to the Admiralty they were, 'very nearly thrown out', because the German U-boats had sunk so much shipping it was becoming desperately short. As Admiral Cunningham (who had replaced Admiral Pound as the 1st Sea Lord) retorted: 'You have the effrontery to come here and calmly ask for 65 merchant ships just to take them across the channel and sink them? … Never heard such damned nonsense'. Tennant compounded his effrontery by noting that 'We came here to get a gooseberry and all we seem to have got is a raspberry'. This could have been the end of the project but it was saved by an interjection from Air Marshall Portal to his superordinate Admiral Cunningham. Portal did not try to argue the point with Cunningham – a strategy almost inevitably doomed to disaster – but put his point in the form of a question – a classic technique for addressing a Wicked Problem:

> Suppose one of those infrequent summer gales blows up and suppose all the landing craft are driven ashore. The army could be driven back into the sea. Are we prepared to face the country and say: 'The invasion has failed because we did not give the navy sixty-five old merchant ships'?[68]

Cunningham reluctantly gave way, not because Portal had 'proved' him wrong, but because Cunningham was made to face the consequences – as head of the Admiralty – of his initial decision. In contrast, as we shall see in similar circumstances, many other subordinates on all sides failed to prevent their leaders from making errors.

Again, the notion that Wicked Problems are best addressed through collaborative effort rather than a reiteration of an already successful process is matched here in the importance of the eventual solution requiring the ideas of many people. Thus, for example, the outer breakwater a mile beyond the floating harbours – the Bombardons – were the original idea of Lt Robert Lochner who had experimented in his own trout pond in Haslemere, Surrey, and then got Dunlop make three giant rubber lilos, 200 foot long and 15 in diameter to test his ideas about wave suppression.[69] Eventually they were fabricated in steel and tested to survive expected wind conditions, which they did. But they did not survive the gale of 19 June.[70]

Thus each Mulberry harbour comprised an outer floating breakwater, anchored to the seabed, then an inner breakwater of sunken block-ships and concrete phoenix caissons (designed initially by Brigadier Bruce White), and finally the floating piers and pier heads. The pier-heads were 200 feet long, 60 feet wide and 11 feet deep and they sat on movable legs, or 'spuds' which were 89 feet tall and 4 feet by 4 feet square. The design and prototype for the pier head took four months; the construction time for the real thing was just four weeks.[71]

The overall size of the project was also astonishing – linked together the units would form two artificial harbours the size of Dover harbour: one for the US and one for the British beaches. Some 150 floating concrete caissons – called phoenixes – in six different sizes from 25 to 60 feet high with some weighing 6,000 tons were required, and the entire project consumed half a million cubic yards of concrete, 30,000 tons of reinforcing steel, and 20,000 tons of timber for shuttering. All of this material was in short supply and even the 25,000 people working on the project had to be supplemented by another 40–45,000 draftees, mainly working on the River Thames where two thirds of the caissons were built.[72] They were developed across Britain in great secrecy, to the extent that even those building them were unaware of their purpose. Building them in separate sections in individual dockyards enhanced the secrecy. Furthermore, when the project was completed, the builders were given a day off with pay and removed from the dockyards when the caissons were floated off.[73]

Despite all this research, planning and construction, Admiral Ramsay was still sceptical, and in January 1944 spoke of the artificial harbour as 'in the realm of fairyland ... [it] may or may not be a practical proposition'.[74] Ramsay's scepticism appeared to be well founded when it became clear that the design had failed to consider the mechanisms for towing the elements across the channel, so the Admiralty took it over.

Being so large (Cornelius Ryan suggested they resembled 'a five story block of flats lying on its side')[75] these units had to be towed by sea weeks before the invasion and hidden in harbours around the south coast by flooding them. The whole system was sea-tested on 1 April 1944 when a gale hit one of them in Weymouth Bay but the test – unlike the real thing – was a success. But this was by no means the end of the problems, for the pumping gear supplied by the War Office to raise the structures failed when one section sank and could not be refloated on 20 May – three weeks before D-Day. The Admiralty Salvage Department also took over this element and completed it just days before 6 June.[76] Even the Mulberry crews were not ready until 4 June – just 24 hours before the original D-Day. But building the devices was just the first of three problems. The second was where to put them off Normandy, and the third was getting them there.

The resolution of the second problem began with the formation of the British navy unit 712th LCP(SY) Flotilla (Landing Craft, Personnel (Survey)), because there were no hydrographic surveys in existence, apart, that was, from the last French survey of the area – in 1836. As a consequence, several secret operations were carried out to map and measure the seabed.[77] The nine members of the 712th LCP(SY) trained in hydrographic surveying in Southampton waters in 1943. Using a wooden hull – to avoid distorting the magnetic signals – the boat was equipped with an echo sounder and a depth measuring device, and it began charting the Normandy coast in minute detail. The LCP(SY) was towed across the channel by three MGBs (Motor Gun Boats) and made its own way to the beach area where the surveying work and beach sampling were carried out between midnight and 0400 am from November to December 1943. One particular problem (a potential peat bog) required one more trip over New Year's Eve 1943 when unfortunately an auger (the boring tool) was lost. Luckily, it was picked up by a French civilian who realized its significance and hid it.[78]

The third problem involved towing the 'phoenixes' across the channel separately. This required 160 tugs – almost all there were in the possession of the Allied nations – plus 40 related vessels and 10,000 personnel to bolt them all together. The American construction, Mulberry A, built off Omaha Beach by No. 108 Construction Battalion (Sea Bees), was destroyed in the great storm of 19 June which reached force 7 (29–36 mph) and from then until the opening of French ports US supplies were landed directly on the beach. Unlike the British Mulberry at Gold Beach, the American design included a 200 foot gap within the phoenixes to allow small craft through; this also let the storm waves through that unhinged the entire harbour.[79] Such was the destruction that there were not enough spare sections to rebuild the American harbour and, since Cherbourg was about to fall anyway and beach landings were viable, it was decided to abandon the US Mulberry.[80] In fact the British Mulberry also had a temporary 40 foot gap but this was a consequence of having to sink eight of the nine block ships before the ninth, the French battle ship Courbet, arrived. A misjudgement on the size left a gap that was eventually filled by a small tenth ship from England.[81]

Photo 10.2 View over Arromanches from St Côme

Photo 10.3 Remains of floating harbour at Arromanches

Those three problems were balanced by four advantages embodied in the Mulberries. The first was the amount of materiel landed: after the great storm, when the British Mulberry B off Arromanches on Gold Beach returned to full operations, it carried 11,000 tons a day. By the end of August the British had landed 830,000 troops, 203,000 vehicles and 1.2 million tons of stores, and half of this had come directly through Mulberry B, built under the guidance of Rear Admiral William Tennant who had been prominent in evacuating British troops from the East Mole (a concrete breakwater) at Dunkirk.

Second, even when supplies could not be landed onto the Mulberries, their presence enabled the landing of supplies directly from the ships onto the beaches. Indeed, the Americans landed almost twice the amount landed through the Anglo-Canadian Mulberry directly onto Utah and Omaha beaches.[82] Charles Wales, a DUKW driver with the RASC, recalled that while the seas could be as high as 15 feet outside the breakwater, inside the surface 'was just very choppy'.[83]

Third, the very existence of the Mulberries seems to have been crucial in giving the planners confidence that supplies could be handled in the necessary bulk. Perhaps more significantly, the secrecy surrounding the harbours also persuaded the Germans that the landings must occur at a major port: as Albert Speer, Germany's Armaments and War production Minister suggested after the war, the artificial harbours were the 'single brilliant technical device' that swung the balance of advantage decisively in the Allies' favour.[84] Yet Lord Haw Haw (William Joyce) had boasted on German radio on 21 April 1944 that 'We know exactly what you intend to do with those concrete units'.[85] He was almost right, though the Germans had guessed that they were self-propelled floating quays for use within a captured port to compensate for the damage that would inevitably be done to any existing facilities by bombardment or sabotage. That misunderstanding cost the Germans dearly and may well have persuaded them that there was no desperate rush to remove the Allies in Normandy; since the Allies had no hope of capturing Cherbourg in the immediate future they would be vulnerable for weeks not just days – wouldn't they?[86]

10.6 Landing craft

Actually getting to the beaches, never mind the right part of one partic-ular beach, proved immeasurably more difficult than the planners had originally anticipated but all of this could be resolved through the use of pre-existing Tame procedures. With the US Navy heavily involved in the Pacific Ocean against Japan, the British navy took prime responsibility for the transportation, and the operating procedures had been established for many years through the experience of previous amphibious opera-tions: HWOST (High Water Mark of Ordinary Spring Tides) marked the dividing line above which the navy's role ceased and the army's respon-sibility started.

Responsibility for actually providing the landing craft mainly fell on American shoulders, since most British capacity was involved in the repair and construction of merchant ships and warships. However, Admiral

King remained wedded to the Pacific theatre and ensured that most American built landing craft were diverted there: on 1 May 1944 only 2,493 of the 31,123 existing US landing craft were destined for Overlord.[87] Eventually, General Marshall intervened to force Admiral King to release some of the landing craft being stockpiled for the Pacific campaign but only on 15 April did King release a number of naval ships for support (3 battleships, 2 cruisers and 22 destroyers).[88]

Paradoxically, then, one of the most critical factors in determining the date of the invasion was the provision of such landing craft, allegedly because the difficulties of design and production ensured that not until 20 March 1944 were the theoretical numbers settled, and not until May 1944 were sufficient numbers of such craft actually available. Yet the numbers available in the Pacific were more than adequate for both theatres so the most significant problem was not the technical problem of production but the political problem of distribution. The numbers had to be huge because Eisenhower required 175,000 troops (of whom 2,000 were allocated just to provide record keeping), 1,500 tanks, 3,000 artillery pieces and 10,000 vehicles to be on French soil in the first 24 hours.[89]

The naval plan required 4,126 landing craft (of which 98 per cent actually sailed on the day), 736 support ships and 864 merchant ships. All of these were to be protected by 1,213 warships of various sizes. Of the latter, 189 minesweepers would sweep the channel of mines (29 mines were swept) in the biggest minesweeping operation of the war to provide 12 safe lanes initially 15 miles wide broadening to 30 miles nearer Normandy.[90] There were also six battleships, two monitors (heavily armoured gunships), 23 cruisers and 56 destroyers that would provide fire power to destroy beach defences and gun-emplacements that might endanger the landings.[91] Specialized landing craft and transport vessels were also required in large numbers, and from the base line of just six in 1939, owned by the largest navy of the time, the British Royal Navy, the requirements were clearly large.

The 229 Landing Ship Tank (LSTs) were the largest, at 4,000 tons and 327 feet long with a maximum speed of 10 knots. Depending on the precise size (the British built versions [the Mk1] were 288 foot long, the US built versions [known as the Mk2] slightly shorter) they could carry between a dozen and 18 tanks, or between 500 and 1,400 tons of stores, or 25 3-ton trucks. And since the ships were flat-bottomed they could be landed directly on shallow beaches, usually grounding in a metre of water. The American version carried traffic lights for unloading instructions: red – unhook your vehicle from the chains it was held by for the voyage; amber – start your engine; green – bow doors open and go![92]

The first 200 LSTs to land in Normandy also carried emergency medical kits which were dumped ashore before any hospitals were set up (from D-Day+2). LSTs also ferried casualties back to England, some of whom were operated on in transit within a small operating theatre at the back of the tank deck. By D-Day+9 air transport for the critically wounded was available from Normandy. By 26 July 38,581 casualties were evacuated by sea and 7,719 by air.[93]

In fact, the precise loading capacity was critical. Admiral Ramsay was appalled to see what he regarded as the army overloading some of smaller Landing Craft (Tank) LCTs destined for Sword Beach and the following day one capsized in Portland harbour, having been loaded with 12 tanks and 70 soldiers instead of the D-Day regulation of 11 tanks and 55 soldiers.[94]

LCLs (Landing Craft Large) were the next largest specialist vessels at 110 feet long, capable of carrying about 200 troops or up to 8 tanks or 75 tons of material. These were also capable of direct beach unloading. Wherever possible 'balanced loading' was adopted which ensured that, for example, guns and their ammunition went together to avoid the problem encountered in Norway – where anti-aircraft guns were shipped separately from their ammunition and the loss of one disabled the other.[95]

Some 245 LCIs (Landing Craft Infantry – or 'Elsies' as they were nicknamed) were the next largest, and the second variant of the latter could also carry 210 troops (rather than the original 182) which discharged them on two ramps on either side of the conventional bow that allowed them to travel at 14 knots. Thus the trip across the Atlantic for American built LCIs – loaded with extra food for the hungry troops and civilians in Britain – could take three weeks.[96] Lieutenant Charles Ryan of the 18th regiment, 1st Division, described the LCI as: 'a metal box designed by a sadist to move soldiers across water while creating in them such a sense of physical discomfort, seasickness, and physical degradation and anger as to induce them to land in such an angry condition as to bring destruction, devastation, and death upon any person or thing in sight or hearing'.[97] Or, in the rather more succinct words of Corporal Hughie Rocks of The Queen's Own Rifles of Canada: 'I don't care if there are 50 million Germans on the beach; just let me off this goddam boat!'[98] But the seasickness was hugely debilitating for many, including Francis Lambert of the US 4th Infantry:

> Everyone got sick. The vomit bags filled. It was impossible to empty them overboard into tricky winds. The chemically impregnated fatigues chafed our necks and wrists. Grunts and groans pre-empted conversation. Our officers tried to boost morale, but gave up. Each bore the misery in his own way.[99]

In descending order of size, then, came 911 LCTs, which had first been used in November 1940 and by the time of the Dieppe raid the third – stretched – variant was in use. In June 1942 the first of 787 Mk4s was in use and the American built version (built in three sections for re-assembly in Britain) was known as the Mk5.[100]

Some 481 LCMs (Landing Craft Medium) were next in order of size, followed by 1,089 LCVPs (Landing Craft Vehicle and Personnel [Higgins Boat]), with some armour plating on the British version – the LCA (Landing Craft, Assault) – after the Dieppe fiasco where plywood craft had been used. The Anglo-Canadian LCAs carried 20 soldiers and were crewed by two Royal Marines, one to operate the ramp and the other to operate the engine and steering. LCAs were built across Britain in numerous factories, many of which had previously built furniture. The largest single producer in Britain was J. Bolson & Son's shipyard at Poole that had previously made leisure boats and yachts. At the height of production Bolson's produced one LCA per day and adopted what was – for then – a revolutionary production strategy: the assembly line and specialized division of labour was replaced by single work squads who produced a complete boat.[101]

Of a different order were the Rhino ferries – 176-foot pontoon barges that could carry 40 vehicles under tow by LSTs until the run in, when outboard motors were used. One of their purposes was to off load the LSTs which were considered too fragile to land directly onto the beach, but the Rhinos proved far too slow and, after it was established that LSTs could, after all, beach safely, the Rhinos were deployed as floating pontoons.[102]

In addition to these landing craft there were also LCRs (Landing Craft Rocket), LCG(L)s (Landing Craft Guns, Large), which carried two 4.7 inch guns manned by Royal Marines), LCFs (Landing Craft Flak)[103]), and last – but definitely not least – the LCB (Landing Craft Bakery) which cooked fresh bread offshore throughout D-Day. A whole range of variously sized merchant and passenger ships were also reconfigured for carrying troops and materials to be unloaded out at sea by winch or down scrambling nets etc., and delivered by the smaller landing craft. But perhaps the most unusual was the DUKW or 'Duck', an amphibious duplex drive 2.5 ton-truck that could manage 50 mph on land and 6.5 mph on water.[104] The US also provided 60 US Coast Guard patrol boats to operate as rescue boats. So effective was the air-sea rescue system that at least one fighter pilot, a Norwegian Wing Commander, was shot down in the Channel in the early hours of 5 June and was rescued, returned to base in time to fly a second mission on the same day.[105]

But perhaps the most pressing problem as far as the actual landings were concerned was the deployment of armour, especially tanks, to protect the troops as they disembarked under fire. There was already plenty of information available from Dieppe about what was likely to happen when unarmoured troops landed on exposed beaches facing a heavily gunned and emplaced enemy, but the experience of the American Marines and Army in the Pacific provided not just further evidence of the problems – but a possible solution: the Amtrac.

10.7 (Not) Learning from the Pacific

In the invasion of Betio Island in the Tarawa Atoll in the Pacific, between 20 and 23 November 1943, the US Marines faced 26,700 Japanese troops, 1,000 Japanese labourers and 1,200 Korean labourers ensconced, it was alleged, in the most heavily fortified area in the world. At just two miles long and one mile wide, the Japanese had installed 14 large coastal defence guns, 40 other artillery pieces and more than 100 machine guns firing through a four foot coconut log wall. In all there were 500 pill-boxes. As the Japanese commander, Rear Admiral Keiji Shibasaki, boasted, 'A million men cannot take Tarawa in a hundred years'.[106] Some of the emplacements had concrete walls eight-feet thick which proved to be impervious to the largest naval shell fire despite the pre-landing bombardment from the sea and air that saw, on average, ten tons of high explosives fall on each of the 291 acres.

The US 2nd and 8th Marine Divisions were carried to the beaches either on the conventional LCVP (Higgins Boats) or the LVTs (Landing Vehicle, Tracked). The LVTs or Amtracs (Amphibious Tractors), or Alligators as they were known, had originated in civilian tractors built for working in the swamps of the southern states. In 1936 Donald Roebling, an engineer who had retired to Florida, witnesses a disastrous hurricane and re-designed a vehicle with his son, John, that they had first dreamt up in 1934.[107] The tracked vehicle, the 'alligator', was one of the few that could traverse the Florida swamps or the marshy everglades to rescue the beleaguered population on behalf of the Florida Red Cross. That rescue mission was covered by *Life* magazine in 1937 and the article was read by one individual who immediately saw a greater use for it: the Commanding General of the US Fleet Marine Force in the Pacific. Using diagonal track cleats and an aluminium construction, the Roebling alligator or amphibian was first prototyped in 1939 and could reach speeds of 10 mph on land and 25 mph in the water. It had a cruising radius of 400 miles and steered either by disengaging the tracks on one side or by reversing the tracks on one side. The prototype drew only five feet of water fully laden with well over 20 people and could drop 6 feet from land to water without capsizing. The provisional cost was put at £3,600 and by 1940 the US Marine Corps was convinced the vehicle was critical for them. In November 1940 the United States Navy and United Sates Marine Corps ordered 200 to be made with light steel rather than dura-lumin and by 1941 the first 100 were delivered. By the end of the war 18,620 had been made.

The first military Amtrac – LVT1 – was one of 1,225 built by Roebling and FMC (Food Machinery Corporation) in July 1941. It had a capacity of 24 troops plus three crew and it travelled at 6 mph in the water and 12 mph on the land. The slow speed of the vehicle and the short life of the tracks led to a two months delay while the design was redeveloped at the California Institute of Technology. In June 1942 demonstrations of the new prototypes were held for the US Navy, Army and Marine Corps.

Most of the LVT1s went to the US Navy and Marine Corps but 485 went to the US Army and 55 were sent to the Anglo-Canadian forces. Its first operational use was at the battle of Guadalcanal on 7 August 1942 and some – especially those for transporting personnel rather than materiel – were fitted with appliqué armour. Of the 2,936 LVT2s, 1,507 were used by the US Navy and 100 sent to the Anglo-Canadian forces. From 1943 the LVT3s had their engines moved forward so that a rear-loading ramp could be used but the most popular British use was of the LVT4 which could carry 30 soldiers, had a rearward loading ramp, and could mount four machine guns. Most of the LVTs used in Europe, however, known in Britain as the Buffalo, were unarmoured with a trap-door exit at the front. As many as 500 were sent to Britain or Canada.

But Tarawa, in November 1943, was the first assault which used Amtracs in large numbers to carry troops.[108] Fitted with propellers and tracks these Amtracs could travel at four knots in the water and 20mph on land – and they had rearward facing doors. Critically, this meant they did not have to disgorge their vulnerable contents straight into the sights of enemy gunners at the water's edge, but could travel across some reefs, sand and barbed wire right up to the enemy emplacements and unload their occupants from the relative safety of the back of the vehicle. The Marines' General Smith had demanded more Amtracs to carry his troops forward but Admiral Turner, the amphibious force commander had overruled his request, insisting that the LCVPs were quite adequate for the task. Given that Rear Admiral Kingman, the commander of the ships, had promised to 'obliterate' Betio before any Marine landed, Turner presumably thought Smith's request unnecessary. Nevertheless Turner eventually accepted the request and 50 more Amtracs were delivered before the invasion bringing the total to 125 – just enough for the first three assault battalions, but leaving the follow up units to land in LCVPs.

The execution of the plan left much to be desired – and much to be learned for Overlord. The disembarking Marines were forced to delay their exit from the carrying ships when it was realized that they were directly under the bombing route. Then the failure to co-ordinate the naval and airborne bombardments led to both a 35 minute gap between the two and a radically shortened aerial assault. As the Marines approached the beach, the fires caused by the bombardment prevented the naval ships from firing right up until the landing and although communications lines were cut precious little material damage had been done to the defenders. Thus at a distance of 3,000 yards the line of 125 Amtracs came under direct fire from the beach guns which destroyed half of them. Meanwhile, the LCVPs could not even cross the reef, leaving the follow-up forces to wade ashore or transfer into one of the few remaining Amtracs returning from the beach. The only area where the defensive ring was penetrated was on Red Beach 3 where two destroyers put the large Japanese guns out of action, allowing the Amtracs to move through the sea wall. Eventually, after three days of fighting, the defenders were overcome. Only 146 of the 4,700 survived (including just 17 Japanese). Of the 12,000 attacking Marines 1,027 were dead or missing (as were 29 Naval personnel), 2,292 were wounded. But significant lessons had been learned and on 1 February 1944 these new techniques and technologies were deployed against Kwajalein Atoll when all the infantry from the 7th Infantry Division landed in Amtracs, and after three days and 334 deaths the atoll was captured.[109]

For the rest of the Pacific war vital lessons were learned: Amtracs were fitted with thicker armour and some upgunned to carry 37mm or 75mm guns in turrets while those invading Okinawa on 1 April 1945 often carried four 30 calibre machine guns – but only two Amtracs were shipped to Normandy and both these appeared on Utah. Thus although it had been clear from the Pacific and Dieppe, that conventionally propelled and unarmoured landing craft with bow-facing doors exposed the assault waves to considerable enemy fire, and although no vehicle was immune to artillery fire, an armoured Amtrac with a rearward opening door would enable troops to be carried across the most exposed part of the assault – the beach. Such vehicles were already available by D-Day because 500 LVT(A)1 – Amtracs with an enclosed and armoured hull supporting a 37mm gun – were supplied to the US Navy and Army between 1942 and 1944. Indeed, they were used again en masse at Saipan in the middle of June 1944 when 150 LVT(A)1s were deployed in support of the 600 LVTs carrying 8,000 US Marines in the first wave on a four mile assault of the beach. Even more useful was the LVT(A)2 which was like the LVT(A)1 except the armour was increased and the 37mm gun removed – thus providing a well armoured personnel carrier – of which the US Army used 200 between 1943 and 1944. The final LVT variant before 1945 was the LVT(A)4 which carried a howitzer rather than a 37mm tank gun. In fact they had originally been used just for carrying stores and troops and were photographed in *Parade* on 15 August 1942 carrying troops – so their availability was clearly not unknown to the Overlord planners.[110]

Nor was the utility of this vehicle questioned by those using them in combat. When the 10,000th LVT rolled off the assembly lines at FMC on 14 May 1945, Vice-Admiral Cochrane, Chief of the (US) Bureau of Ships, said:

> There is not the slightest shadow of doubt that the overwhelming victories of our forces at Tarawa, Kwajalein, Saipan, Tinian, Guam, Palau and Iwo Jima could not have been possible without the Amtracs. It is only they that could navigate the coral reefs which the Japanese thought were their sure defence. It follows, there-fore, that the war against Japan would be far from its present reassuring stage had it not been for the thousands of Amtracs turned out by your company.[111]

If the failure to learn the lesson of the Amtrac in the Pacific cost the assault troops off Omaha dearly, did the Allies learn much from the other aspects of amphibious assaults in the Pacific prior to D-Day?

Well, duplicates of Betio's defences were built in Hawaii on Kahoolawe Island and it became clear that only rocket carrying aircraft, and armour piercing naval shells fired as howitzers with a very high angle of descent, had any chance of penetrating them. That lesson also seems to have bypassed most of the Normandy planners, but not all of them. Major General Corlett, for example, had commanded the US 7th Infantry Division against Japanese forces on the Kwajalein atoll which had fallen for a fraction of the cost in casualties of the attack on Tarawa and he had suggested the D-Day assault use the new Amtracs.[112] But Corlett was, in his own words, 'squelched' by both Eisenhower and Bradley when he suggested it to them in a meeting.[113] A response that Corlett put down to himself being 'A son-of-a-bitch from out of town'.[114] Admittedly, it was probably too late to provide large numbers of these vehicles but even a few would probably have proved invaluable and two were certainly operating off Utah Beach (one of them is still there). After all, at least 24 were stockpiled in England by 23 March 1944 (the photo of them was embargoed until after 6 June 1944).[115]

Even after Omaha the western theatre commanders avoided any significant deployment of Amtracs, though three 'Buffaloes' as the

British called them – were used on 1 November 1944 by 41, 47, and 48 Royal Marine Commandos, supporting the 1st Canadian Army in clearing the Westkapelle end of the Dutch island of Walcheren which blocked the route to the sea from Antwerp.[116] Thus the poverty of naval and air bombardments against deeply entrenched beach artillery and the advantages of Amtracs over unarmoured personnel landing craft were never learned by the military leaders – except by those who became casualties on the Normandy beaches on D-Day.

10.8 The Armada

With the initial 'assault' formations and the 'pre-loaded, follow-up formations' on board in their harbours by 3 June (the subsequent formations were held back further inland), the ships began leaving by early morning 5 June. 'U' (Utah) left from Torquay region, 'O' (Omaha) left from around Weymouth and Poole, 'G' (Gold) left from Southampton, 'J' (Juno) left from Portsmouth, and 'S' (Sword) left from Shoreham. Force 'U' was the furthest from its destination, the most dispersed and the least prepared. There is no large port in western England so the embarkation took place from nine small ports, and, since the landing craft for 'U' were the last to arrive in England, many people had received little or no training in them.[117] Paradoxically, the American landing at Utah Beach incurred the least casualties of any Allied landing on D-Day.

They all headed for their rendezvous point in the channel just south of the Isle of Wight, Area Z to the Admiralty but colloquially known as 'Piccadilly Circus'. The commanders of the ships opened sealed envelopes once clear of the harbours, which revealed their true destinations for the first time and headed south through the night in the ten swept channels – one fast and one slow lane – towards Normandy. Such was the combined effect of the tide and the wind that some ships had to allow a 40 degree directional compensation to maintain their direction – usually due south.[118] The leading minesweepers reached Barfleur at 2000 on 5 June and by 2200 it was possible for those on board to pick out individual houses on the Normandy coast though no German gun opened fire until first light the following morning.

But getting the minesweepers in position was relatively easy; sweeping 10 paths in the dark, and in radio silence, was a much tougher job, especially when entangled or cut mines would themselves be difficult to see. To ensure a co-ordinated movement, all the minesweepers had to change direction simultaneously and that required someone on each ship to look out for and see a signal light from the central ship. The first full-scale rehearsal for this complicated operation took place on 15 March 1944 when it took 90 minutes to turn the ships around and sweep in the opposite direction. Two weeks later a second rehearsal was cancelled for 24 hours due to bad weather – just as on D-Day – but when it was resumed on 30 March it was supposed to take place ahead of a bombarding force. Several breaks in the sweeping wires prevented that but the exercise did include laying smoke screens and anchoring along a perimeter boundary to defend the assault forces, just as required on the evening of 6 June. When the minesweepers got to D-Day the average turn round time for a sweep was 68 minutes.[119]

In fact, a line of extra mines was laid parallel to the coast in the early part of 1944 but the Germans were concerned about their own shipping requirements and assumed that the danger would have passed by the summer of 1944; hence the mines automatically flooded themselves and sank to the bottom at the end of May. There were additional mines ready to be laid in Le Havre but the German minelayers had been sunk by the Royal Navy and the mines remained on land. Conventional contact mines – of the horned buoy variety still in evidence in British seaside towns as charitable containers – exploded when the acid-filled glass tube inside each horn was struck, releasing the acid into a central battery which completed the necessary circuit to detonate the explosive. They were usually anchored to the seabed by a thin wire so that it 'floated' just below the surface. Thus 'sweeping' such mines involved cutting the wire with a wire hauser towed by the minesweeper that was deflected away from the ship a little. The cut mine would then float to the surface where it was destroyed by surface gunfire. Sweeping an entire area required a serried array of mine sweepers operating on overlapping sweeps, followed by 'dan (buoy) laying' ships, usually trawlers, which would mark the limits of the sweep. It may have been one such trawler that Brendan Maher's minesweeper came across winching a jeep out of the water off Sword Beach on D-Day. Maher's own commanding officer, Lt Hutchins, aware that almost all matériel on D-Day was declared 'expendable' to prevent people from stopping on their way to the beach, hailed the trawler's captain: 'You don't have to rescue that you know', he shouted. 'I'm not rescuing it', replied the trawler skipper. 'I've never had a car in my life, and now I've got one. This one's coming home with me!'[120]

Besides the more unusual magnetic mines, which could be cleared by wooden minesweepers or metal ships fitted with a degaussing band to neutralize its magnetic properties, the Germans had also developed magnetic mines which only exploded after the twelfth ship had passed over it. Additionally, an acoustic mine, the 'oyster mine', which operated when the sound of the ship's engines and a change in water pressure occurred simultaneously, had been constructed.[121] These could not be swept by existing equipment and were extremely effective – but Hitler was concerned lest the Allies retrieve such a mine and copy it, so although 2,000 acoustic Oyster mines were stored at Le Havre they were only to be laid in an emergency. Ironically, Goering recalled all the mines in May for redesign and although they were ready for deployment by early June the air interdiction effectively held them up until after D-Day.[122]

Against this mighty armada, the likes of which had never been seen before nor since, the German navy mustered six E-boats from Le Havre which fired torpedoes at the ships at the eastern fringe of the landings, sinking the Norwegian destroyer *Svenner* at 0510 – the only Allied ship sunk by the German Navy on D-Day.[123] HMS *Warspite* then attacked the E-boats sinking one and driving the rest back to Le Havre where they were destroyed by fighter-bomber attacks.[124] Unknown to the Germans – who had assumed that E-boats operated beyond the range of British radar – the British navy had developed ship-based radar that effectively sealed the E-boats in their harbours.[125] Even when the Germans had amassed a sufficiently large number of E-boats to attack the Allied shipping, air attacks usually kept them at bay. For example, on 14 June a large concentration of E-boats was reported at Le Havre and that night 18 Mosquito bombers and 335 Lancaster bombers led by Group Captain Leonard Cheshire, dropped over 1,000 tons of bombs on the flotilla, sinking 3 torpedo boats, 10 E-boats, 2 R-boats, 15 minesweepers and patrol vessels, plus several smaller craft, as well as damaging a further 19 vessels.[126] It was, according to Admiral Kranke, 'a catastrophe. Losses are extremely heavy. It will hardly be possible to carry out the operations planned with the remaining forces'.[127] Not until the night of 6 July was any major assault on Allied shipping carried out when 26 'human torpedoes' – a real torpedo beneath another torpedo with a human pilot rather than a warhead – were launched and two British minesweepers sunk. Two nights later, another 21 'human torpedoes' were launched, sinking one Polish minesweeper; none of the attackers survived. On 3 August, 16 'explosive motor boats' (unmanned boats containing 660 pounds of explosives) were launched at the Trout Line guarding the eastern flotilla. Only one explosive motor boat hit its target (an LCG) while the rest were destroyed. One further major attack occurred on 9 August in which 20 of the attacking 28 boats (16 explosive motor boats and 4 control boats) were destroyed without Allied loss.[128]

10.9 Conclusion

This chapter has focused on the means by which the Allies transported all the troops and matériel across the channel. Given that this was the largest amphibious landing ever attempted – and therefore the most complex single operation ever undertaken – mistakes and failings were inevitable, but by and large this part of the operation was a huge success, primarily because the Allies had developed processes to manage the Tame Problems. Yet not everything was Tame: Air Marshall Portal's interjection to Admiral Cunningham forced his superior to reconsider the block ships that protected the artificial harbours; Churchill's irascible demands forced subordinates to look for solutions not problems; and undoubtedly there were many invisible people who persuaded others to do things they thought were beyond them, all in the name of the war effort.

But not everything either 'went to plan' or 'worked out for the best'. The decision not to use the Amtrac vehicles was to cost the American troops on Omaha dearly, for while the British had their armoured 'Funnies' to protect them, the Americans had precious little. That decision was not rooted in any rational analysis of the Tame requirements but from a mixture of political and cultural issues: since the 'shock and awe' of the pre-invasion bombardment would destroy or disorient the defenders what was the purpose of armoured and tracked landing craft? And if the artillery tests on Japanese defences had proved how little they were affected by conventional bombardment then surely the answer was to use more of the ineffective weapons rather than rethink the problem? Here indeed was a recalcitrant Tame Problem that bore more resemblance to a Wicked Problem – and that would have required a more collaborative effort on the part of formal leaders. Given the political in-fighting that divided the Pacific and European commands it is little wonder that the lessons of the former should find so little application in the latter.

11 Technologies

11.1 Introduction

Getting across the beaches in Normandy took years of planning, training and production. That 24-hour period, which Rommel referred to as the 'Longest Day', proved for many to be their shortest day. In theory Allied material strength, especially that which derived from the Arsenal of Democracy in the USA, could more than compensate for the alleged superiority of the German soldier. And since those soldiers facing the invaders were supposedly second rate the invasion should have been relatively easy. In fact, and with the exception of Omaha, it was, for fewer Allied soldiers died on D-Day than on many of the subsequent days of fighting. But while Allied technology in the form of superior aircraft and artillery, supported by the dominance of the Allied navies, ensured significant advantages for the Allied troops, the latter's poor landing craft, tanks and machine guns proved very problematic. In the main, as the previous chapter suggested, the disadvantages were a product of culture and politics, rather than contingency or misfortune or poorer technologies or inadequate science, because there were alternative and superior boats and tanks that could well have reduced the invaders' casualties even more. That the invasion succeeded is a tribute to those who worked around and against such unnecessary disadvantages.

11.2 The beach defences

Having ensured a method of re-supply through the Mulberries, and secured a protected passage across the channel, the 'only' remaining task was the most difficult of all – breaching the beach defences. Precisely how the invasion force was going to pull off the most complex single operation ever attempted was, to some extent, dependent upon the technologies that the Allies carried with them. Dieppe had revealed the weakness of Allied technology compared to its German counterparts but to what extent had the Allies caught up and surpassed their enemy? As far as Churchill was concerned: 'This war is not ... a war of masses of men hurling masses of shells at each other. It is by devising new weapons and above all by scientific leadership that we shall best cope with the enemy's superior strength'.[1] Churchill recruited Frederick Linderman, Professor of Experimental Philosophy at Oxford University, Millis Jefferis, a major in the Royal Engineers, and Percy Hobart, a recently retired General of an armoured division, to his 'toyshop' and between the four of them many of Britain's 'new weapons' evolved in response to the beach-crossing problems.

The first problem facing the initial assault troops was the obstacles and mines that littered the beach area itself. Any attacking amphibious force would have to face row upon row of defences even before landing on the beach. First, at around 225 metres from the high-water line, 3 metre high iron obstacles tipped with Teller anti-tank mines were supplemented by an occasional example of 'Element C': an array of large steel girders welded together to form a mined obstacle 15 foot long and 12 foot high. Second, at around 200 metres, there were rows of logs, supported by an 'A' frame and tipped with mines and driven into the sand at 45 degrees. Third, at 120 metres, were deployed rows of 'hedgehogs' – constructions of metal rods designed to rip open the bottom of the landing craft.

If the invading troops got through this deadly maze they would then face rows of concertina barbed wire interspersed with minefields and trip-wire mines of various kinds. Rommel had 6.5 million land mines laid along the French coast (1 million a month for four months between February and D-Day), though he had originally wanted 20 million.

Photo 11.1 Anti-tank 'hedgehog'

Where mined beach defences remained submerged specialized underwater demolition teams were to be sent in to make sea-lanes safe and to mark them for the following landing craft. However, safety had a cost: the casualty rate of these teams was amongst the highest of all. On Utah Beach – the safest of all – only 13 of the 40 Underwater Demolition engineers survived the day, and only two of these were uninjured despite the use of Kapok Jerkins, a novel protective suit designed to resist the destructive power of underwater explosions.[2]

Following the underwater demolition squads were the combat engineers. The engineering requirements for D-Day were two: first to open up 50 yard gaps in the wire and minefields to allow initial exits from the beaches. These were to be opened up by special engineering assault gapping teams. Second, behind the gapping teams, support engineering teams would widen the gaps, set up the communications to link the beach to the ships (including radios, semaphores and heliographs with coloured lights to inform the ships what to send in the next wave), and generally ensure an adequate traffic flow.

After D-Day the beach would be cleared by the engineering battalion beach groups who would also be responsible for establishing ammunition and fuel dumps. So important were the engineering tasks that 25 per cent of all the troops landed on D-Day were engineers of some kind. For example, on Omaha the first wave involved 1,450 assault infantry and 546 engineers (including 126 American Navy demolition experts), though the normal proportion was 8 per cent.[3] Omaha was 7,000 yard long with between 70 yards of sand (at high-water mark {HWM}) and 400 yard (at low water mark {LWM}). It was covered by the 5th and 6th Engineering Special Brigade making up the 5,632 members of the Provisional Engineer Special Brigade Group. Another 2,500 engineers landed with other units. (Utah was covered by a single unit, the 1st Engineering Special Brigade).

Omaha's obstacles comprised two main lines: 250 yards from the HWM was a 50-yard deep line of Element C, Belgian Gates, covered with Teller mines. Fifty yards closer to the beach was a 50-yard deep line of wooden posts and ramps supported by three staggered rows of hedgehog obstacles. (Fortunately, there were no Teller mined posts on Utah).[4] By nightfall, about 34 per cent of the combat engineers on Omaha were dead or wounded and 60 per cent of their equipment had been lost or destroyed.[5] Moreover, they had been unable to complete their task of blowing 16 gaps in the beach defences, though four had been opened. Partly this was because the initial bombardment left many defenders alive and fully capable of making the beach a no-go area. This then slowed the demolition down so much that the rising tide covered many other obstacles before they could be dealt with. Partly it was because the fire was so intense that many infantry soldiers crouched behind the obstacles thus preventing the engineers from blowing them up.[6]

In total, around 304 of the large landing craft of various forms were lost or disabled in the initial assault on the Normandy beaches, half to mined obstacles and the rest to artillery and accidents. The numbers included 131 LCTs (97 on the Anglo-Canadian beaches and 34 on the American beaches), and 21 LCI(L) [carrying 200 soldiers] (9 Anglo-Canadian and 12 American). The differential implies that the heavy US casualties on Omaha were caused more by problems on the beach rather than getting to the beach.[7]

Indeed, while the troops tip-toed carefully around the mined obstacles, and even before they tried to cross the triple line of concertina barbed wire that was strung out along Omaha Beach, the whole beach area would be under fire from the gun emplacements and the machine guns. And since these were often set at oblique angles, the defenders were protected from attackers' fire directly in front of them, while being able to provide enfilading fire along a pre-set angle of the beach to the side. Should the attackers appear to be gaining a foothold, the defenders could often retire through a maze of concrete tunnels back to safety some distance from the beach, often to the mortar units whose mortars were already zeroed in onto specific beach positions.[8] In fact one analysis suggests that the most lethal German weapon was the 81mm mortar with an effective range of 2,500 yards which caused three times more casualties than machine gun bullets.[9] Indeed, there are claims that two-thirds of all the Allied casualties in Normandy were due to mortars.[10] Most concerning to the Allied troops seemed to be the fact that the mortar shell, unlike most other shells, was almost inaudible in flight.[11] Certainly very few Allied soldiers were killed or wounded by the German's secret beach weapon – the Goliath (Leichte Ladungsträger [SdKfz 303]) which was a remote (wire guided) controlled tracked container filled with 75kg or 100kg of explosives.[12] But there was another reason for the disproportionate losses at Omaha: the absence of specialized armour used on the Anglo-Canadian beaches – the Funnies.

11.3 The Funnies

It was obvious after Dieppe, at least to General Paget, Commander in Chief of the Home Forces, that the gap between what he called 'the barrage and the bayonet', that is the time between the end of the sea and aerial barrage and the troops engaging the enemy on the beaches, exposed the first assault waves to great danger. In conjunction with Montgomery, Paget and the COSSAC planners decided that as many guns, mortars and rockets as possible should be deployed on the landing craft themselves to provide covering fire right through the initial assault period. This was to take a Tame response – to assume that more of the same would solve the problem rather than to consider whether the problem itself needed rethinking.

General Brooke was also of the opinion that only a heavily armoured assault could ensure a secure lodgement, and he organized the 79th Armoured Division into an experimental unit, under General Percy Hobart. Hobart was Montgomery's brother-in-law, who at the time held the honourable rank of Lance Corporal in the Chipping Campden Home Guard. Hobart was rescued from oblivion, having been removed by Lt General Maitland Wilson with Wavell's support, and he was put in command of the newly formed 11th Armoured Division. However, at 57 he was considered too old to fight and that unit was subsequently led by Major-General Brocas Burrows while Hobart was given a new job: to design and equip with revolutionary weapons the new 79th Armoured Division: 'Hobart's Zoo' as it became known.[13]

Hobart's innovations were as popular with the D-Day troops as he was unpopular with his peers and superordinates. He even admitted as much, for as he wrote to his wife: 'Now I'm damned bad with my superiors'.[14] More importantly for D-Day, Hobart realized that the Dieppe failure had partly been created by the heavy casualties amongst the engineers whose job was to blast a way through the anti-tank obstacles for the tanks. Hobart decided that tanks should clear their own paths – in other words, the leadership would be provided by the tanks not the infantry. It was also important to remember that the Anglo-Canadians were more likely to face an immediate counter-attack by German Panzer forces than the Americans because of the disposition of most German armour at the eastern end of Normandy.[15]

Back in command, Hobart designed and developed a series of vehicles on tank platforms – known as Hobart's Funnies – which the British and Canadians deployed in large numbers and to great effect: in the first five hours on the Anglo-Canadian beaches, 21 lanes were cleared by 'Crabs'. These were Sherman tanks carrying a rotating flail to beat the sand and detonate mines at a safe distance, the 'Crab' or 'Flail' tank used 50 chains arranged around a rotating drum at the front of the tank on two sprockets. A version had been used at the battle of El Alamein and the Sherman Crab was ordered in June 1943. Although effective, the flailing kicked up so much sand that visibility was strictly limited and the gun could not be

fired during flailing. The German response to the Crab involved distributing different versions of their main anti-tank Teller mine so that a second weight or impact was needed to detonate them. Thus the flail would act as the first weight but as the tank moved over the mine it would explode. A larger bar mine was also deployed in Normandy which both caused more damage and had an integral booby-trap device.[16]

But while Crabs may have been lifesavers for the infantry they were deeply unpopular with the tankers who operated them. Those chosen to operate the Crab were seldom enthralled by it, not simply because of the dangers but also because of the status of the technology. As Major Birt of the 22nd Dragoons recalled, 'instead of going into battle in the pride of a cruiser tank formation, we were to crawl into action in what appeared to be the menial task of scavengers and road sweepers, creeping along at a mile an hour'.[17] Indeed, so under-powered was the flail that it had great difficulty operating on a slope of any significance.[18] Leading the way was one thing but there was also a way of leading to think about.

But if the Crabs performed their unglamorous task of mine clearing on the beaches well, far less effective were the rocket-firing boats (LCT(R)) which, on Omaha Beach, loosed their 1,000 rockets at 3,500 metres. In theory the total firepower of the rocket ships was equivalent to 150 broadsides from a destroyer. A full load involved 1080 loaded and 1080 reloads but only the single load was fitted on D-Day because the forecast had suggested 50 per cent of the LCT(R)s would be lost. Each rocket weighed 56 lbs, half cordite propellant and half explosive. That made up 14 tons of warhead per LCT(R) but so powerful was the effect that in training only a few rockets were fired at any one time. Indeed, D-Day was the first time that many LCT(R)s had fired a complete salvo. As they fired it looked as though all the LCT(R)s had caught fire but actually the deck became so hot from the firing that a sprinkler system was fitted to wash the deck. Initially, that water turned to steam making it appear that all the LCT(R)s had caught fire! The directional effort was also hampered by the fact that both engines on the LCTs were right-turning screws as a consequence of the rush to produce them. Thus the LCT(R)s were both unstable, difficult to steer and difficult to aim.[19] It was hardly surprising, then, that more damage seemed to be done to the rocket ships themselves than to the German defenders. Most of rockets landed harmlessly in the sea as the German gunfire forced the ships to fire prematurely.[20]

Indeed, even the 4-inch rockets carried by the Typhoons seemed to cause more fear than actual damage. Only a direct hit could knock out a tank and the RAF estimated that, at most, a rocket had a 5 per cent chance of hitting its target, so unstable was it. Many rocket firers claimed inordinate success rates but the RAF began to assume that only 20 per

cent of the claimed hits were actually successful.[21] Here is an intriguing example of attributed Leadership – for many soldiers seemed to have viewed the rocket-firing Typhoon as their saviour that would *lead* them through the enemy; that this attribution was empirically false does not seem to have made much difference to the troops.

But neither minesweeping Flails, nor rocket ships, nor rocket firing typhoons could cope with the heavily fortified gun emplacements; that was a job for the AVREs. The AVRE (Armoured Vehicle Royal Engineers) – was a Churchill tank fitted with a variety of devices but usually a 'spigot' – a 12.5 inch diameter mortar to fire 7.5 inch 40lb petard (hollow charge) carrying a 26lb explosive charge ('flying dustbins' as they were called). It was designed to destroy concrete fortifications and had a range of 230 yards though 80 yards was regarded as its most effective distance. But again, many of these were not delivered until just before D-Day, and many had not been test-fired before D-Day – an important issue since the AVRE's Petard had the distinct disadvantage of having to be reloaded from outside the turret.[22]

Other AVREs were fitted with assault bridges, or fascines or carried explosive 'snakes'. Some of the 180 AVREs used on D-Day on the Anglo-Canadian beaches were used to carry the demolition engineers, whose job it was to disable beach explosives and defences. Without such armoured protection the demolition engineer's task was virtually impossible – as had already been demonstrated quite clearly in the Dieppe fiasco in August 1942.

Photo 11.2 AVRE Spigot

The US response to the problem of protecting demolition engineers was begun in February 1943 when the US Army Corps of Engineers requested a similar scheme to the British initiative that led to the AVRE. Several experimental Sherman developments resulted, with the gun removed and side doors cut to facilitate movements in and out of the vehicle, but the trials were both slow and unsuccessful. Eventually 100 of the new vehicles were ordered but only two were ever made and neither left US soil. American combat engineers were thus left without any protection whatsoever and they paid the price of political and technological leadership failure.[23]

The British also developed a 'Bobbin' tank which unravelled a long strip of canvas for it and subsequent vehicles to travel over soft sand. A tank was even developed specifically for night-fighting. Code named a CDL (Canal Defence Light), the 13 million candle power lamp, designed by Professor Mitzakis, was fitted to Matilda and Grant tanks and capable of throwing a beam a 1,000 yards long and 350 yards wide. It was demonstrated to Churchill late one evening in 1943 in Penrith when six tanks lit up the Prime Minister as he relieved himself against a bush. Sixty CDLs were landed in Normandy but they were never used for the role intended. According to several tank experts, the CDL would have proved itself very capable, and Mitzakis suggested that it had been kept so secret that even the generals that should have used it were unaware of its capabilities.[24] Finally, and probably most revolutionary of all, Hobart and his team devised the DD amphibious tank (Duplex Drive – or 'Donald Ducks' as they became known).

11.4 The DD tank

The floating tank, originally invented by an émigré Hungarian – Nicholas Straussler – had simply been a tank supported by floats, and several Soviet and German experimental amphibious tanks had been designed (140 were supposed to be converted for Operation Sealion in 1940, the invasion of Britain). In fact, amphibious tanks had been around since the mid 1930s, when the USSR introduced its amphibious T-38.[25] But Delaforce[26] suggests that it was Churchill's idea to support one with a canvas screen.[27] The idea was initially resisted by the Admiralty because the tank had no rudder,[28] but Churchill was adamant that it was essential because the Dieppe raid had shown how costly unsupported assaults by the infantry were. DD equipment was available as early as 1941 and initially a Tetrarch and then a Valentine tank was tested but eventually the Sherman was designated the primary DD vehicle.[29]

The DD tank was a Sherman fitted with twin propellers and a removable canvas 'skirt' that ensured the 33-ton vehicle could float – as long as the sea was not so rough that the waves could swamp the three feet of canvas 'skirt' surrounding the top of the tank. Driven by two contra-rotating propellers, the tank could manage about 5 knots in the water and was steered by a detachable tiller. The detachable screens, inflated with carbon dioxide, raised the tank's height from nine to 13 feet.[30]

Sea trials of DD Shermans began in the summer of 1943 off Stokes Bay near Portsmouth, and by 15 July 500 had been ordered by the British. As soon as Montgomery saw the trails he decided that DD tanks would lead the invasion, and DD tank crews ashore practised underwater escapes in converted swimming pools. After 30,000 practise launchings at sea had resulted in only seven losses he was probably confident that they would survive the sea launch. Thus the conventional assault pattern of infantry supported by tanks would be inverted to one where the tanks would lead and be supported by the infantry.[31] In the event, of the 122 DDs that were sea-launched on D-Day, 39 sank before they beached (many more were landed directly on the beaches).[32] At least one DD tank crew member had to get out of the tank and hold the screen up as they approached Juno Beach on D-Day, so rough was the water.[33]

Despite the secrecy surrounding the DD tank they were not always a surprise: a captured German document revealed that Rommel had fore-warned his troops that, 'when the invasion came the Allies would use all sorts of weapons, including an amphibious tank that actually would float with its body beneath the surface'.[34] Nevertheless, some defenders were surprised. SS-Obersturmführer ((Lieutenant) Hansmann, on reconnaissance for the 12th SS Panzer Division on D-Day behind Gold Beach near Arromanches reported seeing strange sights on that day: 'Imperturbably, other tanks emerge straight from the sea. Is this really happening? At first all you see are the turrets and then the whole tanks emerge like dinosaurs from the primordial deeps'.[35] Relatedly, Sergeant Gariepy commanding the first DD tank to land on Nan Green in front of the Regina Rifles on Juno recalls the effect:

> I was the first tank coming ashore and the Germans started opening up with machine gun bullets. But when we came to a halt on the beach, it was only then that they realized we were a tank when we pulled down our canvas skirt, the floatation gear. Then they saw that we were Shermans. It was quite amazing. I still remember very vividly some of the machine gunners standing up in their posts looking at us with their mouths wide open. To see tanks coming out of the water shook then rigid.[36]

The British and Canadian beaches received a far heavier bombardment than the American beaches partly because the tide turned at the US beaches first, giving less time for a naval assault, and partly because of assumptions about the accuracy of the air bombardment and the quality of the defences and the defenders. Sword received the heaviest bombardment of all, though many of the assault troops there were also surprised at the absence of significant damage. The DD tanks for Sword Beach were launched relatively easily although those that survived the rough weather were overtaken by the infantry landing craft that landed first. But it was not long before the 31 DD tanks and AVREs arrived, and the flail tanks, in particular, quickly cleared a path through the mines. By 0800 there was relatively little firing from the beach area but this had only been achieved at a considerable cost; for instance, only six of the original 20 tanks in A Squadron of the 13th/18th Hussars survived and only two from the 20 of B Squadron left the beach.[37]

On Omaha Beach the two companies of DD tanks (Co. C and Co. B, 743rd Tank Battalion) that were supposed to cover the infantry failed miserably. The 56 Sherman tanks of the 743rd Tank battalion were supposed to lead the 29th Infantry Division ashore to the west of the 1st Division. Some 32 of these were DD Shermans to be launched 6,000 yards from the shore, and 24 were 'dry' Shermans to be beach landed. Eight of the dry Shermans were fitted with dozer blades to help the 146th Combat Engineer Battalion blow holes in the beach defences.[38] The DDs were supposed to 'swim' to the edge of the water by H-5 minutes where they would cover the initial troop landings. But when the 32 DD were launched all but three sank before they reached the beach. Some sank immediately but others were eventually swamped, not just because of the six foot swell that occurred off Omaha without the protection offered at Utah by the Cotentin Peninsular, but also because the strong current and long distance to the beach required the crews to steer the tanks south-west rather than south thus exposing the canvas skirts to the heaviest waves; very few of the crews survived. The three that made it to Easy Green Beach were on LCT 600 where the skipper, Ensign H. P. Sullivan, having witnessed the first of his tanks disappear under the waves, abandoned his orders and drove the LCT straight onto the beach instead.

The LCTs covering the western side of Omaha were under the control of Captain Elder, whose conversation with Lieutenant Rockwell, the flotilla skipper, persuaded him to do likewise. The flotilla, excluding an LCT hit by a mine, landed at 0629 on Dog White and Dog Green sectors under furious attack from the defenders. The first two tanks were immediately hit by German 88mm artillery and this prompted many of the rest to stay deep in the water for protection.[39] Those that did attempt to move inland found themselves unable to cross the shingle.[40]

When the 741st Tank Battalion launched its 32 DD tanks to lead the assaults by the 1st Division to the east on Exit E-1 and Exit E-3 at H-50, allegedly 6,000 yards off-shore, 27 sank while 2 reached the shore under their own propulsion and 3 others were landed directly on the beach after their LCT damaged its unloading ramp. Actually at least two of the DDs must have been launched a lot further out because they were subsequently found nearly *nine* miles (almost 16,000 yards) off-shore.[41] Admiral Ramsay had even warned Admiral Kirk that the 11 to 12 mile launching distance from the beach at Omaha was an unnecessary risk, but Kirk was clearly more worried by the German artillery that could reach ten miles out to sea and sink his ships than he was by the significantly increased risk of swamping to the amphibious vehicles. The problems this left to the 1st and 29th Divisions were, of course, exacerbated by the absence of compensatory armoured forces like the Funnies that led the Anglo-Canadian assaults.[42]

In fact none of the DD-tanks landed exactly when and where they were supposed to on any beach and the post-invasion analysis by the navy suggested that 'ordinary water-proofed tanks, landed on the beach in the normal manner, would have served the purpose equally well. Had the assault been conducted at dusk or in low visibility, on the other hand, DD tanks might have achieved a valuable surprise'.[43] Here, then, was a case where the Wicked approach to a problem failed and a Tame approach might have generated a better result. But out of the water the opposite problem developed – a Tame approach failed when a Wicked one may have proved more successful.

The tanks that were used were regarded as critical to the build up of forces – as well as the initial landing – and it was decided by the American Assault Force to limit their early exposure in the first wave of assault craft to just 15 LSTs (each LST could carry up to 12 tanks limiting the total available to just 180).[44] Ironically, not only did this denude the American assault infantry of vital armoured support – especially in the absence of any other Hobart Funnies – but in the event, the Sherman was to prove no match for the German tanks in any single tank duel, for the German armour was stronger and the German gun more powerful than almost anything the Allies had. In fact, few German tanks appeared on the beaches of Normandy on D-Day but many were involved just behind the beaches and some were involved in the only partially successful counter-attack between Sword and Juno beaches. More importantly, perhaps, the Allies considered the threat of a German armoured counter-attack with days of D-Day to be the most significant threat to the landings. If the Allies could not hold off the Panzers all would be lost. So why, given the superior material resources available to the Western Allies, did they land with so few and such relatively poor tanks? Again, the primary explanation can be traced back to Management, or rather the failure of Management.

11.5 Tanks

Between the wars only the Germans, and to some extent the Russians, had experimented radically with tank design and strategy and quickly recognized that tank design had to be based on a balance between the three critical issues: firepower, mobility and protection. However, like the Russians, the Germans (who had been extremely lax in tank development during the First World War) had decided that the most significant element was the gun. For the British the most significant element was the speed and the protection.[45] The Americans, or at least General Patton, was almost wholly concerned with speed.

The success of the Germans in France in 1940, particularly their Panzer IV, sent shock waves through the Allied armies, especially the still uninvolved Americans who were by far the most reluctant of all major nations to engage in modern tank design or tactics. The existing American tank, the new M2, became obsolete over night and an upgunned M3, the Grant, replaced it with an equivalent 75mm gun. This was the tank which the British ordered in bulk – because almost all their tanks were left in France around Dunkirk. In time the M4 (the Sherman) became the major US medium tank, for all its weaknesses it was available in large numbers (and it provided the base for more variants than any other armoured vehicle) but it was never a match for the best all-round German tank, the Panther, and its larger but earlier stablemate, the Tiger. These were developed in response to the Soviet T-34 which was produced in huge numbers and which outclassed all the Panzers developed up to 1942. More importantly, German success was rooted in tank tactics as well as tank design, for while the Allies deployed their tanks thinly to protect their infantry in long defensive lines, the Germans used their Panzers offensively in large concentrated pockets.

11.5.1 German tank development

German tank (*Panzerkampfwagen* [PzKpfw]) development had continued throughout the interwar period – despite the prohibitions introduced by the Versailles Treaty – thanks to cooperation from the USSR which allowed testing of German 'agricultural tractors' at Kazan between 1926 and 1932. With Hitler's accession to power the secrecy stopped. Given Hitler's aggressive instincts it was probable that German tank design would be built around firepower rather than mobility or protection. However, German tank design mirrored the British division between light, medium and heavy. The Mark I, developed in 1935 was a 5 ton light tank armed with machine guns and the first of 2,000 Panzer Is emerged in 1934. This was followed by the 10 ton Mk II, again armed with machine guns. But Guderian's strategy called for tanks that could knock out enemy tanks and for that a heavier gun was required. This emerged in 1937 with the Panzer IV, complete with a short 75mm gun and then in 1938 in the form of the Panzer IIIs, designed by Daimler Benz, with a 37mm high velocity gun. Both tanks also carried radios – something which Allied tanks omitted until later in the war.[46]

By 1939 the Mk III weighed 15 ton but its final version in 1943 weighed 22 ton, in all 5,650 units were made. The original 37mm gun was gradually replaced by a 50 mm. However, the Panzer IV was designed to accommodate an enhanced gun when it became available – and it did in the form of a 75mm gun just in time for the invasion of France. The latter gun formed the stock weapon of the Mk IV Panzer, designed by Krupp in 1939, and the self-propelled, turretless version, the heavily armoured *Sturmgeschütz* (assault gun). Some 8,500 of the Mk IV were produced by 1945 with the highest monthly production figures (344) – ironically – occurring in June 1944. However, as a consequence of meeting the Soviet T34 in action in July 1941, the Germans sought out a much heavier and better armed tank and the search resulted in two vehicles.

First, was the 56-ton Mk VI, or Tiger, developed by Henschel with an 88mm gun and five anti-personnel S-mine throwers to keep enemy infantry at bay. At 23 mph this was not a quick vehicle but it was heavily armoured and could drive across rivers up to 13 feet in depth, 'breathing' through a snorkel. However it had a limited range of movement (about 40 miles) and was so wide it needed to have its tracks changed in order to fit onto railway wagons. Some 1,354 Tigers were produced and again the maximum monthly production (104) occurred just in time for D-Day, in April 1944. Tigers, though impervious to most Allied tank shells, could be disabled by grenade attacks to the engine compartment and hence they were usually protected by infantry.

The Tiger, armed with a high velocity 88mm gun, could destroy a Sherman at 4,000 yards and it was not uncommon for a single German tank to destroy four or five Allied tanks before being stopped itself.[47] Admittedly, the German tanks were less mechanically robust than the

Allies and usually considerably slower, but since the battleground was not the open steppes of the Soviet Union but the densely farmed, hedged and populated country of Western Europe, the problems of German tank mobility were minimal compared to the problems of Allied tank vulnerability.

The first Allied notification of the existence of the Tiger came in a note on 5 December 1942 and by 11 December 1942 a photograph in the *National Zeitung* had appeared. This was duly distributed throughout the military intelligence and armoured communities. By 30 January 1943 the *Daily Mail* announced the arrival of the 62-ton 'German land-battleship' in Tunisia featuring the 88mm gun and up to seven inches of armour in places (a captured German 88-mm gun was shipped to the US in May 1942). Within the week a secret report on a captured but disabled Tiger in Tunisia suggested that its turret armour – which was only four inches thick – was vulnerable to the 6lb British anti-tank gun at ranges up to 500 yards. The news was carried with glee by the *Daily Telegraph* and the *Daily Mirror* on 5 February, and Brigadier T. Lyon-Smith confirmed that in his opinion a second Tiger had been disabled at 800 yards by a frontal shot from an anti-tank gun. Clearly, the Allies had little to fear from the monster after all. Subsequent analysis of the tank discovered that it had been hit ten times and five of the shots had penetrated the armour. When trial shots were fired at the tank from 300 yards both penetrated through some of the armour but failed to enter the inner chamber and the trial report suggested that, in reality, no frontal attack was likely to succeed. The only real chance was in shooting from the flank against the lesser armoured sides; the 2lb anti-tank gun was only viable from very short range and only against the tracks, and the PIAT (hand-held rocket launcher) was of no use against the Tiger at any range. In effect by March 1943 the Allies knew that the Tiger was immune to their primary anti-tank gun – which was itself superior to the usual armament on Allied tanks – except from the side and at relative short range. It was also suggested that the tank's 88mm gun, or at least the Flak 36 version which is the only one the Allies had tested at this time, could penetrate the typical Sherman's 3–3.5 inch armour of the turret and gun mantle from almost a mile away.[48]

Just how confused the 'truth' about the Tiger was became most clearly manifest when reports began filtering back to London about the despatch of 12 Tigers from 3 Squadron 506th Heavy Tank Battalion whose 16 Tigers were ordered to halt the Allied break out from Anzio towards Rome (which fell almost simultaneously to the D-Day landings). But despite the evidence of several hits to the Tigers – none of which penetrated – the main causes of their defeat had been unreliable tracks and/or unreliable gear boxes. As the Allied report – published in August 1944 – suggested, despite Allied optimism about the vulnerability of Tigers they had simply proved to be unroadworthy in retreat rather than unbattleworthy in defence: in Normandy the latter was more important than the former.[49]

The second German response to the Russian T34 was the 45 ton Mk V, or Panther, developed by MAN with a 75mm high velocity gun and sloping armour like the T34. Not only did sloping armour prove far more difficult to penetrate than vertical armour, but it enabled designers to reduce the weight of armour without sacrificing its defensive capabilities – as long as the shot hit the armour horizontally. Some 4,814 Panthers were built by MAN and Daimler Benz by 1945 and some versions (*Jagdpanther* – tank destroyer) carried the 88mm gun. And as long as the tank was defensively dug in, the thicker armour and, on the Panther, its angular construction, gave greater protection, especially against the lower velocity shells from the Allied tanks: 75 per cent of Allied direct hits failed to penetrate Panther or Tiger tanks and most Panthers and Tigers could continue operating even after one or two penetrating direct hits.[50]

Admittedly the traverse mechanism of the Panther – and for that matter the Tiger – was cumbersome and slow. One Sherman watched by field surgeon Brendan Phibbs managed to fire three 76mm shots into the front glacis plate of a Panther before it fired back – but no shot penetrated, leaving the tanker to scream over the radio net: 'Ping Pong balls, fucking Ping Pong balls' just before the Panther's single shot disabled the Sherman instantly.[51] However, a Panther was destroyed by an M36 tank destroyer with a 90mm gun from 100 yards straight through the same front glacis plate.[52] Even a lone 75mm Sherman could destroy a Panther, but it was a very unusual rather than a common event.[53]

11.5.2 British tank development

British designed tanks were poor compared to their German counterparts though it had led the world in tank design in the early post First World War period. Indeed, a 40-ton Anglo-American heavy tank, the Mk III or Liberty or International Tank, and a flame-thrower tank, were on the drawing boards in good time to lead the planned Allied offensive in 1919.[54] However, with the war's termination the British Treasury, as usual, starved the research and design bodies. In 1936, for example, the Treasury only provided £270,000 towards the design and development of all tracked vehicles, including tanks. The most important tank that was developed, the Vickers Medium Mark 1, was first built in 1923 and still

used as a training tank in 1942. It had what was at that time a high velocity gun, though it was only capable of firing armour piercing shot
intended to destroy enemy tanks. Indeed, the 6lb (57mm) gun used in
the First World War would have provided an adequate platform for inter-
war development – had it not been derived from a navy design and therefore politically unacceptable to the army. Moreover, as with American
doctrine, tanks were regarded by the British High Command as mechanized cavalry, built for speed and mobility, not to attack, or withstand
attacks by, other tanks. As the Secretary of State for War suggested, he
had been forced to make the 'unpalatable' decision to mechanize eight
cavalry regiments – a decision akin to 'asking a great musical performer
to throw away his violin and devote himself to the gramophone'.[55] The
gramophone that then existed in the form of the British Army's tank
strength was probably better described as a pin and a broken shell: of the
375 tanks in existence, only 71 were not officially classed as *already* obsolete.[56] Thus by 1939 the Germans had trained 187,000 tank and truck
drivers while the British only had 550 *tanks* and had to borrow 14,000
civilian vehicles to transport the BEF to France.[57]

The regimental traditions of the British army also inhibited the kind of
co-operation achieved by integrated tank and anti-tank artillery in
German armoured divisions, though the regimental blockage was itself
marginal compared to the simple inadequacy of combined arms training.[58] In effect, the tank, artillery and infantry units by tradition operated independently of each other, thus undermining what chance there
was of transcending superior German armoured units. General Archibald
Wavell confirmed this in his note to General Auchinleck in June 1942
after Tobruk had fallen:

> Inferiority of material probably [was the] primary cause of defeat of our armour
> but inferiority of training and leadership also likely to have been responsible. We
> never get TIME to catch up and our leaders are mostly untrained by German stan-
> dards and most of them have yet to grasp fully the principles of co-operation of all
> arms on the battle field and of concentration of forces though we have done all
> we can to impress these on them.[59]

Not only were there markedly fewer British than German tanks, the
former were also radically under-gunned. The British tank at the time
used a 2lb (40mm) gun designed in the 1930s when tank armour was
relatively thin, but once tank armour improved the gun was obsolete.
Even the replacement 6lb (57mm) was of limited value because most
British tank turrets could not be re-engineered to cope with the increased
recoil. Initially this did not necessarily matter for most 1940 German

tanks were equally poorly armoured and gunned. Indeed the French Somua S 35 – despite overburdening the commander with gunnery responsibility – and British Matilda – despite its poor gun and slow speed – were equal to the Panzer I, II and III in their 1940 format. But the German Panzer Mk IV quickly adopted a short barrelled low velocity 75mm gun, and by the time the British had up-gunned to the 6lb (57mm) gun in 1942 the Germans were already using long-barrelled 75mm guns with much higher velocity. Even the Report by the Select Committee on National Expenditure on 26 August 1942 recognized the error:

> The decision to go into large scale production of 6-pdr guns ought to have been balanced by a plan so timed as to produce tanks to carry the guns when they were ready ... The story of tanks and six-pounder guns seems to show lack of decisive direction, division of responsibilities as between tanks and guns, and failures to consult manufacturers until a late stage in the work on the design have led to failure to make full use of manufacturing resources.[60]

In short, a failure of Management led to a failing tank. Seventeen months later the same committee bewailed 'the avoidable waste of time, money and material resources ... the British manufacturing effort of 1943 has fallen short of realizing expectations or being fully effective ... British tanks issued to British troops have gained a bad reputation both for mechanical reliability and fighting arrangements'.[61]

Leslie Hore-Belisha, the new Secretary of State for War, did at least make some moves in a constructive direction by forming the Royal Armoured Corps, and by the end of the war the number of AFVs (Armoured Fighting Vehicles) had grown tremendously to 31,927 (9,994 armoured cars; 21,933 tanks) – and that was excluding the loss of 17,801 AFVs (1,957 armoured cars and 15,844 tanks). Of course many of the tanks were American in origin (Of a total of 37,777 tanks, 24,670 (65 per cent) were American built) though there were some British designs.[62]

Even if the tanks had been effective the Dunkirk debacle effectively put British armour back by years: 700 tanks and 850 anti-tank guns were lost in Belgium and France in 1940 as were 63,000 other vehicles.[63] Such was the desperate haste to re-equip in late 1940 and 1941 in the face of a possible invasion that all thoughts of a new or improved design were rapidly abandoned and the largest possible quantities of the existing models took priority over anything qualitatively better. Thus the British Army were persuaded to re-equip with what was most quickly available, rather than what was preferable. That meant using 2lb guns even though the 6lb gun was ready for production, simply because the 2lb guns could

Photo 11.3 Churchill Tank

be produced more quickly.[64] And even though the 2lb armament was totally inadequate, the 6lb gun replacement still had no high explosive munitions for use against infantry. As Graham concludes, 'British tank deficiencies were the result of pre-war neglect followed by post-wartime haste'.[65]

A subsequent light tank, the Mk III Valentine, was rather better received than the Matilda, and altogether over 8,000 were made, but it was still regarded as far too slow. In turn this was replaced by the heavily armoured Churchill with various forms of armament and over 5,500 of these were built by the end of the war, primarily by Vauxhall motors.

The main British medium or cruiser tank, the Covenanter, and later the Crusader, provided the equivalent of the heavy cavalry, which would have been fine had the Germans been working on the same pre First World War tactical principles, but they were not and the Covenanter was designed in the maximum speed with the minimum care. As a result over 1,800 Covenanter tanks were built but none entered service because of their notorious unreliability. Its replacement, the Crusader, was also regarded as mechanically unreliable and insufficiently armoured. Despite all these problems, Oliver Lyttelton, the British Minister of Production, was sure that by September 1942 'British weapons were now better than those of the enemy ... . Defects in our tanks had been cured'. Indeed, the War Minister, Sir John Griggs argued that the new Churchill was 'the best in the world'.[66] It was this kind of unwarranted optimism that led to the destruction of so many tanks and tankers in Normandy. As

Gudgin summarizes British tank development, it was 'too little, too late'.[67] Just how little can be assessed by comparing the 1939 with the 1942 tank production figures in Britain. In the former only 969 tanks were made, by the latter 8,600 were produced, and even that was significantly insufficient.[68]

By Christmas 1941, Churchill had already reached the same conclusion, admitting that: 'I am not sure that speed is the supreme requirement of tanks, certainly not of all tanks. Armour and gun power decide the matter whenever tank meets tank'.[69] However, the new tank coming off the assembly lines in Britain at that time was the Churchill – which was already approaching obsolescence in the face of rapid German advances in gun power and armour. A vote of censure was demanded by some in the House of Commons and Churchill went ahead with the Dieppe raid, in part to test the new armour available: all three flame-throwing tanks were captured and all 28 Churchill tanks were either destroyed or captured. In September 1942 the Select Committee on National Expenditure produced a damning report of the tank and gun design and utility and Churchill admitted that the report was 'a masterly indictment which reflects on all who have been concerned at the War Office and the Ministry of Supply. It also reflects upon me as head of the government and upon the whole organization ... the committee have certainly rendered a high service in bringing this tangle of inefficiency and incompetence to my notice'.[70]

Yet the British did have a gun capable of taking on the German tanks, and it was ready by June 1941, this was the 17lb anti-tank gun. British tank design was undertaken at Chobham, separately from gun design which took place at Woolwich, and far more emphasis was placed on designing the tank than designing the gun. However, a technical report in November 1942, allegedly signed by Montgomery, had suggested that the already fitted 75-mm gun was 'all we require' so the 17lb gun was initially consigned to the artillery.[71] However, on Christmas day, 1942, Churchill called for the then secret 17-pound gun to be adopted as soon as possible.[72] It was ironic, then, that by August 1943 Montgomery noted in a report to the Vice Chief of the Imperial General Staff in London: 'It is gun power that counts in battle ... We must produce a tank with a gun as primary armament which is superior to the present 88mm of the enemy.[73] This was to be the Firefly.

The Firefly had been developed from the experiments of Major George Brighty, who had insisted – contrary to almost everyone else – that the Sherman's 75mm gun was (a) inadequate and (b) could be replaced by the British 17lb anti-tank gun, even though the Sherman's turret was objectively too small to cope with the assumed recoil action of

Photo 11.4 Sherman Firefly Tank

the latter gun. By re-engineering the turret and moving the tank radio into a new external compartment, the large gun was fitted into a Sherman M41AC from late 1943 but there simply were not enough of them available by D-Day.[74]

However, three problems remained: first, the tank was still poorly armoured compared to the Panthers and Tigers it would have to face. Second, because of the long barrel, the Firefly could not operate as an amphibious tank – the barrel poked through the canvas screen thus losing all buoyancy. Third, although the Firefly could, in theory, outgun even the best German tanks when it fired Sabot ammunition, these were armour-piercing shells and, while effective against other tanks, this limited their use in infantry support operations.[75]

Montgomery must shoulder a considerable portion of the blame for the British landing on D-Day with the American Sherman which was under-gunned and under-armoured. Yet, Montgomery (who had complained bitterly about the state of weapons in 1940)[76] was positively glowing in his fulsome praise for British tanks only two months after D-Day:

> We have had no difficulty in dealing with German armour once we have grasped the problem. In this connection British armour has played a notable part. We have nothing to fear from the Panther and Tiger tanks; they are unreliable mechanically and the Panther is very vulnerable from the flanks, our 17-pdr gun will go right through them. Provided our tactics are good we can defeat them without difficulty.[77]

Photo 11.5 Sherman M4 Tank

Unfortunately, Montgomery forgot to inform the Germans who were often mystified as to why the greatest industrial powers on earth should attempt an invasion with such a poor tank as the American M4 Sherman.

11.5.3 American tank development

Given the superiority of many Allied weapons and technologies, especially in aircraft and radar, it seems surprising that tank technologies were woefully inadequate. Certainly, Patton, the doyen of American tank warfare, suggested that it wasn't the tank that won the war but the artillery.[78] And Blandford suggests that the artillery, the 'queen of the battlefield', broke up every single German counter-attack on D-Day.[79] Graham suggests that a long learning curve was necessary for the Allies, and especially the British, to realize where their relative strengths lay: 'We only won our battles when we learned to concentrate our forces and do what we did best, which was bury our opponent under tons of high explosive'.[80] But, as I have suggested above, the culture and the Leadership of the British military establishment were the real problems. On the American side, too, Patton's diminution of the role of the tank should be seen for what it was – an attempt to obfuscate his own role in emasculating American tank design.

If British tank development was poor, on the American side, things, if anything, were worse. The only American tank of the First World War was the Ford Three-ton Tank, based on the chassis of a Model T and using two of its engines, it carried a single Browning machine gun and

15,000 were ordered – but only 15 produced before the end of the war. With the Tank Corps officially disbanded in 1920 and only a small Tank Board in existence after 1922, US tank development between the wars was negligible. This was made worse by a War Department policy of restricting tank development to a maximum weight of 15 tons which meant that all development of light tanks had to go under the name of 'combat cars'. This basically resulted in the US being the least advanced in tank design and development of all major nations by 1939.

Indeed, not until the 1940 Blitzkriegs did Congress relent and start supporting the development of tanks. In 1940 only 330 tanks were built, but this increased to 4,052 in 1941, to 24,997 in 1942 (more than the entire German tank production between 1939 and 1945), and to 29,487 in 1943. In total the US produced 88,276 tanks and 3,816 self-propelled anti-tank guns.[81]

US tank doctrine was rooted in the assumption that tanks should not engage in tank destruction but operate like mechanized cavalry, bursting through enemy lines to disrupt their logistical supply and generating the kind of shock to the enemy's will to continue which the German *blitzkrieg* seems to have brought about. In contrast, it was the job of the massed *tank-destroyers* to destroy tanks, hence tanks did not need heavy armour or armament; speed and mobility were their essential requirements.

US tank design was notoriously different from all others: it produced very tall tanks which were thinly armoured, weakly gunned but were also quick, relatively reliable and mechanically robust – in other words mechanical horses. In 1939 the annual research and development budget for tank development was just $85,000.[82] But it wasn't just parsimony that hindered the US tank, it was cultural conservatism.

A revolutionary suspension system had been developed by J. Walter Christie that provided for large vertical wheel movements and thus a more flexible and a faster ride than anything the US had. It also facilitated a wider track to distribute the weight better, but after producing a small number of experimental versions in 1931 and 1932, the Ordnance Department rejected the original design and replaced with a variant known as the T3 (T for Test model). Christie subsequently sold two M1931s to the Soviet Union who copied the suspension directly for the T34 and scrapped everything else. The T34 was the tank that shocked the Germans in 1941 and persuaded them to launch the Panther and the Tiger in response.[83]

The Polish war had demonstrated to Guderian, the German tank expert, that none of the four light tank divisions (armed only with machine guns) had been successful and therefore heavier tanks and up-gunning was essential for any further invasions.[84] The results were evident in France but despite the role of the Panzer Mk IVs with their 75mm guns, a deal was signed between Knudsen (ex-General Motors), the head of US military production, and Keller, head of Chrysler, for 1,000 M2A1s – a marginally improved variant of the already obsolete M2s; fortunately Chaffee cancelled the order with almost his first decision. Chaffee replaced the order with one for 1,000 M3s (called the Grant in the USA and the Lee in Britain), an up-gunned variant of the M2A1, now carrying a 75mm gun. But the only comparison between the US and German 75mm was the calibre, for the American version was a low velocity gun based originally on the 1897 French field gun and its penetrative power was limited. Nevertheless, over 6,000 M3s were built between 1941 and 1942.

Chaffee recognized the M3 was only a stop-gap vehicle and he simultaneously ordered the design for what was to become the M4, the Sherman. But so much design work was required to turn the M3 into an acceptable tank that designing the M4 did not formally begin until April 1941. Given the obvious necessity to develop the M4 at speed, as many elements of the M3 as possible were incorporated into the design and that limited the possibility of up-gunning the vehicle easily because the turret ring remained basically the same size. But by May 1941 a wooden mock-up had been built, by September 1941 it was in prototype form, and by July M4 production began delivering the first of 40,000 finished vehicles.[85]

The M4 also provided the gun carriage for many variants of vehicles, from flame throwers (not used until July 1944 on Guam) and mine-clearers to the M10 Gun Motor Carriage or Tank Destroyer, or the M36 90mm up-gunned variety, the Wolverine. However, the tank destroyer also symbolized the confusion on the part of the US as to the role of tanks, for it set in aspic the assumption that the main effort should be spent on developing the Sherman and this was never designed to engage enemy tanks.[86]

Production facilities were certainly not the problem for Detroit could – and did – churn out tanks faster than the *Wehrmacht* could destroy them. Altogether the US produced 88,000 tanks during the war, the British produced around 30,000, and the Soviet Union about 105,000, as against the German production total of 62,000.[87] So the Tame Problem of production had indeed been resolved by the Allies. Nor was the inability to make and execute quick decisions the problem: the conversion of ordinary Sherman tanks to their amphibious DD format was ordered and organized by the British in July 1943. Yet by January1944 British factories had converted so few that Hobart arranged a demonstration of their abilities to Eisenhower. On 27 January 1944 Eisenhower watched the demonstration and the following day an engineer left with the drawings for the USA. Within a week US factories were converting their own Shermans as they came off the production tracks, and within two months 300 DD Shermans were completed.[88] The failure was more one of politics, imagination and Leadership.

It is a commonplace to assume that, irrespective of the cultural predilections of the US military and its search for a mechanical horse rather than a tank-buster, the Sherman led the invasion on D-Day because it was the only tank available at the time. Thus, although the M26 Pershing proved to be a superior tank and the only Western Allied tank capable of taking on the Panther and Tiger with equanimity, its design came too late. This, as I shall suggest, is simply wrong. The Sherman was chosen for political and cultural reasons at a time when the Pershing was already available and could have been produced in large numbers to lead the Normandy invasion. It was not an inevitability, then, that the D-Day troops landed with inadequate armoured leadership in the form of tanks, it was the direct result of Leadership decisions.

Forty certainly suggests that the Shermans were designed to cope with conditions that would involve crossing 'innumerable rivers on temporary bridges because the original ones would be destroyed. Thus their tanks could not be too heavy'.[89] Moreover, he continues, the US used tanks in long range penetrations of enemy lines to destroy their lines of supply, for which speed and mechanical reliability were more important than strength and shooting power.[90] But this smacks of rationalization for the Sherman was designed when there was little in US strategic planning to suggest that they were ever designed for Western Europe after bridge destruction. Anyway, even if this were the case, one wonders why the Germans never realized the utility of such lightweight tanks, and why the US eventually decided to put the heavy M26 Pershing into production towards the end of the war and managed – by the remarkably simple process of lashing large pontoons together – to get even the heaviest Allied tank across water.[91]

Since the M4 Sherman was specifically designed *not* to fight enemy tanks it had just 75 mm of armour plating, and usually had a low velocity 75-mm gun that could not penetrate the frontal armour of a German Tiger tank at all. Nevertheless, because the Sherman was designed to race through enemy lines it was fitted with a gyro-stabilizer enabling the gun to be fired accurately whilst on the move – something no German tank could do. But being able to hit targets on the move was irrelevant if either the target wasn't moving or the rounds simply bounced off – as most rounds from the Sherman's 75mm gun did. It was not, unfortunately, the same the other way round.

Albert Speer's claim that one Tiger II was the equivalent of 25–30 Shermans was undoubtedly exaggerated, but there were many US tankers who estimated that a Tiger was equivalent of around 8 Shermans, while a Panther was the equivalent of 4 Shermans. Or, as one German tanker remarked: 'Why does the country of Detroit send their men out to die in these things?'[92] As Lawrence Butler remembered sceptically: 'We won the war by losing more tanks and cluttering up the battlefield'.[93]

The Germans referred to the Shermans as 'Tommy-cookers' and not to be outdone, the cynical Allies went one better, calling them 'Ronson Burners' after the contemporary advert suggesting that a Ronson cigarette lighter always 'lit first time'.[94] Research prior to the invasion confirmed what many Allied tankers already knew from their colleagues in North Africa: 60 per cent of Allied tank losses were caused by a single shot from a high velocity 75-mm or 88-mm enemy gun and 66 per cent of all Allied tanks hit 'brewed up' when hit. The consequential metal slivers both killed and injured the occupants and these set the tank alight either by igniting the 50–90 rounds of stored ammunition or severing fuel and electrical cables and igniting up to 200 gallons of fuel. In fact, it was more often the stored ammunition that started the fire rather than the fuel. When armour piercing 'solid shot' penetrated a tank from long range it often partially disintegrated showering the unfortunate occupants with red-hot metal slivers that ricocheted around the compartment. The results could be horrific, as Major John Leytham, 82nd RE Assault Squadron discovered when recovering a disabled Sherman in France:

> Once an armoured piercing shell enters the turret of a tank, it acts in a manner similar to a domestic incinerator. The occupants of the turret are quickly smeared around the walls of the turret. I had given orders after the recovery that none of my men should look inside. A number were foolish enough to disobey my orders. It did not improve morale. Vehicles like this should be taken back to the rear workshops where the experts spray the inside with creosote. After a suitable interval they scrape off the remains from the walls of the turret.[95]

From very close distance a solid shot might go right through the tank without injuring anyone, though it would often disable the tank if it hit important devices on its passage.[96] Of course, if a shot hit the engine or fuel tanks there was almost inevitably a fire and the heat was so intense that it would often anneal the armour, making the tank irreparable. Yet even though Allied armour piercing shot could not penetrate a Panther or Tiger from the front, American gunners were often taught to use high explosive shells simply to kill any German infantry that supported the tank.[97]

The main offensive problem for the Sherman's original 75mm gun was not so much its size as the muzzle velocity. At 2,050 feet per second the Sherman's muzzle velocity was greater than the original short barrelled Panzer Mk IV's 1,500 feet per second but nowhere near the replacement long barrelled Panzer Mk IV's 3,000 feet per second. Even the up-gunned Sherman, the M4A1 with a 76mm gun, still only had a muzzle velocity of 2,650 feet per second. Between 10–15 per cent of the Shermans on D-Day were M4A1s and almost all replacements after D-Day were of this up-gunned variety though many US commanders at all levels remained sceptical of the new gun and focused upon its marginally poorer High Explosive shell rather than its much better armour piercing shell.[98]

But why did the US insist on developing such a low velocity gun? The answer seems to be that the artillery demanded a gun that would equate with *their* needs – that is a gun capable of firing at least 5,000 rounds before being replaced. There was a parallel dispute over the barrel performance of the artillery's own 105mm howitzers which had begun to fire erratically after just 3 months in service. These barrels were supposed to fire at least 7,500 rounds before being replaced – but that was at a rate of no more than 4 rounds a minute at any time. In fact the guns were firing 10 rounds a minute and the consequent overheating was distorting the rifling of the barrel.[99] Thus the Sherman 75mm barrel was designed to fire like an artillery piece – even though the life span of a Sherman was markedly shorter than an artillery piece and the chances of any tank firing 5,000 rounds without getting hit were negligible, especially when, overall, a new tank could look forward to surviving – on average – no more than 7 days of combat.[100] That would mean a Sherman would need to fire its gun every two minutes continuously for all 189 hours just to warrant a new barrel! In effect, the Sherman's gun velocity was sacrificed to long term reliability; the tank seemed to have been designed by a committee composed of cavalry officers and artillery officers instead of tankers. Small wonder that the US 3rd Armoured Division lost 1,340 Shermans in Europe between D-Day and the end of the war – a total loss of 580 per cent of the original number landed in Normandy.[101]

The superior muzzle velocity of the Panzer Mk IVs, Panthers (Panzer Mk V) and Tigers (Panzer Mk VI), should also be viewed in conjunction with their better angled and thicker armour. The Mk IV had four inches of armour behind the vertical plate of the tank's glacis, the Panther had 3½ inches on a 38 degree glacis. Only on top of the turret and from the rear were German tanks really vulnerable to Allied attacks – especially from Allied 105mm howitzers.[102] In contrast, the Sherman has just 2½

inches of armour on a 45 degree glacis, 2 inches on the side of the hull
and between three and five inches on the turret and the gun mantle. This
was adequate to protect the crew against small arms fire but not much
else. Ironically, an Anglo-American meeting on 20 March 1942 had
discussed the need for a heavily armoured variant of the Sherman and the
decision to go ahead with it was taken in May 1942. But it was not until
June 1944, *after* D-Day, that the first of the 254 M4A3E2s arrived,
complete with improved engine and suspension, in addition to the
thicker and better angled armour (100mm at 60 degrees in front of the
driver).[103] At 47 tons the Assault Sherman proved to be difficult to maintain and unreliable – but then it should only have been employed for D-
Day assault itself so neither of these problems was cause not to employ it
in the invasion. An alternative would have been the M4A35 which was
more heavily armoured than the M4 but not as unwieldy as the
M4A3E2. In the event these were available in May 1944 but again they
were not delivered until the autumn of 1944.[104]

Although the M4 Sherman weighed 37½ tons (15½ tons more than
the Panzer Mk IV) it was massively outweighed by the Panther at 52 tons
and the Tiger at 56 tons. But although the Panther was heavier it was not
less mobile because its wider tracks distributed the weight better. The
Sherman produced about 7 lbs. per square inch on the ground – about
twice that of the German tanks and hence decreasing the relative
manoeuvrability of the Sherman in soft ground. When the 3rd (US)
Armoured Division took part in the assault on the Siegfried line in
November 1944 the mud literally stopped the Shermans in their tracks.
As a result, within 26 minutes of the assault beginning, 48 of the original 64 Shermans had been hit – though 40 of these were subsequently
recovered and 35 refitted.[105]

On the other hand, the tracks of the German tanks were made of steel
and rapidly wore out on road surfaces – hence their need to be transported by rail wherever possible – while the Shermans used rubber cover-
ings that could be reversed after wearing out thus providing for much
greater wear. For example, a set of Sherman tracks would last around
2,500 miles while a set of German tracks lasted about 500 miles.[106]

But if the Sherman failed to live up to its design specifications for a
highly mobile tank its legendary reliability was also questionable.
However reliable the Sherman may have been, to have travelled the
1,460 miles from Normandy almost to Berlin required over 10,000 of
the 17,000 troops in the division to be engaged directly (as mechanics)
or indirectly (as tank crew responsible for tank performance) on maintenance and it was this huge support system that enabled such a poor tank
to cope with everything that the weather, the ground and the Germans

could throw at it. For example, Cooper calculates that an armoured division involving perhaps 1,200 vehicles, half of which were tanks or other combat vehicles, would experience as many as 200 breakdowns for every 60 miles travelled in an unopposed night march.[107] Thus, while breakdowns among all tanks on both sides were common, the difference was that the Allies had a far more sophisticated system for recovery and repair than did their enemy. The consequence was a long 'service tail' and Mitchell suggests that for every one soldier actually fighting at the front, 12 more were 'servicing' that soldier behind the lines.[108] But the 'tail' of the Allied, and especially the American, forces was not simply composed of non-combatants back in the stores but a critical factor in Allied armoured success.

The Pershing was the American equivalent of the German Panther: it weighed 47½ tons, it had 4 inches of armour on its 45 degree glacis plate, with six inches on the turret and a five inch gun mantle. It mounted a 90mm gun with a muzzle velocity of 2,850 feet per second, it rode on Christy suspension, and, with its consequently wider tracks and bigger engine than the Sherman, it was both faster and more manoeuvrable than it. In short, the Pershing was the solution to the Panther problem. So why did the Sherman survive?

When the belated development of the M26 Pershing heavy tank took place it was all but too late but it need not have been so. Major General George A. Lynch, the Chief of infantry in 1940, had proposed the establishment of heavier and more powerful tanks and suggested that tank-destroyers lacked the mobility necessary to fight against mobile enemy armour but he had been overruled by McNair, Chief of Staff of General Head Quarters who amongst other things, considered the provision of mass tank-destroyers a cheaper, as well as a more effective, solution to the problem of German armour.

But despite opposition an M26 prototype was available in December 1941, just three months after the Sherman prototype was developed. In the beginning it appeared that the heavier tank would displace its lighter counterpart because an initial order of 5,000 M26s (250 a month) was quickly placed after the prototype was assessed. However, this order was radically reduced to a total of just 115 in September 1942, and further reduced to just 40 in December 1942 after an unfavourable review by the Armoured Force Board (AFB). In the event 40 Pershings were built from this initial order, all by Baldwin Locomotive, but these only appeared because General Barnes, supported by the Ordnance Board but in the teeth of opposition from the AFB, demanded them. Only in 1943 was production actually started and another possible order for 500 was quashed after the Armoured Force Board demanded that Shermans be fitted with the available 90mm guns while the Commander of the Army Ground Forces demanded a block on such a development since it would 'encourage tank units to stalk enemy tanks' – a job best left, according to doctrine, to the tank destroyers. As General McNair (the arch-proponent of tank-destroyers) wrote to Marshall in November 1943 to decry the utility of the alternative T26 Pershing tank that was a match for the Panthers and Tigers: 'There can be no basis for the T26 tank other than the conception of a tank versus tank duel – which is believed unsound and unnecessary. The primary mission of tanks is the destruction of those hostile elements which are vulnerable to them – not anti-tank guns'.[109] So while the Germans – in response to the attacks by the well armoured and gunned Soviet tank, the T34 – began building even better armoured and gunned tanks, such as the Panther and the Tiger, the American designers divided their resources between new tank-destroyers to break up German Panzer formations, and tanks to exploit the apparent gaps that the tank destroyers would create. Here is an interesting case for the Tame/Wicked division. The decision to continue with the Sherman certainly smacks of a Tame approach because the Pershing was, for the US army, a total break with traditional doctrine and thus fits neatly within the Wicked criteria.

The final chance to provide a viable tank to lead the D-Day invasion occurred in January 1944 at a demonstration held on Tidworth Down for all the Allied commanders to evaluate their weaponry. After the small arms and artillery was demonstrated the Sherman was shown, followed by a film of the M26, the Pershing. No working model of this tank existed in the UK at the time but the American ordnance and armoured forces board had tested and approved it and the main production site, the Tank Automotive Centre in Detroit, was ready to go into immediate production and its production schedules implied that it would be ready for D-Day. At the demonstration the most senior armoured commander was General Patton. Despite opposition, particularly from the American General Rose, who wanted the Pershing to replace the Sherman, Patton's view prevailed and the production of the Pershing was subordinated to the Sherman. As Cooper concludes: 'This turned out to be one of the most disastrous decisions of World War II'.[110] In effect Patton's Tame conception of the tank as (lightly) armoured cavalry – with an emphasis on speed – stymied the possibility of considering the tank as a new mode of warfare.

Nonetheless, as soon as the Shermans landed in Normandy the vociferous complaints of the tankers and the field commanders rose to challenge Patton's support for the Sherman. After just five miles into Normandy the 3rd Armoured Division lost 87 Shermans and requested that Washington reverse its decision to place Sherman construction ahead of Pershing. Even the AFB who had fought so hard to ensure the Sherman prevailed over the Pershing subsequently complained to the Ordnance Department – ironically the only institutional supporter of the Pershing – that the army was having 'to close to short ranges in order to destroy opposing tanks. The destruction of the enemy has been accomplished at great cost in tank materiel and personnel and is reflected in the current critical shortage of tanks'.[111]

At last, but after D-Day in June 1944, an order for Pershings was finally placed, but even then it was delayed until December 1944 by an attempt by the Army Ground Forces to change the gun back from a 90mm to a 76mm weapon. The other concern with the Pershing was that the AFB wanted to ensure that no weapon system entered service until it had been thoroughly tried and tested. In fact several weapon systems entered combat in precisely this format but the AFB was assiduous in demanding a delay to the T26 while all its technical problems were resolved. In contrast both the Panther and the Tiger entered service in experimental formats and still managed to inflict severe damage on the Soviet Red Army. The Soviet's T-34 was admittedly built extremely quickly and had a poor finish – but then it was not expected to last more than 14 hours. The Sherman was tested to a 40-hour reliability minimum – though again many did not last that long.[112]

Once the US Army had demonstrated the weakness of the Sherman in a test in early July 1944, Eisenhower reacted quickly to solve the problem, but by then beefing up the Pershing order would take a further four months, until November 1944, to roll off the production line. But this is to ignore the test in January 1944 which had already shown what the Pershing could do, and it could have been ready for D-Day (over five months away) – if Patton had not decided against it and in favour of the Sherman. Small wonder, then, that Patton's response to Eisenhower's request for reports about the Sherman was that it was perfectly adequate for the job, especially given its speed and mobility.[113]

Of course, the *bocage* of Normandy undermined the significance of mobility and enhanced the importance of (German) armour and gun power, but even as the battle moved to the Roer plain in November 1944, the mud proved impassable to the Shermans because, despite being lighter than their German opponents, the narrow tracks of the Sherman converted the smaller weight into a greater pressure through the tracks. But it still took two further events to push the US authorities into mobilizing all their resources for the production of Pershings. The first event was the Germans breakthrough in the Ardennes, which began reducing the Shermans to shreds in huge numbers and at this point the

US General Staff intervened and demanded immediate production at the original specification. The second and related event was the media coverage of the Sherman, for complaints about it grew to a crescendo during the battle of the Bulge in the winter of 1944–5 when, for probably the first time, Allied armour faced mass German armour – and suffered considerably.

The first 20 Pershings arrived shortly after the Battle of the Bulge was over, in February 1945, and they were divided equally between the US 2nd and 3rd Armoured Divisions. In an early engagement on 26 February one M26 destroyed two Tigers at 1,000 yards; admittedly these were flanking shots and the M26 90mm gun was the same as that used by the M36 tank destroyer but, nevertheless, it was a remarkable achievement for an Allied tank.[114] It was also cause for a media celebration as *Washington Post*, noted in its 22 March 1945 edition:

> A Bronx Cheer comes out of Germany to greet the news that the Pershing tank has gone into mass production. It is the opinion of the men at the front, apparently, that they will get the new tank in numbers when it is no longer needed, i.e. when the war is over ... an investigation is thoroughly in order. It should take up the reasons for the long delay in getting the Pershing in production. It should likewise find out why our tanks are inferior to the enemy's.[115]

Expecting something like this, in early March 1945, Marshall asked Eisenhower for his views on the Sherman, given the increasingly bad publicity it was having at home – including a vociferous campaign for a congressional enquiry. Eisenhower replied that, of course, the Sherman could not outgun the Panther in a 'slugging match' but it could succeed by using 'tactics' – that is outflanking the Panthers. But his next response is more important, for he stated that 'with the imminent addition of the more powerful M26 (Pershing) tank to the Army's arsenal, it would soon be superior in every way'.[116] Eisenhower then queried Major-General Rose (US 3rd Armoured Division) and Brigadier-General White (US 2nd Armoured Division) about the Sherman. Their collective reply was that, wherever possible, they used artillery and aircraft to destroy Panthers, not Shermans, though Eisenhower suggested that most of their concerns were restricted to the rare occasion – in his estimation – when a Sherman met a Tiger or Panther head on. He even went on to suggest that, with hindsight, things could have been handled differently but the Sherman had been the only available tank in 1944 and early 1945. This, as I have already suggested, was simply not true, but for Eisenhower the point was that the weakness of the Sherman was not a problem until the American press made it a problem. Moreover, Eisenhower had admitted to Marshall on 21 February 1943 that 'we are still too weak in AT [anti-tank] and AA [Anti-Aircraft], and we still don't yet know exactly how to handle the Mk VI tank [Tiger]'.[117] But within two months Eisenhower saw for himself three Tigers destroyed by the British in North Africa. He did not establish what kind of weapon had destroyed them, though it was very unlikely to have been another tank and much more likely to have been an artillery shell. Thus the 'problem' of the Tiger was apparently resolved because Allied tanks did not need to be up-gunned or armoured if the artillery could take care of them. That was fine if the troops were defending against an attacking Tiger with anti-tank guns in position, but it was not much comfort to attacking infantry or tankers facing dug-in Tigers and Panthers.

Thus the viability of the official US doctrine on tank warfare *may* have been appropriate for a war of manoeuvre where the speed and apparent reliability of the Sherman would simply outpace the ability of the German armour to retreat and regroup in strength. However, two points are worth considering here. First, the top speed of the Sherman was 26mph; the Panther could move at 35 mph and even the Tiger could manage 23mph.[118] Given that the mechanical reliability of the German tanks was unknown at this time, it seems foolhardy at the very least to assume that the Sherman could simply outpace its opposition so that heavy armour and guns were unnecessary. Second, the critical issue here was that D-Day itself was not a war of manoeuvre – at least not on Omaha Beach and not subsequently in the Normandy *bocage*. There it was a war of attrition in which armoured firepower was crucial – and crucially missing from the Allied forces. In the absence of many of Hobart's Funnies, and totally reliant on Shermans that were vulnerable to German firepower, and knowing that the beach was heavily defended and that traditionally the Germans did not retreat, it should have been clear that there was never going to be an immediate breakthrough by highly mobile tanks – unless all or most of the defences and defenders were neutralized by heavily armoured and gunned tanks. Furthermore, even a breakthrough from the beach was a breakthrough into the *bocage* – the kind of territory that 'highly mobile' tanks were virtually irrele-vant. Indeed, the *bocage* countryside of Normandy was almost exactly designed to provide advantage to whichever side operated the best protected and best gunned vehicles, and to significantly disadvantage any vehicle that sacrificed these elements of tank design in favour of speed and reliability.[119]

This is not a question of using hindsight – it is a question of evaluat-ing the limits of the official tank doctrine. That doctrine was flawed under the best of circumstances – as opponents of Patton, especially General Rose, voiced at the time of the decision to produce Shermans rather than Pershings. But in the initial phase of the assault there was never any possibility of deploying the official doctrine – how could tanks not engage other tanks – or worse, gun emplacements? Without the extra armour provided by Hobart's Funnies on the Anglo-Canadian beaches they too would have suffered much higher casualties. And had the Utah forces landed on the correct beach, and not fortuitously against the weakest part of the entire beach, casualties there would have been much higher too. In sum, the doctrine was flawed and the assault phase was tragically inadequate to the task. However, the one thing where the US had a significant advantage over the Germans was in its production capacity – providing it could produce tanks more quickly than the Germans could destroy them. In short, the Tame response to the problem did eventually manage to overcome the problem but at considerably higher cost than necessary. Anyway, should not the weaknesses of the Allied tanks on D-Day and in the first stage of the invasion in Normandy have been more than compensated for by their grossly superior naval gunfire and air bombardment support?

11.6 Naval gunfire and air bombardment

In theory the significance of competing tank and gun performances should have been of marginal significance because the naval and air bombardment was to have been so great that few, if any, of the defenders would be either alive or sufficiently conscious to have fired upon the attackers. This theory bore a remarkable resemblance to the theories developed by General Haig as to the guaranteed success of his offensives in the First World War and was probably about as realistic. Yet, ironically, the planners for D-Day assumed a casualty rate that implied the initial bombardment would not succeed in silencing the defenders of the Atlantic Wall.

At 0520 that aerial bombardment began, and at 0535 the German coastal batteries began firing upon the shipping – much to the relief of the warships who were forced to hold their fire until 0550 unless fired on to avoid hitting the aircraft. In fact at least two Allied aircraft were shot down by 'friendly fire' from the warships. Some of the shells from the largest ships were enormous. HMS Rodney, for example, had nine 16-inch guns firing and prompted one of Howard's soldiers at Pegasus Bridge to exclaim: 'Blimey, sir, they're firing jeeps'.[120] Jeeps they may have been and accurate they often were, but even the enormous naval guns generally failed to destroy many of the German casements, so strong were the protective encasements of steel and concrete. As

Ambrose concludes: 'From the point of view of the soldiers going ashore, the great naval bombardment was as ineffective as the great air bombardment'.[121] Dieter Hartmann-Schultze was an anti-tank gunner with the German 711th Infantry Division on Sword Beach and found himself bombarded for an hour by the armada of naval ships off the cost at first light. When the bombardment finished he emerged from his shelter and 'found to our amazement that only one gun had been damaged, even though a huge number of shells and bombs from planes had fallen about us'.[122] Hans Ulrich Hanter, of the neighbouring 716th Infantry Division also emerged to find that 'although some positions were destroyed, many remained virtually undamaged, strangely enough.[123] This was hardly a novel experience, at least for the British – almost every failed offensive in the First World War had failed because of an inadequate artillery bombardment and a failure to understand the strength of German fortifications.[124] Indeed, the experience of the US forces in the Pacific theatre had long suggested that naval and aerial bombardment was inadequate to completely destroy coastal fortifications.

However limited was the effect of the naval bombardment even fewer of the fortifications had been destroyed by the pre-invasion air bombing. The official diary of the Royal Winnipeg Rifles assaulting Juno Beach notes that at 0900: 'The bombardment ... failed to kill a single German or silence one weapon ...'[125] It certainly did not knockout the heavy battery at Mont Fleury firing on Juno Beach. Actually, the defenders assumed the smoke and the absence of direct attacks upon them implied that a landing was, or perhaps would be, occurring elsewhere on the coast. Even when the far more accurate naval bombardment persuaded the defenders that an invasion was planned for them the effect appeared marginal: only around 14 per cent of the bunkers were destroyed. Nevertheless, the shock of the bombardment left many defenders disoriented and prevented some the inland batteries from firing accurately since their 'spotters' were now amongst the quivering defenders.[126] Despite all this, 90 of the 306 landing craft destined for Juno Beach failed to get there, as did half the DD tanks and 85 per cent of the Royal Marine Centaur tanks, mainly destroyed by mines or the very artillery that was supposed to have been silenced.[127] Even the tanks that did make the beach were not necessarily welcomed by the invading troops: Captain Daniel Flunder blew the track off one of his own tanks when it began crushing his troops in front of it as it progressed up the beach and refused to stop.[128] But blundering and inadequate Shermans were just one of the problems facing the Allies, another was their other weapons.

11.7 Other weapons and support systems

In fact, just as the Sherman's successes were deeply rooted in the support services that followed them, so the critical advantage that the Allied armies (as opposed to air forces or navies) had over their German counterparts tended to be in the more mundane spheres of logistics rather than conventional gunnery. For example, each American infantry division was accompanied by a field artillery battalion comprising approximately a dozen howitzers and 100 soldiers. This was not remarkably different from its German counterpart – but the latter had usually to rely upon horse drawn transport for munitions, while the American battalion could rely upon a two and half ton truck ('deuce and a half') and trailer for each gun, and another 100 plus vehicles of various kinds to ensure that neither running out of ammunition nor mobility was usually a problem (except in the early part of the European campaign). In the German static battalions, such as those attached to the 716th Division there was no motorized transport and no horse drawn transport either.[129]

Despite this, the basic field artillery guns of the Allies, the British 25-pounder and the American 105-mm, had very limited impact upon troops that were dug in, even in conventional slit trenches in the earth. Most of the evidence suggested that a conventional shell (that is not an 'air-burst' exploding in the air before impact) had to land within a metre of an adequately dug-in position to transmit a shock wave sufficient to kill or disable the occupant.[130] Most of the European conflict was fought using time-fire fuses that could be adjusted before firing to explode at a predicted time after firing. Achieving an airburst over infantry required sighting of the explosion but a proximity, VT or pozit, fuse existed amongst the Allies' arsenal which carried a battery powered radar system that ensured an explosion at a preset height above the ground. The pozit fuse had been used in the Pacific war by the US navy for two years before it found its way to the European land war and it was first used in the counter-attack against German forces in Houffalize on 3 January 1945.[131] Allied commanders were always concerned less the Germans should manage to secure and copy proximity fused munitions and Spaatz certainly thought that German flak units had used them in the Autumn of 1944 when Allied air losses suddenly increased.[132] A cheaper and unofficial alternative was to delay the explosion of a conventional 75mm high explosive shell by turning the 'delay' screw with a sixpence or screwdriver. The shell was then fired into the ground a little way in front of the target and it would ricochet about ten feet above the ground over the target before exploding.[133]

The most frightening weapon for most Allied infantrymen in the ETO seems to relate to the noise rather than the lethality of the weapon. For example, the wailing of Stuka bombers and the screaming of the 'Moaning Minnies' (*Nebelwerfer*),[134] – multiple-barrelled mortars whose wailing sounds in flight generated very high levels of anxiety amongst Allied troops. In fact, one of the ways that veterans managed to survive unscathed longer than replacement troops was the ability they developed to distinguish between the sounds of different incoming shells. Some shells, however, were literally inaudible to those they were about to hit. For example, the German 88mm shell, in a flat trajectory, travelled about 300 yards ahead of its sound. Or, as one British veteran explained to his new troops in Normandy: 'The shell explodes, you hear it coming, and only then do you here the report as it's fired'.[135] The ability to distinguish such sounds also told the listener whether the weapon was German or Allied and the direction from which it was fired.[136]

In terms of lethality even machine guns were being displaced in the Second World War by artillery of some form as the primary cause of injury or death, and one survey suggested that less than a quarter were killed or wounded by a bullet.[137] In fact, at the level of machine guns the Allied weapons were markedly inferior: the American Browning Automatic Rifles fired between 300 and 600 rounds per minute depending on the model from a 20 cartridge box magazine. The British Bren gun, based on a Czech ZB 26 design, fired 500 rounds per minute from a 30 cartridge magazine, while the German MG-42 Spandau fired at 1,200 RPM from a 50-round belt.[138] Allied soldiers frequently referred to the German MG-42 as sounding like cloth being torn, so quick was the rate of fire, whereas their own guns 'chattered'. Not only was the firing rate so much faster, the MGs seldom seemed to run out of ammunition – primarily because many ordinary infantry soldiers carried spare boxes of MG ammunition.[139] Such a firing rate did tend to overheat the barrel of the MG-42 quickly and this led to the bullets spinning wildly as they emerged from the barrel – but being hit by a vertical bullet was still lethal. The consequence of the accuracy, range and rate of fire of German machine guns was that a single MG42 could effectively cover around 300 yards of beach from a position on the bluffs above Omaha.[140] So why didn't the Allies develop similar weapons?

Once again the question is best answered by reference to cultural considerations – in this instance because the Allies' infantry doctrine was wedded to the notion of mobility rather than firepower, and since machine-guns were heavier weapons than rifles, and required some riflemen to carry ammunition rather than a rifle, the mobility of units armed with machine was clearly hampered by the presence of machine guns.[141] Indeed, British infantry sections comprised just eight soldiers – one Bren gunner and seven riflemen; by comparison the smallest German section involved 13 men, providing them with sufficient firepower to act independently of any supporting section, unlike the British section.[142] It is ironic, then, that what usually hampered the mobility of Allied soldiers was the presence not the absence of machine guns, in most cases German machine guns.

At the level of ordinary infantry rifles both the Germans and the British used bolt action weapons which required the user to fire one round at a time and to pull back the bolt to reload the next bullet from the magazine. The American standard rifle was the M1 Garand, a semiautomatic weapon that would fire a bullet from the eight-round magazine each time the trigger was pressed until all eight had been fired, at which point the cartridge clip was itself ejected. Some troops carried the lighter M1 carbine which fired smaller calibre ammunition and had half the range of the Garand. The M1 Garand was generally held to be the best infantry rifle of the war, but it was not without its critics or competitors.[143] *Life* magazine, a supporter of the rival Johnson rifle, insisted that 'it would be tragically dangerous to go to war with the Garand'.[144] Official US Army manuals suggested – again before the war – that the rate of fire of a rifle squad (11 soldiers) armed with M1s was so great that enemy troops would not be able to keep their heads out of their foxholes for more than an instant.[145] This was ironic given the fire power that the comparative troops could generate, simply because the average German unit had so many more machine guns than the average American (or even Anglo-Canadian) unit – a lesson that only the Germans, apparently, had learned from the First World War. For example, the rate of fire per minute from an M1 Garand was 32, and from the Carbine version 40. This was, indeed, much faster than the German Mauser – originally used in the Franco-Prussian War of 1870–1 – at just 15. But the firing rates of the submachine guns of both sides reversed the advantage: the German MP 40 firing rate was 200 rounds per minute (RPM) and the American Thompson was 100 RPM (the American BAR was 500 RPM). At the machine gun level the difference was even greater: the US Browning could manage 500–525 RPM depending on the model, but the MG 42 could spew out 1,200 RPM. This difference was compounded by the number of troops carrying automatic weapons. For instance, of the 14,281 soldiers of the US 29th Infantry Division who landed on Omaha, 11,706 carried rifles, 93 carried Thompsons, 143 BARs, and 157 carried Browning machine guns. That equated to a combined theoretical small arms fire power of 677,540 RPM (assuming – generously – that all the rifles were the faster firing carbines). Against them the 13,027 soldiers of the German 352nd Infantry Division, carried 9,569 rifles, 1,592 MP 40 submachine guns and 718 MG42 machine guns. That equated to a combined theoretical firepower of 1,323,535 RPM. In other words, the small arms fire power of an average German infantry division was almost twice that of its larger American counterpart. The equivalent firepower of the 15,976 members of the German 3rd Parachute Division was even greater at 2,082,535 – that is, over three times greater than the average American infantry division.[146] In short, in terms of small arms fire the American forces were quite simply outgunned, and their British allies even more so. Fortunately for the Americans facing them, the German 3rd Parachute Division only had 70 per cent of its allotted weapons on D-Day – but even then it remained better armed. It is hardly surprising, then, that the Allied infantry so frequently went to ground and called for artillery support when under fire from German positions – they were simply outgunned.

McManus is scathing about the assumption – rooted in Marshall's (1947) early post war writing – that the ordinary infantry soldier was reluctant to fire unless armed with a fully automatic weapon.[147] McManus suggests the 'myth' of the 'ratio of fire' theory was never based in any form of evidence and was quite contrary to the truth. On the other hand, there does seem to have been an 'unwritten soldiers' maxim: 'if you shoot at them, they will shoot at you'. That may explain some of the reluctance of the Allied troops to fire: since the German machine guns were superior to the Allies in both quantity and quality, to fire upon a German position was to bring down upon the head of the initial shooter an avalanche of return fire. Equally important, American gunpowder produced a blue flash and smoke – providing the Germans – who used smokeless and flashless powder – with an excellent way of spotting them.[148] Thus, unless the initial shooter was certain of eliminating the target, or generating a heavier firepower, it was not always sensible to open fire.[149] The consequence was that for all that US manuals spoke of 'winning battles through dominant fire-power', neither the infantry nor the tanks, could match their German counterparts and they had to rely upon artillery or aerial supporting fire to even up the odds. It was not, then, that Allied infantry were unusually reluctant to advance without fire support – their planners had left them with almost no choice.

Moreover, even though the Allied infantry was far more mechanized that the German equivalent and the M-15 and M-16 half tracks provided an armoured assault unit that the opposition could never match, the self-evident superiority of German tanks and German infantry weapons began gnawing away at the Allies' confidence that the material power of the US would guarantee victory.[150] Admittedly the sky was often empty of the *Luftwaffe* and most Allied troops did not meet large numbers of Panthers or Tigers. Indeed, at least one member of the 116th Infantry Regiment's anti-tank company who landed in Normandy and fought right through to May 1945 never saw a German tank.[151] But 'Tigerphobia' – the assumption that every German tank was a Tiger, and thus unstoppable, was common.[152]

Fortunately, the superior development of field communications on the Allied side ensured that immobilized infantry could call down artillery or aerial bombardments with relative ease. Using either the hand held six pound SCR-536 (Signal Corps Radio) Walkie-Talkie sets with a range of a mile or less, or the back packed SCR-300 weighing 32 pounds with a range up to five miles, these FM (Frequency Modulation – static-free) line-of-sight radios were god-sends to under-gunned infantry units. Each rifle company carried six walkie-talkies or carried miles of telephone cable for phone connections back to their HQs. However, there was a price to pay for this – and it was the ability of the Germans to eavesdrop on US radio communications that cost a considerable number of Allied lives.

Nonetheless, within 48 hours of H-Hour, two submarine cables had been laid from the command ships off shore to the shore-based units. Most of the Forward Observations Officers (FOOs) spotting for artillery on land used High Frequency devices but the multi-channel Very High Frequency radios – which were less susceptible to atmospheric conditions – had just been developed and some were deployed with the invasion forces, along with civilian technical support. By 8 June a line of sight connection had been established between Omaha Beach and a watch tower on the Isle of Wight (originally used to watch for the Spanish Armada) and this allowed aerial photographs to be developed in England and transmitted by radio facsimile to Normandy for rapid assessment and decision-making. To that effect, once a photo plane had landed in Britain and its film had been developed, the results could be at Omaha Beach within seven minutes. That basically provided an hour by hour update on the state of German defences and troop movements.

In contrast German field communications, which had been dependent upon the new 1,000 mile underground cable along the French coast, were quickly reduced to using the outdated and frequently sabotaged French telephone system, and the *Wehrmacht's* own mobile radio system. These vehicles became a primary target for the Allied fighter-bombers in Normandy: both von Schweppenburg's and Sepp Dietrich's units lost 75 per cent of their radio vans in the first few days of the invasion, making co-ordinated counter-attacks difficult, and cutting off the beach head from the Cotentin peninsular. That also necessitated German command-ers physically moving between areas to co-ordinate developments, and the inevitable result was a greater exposure to Allied air attack: both Rommel and Marcks were attacked in this manner and the loss of both these commanders severely inhibited the ability of the German army to respond.[153]

11.8 Conclusion

It is often assumed that D-Day was successful because the preponderance of Allied technology made such a victory inevitable or because a series of lucky breaks undermined the German defences and facilitated the Allied attack. Certainly many Allied soldiers seemed to have felt an enormous confidence in the veritable cornucopia of technology. Surely no-one could resist the Arsenal of Democracy? But this optimism was premised upon a conventional notion of US material superiority and an inordinate and naïve faith in the utility of machines to tame the opposition. This chapter, however, has suggested that the material strength of the Allies was far from self-evident once the technology was deployed in the water or on the ground. Just a few examples will re-illustrate the problems that the scientists, technologists and above all, military leaders, left the Allied soldiers to deal with in Normandy.

First, the landing craft that the initial assault waves landed in were simply inadequate to the task. This was already obvious from the Pacific assaults and, in that theatre of war, a partial solution – the Amtrac – had already been deployed to resolve it. Only two Amtracs were available for D-Day off Normandy and the consequence was a litany of death on Omaha. Moreover, subordinate officers had appealed to the commanders to reconsider the issue but had been overruled by leaders who should have known better. Second, the Pacific war – to say nothing of the entire First World War – had also demonstrated that naval and aerial bombardment of reinforced defensive positions was unlikely to succeed, either in destroying the defenders or even undermining their ability to resist. Third, the Funnies that so ably assisted the British and Canadians on the eastern beaches were noticeably absent from the American beaches – as are reasons for their absence. The consequence of this tragic oversight by Bradley was the bodies littering Omaha on D-Day. Fourth, the tanks that were to lead the charge through the German defences and strike terror into the heart of the defenders, instead struck terror into the hearts of the users and form a considerable part of the explanation for the Normandy stalemate. Worse, the poverty of Allied tank design – and British tank designs were worse than US tank designs in the main – was all so unnecessary. A tank capable of withstanding the attacks of the Tigers and Panthers in Normandy was available and could have been usefully deployed across the beaches on D-Day to deal with the German emplacements. But, thanks to doctrinal cultures, and Patton's disastrous decision-making, the Pershing did not arrive in Europe until the war was almost over. Fifth, the inadequacy of Allied automatic small arms, especially in numbers, left troops immensely vulnerable to equivalent sized German units. Once again, someone had failed to learn the lesson of the last war and had conflated mobility with light weapons. Paradoxically, where lightness was critical – for the initial assaulting infantry – the Allies seem to have reversed their initial logic and weighed them down so much that many could hardly move and many drowned in the tide, pulled under by three days of rations on a day when the majority of survivors did not even eat.

In sum, the three main problems: getting to the beach, getting across the beach, and getting off the beach, were all resolvable – had various leaders made appropriate decisions – but only in small sections did the solutions arrive. And in each of the cases where errors were made, it is a cultural explanation that provides the better understanding of Leadership decisions than a contingent rational approach. Treating problems as Tame rather than as Wicked, and assuming that superordinates always knew best doomed many soldiers to unnecessary deaths or injuries. Sometimes, as in the provision of a breakwater for the floating harbour, the subordinate's case succeeded, but more often than not the subordinate was over-ruled and dire consequences usually followed. Fortunately for the Allies, they had sufficient superiority elsewhere, notably in the airforces, the navies and the artillery, to compensate for these Leadership errors.

Part Four

Commanding in Crises

Introduction

If the primary Wicked Problem for the political and military leaders of the Allies on D-Day was where and when to invade, and the Tame Problem was how to build and supply sufficient matériel to get the troops to the beach, what happened when the troops actually got to the beaches or dropped out of the planes? At this point it is worth reconsidering the third category of decision-maker – the Commander. As suggested in Chapter 1, Commanders operate when a self-evident crisis occurs and there is general uncertainty – though not ostensibly in the head of the Commander who provides an 'answer' to the crisis. There is no time for discussion or dissent or worrying about Management 'procedures' if they delay resolution, and thus a crisis legitimizes coercion as necessary in the circumstances for public good. Of course, if the Management of Tame Problems has been successful then few crises will actually occur, but in war there are always likely to be crises. So how good were the commanders and how could Command be instilled into the commanders?

In what follows I compare the way this developed for the three primary groups involved: Anglo-Canadians, Americans and Germans. But first let us consider the theoretical role of the commander in general.

12 Commanding

12.1 Commanding soldiers to kill

The capacity of soldiers to kill on order and to remain doing so has always proved troublesome for higher command, because an army may be 'a dumb beast which kills when it is set down but its soldiers also feel pain'.[1] Looking back at D-Day one quote always comes to mind: 'A rational army would run away'.[2] Yet, by and large, armies do not act in this way and certainly the vast majority of all troops involved on both sides carried out their duties on D-Day. Keegan[3] suggests several other reasons why, in the main, most soldiers do not run away, despite the danger involved in staying put in a crisis:

- *coercion* – the fear of something worse happening if you do run away, usually via your own military police, quite possibly resulting in your execution and definitely resulting in your enduring shame
- *inducement* – the rewards of success in battle, be they looting or prize money or simply survival
- *narcosis* – the use of chemical stimulant, notably alcohol to suppress fear
- *mimicry* – the copying of heroes, leaders or even enemies in an attempt to redefine oneself
- *frenzy* – the blood letting that can and does occur when emotional balance is unsettled by particular events, originally associated with Nordic *berserkers*
- *stardom* – the desire to perform on a battlefield to be the envy of the onlookers and finally,
- *honour*.

Of all these reasons the coercion of discipline is often the one most commonly considered. Military discipline is usually the most compelling available: after all, what commanders require their subordinates to do is often perceived by those subordinates as suicidal, hence the coercive disciplinary system. But battles are often amongst the most indeterminate activities, and although they may appear to require a functional discipline amongst massed ranks of soldiers to cope with this, in fact, the chaos of battle ironically requires the radical deployment of initiative – relatively unconstrained by any notion of hierarchical discipline. It is the resolution of this paradox that defines the better performance in battle – and distinguishes most German units from most Allied units. Nonetheless coercion was most certainly available to the commanders of all sides in compelling their subordinates to stay put. Stanley Whitehouse experienced this when digging in off Sword Beach and told to expect an imminent German counter-attack: 'We were startled by a big brawny military police officer who crouched along side us. "Orders are – there is to be no Dunkirk this time … You must stay here and fight it out. My men are between you and the beaches, with orders to shoot anyone leaving his post. OK?"[4] Though there are no records of anyone being shot by the British military police in this way – and in this case the attack never came – it is unlikely that such an 'execution' would be recorded should a crisis have developed and the military stepped in to prevent another Dunkirk.

It is also worth pointing out the desire of many subordinates to fight for commanders – at any level – whom they regarded as being able to maximize their chances of survival by their personal reputations as efficient and effective commanders. For Whitehouse, Corporal Smith, 'was the epitome of an infantry NCO … he led from the front, yelling and cursing, waving his Tommy gun, and shooting and coshing everyone in sight. I heard other squaddies say: "I wish I could get in Smudger's section. He's a useful bloke and would look after you"'.[5]

In the *Wehrmacht* on the Russian front, Private Sajer had parallel thoughts as his company commander spoke to his comrades: 'I would burn and destroy entire villages if by doing so I could prevent even one of us from dying of hunger … We are trying to change the world, hoping to revive the ancient virtues buried under the layers of filth bequeathed to us by our forbears … life is war, and war is life. Liberty doesn't exist'. Upon hearing this, Sajer reports, 'we loved him and felt we had a true leader, as well as a friend on whom we could count'.[6]

Similar sentiments were sometimes developed about Allied field officers (very seldom about staff officers who seldom 'strayed' into the front line). For example, Private Albert J. King from the 1st Worcesters served with the 43rd Infantry Division, and his company was commanded by Major Grubb. When a group of replacements arrived in France, King overhead one of them question his colleagues about Major Grubb's sanity. The reply reproduced that same bonding that Whitehouse witnessed: 'Grubby? He is mad, mad as an effing hatter, but his company will follow him anywhere. If you're not prepared to do that, piss off to some other company'.[7] Grubb was surprised by some of his own reactions to battle:

> It may now seem rather an incomprehensible thing to say, but it [fighting] could be great fun. What was really tiresome was when the shells came, then you had no chance ... but a little gentleman's war was a great deal of fun ... You really were, you became a little elated, unbalanced even. On reflection it appears odd that you could enjoy such a thing, but it is an example of an extraordinary reaction of the body that I think is largely due to the generation of adrenaline. In moments of intense danger, one became elated to such an extent that it bordered on insanity.[8]

Grubb was eventually sent back to Britain to run a Battle School and leaders like him rapidly became thin on the ground, causing considerable problems for senior commanders. Lt Colonel Hart Dyke, of the Hallamshires, the British 49th (Polar Bear) Division, regarded himself as:

> Fortunate to have so many men with the stuff of leadership in them. They were like rafts to which all the rest clung for support. It was these men, the pre-war territorial nucleus of our battalion – the Hallamshires – who provided the warrant and non-commissioned officers with the exception of course of the officers ... It was now getting most difficult to find men to accept the added responsibility and danger of leadership. There was little to offer in return for what one asked of them. Rank and money meant little these days. A dozen times they had escaped improbably. Long ago the few surviving men in the rifle companies had been bound to realize the odds against them remaining unharmed. But the honour and good name of the battalion meant much to them.[9]

This respect for commanders who took a positive interest in their subordinates seems to have been universal but rarely extended higher than a captain, for as one US soldier proclaimed: 'A lot of guys don't even know the name of their regimental commander'.[10] And in an army where 'unearned' respect for hierarchy was almost always subordinated to 'earned' respect for what was regarded as inspirational Command, war was not something that necessarily engendered a positive regard for the officer corps.

Clearly, not everyone involved in the fighting was driven by an ideological desire to fulfil their commander's desires, and there were probably few on the Allied side that were politically motivated and fought specifically to rid the world of fascism. There were, however, many committed troops on both sides, especially the German SS units, and there were also many that were turned into inveterate haters of the enemy by witnessing the deaths or injuries inflicted upon their close friends and colleagues.[11]

But the popular assumption that war is only possible because of effectively coercive disciplinary systems runs contrary to the evidence which suggests that many (though by no means all) soldiers 'enjoy' some or several aspects of combat. Grey suggests that three reasons predominate in trying to explain what might be called 'the irrational commitment to stay': the spectacle, the comradeship and the destruction.[12] Since all three provide 'attractions' that are seldom found outside war, at least not together, war embodies a magnet that holds soldiers to its chest in a literal death grip.

For many combatants on D-Day the spectacle of the vast armada of ships and the realization that history was unfolding before their very eyes was incredibly powerful. 'Looking back on Normandy,' recalled Stan Leech, a beach signaller, 'the impression which remains is how *interesting* everything was, not how frightening. I'm no braver or more cowardly than anyone else, but I was so caught up in the excitement of it all. Everything was new'.[13]

But there were probably many more that fought on because they felt it their duty to those with whom they had trained and fought. Stanley Whitehouse, for example, remembers that:

> Luckily the old Bucks Battalion platoon that had been together for more than two years remained virtually intact, which was a tremendous fillip … . They were all trusted mates who could be relied on when we were in a tight spot. A platoon is like a large family of about forty men, living, eating and sleeping together for month after month. They laugh and cry over shared experiences, get drunk together and fight the common enemy. Is it any wonder then that such powerful bonds are forged between them, bonds stronger than even those between blood brothers? Truly they are ready to die for each other – and sometimes do – and when a member of the 'family' is killed or maimed the rest feel a deep anguish and express a blind hatred for the perpetrators.[14]

Hitler's own *Weltanschauung* or 'worldview' was, to some extent rooted in his fond memories of the trenches in the First World War and, as shall become clear, there are several examples of soldiers joining and remaining in an army because they manifestly enjoy killing without necessarily exhibiting the characteristics associated with *berserks*.[15] This is hardly a novel idea; historically many societies have been framed around warrior cultures that glorified war and Hitler's leadership was certainly premised on this philosophy: exploiting the solidarity of soldiers. And we need only return to the last hour of the First World War – when the armistice due at 1100 was common knowledge – to see both sides engaging in militarily 'unnecessary' deaths. Many of the Allied gunners fired right up until 1059 (though Captain Harry Truman stopped his shelling near Verdun at 1045). Elsewhere, Brigadier General Bernard Freyberg led a cavalry charge at 1055; the Germans fired gas and incendiary shells onto the hospital at Mézières until 1059; and at 1058 John Price, a private in the Canadian army, became the last Allied casualty of war when he took his helmet off to take some flowers from Belgian children and was promptly shot through the head by a German sniper. Even as the armistice began, a platoon of the 2nd Middlesex Regiment had to be restrained from attacking a nearby German post where they wanted to 'kill a few more Germans while they had the chance'.[16] These are not necessarily acts induced by any of the causes on Keegan's list; they may be the acts of individuals who appear to enjoy war, who gain pleasure from killing.

This, in itself, may lead to subsequent acts of violent revenge where a close comrade is killed or wounded. 'Good friends died at Mouen', wrote Private Kings, a Brengunner with the 1st Worcesters,

> I was both sad and angry, my hatred for the enemy had become very personal now. I felt no compassion at all; my one thought now was for retribution. I felt that as a Brengunner I had a special job to do; that was to reach one's objective as quick as possible, dig in and be in a position to defend against counter-attack and kill as many Jerries as possible. To this end killing was almost an obsession.[17]

When Brendan Maher's ship came under air attack off the Normandy beaches on D-Day+3, he was positively ecstatic: 'The thrill of opening up at enemy aircraft was unbelievable. I found myself jumping up and down with excitement and cursing the gunner for not bringing one down'.[18] These cases suggest, as Bourke does, that some soldiers enjoy 'the pleasures of killing', and there are enough violent sports, violent games and acts of violence to suggest that an adrenaline buzz from physical combat is not the preserve of the mentally unbalanced.[19]

A more gentle man than Sapper Anderson of the British 653rd Engineers would be hard to find but when the war ended on 8 May he was not simply relieved: 'to be honest some of us felt a sense of disappointment that we had come to the end of our exciting adventure'. Under air attack on New Year's Day 1945 he and a corporal 'got hold of a Bren gun with tracer bullets in the magazine, and when the next aircraft came over us, we fired at it. It was very low flying and we could see the tracer bullets go into the engine nacelle. Immediately white fumes came from the aircraft and the pilot straight away climbed up to a greater height until he vanished over the horizon. At that time we rejoiced that we might have killed him but now I hope that he got back to his side without serious injury'.[20]

Thus not all war is perceived by all combatants as dreadful and as deeply repulsive because many combatants look back fondly to their fighting days as the times when they were most 'alive' – if indeed they were. This may be derived from the common reports from the front that the intensity of life is multiplied by war to the extent that every moment is qualitatively different from every moment in peace. Critically for us this implies that Command in war does not necessarily derive from harsh disciplinary systems, though it may. Successful commanders, then, may be those who recognize these primary drivers of soldiers' motivation and exploit them. In effect, their soldiers teach them to be commanders by responding or not responding to particular acts of command.

That great friend of the lowly American soldier – or 'dogface' – Ernie Pyle, was quite clear that 'There is an intoxication about battle, and ordinary men can sometimes soar clear out of themselves on the wine of danger-emotion'.[21] That emotion is not even dependent upon actual combat but can be readily perceived in those who are about to go into combat: watching a unit of British Commandos, Eric Sevareid noticed the intensity of the moment:

> I stood beside a Commando major and watched the assault troops take formation … Now and then [the major] reached out and touched a passing soldier; just touched him, saying nothing … . I knew suddenly that I was looking into his open heart and that I understood how he felt. The war had become his very life; these men were all his world. Here with them, under the dark moon, in the middle of the hellish noise, he was intensely alive. Elsewhere he was half-dead.[22]

Delaforce, quoting Lt General Brian Horrocks, puts forward the strongest claim to this paradox at the heart of war: 'Nobody enjoys fighting. Yet the forward area in any theatre of war, the sharp end of the battle, as we used to call it, is inhabited by young men with a gleam in their eye, who actually *do* the fighting'.[23] Indeed, it often seems that the lives of every soldier in combat are focused wholly and intensely on the present, for they cannot remember anything before the war and there often appears to be no future other than war.

There is also the delight in destruction – of property and people – that provides the most difficult issue for civilians to understand. The unmitigated pleasure in wanton destruction encapsulated by the destruction of civil property in the form of 'mindless vandalism' continues to bemuse and outrage people, but there are self-evident traces back into the actions and emotions of those involved in its military equivalent. Bert Damsky from the US 1st Infantry Division, then across the beaches, and across France into Germany, entered a German house set for dinner. There his unit ate the fine food and drank the fine wine from a clean white tablecloth and off fine china plates. And when they had finished they wiped their mouths on the tablecloth and proceeded to smash all the plates against the wall and rip the tablecloth to shreds – 'It was', exclaimed Damsky, 'a really great feeling'.[24]

However, much of these 'attractions' quickly wane as the spectacle becomes commonplace, as the excitement of danger turns into the dread of death, and as the destructive impulse draws closer to the perpetrator. Once a soldier has been to hell and returned it was usually difficult to retain any of the assumptions that war could be a 'glorious adventure'. Sergeant Bob Shelldrake, with the British 55th Antitank Regiment, 49th Division, had seen enough at 'hell-fire corner' near Rauray in France in the summer of 1944 to obliterate any such assumptions:

> Dead strewed the road – who was fool enough to stay there long enough to move them? As tanks and carriers passed to and fro they champed over those bodies churning them to a pulp of flesh and rag. I saw a carrier make a skid turn on the corner and strip the skin backwards over a ghastly trunk until the flesh lay exposed, vividly pink and shining for the brief moment it arched as if in living torment before it slumped back into the ignominy and desecration of the mud. So this is war – here was no glory, no proudness of scarlet uniforms and military music, but a bloody mashing and pulping of human beings. The ordinary man's war cannot be glorified, necessary it may be, but it is vile in the extreme.[25]

That 'vile necessity' was certainly a strong motivator for many who could see no pleasure in war but were sucked into the maelstrom by all kinds of forces, including duty and outrage. As Drez concludes about the American volunteers: 'They came for all the reasons under the sun' – though Pearl Harbour was a particularly significant one.[26]

But importantly, perhaps the most influential issue beyond Pearl Harbour was the 'lead' played by the movies. Many soldiers spoke of their experiences in terms of the films they had seen – which often made the experience either less alien or quite unreal, as if they were actually in a movie about war rather than in war itself. However, the actual experience of combat often generated a marked distancing from such glossy representations of heroic deeds and a considerable antipathy towards those who continued to peddle them. Hence when John Wayne – who was refused entry to the armed forces because of his age (34), his three children[27] and his injured shoulder – arrived in Hawaii to perform for the wounded survivors of Okinawa he was met by a 'stony silence' and then booed off the stage.[28] As Edwin Hoyt suggested: 'There was nothing a [Bogart or Wayne] could suggest about toughness that matched the reality of combat'.[29] And for many soldiers it was not macho heroism that kept them at the front subject to incessant dangers but the fear of shame.

American Private Eustis, for example, was not concerned about possibility injury or death but with something far more personal: 'how well I acquit myself when I come up against the real thing'.[30]

12.2 The stages of combat

That 'reality of combat' suggested that most soldiers went through a three phase experience as frontline fighters and the different phasing suggests that successful combat commanders may have been the ones who recognized the phases and acted appropriately.

First, there was an 'adventurous' stage where youthful ardour and the novelty of the situation propelled soldiers into situations that others would have shirked. At this stage many individuals seemed to have believed themselves destined to survive even if – and perhaps because – so many fell besides them. Stanley Whitehouse, recounting his experiences from D-Day to the German surrender captures this well for: 'Naively, I still regarded the invasion as a big adventure'.[31] Ellis also suggests that the first few days of combat tended to generate both very high levels of stress and of a consequent selfishness in most individuals.[32]

Second, for the first weeks and perhaps a couple of months following the initial experience of combat, a sharpened sense of effectiveness and efficiency exists as individuals learned from their own and others' mistakes about how to survive and perform under fire as a team rather than as an individual. At this stage soldiers became very aware that luck was in finite supply and that survival depended upon skill – often manifest in the ubiquitous 'infantry crouch'. 'I wasn't scared until the third day,' recalled Lieutenant Elliott Johnson from the 4th US Infantry Division.[33] Unfortunately it did not take much longer to realize that skill was almost redundant – and hence so was avoiding making a mistake; the only thing that mattered was luck![34] Ernie Pyle had certainly come to that conclusion as he left the European war, admitting that 'I feel that I've used up all my chances'. He had; in the middle of April 1945 Pyle was shot on Ie Shima, Okinawa.[35]

Third was an almost universal stage, variously known as battle weariness or battle fatigue, 'bomb-happiness' or 'shell-shock'.[36] At this stage the stress of continuous combat or simple exposure to uncertainty sapped the confidence of soldiers and inverted their initial optimism to fatalistic pessimism: they knew they would die if they did not get out soon. As troops of the 1st Canadian Army reported: the only way one could get out of a battle was death, wounds, self-inflicted wounds and going 'nuts'.[37] General Bradley concurred, 'behind every river, there's another hill and behind that hill another river. After weeks or months in the line only a wound can offer him the comfort of safety, shelter and a bed'.[38] At this point soldiers adopted what was known as 'the death wish walk', or the 'two thousand yard stare', often appearing completely oblivious to the dangers around them. After six months of continuous combat Stanley Whitehouse approached breaking point: 'the gnawing, nagging fearfulness that filled my waking, and often sleeping, hours'.[39] He was not alone, for perhaps as many as one in five non-fatal casualties were suffering from some form of shell-shock; and the longer troops stayed in the combat zone the more likely they were to succumb. Indeed, had it not been for the continuous replacement of wounded or dead troops, Ellis suggests that many units would not have been able to continue.[40]

It should also be noted that it was unusual to get leave more than once every 6–8 months in the British army and complete rotation out of combat altogether was not practised by any army at this time – except those beyond the European theatre who could be abroad for four years or more.[41] Any of those soldiers diagnosed as suffering from combat fatigue were simply sent to the rear for a few days 'R&R' (rest and recuperation), and then returned to the front line to resume their role. Indeed, this seems to have worked and there is some evidence that suggests that troops sent too far from the front, or for too long, were more unable and unwilling to return to duty.[42]

The US Army suggested that the average GI could take between 200 and 240 days of combat, though many GI's recognized the 'stare' after just two weeks. A team of psychologists following the US Army through Normandy suggested that after a month the soldier's effectiveness declined markedly and that within 6 weeks they were 'close to a vegetative state'.[43] In fact, most US Marines served around 120 days in combat through the war in the Pacific and their European theatre comrades could look forward to about 60 days of continuous combat before relief, compared to about 12 days in the British Army. The results are relatively clear: in Europe fully a quarter of all US combat soldiers apparently suffered some form of nervous medical condition.[44]

The temporal change between the naïve but excited rooky and the 'old hand' was particularly obvious to the American troops fighting for the first time next to the experienced British troops in North Africa. Cooper recalled a friend telling him: 'The difference between the Americans, who had been in combat only a short time, and the British, who had been there for two years, was that the Americans fought today so they could go home tomorrow, and the British fought today and hoped and prayed that they would be alive to fight again tomorrow'.[45]

Sometimes the stress manifested itself in bizarre behaviour. Hedley

Bunce, a sergeant with the 3rd Monmouthshires recalls one of his fellow sergeants asking him how to say: 'Do you speak French?' Bunce assumed he meant 'English' but told him what he wanted to know. Next day, after Bunce had heard the man practising the phrase, he witnessed him walking up to a French farmer:

> 'Parlez-vous Français?', asked the sergeant.
> 'Oui Monsieur', replied the farmer.
> 'OK then', continued the sergeant, 'Let's have some bloody eggs'.[46]

Combat commanders who remained oblivious to these problems were unlikely to get the best efforts from their subordinates. Major D.J. Watterson, 2nd Army's Adviser in Psychiatry, suggested that by August 1944 the stalemate in Normandy was reaching a crisis:

> The high optimism of the troops who landed in the assault and early build up phases inevitably dwindled when the campaign for a few weeks appeared to have slowed down. Almost certainly the initial hopes and optimism were too high and the gradual realization that the 'walk-over' to Berlin had developed into an infantry slogging match caused an unspoken but clearly recognizable fall in morale … . [but] for every man breaking down there were certainly three or four effective men remaining with their units.[47]

The problem was not simply being under fire but the very high level of anxiety generated by the uncertainty of war – about where the enemy was, about when they would fire, about what would happen and so on – the classic conditions of a long run crisis. Indeed, where green troops seemed often as not to be driven on by curiosity, veterans were often held back by uncertainty. Manifestations of stress were not limited to mental uncertainties: over half the troops questioned in one questionnaire suggested that they had, on at least one occasion, been unable to perform adequately through extreme fear. Twenty per cent even admitted to wetting or soiling their pants. Yet it was this very fear that drove many on, for the fear of appearing cowards in front of their comrades was even greater than the fear of injury or death.[48] Phillip Brown, in combat in France noted that everyone was afraid almost all of the time, 'no one that I have ever talked to has admitted to being unafraid. Whatever requisite a man must possess to be known as a brave man, the absence of fear is certainly not one of them'.[49] In effect being brave meant being able to operate even when scared, it did not mean being unafraid, and being afraid did not mean being a coward.

This fear often seemed to generate a dreamlike state amongst troops so that nothing seemed real and that very trance would enable them to switch off and operate automatically as their training had taught them and as the disciplinary system always intended. Frank Burnett captured this strange life of an infantry soldier after a long exposure to combat:

> The infantryman becomes supremely indifferent; his intellect only *records* events, it makes no decisions for him. Drying his feet becomes as unpleasant as getting them wet. Standing in the rain is of no more consequence than sitting in a shelter. Cold food provokes no more excitement than no food at all. Mechanically the body tries to do what instinct tells it is best. But there is no reality; everything is done in a ... monotonous dream.[50]

Under such conditions John Stirling, a captain in the Royal Dragoon Guards, was certain that only the completely insensitive had no fear. Thus what marked out a combat commander was the 'person whose men never guess that he is as much afraid as they themselves and therefore follow him into the present danger instead of following their natural inclination to safety and self-preservation'.[51] In fact, the pretence of bravery often generated a collective strength amongst groups as each frightened individual masked their fear with a surface bravery that others took as genuine bravery. Everyone subsequently tried to emulate the bravery they saw around them and the result was, collectively, a 'brave' unit of frightened individuals. Hence Ellis suggests that while individuals went through personal stages of terror, the collective morale of a unit tended to rise and fall collectively.

Indeed, there are several examples where units from all armies panicked and fled the battlefield or refused to engage with the enemy – though they were very rare in comparison to the numbers of troops who did go forward when required to do so.[52] Three Australian Battalions of the 22nd Brigade in Singapore 'deserted' or 'escaped' depending on one's definition of their action in Singapore in 1942. In February 1943, in Tunisia, elements of the 1st US Armoured Division panicked in the face of an attack by Rommel's *Afrika Korps* – as had the British 1st Essex Regiment in November 1940 at Metemma. And in May 1941 the 22nd New Zealand Battalion were one of the few units to remain disciplined enough to control the frenzied evacuation from Crete by British troops, particularly two platoons of Marines near Maleme who refused to stand and fight. On the Salerno beachhead 700 replacements for the 51st (Highland) Division (who had lost two thirds of their original members in France in 1940 and were now due to return to England) were reposted to different units and refused to go. 192 were tried as mutineers and found guilty but returned to their original units.[53] In the same area tanks and troops of the US 5th Army fled before a German attack,

as did the British 6th Grenadier Guards and the 8th Royal Fusiliers.[54]
Just after D-Day a Canadian paratroop battalion went on hunger strike
in protest against the harsh discipline imposed by their new commander.
Later in the campaign for Caen, on 11 July, a section of the British 5th
Duke of Cornwall's Light Infantry (DCLI) fled before a German
counter-attack:

> They had come running back in panic through the ranks of the (4th) Somersets.
> A wounded officer of the DCLI had been trying to prevent them; he had been hit
> in the jaw, so that part of his face had dropped, and he was waving a pistol and
> trying to shout, making horrible sounds ... Some of the Somersets were so badly
> rattled that one sergeant had leapt into a sitting position on his slit trench, pointed
> his rifle down the line of his own men, and shouted that he 'would shoot the first
> bastard who moved'.[55]

As one unnamed British officer explained about his battalion in
Normandy: 'It is no longer a battalion but a collection of individuals.
There is naturally no esprit de corps for those who are frightened (as we
all are to one degree or another) to fall back on. I have twice had to draw
my revolver on retreating men'.[56]

Thus effective commanders in a crisis take coercive action against their
own followers but the problem is not explaining why these incidents
occurred and how they are resolved but why they occurred so rarely.
After all, it was widely known that the British and Americans were very
unlikely to shoot deserters – in contrast to the First World War when the
British alone found 31,000 soldiers guilty of desertion and executed 266.
Indeed, desertion, or absence without leave (AWOL) was the largest
single offence heard by the British Army Courts Martial. In 1940–41
12,000 soldiers were found guilty, rising to 20,000 by 1943–44. In
effect, desertions rose not with defeats but with the prospect of final
victory.[57]

The same cannot be said for the German army, though disciplinary
problems only became significant towards the end of the war. Twenty
thousand German soldiers were executed during the war, primarily on
the eastern front.[58] In Operation Barbarossa, for example, members of
the SS *Kampfgruppe Nord* deserted before a Soviet counter-attack at
Salla.[59] Even the soldiers on the western front became a target for the SS
in the last few months of the war when many were executed for desertion.[60] 4,000 were shot between January and September 1944, 1,605 of
these for desertion.[61] And by this time many Allied soldiers began to
recognize that the replacement German troops were neither trained,
armed, nor led as well as had the initial *Wehrmacht* soldiers.[62]

12.3 Combat and ideology

It also seems to have come as a shock to both sides when the stereotyped enemy failed to correspond to the assumed pattern. Fred L. Rau with the USAAF recalled a young *Luftwaffe* pilot, captured on his first mission at Christmas 1944 stating that 'Hitler is a madman and a butcher' but explaining that did not fight for Hitler, but for Germany.[63] Contrarily, the German photographer, Hans Ertl, was clearly surprised by the attitude of the British officers he witnessed being captured in Normandy:

> Whereas the ordinary British soldiers willingly replied to the questions put by our interrogators, the officers behaved in a downright arrogant, even insolent, manner. There was no more of that 'the fight is over' attitude; no longer any trace of the fairness and comradeship which I remembered from the battles in Africa in 1941. There, the first thing you did was offer the captured enemy a cigarette in order to smoke a 'pipe of peace'. Here, you had to reckon with one of those hate filled British officers possibly knocking the proffered cigarette out of your hand, deliberately to provoke a serious argument.[64]

There were, however, few ideological zealots in the Allied armies whose perspective ranged far beyond the day to day living and dying that surrounded them. And that was especially true for the North African war, often fought out in vast empty spaces without many civilian spectators or casualties. Indeed, this may be one reason that Rommel was so often regarded by the British troops as a 'professional' soldier – who played by the rules – rather than a soldier who never spoke out against Hitler's policies, unless they seemed to place German success in jeopardy. And it was Rommel who volunteered to become the military adviser to the Nazi Party's SA in 1933 – hardly the action of a professional soldier disinterested in political machinations.[65] Yet for most soldiers such issues were far beyond their everyday experience:

> For the average soldier, once he was in combat, his view became microcosmic, and he lived only from day to day, barely daring to think about the end of the war, increasingly unconscious that life had any meaning beyond the unremitting ghastliness of endless combat. The soldier became increasingly bound up with his tiny fraternity of comrades who shared his suffering, and they alone came to represent the real world. In the last analysis, the soldier fought for them and them alone, because they were his friends and because he defined himself only in the light of their respect and needs.[66]

Or as the British Second Army's psychiatrist suggested in July 1944, 'The emotional ties among the men and between men and their officers

... is the single most potent factor in preventing breakdown'. A feeling shared by Major Paddy Boden of the Rifle Brigade writing of the desert war in which 'A large body of men sharing a common experience over a period of months and even years, isolated from all contacts with their home country, developed a set of customs, habits and even jargon of their own'.[67] This 'brotherhood of the damned' as Ellis calls it, positively revelled in, rather than chaffed at, their isolation, just as the soldiers of the New Model Army had done in England 300 years earlier.[68] Indeed, the more isolated and terrible became the situation the more united the combat unit became, seeking solace in their solidarity and comfort in their community. For, as one American put it,

> It is just those men whose lives are most miserable, the very toughest soldiers, those whose job is to kill, maim and destroy, it is just those men who are the most gentle, considerate and moved by feelings of sympathy for others ... War binds men more tightly together than almost any other branch of human activity ... and the paradox is that war, that institutionalization of hate, is rooted in its opposite, for only the love of one soldier for another keeps armies coherent.[69]

Of course, part of the pressure to 'soldier on' was derived from the fear of letting these same comrades down and appearing a coward – a fate worse than death for many. It was also the case that one's comrades provided rationales and excuses for behaviour that would otherwise be deemed 'excessive', such as the killing of surrendering troops. But Ellis summarizes the main positive point: 'not a billion cheery exhortations, a million sergeant-majors or a thousand scaffolds could have made a jot of difference'.[70] A US Marine wounded on Okinawa put it more bluntly: 'Men ... do not fight for flag or country, for the Marine Corps or glory or any other abstraction. They fight for one another'.[71] Or in Henry V's words (via Shakespeare), on assuring all those that wanted to leave before Agincourt that he would not stop them. For 'We would not die in that man's company that fears his fellowship to die with us'.[72]

Lewis Mumford concluded, on the basis of his soldier son's letters, that combat soldiers 'knew comradeship and experienced love, sometimes to a degree far beyond their civilian experience ... . War, which plainly brutalized men, also raised some of them to a saintly level'.[73] But that brutality also left soldiers with only a fleeting concern for their comrades once dead or wounded: few hospitalized soldiers actively sought a quick to return to their units and few units seemed to have made enquiries as to the health or imminent return of such soldiers.[74] As Levi suggested with regard to survival in the concentration camps: 'Our wisdom ... lay in not imagining the future'. For the Allied troops in Normandy survival and possibly getting home was what drove most of the troops on and if that meant, as Patton had suggested, going through Berlin first, then so be it. To the chagrin of many anti-Nazi-German-Americans or Jewish Americans in the war, most GIs did not hate the Germans, at least as long as they were not directly involved in combat and had not seen their friends killed or wounded.

12.4 Conclusion

It would seem self-evident that the motivation to stay and fight amongst troops of most kinds was composed of a relatively small number of crucial factors. For most it seems to have been ideological glue rather than physical force that kept them. A significant proportion of German troops it seems to have been ideologically attached to Hitler, or at least to the German state, though such 'political' unity was probably relatively rare amongst the Allied troops, at least the main groups. However, the centripetal force that glued the Allied troops together was just that – the group – and it was recognizing the group cohesion that enabled many commanders to coerce those thinking of deserting during moments of crisis. Under extreme conditions of privation and danger the sinews of mutual dependence seem to have spawned in most places and bound soldiers together in a very powerful emotional grip. That also implied that successful Command depended upon understanding these motivations and working with them rather than against them so that the groups facilitated the superordinate's command instead of undermining it.

In this chapter there have been several examples of how followers attach themselves to particular commanders that appear to embody this relational sensitivity and few that reproduce the convention that soldiers are driven by fearing their commanders more than they fear the enemy. We have also compared the combat philosophies of the warring groups and considered how these provided different frameworks for Command. For the most part the German model of Command was aligned with the propositions outlined in the previous chapter to some degree: the difficulty of providing top-down, rule based and plan driven Leadership in a situation of radical instability encouraged them to adopt a system rooted in *Auftragstaktik* (mission) rather than the Prussian *Befehlstaktik* (an uncompromising order), so that 'Intention' displaced a 'direct order'. As we shall see in the next chapter, the Allied elite units tended to copy this, but not so the main infantry units that did most of the actual fighting.

13 The Airborne Assaults

I have to announce to the House that during the night and the early hours of this morning the first of the series of landings in force upon the European continent has taken place … . So far the commanders who are engaged report that everything is proceeding according to plan. And what a plan! This vast operation is undoubtedly the most complicated and difficult that has ever taken place. It involves tides, winds, waves, visibility, both from the air and sea standpoint, and the combined employment of land, air and sea forces in the highest degree of intimacy and in contact with conditions which could not and cannot be fully foreseen.

Churchill, 6 June 1944

13.1 Introduction

This chapter focuses on the air assault. It begins with a review of the strategy and then details the actions of the three Allied elements (US 85th and 101st Divisions and the British 6th Division) and the responses of the Germans to these initial attacks. It will become clear that much of the plan went awry early on the morning of D-Day for the Allies as paratroopers and gliders landed in the wrong place and generated an array of Critical Problems for all concerned. Nevertheless the scattering of troops, while it inhibited the execution of Allied assaults on specific targets, also confused the German defenders. Most of the goals of the air assault were achieved on the day but a critical element in their achievement was the catastrophic failure of the German command system. Historically the German army had moved a long way from its authoritarian and hierarchical Prussian origins and developed a system of *Auftragstaktik* – mission control – that replaced *Befehlstaktik* – an uncompromising order. This inversion had been in response to Prussian defeats at the hands of Napoleon and the subsequent displacement of 'direct orders' by 'mission goals' had proved the basis for the success of the Blitzkriegs in Europe. However, Hitler's increasing interventions in military decisions, especially from late 1941, undermined the value of *Auftragstaktik* and overlaid it with a new form of *Befehlstaktik*. This, as we shall see, effectively compromised the efforts of the German field commanders to respond to the first developments on D-Day and provided the Allies with enough time to establish a foothold on the French coast which proved to be the bridgehead to Berlin. In effect as the crisis developed for the Germans their commanders failed to provide the directive orders that might well have undermined the invasion. On the Allied side as the scattering of the paratroopers itself generated a whole series of local crises, the Allied commanders on the spot generally reacted well to the situation and transcended the potential catastrophes that faced them.

13.2 Strategy

Bradley's decision to launch an assault on Omaha with the 1st Division was premised upon using airborne troops to minimize the chances of German reinforcements reaching the beachhead and there were some on the British side who regarded such a plan as both folly and as typical of the American's desire for a head-on clash with the *Wehrmacht* that would prove extremely bloody. Leigh-Mallory in particular advised against the American drop: the anti-aircraft artillery (AAA or Flak) was intense – hence the decision to fly across the Cotentin peninsular from west to east rather than down it from north to south – plus the flooded areas, posed considerable dangers. In mid-April 1944, at St Paul's School,[1] Leigh-Mallory had demanded the cancelling of both American airdrops behind Utah Beach telling Bradley that 'Your losses will be far more than what your gains are worth'. 'Very well sir (Bradley replied) 'if you insist on cutting out our airborne attack, then I must ask that we eliminate the Utah assault. I am not going to land on that beach without making sure our airborne people have the four causeway exits behind it'. Leigh-Mallory – with the stakes now at crisis level because the capture of Cherbourg depended upon the Utah landings and the success of the entire invasion depended upon the capture of the port, turned to Eisenhower and said: 'If General Bradley insists upon going ahead, he will have to accept full responsibility for the operation'. This response was an error because Bradley's reply captured the essence of his command and undermined Leigh-Mallory's criticism: 'That's perfectly OK', said Bradley, 'I'm in the habit of accepting full responsibility for my operations'.[2] So, despite Leigh-Mallory's warning of a 50–70 per cent casualty rate (50 per cent of the parachutists and 70 per cent of the glider troops) the mission went ahead.

As Bradley had noted, the airborne strategy was directed at denying the Germans control over the space immediately behind and to the flanks

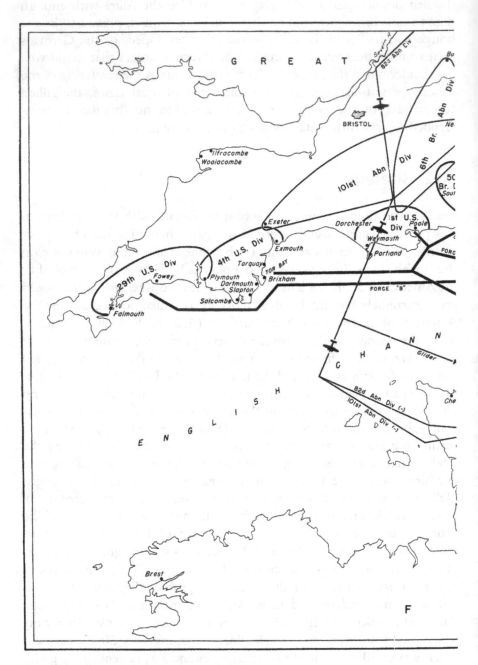

Map 13.1 Allied assault routes, 6 June 1944

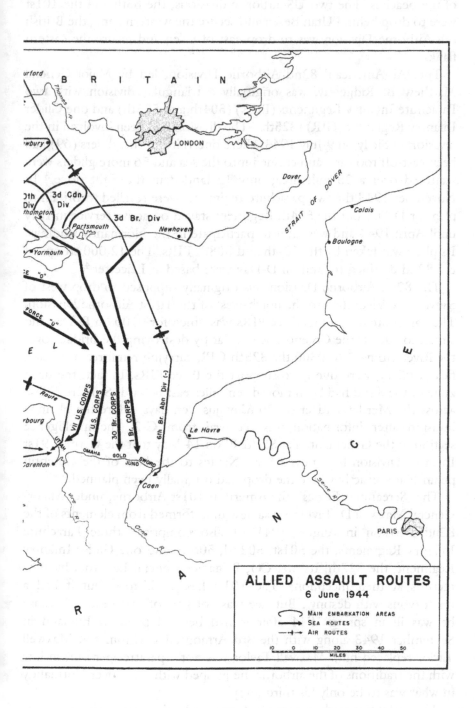

ALLIED ASSAULT ROUTES
6 June 1944

of the beaches. The two US airborne divisions, the 85th and the 101st were to drop behind Utah Beach and secure the western flank, the British 6th Airborne Division was to drop east of Caen and secure the eastern flank.

The 'All-American' 82nd Airborne Division, led by Major-General Matthew B. Ridgeway, was originally a triangular division with two Parachute Infantry Regiments (PIRs) (504th and 505th) and one Glider Infantry Regiment (GIR) (325th). The division had been involved in the invasion of Sicily on 9 July 1943 where one-third of the gliders (69) had been cast-off too early and crashed into the sea and 56 more gliders were scattered over a 25 mile area; only 12 landed in the right place.[3] In November 1943 the two parachute regiments were recalled to Britain to plan for D-Day but the 504th Regiment stayed on active service in Italy until April 1944 and was unfit to participate in the Normandy landings. Its place was taken by the 507th and 508th PIRs. The 12,000 troops of the 82nd destined to land on D-Day were based at Leicester.[4]

The 82nd Airborne Division was originally supposed to drop west of Sauveur Le Vicomte – to the north-west of the 101st Airborne Division. The parachute drop of its three PIRs was timed for 0100 on D-Day and aimed to cut off the Cotentin peninsular by destroying the bridges over the River Douve.[5] At 0300 the 325th GIR, carrying reinforcements and field artillery, were due in to support the three PIRs. In fact, the drop zone of the 82nd had been moved ten miles east towards St Mère-Eglise across the Merderet River on 26 May, just ten days before the planned invasion after information was received from G-2 (the intelligence section of the General Staff at SHAEF) on 14 May that the German 91st Infantry Division had moved from Nantes to the base of the Cotentin peninsular – exactly where the drop had originally been planned.[6]

The 'Screaming Eagles', the American 101st Airborne, under Major-General Maxwell D. Taylor, was a new unit, formed from elements of the 82nd Division in August 1941. It also comprised three Parachute Infantry Regiments, the 501st, 502nd, 506th, and one Glider Infantry Regiment, the 327th. Its first CO, Brigadier General Lee, told his new recruits at their inception: 'The 101st has no history, but it had a rendezvous with destiny'. But Lee was not part of that destiny because he was ill in spring 1944 after it had been shipped to England in September 1943 along with the 3rd Armoured Division, and Maxwell Taylor replaced him. Maxwell Taylor was not a paratrooper but, in line with the traditions of the airborne, he jumped with them over Normandy in what was to be only his third jump.

The 101st was to drop north of Carentan behind the Utah Beach area to secure the exit routes or 'draws' and the key bridges at Carentan –

which were the links between the two American beaches and a key area for cutting off the Cotentin peninsular and attacking Cherbourg.[7] The area had been heavily mined making control over the exit routes of critical importance.

Major-General Richard Gale was in command of the British 6th Airborne.[8] Gale had won the Military Cross in the First World War and took over the newly formed 1st Parachute Brigade in September 1941. Besides protecting the eastern flank of the Allied invasion beaches, the 6th Airborne Division had three specific *coup de main* (surprise) missions. First, it had to disable the Merville battery which was thought to be capable of shelling Sword Beach with its 150mm guns. Lt Colonel Otway and the 9th Parachute Brigade supported by some of the 3rd Parachute Brigade would be responsible for this. They would be reinforced by three Horsa Gliders, each carrying 30 members of 9th Parachute Battalion to assist in the assault at 0430. Second, it had to capture the bridges over the Orne River and the parallel canal that protected the eastern flank of the invasion. The intact bridges would then allow Allied reinforcements to deploy to the east and secure the flanks of the beach-head from enemy incursion. Six gliders under Major John Howard, carrying 180 troops of the 2nd Oxfordshire and Buckinghamshire Light Infantry and 249th Field Company Royal Engineers, had the unenviable task of capturing two bridges east of Caen, one over the Orne River and one over the canal at Bénouville. The latter was subsequently known as the Pegasus Bridge after the cap badge of the 1st and 6th Airborne Divisions.[9] They would be reinforced by No. 4 and elements of No.10 Commando that would land on Sword Beach and destroy the coastal defence battery at the site of the former Casino before marching the six miles inland to the bridges. A third task was the destruction of four bridges over the River Dives at Robehomme, Bures (two bridges) and Troarn, and one bridge over the stream at Varaville. All these blown bridges would impede enemy reinforcements from the east and were to be executed by a mixed Anglo-Canadian unit led by Major Tim Roseveare.

13.3 The 82nd Airborne

The 20,000 paratroopers of the British 6th Airborne, and the US 82nd and 101st Airborne Divisions, left Britain from 22 airfields on board 1,200 transport planes (primarily C-47 Dakotas) and 700 gliders – the largest airborne assault in history.[10] Some aspects of this operation could not be tamed – that is practised for – and the pilots of the paratroop carriers had obviously not trained under 'realistic' conditions because these could not be reproduced without endangering the lives of all concerned. Thus, once the anti-aircraft flak started, many of the pilots increased speed from the 90-mph they were supposed to drop the paratroopers at, to around 150-mph. They also began flying as erratically and as low as possible to avoid being hit; often lower than the 600–700 feet regarded as the minimum safe height. Additionally, fog, low cloud cover and inexperienced pilots all contributed to a very wide dispersal pattern across the Cotentin peninsular, not helped by the pathfinder groups, which were to guide the main body of troops in, often being off course in the first place. For instance, only one of the 18 US pathfinder teams landed on their targets, with one landing in the channel.[11] The consequence, of course, was that neither the pilots nor the paratroopers knew where they were any longer, the jump patterns mirrored the chaos and many of the weapons and ammunition bags attached to the paratroopers broke loose.

Some soldiers from the 82nd Airborne Division, who were supposed to land further east of the 101st Airborne Division, were dropped in the wrong zone completely, landing amongst troops from the 101st and vice versa. Indeed it has been claimed that 75 per cent of the 13,000 American paratroopers landed so far from their targets that they played no effective part in any of the planned attacks.[12] Many landed in the flooded areas, particularly behind Utah Beach near the Merderet River which although often little more than a metre deep in water, was deep enough to drown many paratroopers weighed down by up to 100lbs of equipment and smothered by their own parachutes. The intelligence report in April 1944 had merely suggested that the ground was 'probably soft' but the area had been flooded in July 1943.

Major-General Ridgeway was always well aware of the chaos that attended an airborne landing – and hence the need for strong commanders, compared to the managed order accompanying a conventional infantry unit:

> The infantry unit goes into battle with its communications and its command structure at its best. The radios are all functioning, the command chain is intact. The commander knows where all his people are, and what's happening to them, and he can exercise an excellent degree of control. The exact opposite is true of an airborne division. When its people hit the ground they are individuals, and a two star general and Pfc [Private first class] are on exactly the same basis. You have no communications whatsoever for some little time, particularly when you have jumped at night. You don't know where you are. You don't know who's around you, friend or foe.[13]

Similarly during the Sicily drop on 9 July 1943 the 3,400 paratroopers under Brigadier-General James M. Gavin (later second in command of the 82nd under Ridgeway) landed in a random pattern that did little to assist the main assaults on the beaches. Indeed, in a prequel to the Normandy drop, within 4 hours of the airdrop on Sicily only 20 paratroopers had arrived at Gavin's rendezvous point. The result confirmed to Eisenhower that airdrops were inherently problematic. As he concluded in September 1944, just three months after the drop: 'I do not believe in the airborne division ... I seriously doubt that a division commander could regain control and operate the scattered forces as one unit'.[14] Marshall, however, could not have been more enthusiastic, even suggesting at one time that the main Normandy attack should be airborne, while the amphibious assault should be merely supplementary.[15] The hazard were not necessarily restricted to the high casualties that Leigh-Mallory expected but more probably in that the drops would not be able to achieve the accuracy they needed to execute their respective missions. For many, though not for all, this proved to be the case.[16]

The 505th PIR was supposed to land around eight miles south of Ste Mère-Église, but some of them landed right in the middle of the town – including Private John Steele whose famous landing on the steeple of the church is still commemorated today. Steele was a member of F Co. 505th PIR and six or seven of the others were killed in the air or immediately on landing. Private Kenneth E Russell also hit the church and was stranded on a lower part of the roof, though he managed to cut himself free and escaped.[17]

In fact only one battalion sized unit remained intact from the American drops – Vandervoort's 2nd Battalion of the 505th – and with the help of this unit the 3rd Battalion under Lt-Col. Krause took Ste Mère-Église at 0400 from German defenders who had assumed the initial assault was all that there was. The first French town had been liberated. The Americans went on to cut the Cherbourg-Carentan road.[18]

Meanwhile Ridgeway had landed alone and the first person he met was Captain Willard Folmer – the same person he had met first when Ridgeway had jumped in Sicily.[19] As Ridgeway himself later commented about his own position near Ste-Mère Église (which was almost exactly where he had planned to set it up): 'The Germans were all around us, of course, sometimes within 500 yards of my command post, but, in the fierce and confused fighting that was going on all about, they did not launch the strong attack that could have wiped out our eggshell perimeter defence'.[20] 'Command post' is probably something of an exaggeration: according to Sergeant Leonard Lebenson, when he arrived, there were only six people for Ridgeway to command.

Ridgeway's scattered troops from the 82nd were unable to mount any major attack upon German positions but ironically the very same distribution led the Germans to assume a much heavier airborne attack than had actually occurred, not just because the 82nd seemed to be everywhere but because they cut every telephone line they found, making it very difficult for the Germans to verify the position and density of the paratroopers.

But the post-jump crisis also left the Americans very short of troops and bereft of any heavy weapons, such as the 57mm anti-tank guns. In theory, the guns were due to accompany the 4,000 reinforcement glider troops, the first wave (of four) being due to arrive at 0407 in 52 Waco gliders. But 15 of these were lost before landing, only 24 landed in the drop zone, and many of those that landed broke up against the hedgerows of the *bocage*. As a result, Ridgeway still had no communications with the beaches or with England or the floating HQ ships off the coast. Even by 8 June there were still only 2,100 available troops from the 82nd Airborne, though over 6,000 had left England (the official casualties totalled 1,259), and German radio quickly reported that the invading division had been destroyed.

What Ridgeway found most galling was that he could do so little about any of the situations his troops found themselves in as they tried to take and hold the causeways against German movements towards the coast because he could only communicate in person and because the area was so vast. His comments personify the critical role – and limits – of the commander in a crisis:

> There was little I could during that first day towards exercising division control. I could only be where the fighting seemed to be the hottest, to exercise whatever personal influence I could on the battalion commanders as they drove on towards the causeways … . Far in the night I was roused by someone shaking me. It was a messenger from one of the battalions fighting towards the river crossing. The Germans, he said, were counter-attacking in strength across the causeway. I couldn't see what in the hell I could do about that single-handed. So I sent word back that the battalion was to hold if it could. If this was impossible then it could pull back. Then I turned over and went back to sleep.[21]

Ridgeway may have been responsible for the 82nd Airborne at this point, but he was not physically leading them.

On 9 June Ridgeway ordered a combined unit of the 507th and 508th PIRs to retake the bridge over the Merderet River at La Fière, one of the few routes west across the flooded base of the Cotentin peninsular.

The bridge had been taken by 400 soldiers from all three of the 82nd's regiments but lost when the 12 paratroopers left to guard it were overrun by a German counter-attack. It took four days to win back the bridge.[22] By D-day+3 contact had been made between the 82nd and

Photo 13.1 Bridge over Merderet River at La Fière

forward units of the 4th Division who had landed on Utah but the fighting to control the four main causeways across the flooded land was extremely bloody. It was another three days before Ridgeway managed to integrate the isolated units under his command and dispose of the German 91st Air Landing Division which was defending the area.

In Ridgeway's opinion, command was critical to the eventual American success:

> The place of a commander is where he anticipates the crisis of action is going to be, and it was obvious to me that these causeway crossings were the spots of greatest hazard. Each time, therefore, before we attempted the crossing, I would go down, preferably at dark, by day if I had to, personally to reconnoitre each crossing before I sent any element of my division across. There were four of these crossings and by far the toughest was the causeway across the wide and sluggish Merderet at La Fière ... . We lost a lot of men there and I think the final assault on June 9 unquestionably would have failed if all the commanders from division to battalion had not been there in person to shove the troops across ... . The first men came down to the crossing, shoulders hunched, leaning forward as if they were moving into a heavy wind. Some of them began to go down, and the others hesitated. Then they turned and started back, instinctively recoiling from the sheer blasting shock of the concentrated enemy fire. I jumped up and ran down there. The men were milling around in the cut. Jim Gavin, my Assistant Divisional Commander, whom I had put in charge of this operation, was there, with the regimental CO ... and the battalion commanders. And there in the cut at the head of the causeway, we grabbed these men, turned them around, pushed, shoved, even led them by hand until we got them started across.[23]

The division continued to move west and enabled the US 9th Infantry Division to cut off the peninsular. It was eventually withdrawn after 33 days on 9 July.[24]

13.4 The 101st Airborne

The experience of the other American Airborne Division, the 101st, was very similar but that of the commander quite different. The 101st, was due to land in four concentrated groups but instead they were spread over 300 square miles of Normandy with 35 'sticks' (plane-load) outside their designated drop zones, and some people 20 miles from their drop zone.[25] This was partly because only 38 of the 120 pathfinders were themselves put down on target.[26]

Some of the 101st paratroopers jumped from a height so low that their parachutes could not open; others survived, but only just. Ken Cordy remembers the jump sequence thus: 'I was dumped out, hit the ground, and then got the opening shock of my chute'.[27] Private Donald Burgett dropped from 300 feet and just managed to get his chute open before he landed but the rest of his comrades were not so lucky: 17 other paratroopers dropped into the same field as he did but none with their parachutes open.[28]

The 101st was to due to drop behind Utah Beach, destroy the coastal battery at St Martin-de-Varreville, capture the exits from the beach, and link up with the sea-landed troops and the 85th Airborne a little further inland. Only exit 1, the most southerly, at Poupeville, caused any problems and that was taken when troops from the 2nd battalion, 8th Infantry Division from Utah Beach attacked the village from the seaward end.[29]

Once again the Germans were unable to take advantage of the situation because the scattered troops, the use of dummy paratroopers, and the effective cutting of many telephone lines by the French resistance, left them unable to assess the picture with any accuracy. The confusion was only to be expected for even by the end of D-Day only 1,100 of the 6,600 soldiers of the 101st had assembled.

Taylor, in command of the 101st, like Ridgeway, found himself in a field – though he did have a cow for company which at least meant that the field was not mined. Like Ridgeway, Taylor also found himself travelling to the front line, but intriguingly he appears to have been doing the trips for the opposite reason:

> In my experience, the history books that depicted the role of the general as being that of galvanizing his men into action were all wrong. I found more often than not that I went up to the front lines not to urge on the troops but to escape the worries

of the command post where all battle noises sounded like the doings of the enemy, and where it was easy for the commander to give way to dire imaginings. A visit to the men of the 101st under fire never failed to send me back to the command post, assured that the situation was well in hand, and that there was no cause for worry.[30]

This is intriguing because it implies that perhaps command as tradi-tionally understood – heroic individuals commanding from the front – was less relevant than we may imagine. Ridgeway embodied this but Taylor's approach was both the opposite and equally effective. Indeed, this is much closer to what Heifetz calls 'getting onto the balcony' now and again to get a strategic perspective on the dance floor.[31] Perhaps, after all, it is what the soldiers and local commanders at the front are doing that makes the difference, not what the formal commanders are doing. As Taylor continued, the scattered distribution of troops also left the 101st with command problems but these seem to have been solved on the spot: 'In the course of the day the men had shown remarkable initiative in forming small task forces under the officers or non-commis-sioned officers who happened to be present and then heading for the nearest division objective.[32]

Carentan was defended by von der Heydte's 6th Parachute Regiment (2nd Parachute Division), and after three days, on his own initiative, he decided to pull out of the city.[33] On 13 June a counter-attack by von der Heydte's paratroops, supported by armour from the 17th SS *Panzergrenadier* Division, came close to retaking the town but they were eventually stopped by tanks from the US 2nd Armoured Division. It was surprising that the 17th SS managed much at all: one third of the 'motor-ized' grenadiers had bicycles, and most of the division was stranded near Vers for two days from 10 to 11 June through lack of fuel. Von der Heydte was certainly unimpressed by their performance (as they were by his), and they were so short of ammunition for their heavy weapons that only a desultory barrage preceded their attack upon the 82nd and 101st Airborne Divisions on 13 June.[34]

About 6,600 paratroopers of the US 101st dropped but only 4,600 landed within their allotted drop zones; many of the rest were killed or captured on landing. By the end of D-Day there were still only 2,500 troops assembled properly and only one of the three senior officers was present, nevertheless, by the afternoon some troops had already linked up with the 4th Infantry Division who had landed on Utah early that morn-ing. By the end of June, 4,670 casualties had been taken and though it eventually accomplished its missions, including taking Carentan on 12 June, its most significant battle lay six months after D-Day when it made a successful stand at Bastogne during the Battle of the Bulge.[35]

334

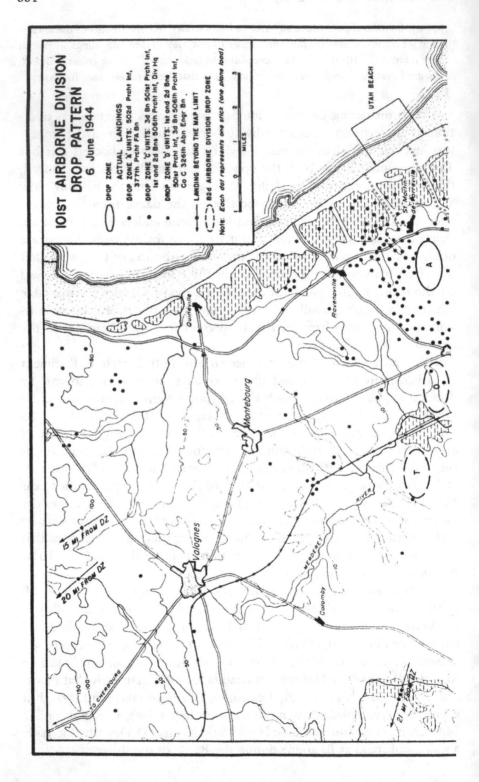

101ST AIRBORNE DIVISION DROP PATTERN
6 June 1944

○ DROP ZONE

ACTUAL LANDINGS
• DROP ZONE 'A' UNITS: 502d Prcht Inf, 377th Prcht FA Bn
• DROP ZONE 'C' UNITS: 3d Bn 501st Prcht Inf, 1st and 2d Bns 506th Prcht Inf, Div Hq
• DROP ZONE 'D' UNITS: 1st and 2d Bns 501st Prcht Inf, 3d Bn 506th Prcht Inf, Co C 326th Abn Engr Bn

•—•—• LANDING BEYOND THE MAP LIMIT
⊂⊃ 82d AIRBORNE DIVISION DROP ZONE

Note: Each dot represents one stick (one plane load)

MILES
0   1   2   3

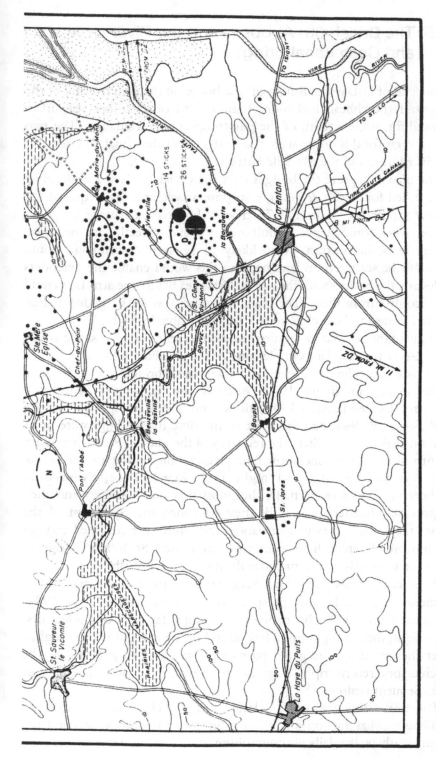

Map 13.2 101st Airborne Division drop pattern, 6 June 1944

13.5 The British 6th Airborne and the River Orne and Caen canal bridges

By the end of D-Day the British 6th Airborne on the eastern flank of the Normandy beachhead had more than a third of its troops still unaccounted for, while a tenth of the paratroopers were casualties. The two main targets for this group were the bridges over the Canal de Caen and the river Orne, and the Merville battery.[36]

The plan to capture the bridges over the Canal de Caen and the river Orne called for a *coup de main*, a surprise attack, and that required the *instant* appearance of around 75 troops. In effect, an attack by glider troops who could arrive simultaneously and directly at the spot. Paratroopers, in contrast, were likely to be seen descending, would inevitably be scattered on landing, and this would enable the defenders to destroy the bridges with the pre-laid charges before the attackers could wrest control from them. The plan, therefore, was for six gliders led by Major Howard to land close to the bridges (three by each).

Many of the air assaults required numerous rehearsals across the country.[37] Geoff Barway, for example, one of the six glider pilots involved in the attack upon the Orne river and Caen canal bridges, began general glider training in August 1942. But like the rest of the British 6th Airborne (formed in April 1943) he was not given any specific training until February 1944, and for most of the time the landings were practised on airfields to facilitate the recovery of the gliders. From then, with the 6th Airborne now operational, he practised the landing on the bridge forty-two times by day and night from March 1944, flying from Netheravon, Wiltshire. Initially, the pilots flew empty gliders and then progressively heavier loads until they contained the equivalent of the troops they would carry to Normandy; they even wore coloured goggles to simulate different light conditions and used St John's bridge at Lechlade to practise the actual assault in Operation Mush.

Another of the six pilots, Staff Sergeant Roy Howard, also practised at Netheravon, but did not begin specialized training until 21 April 1944. From then until D-Day he made one landing a day from 6,000 feet first in daylight, then at night using lights, and finally at night without lights. After the first drop, the glider pilots were expected to get back to the beaches for a return trip to England, from where they were to take part in subsequent airdrops.[38]

The final training involved a large-scale model of the site down to details as small as the position of individual trees. The model was updated continuously by the daily photographing of the area, and it even included

Photo 13.2 St John's Bridge, Lechlade, site of Exercise Mush by 6th Airborne in preparation for assault on Pegasus Bridge

a cine film of the landing using a camera slung from ropes above the model for the pilots to use. In fact, Major Howard himself did not know of the model until a week before the invasion. Morrison's No. 5 Flight watched the film three times.[39]

Even all this training and intelligence was likely to prove inadequate because on 17 April 1944 British intelligence were shocked to discover that anti-glider poles were being erected all over the designated gliding landing areas. This made it necessary to clear landing zones of 1,000 yards by 60 yards and to illuminate them with lights. The 6th Airborne Division then felled 100 trees in the New Forest and erected them in the same pattern to establish the best way to clear them. In the end it was decided that the best clearance involved digging out a hole round the base 6 inches deep and 12 inches out for the pole, laying a bicycle inner tune filled with 5lb of explosive in the hole and six squads of twelve soldiers could clear the necessary number of poles in the time allotted: 90 minutes. On D-Day the times were bettered, despite being under fire, because the poles were of smaller diameter than had been assumed.[40]

The sudden appearance of anti-glider poles around the bridges just days before the invasion, then, did not deter the pilots and four of the gliders landed to plan – one landed by the wrong river eight miles away but these four were exactly on target. One authority[41] suggests that Howard's glider hit the ground 47 yards from the canal bridge and one that he was 47 feet away.[42] While Howard himself thought it was about 50 yards – and his descent had required two people to run to the back of the glider to rebalance it.[43] Whatever the distance Leigh Mallory later called it 'the finest feat of airmanship in the entire war'.[44] The first glider, No. 91, flown by Staff Sergeants Wallwork and Ainsworth, landed at 0016 and 23 members of the 2nd Battalion, the Oxfordshire and Buckinghamshire Light Infantry (52nd Foot) and five sappers from 2nd Platoon, 249th Field Company Royal Engineers, exited the plane.

On hearing the gliders land Wilhelm Furtner and Helmut Romer, the German sentries on the canal bridge, assumed a bomber had crashed and were taken totally by surprise. So despite landing so close to their target, and despite the sentries being aware of a plane crash-landing, the exiting glider troops were met by silence. 'It seemed quite unbelievable', recalled John Howard clearly expecting a chaotic situation, 'there was no firing!'[45] No. 1 Platoon, under Lt Brotheridge, stormed the bridge, putting the machine gun post on the northern edge out of action, and then raced across the bridge sending the two sentries scuttling back to the west end near the café under fire. They immediately knocked out the 50mm anti-tank gun – which was unmanned at the time because the garrison commander, Major Hans Schmidt, had stood down many of his soldiers and was himself asleep with his girlfriend in the nearby village of Ranville.

Within five minutes the other gliders had landed and D Company had taken its objectives suffering just one death on landing (L. Corporal Greenhalgh) and one further death in the assault against the 50-strong German garrison (Lt Brotheridge). Many of the German defenders, though not their NCOs, seemed to have fled in terror.[46] Heinz Hickman and four other members of the German 6th Independent Parachute Regiment had been about to cross the canal bridge from the west when they heard the firing and took up defensive positions, but not for long: 'I am not a coward but at that moment I got frightened. If you see a Para platoon in full cry, they frighten the daylights out of you … the way they charge … the way they fire, the way they ran across the bridge … . Then I gave the order to go back. What could I do with four men who had never been in action?'[47]

The attackers knew that the demolition charges were set to be activated from the pill box because Georges Gondrée, the owner of the café on the bridge, had already informed the French Resistance who had passed the information back to London.[48] But although the wiring was in place, the charges had been removed to prevent accidents or sabotage and were stored in a house by the canal-bridge.

Shortly after the assaults Major Schmidt returned from Ranville in an open half track with a motor cycle escort and the group was fired on by the troops on the canal bridge. The motor cyclist was killed and his bike went into the river but Schmidt's vehicle ploughed across the river bridge only to be stopped at the river bridge's west end by more firing from Sweeney's platoon. The captured Schmidt then proceeded to lecture Captain Vaughan, the Medical Officer, about the futility of the attack and the inevitable victory of the 'master race', ending his diatribe with a request for Vaughan to shoot him. 'This I did,' remembers Vaughan, 'in the bottom with a needle attached to a syringe of morphia. The effect of this, it seems, induced him to take a more reasonable view of things'.[49]

At 0050, just half an hour after the attack on the bridges had started, and right on time, the first of the 2,200 reinforcing paratroopers from 7th Parachute Battalion could be heard circling overhead. But the poor visibility and high winds scattered them all over the countryside and it was another 90 minutes before they arrived, and even then only one third turned up and without any heavy equipment. Before they had arrived the first German counter-attack had been launched at 0130 from the Bénouville direction in the form of a Panzer Mk IV. This could only be stopped by Sergeant Thornton firing the only available PIAT:

I don't mind admitting it, I was shaking like a bloody leaf as this bloody great thing appears. The lads behind me were only lightly armed with Bren guns, rifles and grenades. They wouldn't stand a chance if I missed and the whole operation would be over. I was so nervous I was talking to myself, 'This is it! You mustn't miss'. The first tank, a MK IV, had begun moving slowly down the road. I pulled the trigger on the PIAT. It was a direct hit. Machine gun clips inside the tank set off grenades which set off shells. There was the most enormous explosion, with bits and pieces flying everywhere, and lighting up the darkness. To my delight the other tank fled ... .[50]

In fact the tank partly blocked the road but, more importantly, an early flight by an Army spotter plane had seen further tank movements and radioed the co-ordinates back to HMS Warspite. After a few salvos the German armour retreated.[51] Thornton's attack and the naval gunfire persuaded the Germans that the bridges were held by a strong group that could only be assaulted with reinforcements and in daylight – several hours away. In that time the owners of the café, George and Thérésa Gondrée, offered their building for use as a hospital – and dug up and distributed the 98 bottles of champagne George had buried in the garden in 1940.

The unreality of war continued the next morning when two Italians, working for the German Todt Organization, were discovered in the hedges nearby; they were fed, and turned loose. They immediately resumed the job for which they had turned up: erecting anti-glider poles on the fields where the gliders had just landed.[52]

Lovat's Commandos of the 1st Special Service Brigade were the first sea-borne troops from the Anglo-Canadian beaches to link up with the airborne troops and did so at about 1330 to the sound of Lovat's piper, Bill Millin, playing 'Blue Bonnets over the Border'. Contrary to the film version in *The Longest Day*, Millin did not pipe the Commandos over the canal bridge despite the enemy fire but actually stopped playing 100 yards short of the bridge and ran across it with Lovat.[53] As they got to the end of the canal bridge, Lovat turned to Millin and said, 'Right, play now and keep playing all along this road until you come to another bridge and keep playing right across – no matter what just keep playing'.[54] In fact some Commandos were killed on the bridge as they crossed and subsequently steel helmets rather than green berets were often adopted.

The attackers who captured the Dives bridge were even more fortunate, for that bridge had been the subject of an unannounced night-time training exercise the previous month when, in the confusion, two German 'attackers' were shot dead and an investigation carried out. Little wonder that when another night-time attack occurred the defenders were reluctant to open fire again.[55]

13.6 The British 6th Airborne and the Merville battery

The other critical task allotted to the British 6th Airborne was the elimination of the Merville battery which comprised 150mm guns with a range of over 8 miles and thought capable (erroneously as it turned out) of bombarding Sword Beach.[56] The battery had been the target of over 1,000 bombs before the raid, but only 50 landed near the target and only two landed on it, one of which cracked casemate No. 1.[57]

The task of destroying the battery from the land fell to Lt Colonel Terence Otway's 9th Parachute Battalion which included 690 paratroopers and 60 glider troops – almost 10 per cent of the total strength. Otway had an area four miles south of Hungerford near Newbury, Berkshire, landscaped until it resembled the battery – and had just two months to perfect their attack – which they practised in full nine times, mainly with live ammunition by day and night. Otway had asked for 75 volunteers from the existing British 6th Airborne and deselected the extra number who stepped forward by rejecting all those who were married. The troops were not briefed as to the precise location of their target until the beginning of June and all individuals were required to submit a sketch to their superiors showing, from memory, their precise location and task.

But some old hands had long understood that no amount of training was ever going to ensure perfect execution. Brigadier James Hill, in over-all command of the Merville operation, told his officers the day before the assault: 'Gentlemen, in spite of your excellent training and orders, do not be daunted if chaos reigns. It undoubtedly will.'[58]

The raid was supposed to be guided in by ten members of the advance party who were to land at 0020 and ten minutes later 100 Lancaster and Halifax bombers would drop 4,000lbs of bombs on the battery to 'soften up' the defenders. The advance party would then cut the wire around the battery, secure access through the minefield and determine whether the bombing had put the guns out of action. Another section from the advance party was to set up the rendezvous for the rest of the battalion which would be dropping at 0050, along with five gliders carrying jeeps, anti-tank guns to destroy the doors of the casemates, mine detectors and luminous tapes, mortars to illuminate the attack, machine guns to guard the flanks from counter-attack, bangalore torpedoes – whose detonation would mark the beginning of the attack – and explosives to destroy the guns. By 0235 the battalion should have assembled and by 0400 they should have been ready for the assault. At 0430 three more gliders would land between the casements carrying troops with flame throwers to lead the assault and if no success signal was received by 0500 HMS *Arethusa* would begin shelling the area from the sea at 0515.

Things went wrong almost immediately. First, the majority of bombers missed their target, bombing the nearby village of Gonneville-sur-Merville (now Gonneville-en-Auge) to the south of Merville battery instead. Second, many of the paratroopers were widely dispersed by the weather conditions and by the evasive action taken by the pilots to avoid flak. Third, much of the matériel had been lost in the drop because all five transport-gliders had ditched in the channel. This left the attackers with little. For example, they only had one bundle of bangalore torpe-does and one heavy machine gun, but they had no jeeps, no mine detec-tors or tapes, no anti-tank guns, no mortars nor indeed did they have the remaining two thirds of the troops who had failed to turn up at the rendezvous. Fourth, the advance party had managed to make a path through the minefield but it could not be marked by tapes, nor could the attack be illuminated because the mortars were also missing. Fifth, the absence of flame-throwers or explosives made both the assault precarious and the destruction of the guns difficult.

Otway's own descent was precarious and he watched the leader of the parachute stick behind him land in a bog and go straight under the surface, leaving only the top of his parachute as a marker. By the time he was retrieved he was dead.[59] By 0250, with just over 150 soldiers Otway headed for the battery and awaited the glider assault troops. In theory the gliders were to land on top of the battery but in practice the radio beacons to guide them were destroyed on landing and the signal flares to guide them in were missing. Thus three of them landed some distance away. The fourth, hit by anti-aircraft fire, landed within 200 yards of Otway's assault position – having narrowly missed crashing straight into them – and managed to keep German reinforcements away from the area. The fifth glider had been over-laden and forced to land back at Brize Norton.[60]

Despite the crisis that faced the paratroopers, the assault was successful, but the cost to both sides was high: 110 of the 200 German defenders[61] and 65 of Otway's 155 attackers were dead or injured. Some had stepped on the mines because the pathways were not marked by tapes, some had been shot by German machine-gun fire, some injured or killed in the hand to hand fighting inside the four casemates, and others were hit by the artillery fire laid down by the nearby Cabourg battery. This had been telephoned for by Raimund Steiner, the Merville Battery Commander, who was actually in the observation bunker on the beach 1.5 miles away at the time of the attack.[62]

The guns turned out to be 100mm not 150mm, and there is still some dispute about whether all the guns were disabled – though even without explosive charges it seems that at least some were put out of action with gammon grenades.[63] The only thing left to do was to notify the *Arethusa* to prevent friendly fire. That notification should have come from a naval signaller but none had arrived so the first alternative was a carrier pigeon, carried by Lt Loring, which promptly flew off to England rather than the *Arethusa*. Fortunately, the second alternative signal – yellow flares – were spotted by a circling reconnaissance plane.[64]

When Otway's troops withdrew from the battery it was retaken by a unit of the German 736th Grenadier Regiment who, in turn were routed by another British attack on 7 June by two troops of No. 3 Commando under Major Pooley. The Commandos were themselves counter-attacked and half of them killed, including Pooley, posthumously awarded the George Cross and subsequently buried in Bayeux. The battery remained disputed territory until late June.[65]

13.7 The German response to the airdrops

The confusion that reigned amongst many of the Allied paratroopers and glider troops was mirrored by the German defenders on the ground. The common assumption remained that the airdrop was merely a feint to draw attention away from the real invasion at Calais. And although reports of Allied troops in the area emerged soon after the landings, the apparently random pattern of the drops made it exceptionally difficult for the Germans to make an appropriate response. Furthermore, since most of the senior commanders were away, whatever the response was – and contrary to traditional Germany military philosophy of Mission Command – it would have to await further orders from above.

Colonel Hans von Luck, CO of the 125th *Panzergrenadier* Regiment (part of General Feuchtinger's 21st Panzer Division) typified the dual reactions of the German troops on the ground on the night of the airborne landings. First, an immediate willingness to engage the invaders in response to the apparent crisis, but second a refusal to do so without permission from above: 'I gave orders without hesitation, recalled von Luck, "All units are to be put on alert immediately and the division informed. No. II battalion is to go into action wherever necessary" .... . In the meantime, my adjutant telephoned the division. General Feuchtinger and his general-staff officer had not come back yet (Feuchtinger was seeing his girlfriend in Paris). We gave the orderly officer, Lieutenant Messmer, a brief situation report and asked him to obtain clearance for us for a concentrated night attack the moment the divisional commander returned'.[66] Von Luck, then, while willing to engage the invaders with his own local forces would not move in any concerted manner until Feuchtinger agreed, and Feuchtinger was absent and had forgotten to take a radio with him. Dollman (CO of the 7th Army) was also missing – at the war game in Rennes. Even when Feuchtinger returned, von Luck still had to wait because Feuchtinger had to wait for Rommel's clearance.

Since I had been told that I was to make no move until I heard from Rommel's headquarters I could do nothing immediately but warn my men to be ready. I waited patiently all that night for some instructions. But not a single order from a higher formation was received by me ... I finally decided at 6.30 in the morning that I had to take some action. I ordered my tanks to attack the English 6th Airborne which had entrenched itself in a bridgehead over the Orne. To me this constituted the most immediate threat to the German position.

Hardly had I made this decision when, at seven o'clock, I received my first intimation that a higher command did still exist. I was told by Army Group B that I was now under the command of the Seventh Army. But I received no further orders as to my role. At nine o'clock I was informed that I would receive orders from 84th Infantry Corps and finally at ten o'clock I was given my first operational instructions. I was ordered [by General Marcks] to stop the move of my tanks towards the Allied airborne troops and to turn west and aid the forces protecting Caen ... . By this time the enemy ... had made astonishing progress and had already occupied a strip of high ground about ten kilometres from the sea. From here the excellent anti-tank gunfire of the Allies knocked out eleven of my tanks before I had barely started ... . By the end of that first day my division had lost almost twenty-five per cent of its tanks.[67]

This marked inertia amongst the German High Command was in clear opposition to the traditional policy of subordinate initiative, especially in a crisis, but that had been stripped away by Hitler's determination to maintain control over the Panzer reserve, by the division of responsibilities between Rommel and von Rundstedt, and – the critical point – by the unwillingness of local and subordinate commanders to take the action that they knew to be required irrespective of orders to the contrary. In fact, Feuchtinger was cajoled by Major-General Richter, CO of the neighbouring 716th Infantry Division, to attack the airborne landings at 0120 and the standing orders *required* Feuchtinger's compliance because although the 21st Panzer Division was under (Hitler's) OKW control, this control shifted to Richter's 716th Infantry if the area came under attack – which it most clearly was.[68] Feuchtinger, however, preferred to obey another standing order that contradicted the former one and demanded no action without the authorization of Army Group B, under Rommel. Yet Rommel had also issued a general directive demanding an immediate attack by all forces available should an airborne landing occur and, according to General Speidel, Rommel's Chief of Staff, Feuchtinger was well aware of this – even if no other officer except Speidel was. Perhaps this should not be such a surprise because Feuchtinger had no combat experience, little tank experience, and owed his position to his organizing of Nazi Party rallies and thus the close appreciation of Hitler. As Mitcham concludes, Feuchtinger was 'one of the least qualified and least successful of the German tank commanders'.[69] And the greatest irony was that the chief architect of this shambles, Hitler, had issued a directive on 23 March 1942 which specifically warned against what eventually happened: 'The preparation and execution of defensive operations must unequivocally and unreservedly be concentrated in the hands of one man'.[70]

Whoever was responsible for this calamitous state of affairs it provided the Allies with several hours of freedom of movement before any significant German response occurred – and this despite Hitler's own briefing just before the invasion that 'the enemy's entire landing operation must under no circumstances be allowed to last longer than a matter of hours, or, at most days'.[71] As von Luck went on: 'I am quite sure that had we been able to make a counter-attack at once, in the direction of the coast and Pegasus Bridge, it would have been successful'.[72] He was probably right and, as Carell insists, 'this diversion of German reserves away from the coast was probably the most important contribution by the British 6th Airborne in the early hours of 6 June'.[73] It would be difficult to conjure up a more Critical Problem for the German army than had occurred in the very early hours of 6 June, and the response required by a successful commander would have been a decisive act to attack the invaders at whatever point was deemed crucial, but the failure to act at all for several hours irredeemably undermined the German defence: at the crucial moment the commanders – at each and every level – had failed.

Colonel Oppeln-Bronikowski, commander of the 98 obsolete tanks and 26 self-propelled artillery guns in the 100th Regiment of the 21st Panzer Division was another of those ordered to change direction four hours after his first move against the paratroopers on the Orne river. He had been ordered to maintain radio silence and thus unable to pick up the orders from Feuchtinger to change direction earlier. Oppeln-Bronikowski should probably have not been in command because a few weeks before the invasion Rommel had visited the HQ of the 21st Panzers at Falaise – but first found no-one there – and then discovered Oppeln-Bronikowski drunk.[74] Oppeln-Bronikowski was later joined by the 192nd *Panzergrenadier* Regiment and the 736th Grenadiers for the push towards the beaches in daylight – a move that left the 21st Panzers with only 60 tanks after air attacks by the time they made contact with the invaders.

A rifle company of the 192nd *Panzergrenadiers* reached the beach at Lion-sur-Mer almost unopposed between 1900 and 2000 on D-Day, but as the leading half dozen tanks approached they were attacked from the east on Sword Beach by the British, from the west on Juno Beach by the Canadians, and again from the air by Allied aircraft. Within minutes, 16 of the second rate tanks of the 21st Panzers were hit – even before their own guns were within range of their persecutors. Moreover, as the tanks reached the coast at 2100 a huge glider force landed virtually on top of them, encouraging the tank commander to order a halt. As von Luck stated later, 'From the hills east of Caen, we saw the gigantic Allied armada, the fields littered with transport gliders. In view of this superiority, I thought, on seeing the landing fleet, there was no longer much chance of throwing the Allies back in to the sea'.[75]

Lt Franz Grabmann, also with the 21st Panzers as it headed for the sea, had a similar experience. He been told by a returning motor cyclist that the leading units were already there '... which was heartening news. Then, like a thunderbolt from the sky came a great aerial column of planes and gliders which, despite our flak, proceeded to land before us about the area. We were so disheartened we felt we could not continue'.[76] In fact, the gap between the beaches remained in German hands for a short while but it was not to become the spring board for a major counter-attack[77] and by the end of D-Day the 21st Panzer Division had lost 54 of its 124 tanks.[78] The only German division that was moved to Normandy from outside, the 346th Infantry Division stationed west of Dieppe, was ordered to Sword Beach area but it was too little and too late.[79]

General Bayerlein, commander of the *Panzer Lehr* division at Le Mans, 130 miles from the coast, was also informed of the invasion at 0200 and was also ready to move against the invaders by 0500. Since it was already starting to get light by then any movement would be vulnerable to air attack – but the low cloud that existed on the morning of D-Day would have effectively rendered the movement invisible. However, *Panzer Lehr* was unable to move until personally released by Hitler at 1540. Given the improved visibility and the clear presence of Allied aircraft, Bayerlein then requested a delay until dark. This was denied and the division was ordered by Hitler himself not just to move immediately but to ensure that the invaders were repulsed by that evening. *Panzer Lehr* began its move north as ordered by Dollmann, commander of the 7th Army, and from Chartres to the beaches *Panzer Lehr*'s Captain Hartdegen, General Bayerlein's orderly officer, recalled being attacked on ten separate occasions from the air.[80] By the end of the day *Panzer Lehr* had still not reached its destination but had lost 40 fuel trucks, 50 other trucks, five tanks, and 84 half-tracks and self-propelled guns.[81]

Not far behind *Panzer Lehr*'s state of readiness was the 12th SS *Hitlerjugend* (HJ) Division. At 0230 the 12th SS HJ made a reconnaissance to the east of the Dives river but was ordered at 0545 to concentrate around Lisieux – almost 40 miles east of Caen by road and in the wrong direction – despite the fact that the commanders of the HJ already knew where the invasion had occurred. Unable to contact the 1st SS Panzer Corps commander, Dietrich, to suggest a change of direction, the HJ duly obeyed orders and set out at 1000 hours. At between 1500 and 1600 the orders were changed and the division redirected to where they should have been going in the first place, west of Caen. By the time the HJ were in the right place to attack the Allies they had spent almost 24 hours in a fruitless movement across Normandy.

Witt's 12th SS HJ and Feuchtinger's 21st Panzers had just 160 tanks between them and less than one third of the 12th SS's infantry had arrived, so great was the air pressure on German movements. They wanted to wait for *Panzer Lehr*'s arrival before mounting a three-division counter-attack but were ordered to ensure that Carpiquet airport remained in German hands and attacked at 1600 on 7 June. Three hours prior to this Canadian infantry from the Nova Scotia Highlanders and tanks from the Sherbrooke Fusiliers began approaching Carpiquet airport and ran straight into Kurt Meyer's 25th SS *Panzergrenadier* Regiment (part of the 12th SS HJ) waiting for the German counter-attack to take place. In the ensuing 6 hour battle the Canadians lost 302 casualties (including 110 dead) and 128 as prisoners and 21 tanks; the Germans lost 300 casualties (including 73 dead) and 9 tanks. By D-Day+3 the 12th SS HJ had suffered 725 casualties, including 186 dead.[82,83] The Germans had prevented the Allies reaching either the airport or Caen but the Allies had prevented the Germans from reaching the coast. *Panzer Lehr* had been delayed by the destroyed bridge at Thury-Harcourt and eventually reached Caen in the morning of 8 June.[84] But the willingness of the German troops to commit themselves to battle could not compensate for the farcical nature of the German higher command.

In the event Von Rundstedt was the only senior officer around at the time of the invasion (Rommel wasn't even informed of the invasion until one hour after the Allies issued the official communiqué at 0930 – eight hours after the first capture of Allied paratroopers).[85] Within two hours of being notified von Rundstedt had ordered *Panzer Lehr* and the 12th SS HJ to move towards Caen. Von Rundstedt was well aware that formal permission from Hitler was necessary for such an order, but since the movement made good military sense his request to OB West was more in terms of fulfilling the bureaucratic niceties rather than formally asking whether he could mobilize the Panzers. But that order was countermanded by Jodl, head of the OKW (*Oberkommando der Wehrmacht*, German High Command) at about 0600 on 6 June – at the same time as a message arrived at OB West from Normandy reporting very heavy fire and large seaborne landings. Jodl reminded Von Rundstedt that Hitler alone could order their movement – and Hitler had only gone to sleep at 0400 and would remain asleep until 1030 – giving the Allies four and a half hours of extra freedom. 'According to reports I have received', insisted Jodl, 'it could be a diversionary attack … part of a deception plan. OB West has sufficient reserves right now … . OB West should endeavour to clean up the attack with the forces at their disposal … . I do not think this is the time to release the OKW reserves … . We must wait for further clarification'.

That decision to avoid a decision – so important for Wicked Problems – was manifestly inappropriate when facing a Critical Problem. Kurt Zeitzler, Chief of the General Staff of the army, clearly thought Hitler's response to the invasion news was just such an inappropriate response, 'that was typical. The invasion has begun. Time is of the essence. Instead of rushing officers to the front in an aircraft, instead of flying to the west immediately in person, instead of taking decisions or giving your commander in the west a free hand, every situation is discussed at length. We wait and hesitate. We'll miss the right moment to strike back and then it will be too late.'[86] Thus 160 German tanks were stood to, fuelled and ready to move, and they sat there waiting. Not until 1540 did Hitler order the 12th SS *HJ* and the *Panzer Lehr* to resume the movement towards Caen that Von Rundstedt had ordered and OKW stopped.[87] 'It was what General Warlimont called 'the chaos of leadership in the Leader State'.[88] The decision – to leave things as they were – according to Lt General Zimmerman, chief of operations, left von Rundstedt 'fuming with rage, red in the face, and his anger made his speech unintelligible'.[89] Yet the specific question of releasing the OKW Panzer divisions was not even raised at the conference called on D-Day and von Rundstedt failed to try and make direct contact with Hitler on 6 June.

Inevitably, the hopelessly byzantine command structure hamstrung the flexibility of the commanders on the ground. As Ambrose concludes:

> The truth is that despite individual acts of great bravery and the fanaticism of some *Wehrmacht* troops, the performance of the *Wehrmacht* 's high command, middle-ranking officers, and junior officers was just pathetic. The cause is simply put: they were afraid to take the initiative. They allowed themselves to be paralyzed by stupid orders coming from far away that bore no relation to the situation on the battlefield ... . The contrast between [the Allied leaders] in adjusting and reacting to unexpected situations, and their German counterparts could not have been greater.[90]

And where stupidity fell away, naiveté replaced it: between 1430 and 1500 on D-Day the 1st SS Panzer division LAH was ordered to remain in Belgium. On 9 June German intelligence reported that the main Allied landing would occur on 10 June in the Pas de Calais region and 1st SS Panzers were moved to Bruges to prepare for an attack that never came. The attack had already occurred over 200 miles away. As Rommel drove back to Normandy his diagnosis of the situation to his driver, Hellmuth Lang, was dire: 'If I was commander of the Allied forces right now I could finish the war in fourteen days'.[91] General Erich Marcks, commander of the LXXXIV Corps until his death on 12 June, would have agreed for he had thought that 10 June was the last date to defeat the invasion.[92]

13.8 Conclusion

Rommel was unduly pessimistic for it took another 11 months to finish the war in Europe but nevertheless he recognized that a fatal blow had been struck against Fortress Europe from which it would be almost impossible to recover. What is intriguing about the air drops is that they embody a microcosm of the critical difference between the Allies and the Nazis. While the latter's success in the first two years of the war had been grounded in *Auftragstaktik* – mission control – that replaced *Befehlstaktik* – an uncompromising order, that flexibility at the local level had been progressively undermined by Hitler. Ironically, while the conventional units of the Allies tended to follow in the tracks of *Befehlstaktik* their more elite units, including the airborne divisions worked through *Auftragstaktik*. This may have partly due to the nature of their tasks but also derived from their cultural preference for devolved control. On D-Day the massive dispersal of paratroopers and glider troops effectively forced Allied commanders to work through small and often informal structures. In contrast, where *Auftragstaktik* was precisely what the situation required from the German commanders their slide back into *Befehlstaktik* destroyed what chance they had for throwing the invaders back into the sea. That chance was significant: if the Panzer divisions had moved towards the coast when they were first ready all the landings could have resembled Omaha and the whole operation might have been in jeopardy. As it was the Allied confusion in the air mirrored the German confusion on the ground, giving the seaborne troops a fighting chance of gaining and retaining a foothold in Normandy: Command – good and bad – not luck, was the springboard to success.

14 The Amphibious Landings

14.1 Introduction

One of the essential aspects of a crisis is its unanticipated nature, and the shock to the Germans of the armada's sudden appearance was colossal, for the sheer size and scale of the operation seemed overwhelming. 'There were so many vessels', recalled Sergeant Richard Heklotz of the German 110th Field Artillery, 'so many ships, that there was nowhere on the horizon that you could look and not see some type of vessel'.[1] But as Omaha Beach was to prove, surprise and materiel were necessary but not sufficient to secure the landings; that required Command too.

The Allied policy of the assault teams had been that an officer should be the first off the landing craft and, as in the assaults from the trenches in the First World War, this was partly responsible for the junior officers' high casualty rate: although they comprised just under 1 per cent of the total numbers in the army, they made up 3 per cent of the total casualties.[2] But the reason for requiring such a heavy sacrifice reflects back upon the general Allied assumption amongst all except the elite troops, that without Command from the front the ordinary soldiers could not be persuaded to go forward. Turner is certainly clear that getting the troops off the beach was only secured through one particular phenomenon:

> The decisive factor proved to be leadership. Where did they go from there? No one could see how to advance straight over the top. Then a young lieutenant and a sergeant, already wounded, suddenly stood up, disregarded the frequent firing, and calmly walked over to look at the wire beyond the embankment. Somehow they were not hit. The lieutenant returned and, hands on hips, looked down at the men lying behind the shingle. "Are you going to lay there and get killed, or get up and do something about it?" he called across to them. None of them moved, so, with the sergeant, he got the explosives, walked back to the obstacles, and blasted a way through the wire. At last the men stirred, and the lieutenant led the way in single file under continuous fire up a path prickling with mines. So, slowly, they got to grips with the enemy defences which covered the beaches.[3]

But the related consequence of an over reliance upon formal commanders was that when those leaders were incapacitated, the rest of the group often moved into 'learned incompetence' – they only knew how to follow. Private John Mather, a combat engineer who cleared a path up the bluff, came across one group of soldiers where the Lieutenant was trying to persuade his company commander to move forward. But 'the CO was in a state of shock; he had lost half his men. He looked like hell and was very dispirited. I asked the Lieutenant if there wasn't something we could do but he couldn't get the CO to take action. So we sat in our holes and listened to the sound of the mortars swishing overhead and watched the tide go out'.[4] It is also important to note that the commanders who seemed most successful on the day were the kind that embodied rather than simply articulated the action required. In other words, if commanders wanted followers to do something other than what they were currently doing, then the commanders had to show them how to do it not just tell them what needed doing; they had to command from the front. Sergeant John Ellery certainly felt this way:

> I read about a number of generals and colonels who are said to have wandered about exhorting the troops to advance. That must have been very inspirational. I suspect, however, that the men were more interested and more impressed by junior officers and NCOs who were willing to lead them rather than having some general pointing out the direction in which they should go. I didn't see any generals in my area of the beach, but I did see a captain and two lieutenants who demonstrated courage beyond belief as they struggled to bring order to the chaos around them … . I don't see how the credit can go to anyone other than the Company grade officers and senior NCOs who led the way.[5]

McManus is equally adamant that it was the NCOs that made the difference, rather than the officers: 'With surprising frequency combat soldiers looked to their sergeants for leadership day and day out in combat. A major reason for that was the turnover in officers. Another reason was that NCOs were usually closer to the men'. Indeed, the closer one got to the front line the greater the respect for the officers who actually fought there became. And since casualty rates amongst combat officers were extraordinarily high, many units fought without officers under the command of NCOs, or whoever took control if there were no NCOs left alive.[6] But were the experiences of the troops on different beaches identical?

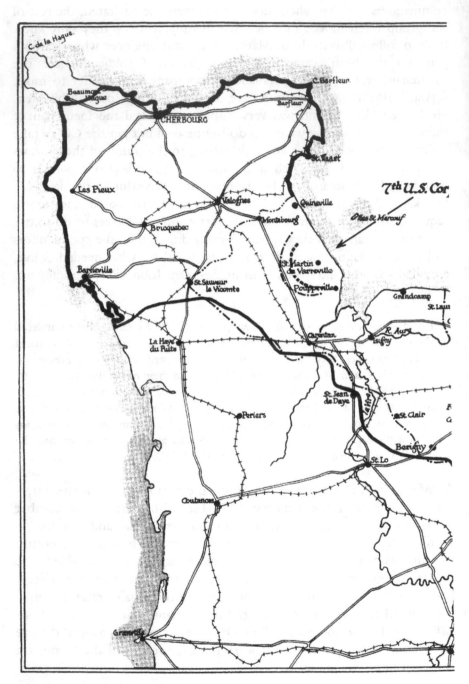

Map 14.1 Sketch map of military advance, 6–30 June 1944

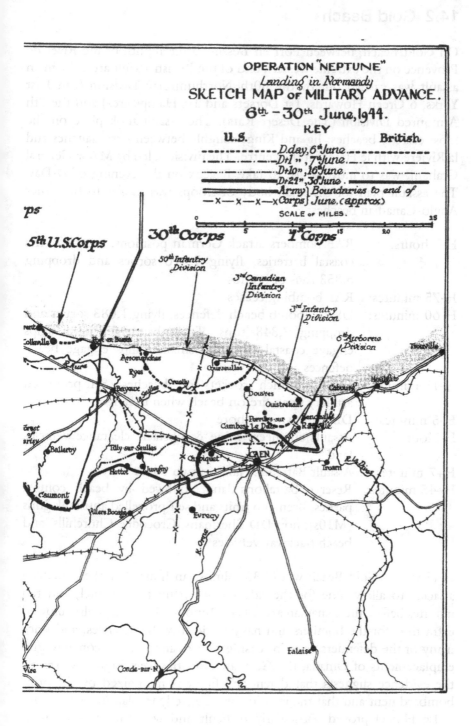

OPERATION "NEPTUNE"
Landing in Normandy
SKETCH MAP of MILITARY ADVANCE.
6th – 30th June, 1944.

KEY

U.S.		British
	D.day, 6th June	
	D+1 ", 7th June	
	D+10", 16th June	
	D+24", 30th June	
	Army) Boundaries to end of	
	—x—x—x—x Corps) June. (approx)	

SCALE of MILES.

14.2 Gold Beach

On Gold Beach, between Port en Bessin to the mouth of the River de Provence on the extreme western end of the British assault area, the main assault was carried out by the 50th Northumbrian Division (5th East Yorks, 6 Green Howards, 1st Dorsets and 1st Hampshires) and the 7th Armoured Division (The Desert Rats). The assault took place on the most easterly beaches: Jig and King, roughly between Arromanches and la Rivière with le Hamel at the centre. The division, led by Major-General Graham, was to move south to take Bayeux on the evening of D-Day. The assault plan for the main body of troops was similar to the other Anglo-Canadian beaches:

H-7 hours:	RAF bombers attack German positions, especially the coastal batteries, flying 1,316 sorties and dropping 5,853 tons of bombs
H-75 minutes:	RAF bombing ceases
H-60 minutes:	USAAF bomb beach defences, flying 1,083 sorties and dropping 7,348 tons of bombs; larger naval ships engage coastal batteries, smaller ships engage beach defences
H-15 minutes:	LC(R)s launch rockets on beaches; Self-propelled artillery open fire on beach when in range
H-5 minutes:	DD tanks swim ashore
H Hour:	Assault engineers mine & obstacle clearance vehicles land
H+7 minutes:	Assault Battalions land in two waves
H+45 minutes:	Reserve battalions land, followed by beach control parties, Bren gun units and self-propelled anti-tank guns (M10s), non-DD Shermans, Crocodile Churchills, and beach trackway vehicles[7]

H-Hour on Gold Beach was 0735, almost an hour after the American attacks, to allow time for the tide to sweep up the channel, and ten minutes before the Canadian assaults on Juno further east. It also allowed extra time for the bombers and navy to destroy the defences, and since many of the defenders were in seaside houses and not the concrete gun emplacements of Omaha, the German casualties were higher. Certainly the evidence suggests that defender's fire was minimized by the prior bombardment and that the invasion went exactly to plan in some areas.

Le Hamel proved particularly difficult and was not captured until around 1600. Partly this was because low cloud cover had prevented accurate bombing and the 75 tons of bombs planned for the area were dropped 3,000 yards south of the beach. Also missing was the 147th Field Regiment of self-propelled artillery that should have shelled Le Hamel on approach from the sea.[8] However, the navigating and controlling craft were both delayed and, as a consequence, the 147th fired on the beaches to the east of Le Hamel. It was also the case that the German gun emplacements were almost immune to the low trajectory shells fired from the destroyers off the beach and the first three of four Flail tanks were hit by fire from the anti-tank guns. Finally, no requests for additional shelling were made by the attackers, the 1st Battalion the Hampshire Regiment – because both the commanding officer and second in command were killed in the initial assault and because the Battalion had landed several hundred yards east of their designated landing position – in fact precisely where the Dorsets should have landed. They had also lost all their radios and could not, therefore, call for supporting fire from the naval ships – though someone in authority could presumably have contacted their nearest associates with a radio.

Particular problems derived from the 75mm casemated gun on the seafront which destroyed at least six Allied tanks before being put out of action. Eventually, a combined bombardment by the destroyers and several LCFs and LCGs, using 4.7 inch guns, co-ordinated with a land assault from the west by the 1st Hants, successfully stormed the defences but the area was not completely secured until 2000.[9] On the beach itself most of the initial work had been completed by 2030, when 1,200 yards of beach was open and by the end of D-Day+1, by when 2,000 obstacles had been removed or destroyed and two miles of coastline were declared safe.[10]

As on Omaha Beach, one of the reasons that the Allied soldiers *eventually* made progress against a seemingly impregnable enemy defence system was simply that the defenders ran out of ammunition. For example, Fritz Buchte, manning an MG42 machine gun, 'ran out of ammunition so one of my helpers at the gun ran off for more but never returned. We were obliged to use rifles and grenades, but this was very hard as the British tanks and infantry were shooting at us and some got behind us. Suddenly our sergeant appeared and said, "It's no use, we're surrounded! We must surrender!"'[11] Hans Ludwig Weiner, of 716th Infantry Division, had also surrendered when he ran out of ammunition – though he too was surprised that the British troops moved so slowly up the beach, as much as anything because of the preposterous amount of material they each had to carry.[12] Even the casemated positions on Le Hamel did not stock enough ammunition to hold up the British attackers. Peter Wolf Agnussen of the 711th Infantry Division held on until two AVRE

Petards began mortaring his emplacement in the sanatorium at the same time as his ammunition ran out in the early afternoon. Only when the situation appeared hopeless did the German captain, in consultation with his sergeant, accept that surrendering was acceptable.[13]

In other areas the plan went awry almost immediately when conditions at sea were so rough that it was decided not to launch the DD tanks at sea from where they were supposed to spearhead the infantry, but to land them directly on the beach, *behind* the infantry. The original plan had been to deploy three squadrons of DD Shermans from the 4th/7th Royal Dragoon Guards but the introduction of five Fireflies to A Squadron, left B Squadron's DD Shermans to land 5 minutes before the 6th Green Howards on King Green, and C Squadron's tanks to land 5 minutes before 5th East Yorkshires on King Red. A Squadron's Fireflies plus the conventional Shermans would land directly on the beach at H+45 minutes alongside the third infantry battalion for King sector, the 7th Green Howards. In the event all the tanks were landed on the beach or a few hundred yards offshore because the local naval commander decided the sea was too rough to launch the DD Shermans out at sea: in effect, recognizing the beginnings of a crisis, the commander took decisive action in contravention of the plan. As a result only two tanks were lost in the water; both had sunk in shell craters. A Squadron's tanks, followed by 7th Green Howards, then pushed inland past Crépon, through Creully and into open country – where they were attacked by German anti-tank guns and by 'friendly-fire' from HMS Orion and a passing American Thunderbolt plane. The plane missed but four tanks were destroyed by the fire of the ship.[14]

Once ashore the flail tanks in particular served to beat paths through the minefields allowing the assault engineers to clear and mark the paths for infantry to leave the beach area relatively quickly in most places. Each of these clearing operations was to be carried out on the Anglo-Canadian beaches by a Composite Beaching Team of Flails, AVREs, and Assault Engineers. 'To the best of my knowledge', wrote Lieutenant Frank Pearson of the Assault Pioneer Platoon of the 2nd Devons, 'and against all that the history books say, most of the 231st brigade and the forward elements of the 50th Division followed in the wake of that one flail tank.[15] Turner suggests there were three flail tanks initially involved but whatever the numbers the flailing appeared to be successful.[16]

The importance of individual tanks is replicated in the command decisions of individuals. For example, on Jig Sector the Hampshires, Dorsets and Devons estimated their casualties at 171 out of the initial assault involving 4,000 soldiers until 0820.[17] Corporal John Mclaughlin with the 1st Battalion of the Hampshires landed at around 0730 and found himself at the head of a group as machine gun bullets killed three of his comrades. They were stopped half way up the beach and McLaughlin spotted a gap in the sea wall. 'So I shouted "Come on!" and started moving towards it; the others followed reluctantly'.[18] Similarly, when Lt Colonel Hastings's (Green Howards) landing craft hit the beach nothing happened. The ramp stayed up and no-one moved to open it in the light of the heavy fire that was coming in their direction. However, as the craft swung slowly towards an obstacle with a teller mine attached, the ramp was kicked open by a soldier. Still no-one moved. So Hastings walked to the front, sat down on the prow, edged himself slowly into the water and walked towards the beach – followed, slowly, by the rest of the unit.[19] Further along the coast, on King Beach, two Flail tanks and two AVREs had been knocked out by a casemated 88mm gun built into the seawall (WN 33) and supported by an anti-tank gun, three machine guns and a mortar pit which had held up the East Yorks on the beach. After hits from a destroyer and an LCG(L) the guns were eventually put out of action by a Sherman from the Westminster Dragoons at around 1000.[20] La Rivière proved an equivalent problem on King Beach for the 5th Battalion East Yorkshire Regiment. A fortified position on the front at La Rivière was decimating the AVREs with an 88mm gun, and the infantry with machine guns, as they came up the beach. Not until one AVRE managed to approach it from the blind side, and fired directly into the aperture, was it put out of action.

The 50th Division as a whole suffered around 1,000 dead, wounded and missing – though this was considerably lighter than had been expected.[21] The capture of the four 122mm gun battery at Mont Fleury by D Company of the Green Howards was one example where casualties should have been high but were actually very light.

Company Sergeant Major (CSM) Hollis, having shot up an apparent pill box on the run into the beach at King Red – which turned out to be a tramcar shelter – made good his practice when he single-handedly captured between 25 and 30 Germans in the two real pill boxes guarding the approach to the battery. But the manner of his doing again reflects on the more traditional British soldier's conventional penchant to wait for orders. Moving off the beach with Major Lofthouse of Company HQ, Hollis came under fire from a machine gun post behind them and, in the words of Dunphie and Johnson, '*Not waiting for orders* he [Hollis] charged the pillbox alone' (my emphasis).[22] Hollis successfully routed the occupants and did the same for another pillbox, capturing as many as 30 prisoners on the way.[23]

When the two platoons reached the Mont Fleury Battery they found it abandoned, apparently as a result of the air and sea bombardment, though there was no evidence of any German casualties. At this point in the day of the 850 Green Howards who had started the day over 840 were still functioning effectively – though most of the casualties were officers or NCOs.[24] Estimates for the total casualties on Gold Beach vary but they were probably around 300 on the beaches themselves (roughly 200 Green Howards and 100 East Yorks) and about 1,000 for the whole of D-Day.

By the end of D-Day the Green Howards were just one mile short of their planned objective, the Caen-Bayeux road. This was achieved the following day but their relative success and security were rudely shattered on 11 June when they attacked hill 102, south of Cristot. Unbeknown to the attackers, a unit of the 12th SS *HJ* had recently moved onto the hill and the failed attack cost the Green Howards 250 casualties, including one officer from the 4th/7th Royal Dragoon Guards who was captured by the 12th SS and, though wounded, was tied to a tree branch and dragged into the open each time British artillery opened up on German positions. The officer died after about three hours.[25] The hill, overlooking Caen, was not taken until 25 June, D-Day+19.

At the extreme west end of Gold at Le Hamel No. 47 Royal Marine Commando landed and trekked west to take Port-en-Bessin. In fact they found themselves heading for the wrong beach and as they moved parallel to the coast to correct their approach four of the 14 landing craft were sunk. Despite some hostile fire (one Commando suggested to his comrades that 'perhaps the beach was private') 47 Commando took the beach area with minimal casualties but lost 50 per cent of their number taking Le Hamel and Port-en-Bassin. As a result they did not take the port – wanted for its primary role as an oil terminal – until the following afternoon. The latter was also the point at which the US and British assault areas joined and it was finally captured at 0400 on 8 June, though the first contact between US and British troops occurred on the evening of 7 June. The port was found to be capable of disembarking stores at a much higher rate than assumed and by D-Day+6 it was handling 1,000 tons a day.[26] By nightfall, about 25,000 troops had landed on Gold Beach.

14.3 Juno Beach

Of all the units training for D-Day the Canadian forces destined for Juno Beach had begun first, as early as October 1942. Juno Beach was situated to the east of Gold Beach and the west of Sword, and was divided between Mike (Red and Green) and Nan (Green, White and Red) beaches. The 3rd Canadian Infantry Division which provided the assault troops was divided between the Canadian 7th Infantry Brigade (under Brigadier H. Foster), supported by two squadrons of the 6th Canadian Armoured Regiment, and the 8th Infantry (under Brigadier K. Blackadder), supported by 10th Canadian Armoured Regiment. Behind these initial assault units came Brigadier D. G. Cunningham's reserve 9th Canadian Infantry Brigade supported by the 27th Canadian Armoured Regiment.

The 7th Infantry Brigade was divided into two. First, the Royal Winnipeg Rifles, supported by A Squadron the 6th Canadian Armoured Regiment, on the western flank, who were to land on Mike Green and Mike Red, capture Courseulles and move south to Pierrepont. Second, the Regina Rifles, supported by B squadron of the 6th Canadian Armoured Regiment, on the eastern side, who were to land on Nan Green, take the eastern section of Courseulles and move south to Reviers.

The 8th Brigade, further east still, comprised The Queen's Own Rifles of Canada (QORoC) destined to land on Nan White and capture Bernières, Beny-sur-Mer and move south to Anisy. On Nan Red, the most easterly beach, the North Shore Regiment was to take St Aubin-sur-Mer. The reserve 9th Brigade would then land on Nan White, pass through the positions of the 8th Brigade and move south. In addition, the Canadians were to cut the Caen-Bayeux road at Bretteville-l'Orgueilleuse, destroy the bridges on a ten mile section of the Orne river, and link up with the British 3rd Infantry Division to their east on Sword.

The assault troops had to delay their landing for around 10–15 minutes due to rough seas and to ensure the tide could lift them over a reef a mile off shore.[27] In addition, one of the assault groups (J1) had approached the beach down the wrong mine-free channel to the west of their intended channel adding a further delay.[28] The cumulative delays meant that when the landing craft beached the tide was so high the beach obstacles could not be cleared properly. Fortunately the obstacles were rather more sparsely deployed than had been feared and so casualties from the Teller mines were limited on the approaches, though many craft were lost when they tried to reverse out from the beach. As a result, fully 20 out of the leading 24 craft were sunk, as were 25 per cent (36) of the landing craft in the first wave, and 90 of the 306 landing craft used on Juno that day.[29]

The 19 DD tanks of B Squadron 6th Armoured Regiment heading for Nan Green to lead the Regina Rifle Regiment ashore, east of the river, were supposed to launch at 7,000 yards but it was decided that the

weather was too rough and their launch was delayed until 4,000 yards
from the beach. 14 of B squadron's 19 DD tanks heading for Nan Green
reached the beach before the AVREs and the infantry of the Regina Rifles
at about 0800, roughly 15 minutes before the assault troops. This seems
to have been a result of B Squadron taking matters into their own hands
– that is recognizing a crisis and taking command of the situation – they
launched prematurely when an unsupported landing looked decidedly
unhealthy for the infantry. Sergeant Leo Gariepy's DD tank appears to
have been the first to land but the Regina Rifles still came under heavy
fire from beach emplacements. Gariepy stopped his tank just beyond the
sight of one such German gun, opened a bottle of rum which the tank's
crew demolished at speed, then reversed towards the emplacement firing
12 rounds into it. The German gun did not fire again.[30]

The preliminary bombardment had not eliminated the opposition but
the assault went largely to plan – though the delayed assault meant that
many obstacles were covered by the water by the time the engineers
landed to open up the gaps. As a consequence many troops were pinned
down on the beach, notably by machine gun fire and the two strong
points harbouring a 75mm and an 88mm gun. Eventually these were
both knocked out by DD tanks – though not until the former gun had
already fired around 200 shells – despite the evidence of multiple – but
ineffective – hits from the preliminary naval bombardment.

The sighting of the German beach artillery, which restricted it to enfilading fire, made the defenders virtually invulnerable to long-range shell
fire from the sea. But it simultaneously made the defenders vulnerable to
head-on assaults from tanks precisely because the defenders could not
bring their guns to bear directly in front of them. In the words of
Sergeant Gariepy leading the first DD tank onto Nan Green, 'My target
was on the seafront. A 75mm which was in a position of enfilade fire
along the beach like all the guns. The houses along the beach were all full
of machine-gunners and so were the sand dunes. But the angle of the
blockhouse stopped them firing on me. So I took the tank up to the
emplacement, very close and destroyed the gun by firing at almost point-
blank range'.[31] The removal of strong points by this method proved
costly but effective. Sergeant Wood of C Squadron 22nd Dragoons on
Sword Beach was involved with a pillbox housing mortars, as Major Birt
recounted: This was fierce shooting at close range; like so much of the
fighting on this beach, tanks ran for the gun emplacements in a grim race
to put their shells almost point-blank through the mouths of the concrete
'boxes' before they themselves were put out of action'.[32]

After this the Crabs cleared the mines, the AVRE fascines filled the
anti-tank ditch, the armoured bulldozer cleared the path and by 0900

both exits to east Courseulles were open.[33] Unfortunately, though, the Regina Rifle's A Company, having suffered the most casualties in the assault upon the beach strongpoint, failed to leave a defending force behind when they moved south and it was reoccupied by the Germans who resumed their attack upon the subsequent waves of Canadians.

The exit on Mike Green was opened by 0930 but the delays meant that the DD tanks could not support the infantry moving inland for one and a half hours. At H-Hour+2 the beach remained completely congested. However, by 1700 Courseulles was declared safe and the Reginas pushed south towards Reviers, losing five of the remaining DD tanks on the way. Nevertheless some of the DD tanks of the reserve C Squadron of the 6th Armoured Regiment led by Lt McCormick probably got the furthest south of any Allied troops on D-Day, approaching their objective of Bretteville-l'Orgueilleuse before pulling back.[34]

Alongside B squadron's tanks supporting the Regina Rifles, the tanks of A squadron were to lead The Royal Winnipeg Rifles onto Mike Red and Mike Green after being launched only 1,500 yards out when enemy fire was becoming more accurate. Only 10 were launched at sea, seven of which reached the beach. Most of the rest were launched directly on the beach but all of the DD tanks of this squadron landed after the infantry.[35] The other specialist armour, in the form of two LCTs carrying AVREs, armoured bulldozers, Sherman and Centaur tanks, was also slightly delayed and the troops landed first under heavy fire from the German defenders in the French houses and under great threat from the underwater obstacles. Many vehicles failed to reach the beach, unloaded in water too deep and too rough, and one example typifies the ambiguity of Command: a motorized mortar platoon of the Royal Winnipeg Rifles was ordered off an LCT and the first vehicle plunged into four meters of water, never to emerge again. The skipper of the LCT then ordered the second vehicle off but the sergeant refused, even when threatened with a court martial. Eventually the skipper acquiesced and landed on the beach to disembark the vehicles safely.[36]

The slight delay in the assault on Mike Beach also enabled the German defenders to emerge from their bunkers and prepare for the assault, though the official report suggests that, thanks to the determination of the assault troops and the coxswains, the accuracy of the supporting artillery – including the eight LCTs Rocket,[37] and the weakness of the enemy fire, casualties were relatively small in the initial assault.[38] This was helped through the absence of the *Luftwaffe* and the relatively little shelling from inland batteries.

On Mike Red and Nan Green, the defensive fire really began when the landing craft touched down. B Company of the Royal Winnipegs found their section of Mike Red under heavy mortar and machine-gun fire, losing 26 soldiers in the initial assault and over 100 more in the rest of D-Day. A and C Companies of the Royal Winnipegs were also pinned down on the beach for two hours, despite being reserve units following on behind the first assault waves that had already moved inland. But within a further hour almost all the beaches were secured.[39] Even then casualties could be high for incoming troops. D Company suffered more than their predecessors even though they landed just before 0900 when several of their landing craft struck (now submerged) mined obstacles.[40]

The experiences of those attacking Bernières behind Nan Red and Nan White beaches in the 8th Brigade were rather different from their colleagues further west. Both squadrons of DD tanks from the 10th Armoured Regiment (The Fort Garry Horse) waded, rather than swam, to shore because of the weather conditions, and they were consequently slightly behind the infantry which were also in front of the AVREs. Worse, the naval and air bombardment once again seemed to make little impression on the defences.

The main strong point (WN 28) facing the Queen's Own Rifles (QOR) on Nan White at Bernières comprised two anti-tank emplacements, seven machine gun posts and two mortar posts. The prior bombardment had damaged a claimed 90 per cent of the buildings in the area but had not hit the strong point and the Queen's Own Rifles lost 36 soldiers and took a further 29 wounded in storming it without tank support. The QOR also had to storm two 50mm anti-tank positions and lost heavily again in the absence of tank support. What made the position even more difficult was that the AVRE's could not launch their petards against them because the infantry were already too close to the strong-point. The solution was provided by one bulldozer driver: he filled one of the strong-points up with sand and suffocated the incumbents.

Nonetheless huge congestion stymied the attempts of the Canadians to move south at speed from Bernières, not simply because of the sea-wall breaching problems or the very limited beach area available at high tide, but because the entire reserve Brigade was ordered to land here on Nan White and not on Nan Red where the North Shore Regiment was taking heavy casualties, particularly from the St Aubin-sur-Mer strong-point.[41] This essentially meant that all traffic had to travel along a single road to Bény-sur-Mer that was captured by mid-afternoon.[42]

On Nan Red at St Aubin-sur-Mer, the North Shore Regiment and 48 Commando faced stone and brick buildings reaching down to the sea behind the seawall.[43] This is also the area where what is probably the most famous cine film of the D-Day landings was taken: *True Glory*. It shows the second wave of assault troops, either A or B Company of the

North Shore Regiment on Nan Red at La Rive who touched down just after 0800. A still from the film is reproduced, next to the house as it currently exists, in Photos 14.1 and 14.2.

So poor had the pre-assault bombardment been that Lt Colonel James Moulton of 48 Commando subsequently found only two houses along the front had been hit by anything other than fire from the assaulting troops. WN 27 dominated the beach with its 50mm anti-tank gun which had fired around 70 shells and hit several DD tanks before it was finally

Photo 14.1 'True Glory' House, D-Day 1944

Photo 14.2 'True Glory' House today

put out of action by AVRE petards and DD tanks at about 1115, after four hours of resistance. St Aubin itself was not captured until the evening.

On the west side of St Aubin, on the limits of Juno, the 4th Special Service Brigade of 48 Royal Marine Commando were to land after the North Shore Regiment and move westwards to link up with 41 Commando moving towards them from Sword Beach. No. 48 Commando had assumed their approach would be covered by the preliminary assault of the Canadians but in the event two of the six Commando boats were caught by the beach obstacles, and all were ferociously attacked by the machine guns and mortars on shore. Thus 45 minutes after the 8th Canadians had stormed across Nan Red Beach No. 48 Royal Marine Commandos suffered heavy casualties from German beach defences that appeared to have recovered from the initial shock and had not been originally eliminated. In theory they should have been covered by smoke mortars fired from their own boats but so quiet was the run-in that just after 0730 the mortar troops had dismantled their weapons and stood ready to land with the rest of the Commandos. By the time they had resumed their firing positions many of the casualties had already been caused. As they moved inland they had already lost half their strength with 75 per cent of these casualties occurring on the run-in to the beach itself, many from drowning.[44] But progress away from the beach through Langrune-sur-Mer was still dangerous for many of the houses had been wired with booby traps by the defenders and winkling them out took an inordinate amount of time and effort.

Overall, the landings on some areas of Juno Beach that were adequately covered by the defenders were very costly. Between 1,000 and 1,200 casualties were taken from the 21,400 who landed at Juno (5 per cent [12 per cent were expected]) of whom 340 were dead compared to 2,200 casualties of the 40,000 at Omaha (5.5 per cent).[45] However, since there is considerable uncertainty about both the number landed and the number of casualties we should treat all these figures with some scepticism. Certainly for those involved in clearing the obstacles from the beaches the prospects were bleak: of the 100 members of the 6th Field Company, Royal Canadian Engineers, only 26 were still working at the end of the day. And of the 36 soldiers in No. 10 platoon, A Company of the Queen's Own Rifles of Canada (QORC), only nine got off the beach.[46] The casualties of both brigades were roughly the same: the QORC lost 143, the Royal Winnipegs had 128 casualties, and the North Shore Regiment lost 125.[47]

Yet some individuals on Juno went to extraordinary lengths to get onto the beach. Major de Stackpoole of 48 Royal Marine Commandos found himself in the water after his LCI was hit. Fifty of the survivors were picked up by an LCT which, it turned out, was under orders to return to England, and the skipper refused all the requests from the Commandos to take them to the beach first. Thereupon de Stackpoole, already wounded in the thigh, dived overboard and swam to shore.[48]

Les Wagar, a rifleman in Company C in the QORC was not that keen, but neither did he need to be told what to do: 'The ramp dropped and we poured off in single file into waves up to our waists, running. Idiot orders were being shouted: "Off the beach! Off the beach! Get to the Wall!" Relieved someone's tension I suppose. But I don't know anybody who had to be told what to do on that beach'.[49] By 0900 the assault was still taking heavy casualties but, bizarrely, within another 40 minutes a beachside café had opened for business amidst the continuing carnage.[50]

The German response inland of Juno was, at best, tardy. The Allies were very concerned about the possible movements of the 21st Panzer Division south-east of Caen and the 12th SS HJ Panzer Division, and intercepted radio traffic had suggested reconnaissance patrols of the 21st were on the move by 0640. But no major movement of armour was detected by the Allied air reconnaissance until the afternoon. In fact the British 6th Airborne drops over the Orne had already severed all telephone links between Caen and Ranville (just to the east of Pegasus Bridge) so the 21st *Panzergrenadiers* preparing to defend Caen on D-Day had no idea whether the bridges had indeed been taken by the British.

Furthermore, such was the state of confusion on the morning of D-Day that SS-Obersturmführer Hansmann of the 12th SS Panzer Division had to drive 80kms north to Bayeux before he knew that the landings were by sea as well as air. At 0745 he arrived just inland of Arromanches to see the British landings and was convinced that 'That this must be the invasion! What else can it be? Soon there will be more ships than water! But who will believe this, if he hasn't seen it himself?'[51]

Hansmann's CO, Fritz Witt, with his deputy Kurt Meyer, led the 12th SS HJ Panzer Division, which had been stationed at Lisieux, 28 miles east of Sword Beach, and did not reach Caen until midnight on 6 June. The 12th SS HJ had been formed on 24 June 1943 and spent a year in Belgium training with cadres drawn from the 1st SS *Leibstandarte* Adolf Hitler (LAH). In April 1944 the 12th SS HJ had moved to Lisieux and from there, on 6 June, they proceeded north to Caen from where, according to Matthias Jubell, one of the thousands of 18 year old privates, they would drive 'the small Allied landing force into the sea'.[52] But the fuel shortage that had resulted from Allied strategic bombing was exacerbated by the siting of most reserve stocks in 15th Army area and it proved almost impossible to secure provisions on 6 June with Allied fighter-bombers constantly patrolling the skies.[53]

It was 1515 before reports suggested the 12th SS were on the move – a mere 15 minutes after the leading reconnaissance units left Lisieux – and by the time they got to Evrécy, a couple of miles south-west of Caen, they were almost out of fuel and had been attacked many times by Allied fighter-bombers. The 5th SS Artillery of the division, for instance, lost three of its 15 howitzers on the journey. Worse was to follow for those Allied fighter-bombers had also destroyed the fuel dump at Evrécy. Nevertheless, the 12th SS HJ attacked the Canadians moving inland from Juno Beach, only to find themselves counter-attacked by a naval and aerial bombardment that forced the Germans to retreat. By that time the 5th SS Artillery had lost another three guns. They dug in for the night and when the Canadian attacks resumed, soon found themselves out of ammunition, having to wait 2 hours for replenishments to arrive.[54]

On D-Day+1 the expected German counter-attack also finally materialized first at Buron, north-west of Caen, where 23 captured North Nova Scotian infantry were executed by the 25th SS *Panzergrenadier* Regiment of the 12th SS *HJ* Panzer Division under Kurt Meyer.[55] The following day the Royal Winnipeg Rifles were attacked at Putot, just south of Caen-Bayeux road, west of Bretteville. This time 40 Canadian POWs were executed, again by 25th SS *Panzergrenadiers* of the 12th SS *HJ*.[56] At least 18 were executed in the garden of Kurt Meyer's own HQ building at the Abbaye d'Ardenne, seven of them at Meyer's direct order.[57] But murdering POWs was never going to stop the Canadians and by the end of D-Day around 21,400 troops had landed on Juno Beach.

14.4 Sword Beach

At Sword Beach, in particular Queen Red and Queen White, covering the most easterly end of the assault area, the defences were expected to be the toughest, with the large guns at Le Havre and the large number of boats expected to cause problems for the British attackers. Furthermore, south of Sword lay Caen, and Caen was deemed to be the funnel through which all German reinforcements would have to pass.[58] For this reason a very large naval bombarding force was stationed opposite the beach. The British 3rd Division was primarily concentrated just east of Lion-sur-Mer on Queen Beach, a narrow area just to the west of Ouistreham situated between the deep shelving beaches of Roger Beach and the cliffs of Peter Beach to the west – an area more appropriate for a brigade. So narrow was the area that two midget submarines were deployed to mark the boundaries offshore. The 1st Battalion of the South Lancashire Regiment was to land on Queen White while on their east the 2nd Battalion of the East Yorkshire Regiment was to land on Queen Red Beach nearest to Ouistreham. The dividing line between the two beaches was exactly where the German strong-point WN 20 lay and both brigades were required to ensure its destruction. The Division was then to move rapidly south via Périers-sur-le-Dan to take Caen.

For D-Day about 5,000 Commandos were involved in the Special Services Group, headed by Major-General Sturges, Royal Marines (RM), and subdivided into two groups. The 1st Special Service Brigade under Brigadier Lord Lovat (Nos. 3, 4, 6, 10 and 45 RM) landed on Sword near Ouistreham on D-Day, silenced the coastal battery, and headed for the drop zones of the British 6th Airborne to support the eastern flank of the landings and protect the bridges over the Orne River and the Caen Canal. The 4th Special Services Brigade under Brigadier Leicester (all RM units – Nos. 41, 46, 47, 48 RM Commando) landed on all three Anglo-Canadian beaches: No. 41 and No. 48 were to land separately on Sword at Lion-sur-Mer and Juno at St Aubin respectively and head towards the radar station at Douvres. However, both groups were delayed and no link up was achieved. The following day the two units met but by then the group was too weak to attack the station which was eventually captured by No. 41 on 15 June.[59] Strong point WN 20A was also to be taken by 41 Commando on their way to join up with 48th Commando. In the event the assaulting group failed to take WN 20A until D-Day+2 and it was into this gap that the primary German armoured counter-attack was made.

One 'troop' (No. 4) captured the gun battery at Ouistreham before returning to link up with Lovat while No. 6 went straight to the bridges. The Ouistreham battery housed six 155mm guns and No. 4 troop was accompanied by two troops of French Commandos under Commandant Kieffer.[60] The Grand Bunker at Ouistreham, which is still clearly visible from the ferry, and which controlled the local anti-aircraft fire, was captured with 52 German POWs on D-Day+3, after all the guns it controlled had been silenced.[61]

Ironically, while these Commandos were probably the best prepared and trained British troops, their army colleagues in the 3rd Division were probably the least prepared. They had only begun training in December 1943 in Scotland where poor weather had hampered preparations. Not until the end of March was it possible to practice close-support fire and a beach assault simultaneously.[62] Indeed, some tanks had never practised disembarking from an LCT until D-Day.[63] It was fortuitous, then, the pre-assault air and sea bombardment of Sword was the most effective of all the D-Day bombardments. Until one minute before the first assault troops landed even Admiral Vian's own ship, the cruiser *Scylla*, closed to within 5,500 yards of the beach to provide intensive fire on the beach defenders.[64]

Although the sea was deemed too rough to launch the DD tanks – it was blowing a force 5 – 34 out of 40 tanks were in fact launched 5,000 yards out (one DD tank tore its canvas surround and the rest from the LCT were landed directly on the beach half an hour late). Three of the DD tanks sank (one rammed by a passing LCT carrying AVREs) but 31 made it to the beach, along with the AVREs and Flail tanks – all ahead of the infantry who had been ordered to stop and allow the tanks through – 'a decisive factor in the success of the assault' according to Rear-Admiral Talbot and another example of the decisive role a commander can make in the midst of a Critical situation.[65] Five DD tanks were quickly swamped by the rising tide but critically, these tanks destroyed three or four 75mm guns, four or five 50mm guns and many 20mm guns. All of these had been reported destroyed after direct hits from the destroyers but, again, the German fire was enfiladed onto the beach and they were almost immune to seaward fire. On Sword Beach, then, the possibility of heavy British casualties was limited not just by the prevalence of technologies that the American forces were denied through poor Leadership, but also through the decision of the assault commander to delay the troop landings until that technology had already landed and dealt with as many enemy positions as possible. By the end of the beach battle 23 of the 31 DDs were still running, but only 3 of the original 17 AVREs.[66]

The leading companies of the South Lancashire Regiment landed on Queen White at 0720 and by 0810 had taken control of the beach, suffering 37 dead or missing and 89 wounded. Dennis Cartwright was probably typical in his reaction to enemy gunfire: he hit the deck. But his reaction to local commanders is also typical:

> Urged on by NCOs, we forced ourselves out of cover … . Then the lieutenant said, 'Come on lads, follow me!' So we did, and ran slap-bang into heavy fire from a Jerry machine-gun we hadn't seen. I went down in sheer terror and heard chaps bawling like kids who'd been hit. There were bangs and shooting and when I dared to glance up I saw our lads rushing on past a Jerry strong point, so feeling a bit of a twerp I followed.[67]

Charlie Hansen had a similar experience, lying on the beach criss-crossed by fire. 'After about ten minutes our NCO got us to move'.[68] Many would have been suffering in front of WN 20, the German strong point marking the boundary between Queen Red and Queen White Beach. WN 20 was not a single casemated gun but an array of 20 well constructed defences and weapons, including: a 75mm gun, two 50mm anti-tank guns, three 81mm mortars, and six machine gun posts of various calibres, some with multiple guns. WN 20 was eventually overrun by infantry from four different units after three hours and after sustained attack from the navy, from tanks and from self-propelled artillery.[69]

The second wave on Sword Beach, the 185th Brigade, comprised the 2nd Battalion King's Shropshire Light Infantry, the 2nd Battalion the Royal Warwicks, the 1st Battalion the Royal Norfolks and the Staffordshire Yeomanry's 6 pounder Sherman tanks. The latter, however, was very delayed both at sea and on the beach. Even seasoned sailors like Brendan Maher, who had been at sea for the best part of two years, found the sea too much and was 'violently sea-sick'.[70] For Albert Pattison, platoon sergeant with the 1st Suffolks, it was 'the worst 48 hours of my life ... worse than swimming 2 miles off the Dunkirk beaches in 1940'.[71] Rex Williams with the Shropshires also found disembarking very difficult after the sea-sickness and with the great weight he had to carry:

> We were so overloaded with gear I almost overbalanced into the water. But I made it. My legs felt like jelly through nerves. I tried to run up the beach but it was no use. I just couldn't. So I said out loud, 'Fuck it!' and simply walked until I was with a bunch of the lads lying down near a Sherman ... we kept our heads down as there was stuff flying about. Then a lieutenant I didn't know told us to get off the beach and into the grass and sand dunes.[72]

Note here, once again, the temptation to stay down is only transcended by a direct command from someone in higher authority. Moreover, this was not simply a response to the terror on the beach but had clearly been embedded in the training because when Williams followed the Lieutenant off the beach they came up against a German machine gun post which they knocked out but the officer was killed in the attack. 'The corporal looked around for another officer ... We had no idea what to do next and we couldn't see our own sergeant. But then a sergeant-major ran up, sized up the situation and told us to follow him'.[73] As Blandford surmises: 'Those first British shock troops surviving the actual landing did indeed lie up on the beach in great relief and thankfulness, most unwilling to leap up and face acute danger again at once. The relieving lethargy that followed miraculous survival was strong and inevitable ...'[74] Even some of the Commandos seemed unable to act in the absence of an officer or NCO. Tim Holdsworth with 41 RM Commando lay immobilized behind a burning Sherman just off the beach. 'After a few minutes an officer appeared and showed us how to get behind the wall and into some undergrowth, so we followed him in fear, but he seemed to know what he was doing'.[75]

Later in the Normandy campaign the same problem recurred. Jim Fiske of the 1st Gordon Highlanders was being led inland when 'our lieutenant got hit not far from us; he shouted at us to keep going so we did ... We reached these houses with fire coming at us from all directions ... There was a high grey wall and I huddled against it with my mate Tommy and we waited. We had no orders and didn't know which way to move'. Not far away Angus Jones of the Glasgow Highlanders faced a similar problem: 'As soon as we reached the ruins we set up for defence and waited for orders, but none came until a sergeant-major we didn't know ran up and said, "Don't hang about lads – get on!" So we did.[76] Edward Devlin, a member of the Royal Scots, was also critically depend- ent on his officers and NCOs: 'Our officers had vanished long before among some ruins and only our sergeants kept us going'.[77]

The 1st Special Service Brigade Commandos under Lord Lovat, responsible for fighting through the defences to reach the 6th Airborne troops at Pegasus Bridge and over the River Orne, landed at the extreme east of Queen Beach in 22 boats, five of which were destroyed on the run-in.[78] Lovat was impressed by the actions of a certain Monsieur Lefèvre, a Resistance leader, who had braved the shell-fire at Ouistreham to cut off the cables that would have initiated static flame throwers on the beaches.

Lovat, though, had little respect for the 3rd Division troops that preceded him 'Barely clear of the creeping tide, soldiers lay with heads down, pinned to the sand. Half way up the beach others dug themselves into what amounted to a certain death-trap'. When the Commando Peter Masters, carrying his usual materials plus a 200-foot hemp rope and a bicycle clambered down the side of his LCI on Queen Beach on Sword, he was astonished to see ordinary soldiers digging in on the beach itself. 'I even saw two men trying to dig in – in the shallow water ...'[79] Here is a classic case of risk-taking: despite the undoubted desire to dig for cover those who did seemed much less likely to survive than those who took the apparent risk of running across the beach.[80]

The difference between the Commandos' training, that instilled a sense of urgency and movement to minimize casualties and, and the army infantry training, that focused on minimizing casualties by cautious advance – and even that only under direct orders – is manifest in the two different approaches taken to the mined beaches. While the infantry stayed on the beach waiting for the all-clear from the mine-clearance units, the Commandos were more likely to risk the mines – thereby avoid- ing the artillery and small arms fire on the beach. Again, this is not about different levels of bravery but about different training and different assumptions about where the greatest danger lies – and that was usually from artillery and small arms not from mines. That became most transparent when the 3rd Division moved inland.

Two strong points lay south of Sword at Colleville-sur-Mer between the invaders and their target, Caen. Codenamed 'Morris', comprising four 105mm guns, three of which were casemated, and 'Hillman' with 12 smaller gun emplacements, defended by 150 soldiers. The 67 defenders of Morris quickly surrendered, apparently having suffered enough from the attentions of the Allied navies and air forces in the previous days. The attack upon Hillman, however, was stymied from the outset when the Forward Observer (Bombardment) was killed with his team, essentially meaning that no external artillery fire could initially be called down. The 1st Battalion the Suffolk Regiment, which landed at 1100 on D-Day, was responsible for taking Hillman and it took a seven-hour assault with 40 casualties, 20 of which were deaths. Eventually, 270 Germans surrendered at Hillman. The delay then reverberated backwards through the Norfolks and the Shropshires so that all the groups concentrated on digging defensive positions rather than maintaining the assault inland.

By 0930 Hermanville-sur-Mer, a couple of miles inland, had been captured but the 1st South Lancs who led the advance on Caen came up against the 21st Panzers at Périers, a couple of miles short of Caen. Here they stopped and dug in, waiting for the King's Shropshire Light Infantry (KSLI) to support them, who were a couple of miles behind them at Hermanville waiting for the 65 tanks of the Staffordshire Yeomanry, who were a couple of miles back, stuck in a traffic jam on the beach itself for over an hour. Indeed, the 9th reserve Brigade did not land until 1200.

Eventually the tanks caught up and progress was made as far as Biéville by 1600 where the British dug in at the approach of 21st Panzer Division. The Germans mustered around 90 tanks and two regiments of *Panzergrenadiers* in total and, wrongly assuming that their own 88mm guns still held the ridge, around 40 tanks charged headlong into the defensive screen thrown up by the Staffordshire Yeomanry's tanks, the 20th Anti-Tank Regiment's 17lb Self-propelled anti-tank guns, and 6lb anti-tank guns of the Shropshire light infantry. Four German tanks were quickly destroyed and the attack broke off, to be repeated twice more that afternoon, each time suffering significant casualties to the British anti-tank guns. By nightfall the German commander of the 21st Panzer Division, who had started the day with 124 tanks, had only 70 left.[81] By nightfall the leading elements of the KSLI had also reached Lebisey, just a mile short of Caen's northern suburbs but under attack from both sides, without reinforcements, and having already taken 113 casualties, the KSLI pulled back to Bieville just before midnight.[82]

Many have insisted that such 'defensive posturing' by the British troops landing on Sword cost the Allies the momentum that might have taken Caen and it may be significant that this Division had no experience of a sea-borne assault.[83] Belchem, for one, blames the officer corps, but not the troops, for the limited success on this front, and Lovat had little time for either group. Montgomery – who sacked Lt General Bucknall, the CO for Gold Beach – had originally claimed that Caen was the primary British objective for D-Day, though it took six more weeks to achieve in conjunction with a break out to the west by the American forces that moved rapidly south from their beachhead. However, it is also the case that this sector faced the only serious armoured counter-attack of the day – and held it off. Von Schweppenburg was very clear from his position as the organizer of German defences around Caen about what was possible:

> The British and Canadian troops were magnificent ... However, after a while I began to think, rightly or wrongly, that the command of these superb troops was not making the best use of them. The command seemed slow and pedestrian. It seemed that the Allied intention was to wear down their enemy with their enormous material superiority.[84]

The Germans also began to suffer critical losses in their leadership through air attacks: on 11 June von Schweppenburg's HQ at La Caine was bombed (by 17 Mitchell bombers of the RAF's 320th Squadron {Dutch}) following an Ultra intercept, and though von Schweppenburg was only injured, about 20 other staff including his Chief of Staff were killed, and the co-ordination of the Panzer divisions disrupted for two weeks.[85] The following day, 12 June, General Marks was killed in an air attack, and two days later General Witt, CO of the 12th SS, was killed by naval gunfire at his HQ at Venoix near Caen.[86] In short, three of the defenders' most important commanders had been killed or put out of action within a week of the invasion.

Nine days after D-Day (15 June), the Germans regained control of the east bank of the River Orne and began shelling Sword so accurately that all landings there were halted and transferred to Juno Beach. Conditions continued to deteriorate for the Allies and on 1 July Sword was officially 'closed' and all activities transferred further west. But this was not regarded as a significant problem because the date also marked the end of Operation Neptune – the naval aspect of Overlord, and with five more days (5 July (D-Day+29) the millionth Allied soldier had stepped ashore.[87] By 18 August 1.9 million soldiers, over 400,000 vehicles and 2.5 million tons of supplies had been landed in France.[88] Of those that landed on D-Day, by far the easiest assault occurred at Utah Beach.

14.5 Utah Beach

Utah was to be attacked by the US 4th Infantry Division, minus all those killed in Exercise Tiger of course, and supported by one battalion of the 90th Infantry Division. They were to be followed up by the 9th and the 79th Infantry Divisions. The confusion at Utah Beach was as great as anywhere else. At about 0555, around 7,500 yards off-shore, PC (Patrol-Craft) 1261 destined to act as primary guide for the 2nd Battalion, 8th Infantry Regimental Combat Team (RCT – an oversized regiment) heading for Uncle Red Beach was sunk, and the secondary PC was still stuck in the transport area with a fouled propeller. The two PCs guiding the 1st Battalion 8th Infantry then led all the landing craft in but in the reorganization, and the confusion caused by smoke on land and just off shore, the majority of the landings occurred at Exit 3 – about two thirds of a mile south of the intended target (Exit 2).[89] This was a most fortunate error for several reasons. First, Exit 2 lay opposite a sand bar that would have made the landing more difficult and the run-in across the beach area longer – though why it was chosen in the first place is not obvious. Second, Exit 3 had received the heaviest bombardment and the defences here were in a markedly poorer shape than at Exit 2.

With greater protection from the Cotentin peninsular than at Omaha, two squadrons of DD tanks were successfully launched 3 kilometres off Utah Beach and 28 of the 32 made it ashore, although they were 15 minutes behind the infantry who were just one minute behind schedule when they landed. As troops of the 1st and 2nd Battalion, 8th Infantry made a relatively easy run across the beach with no small-arms fire and relatively little artillery fire, they cheered at their successes – only to discover that they had, by chance and in a smoke screen, come ashore not on Tare Green and Uncle Red beaches respectively but almost 2,000 yards further south than planned, on Uncle Red and Victor respectively.

There could have been many more casualties on Utah. The area actually had 28 German resistance points along the beach itself, with 111 medium to heavy calibre guns, and subsequent analysis suggested that 75 per cent of these guns were still operational at the time of the assault; indeed, half were still working *after* the assault.[90] 67 of the 360 heavy bombers that targeted Utah failed to release their bombs because of the

Photo 14.3 Utah Beach, near Exit 5

poor visibility and one third of the medium bombers also missed their targets.[91] However, it appears that the air and sea bombardment effectively neutralized the vast majority simply by killing or wounding the gunners or by paralysing them through shock. Luckily, Exit 3 was also the spot where the B-26 Marauder bombers had done the most damage. Certainly Lieutenant Jahnke of the German 709th Infantry Division's strongpoint W-5 was, like most of his troops, devastated by the bombardment, and only one 88-mm gun and one old French tank turret was left in working order as the Americans hit the beach. The 88-mm jammed after firing one round and the turret was quickly destroyed, as was the rest of the bunker.[92]

Not only were there less beach obstacles at Exit 3 but it was further from the four 210mm guns at Crisbecq (St, Marcouf), and the four 105 mm guns at Azeville. More important than the extra mile of safety, there were fewer artillery observers here so the long-distance shelling was less accurate. Moreover, the removal of the artillery spotters immediately on the beach by the pre-invasion bombardment meant that the German artillery continued to fire on pre-planned targets on the beach area where the invaders might have been expected to land – not where they actually landed. Thus for three hours the German guns fired safely into the sand where they should have landed, while the American invaders continued pouring ashore 1–2,000 yards further along the beach. Even where the defenders' guns were accurately zeroed in on the position at which the attackers landed, their guns had been set to fire on the high water mark, when in fact the landings began just an hour after low water.[93]

Despite this apparent good fortune, the 'luck' of the Americans was as much to do with German command errors and Allied skill as anything else. Very early on the morning of D-Day 19 members of the 2nd battalion, 506th PIR, 101st Airborne, were captured by members of the W5 Resistance Nest under Lieutenant Jahnke at Exit 3. At 0245 the American prisoners asked what time it was and, when being told the answer, suggested that they should be evacuated – precisely why was not explained but it should have been enough to confirm to the German occupants that W5 was a likely target – and soon.[94] Ninety minutes later the first shells began landing around Janke and he immediately telephoned an order for a barrage on the beach from the gun battery situated three kilometres behind him. However, the naval shelling had destroyed the telephone system by then so he sent a motorcycle despatch rider with a very clear message: beach barrage to be laid down on my signal of two green flares. When the landing craft arrived Jahnke fired two green flares but no barrage arrived because the despatch rider had been killed by a marauding fighter-bomber.[95] Jahnke's inability to comprehend why the paratroopers were so nervous in his bunker and his consequent delay in ordering a barrage, coupled with that single fighter attack, probably saved hundreds of American lives but the actions of General Roosevelt were also important.

General Theodore Roosevelt, son of the late president, had originally been refused a place in the landings because of his age (he was 56) and ill-health. However, he had taken part in more amphibious landings than almost any American fighting in Europe (North Africa, Sicily and Corsica). In contrast to the indecisive command of Lieutenant Jahnke, General Roosevelt rallied the 'lost' troops, and quickly assessing the Critical nature of the situation declared 'We'll start the war from right here'[96] and ordered the follow up troops to land where he was, not where they were supposed to. Harper Coleman, from the 2nd Battalion of the 8th Infantry RCT, remembers being harangued by General Roosevelt. 'If we were afraid of the enemy, we were more afraid of him, and could not have stopped on the beach had we wanted to'.[97] A month later, on 6 July – and the day before Eisenhower was to announce he had been given command of the 90th Infantry Division – Theodore Roosevelt died of a heart attack. He was awarded a posthumous Medal of Honour and is buried in the American Cemetery above Omaha Beach, next to his younger brother who died in France in 1918.

The first gaps in Utah's beach defences were opened up by 0715, and by 0930 the entire beach area was declared free of obstacles. Later that

morning the bulldozers cleared paths through the dunes.[98] St Martin de
Varreville was in US hands by 0745. By 1000 the infantry was pushing
inland from the beaches and by 1300 they had linked up with elements
of the US 101st Airborne who, of course, had confused the enemy and
prevented any major strike against the beaches. By nightfall the 4th
Infantry was eight miles inland.

The only real problem at Utah was the overcrowded beaches with
23,000 troops and 1,700 vehicles all trying to get off the beach.[99]
However, much to General Collin's disgust, Admiral Moon unilaterally
suspended unloading that night on Utah after losing a small number of
navy vessels in the initial assault. Collins apparently exploded at Moon
and told him 'Let the navy expend its ships if that's what it takes. But
we've got to get the build-up ashore even if it means paving the whole
damn Channel with ships'.[100] The unloading resumed.

By the next day the 4th Division reached St Mère Eglise and advanced
towards Cherbourg. That advance proved very difficult and the division
was ordered to halt until reinforcements arrived. Eventually the division
entered Cherbourg and was also the first US unit to enter Paris. As a
whole the 4th Division's landing at Utah was remarkable for the limited
number of casualties (around 200 including 60 lost at sea), indeed, it had
lost 20 times more in the disaster of Operation Tiger at Slapton Sands.
By D-Day+1 32,000 soldiers had landed on Utah. But their luck would
not hold: a year later, in May 1945, the 4th Infantry Division alone had
suffered 34,000 dead and 22,000 wounded in the final campaign against
Germany.[101]

14.6 Pointe du Hoc

Between Utah and Omaha lay the Pointe du Hoc where the cliff ostensibly housed concrete bunkers containing six 155mm guns that could hit
both American beaches.

Companies D, E and F of the US 2nd Ranger Battalion, led by their
Commanding Officer, Lieutenant Colonel James Earl Rudder, had been
given the task of landing on a narrow shingle beach, scaling the 30 metre
cliffs with 200 Rangers, and destroying the guns. As Rudder admitted
later to Bradley, 'First time you mentioned it [in January 1945 at
Bradley's London HQ – 20 Bryanston Square], I thought you were
trying to scare me'.[102]

Later, Admiral Hall's Intelligence officer had also suggested the task
was impossible, in his words to Rudder, 'Three old women with brooms
could keep the Rangers from climbing that cliff'.[103] The remaining

Photo 14.4 Pointe du Hoc, gun emplacement

Photo 14.5 Looking east from Pointe du Hoc along Baker Sector

companies of the 2nd Battalion (A and B), plus the 5th Battalion led by Lt Colonel Max Schneider, were to wait off-shore until Rudder signalled he had taken the Pointe du Hoc. If that signal did not appear by H-Hour+30 minutes Schneider was to land behind the 116th RCT on Omaha at Dog Green and make his way via the Pointe de la Percée to the Pointe du Hoc overland.

In fact Rudder was not supposed to have led the assault and his CO Major-General Huebner had responded with alarm to his request to do so, saying that 'You can't risk getting knocked out in the very first round'. Rudder was unimpressed: 'I'm sorry, sir', he allegedly replied, 'but I'm going to have to disobey you. If I don't take it – it may not go'.[104] In the event Rudder did lead the assault but only because the officer who was supposed to have led it got drunk on board the transport ship and Rudder had to take over.[105]

The Rangers had prepared by scaling equivalent cliffs on the Isle of Wight and practised the climb using the three rocket-propelled grappling lines or rope ladders fired from each of the ten LCAs involved. Their other specialist equipment included 100 foot extension ladders from the Merryweather Company, suppliers to the London Fire Brigade, mounted on four DUKWs, and ten hand-carried 112 foot extension ladders in 16-foot lengths, four of which were not for scaling the cliff but were fitted with two Lewis machine-guns mounted on the top, attached to the LCTs and designed to provide 'high wire' support for the climbers.[106]

In early April 1944 the area was bombed, and then on 15 April and 22 May. Since the Allies did not want to draw too much attention to the area it was not bombed again until the evening of 4 June – when the RAF dropped its heaviest tonnage of bombs on any night of the war – and at 0550 on 6 June the USS *Texas* bombarded it with approximately 250 14" shells.[107] At 0610, just for good measure, 18 medium bombers from the 9th USAAF bombed it. By the time the Rangers landed the equivalent explosive power of Hiroshima had been dropped on the Pointe du Hoc, and much of the damage remains to this day.

Photo 14.6 Pointe du Hoc, shattered gun emplacement

Defending Pointe du Hoc from the 200 Rangers were 210 soldiers of the 716th Coastal Defence Division, of whom 125 were infantry from the 726th Infantry Regiment protecting the 85 members of the 1,260th Coastal Artillery Regiment.

Typically for the day, nothing went to plan. The rangers approached in ten LCTs guided by three small British gunboats. Even before they landed 10 per cent of their group were already heading back to England after their boat sank, as did one of the two boats carrying their equipment and ammunition. The remaining eight boats eventually landed at 0708, 38 minutes late after the coxswain of the lead British gunboat (of three) had mistaken the Pointe-de-la-Percée for the Pointe du Hoc. As a result two things happened. First, the bombardment had stopped, allowing the defenders to return to their guns and fire upon the attackers, at least until 0710 when *Satterlee* moved back in and resumed the bombardment. As US naval staff admitted afterwards, 'naval gunfire support should conform to the movement of the landing boats rather than adhere to a pre-determined time schedule'. In fact, Rear Admiral Vian had stated *before* the assault that 'fire (should) not be checked or shifted at the pre-arranged time of touchdown unless the craft have, in fact, arrived at the beach'.[108] Second, the delay meant that the main group of Rangers waiting off Omaha never received the signal to divert to the Pointe du Hoc if the attack was successful until it was too late. This group, assuming a failed attack – which would generate a heavy naval bombardment on the Pointe, landed on Omaha instead.

The rocket-propelled grappling hooks generally failed to operate properly, probably because the attached ropes were wet and thus too heavy but all but one of the landing craft managed to get at least one rope up to the top. The Rangers had managed to climb up by situating sections of the scaling ladders on top of the 40 feet mound of debris brought down by the bombardment. They then gradually added additional sections through individual Rangers cutting out standing positions in the cliff face and holding a ladder section while the next Ranger climbed up it and repeated the process until they worked their way up to the top. But within 20 minutes of landing beneath the Pointe du Hoc the first Rangers had reached the top of the cliff.

As ever, macabre humour was remembered. Pte Harry Roberts climbed the cliff by rope, after having two ropes cut by the Germans and was apparently the first Ranger to the top. Close behind him was Sergeant Gene Elder who called down to those following him: 'Boys, keep your heads down, because headquarters has fouled up again and has issued the enemy live ammunition'.[109] In fact most of the immediate defenders had temporarily disappeared, except for those manning a rein-forced Observation Point who were quickly silenced.

Another irony was that the 155mm guns were not in their bunkers – telephone poles had replaced them. The guns had been moved to a nearby apple orchard three days earlier to avoid the recent air raids in the area and were aligned to fire on Utah Beach. Once discovered, however, the three guns that had not been damaged by the bombardment were disabled by thermite grenades – just as the gun crews lined up for inspec-tion at 0900 – the first mission accomplished by American ground forces on D-Day. The Rangers then moved on to the complex of bunkers until reinforcements arrived. In fact, at midday Rudder's message back to General Huebner via the *Satterlee* read: 'Located Pointe du Hoe (sic) – mission accomplished – need ammunition and reinforcement – many casualties'. Huebner's reply reflected the tragedy unfolding at Omaha: 'No reinforcements available'.[110]

Those reinforcements should have been the 5th Rangers Battalion, which diverted to Dog Green on Omaha while Company C and the rest of the 2nd Rangers attacked Pointe at Raz de la Percée – where Rudder had been inadvertently led at first. They were awaiting a signal from Rudder that would call them over to reinforce him should he have trouble – which he did. Unfortunately Rudder's delayed landing and consequent bitter struggle up the cliffs meant that by the time the signal for help was sent they were already committed to Omaha. Thus the reinforcements that

Photo 14.7 Pointe du Hoc from west showing Rangers Memorial

were due at 1200 on D-Day did not arrive until 1200 D-Day+2. At that point Rudder's Rangers had fought off five counter-attacks, with the help of naval gunfire from the ships offshore, and only 50 of the 200 Rangers were still capable of fighting.[111] Even then some of the tanks involved began shelling the area on the assumption that all the Rangers must have been killed.[112] Having just driven off Omaha the tankers could be forgiven for that assumption.

14.7 Omaha Beach

Omaha Beach is the 7,000 yard crescent of beach encompassing Colleville-sur-Mer and Vierville-sur-Mer, linking Utah in the west with Gold in the east. A 300 yard beach exists at low tide with a very gentle gradient (1:188) rising to 1:47 at the high water point and 1:8 to the shingle beach (now disappeared).[113] Beyond the beach is a marshy area running up to the bluffs that are not accessible to vehicles. Five 'draws' or valleys provided the only access for these and only one metalled road existed at the time, through Vierville-sur-Mer.

If death on the other beaches and on the Pointe du Hoc was a 'random harvest', on Omaha it was a 'grim reaping'.[114] The total casualties for Omaha on D-Day itself were about 2,000 (almost 40 per cent of the total invasion casualties of about 4,900). In effect, Omaha took twice the number of casualties it should have done if the numbers were even distributed between the five beaches, though proportionately it was only marginally more than the Canadian casualties on Juno. General Bradley, speaking 30 years after the event, called it 'a nightmare'.[115] In a typically plain-speaking conclusion Ambrose suggests that 'The plan had called for the air and naval bombardments, followed by tanks and (bull)dozers, to blast a path through the exits so that the infantry could march up the draws and engage the enemy, but the plan had failed, utterly and completely failed'.[116] What made it particularly ironic was that Bradley had always assumed that the major problem was not forcing a landing but securing it. As he told the journalists on board the USS Augusta on the 4 June – what should have been the eve of D-Day:

> We're going to face three critical periods in this invasion. The first will come in getting ashore. It'll be difficult – but we're not especially worried about that part of it. The second may come on the sixth or seventh day when the other fellow gets together enough reinforcements for a counter-offensive. This counter-attack will probably give us our greatest trouble. Then, once we hurdle the counter-attack, our third critical period will come when we go to break out of the beach-head ... .

You've got to remember that just as soon as we land, this business becomes primarily a business of build-up. For you can almost always force an invasion – but you can't always make it stick.[117]

This is a crucial statement because it explains why Bradley was so reluctant to use the 'funnies', the specialized assault armour, used by the Anglo-Canadian forces: since the landing itself would be tough but viable, the real problem was in getting sufficient conventional armour, artillery and troops on-shore with a week. Thus to displace precious space for armour and troops with 'funnies', that had a very limited role, was perceived as counter-productive.

Bradley's summation of German strategy is also important because it mirrors von Rundstedt's but inverts Rommel's – and it was Rommel who was in control of the beaches. Hence Bradley's evaluation of the German and his own strategy ultimately under-resourced the landings themselves and, in part, made the Omaha assault much more costly than it need have been.

On D-Day itself, off Omaha Beach, Bradley sent his Chief of Staff, Major General Kean, to assess the situation personally. His report supported this critical lacuna in Bradley's plan. When Kean returned to the USS Augusta Bradley asked him 'What do they need most?' 'Bulldozers', Kean answered, 'bulldozers and artillery'. They're badly pinched for both'.[118] Given the colossal number of 'Funnies' available to the Anglo-Canadian beaches, the Americans on Omaha had just 16 bulldozers available in the morning: of these only six reached the beach and only three survived. By contrast, the two British beaches alone had 196 'Funnies' in eight mixed groups with a combined total of 50 Crab tanks (12 of which were destroyed), 120 AVREs (22 of which were destroyed), eight Fascines, ten SBG bridges and eight bulldozers.[119] Chester Wilmot was clear that the Funnies had played a crucial role on the Anglo-Canadian beaches:

Apart from the factor of tactical surprise, the comparatively light casualties which we sustained on all beaches except Omaha, were in large measure due to our success of the novel mechanical continuances which we employed, and to the staggering morale and material effect of the mass of armour landed in the leading waves of the assault … . How many lives were saved on other sectors by the 79th Armoured Division nobody can tell but if it had not been for the specialist armour, the spearhead of the assault, progress on the British and Canadian beaches might have been almost as slow and expensive as it was on Omaha.[120]

The consequence for Omaha was not simply that the assault troops and combat engineers had no protection in their movement *off* the beach but that the initial paths *across* the beach were confined to the width of the individual who removed the mines by hand. Thus on the Anglo-Canadian beaches the infantry could move across the beach in relatively dispersed form, providing a disparate target for the defenders. But on Omaha the troops had to either risk falling victim to a mine or moving in single file across the beach – a slow process that inevitably led to bunching and providing an easy target for the defenders. And whatever else hampered the assault it was not a lack of bravery on the part of the Combat Engineers who were trained to clear the obstacles: of the 272 joint Army-Navy demolition engineers on Omaha Beach, 111 were dead within 30 minutes.[121]

The only specialized armour employed on Omaha was the DD tanks and the bulldozers. But to use the amphibious Shermans the surface wind should not have been more than 12 mph onshore and 18 mph offshore. Additionally, visibility of not less than 3 miles was needed to facilitate the naval bombardment; and a cloud base of not more than 3,000 feet to help the bombers. Yet, according to Rear-Admiral Hall, naval Commander, Force O, the 'sea was choppy, with wind force 5 from the south-west. The sky was partially overcast with visibility about ten miles'.[122] That translates to between 17 and 21 knots or 20–24 mph; in short, the winds at Omaha were between 10 and 33 per cent higher than planned. Worse, the waves were up to two metres high which would threaten the tanks and landing craft, the cloud base would partially obscure the beach targets from the air; and although the ships would have been able to see their targets – that visibility would only last until the smoke from the initial shelling covered the area.

Bradley was well aware of the problem as he approached the coast in the USS Augusta and recalled a conversation with 'Tubby' Thorson his G3 (Battle Planning Officer):[123]

Thorson: I don't like it General. The DDs are going to have one helluva time in getting through this sea.
Bradley: Yes Tubby, I'm afraid you're right. But at this point there's nothing we can do.
Thorson: Any sign of a let-up in the surf?
Bradley: Not yet. Kirk tells me the DDs may be swamped in these seas if they're launched from the LCTs. Either the LCTs cart them ashore – or we'll have to count with getting along without them.[124]

The plan was relatively clear: a 40-minute naval bombardment was designed to neutralize specific targets followed by a 30-minute air assault. Once the initial assault troops had landed (the 16th RCT of the 1st Division and the 116th RCT of the 29th Division), the 1st Division (known as the 'Big Red One' from the red numeral on their shoulder flash and helmets) would move inland and east to link up with the British at Port-en-Bessin, while the 29th Division (known as the Blues and Grays from their recruitment across the old north-south dividing line) would move inland and west to the Vire estuary. Of the eight sectors of the beach, the 116th RCT, aided by C Company of the 2nd Ranger Battalion, were responsible for the five eastern sectors: Charley, Dog Green, Dog White, Dog Red and Easy Green. The 16th RCT took the three western sectors: Easy Red, Fox Green and Fox Red.

The beach was a nightmare for attackers and a dream for defenders: it was difficult to outflank, the bluff provided good views for the defenders of the attackers, there were more mines here than at Utah and it was more heavily fortified with 12 reinforced gun emplacements situated on either sides of the five available 'draws' or exit routes to the hinterland. The five draws were also covered by *Stützpunkt*, strongpoints of mutually supporting Resistance Nests. For example, the Vierville Draw was covered by 70 soldiers of the 3rd Battalion, 726th Infantry Regiment and comprised six resistance nests.[125] Overall there were 21 Resistance Nests overlooking Omaha Beach, though not all were concrete or bombproof. Nevertheless, the entire beach was covered by a terrifying array of defences: eight concrete bunkers with large calibre artillery (75mm +); 35 pill-boxes with smaller artillery and automatic weapons; four separate batteries of artillery; 18 anti-tank guns; six mortar pits; 35 rocket launching sites; and 85 machine-gun nests.[126] Many of the machine guns were targeted sideways to provide enfilading fire whilst being protected to the front by concrete. Hence many of soldiers wading through the surf were being fired at but could see nothing to fire back at: either the defenders were in hidden bunkers or the solid concrete gun emplacements were simply impermeable to rifle and machine gun fire. And, since the DD tanks had failed to negotiate the rough sea, bullets were just about all the attackers had. Indeed, the gun emplacements were often impenetrable to naval gunfire too. Major Pluskat took several direct hits on his bunker from sea and air but when the shelling stopped not one of his 20 guns was damaged and no single injury had been caused.[127] Everitt Schultheis from the 467th Anti-Aircraft Battalion watched as a heavy cruiser pounded a concrete gun emplacement directly in front of his LCT but to no avail:

> From our vantage point, the projectile(s) appeared to be about the size of a domestic water heater. Every round fired struck the target, but the shore battery continued to fire. The navy ceased fire and we were able to see one of our GIs begin working his way up the cliff, dragging a long pole with satchel charges in it

... He stuffed his charges into the firing slit, then tumbled down the bluff. Seconds later, dust and black smoke erupted from the gun emplacement, effectively silencing the shore battery.[128]

But before all the batteries were silenced around 2,000 attackers were dead from the two divisions.

14.7.1 The 116th RCT of the 29th Division

In overall command of the 29th Division was General Gerhardt but his assistant, Brigadier General Cota, was to land first with 116th RCT and assist the 1st Division's commander, General Huebner, with the combined assault by both RCTs until Gerhardt landed later in the day. In fact Admiral Ramsay (Allied Naval Commander in Chief) and Rear Admiral Kirk (Commander of the Western Task Force) were extremely hostile to each other. Given the predominance of the British naval effort in the invasion Eisenhower had accepted that there would be no 'joint' naval command and that the US naval effort would be subordinated to Ramsay's command, but there was a remarkably degree of personal enmity between the two 'allies'. On 6 May Ramsay wrote in his private diary about 'two hysterical letters from Alan Kirk ... he has quite lost his sense of proportion besides being rather offensively rude. My opinion of him decreases steadily. He is not a big enough man to hold the position he does'. For his part, Kirk recalled how Ramsay 'had become very testy and very difficult about the American effort'. The issue was not simply one of differing personalities but rather a contradictory perspective on planning. The British had traditionally been very hierarchical with all planning undertaken by the Admiralty, leaving subordinate commanders to do little except execute the plans as required. But the American naval system was far more flexible, with the naval hierarchy issuing outline plans and leaving their subordinates to fill in the details as they saw fit.[129]

Those details for Omaha, for instance, were incredibly complex. At H-Hour minus five minutes 32 DD tanks would swim ashore on Dog White and Dog Green. At H-Hour 16 LCT(A)s (Landing Craft Tank [Armoured]) carrying two or three tanks each with 95mm guns would land having continued firing as they approached the beach directly from their landing craft. At H-Hour the 4 LCTs of the 1st Battalion's Company 'A' were to land carrying 'tank dozers' to clear the obstacles prior to further landings and before the tide covered them again.

The plan did not call for all of the 1st Battalion's four companies to land at once but for one of the 1st Battalion (A Company), and three of the 2nd Battalion (E,F, and G Companies). At H+1 minute Companies

A, G, F, and E were to land on Dog Green, Dog White, Dog Red, and Easy Green respectively. Each company comprised around 200 soldiers and each LCVP carried one officer and 31 soldiers. These were to be followed by various specialized units, engineers, anti-aircraft batteries, light artillery etc., and some 50 minutes later, the second wave of infantry would arrive in the shape of the Companies I, K and C. The first heavy artillery would arrive on the DUKWs at H+110 minutes and by H+180 minutes the navy salvage vessels would arrive to clear any broken or destroyed vehicles as the infantry companies moved deep inland. That was the theory and it was a theory suitable for Tame Problems.

Indeed, some soldiers were sure that the precise scheduling of D-Day almost in itself would ensure victory. In the words of Private Barnes, Company A, 116th Infantry RCT: 'It seemed so organized that nothing could go wrong, nothing could stop it. It was like a train schedule'. But Cota had warned his troops that little would go to plan:

> This is different from any of the other exercises you've had so far. The little discrepancies that we tried to correct on Slapton sand are going to be magnified and are going to give way to incidents that you might first view as chaotic ... The landing craft aren't going in on schedule and people are going to be landed in the wrong place. Some won't be landing at all. The enemy will try, and will have some success, in preventing our gaining a lodgement. But we must improvise, carry on, not lose our heads. Nor must we add to the confusion.[130]

Captain Miller of the 175th Regiment agreed, and suggested that his troops forget about the operational plan for the regiment, which was thicker than a telephone directory and could not be torn in half: 'Forget this goddamned thing. You get your ass on the beach. I'll be there waiting for you and I'll tell you what to do. There ain't anything in this plan that is going to go right'.[131] He was right – but the problem was if he didn't survive the landing the ordinary soldiers would be completely bereft of command, so dependent were they upon their officers and NCOs.

At 0250 the ships of Force O began anchoring 11 miles from the beach, and at 0315 the troops began debarking to the landing craft, most in sections of 31 people including one officer at the bow (which explains their terrifying casualty rate) followed by a five soldier rifle team, a team of four wire cutters, two BAR teams with two soldiers each, two Bazooka teams of two soldiers, a single mortar team of four people, a two soldier flame-thrower team, five members of the demolition team using Bangalore Torpedoes, a medic and an assistant team leader. Since they assumed that no re-supply would be available for 48 hours each soldier had to carry two days food and ammunition. With six or seven sections to a company, and 30 LCAs on each of the three ships carrying one of the three battalions of the 29th Division, the craft headed for Omaha Beach at a steady nine knots – at least two and a half hours' standing ride, but for many it was to be much longer.

The naval assault was executed on time but it appears that little damage was done. Worse, the bombing aircraft were ordered – much to Bradley's dismay who was unaware of the decision at the time – to delay their bomb drop by 30 seconds because the early morning mist and the smoke from the naval gunfire effectively obscured the target and the USAAF wanted to avoid any 'friendly-fire' incidents.[132] So far adrift were the bombs from their targets that only two sticks of bombs landed within four miles of the coastal defences.[133] Here is an example of a crisis being generated because of the fear of being held responsible for what might have been an error of judgement. The consequence was that almost no damage was inflicted on the defenders. As a direct result many of the German artillery spotters remained untouched in the bluffs. As the official report suggested, 'the (German artillery) fire was obviously observed because enemy batteries would be silent until craft beached, when there would be a few quick salvos, usually right on target'.[134]

The assault plan began fraying the moment the bombers missed their targets and the DD tanks sank in the choppy water. Many of these first assault troops died, partly because the division's armour and communications failed miserably: 57 of the 96 DD tanks allocated to Omaha sank, as did most of the radios, and ten of the first landing craft containing 310 soldiers.[135] The 743rd Tank Battalion was supposed to land 32 DD Shermans from the 8 LCTs in Companies B and C from 6,000 yards off shore. But after all but five DD Shermans from the adjacent 741st Tank Battalion covering the 1st Division's beaches had sunk, the CO of the 743rd recognized the Critical situation and ordered his DD Shermans directly onto the beach. One of the 743rd's LCTs was hit and destroyed as it neared the beach and all four tanks were lost, but the other 28 tanks hit the beach.[136]

The artillery support for the 116th RCT was as sparse as the DD-Tank support. The 111th Field Artillery Battalion had twelve 105mm howitzers on 12 DUKWS and at about 0730 liaison officers were to land and establish firing positions for the guns to support the infantry, assumed by then to be moving inland beyond the bluffs. Each DUKW also carried 14 artillery soldiers, 50 rounds of ammunition, sandbags and other extraneous material – but that gave the DUKWs little between the top of the boat and the water. The liaison officers tried to warn the DUKWs to stay off the beach since the fire was too intense but no radios could be found. Not that sighting the guns was the major problem because by 0900, 11 of them were at the bottom of the sea. They had been unloaded in their DUKWs from the LSTs at 0200 and seven had sunk as they waited for the run into the beach. On that run one more sank, leaving just four and three of these were hit by gunfire. The remaining DUKW, with Captain Shuford on board, was prevented from landing in the 29th Division area by a control boat and moved onto the 1st Division area – where the same thing happened. Shuford eventually landed his exhausted troops on a Rhino offshore and the howitzer ended up with the 1st Division.[137]

At first Omaha looked like it was going to replicate Utah for there was almost no German fire as the 48 craft of the 116th RCT's first assault wave approached. Captain Sabin of the US Navy remembers there being 'no sign of life or resistance ... . There was an intense quiet, so quiet it was suspicious'.[138] But up to 800 defenders had other ideas.

The detailed plan to assign particular companies to particular beaches at particular times was almost immediately invalidated because the currents that moved across the beach drew most of the assault craft off course. At 0600 the leading boats reached the official Line of Departure, 2½ miles off shore, when they were to form their final assault lines at the designated time of departure – 0613. At that time 24 boats carrying the four first wave companies (A,F,G and E) set off in a line 1½ miles long, led by the LCTs carrying the 741st and 743rd Tank Battalions of Shermans. Within 30 minutes all four leading companies were to have landed, followed by a further eight companies within the next 30 minutes. Within two hours the entire 116th RCT was to be ashore.

Half a mile from shore nine LCT(R)s loosed their salvos of rockets but already the casualties were mounting and no German shot had come near them as yet: LCA5 from Company A had been swamped 1,000 yards off shore and as they got past the 500 yard mark enemy fire began, sinking another LCA from Company A. The remaining four boats grounded precisely where they were supposed to, just east of the Vierville draw on Dog Green – right in front of the best defended area of the beach. In LCA 1015 every member of the 32 occupants died. By the time they landed most of the soldiers had been in the small landing craft for at least four hours and many were sea-sick. In fact, so bad were the conditions that a colonel recalled seeing some of his men in their waterlogged landing craft who 'just lay there with the water sloshing back and forth over them, not caring whether they lived or died'.[139] Ironically, because the guide boat for Company A – one of the few guide boats left afloat – landed exactly where it was supposed to, right under the barrel of an 88mm gun emplacement, its enfiladed direction prevent it from firing directly upon them and they managed to signal their company in with flags. However, the result was a disaster because Company A was now isolated in its accurate landing with Companies G and F well down the beach leaving the defenders around Vierville to converge on A Company. As one correspondent noted at the time, there was 'a line of American soldiers waist deep in water and immobilized by fear. Descending arcs of tracers were entering the water around them, and they could not bring themselves to move. They seemed as permanently fixed in time and space as those marines in the statue of the flag-raising on Iwo Jima'.[140] According to the official history, 'As the first men (of Company A) jumped, they crumpled and flopped into the water. Then order was lost. It seemed to the men that the only way to get ashore was to dive in head-first and swim clear of the fire that was striking the boats. But as they hit the water, their heavy equipment dragged them down, and soon they were fighting to keep afloat'.[141] All the US soldiers wore M26 Life Preservers but unfortunately they could not support a fully laden soldier and to remove much of the equipment a soldier had first to ditch the life preserver.[142] The irony was that these had replaced the cork lifejackets used in Sicily: these could support a soldier but a jump from a ship at any height above the water often resulted in a neck injury or death as the cork caught under the wearer's chin on entry.[143]

Ten minutes later no officer or sergeant on A Company remained both alive and uninjured. By the end of 15 minutes, A Company has still not fired a weapon.

> No orders are being given by anyone. No words are spoken. The few able-bodied survivors move or not as they see fit. Merely to stay alive is a full-time job … . Above all others stands out the first-aid man, Thomas Breedin. Reaching the sands he strips off pack, blouse, helmet and boots. For a moment he stands there so that others on the stand will see him and get the same idea. Then he crawls into the water to pull in wounded men about to be overlapped by the tide. The deeper water is still spotted with tide walkers, advancing at the same pace as the rising water. But now, owing to Breedin's example, the strongest among them become more conspicuous targets. Coming along, they pick up wounded comrades and float them to the shore, raftwise[144]

Some 96 per cent of the 200 men of A Company were killed or wounded on D-Day and the eight uninjured survivors – who had hardly fired a shot – were huddled under the sea wall trying to secure some protection from the defenders and Lieutenant Nanace was the only officer left alive.[145]

The first assault wave of the 116th (Companies A, G, F and E) accompanied by Company C of the 2nd Rangers – or what was left of them – were now either on the beach or at the water's edge. To all intents and purposes they had 'failed' and the plan that should have tamed the problem of the landing had disintegrated; they were now in crisis.

On time, at 0700, Company B landed directly behind what was left of Company A, led by Captain Zappacosta on the command boat. SLA Marshall claimed in an article in *Atlantic Monthly* in 1960 that Zappacosta drew his pistol on the British coxswain after the latter refused to take the boat into the beach on the border of Dog Green and Charlie opposite Exit E-1, the Vierville draw. The coxswain, in Marshall's account, changed his mind but Zappacosta had his terminated as he was shot leading the charge off the boat. Only one soldier made the shoreline alive and uninjured, that was Private Robert Sales who slipped on exiting the boat and fell into the water before the machine gun raking his boat killed or injuring all his companions. It took Sales two hours to get from the boat to the beach and he remained behind a floating log with two wounded companions until nightfall.[146] Sales, however, suggested that Marshall fabricated the whole story – as he had with his earlier claims that few soldiers fire their weapons in action.[147]

Lt Walter P. Taylor of B Company 116th Infantry, leading the boat next to Zappacosta's, landed in a relatively quiet area – he only lost four dead and two wounded to machine gun fire in the run across the beach and led his team straight up the cliffs into Vierville and on to the Château de Vaumicel (the most southerly point achieved by US beach forces on the eastern flank of Omaha on the day) where they captured 26 Germans before being counter-attacked and being ordered to fall back to the beach area. Staff Sergeant Price, one of the assorted individuals who joined Taylor's team on the beach, recalled why he had chosen to follow him: 'We saw no sign of fear in him. Watching him made men of us. Marching or fighting, he was leading. We followed him because there was nothing else to do'. Marshall subsequently called Taylor 'one of the 47 immortals of Omaha who, by their dauntless initiative at widely separated points along the beach, saved the landing from total stagnation and disaster.[148] Note here that this would fit well with Marshall's predilection for heroes as the explanatory factor in military success and should be taken as a warning against the assumption that success can only be achieved through such individual acts of bravery – when in reality much of the success on D-Day was probably down to the mundane acts of the many as much as the heroic acts of the few.

Private J. R. Slaughter of D Company 116th also experienced a less than enthusiastic British coxswain calling out that he was lowering the ramp at 300 yards as the landing craft came under direct fire. When Sergeant Norfleet demanded that the boat go further in the coxswain refused – until Norfleet took out his pistol and held it to the coxswain's head.[149] Given the hundreds of landing craft involved it is probably more surprising that the majority of Coxswains unloaded their troops at the appropriate spot without the need for such coercive 'encouragement' from the local commander. As Admiral Ramsay wrote afterwards the vast majority of the landing crews performed admirably and he praised the 'courage and devotion to duty on (their) part ... the assault proceeded to plan not necessarily because it was a good plan, but because every single individual taking part had confidence in it and was determined to achieve his objectives'.[150] One such individual was the Coxswain of LCA 786, Corporal George Tandy of the Royal Marines, who had his steering wheel shot away long before he reached the beach but he steered the remains of the rudder with his foot for four hours as he delivered his soldiers to Sword Beach.[151]

Worse still, the self-evident confusion and death on the beaches made the coxswains of the second wave of landing craft much more wary about landing than had the previous wave. There had been some discussion about who had the authority to order a launch at sea – the captain of the landing craft/ship or the captain of the tanks – and it was eventually agreed that the latter would be responsible – though this did not prevent some LCT captains from demanding premature launches when the turmoil on the beaches became apparent, nor did it cover the launch of troops from landing craft.[152] In fact, the rule was that the naval officer was in command as long as the boat or ship was at sea, but once it hit the land the army officer was in control. In practice this did not always clarify the responsibilities because it wasn't always clear whether the boat or ship was permanently in contact with the land or just floating on and off.[153]

Yet for many troops anywhere was better than staying out at sea. For as Sergeant Benjamin McKinney, a combat engineer with C Company recalled: 'I was so seasick I didn't care if a bullet hit me between the eyes and got me out of my misery ... it looked as if all the first wave were dead on the beach'.[154] At 0641 Patrol Craft 552, which was completing the 1st Division's operations journal as it happened, noted: 'Entire First Wave Foundered'.[155]

The second wave of the 116th (Companies B, C, D, H, I, K, L and M) began landing from 0700. Zappacosta's Company B had been decimated on Charlie, but Company C was relatively unscathed thanks to the smoke across the beach on Dog Green. Company D suffered casualties from mines, and Company H was caught on the boundary of Dog White and Dog Red by machine gun fire. But Companies I and K on Easy Green, and Companies L and M on Easy Red (1st Division's designated beach) arrived a little later at around 0720 and managed to cross the beach without suffering huge numbers of casualties.

Ten minutes later General Cota and Colonel Canham landed under smoke amongst Company C and a few wayward Rangers. Within 30 minutes soldiers were moving up the bluffs.[156] Cota had landed with Colonel Canham on LCVP 71 which struck a mine on the way in; luckily the mine fell harmlessly into the sea, though Major Sours was killed as the occupants ran for the sea wall.

As Cota's aide-de-camp described it: 'Although the leading elements of the assault had been on the beach for approximately one hour, none had progressed farther than the seawall at the inland border of the beach. [They] were clustered under the wall, pinned down by machine-gun fire, and the enemy was beginning to bring effective mortar fire to bear on those hidden behind the wall.[157] Cota was faced with a motley collection of troops from different companies of the 29th Division, interspersed with some misaligned Rangers and communication was almost impossible in the noise and because the beach was divided by wooden 'groins' that ran perpendicular to the sea wall straight back to the water at about every 50 feet. The shelling was intensifying by the minute and, according to Captain McGrath, 'so many shells were ranging along the crest of the hill that a man standing there felt as if he could reach out and pick them out of the air'.[158] Those that remained at the water's edge at high water were now just 50 yards from the seawall.

At this point in time the organization on Omaha had simply ground to a halt: troops continued to unload into the surf, and continued to be shot or blown apart by the defenders and those that reached the beach or the sea wall or the bottom of the bluffs, simply stayed put, unable or unwilling to take the next step. That next step would only come when sufficient numbers of people had decided to take it.[159]

When Brigadier-General Cota got to the wall, and realized that attacking the draws directly was suicidal, he decided to move straight up the bluffs through the minefields. In the face of such a growing crisis, Cota allegedly stood up to leap the wall, and personally directed the BAR (Browning Automatic Rifle) to fire at the bluffs whilst fixing a bangalore torpedo to blow a gap in the barbed wire. Three men were killed and two wounded by mortars in the action but the first breakthrough had been made. Behind them, the next waves were piling in on the shore and, at last, provided such a large target for the defenders that their fire could no longer be concentrated against isolated pockets of invaders.

By 0900 Cota had made it up the bottom of the bluff where little fire occurred because most of the defender's fire was zeroed in on the beach. He moved up via Les Moulins above Hamel-au-Prêtre where he headed toward Vierville to attack the German defences from the rear. Also entering the village were several members of Company C and at about the same time the USS *Texas* fired six 14 inch shells into the draw, making the pavement rise in the village according to Lt Shea who was accompanying Cota.

By the time Cota got to the beach at D-1 on the border of Charlie and Dog Green (sometime after 1230 when the naval bombardment had stopped), he had only five soldiers with him but they took the surrender of the German forces, forcing one of them to lead the way through a minefield, and began the task of moving the rest of the 116th RCT, soon to be reinforced by the 115th RCT (which began landing from 1030), through the draw and up towards St Laurent. The village held out until the following day.

But first Cota had to clear the exit at Vierville, then blocked by an anti-tank wall and the troops close by explained that there was insufficient explosives to blow it up. Cota, replicating his commander-in-a-crisis mode of earlier, then, allegedly, went down to the beach to a bulldozer piled high with TNT and, eventually, managed to command a soldier to drive it up to the anti-tank wall for the engineers to use.[160]

Colonel Canham played a similar role. Though wounded, and with his right arm in a sling, he carried his pistol in his left and railed at his troops – and especially his subordinate officers – to get moving. 'They're murdering us here,' he allegedly yelled, 'let's move inland and get murdered'.[161] Private John R Slaughter of D Company 116th remembered him not shouting at the ordinary soldiers but at their officers who were just as frozen to the beach as everybody else was:

> He was yelling and screaming for the officers to get the men off the beach. 'Get the hell off this damn beach and go kill some Germans'. There was an officer taking refuge from an enemy mortar barrage in a pillbox. Right in front of me Colonel Canham screamed, 'Get your ass out of there and show some leadership'. To another lieutenant he roared, 'Get these men off their dead asses and over that wall'.[162]

Canham then led his followers up the bluffs to the east of the Vierville draw on Dog Green and proceeded into Vierville where he met up again with Cota. Canham then moved eastwards to take the German defences at Les Moulins from the rear.

Further along the same beach Private John MacPhee struggled to the beach to find: 'officers sitting there, stunned. Nobody was taking command.[163] This was hardly surprising: I Company had taken over 33 per cent casualties; F Company, which had been on the beach for 45 minutes and had taken 50 per cent casualties, no longer existed as a fighting unit.[164] Samuel Morison, one of the authors of the official US history of the campaign noted: 'All along Omaha there was a disunited, confused

Photo 14.8 Looking west from WN-71 onto Dog Green at Vierville

and partly leaderless body of infantry, without cohesion, with no artillery support, huddled under the seawall to get shelter from the withering fire'.[165]

Two aspects are important here. First, the noise of battle would have made anything other than a direct shout into the ear of an individual probably irrelevant. Thus, any kind of 'speech' to a company of soldiers was simply out of the question.[166] Second, Canham focuses upon those he clearly assumes responsible for the inertia: his own officers, not his ordinary soldiers. The role of the latter is to do what their officers tell them – and if their officers don't tell them what to do they don't do anything except try and stay alive. Thus although the *cause* of the immediate problem is very probably the responsibility of senior leaders elsewhere who have misorganized the bombardments and the design and deployment of supporting armour, the immediate solution is laid at the feet – literally in this case – of the local commanders. Once again, the failure of senior leaders can only be rescued – if it can be – by the acts of subordinate commanders. It should also be noted that the 29th Division had never before been involved in combat – and to some extent this might explain their initial inertia. Inexperienced troops and officers may have been relatively eager to get to the beaches but were immobilized by their inexperience once they were in difficulties.

Company F tried to made good use of the smoke then arising from the bluffs but their boats landed right in front of German resistance nests and they took more casualties as they moved to the shingle line. Sergeant

Bare of F Company tried to get his soldiers off the beach 'but it was horrible – men frozen in the sand, unable to move. My radioman had his head blown off three yards from me. The beach – barely 30 metres wide in places – was covered with bodies – men with no legs, no arms – God it was awful. It was absolutely terrible.[167] Sergeant Warner Hamlet of F Company demanded that those around him get up and run for the sea wall. But to do that meant risking the bullets, fighting through the barbed wire by hand and running across the shingle that was being peppered by mortars.

Even when troops managed to land and reach the bluffs relatively intact their problems were not necessarily over. Company G's six LCVPs had drifted just east of Les Moulins on Easy Green, but the soldiers had been protected from German attack when crossing the 350 yards of sand by the smoke emanating from the grass fires in the surrounding bluffs. Most of them made it to the seawall but military inflexibility acted to decimate them. When they realized they were 1,000 yards east of their designated landing spot (Dog White) they were ordered to more west 1,000 yards, a process that took them two hours and cost them many casualties.[168]

Slowly groups began to move across the beach, over the wall and up into the bluffs. Private John Robertson with Company F landed on Dog Red, opposite D-3, the draw at Les Moulins, and was content to lie flat against the sand until a Sherman headed straight for him from the water, at which point he ran for the sea wall, after all 'crossing the beach looked like suicide, but better than getting run over'.[169]

Major Sidney Bingham, CO of 2nd Battalion, 116th, had four of his company commanders dead or wounded and rest scattered across the beach and insists that 'The individual and small unit initiative carried the day. Very little, if any, credit can be accorded company, battalion or regimental commanders for their tactical prowess and/or their co-ordination of the action'.[170] In other words, what mattered was not so much the visible and heroic actions of the commanding officers, but what the lower ranking officers, the sergeants and so forth actually *did* – as opposed to said. Further evidence for this is provided from the ordinary soldiers, in this case by Private Carl Weast: 'It was simple fear that stopped us at that shingle and we lay there and we got butchered by rocket fire and by mortars for no damn reason other than the fact that there was nobody there to lead us off that goddamn beach. Like I say, heh man, I did my job, but somebody had to lead me'.[171]

Sergeant William Lewis was another of those waiting to be led over the shingle where he lay prone trying to stay alive as long as possible. Then Lieutenant Leo Van de Voort shouted at him: 'Let's go, goddam, there ain't no use staying here, we're all going to get killed!' Van de Voort immediately set off up the beach, silenced a gun emplacement with a grenade and took half a dozen prisoners, prompting Lewis to think 'hell, if he can do that, why can't we. That's how we got off the beach'.[172] The significance of exemplary commanders' action seemed to be critical, not just in that commanders took control or demonstrated their personal bravery but more simply in the evidence that taking action did not necessarily mean being shot – while staying on the beach appeared increasingly suicidal. It was what Sun Tzu would have referred to as 'Death Ground' where 'Blocked by mountains to the fore and rivers to the rear, with provisions exhausted. In this situation it is advantageous to act speedily and dangerous to procrastinate'.[173]

Later assault troops tended to receive lighter casualties but this was probably due to the increasing number of targets available to the defenders and the value of some smoke from grass fires on the bluffs, rather than to any degree of successful penetration by the attackers.[174] Of the 16 lanes that should have been opened up only four were completely cleared and one German machine gunner fired 12,000 rounds until he was overrun in the afternoon of D-Day.

There was still some fire on Easy Green, where the 115th landed but far less than had opposed the first assault troops there in the morning, and the gaps blown by the 1st Division assault units were sufficient to allow the troops to disembark in relative safety. The 1st Battalion, landing at 1000 was to move through Exit E-1 around the rear of St Laurent behind Les Moulins – which it did by 1800 – while the 2nd and 3rd Battalions landing at 1030 provided a frontal assault in the late afternoon. At 1137 a report reached the 1st Division's HQ saying that German troops were surrendering but it was another two hours, at 1341, that Dog was declared clear of opposition.[175]

Some 34,000 of the expected 55,000 designated for this part of Normandy were on land by nightfall, though 2,400 were casualties, a rate of 7 per cent that was still below the expected 12 per cent. However the 116th alone had lost over 800 soldiers.[176] As Private Paul Calvert of the 166th recalled: 'The end of the day saw this group completely fatigued, demoralized, disorganized and utterly incapable of concerted military action'.[177]

Gerhardt tried ruthlessly to drive his 29th Division in Normandy but being in command does not necessarily ensure compliance. As the 29th Division stumbled to a prolonged halt outside St Lô Gerhardt tried again and again to drive his unit commanders to take the town but with little initial success. The soldiers even stopped calling him 'Uncle Charlie' and insisted that he was no longer a divisional commander but a 'corpse'

Photo 14.9 29th Division monument built into WN-71 at junction of Charlie and Dog Green

commander, given the number of corpses his strategy was generating. By this time (mid-July) the 3rd Battalion of the 115th Infantry Regiment, 29th Division, only had 177 of the original D-Day 900 soldiers left. One platoon had just three of the original 41 left. Even then Gerhardt was uncompromising in his determination to hold on to St Lô once it had been won. As the German's 3rd *Fallschirmjäger* Division (paratroopers) counter-attacked on 17 July Gerhardt told Major Warfield of the 2nd Battalion (115th) to 'expend the whole battalion if necessary, but it's not to get there'.[178] What was left of the battalion, along with the rest of the 29th Division was replaced by the 35th Division on 20 July.

14.7.2 16th RCT of the 1st Division

The experience of the 16th RCT of the 1st Division was very similar to that of the 116th, further west. Many of the units were blown east of their allocated landing spots, landing on Fox Green where they were decimated by WN62 with two 75mm guns, three mortar positions and four machine gun posts. Lt Frerking occupied the main bunker at WN62 and provided firing instructions for the artillery battery at Houteville five miles south. He also controlled the machine gunners and ordered them to wait until the boats touched down, approximately 400 yards from the bunker.[179] Nearby, with an 88mm gun, WN61 covered Exit E-3 north of Colleville. WN61 was put out of action at 0710 by Sergeant Sheppard's Sherman DD tank from the 741st Tank Battalion.

Photo 14.10 Leaderless American troops under the cliffs at Colleville sur Mer

Near Exit E-1 Lt Commander Joseph Vaghi, beach master of Easy Red, landed 500 yards short of the cover provided by the sand dunes but having reached the high water mark found himself, like everyone else, simply unable to move for the machine gun fire emanating from the bluffs and from WN 64 and WN65. At 0800 Colonel George Taylor, the 16th RCT's regimental commander landed and, after working his way up to this line of troops trying to find cover from the fire, stood up and demanded his troops move forward. An officer, perhaps Colonel Taylor, told Vaghi to use his megaphone and tell the soldiers to 'move forward'. At that point a sergeant pushed a bangalore torpedo under the concertina barbed wire and told his unit to 'follow him' through the gap. They did and ran straight onto the mined plateau before the bluffs where many were killed or wounded.[180]

Around this time Taylor (though there are suggestions it was Cota leading the 29th Division) uttered his now-famous remark: 'There are only two kinds of people on this beach: the dead and those who are about to die. So let's get the hell out of here!'[181] Clearly, given the noise and danger, only a handful of people would have heard Taylor – Lt Jack Carrol heard it but he was only 5 yards away – and probably just a few were motivated by it to do something. But it may be that even a few individuals changing their actions – and showing a successful run across the beach was possible – would have been enough to persuade others to do the same, this starting a small 'social avalanche' of troops towards and up the bluffs. Carrol followed another young officer up the bluffs past mines that had already killed and maimed countless soldiers and when they came to the last few yards before the cliff top the officer threw himself on the ground detonating a mine and killing himself.[182]

Not everyone was persuaded: Captain Friedman, now motivated to move, came across three soldiers lying prone while the rest were making an effort to advance. After they refused to move Friedman drew his pistol and threatened to use it on them – prompting one to turn on him shouting: 'Captain, are you out of your fucking mind?'[183]

Those that got to the Atlantic Wall found little respite and no commanders: all the officers that had been in the first wave were either dead or injured. So even the soldiers that were not already dead or wounded seemed to lie on the beach or crouch behind whatever obstacle they could find, hoping they would not get shot. It was as if their entire world had been shrunk in time and space to a tiny envelope of sand. As Bill Friedman with the 16th Infantry Regiment on Omaha Beach recalled:

> For one so intimately associated with the assault landing, my experience was confined to a few yards of the beach – at least for the first two hours. Along with thousands of men escaping from the assault landing craft, I lay immobile behind the largely imagined protection of the famous shingle ledge at the beach's high water mark. All I could see was a long line of men taking cover each side of me, and a bluff to my front. I really had no desire to see more. As for understanding or appreciating the great forces, Herculean efforts, good and bad guesses, brilliant strategies (and there were those too), unit and individual actions, and the astronomical number of interrelated events, I had not the foggiest ... . We were totally immobilized. I did not know what to do or where to go. I remember looking at the sea and the water was red, there were bodies and equipment just rolling in the surf ... . Along the line of men on the shingle I saw people jerking as they were hit with the impact of bullets and shrapnel. Somehow it didn't count ... . I was reassured because I was shoulder to shoulder with other men. There was something reassuring about having warm, familiar human bodies next to you ... even if they're dead ... . At one point I was still lying down and shouting in the ear of the Regimental S4. He was a major. My mouth was next to his ear; it was so noisy he could not hear me otherwise. While I was trying to make myself understood above the din, a bullet struck him dead.[184]

Sergeant Norfleet, also trapped at the water's edge, had no intention of staying there and did not need any heroic commanding officer to tell him what to do, indeed: 'The decision not to try never entered my head ... I noticed a GI running from right to left, trying to get across the beach ... . An enemy gunner shot him as he stumbled for cover ... I believe I was the first in my group telling Private Walfred Williams, my Number One gunner, to follow'.[185]

At 0809 a control craft radioed back that 'All of DD tanks for Fox Green Beach sank between disembarkation point and line of departure'. At 0849 the report suggested the troops were 'Held up by enemy MG (Machine Gun) fire. Request fire support'. An hour later it was that 'Firing on beach Easy Red keeping LCI's from landing'. Within minutes the situation had worsened: many wounded at Dog Red Beach need immediate evacuation. Many LCTs standing by buoy but cannot unload because of heavy shell-fire on beach'.

Captain Joe Dawson, commanding officer of G Company and part of the 16th Infantry RCT thought that he clearly was in what Sun Tzu would have called 'Death Ground' for there was 'nothing I could do on the beach except die'. And this fatal pessimism seemed to immobilize many. But Private Shroeder, who had already spent an hour at the sea wall and was similarly frozen to the ground, suddenly saw an ordinary rifleman stand up and run for the bluff, zigzagging as he went. 'He made it to the bluff. So we all felt a little better to see that we had a chance, we were going to get off'.[186]

Similarly, Anthony Stephano came ashore at 0830 with C Battery of the 11th Field Artillery and was quickly followed by his commanding officer Lt-Colonel Mullins who had already been wounded. As Stephano recounts: Mullins 'saw immediately that the beach was no place for artillery – in fact the 16th Battalion lost all six of its howitzers as the DUKWs carrying them were swamped by the waves'.[187] Then,

> Mullins began to put some fight back into the little knots of stunned, inert riflemen along the sea wall. Most of them had lost their weapons or dropped them in the sand. Lt-Colonel Mullins crept along. Talking to one man after another. While he was urging one small group to clean their guns and start returning the fire from the bluffs, a sniper's bullet drilled through his hand. Mullins ignored this second wound as he had the first one, and started moving a pair of amphibious tanks into decent firing positions ... a third bullet hit him in the stomach ... and he died.[188]

Harley Reynolds of the 1st Infantry Division similarly witnessed a soldier pushing a bangalore torpedo under a beach obstacle while under constant fire:

> He pulled the string to the fuselighter and pushed himself backward. The first didn't light. After a few seconds the man calmly crawled forward, exposing himself again. He removed the bad lighter, replaced it with another, and started to repeat his first moves. He turned his head in my direction ... when he flinched ... and closed his eyes looking into mine. Death was so fast for him.[189]

But despite the efforts of individual and isolated groups of soldiers to fight their way directly up the bluffs, no exit routes had been cleared and as the tide crept up the beach the jumble of vehicles and the remains of the 5,000 soldiers landed so far grew worse by the minute. At 0830 the commander of the 7th Naval Beach Battalion, without informing Bradley, ordered the suspension of vehicle landings (though not troops) and the removal of all beached landing craft that could move. As a result hundreds of craft began milling around just out of range of the defenders' fire. It looked to the invaders that they had failed and the defenders thought so too – as Private Franz Gockel recalled: 'we believed the Americans were initiating a withdrawal'.[190]

By 0915 the conditions were so bad that Bradley considered calling off the invasion and landing the rest of the troops at one of the British beaches. Man suggests that Bradley actually asked permission from SHAEF to suspend the landings at Omaha and move them elsewhere but that the message did not arrive in the UK until the afternoon – by which time it was irrelevant.[191] The delay seems incredible but when Eisenhower eventually met Bradley in Normandy on D-Day+1, he admonished Bradley for not keeping him in touch:

Eisenhower: Golly Brad, you had us all scared stiff yesterday morning. Why in the devil didn't you let us know what was going on?
Bradley: But we did, we radioed you every scrap of information we had.
Eisenhower: Nothing came through until late afternoon – not a damned word. I didn't know what had happened to you.
Bradley: But your headquarters acknowledged every message as we asked them to. You check it when you get back and you'll find they all got through.

It subsequently turned out that Bradley had indeed sent all the messages but the transcription service simply became overloaded and eventually incurred a 12-hour delay in reporting messages.[192]

Bradley wrote later, 'as the morning lengthened my worries deepened … From (the) messages we could piece together only an incoherent account of sinkings, swampings, heavy enemy fire, and chaos on the beaches.[193] In fact there was no method or sense in stopping the invasion: to return across the beaches would have massively increased the casualties and anyway there were not enough empty landing craft to take people off, to say nothing about contacting those who were already inland. Nor could he seriously consider his alternative of sending the remainder elsewhere to another beach for this would have left the landed troops too vulnerable to a German counter-attack.

At 0930 Bradley sent Colonel Benjamin Tallen to assess the situation and he returned within the hour to report the general chaos and confusion and that only on Easy Red had the obstacles been cleared but that a line of traffic at this exit made an easy target for German artillery.[194] Bradley now had three assault waves bunched up behind the initial one and he had a further 25,000 troops and 4,400 vehicles waiting.

Here indeed was a crisis in search of a decisive commander; in this case the metaphorical cavalry arrived, not on waves of horses but the backs of the waves: the destroyers were moving in. The destroyers standing off shore had been ordered to cease firing directly on the beach as soon as the first waves landed at 0630 until ship to shore communications was established. But 75 per cent of the 116th RCT's radios had been lost in the water. But by 0810 it was clear to some destroyer captains that the situation on the beaches was intolerable. The destroyers began shelling identifiable targets and were then ordered by Captain Sanders, commander of the destroyer group on the USS *Frankford*, to move closer still. His order was reinforced by a message from Admiral Bryant on the USS *Texas*: 'Get on them men, get on them. We must knock out those guns. They are raising hell with the men on the beach, and we can't have anymore of that. We must stop it'.[195]

So close were they that the USS *Shubrick* even fired four of its 5 inch shells at a lone German officer believed to be spotting for his own artillery in the area. Charles Murphy was just one of hundreds pinned down by fire from a pillbox when a destroyer moved in: 'He couldn't have been 200 yards off the beach. He pumped four rounds right into that brazier (of the pillbox). Boy that was the end. Then things started moving fast. I loved the Navy from then on'.[196]

Opposite Dog Green, where the 29th Division were landing, the USS *Carmick* spotted Shermans pinned down by a gun built into the cliff. The tanks fired at the cliff but their shells could not penetrate the emplacement. However the destroyers much larger guns could and taking their lead from the tank the destroyer quickly silenced the German position and then tracked the tank shells marking out the next target.[197]

The casemated 88mm gun on the eastern side of Exit 1 on Easy Red (WN65) was another destroyer target. It had been pounding the landing craft and troops all morning and eventually an army-navy beach team landed with radio contact to the ships. Don Whitehead takes up the story:

> We saw the destroyer come racing towards the beach and swing broadside, exposing itself to the fire of the batteries on the bluff. One shell from the destroyer tore a chunk of concrete from the side of the blockhouse. Another nicked the top. A third ripped off a corner. And then the fourth shell smashed into the gun-port to

silence the weapon. Always, in my mind, the knocking out of this gun was a major turning-point in the battle in our sector ... . As I saw it, that was when the battle of the beach was won – seven hours after the first wave hit the beach.[198]

WN64 and WN65, covering Exit E-1 on Easy Red proved a formidable obstacle and several destroyers began shelling the area from 1000. The USS *Frankford* began shelling the beach first and by 1021 it had destroyed a pill box on the beach. 15 minutes later a mortar position on the bluffs above E-1 was located and destroyed after five salvos. The destroyer then located and destroyed the site of two machine gun positions. Meanwhile, the USS *Harding*, a little further east on Easy Red, spotted fire from WN62 and demolished it at 1050 – just as its commanding officer, Lt Frerking ordered its evacuation because of the accuracy of the naval gunfire.[199] Under this covering fire from the destroyers off the beach Lt Spaulding's Company E soldiers from the 16th RCT outflanked WN64 and stormed it from the rear, taking 21 prisoners and killing 40 defenders in the process.

Indeed, it was just at the time that several small pockets of soldiers had reached the top of the bluffs and were beginning to flush the defenders out of the trenches and the pill boxes that infested the entire area that Bradley was informed that the situation on Easy sector was critical. Vierville had been taken and units of the 18th Regiment were beginning to land behind the initial assault groups. Such was the success of these small groups that by 1200, although mortar and artillery fire from

Photo 14.11 Exit E-1, Omaha Beach, looking south

Photo 14.12 WN-64, Exit E-1, Omaha Beach

Photo 14.13 Exit E-1, overlooking WN-64 from the north

behind the bluffs onto the beaches remained intense, several machine guns had been silenced by the destroyers.

At about the same time as the destroyers moved in so did the 18th RCT of the 1st Division, this time onto Easy Red sector of Omaha Beach. This sector should have received the largest number of invading troops but the currents and confusion meant it was almost untouched as the 18th RCT moved in – much to the dismay of the coxswains who had been ordered not to land on the sector because of the unexploded mines and obstacles. In the attack that followed, 22 LCVPs, 2 LCIs and 4 LCTs were lost to mines or artillery fire and casualties amongst the invading troops mounted rapidly: F Company, for example, lost all its officers and half its NCOs on the first day. On the beach itself the demolition engineers had by this time cleared 13 lanes and removed one third of the obstacles.

The 18th RCT was still under fire from WN65, on the western edge of Exit E-1 (still) housing a 50mm gun. Two half tracks of the 467th Anti-Aircraft Artillery Battalion engaged the strong-point from the water with their 37mm and .5 inch machine guns but to little effect. Then destroyers were called in to shell the position as ground troops moved forward but their movement off the beach was held up by mines, barbed wire, anti-tank obstacles, sand and shingle. Eventually, and under intense fire, two bulldozers, driven by Private Vinton Dove and Private William Showmaker, both from C Company, 37th Engineer Combat Battalion, cleared a path through the shingle and filled in the anti-tank ditch between WN65 and the beach E-1 after 40 defenders of WN65 had been killed, the 20 survivors surrendered by 1200 to members of E Company 16th RCT. The two drivers were later awarded DSCs for now Exit E-1 was secure (Fowle, 1994: 216; Ramsey, 1995: 359). By 1300 Exit E-1 (where several of the gun emplacements were still incomplete by D-Day) was open – and at this precise time General Marcks dictated a note to Army Group: 'Landing near Vierville as good as repulsed'. It was not.

With D-3 also open by 1130, two exits were now clear, though Easy Red became the primary exit beach and most of the vehicles getting off Omaha Beach that day went through E-1, including the third of the 1st Division's RCTs, the 115th which landed as the 118th were moving out.

Several advance units were now making significant headway and had already climbed the bluffs and penetrated the defences roughly midway between Exits D-1 and D-3 (three Companies of the 16th RCT), between Vierville and Les Moulins, and between Exits E-1 and E-3 (five Companies 116th RCT), between St-Laurent and Coleville, and also just to the east of Coleville (three Companies of the 16th RCT).

At 1500 Bradley sent another staff officer ashore to assess the situation, who returned to note that progress, albeit slow and bloody, was being made.[200] Half an hour later command posts were being established on the beach and by late afternoon some of the delayed tanks had arrived and gradually the Americans inched their way up the cliffs and over the sea wall to the road that ran parallel to the beach. Exit E-1 was open to tracked vehicles by mid-afternoon and three tanks from the 741st Tank battalion attacked St-Laurent. By 1700 exit D-1 was opened after destroyers had eliminated the casemated artillery at the Pointe de la

Percée around noon, though the beach was still under heavy fire.[201] Eventually 121st Combat Engineers were responsible for its capture but some of their members had landed as far away as Exit D-3 and 75 per cent of the equipment had been lost on landing. Consequently it took them much longer than anticipated to accumulate sufficient troops and explosives to overcome the defenders.[202]

Gradually the Americans worked their way up the bluffs inland but by 1900 the line of objectives for D-Day on Omaha Beach had still not being achieved and 50 tanks had been lost, with 50 landing craft sunk.[203] But the troops were ashore and 18 different fire-fights were continuing around the three villages of the area. By about 2030 hostile action against the beach area controlled by the 1st Division had ceased and the Commanding General, First Division, and his staff established their HQ on the beach.[204] For the next two days after D-Day, as Captain Friedman of the 16th RCT recalled, 'we pretty much just licked our wounds and tried to find out who was alive'.[205]

On the evening of 7 June the first units of the 2nd Infantry Division began landing on Omaha, and within 24 hours they were all ashore, moving inland through the boundary line between the 29th and the 1st Infantry Divisions towards Trévières and on to the relatively undefended Cérisy Forest, north of Balleroy.[206] By the evening of 8 June the US forces from Omaha and the British forces from Gold had linked up, forming an uninterrupted territory from Ouistreham to Vierville. But the congestion on the Anglo-Canadian beaches delayed the reinforcing armour, and the deployment first of the 21st Panzers to stall the British off Sword Beach and the arrival of the 12th SS HJ to stall the Canadians off Juno, effectively stymied Montgomery's attempts to take Caen for weeks.

Nonetheless, D-Day had proved remarkable successful, with the single exception of Omaha, and even that had been saved from catastrophe by the individual and collective acts of American soldiers on the ground and Allied sailors and flyers in the sea and air. In particular, the destroyers seemed to have played a pivotal role in reducing the defensive fire of the opposition. By the end of the day each of the 11 destroyers off Omaha Beach had fired between 400 and 1,200 five-inch shells at the beach targets. Lieutenant Joe Smith, a Navy beachmaster was not alone in his conclusion: 'There is no question in my mind that the few Navy destroyers that we had there saved the mission'.[207] His opinion is supported by Colonel S.B. Mason who inspected the German defences at Omaha after the invasion and suggested that they were impregnable to conventional army artillery and that only the Navy's pounding had loosened them enough to enable the troops to break through. But heavy shelling by the sea-borne cavalry alone had not won the day. That also required ineptitude on the part of German senior commanders.

14.8 German responses on the beaches

Initially it appeared not just to Bradley but also to the Germans that the invasion was lost. Sometime between 0800 and 0900 Colonel Goth, commanding WN76, the fortifications overlooking Omaha Beach at the Pointe et Raz de la Percée near Vierville, sent a report to Lt Colonel Ziegelmann, the 352nd's Operations Chief:

> At the water's edge the enemy is in search of cover behind the coastal-obstacles. A great many motor vehicles – among them ten tanks – stand burning on the beach. The obstacle demolition squads have given up their activities. Disembarkation from landing boats has ceased ... the boats keep farther out to sea. The fire of our battle positions and artillery is well placed and has inflicted considerable casualties on the enemy. A great many dead and wounded lie on the beach.[208]

But this was before the destroyers moved in. And it was not just the aggressive action of the navy that undermined the German defences on Omaha, for at the very same time the destroyers began their assault over the heads of the troops pinned down on the beach, the German defenders were beginning to run low on ammunition. For example, the 1st Battery of the 352nd Artillery regiment behind Omaha Beach had seen their ammunition stockpile reduced by 50 per cent just a fortnight before D-Day to make it more 'secure'. Major Werner Pluskat, in command of four of the batteries, had told General Marcks that should an invasion occur his guns only had enough ammunition for 24 hours, to which Marcks had replied: 'If an invasion ever does come in your area you'll get more ammunition than you can fire'.[209] But when a truck carrying the shells back to the front was sent during the attack it was itself destroyed by naval shell-fire before it reached the battery. Private Severloh fired 12,000 rounds[210] of ammunition from his MG42 machine gun post on the bluffs above Omaha and was forced to use tracer-fire, normally used for night firing when he ran out of standard ammunition. As a result the eight destroyers out to sea could, at last, pinpoint him and quickly destroyed his gun position. At the same time, all the other guns in Resistance Nest 62 ran out of ammunition and the gun crews withdrew inland.[211]

Furthermore, because the Germans had been ordered not to retreat they could continue to fire upon the attackers – at least until the ammunition ran out – but could not mount any kind of counter-offensive in depth, particularly when so few senior commanders were available and the defenders were strung out across the entire coastline and unable to move for fear of drawing down naval or aerial bombardment. Indeed, when the firing on the beach lifted a little on Dog White at around 1000 many of the troops were thankful but bemused as to why. Later, some of the defenders were interviewed by Roy Stevens and they declared that it was not the encircling troops that worried them but 'we got scared with all those boats out front, and we just got up and left'.[212] Private Franz Rachmann, from the German 352nd Division was firing one of the machine guns that was massacring the Americans on the beach and he also suggests that the infinite mass approaching him was crucial to their success; as he recalled 'I shoot, I shoot, I shoot! For each American I see fall, there came ten hundred other ones!'[213] But the impression of the German troops at the front line was not that taken by their commanders back at headquarters.

Despite this gradual attrition of the defenders, the reserves of the 352nd Division were redirected away from Omaha. Some went to execute a counter-attack against the Rangers holding Pointe du Hoc while the bulk went to the British beaches after a report arrived at 0800 suggesting a breakthrough at Arromanches. A report sent at 1100 to the HQ of the German 84th Corps at Littry still suggested that the Omaha landing was repulsed and General Kraiss, the CO of the 352nd, sent two battalions (around 1,000 troops) of reinforcements to the British sector where the need appeared greater.[214] Such a decision was always likely given the confusion that prevailed: at 0900 Lt Ulrich Radermann of the German 5th Parachute Division had arrived at the HQ to find out what Kraiss wanted the 5th Paras to do – for their CO, General Meindl, had yet to receive any orders. 'When we reached 84th Corps HQ we found panic and a complete lack of decision-making. I did not know what to make of it, and when I tried to telephone my own HQ at Rennes and speak to General Meindl it proved impossible to get through. I decided all I could do was try to investigate the situation for myself'.[215] By the time the two battalions of troops arrived at Gold Beach they were too late and too decimated by air attack to make any difference; in effect, the poverty of German Command allowed the invaders at Omaha just enough space and time to secure a footing.

By 1300 Exit E-1 was finally opened up but at precisely this time General Marcks dictated a note to Army Group: 'Landing near Vierville as good as repulsed'. It was not. Even General Salmuth's offer of troops from the 346th Infantry Division was turned down: 'We don't need them', he was told.[216] Kraiss also had access to *Kampfgruppe* (Battle group) Meyer which could have been called up to Omaha, but Kraiss was more concerned about the paratroopers to his west and at 0310 had ordered Meyer to deploy his three battalions of 915th *Panzergrenadiers* from their base at Bayeux westwards to the River Vire to protect his flank. When the landings had started Kraiss had halted the movement of Meyer's *Panzergrenadiers* and about an hour later one of the two battalions (II/915th) was ordered north to Colleville sur Mer where Allied forces were reported to have broken through near WN 60, WN 61 and WN 62 (Fox Beach). The II/915th should have arrive just east of Fox Beach by 0930 – in time to stem the 1st Division's advance up the bluffs – but, thanks to Allied air attacks, it arrived about five hours later and five hours too late.[217]

At around the same time that Bradley was considering withdrawing from Omaha, von Rundstedt reported to Hitler's HQ: 'Still no clear picture whether we are seeing the diversion or the main attack'.[218] Quite what criteria von Rundstedt was using is unclear but the size of the invasion force should have suggested by this stage that whether another attack at Calais was planned or not, this was a serious and substantive attempt to land a large body of troops – and that should have initiated the immediate movement of local Panzer reinforcements. Equally important, the 7th Army, on the basis of reports from the 352nd Division at Omaha, suggested that the main thrust of the attack must be at the British beaches and not across the Cotentin peninsular to capture Cherbourg – as they had assumed after the initial airborne landings – because the Americans were only attempting a sea-borne landing at Omaha and this was being repulsed. As the War Diary of the 7th Army states, 'From 0600 hours the seaborne landing began, with its main thrust between the Orne and the Vire.[219] At 1620 the 7th Army HQ had still not heard of the attack on Utah Beach, so severely disrupted were the communication by the bombardment and the paratroop drops.[220] Indeed, it could report that: 'Operationally there is at present no particular cause for concern since, to cut off Normandy, the east coast of Cotentin has still to be taken. It is noticeable that here airborne troops have been committed without direct support from the sea ... Since 16.30 (however) the enemy has carried out heavy follow-up landings from the sea in the Madeleine sector' (Utah Beach).[221]

On the day after D-Day, Ziegelmann proceeded from the 352nd's HQ in Molay-Littrey, nine miles south of Omaha, and should have arrived 30 minutes later at WN 76 (overlooking Omaha Beach at the Pointe et Raz de la Percée) – but it took him 5 hours because of Allied fighter attacks. 'The view from WN 76 will remain in my memory forever' he wrote. 'The sea was like a picture of the "Kiel review of the fleet". Ships of all

sorts stood close together on the beach and in the water, broadly eche-
loned in depth. And the entire conglomeration remained there intact
without any real interference from the German side! I clearly understood
the mood of the German soldier who missed the Luftwaffe. It is a
wonder that German soldiers fought hard and stubbornly here'.[222]

But the future could only get worse for the Germans, for whom no
hope of reinforcement or relief was now available. The German 352nd
Division had suffered about half the absolute US total of casualties on D-
Day at 1,200 but this was three times the number of relative casualties at
20 per cent of the total strength available. By 9 June the entire Omaha
coastline was in US hands and the 116th was rested. Ziegelmann calculated that by that time the fighting strength of the 352nd Division had
been reduced by two thirds and it was now defending a corps area
(requiring two divisions {six regiments}) with the equivalent of just one
regiment. (By 13 June the 352nd Divisional strength was down to 25 per
cent; the following day the 29th Infantry Division had suffered 2,400
casualties, 17 per cent of its initial strength; within four more days 25 per
cent (3,500) of the 29th's initial strength had become casualties, with
1,000 deaths. By the end of July 90 per cent of the 29th Division's rifle
companies – 5,211 soldiers – had become casualties.[223]

On the evening of 9 June Kraisse ordered his remaining defenders to
retreat – contrary to Hitler's orders – to the line of the River Elle – a
night march of between seven and 16 miles depending on the sector –
and to dig in and await reinforcements. These were on their way. On 6
June the 984th Infantry Regiment of the 275th Infantry Division
stationed in Brittany began moving east with the *Kampfgruppe Heintz*.
The two day journey of 125 miles by rail took seven days as most of
the travelling had to undertaken at night on foot. The 3rd
Fallschirmjägerdivision (3rd *FJ* {Parachute} Division), which was only
raised in November 1943, was directed to support Kraiss on his western
side, did not even start their 190 mile move from western Brittany until
the evening of 7 June and there was only enough transport and fuel to
carry a third of the troops, the rest had to go on foot.[224]

Still the Germans refused to deploy their forces in the north to help in
Normandy. Even General Bradley could not believe that the Germans
would remain fooled by Operation Fortitude for so long:

> In devising this cover plan, we had hoped for no more than a modest delay, a week
> or two at most, until we had sufficient divisions ashore to secure the Normandy
> landing. Even now [1951], I cannot understand why the enemy believed for so
> long in so transparent a hoax. For once we landed in Normandy, only a fool could
> have thought us capable of duplicating so gigantic an effort elsewhere.[225]

Luckily for the Allies that fool was Hitler but there were, by this time, many on the German side who did know that the Normandy invasion must be the main force of the attack. Major Hayn of the 84th Corps, for example, reported at a meeting on the evening of D-Day that: 'Three airborne divisions have been positively identified. That's three quarters of all the parachute units known to be in England. As well there are US elite formations of the 1st and 4th Divisions. It is incomprehensible that over there they would sacrifice their best attack units for the sake of a mere diversionary manoeuvre'. Major Wiegman reported from the Caen area that 'The British 3rd and Canadian 3rd Divisions had been identified by about noon. We know that the 50th London and 7th Armoured Divisions are also there. All that's missing is the 51st Highlanders and the 1st Armoured Division and we'll have Montgomery's entire 8th Army from Africa at our throats! If this isn't the invasion what are they going to come with?'[226]

14.9 Conclusion

The intention on D-Day was to achieve a solid area approximately 10 miles deep and 60 miles wide. The width was achieved but there were large gaps in it: between Omaha and Utah (11 mile gap), Omaha and Gold (7 mile gap), and Juno and Sword (3 mile gap) but, apart from the isolated 192nd *Panzergrenadiers* in the latter gap the discontinuous line was not a critical issue because the battlefield as a whole had been isolated.[227]

No single corps had achieved its aims. The British 30th Corps on Gold had not reached Bayeux; the Canadian half of the British 1st Corps on Juno had not reached the Bayeux-Caen road nor linked eastwards with their counterparts on Sword – who were still short of Caen. On the American side the 7th Corps on Utah had failed to secure the line of the Merederet river nor linked up with the 82nd Airborne at St Mère Église and, most critical of all, the 5th Corps on Omaha was only just beginning to make significant progress inland and the Rangers at the Pointe du Hoc were only just hanging on.

Yet although no group had achieved its targets completely all had a secure foothold and the impregnable Atlantic wall had only lasted between one hour (Gold, Juno, Sword and Utah) and one day (Omaha). The British had reached the outskirts of Bayeux but neither taken it nor Caen, nor cut the N-13 road that linked them; the Canadians at Juno had achieved the greatest distance inland (6 miles) but had not taken the airport at Carpiquet and had suffered the second largest number of relative casualties.[228] The Americans at Omaha were less than one and half miles into France but they had secured that against the heaviest absolute casualties. The Utah attackers had reached the airborne divisions but had not taken the roads at Carentan to cut off the Cotentin peninsular.

At the gap between Sword and Juno, at 1600, the Germans launched their only significant counter-attack of D-Day but the expected German counter-attack in force never came. The Panzer groups were either too far away to intervene, or held back for the 'real' invasion at the Pas-de-Calais, or immobilized by the confused and dislocated command structure or the information to mount such a co-ordinated attack was simply not available – the telephone system had been badly affected by the air and naval attacks and the Resistance sabotage and, in the absence of the Luftwaffe, no aerial reconnaissance was possible. As an American fighter pilot quipped: 'the *Luftwaffe* had Leftwaffe'.[229] A *Wehrmacht* equivalent was that 'if the plane was silver it was American; if it was blue it was British; if it was invisible it was German.[230] All the Germans could really be sure of was that the Allies seemed to be everywhere, and in the Cotentin peninsular where the US Airborne had dropped, they were everywhere and nowhere simultaneously – how could a counter attack be organized if there was no known concentration of troops to attack?

It is often suggested that a critical success factor in the Allied landings on D-Day was surprise, yet just after D-Day von Rundstedt claimed that this was of marginal significance. Indeed, in his perspective, there was no surprise:

> The enemy hoped to take us by surprise! In that attempt he failed ... [the] airborne landings failed to achieve surprise because officers and men had expected them for weeks and had made appropriate preparations. As a result enemy parachute and airborne troops suffered heavily, even extremely heavy casualties ... They did not succeed in breaking up the coastal defences from the rear ... [However] the enemy succeeded, by concentrated and ceaseless attacks from the air, in disorganizing our supply to such an extent and to cause such losses of railway rolling stock and vehicles that supply has become a serious problem ... . It is all a question of air force, air force and again air force.[231]

In retrospect there were clearly errors on the Allied side: the night airborne landings had achieved little for the cost in lives yet the previous airborne attacks on Italy had already demonstrated airborne landings were extraordinarily difficult to deploy accurately. The amphibious armour proved all too vulnerable to the choppy waters they were launched into but then the maximum strength of the wind in training had been force four while on D-Day the wind was between force five and force six. The planners had over-concentrated upon D-Day itself to the extent that the task was restricted to a successful landing, rather than the landing being a preliminary event to the main task – the invasion of Europe and the destruction of Nazi Germany. At a local level the result can be seen by the large numbers of troops for whom surviving the landing itself was the primary task of the day, rather than moving inland to drive the German defenders back. At a strategic level the problem became more evident as the troops were forced to fight through the *bocage* countryside, metre by metre rather than across the more open plains of central France. A war of movement may have rebalanced the disadvantages of the Allied tanks against their German counterparts but a battle of almost static attrition was always going to favour the Panthers and Tigers of the *Wehrmacht* and the SS. The planners had also assumed that the Germans would retreat to regroup and counter-attack but this had not happened in Italy and Hitler's order not to retreat had prevented any change in strategy; the result was a much tougher battle for the beaches and the immediate hinterland than the Allies expected. But once the crust of the German opposition was broken the movement through central France itself proved to be relatively quick. And despite the pleas of both Rommel and von Rundstedt, Hitler refused either to release the 20 divisions of the 15th Army for a counter-attack or to allow the 7th Army to retreat to build up reserves and counter-attack itself. The beach landings were, in the end, won and lost through Leadership, Management and Command.

Part Five

Retrospective

15 Post-D-Day

15.1 Allied casualties on D-Day

If all the British military casualties of the 20th century marched past the Cenotaph in columns it would take three days and three nights. In the First World War about three quarters of a million British deaths occurred.[1] In the Second World War that number decreased to around 145,000.[2] Including all the casualties in all the theatres of war between 1939 and 1945, over 23,000 people died every day. Overall, almost 7 per cent of US forces did not make it through the war unscathed. Two per cent died in action, 1 per cent died from wounds or disease and 4 per cent were wounded but lived. In contrast, by July 1944 over one third of the German army had been wounded once, 11 per cent had been wounded twice and 11 per cent had been wounded three times. The casualty rate amongst German officers was even greater: on average each officer's position was refilled nine times.[3] Most of these casualties had been incurred in the east not the west, indeed, 3 million of the 4 million German casualties had been inflicted by the Soviet Union.[4]

The Allied planners for D-Day calculated that on D-Day itself the initial assault divisions would suffer 15 per cent casualties, with the actual first wave RCTs suffering 25 per cent. Seventy per cent of these would, they assumed, be wounded, 30 per cent would be dead, missing or POWs. The follow up divisions would, they assumed, suffer 8 per cent casualties overall, with the combat regiments taking 15 per cent.[5] By the end of D-Day the Allies had landed something in the region of 175,000 soldiers[6] on the beaches and 22,000 inland by air.

Casualty figures are notoriously unreliable: there are no official German figures for D-Day itself, and of the three main Allied forces only Canada collected data from individual soldiers. Overall Allied casualties seem to be somewhere between 8,443 (4.3 per cent) and 10,865 (5.5 per cent) depending on whose figures are accepted. Roughly one-third of these were deaths.[7] Whatever the number it was still far smaller than the 29,500 the planners had assumed.[8] Churchill had feared 70,000, and the generally expected number had been half this at around 35,000. In fact

SHAEF's secret prediction had been the most accurate at 10,000 dead.[9] Ambrose estimates that perhaps 10 per cent is a more accurate account.[10]

Within two weeks of D-Day the Allies had 20 full divisions in Normandy against the Germans rapidly depleting 18 divisions.[11] According to the Official US statistics the 101st Airborne's casualties were 1,240, including 182 confirmed dead and 501 missing (presumed captured or killed). The 82nd Airborne's casualties were 1,259 including 156 confirmed dead and 756 missing (presumed captured or killed).[12] Of the 11,770 troops who fought for the 82nd Airborne Division for the 33 days it was in action in Normandy (i.e. including replacements) 46 per cent were casualties, of whom 1,982 were either killed in action (KIA) or missing in action (MIA); 17 per cent did not get back to England.[13]

The US 4th Infantry Division losses at Utah were put at 197. The casualties at Omaha for the 4th Division and the 29th Infantry were approximately 2,000 on the first day and by D-Day +1 between 3,500 and 4,200 were dead, wounded or missing.[14] Within five days the 1st Division had suffered 1,638 casualties (1,083 wounded; 555 dead or missing), while the 29th Division suffered 2,210 casualties (1,027 wounded; 1,183 dead or missing [includes 7 POW]). Non Divisional casualties amounted to 1,373 (656 wounded; 717 dead or missing) for the same period to 10 June (Hall, 1994: 138).

The 116th RCT of the 29th Division took the highest casualties of any US regiment in the war. The Division itself took 28,766 casualties in the

Photo 15.1 American cemetery at St Laurent

242 days it was in the line, a 204 per cent casualty rate. When the 115th Regiment of the 29th Division was awarded a Distinguished Unit Citation in March 1945 General Gerhardt wanted each company flag holder to be a D-Day veteran; six of the 12 companies could not find a single representative riflemen left.[15] The most significant naval casualties amongst the US navy were the 46 (13 dead and 33 injured) members of the *Corry* sunk by a mine.[16]

On Juno Beach the Canadians suffered 805 casualties to add to the 146 suffered inland. There were another 243 casualties in this area from the British Commando units involved on or near Juno, to bring the total for the Juno area to at least 1,204 (and this excludes casualties taken by the Commando units operating inland). The Canadian 3rd Infantry Division suffered over 2,800 casualties in the first five days. On 7 June alone, the Nova Scotia Regiment suffered 242 casualties (84 dead), and 377 casualties were taken in the battle for Carpiquet airport with the 12th SS. On D-Day itself 335 Canadians were killed; most of these are buried amongst the 2,044 others at the Canadian Cemetery at Bény sur Mer. There are nine pairs of brothers here and one set of three – the Westlakes, as well as a father and son (Edward and Alfred Mantle) who died in the two world wars.[17]

On Gold Beach itself the British suffered 413 casualties. The 1st Hampshires, who landed on Gold with a complement of around 600, lost 231 dead and 1,050 wounded between D-Day and 17 November. In effect the battalion was wiped out twice.[18] On Sword the beach casualty figures totalled 630.

The British 6th Airborne Division suffered around 1,500 casualties, on D-Day and 4,500 in the Normandy campaign as a whole, including 821 dead.[19] Gale's parachute battalion incurred 141 casualties out of 160 participants just in the counter-attack against Breville on 12 June, while the British 6th Airborne as a whole lost 4,457 casualties (1,748 dead or missing and 2,709 wounded).[20] The 2,500 members of the 1st Special Service Brigade of Commandos under Brigadier Lord Lovat suffered 967 casualties (29 per cent) between D-Day and late August when it was withdrawn (Oakley, 1994: 248). Of the 87 members of No. 3 Troop, No. 10 Commando on active service, 41 (47 per cent) were casualties (19 were killed in action, 22 wounded).[21] The 15th Scottish Infantry Division lost 2,720 soldiers in six days and half of the rifle companies were amongst them.[22]

Despite Leigh-Mallory's concerns, the loss of aircraft carrying the airborne forces was relatively low, at about 5 per cent.[23] The RAF lost 10,000 fighter aircraft in the war and 3,600 pilots. The US lost 5,739 pilots in Europe and the Mediterranean.

Photo 15.2 British cemetery at Bayeux

15.2 Allied casualties beyond D-Day

Allied battle casualties from 6 to 30 June 1944 were approximately 62,000 with 79,000 replacements. The US had suffered 37,000 casualties The Anglo-Canadians had taken around 25,000 casualties (3,356 dead, 15,815 wounded and 5,527 missing, most of whom were presumed to be prisoners).[24] By then the Allies had landed 875,000 troops, 150,000 vehicles and 570,000 tons of stores and the British 24,698 casualties.

By the end of the battle for Normandy, usually taken as 15 August with the fall of Falaise, Montgomery's 21st Army Group had suffered 83,000 casualties, including 16,000 deaths, mostly suffered by the combat arms comprising just 56 per cent of the total numbers.[25]

Ironically, for all that Montgomery tried to avoid replicating the bloodbath of the First World War, the Normandy campaign overall sustained casualty figures on a par with and sometimes well above, those suffered on the Western Front between 1914 and 1918. On average, British involvement in the battle of Ypres in 1917, including Passchendaele, resulted in 244,000 casualties or 2,121 a day. The battle for Normandy resulted in 200,000 casualties, a rate of 2,354 a day. However, many of the troops involved still believed that their own experience in Normandy had been nothing like those of their fathers in the fields of Flanders 20 years earlier.[26] For example, by 3 September 1944 there were approximately 240,000 Allied and 200,000 German dead, wounded or missing [the Germans also lost an additional 200,000 as POWs]).[27] By late October 1944 Eisenhower was to admit 'that 2,500 Americans are falling in battle every day'.[28] By early 1945 this number had increased, and in the third week of January 22,825 became casualties.[29] By comparison, in May 2007 the *total* number of US casualties in Iraq in the four years plus since the invasion (March 2003) is 25,225 including 3,509 deaths. Put another Allied casualties in Normandy were more than 140 times those suffered in Iraq.

Equally significant, most of these casualties were to the minority of troops making up the infantry rifle companies.[30] This was already obvious in 1943 when a study of US casualties suggested that 70 per cent were taken by the infantry,[31] and the Normandy campaign was expected to result in a similar figure.[32] That figure, if anything, increased to almost 80 per cent by the end of the war.[33] The Canadians had expected around 50 per cent of their casualties to be amongst the infantry but over 75 per cent was the eventual figure.[34] In one case a single US company took 400 per cent casualties and altogether 18 infantry divisions in Europe suffered over 100 per cent casualties.[35]

The probability of disproportionate number of casualties suffered by the rifle carrying infantry was already clear in 1940 to Churchill who suggested that for every infantry division of around 15,500 soldiers a further 20,000 were engaged in servicing them and of the original 15,500 only around 4,000 actually carried a rifle. For the US armies a similar picture emerges with only around 37 per cent of the total number involved in any form of combat (in the Pacific around 18 service troops were needed to keep one combat soldier in the field). The results were predictable: in the British army in the Normandy campaign the infantry comprised 25 per cent of the total but 71 per cent of the casualties. In the American army the infantry soldiers comprised just 10 per cent of the total but 70 per cent of the casualties. In effect, one in three of the Allied infantry that fought in Normandy became a casualty (in the Pacific and Far East campaigns about one in ten Americans became a casualty and one in 15 Commonwealth soldiers). For some US divisions, such as the 4th who landed at Utah on D-Day, almost a fifth were killed by the end of the war and two thirds were wounded. The 29th Division, with a nominal 14,000 troops, suffered 20,111 casualties from D-Day to the end of the European war, including 3,720 dead – the second highest of any US division.

In the 50th Northumbrian Division that landed on Gold Beach, half of all the troops who served (including the 80 per cent replacements) became casualties in the Normandy campaign, while almost 60 per cent of the 15th (Scottish) Division suffered the same fate. Even worse, two thirds of those in the 1st Royal Norfolk Regiment were battle casualties and one in six killed. For officers the rates were yet higher: almost three quarters of all the officers serving with the 15th (Scottish) Division became casualties and over a quarter (29 per cent) was killed.[36]

In the US forces things were little different: in the 1st, 4th, 9th and 29th Divisions, between D-Day and 31 July, 60 per cent of the original rifle companies were no longer serving and 69 per cent of their officers were absent. In June alone the 12th Regiment lost three quarters of its officers and almost two thirds of its enlisted soldiers. On average, platoon leaders (lieutenants) lasted about three weeks in Europe. Battalion commanders lasted a little longer: two of the nine battalion commanders (majors or lieutenant colonels) of the US 29th Division were still in command two months after D-Day.[37] Ironically, one of the most dangerous jobs was being a medic or an 'aidman'. John Worthman, a medic with the US 4th Infantry Division was lucky to remain alive, uninjured and uncaptured for 'Our regiment had 80 per cent of its aidmen lost in Normandy – wounded, killed in action or captured'.[38] And though soldiers in action usually spoke very highly of the bravery shown by most medics, in training medics took a lot of stick. In the British Army medics were members of the Royal Army Medical Corps (RAMC), but, as far as the infantry was concerned, the acronym stood for Rob All My Comrades, after medics in the Napoleonic Wars had been seen robbing their own wounded. Or, in a reversal of the letters, it stood for Can't Manage a Rifle.[39] In the RAMC about 30 per cent were conscientious objectors, though only 3 per cent of the total numbers of British conscripts were conscientious objectors.[40]

Despite these casualty levels courts martial on the Allied side were relatively rare: in the British army during the Second World War 211,684 soldiers were court-martialled, representing between 0.6 and 1.8 per cent of the total serving force and the vast majority of these were for being AWOL (Absent Without Leave) in Britain or for 'borrowing' military vehicles without permission.[41] In the US army around 30,000 soldiers were court martialled for 'serious offences' (robbery, rape and murder) representing about 0.5 per cent of the total force. Some of the D-Day assault troops had been informed that to stop or retreat on the beaches would be a court-martial offence but there is little evidence that this threat made any difference one way or the other.[42] 102 Americans were executed throughout the war (49 of them after the Normandy campaign for raping French women) with all but one for crimes that would have incurred a death penalty in civilian life; only one American was shot for desertion. In both armies desertion was primarily restricted to infantry soldiers and just as these bore the brunt of the casualties so too they – or rather the very young, the weakly integrated and the less educated – tried to escape the conflict, but only in relatively small proportions; perhaps as few as 4 per cent deserted.[43]

The Allies had landed over 2 million troops in 39 divisions, along with 438,471 vehicles. They had suffered 209,672 casualties (including 36,976 dead) and lost 16,714 aircrew in 4,101 aircraft.[44]

15.3 German casualties

German battle casualties are even more unreliable than Allied figures. It is estimated that between 4,000 and 9,000 were killed in the bombing and naval bombardments. German casualties for Omaha Beach on D-Day are unclear, but have been estimated at 1,200.[45] Including POWs, for the slightly longer period from 6 June to 7 July 1944 there were about 81,000 casualties but there were no replacements.[46] When the battle for Normandy formally ended, on 19 August, 20 Germany Army, Corps or Divisional commanders had been killed or captured and 40 divisions destroyed or badly beaten with total losses at around 200,000 soldiers, 1,000 tanks, 3,000 artillery pieces.

By 11 June, 6,000 of the original 10,000 members of the 716th Infantry Division were casualties and the division was withdrawn. Only 180 of the original 15,000 members of the 352nd Infantry Division survived the Normandy battles.[47] By 30 June, 47,515 German casualties

Photo 15.3 German cemetery at La Cambe

had been recorded. Two weeks later another 18,000 had been lost and by the end of July 114,000 dead and 41,000 POWs had been accumulated. The Battle for Normandy cost the Germans approximately 250,000 soldiers.[48]

By the end of June, the 14,634 members of *Panzer Lehr* had been reduced by 20 per cent (1,809 wounded and 1,163 dead and missing).[49] By 30 June the Germans had 400,000 troops in battle (leaving the 250,000 of the 15th Army still around Calais). By 7 July, Army Group B had taken 80,783 casualties and received 4,000 replacements. By 6 August Army Group B had taken 144,261 casualties and received 19,914 replacements. In the six weeks from D-Day the Germans lost 250 tanks, which should not have been a major problem since this coincided with the peak of German tank production – but only 17 replacement tanks made it into Normandy in that period, so intense was the aerial blockade.[50]

By the end of the battle for Normandy 25 of the 38 German divisions had been destroyed. Over 1 million soldiers had fought in German uniforms in Normandy and total German losses, including POWs, are put at around 450,000 troops (250,000 casualties plus 200,000 POWs or missing), 1,500 tanks, 3,500 artillery pieces and 20,000 vehicles.[51]

Of the 18,000 strong SS Divisions, the 1st SS had no tanks or guns left and precious few soldiers; the 2nd SS were a little better off with 450 soldiers and 15 tanks; the 9th SS had 460 soldiers and 25 tanks, the 10th SS had no tanks and the 12th SS HJ had just 300 soldiers and ten tanks.[52]

Only 60 of the German 6th Parachute Regiment's 3,000 soldiers were still fighting by the end of August 1944. Of the 250 members of the 1st Company, 1st battalion, 25th *Panzergrenadiers* that had fought around Caen on D-Day, only five remained. Within three weeks of D-Day *Panzer Lehr* had lost 5,400 soldiers and 160 officers.[53]

Surprisingly few prisoners were taken in the early days of Overlord. The plan had assumed 500 per day for D-Day to D-Day+9 and 1,000 a day thereafter. In fact, by 26 July, after 56 days of battle, the numbers were not the assumed 50,000 plus but less than a quarter of this at 12,153. And of these over 90 per cent were ethnic German. By comparison 'enemy' casualties in Normandy up to 30 June were: 76,996 ethnic Germans (including 1,830 officers) and 3,787 Russians – over 96 per cent German. In short, fewer enemy troops surrendered than had been expected and there seemed little significant difference between the propensity to surrender between the ethnic Germans and their eastern Allies.[54]

15.4 Retrospect

According to Montgomery:

> In spite of the enemy's intentions to defeat us on the beaches, we found no
> surprises awaiting us in Normandy. Our measures designed to overcome the
> defences proved successful. Although not all our D-Day objectives had been
> achieved – in particular, the situation at Omaha beach was far from secure – and
> in all the beach-head areas there were pockets of enemy resistance, and a very
> considerable amount of mopping up remained to be done, we had gained a
> foothold on the Continent of Europe.[55]

One particular reason for the high casualties and tardiness of progress
on the ground was that for all the superiority in matériel and numbers
that the Allies could achieve it was rendered less significant against an
enemy that was well dug-in, well armed and prepared to stay-put.
Ironically, then, it was in some respects a rerun of the First World War –
most of the advantages lay with the defender and it seems that only the
ability to win a bloody battle of attrition ensured a victory for the
invaders.

But success in Normandy was by no means foreordained. Alan Brooke
later accepted that a defeat would have been likely if strong counter-
attacks had been launched at mid-day on the Allied beach-heads –
Rommel had been right – but they were not. Partly this was because the
Allied control over the air and over the immediate hinterland prevented
this but it was also the case that the Germans redeployed their own reinforcement away from Omaha just at the time when the situation was critical for the Americans. Similarly, had the defenders not moved half their
ammunition back to 'places of safety' they would, perhaps, not have had
to withdraw quite so quickly nor use tracer ammunition that enabled the
invaders to spot them more easily.

And for all the information made available for the assault on the
beaches – and this aspect was markedly successful in general – it was in
sharp contrast to the very problematic information available about the
defences and deployment of defenders off the beaches. Even when the
Allies correctly identified their enemies they almost always underestimated
the skill and tenacity with which these enemies held their ground or
counter-attacked when their ground was lost. For all that Montgomery
was the great planner, the plan really only covered the beaches, after that
there was neither a coherent plan nor were local commanders empowered
to use their initiative because the great planner, allegedly, already had an
infallible plan; if only the Germans had allowed it to unfold.

The issue of Leadership has also noticeably shifted from a concentration at the top of the individual political and military leaders discussed in previous chapters to a perspective that focuses on the management of resources and processes and then to consider the significance of Command at the 'sharp end'. Allied organizational superiority lay in strategic not tactical terms and success came through the superior planning and better management of production but this was almost negated by the better tactical fighting abilities of the defenders. However, that superiority at the tactical level was radically undermined by the inept strategic decision-making of the German High Command which more than compensated for the poverty of some Allied technologies, such as tank design. On D-Day it was the tactical Command of junior officers, NCOs and ordinary soldiers that rescued the so called strategic superiority of the Allied senior commanders. In contrast, the strategic failures of the German leadership were not rescued by the German junior commanders – even though many such officers knew what needed to be done. In short, the poor bloody infantry of the Allied side made up for the errors of their senior leaders and managers while the poor bloody infantry on the German side were generally able but usually unwilling to do the same for their leaders. As surely as the junior Allied commanders commanded their troops to success, the senior German leaders led theirs to defeat.

Another way to put this is to consider the result through Archilochus's notion of the Fox and the Hedgehog: 'The Fox knows many things, but the Hedgehog knows one big thing'. In this case the German Hedgehog may well have known more about combat than any other army – indeed, it was the world's greatest army. But hedgehogs are apt to forget that other things matter. In this case the Allied fox may not have been quite as effective as a combat soldier on an individual basis – but success on the battlefield could not be reduced to the martial skills of individuals; it was as much to do with ensuring logistics, securing air domination, removing the u-boat threat, and keeping the Soviet Union on side and in time as it was with individual valour on the battlefield. Indeed, the German penchant for tactical innovation on the battlefield seems to have left them bereft of strategic planning off the battlefield. Such a conclusion might go a long way to explaining the initial success and subsequent failure of the German spring offensive in 1918, as well as the failure of Operation Sealion to invade Britain in 1940, the failure in the USSR in 1941, and the failure in Normandy.[56]

So where does this leave the issue of problems and decision-making? On the one hand it should be clear that problems do not and certainly did not arrive in neat boxes marked 'Tame' or 'Wicked' or 'Critical';

instead they come in a sprawling mass that seeps out of any container and embodies all kinds of elements. Thus if the problems approach is useful it can only be as a heuristic device, not as an attempt to match the so called 'real world'. That said, there are many occasions when the assumption that problems are Tame rather than Wicked encourages an approach best described as 'more of the same' when oftentimes that approach seems entirely redundant. Thus the Allied problems of confusing the Germans as to the landing place and time were not ones that had been faced and solved before and hence the collaborative efforts employed through a Wicked approach seemed eminently appropriate. Yet the German response to the invasion was one closer to the slow and deliberate avoidance of decision-making when the growing crisis actually required a Commander to act as soon as possible. Many German commanders had historically done this but their subordination to Hitler's personal whim effectively undermined their entire response.

On the other hand the Allied Arsenal of Democracy was built using precisely the Management and skills that had solved the relatively Tame Problems of mass production – management skills that the Germans had before the war but could never properly compete given the incompetence and infighting at the heart of the Reich. Thus the Allies, and especially the Americans, mass produced thousands of aircraft but the Germans simply could not produce the thousands of pilots needed to shoot them all down. Similarly, while the German superiority at the level of the individual combat soldier may have been significant – other things being equal – things never were that equal. Indeed, the German penchant for the heroics of combat seemed to have positively enervated their concern for the more mundane aspects of war, like fuel, munitions and food. The enormous administrative tail of the Allied armies, in contrast to the German reluctance to have anyone in uniform who was not actually fighting at the front, essentially meant that the longer any operation went on the less likely were the Germans to be successful. It was not so much Guns rather than Butter than won wars (as opposed to individual battles) but Guns and Butter. As several German machine gunners insisted, it was only when they ran out of ammunition that they stopped firing: logistics as much as heroism proved to be the arbiter of fate in Normandy.

At the same time when the problems facing both sides on D-Day turned Critical it was the German army – historically the more adept at low level Command – which failed to act appropriately, while the Allies – historically poorer at the flexibility required of mission Command – embodied enough junior commanders to get the troops off the beaches and into Normandy.

Here is the final point to reinforce the importance of all three

Photo 15.4 Easy Red, Omaha Beach from the American cemetery

approaches: it was not the ability to lead collaboratively over Wicked Problems that secured success for the Allies, nor the ability to manage Tame Problems, nor even the ability to command Critical Problems, but rather the ability to do all three at different times and in different places. Again this reflects the issue of effective war fighting versus effective battle fighting: being good in a crisis, or good at securing collaborative consent, or good at managing, simply isn't good enough, you have to be good at all three. Those who romanticize the notion of collaborative leadership – that democratic or participative leadership will prevail over all problems – will drown in endless and often unnecessary committees. Those that rely solely on Management – that targets and science can fix everything – will forever be required to rationalize the consistent failures that follow ineluctable from their consistent application of 'the' correct process. Those who believe that the decisive actions of commanders are the guaranteed way to every victory will always want to look anywhere but at the history for the litany of decisive failures. All attempts at the consistent application of the same technique are likely to fail because success on D-Day was secured – but never determined – by a judicious and subtle blend of all three decision-modes: Leadership, Management and Command.

Notes

Chapter 1

1. Quoted in Ramsey, 1995: 568.
2. Brooke, 2001: 554.
3. Gleick, 1987.
4. Durschmied, 1999.
5. Tsouras, 1994.
6. Ambrose, 2000: 345–7.
7. Badsey, 1994a: 38/9; Magenheimer, 1998: 188.
8. Murray, 1994: 35.
9. Mets, 1997: 181–94. It should also be pointed out that, on average, the Western Allies lost six aircraft a day to accidents in 1944 and 1945 (Freeman, 1998: 94).
10. Murray, 1994: 35. In fact the greatest losses of German aircraft occurred right at the end of the war: on 16 April 1944, 724 aircraft were destroyed and 373 damaged; most had not even taken off (Freeman, 1998: 176).
11. Carrell, 1995: 31.
12. The ten batteries were: Ouistrehem (4 × 105mm), Houlgate (4 × 155mm), Merville (4 × 100mm), Mont-Fleury (4 × 122mm), Longues (4 × 150mm), Pointe-du-Hoc (6 × 155mm), Maisy (4 × 105mm and 6 × 155mm), St Martin-de-Varreville (4 × 105mm), Crisbecq (4 × 210mm) and Le Pernelle (3 × 170mm) (Ramsey, 1995: 113).
13. Mets, 1997: 214–15.
14. Cf. Overy, 1995: 160.
15. Man, 1994: 37.
16. Neillands and Normann, 1993: 126.
17. Badsey, 1994b: 54.
18. Ramsey, 1995: 620.
19. Botting, 1978: 161; Man, 1994: 71.
20. Ambrose, 1995: 319.
21. Quoted in Peddie, 1994: 1.
22. Carrel, 1995: 286.
23. D'Este, 1983.
24. Neillands, 2002.
25. Hastings, 1984.
26. Ambrose, 1995; Badsey, 1994c; Carell, 1995; D'Este, 1983; Hastings, 1993; Neillands, 2002.
27. An earlier version of this section was published as Grint (2005b).
28. Bratton et al., 2004: 58–85; Zaleznik, 1977. An earlier version of this section was published as 'Problems, Problems, Problems: The Social Construction of Leadership' in *Human Relations* (2005).

29. Weick, 1993.
30. Rittell and Webber, 1973.
31. Howieson and Kahn, 2002; Cf. Watters, 2004.
32. http://news.bbc.co.uk/1/hi/uk_politics/921524.stm
33. Overy, 2000: 267.
34. Howieson and Kahn, 2002.
35. Heifetz, 1998.
36. Etzioni, 1964.
37. Nye, 2004.
38. Nye, 2004: 1.
39. Dahl, 1961, Schattschneider, 1960, Bachrach and Baratz, 1962; Lukes, 1974.
40. Etzioni, 1964.

Chapter 2

1. Eisenhower to Bradley, quoted in Ambrose, 1995: 107.
2. For a naval example of this see the case study of the consecutive Royal Navy mutinies at Spithead and Nore in 1797: the mutineers tactics are very similar, but the navy's tactics changed dramatically and while the Spithead mutiny ended in a victory for the mutineers, the Nore mutiny ended with 29 executed mutineers (see Grint, 2000: 71–105).
3. Overy, 1995: 141.
4. Quoted in Botting, 1978: 80.
5. Roosevelt's own influence over the war was distributed through two channels: a military line through the Chiefs of Staff, and a civilian line through the secretaries of war and navy and the War production Board and so on (Eiler, 1997: 329).
6. Quoted in Kemp, 1994: 133.
7. Quoted in D'Este, 1983: 50.
8. Eisenhower, 1995a: 10.
9. Quoted in Kemp, 1994: 134.
10. Just how skilful was Montgomery's victory over the Afrika Korps at El-Alamein is difficult to say because the logistical superiority of the British forces was overwhelming: Montgomery accumulated 195,000 troops against the German-Italian forces of 60,000–104,000 (depending on the source) combat ready troops. In addition Montgomery had 1,100 tanks against Germany's 270–496 as well as 900 RAF versus 324 Luftwaffe aircraft (Lewin, 1998: 70; Magenheimer, 1998: 173). Montgomery went on to serve for 50 years in the British Army – the longest service since Wellington. He retired from the army in 1958 and died in 1976 (Ramsey, 1995: 624).
11. Quoted in Kemp, 1994: 134–5.
12. Quoted in Lewin, 1998: 15.
13. Quoted in Gelb, 1996: 329/427–8.
14. Quoted in Lewin, 1998: 146.
15. Quoted in Lewin, 1998: 178.
16. Lewin, 1998: 57.

17. Neillands and de Normann, 1993: 9. Ironically, in 1933, the British government agreed on its priorities for the armed services: first, the defence of possessions in the Far East; second, a commitment to Europe; third the defence of India (Fraser, 1999: 14).
18. Ross, 1997: 2/3.
19. O'Neill, 1994: 580.
20. Quoted in Kimball, 1997: 262.
21. Haffner, S. (2003), *Churchill* (London: Haus).
22. Quoted in Breuer, 1995: 149.
23. Overy 1995: 141.
24. Quoted in Botting, 1978: 49.
25. Quoted in Breuer, 1995: 124.
26. Quoted in Breuer, 1995: 124.
27. Ross, 1997: 98.
28. Gelb, 1996: 303; cf. Badsey, 1994a: 49.
29. Ramsey, 1995: 111.
30. MacArthur became, at 34, the youngest general in the Allied Expeditionary Force in France in 1918. He had worked for President Theodore Roosevelt and his mother was a close friend of the US CO, General Pershing. In 1930 President Hoover appointed him army chief of staff and in 1934 he retired for the first time – ten years early.
31. Jackson, 2006.
32. Badsey, 1994b: 455–7.
33. O'Neill, 1994: 580.
34. Eisenhower to Marshall, 19 February 1944, quoted in Hobbes, 1999: 154.
35. Badsey, 1994c: 11.
36. Copp, 1997: 148.
37. Mitchell, 1997: 310.
38. Pronounced 'duck': (D = 1942 registration year; U = Amphibious; K = all-wheel drive and W for dual rear axles).
39. Bruce, 1999: 78–83, 147.
40. Wilson, 1997: 286. Until 1943 recruits had to have at least 32 natural teeth. This seems to have been a left-over requirement of the American Civil War where soldiers had to bite the end of their cartridges (Wright, 1998: 3).
41. Quoted in Collier, 1999: 114.
42. Quoted in Copp, 1997: 149.
43. Gelb, 1996: 300.
44. Collier, 1999: 8.
45. Collier, 1999: 7.
46. Breuer, 1995: 122–3. The object of Churchill's 'Operation Unthinkable' was to 'impose upon Russia the will of the United States and the British Empire'. It was to involve 100,000 German soldiers. It was to take place on 1 July 1945 with an initial assault by a joint force of 47 Anglo-American divisions between Dresden and the Baltic Sea. Fortunately the British Chiefs of Staff dismissed Churchill's ideas as politically and militarily unachievable (*Daily Telegraph*, 1 October 1998).
47. Quoted in Botting, 1978: 20. France was the only country to sign an armistice with Germany. Germany occupied northern France and the

complete coastline while French colonies remained under French control from Vichy, the capital of the unoccupied southern region.

48. Botting, 1978: 20; Turner, 1994: 13–14.
49. Kemp, 1994: 15.
50. Quoted in Kilvert-Jones, 1999: 29.
51. Botting, 1978: 21, 24–5.
52. The first significant American land offensive of the war was twelve days earlier, on 7 August 1942 at Guadalcanal in the Solomon Islands of the Pacific. The US navy had been attacked at Pearl Harbour on 7 December 1941 and had begun the defeat of the Japanese navy at the Battle of Midway between 3 and 5 June 1942.
53. Ross, 1997: 15.
54. Quoted in Botting, 1978: 22.
55. Quoted in Collier, 1999: 11.
56. Quoted in Collier, 1999: 11.
57. Quoted in Holt and Holt, 1999: 83.
58. Quoted in Collier, 1999: 12.
59. Lewin, 1998: 40–1.
60. Quoted in Collier, 1999: 12–13.
61. Botting, 1978: 25–33.
62. Kemp, 1994:17–18.
63. Quoted in Botting, 1978: 40.
64. Carell, 1995: 8.
65. Botting, 1978: 44–5.
66. Quoted in Hansen, 2006: 37.
67. U boats sank 800,000 tons of Allied shipping in one month during the winter of 1942–3 (Neillands and de Normann, 1993: 11).
68. Quoted in Breuer, 1995: 141.
69. quoted in Gelb, 1996: 279.
70. Drez, 1996: 3.
71. Williamson, 1999: 106.
72. Breuer, 1995: 122/3.
73. Quoted in Breuer, 1995: 142.
74. Overy, 1995: 142/3.
75. Kilvert-Jones, 1999: 12.
76. Fisher, 1994a: 90.
77. Quoted in Breuer, 1995: 140.
78. Quoted in Collier, 1999: 22.
79. Quoted in Breuer, 1995: 147.
80. Ross, 1997: 60–3/119.
81. Breuer, 1995: 154–60.
82. Quoted in Neillands and de Normann, 1993: 42.
83. Evans, 2005: 66.
84. Man, 1994: 26.
85. As on Omaha, so at Salerno, at one point an evacuation of troops was seriously considered as a result of the German pressure (Bruce, 1999: 102).
86. Neillands and de Normann, 1993: 42–3.
87. Bradley, 1995: 322–3.
88. Eisenhower, 1995a: 15.

89. Man, 1994: 17.
90. The planning for the US beaches under Bradley took place in Clifton College, Bristol, the *alma mater* of Haig, and, in hindsight, a worrying start.
91. Pitcairn-Jones, 1994: 30.
92. Belcher, 1995: 517.
93. Collier, 1999: 105.
94. Leigh-Mallory, 1995a: 135.
95. Turner, 1994: 41.
96. Pitcairn-Jones, 1994: 25.
97. Belchem, 1995: 518–19.
98. Neillands, 2002: 39.
99. I would like to thank Mike Harper for pointing out this anomaly.
100. Pitcairn-Jones, 1994: 21–2.
101. Breuer, 1995: 180; Overy, 1995: 157.
102. Doughty, 1994: 25.
103. Ramsey, 1995: 131.
104. Bruce, 1999: 141.
105. Neillands and de Normann, 1993: 57.
106. Pitcairn-Jones, 1994: 24.
107. Pitcairn-Jones, 1994: 14.
108. Ramsey, 1995: 161.
109. Botting, 1978: 61; Man, 1994: 23.
110. Cherbourg, and its 39,000 enemy prisoners of war, was eventually captured on 27 June (D-Day+21) at the cost of 22,119 US casualties (Lloyd-Owen, 1994: 17). The German sabotage of the port involved the sinking of 67 ships and dozens of railway wagons in the harbour. It took over two months to clear the harbour and return the port to normal usage.
111. Botting, 1978: 52.
112. Neillands and de Normann, 1993: 48.
113. Collier, 1999: 27.
114. Mets, 1997: 220. However, when the Americans did break through at the end of July the US forces faced only two Panzer divisions and 190 tanks compared to the six Panzer divisions and 645 tanks defending Caen from the Anglo-Canadian forces. The relative tank numbers are reproduced below:

	Tanks opposite US 1st Army	Tanks opposite British 2nd Army
15 June	70	520
20 June	210	430
25 June	190	530
30 June	140	725
5 July	215	690
10 July	190	610
15 July	190	630
20 July	190	560
25 July	190	645

115. Gray, 2006: 161.
116. Ramsay, 1995: 200.
117. Quoted in Collier, 1999: 141.
118. Stagg quoted in Ramsey, 1995: 162.
119. Botting, 1978: 61.
120. Turner, 1994: 56
121. Bowyer, 1995: 67.
122. Neville Brown, 1994: 588.
123. Carell, 1995: 24.
124. Ryan, 1960: 23.
125. Ryan, 1960: 23/70.
126. Ryan, 1960: 38.
127. Pitcairn-Jones, 1994: 83.
128. Quoted in Drez, 1996: 61.
129. Zimmerman, 1995a: 56.
130. Stagg quoted in Ramsey, 1995: 164.
131. Doughty, 1994: 100. As Stagg wrote in his diary for 5 June, 'When we got back to lunch, the sky was 10/10ths, some of it very low, 800–1,000 ft it seemed, and wind force up to 5–6. What the mischief was going wrong?' On the evening of 5 June there was *still* a dispute between the British and the American forecasts for D-Day (Stagg, quoted in Ramsey, 1995: 169).
132. Quoted in Overy 1995: 158,
133. Quoted in Ramsey, 1995: 167.
134. In the event 42 Spitfires were involved in 76 sorties over the British beaches wholly dedicated to spotting for the naval guns. RAF Mustangs did the same over Canadian and American beaches (Bowyer, 1995: 191/218).
135. Bradley, 1995: 325.
136. Eisenhower, 1995b: 157.
137. Quoted in Collier, 1999: 144. Most of the accounts of Eisenhower's actual words – including his own version – suggest he said 'O.K. Let's go!' However, Alan Michie, London correspondent for the Reader's Digest interviewed Admiral Ramsay immediately after the meeting and Ramsay had difficulty remembering, but finally agreed that it was 'a short phrase. Something typically American'. When asked whether it was 'OK we'll go'? Ramsay denied it but agreed that 'OK, let 'er rip' 'sounded like it'. The military censor refused to pass the phrase and insisted that 'OK let's go' was the phrase, even though Eisenhower subsequently agreed with Michie that 'OK let 'er rip' was what he actually said (see Ramsey, 1995: 167).
138. Quoted in Keegan, 1992: 66. Eisenhower had originally written 'the troops have been withdrawn' but he altered this in line with his acceptance of personal responsibility to 'I have withdrawn the troops' (see the reproduction of the original note in Ramsey, 1995: 324).
139. Bowyer, 1995: 161.

Chapter 3

1. Breuer, 1995: 165; Gleb, 1996: 291. Orange (2006: 148) suggests it was three months rather than one month.

2. Orange, 2006: 150.
3. Salewski, 1994: 272–3.
4. Badsey, 1994c: 212.
5. Neillands, 1995: 104.
6. Man, 1994; 21.
7. Freeman, 1998: 114–15, 158, 170. Preddy was killed by friendly fire from a US anti-aircraft battery on Christmas Day 1944.
8. Mets, 1997: 183–7.
9. Collier, 1999: 41.
10. Collier, 1999: 32; Linderman, 1997: 39, 42. 52,000 of the US's 290,000 battle deaths in the Second World War were to air crew. Only around a of bomber crews managed to complete the initial number of missions – the 'tour' (25, subsequently increased to 30, then 35, and finally 50) to secure release from flying duties, a Distinguished Flying Cross ('The Lucky Bastard Ribbon' as it was called), and a return to the US. In 1943 less than half the crew survived a tour. A greater loss was only imposed upon one group in the US forces: the infantry (Linderman, 1997: 39).
11. Mets, 1997: 197, 211; Hastings, 1993b: 51.
12. Badsey, 1994a: 38/9; Magenheimer, 1998: 188.
13. Murray, 1994: 35.
14. Mets, 1997: 181–194. It should also be pointed out that, on average, the Western Allies lost six aircraft a day to accidents in 1944 and 1945 (Freeman, 1998: 94).
15. Murray, 1994: 35. In fact the greatest losses of German aircraft occurred right at the end of the war: on 16 April 1944, 724 aircraft were destroyed and 373 damaged; most had not even taken off Freeman, 1998: 176.
16. Cooper, 1998: 172, 274, 285.
17. Mets, 1997: 198, 248.
18. Kilvert-Jones, 1999: 17, 38.
19. Breuer, 1995: 165; Hastings, 1993b: 48.
20. Orange, 2006: 148.
21. Turner, 1994: 38.
22. Overy, 1995: 130.
23. Leigh-Mallory, 1995a: 138.
24. Ambrose, 1995: 240.
25. Collier, 1999: 32.
26. Carell, 1995: 31.
27. Hargreaves, 2006: 13.
28. Quoted in Ryan, 1960: 73.
29. Doughty, 1994: 20.
30. Ryan, 1960: 128.
31. Quoted in Bennett, 1995: 69.
32. Quoted in Kilvert-Jones, 1999: 37.
33. Price, 1994b: 488–90.
34. Price, 1994b: 494–5.
35. Neillands and de Normann, 1993: 70.
36. Bennett, 1995: 70.
37. Ramsey, 1995: 432. Bowyer, 1995: 165.

38. Ramsey, 1995: 571. Allied ships were forbidden to shoot at any aircraft during the approach to the beaches, so thick was the sky with aircraft – and all of them likely to be Allied (Kilvert-Jones, 1999: 86).
39. Cooper, 1998: 49.
40. Cooper, 1998: 56.
41. Freeman, 1998: 125, 144.
42. Quoted in Gelb, 1996: 293.
43. Tedder, 1995: 82.
44. Quoted in Hughes, 1995: 127.
45. Quoted in Overy, 1995: 148.
46. Mets, 1997: 255.
47. Orange, 2006: 151.
48. Quoted in Tedder, 1995: 87.
49. Churchill did not give up on this: on 10 July he sent a letter to Tedder asking 'how many Frenchmen did you kill' before D-Day? (Orange, 2006: 151).
50. Leigh-Mallory, 1995a: 140–1, 145.
51. Leigh-Mallory, 1995a: 139.
52. Macksey, 1996: 196; Neillands, 2001: 316.
53. Fisher, 1994b: 411.
54. Mets, 1997: 182–215.
55. Leigh-Mallory quoted in Kilvert-Jones, 1999: 35.
56. ADGB was never a popular term for the fighter pilots it encompassed and on 22 October 1944 the title was replaced by the former term, Fighter Command (Legg, 1994: 126).
57. Leigh-Mallory, 1995a: 145.
58. Freeman, 1998: 116.
59. Leigh-Mallory, 1995a: 146–7.
60. Orange, 2006: 152. German efforts to maintain supply were extraordinary, for example, the bridge at Rouen was destroyed eight times after it was rebuilt seven times.
61. Ambrose, 1995: 97/103.
62. Overy, 1995: 150.
63. Neillands and de Normann, 1993: 46.
64. Keegan, 1992: 179.
65. Man, 1994: 108.
66. Barbier, 2006: 180.
67. Leigh-Mallory, 1995a: 148–9.
68. Bowyer, 1995; 24. Designed by Barnes Wallis, the first Tallboy was dropped on 8 June 1944.
69. Dunphie and Johnson, 1999: 14.
70. Holt and Holt, 1999: 73.
71. The first operational use of the 60lb rocket carried by the Typhoon was probably just before Christmas 1943 (Bowyer, 1995: 234).
72. Bowyer, 1995: 15.
73. The ten batteries were: Ouistreham (4 × 105mm), Houlgate (4 × 155mm), Merville (4 × 100mm), Mont-Fleury (4 × 122mm), Longues (4 × 150mm), Pointe du Hoc (6 × 155mm), Maisy (4 × 105mm and 6 × 155mm), St Martin-de-Varreville (4 × 105mm), Crisbecq (4 × 210mm) and Le Pernelle (3 × 170mm) (Ramsey, 1995: 113).

74. Mets, 1997: 214–15.
75. Darlow, 2004: 160–1.
76. Cf. Overy, 1995: 160.
77. Pitcairn-Jones, 1994: 57.
78. Ramsey, 1995: 419.
79. Quoted in Kilvert-Jones, 1999: 43.
80. Pitcairn-Jones, 1994: 88–9.
81. Bowyer, 1995: 96.
82. Leigh-Mallory, 1995b: 608–13.
83. Hastings, 1993b: 54.
84. Pitcairn-Jones, 1994: 33.
85. Quoted in Kilvert-Jones, 1999: 35–6.
86. Kilvert-Jones, 1999: 36.
87. Bowyer, 1995: 231.
88. Hughes, 1995: 8–9.
89. Pitcairn-Jones, 1994: 105–6.
90. Such spotting had originally occurred in 1915 at Gallipoli, and in July 1943 the Americans had used seaplanes to the same purpose for the Sicilian invasion. But the losses in Sicily were high and fighter-aircraft were used over Normandy after three months training in Britain (David Brown, 1994: 31).
91. Bowyer, 1995: 218.
92. Bowyer, 1995: 224–5.
93. Bowyer, 1995: 38.

Chapter 4

1. Clausewitz, 1968: 162/3.
2. Evans, 2005: 75.
3. Wright, 1998: 285.
4. Quoted in Kilvert-Jones, 1999: 48.
5. Hinsley, 1994: 175.
6. Hesketh, 1999: 70–154; Overy, 1995: 151. There was even an attempt to persuade the Germans that the Mediterranean was the real destination for the invasion force by recruiting a 'double' for Montgomery (Lt Clifton James, then in the Royal Army Pay Corps) to tour Gibraltar and Algiers on 26 and 27 May 1944 in Operation Copperhead (Bennett, 1995: 65) Paradoxically, the Germans seemed to doubt the authenticity of Montgomery's visit, primarily because just a fortnight before hand Tedder, Leigh-Mallory, and several other senior officers had been reported at Gibraltar and it was inconceivable to the Germans that Montgomery would have made the same journey a fortnight later (Hesketh, 1999: 122–4,190). Against considerable opposition, Montgomery insisted that Lt James receive the full pay of a general, then set at £8 a day (Collier, 1999: 78). That was more in a week than most British servicemen earned in a year.
7. Quoted in Badsey, 1994a: 39. A good example of this might be to consider the claims about aircraft losses at the height of the Battle of Britain, 15

September 1940. The Germans claimed to have shot down 170 British fighters – when only 26 were actually lost, while the British claimed that they had shot down 185 German planes, when only 60 were lost. In effect both sides were lying but the German lies (and losses) were bigger than the British ones (Macksey, 1996: 117).

8. Hobbes, 1999: 160
9. Breuer, 1995: 170–1.
10. Hesketh, 1999: 170–80.
11. When Patton took over the 3rd Army in Normandy FUSAG's 'ghost army' was taken over by Lt General L. J. McNair on 14 July. McNair was subsequently killed by 'friendly fire' near St Lô but his death was kept secret to enable the deception to continue. Not until late July did the German High Command eventually accept that there was no FUSAG (Bennett, 1995: 64).
12. Carell, 1995: 16–17.
13. Wright, 1998: 290.
14. Maher, 1996: 67.
15. Hesketh, 1999: 59–60.
16. Hesketh, 1999: 163–7.
17. Quoted in Barbier, 2006: 178.
18. Botting, 1978: 56.
19. Overy, 1995: 151.
20. Keegan, 1992: 63.
21. Quoted in Botting, 1978: 56.
22. Bowyer, 1995: 18.
23. Goldstein et al 1994: 15/109.
24. Badsey, 1994a: 212.
25. Hesketh, 1999: 116.
26. Hesketh, 1999: 121.
27. Breuer, 1995: 143/183–6.
28. Collier, 1999: 120; Gleb, 1996: 301. de Gaulle led the French Committee of National Liberation (FCNL), based in Algiers but Roosevelt in particular refused to recognize its claim to sole legitimate representation of the French people and he forbade Eisenhower from discussing the post-war administration of France with de Gaulle until after the Allies had 'liberated' France. Nevertheless, on 26 May 1944 the FCNL proclaimed itself the provisional government of France (Ramsey, 1995: 158–9).
29. Collier, 1999: 120.
30. Masters, 1997: 141.
31. Ramsay, 1995: 170.
32. Ryan, 1960: 44.
33. Quoted in Collier, 1999: 133.
34. Ramsey, 1995: 157.
35. Ridgway, 1995: 260.
36. Pitcairn-Jones, 1994: 39.
37. Botting, 1978: 94.
38. Bowyer, 1995: 26.
39. Price, 1994a: 211.
40. Pitcairn-Jones, 1994: 85.

41. Quoted in Botting, 1978: 104.
42. Price, 1994a: 1994: 212.
43. French members of the British SAS were to suffer greatly at the hands of the *Wehrmacht* who, in line with Hitler's *Kommandobefehl* of 18 October 1942 and 25 June 1944, regularly executed them. For example, of the 55 individuals involved in Operation Bulbasket 1 and Bulbasket 2, reconnaissance drops in France in support of Overlord, only 2 survived: 31 were captured and executed by 80th *Armeekorps Radfahrschwadron* on 7 July 1944 near Rom. On the other hand, two members of No. 3 Troop, No. 10 Commando were saved from probable execution by the personal intervention of Rommel in April 1944 after they were captured while examining beach defences in France. In fact, Masters (1997: 125–6, 221) suggests that many local German commanders ignored Hitler's order to execute Commandos.
44. The dummies were made in the Littlewoods factory at Carrickfergus. They had first been used in September 1942 by the SAS in Egypt and were last used in Holland in April 1945 (McLeod, 1995: 252).
45. McLeod, 1995: 250–1.
46. Mcleod, 1995: 252; Ambrose, 1995: 216. In Operation Dragoon, the invasion of southern France in August 1944, 300 dummy paratroopers were again dropped and, once more deceived the Germans and delayed the movement of reinforcements (Westall, 1994: 29).
47. Quoted in Macksey, 1996: 113.
48. Russell, 1981: 21–4.
49. The *Abwehr* was not the only German counter-intelligence organization for the *Sicherheitsdienst* (SD), the intelligence system of the Nazi party, also operated against Allied intelligence, though the SD was not as large as the *Abwehr* with its 13,000 employees.
50. Collier, 1999: 71–2.
51. Twenty in Roman numerals being a double X. The Allies were not the only ones to succeed in breaking up a network of agents. The German Abwehr managed to infiltrate the Dutch resistance from 1941 to such an extent that 52 agents (all but one from the SOE and all but six subsequently executed) were captured, as well as 350 local resistance fighters. In addition, thanks to the deception, London provided the Germans with 570 containers of arms and ammunition, thinking they were being dropped to the Dutch Resistance (Miller, 1998: 49–51).
52. Collier, 1999: 77.
53. Breuer, 1995: 60–2. Churchill was extremely worried about aggravating the Irish government throughout the war – just in case Hitler occupied Ireland (as he had intended at one point) and thus hugely increased the risk to Allied shipping from U-boats operating from Irish ports (my own grandfather came across two U-boats in Irish coastal waters while working on a fishing smack during the war). Irish neutrality extended to a multi-national POW camp on the Curragh, known as K-Lines. Prisoners of all sides were allowed into the local pubs and were on their honour not to escape – indeed, so concerned were the British not to upset the Irish that at least one escapee, Bud Wolfe, an American flying with the RAF, was sent back to K-Lines from Belfast by RAF police. So bizarre was the whole set

up that when two Canadian pilots crash landed their plane – in what they thought was Scotland – they staggered to a nearby pub (Lawlor's bar in Naas) to celebrate their miraculous escape only to be faced by a bar full of Germans in uniform (a special privilege granted by the Irish guards because it was one POW's birthday) who demanded that the Allied pilots go drink in their own part of the pub! (Margolis, 1999: 2).

54. Pitcairn-Jones, 1994: 39.
55. Hesketh, 1999: xix.
56. A German 'triple' agent, codenamed 'Teapot' worked in Hamburg, allegedly for the British but actually for the Germans. The British were aware of this and fed him false information (Hesketh, 1999).
57. Russell, 1981: 28.
58. Collier, 1999: 76.
59. Russell, 1981: 28–9.
60. Collier, 1999: 78–9; Hesketh, 1999: 145–8.
61. Russell, 1981: 201.
62. Stafford, 2003: 317.
63. Quoted in Hesketh, 1999: xxv.
64. Quoted in Hesketh, 1999: 209.
65. D'Este, 1983: 157.
66. Quoted in Hesketh, 1999: xxi.
67. There was no formal ceremony for Garbo's MBE, it took place in 1984 – when Garbo revealed himself (*The Guardian*, 27 January 1999; Bennett, 1995: 62). He was never formally awarded with his Iron Cross. The German hierarchy of military medals at the time of D-Day was (in ascending order):

   1. Iron Cross (Second Class; First Class) {there were 3 million holders of the Iron Cross};
   2. Knights Cross (with Oak Leaves; with Oak Leaves and Swords {Michael Wittmann, for Villers-Bocage, and Fritz Bayerlain, for *Panzer Lehr*, were awarded this is Normandy};
   3. Knights Cross (with Oak Leaves, Swords and Diamonds) {Sepp Dietrich won this at Caen});
   4. Grand Cross (Only Goering won this) (Thomas, 1994: 354).

68. Quoted in Kemp, 1994: 144.
69. Pitcairn-Jones, 1994: 70.
70. Collier, 1999: 128.
71. Ramsay, 1995: 200.
72. Ramsey, 1995: 124.
73. Several Allied planes were shot down by friendly fire, though not on D-Day itself. One of the most notorious incidents occurred early in 1945 when Spaatz and Doolittle were shot at by Patton's anti-aircraft gunners. Spaatz complained to Patton on two counts: first, his troops had misidentified a friendly aircraft; second, they had failed to shoot accurately (Mets, 1997: 268). What made the mistake worse was that Spaatz and Doolittle were flying a twin-engined P-38 Lightening – a plane with twin boom that made its silhouette so distinctive that it was often used to fly defensive cover over the beachhead in Normandy – because even trigger-happy army-gunners could not mistake it for a German plane!

74. Quoted in Neillands and de Normann, 1993: 84.
75. Darlow, 2004: 162.
76. Pitcairn-Jones, 1994: 39.
77. Bradley, 1995: 324.
78. Ryan, 1960: 32/46.
79. Blandford, 1999: 52.
80. Evans, 2005: 90.
81. Code books carried by the Royal Navy were kept on the bridge in perforated bags weighted with lead, to be jettisoned overboard in the event of likely capture (Maher, 1996: 65).
82. Russell, 1981: 75–7.
83. Keegan, 1995: 87; Macksey (1996: 128), however, suggests that the commander of Crete, General Freyberg, was fully informed of German intentions.
84. Ambrose, 1995: 85.
85. Doughty, 1994: 85.
86. Bennett, 1995: 66–8.
87. 'Tallboys' were designed to penetrate deep into the soil before exploding and could, in theory, displace 5,000 tons of earth (Ramsey, 1995: 573).
88. Bennett, 1995: 73–5.
89. Keegan 1995: 87.
90. Miller, 1998: 82, 116, 191, 194, 202. The French army before the war had already experienced the kind of political splits that tore the country apart under German occupation: the political left feared the French army would do the dirty work of the anti-republican conservative elements in the establishment while the political right feared that a conscript army would bring political instability into the heart of the state. The result was a conscript army with only one year's compulsory service – a limited term that helped persuade the French officer corps that an offensive strategy against Germany was out of the question (Kier, 1997: 7). The Resistance was also internally split and the relationship between de Gaulle and the communist groups was notoriously bad. When de Gaulle entered Bayeux on 14 June he was, according to the official version, met by thousands of adoring supporters. The local communist group's version is that, at most, 500 people turned up, mostly to find out who this de Gaulle – whose politics they despised – was (Holt and Holt, 1999: 135).
91. Funk, 1994: 139.
92. Maher, 1996: 140.
93. Personal communication, 16 September 1999.
94. Funk, 1994a: 140; Funk, 1994b: 264.
95. Botting, 1978: 56.
96. Quoted in Collier, 1999: 96.
97. Miller, 1998: 47–8.
98. Russell, 1981: 67.
99. Collier, 1999: 97–8.
100. The BBC was originally enlisted to help the various Resistance movements, and the SOE that tried to co-ordinate them, because using a secret transmitter and receiver was markedly more dangerous (Miller, 1998: 43).
101. 'The dice are on the table'.

102. Botting, 1998: 184.
103. Carell, 1995: 27.
104. Botting, 1978: 186.
105. Miller, 1998: 184.
106. Ryan, 1960: 76–8.
107. Ryan, 1960; 203.
108. Ryan, 1960: 206.
109. Reynolds, 1997: 21. In September 1944 Belgian Resistance fighters managed to prevent the Germans from destroying the port facilities at Antwerp as the Allied army approach.
110. The 2nd SS was, in fact, the first *Waffen* SS division formed, but Hitler reserved the first number for the *Leibstandarte*.
111. Even without widespread Resistance activity the flow of reinforcements across France was severely curtailed by the bombing. For instance, the French rails were reporting that by 26 May 1944 only 55 per cent of their journeys could be carried out, but by 5 June this had been reduced to just 10 per cent of their normal journeys. The 1st SS Panzer Division, stationed at Louvain in Belgium tried to travel to Paris after the invasion but all three possible rail routes were blocked by bomb damage and the journey took a week (Mierzejewski, 1994: 449).
112. The SOE was set up by Churchill in the summer of 1940, just after Dunkirk, to launch Commando raids on Europe, or in his more flamboyant words, 'To set Europe ablaze!' (quoted in Miller, 1998: 40). Its more formal remit was to co-ordinate all action, by way of sabotage and subversion, against the enemy overseas'. 10,000 men and 3,000 women volunteered for service with the SOE. The SOE's training school in Scotland was known by the Germans as the 'International Gangster School'.
113. There is a claim that Lammerding had been transporting looted gold on the day of the ambush and had burnt that particular village because he had traced one of his stolen vehicles there; see: www.scrapbookpages.com/Oradour-sur-Glane/Story/MacknessStory.html. After the war Lammerding was condemned to death in his absence at a trial in Bordeaux, in 1951, for the hangings at Tulle, but he was never extradited. He hid, for a short while, in Schleswig-Holstein, before returning to Dusseldorf, where he lived, undisturbed, at the head of a thriving business. He died in 1971.
114. Miller, 1998: 184–5; Williamson, 1996: 240.
115. Ambrose, 1995: 104–5; Botting, 1978: 187. Though there are claims that *Das Reich* went into the Reserve once it reached Normandy – and thus was not in any particular rush to reach the front (see Lucas, 1994b: 499).
116. Williamson, 1994: 170–3.
117. 'The long sobs of the violins of autumn'.
118. Overy, 1995: 158.
119. Zimmerman, 1995b: 317.
120. 'Wound my heart with a monotonous languor'.
121. Quoted in Collier, 1999: 168.
122. Quoted in Ryan, 1960: 84.
123. Ryan, 1960: 33–4.
124. Carell, 1995: 29.

125. Two kinds of rockets were developed by the Allies for aircraft attacks upon shipping and AFVs (Armoured Fighting Vehicles). First, a 25lb solid armour-piercing head. Second, a 60lb semi-armour piercing format. The 60lb version was adopted by most pilots in Normandy. (Ramsey, 1995: 152).
126. Turner, 1994: 95.
127. Carell, 1995: 19.
128. Carrel, 1995: 40.
129. Pitcairn-Jones, 1994: 86.
130. Pitcairn-Jones, 1994: 83.
131. Carrel, 1995: 82.
132. Quoted in Hesketh, 1999: 198.
133. Hesketh, 1999: 194.
134. Ryan, 1960: 123.
135. Quoted in Hargreaves, 2006: 39.
136. Zimmerman, 1995b: 318; Ramsey, 1995: 412
137. Ramsey, 1995: 416.
138. Ambrose, 1995: 186; Neillands and de Normann, 1993: 38/; Overy, 1995: 159.
139. Quoted in Hesketh, 1999: 199.
140. Quoted in Balkoski, 1999: 151.
141. Quoted in Carell, 1995: 100.
142. Quoted in Hesketh, 1999: 228.
143. Heinemann, 1994b: 497–8.
144. Quoted in Hesketh, 1999: 240.
145. Quoted in Kilvert-Jones, 1999: 50.
146. Quoted in Hesketh, 1999: 268.
147. Quoted in Hesketh, 1999: 286.
148. Hesketh, 1999: 361.

Chapter 5

1. Evans, 2005: 66.
2. Zimmerman, 1995a: 53.
3. Montgomery, 1995: 91/116.
4. Quoted in Botting, 1978: 8. (photo on opposite page).
5. Carrel, 1995: 14.
6. *Vergeltungswaffe 1*. Churchill had been warned of such a weapon in the Autumn of 1943 (Delaforce, 1998: 24).
7. Orange, 2006: 152.
8. Quoted in Kilvert-Jones, 1999: 17.
9. Botting, 1978: 9–15; photo Botting: 14.
10. Blandford, 1999: 14.
11. Quoted in Zimmerman, 1995a: 40.
12. Orange, 2006: 152.
13. Overy, 1995: 153.
14. Pitcairn-Jones, 1994: 54.
15. Kilvert-Jones, 1999: 60, 64–5.

16. Griffith, 1996: 31; Parker, 1995: 290.
17. Reynolds 1997: 34.
18. Badsey 1994c 179.
19. Quoted in Zimmerman, 1995a: 45.
20. Ryan, 1960: 24.
21. Quoted in Zimmerman, 1995a: 46.
22. Botting, 1978: 100; Zimmerman, 1995a: 48. Kilvert-Jones (1999: 21) puts the number of mines planned at 200 million.
23. Botting, 1978: 19.
24. Collier, 1999: 86.
25. Quoted in Botting, 1978: 53.
26. Badsey, 1994c: 72.
27. Zimmerman, 1995a: 39.
28. Hitler, 20 March 1944 quoted in Zimmerman, 1995a: 49.
29. Hargreaves, 2006: 13.
30. Hargreaves, 2006: 60.
31. Quoted in Kemp, 1994: 149.
32. Ryan, 1960: 25.
33. Carrel, 1995: 21.
34. Quoted in Neillands, 1995: 97.
35. Hesketh, 1999: 102–3.
36. Hesketh, 1999: 102.
37. Neillands and de Normann, 1993: 30; Carrel, 1995:13.
38. Hitler had invaded France with significantly fewer troops and tanks than the three to one superiority considered the norm in military circles: there were 141 German divisions against 144 Allied Divisions, 7,378 German artillery pieces against 13,974 Allied artillery pieces, and 2,445 German tanks against 3,383 Allied tanks. Only in aircraft did the Germans have a numerical superiority: 5,500 Luftwaffe planes to 3,100 Allied planes (Veranov, 1997: 104; Davidson and Levy, 1996: 63).
39. Overy, 1995: 154–5.
40. Keegan, 1992: 74.
41. Overy, 1995: 153.
42. Quoted in Hargreaves, 2006: 4.
43. Zimmerman, 1995a: 55.
44. Badsey, 1990: 9, 25.
45. Carrel, 1995: 22.
46. Ambrose, 1995: 149.
47. *Panzer Lehr* ('Instructional or Training') Division was composed of many tank instructors or train*ers* not train*ees*, and was the only completely armoured Panzer division in the German army. In May 1944 it had 14,185 soldiers and 449 officers (3 per cent) in two *Panzergrenadier* regiments, one armoured regiment and one armoured artillery regiment. That added up to 183 tanks, 58 anti-tank guns, 53 artillery pieces and 612 half tracks (Heinemann, 1994a: 414). It was stationed at Le Mans in June 1944, almost 90 miles south of the Normandy coast. Despite being the best armoured division in the German army its commander, Lt General Fritz Bayerlain, was worried: the fuel situation was critical, the Le Mans area was dissimilar to any of the likely invasion areas and therefore

prevented realistic training, and the decisional paralysis at the top of the army had generated a rash of different location orders and counter-orders.

48. Quoted in Blandford, 1999: 8.
49. Quoted in Ambrose, 1995: 129
50. Quoted in Lewin, 1998: 182–4.
51. Quoted in Zimmerman, 1995a: 55.
52. Quoted in Blandford, 1999: 9.
53. Schweppenburg, 1999: 413.
54. This, strangely enough, was exactly what Montgomery had planned when he was given command of the British 3rd Division after Dunkirk to prevent the expected German invasion. As he wrote to Churchill on 3 July 1940: 'I was disturbed to find the 3rd Division spread along thirty miles of coast, instead of being, as I had imagined, held back, concentrated in reserve, ready to move against any serious head of invasion (quoted in Lewin, 1998: 35).
55. Quoted in Wright, 1998: 69.
56. Rommel 23April 1944 quoted in Zimmerman, 1995a: 54.
57. Quoted in Collier, 1999: 83.
58. Ryan, 1960: 23.
59. Overy, 1997: 237–8.
60. Quoted in Botting, 1978: 92–3.
61. Quoted in Neillands and de Normann, 1993: 26.
62. Ryan, 1960: 220.
63. Collier, 1999: 36.
64. Quoted in Hobbes, 1999: 154.
65. Quoted in Hobbes, 1999: 155.
66. Goldstein et al 1994: 22.
67. Schweppenburg, 1999: 414.
68. Quoted in Balkoski, 1999: 175.
69. Quoted in Keegan, 1992: 65.
70. Kilvert-Jones, 1999: 164.
71. Quoted in Keegan, 1992: 146.
72. Herbert, 1997: 355–8.
73. Quoted in Salewski, 1994: 273.

Chapter 6

1. Badsey, 1994c: 109.
2. Holt and Holt, 1999: 86.
3. Quoted in Kilvert-Jones, 1999: 46.
4. Goldstein et al. (1994: 92) suggest that 'Hoc' is old French for 'jib' and represents the triangular shape cape.
5. Pitcairn-Jones, 1994: 87.
6. Quoted in Pitcairn-Jones, 1994: 131.
7. Kemp, 1994: 64–5.
8. Ryan, 1960: 150/1; Kemp, 1994: 64–5.
9. Most of the shingle has since disappeared, either filling in the anti-tank ditches or for local building projects.

10. Ramsey, 1995: 377.
11. Whitehouse and Bennett, 1995: 21.
12. Delaforce, 1999: 12.
13. Kilvert-Jones, 1999: 9.
14. Delaforce, 1998: 85.
15. Bruce, 1999: 143.
16. Quoted in Ryan, 1960: 183.
17. Badsey, 1994c: 52.
18. Drez, 1996; 62–3; Rhodes-James, 1998.
19. Quoted in Kilvert-Jones, 1999: 42.
20. Ramsay, 1995: 205.
21. Pitcairn-Jones, 1994: 10–12.
22. Norman-French for grove or copse.
23. Colonel Gordon of the 1/7 Queens fired three PIAT projectiles at point
    blank range at a Tiger in Villers-Bocage, just after Michael Wittman's
    attack, but to no avail (Dunphie and Johnson, 1999: 121).
24. Ford, 1999: 58; Lucas, 1998: 80.
25. Cooper, 1998: 11–12.
26. For a contemporary example see Abrashoff, 2002.
27. Cooper, 1998: 44–52.
28. Quoted in Lee, 2006: 66.
29. Quoted in Hastings, 1993a: 43/176.
30. Quoted in Botting, 1978: 59.
31. Quoted in D'Este, 1983: 71.

Chapter 7

1. Wheeler, 1999.
2. Kier, 1997: 7–9.
3. Fraser, 1999: 12.
4. Bruce, 1999: 98.
5. Fraser, 1999: 146.
6. Forty, 1998: 108.
7. Kier, 1997: 114–15.
8. Quoted in Kier, 1997: 114.
9. Fraser, 1999: 15–17.
10. *Reveille*, 9 November 1942.
11. Quoted in Fraser, 1999: 19.
12. Forty, 1998: 5–37.
13. Badsey, 1994a: 284–5.
14. Fraser, 1999: 25–100.
15. Neillands and de Normann, 1993: 20; Sheffield, 1997: 34.
16. D'Este, 1983: 269.
17. Crang, 1997: 71.
18. French, 2000: 133.
19. Badsey, 1994a: 283.
20. Quoted in Ambrose, 1995: 162/185.
21. Quoted in Lewin, 1998: 25.

22. Quoted in Fraser, 1999: 5.
23. Maher, 1996: 113.
24. Quoted in Neillands and de Normann, 1993: 97.
25. Quoted in Delaforce, 1999: 35.
26. Quoted in D'Este, 1983: 272.
27. D'Este, 1983: 275–6.
28. Maher, 1996: 46.
29. Reynolds, 1997: 45–6.
30. As a typical squaddie's 'joke' went, the Americans had brought with them a new form of women's underwear: 'One yank and they're off!' (quoted in Botting, 1978: 116).
31. Channel 4a, 23 August 1999.
32. Botting, 1978: 116; Long, 2000.
33. Quoted in D'Este, 1983: 283.
34. Quoted in Kier, 1997: 130.
35. Quoted in Kier, 1997: 135. The significance of status in the British Army is hard to overstate and is probably best represented by the 'precedence' that governs which regiment should march in front of which in parades. Thus the Household Cavalry always takes precedence over the Royal Armoured Corps (except when the Royal Horse Artillery have their guns on parade). After the RAC comes the Royal Regiment of Artillery, the Corps of Royal Engineers, the Royal Corps of Signals and the last major units – of course, given that in war most of these people are likely to become casualties and thus not be able to parade – are the Infantry regiments. The training for Royal Marine officers depended, as did most others, on whether one's commission was 'Regular' or just for the duration of hostilities ('Hostilities Only'). Hostilities Only officers received five months training, while regular officers received eighteen months training (Bruce, 1999: 121–2).
36. French, 2000: 18–23; 46.
37. Channel 4b, 12 December 1999.
38. Quoted in Kier, 1997: 131.
39. Nor had British officers had much initiative before this. Wellington, for example, refused to allow his generals to design their own operations (Kier, 1997: 149).
40. Quoted in Kier, 1997: 130.
41. Blandford, 1999: 113.
42. Ferguson, 1998: 305–6.
43. Quoted in Forty, 1998: 11.
44. Hobbes, 1999: 164.
45. It is still questionable whether much changed long after the war was over: until 1969 the most senior regiment in the British Army, the Household Cavalry, avoided using what every other 'cavalry' unit had already accepted: the tank (Kier, 1997: 129). In the 1980s an officer commissioned from the ranks was still commonly referred to as 'not a *real* officer'.
46. Hastings, 1993a: 55. The Romans did not appear to have any systematic method for assessing officers other than by experience. Until the end of the second century AD staff officers had to serve a minimum number of years 'in the field' (Peddie, 1994: 4). Most officers tended to come from the

centurions, battlefield veterans for whom the selection policy was much
more rigorous for, according to Polybius: 'Romans look not so much for
the daring or fire-eating type, but rather for men who are natural leaders
and possess a stable and imperturbable temperament; not men who will
open battle and launch attacks, but those who will stand their ground even
when worsted and hard-pressed and die in defence of their posts' (Quoted
in Peddie, 1994; 29).

47. Quoted in Hastings, 1993a: 173.
48. In the First World War roughly equivalent figures were 60 per cent and 98
per cent (Ferguson, 1998: 348).
49. Masters, 1997: 225.
50. Whitehouse and Bennett, 1995: 30.
51. Quoted in Hastings, 1993a: 177, original emphasis.
52. Quoted in Holt and Holt, 1999: 108.
53. Graham, 1999: 159.
54. Whitehouse and Bennett, 1995: 28; Ellis, 1993: 90; Blackburn, 1998:
102. From August 1941, with Soviet collapse assumed to be just weeks
away, Stalin ordered that any Soviet officer found to have removed his or
her insignia could be shot by other members of the officer's unit
(Magenheimer, 1998: 95–6).
55. Forty, 1998: 107.
56. Balkoski, 1999: 219.
57. Balkoski, 1999: 219. The practice of letting attackers past a thinly held
front line (to avoid incurring heavy casualties from an artillery bombardment) and then attacking them from the flanks and rear had become standard German 'defence in depth' in the second half of the First World War
(McManus, 1998: 207).
58. Cooper, 1998: 73.
59. Quoted in Delaforce, 1999: 66.
60. Forty, 1998: 98.
61. Quoted in McManus, 1998: 206.
62. Masters, 1997: 307–8.
63. Quoted in Linderman, 1997: 186.
64. Kier, 1997: 125.
65. Kier, 1997: 126–7.
66. Fraser, 1999: 97–104.
67. Quoted in Kemp, 1994: 143.
68. Graham, 1999: 135.
69. Quoted in Linderman, 1997: 4.
70. Dominick Graham, 1999: 133.
71. Neillands and de Normann.1993: 84.
72. Quoted in Forty, 1998: 296.
73. Quoted in Delaforce, 1999: 104.
74. Graham, 1999: 155.
75. The term 'Commandos' came from the Boer word *Commandos*
(commands) but Churchill's original suggestion in 1940 had been 'storm
troopers'. When this was rejected for obvious reasons Churchill insisted
that they be called 'Special Service' troops. The 'SS' was eventually
dropped – for reasons that should also have been obvious before they were

so labelled by Churchill – in favour of 'Commando'. On 18 October 1942 Hitler's 'Commando Order' ordered that 'All enemies on Commando-type missions, even if they are in uniform, armed or unarmed, in battle or in flight, are to be slaughtered to the last man. If it should be necessary initially to spare one man or two for interrogation then they are to be shot immediately after this is completed'. After the intensification of the air bombing campaign over Germany, Allied aircrews were added to the list and after D-Day paratroopers and US Rangers became candidates for immediate execution (Bruce, 1999: 49; Linderman, 1997: 97; Ramsey, 1995: 515).
76. Bruce, 1999: 13; Delaforce, 1998: 18.
77. Bruce, 1999: 11–37.
78. Kipling, 1999. In 1946 the army Commandos were disbanded and the Royal marines took over all Commando duties (Forty, 1998: 106).
79. Masters, 1997: 114, 272.
80. Masters, 1997.
81. Quoted in Bruce, 1999: 20.
82. Masters, 1997: 248–9.
83. Quoted in Masters, 1997: 51, my emphasis.
84. Masters, 1997: 82.
85. Quoted in Masters, 1997: 63.
86. Masters, 1997: 74–5, 102.
87. Quoted in Masters, 1997: 143.
88. Keegan, 1992: 115–24.
89. Masters, 1997: 82–3.
90. Wright, 1998: 5.
91. Delaforce, 1999: 3.
92. Wright, 1998: 73.
93. English, 1994: 133–6.
94. Rodney, 1994: 470–1.
95. Douglas, 1994: 472.
96. Including Sergeant Josef Franttisek, a Czech fighter pilot with the RAF, shot down the highest individual number of Luftwaffe planes in 1940.
97. Bowyer, 1995: 20.
98. One South African – Adolph Malan – destroyed the highest number of enemy planes of any RAF pilot {27 solo and 10 shared; Johnny Johnson was higher scoring with 34 solo and 7 shared but he also flew for the Canadian RAF as well as the RAF (Freeman, 1998: 86, 96)} (see Somerville, 1998). In fact, the RAF had not encouraged the keeping of 'tallies' of 'kills' until the Americans arrived and brought with them a rugged and competitive individualism that eventually persuaded the RAF to do likewise.
99. Anderson, 1994a: 91.
100. Anderson, 1994b: 387.

Chapter 8

1. Just before D-Day there were 1,526,965 American troops in Britain, as well as over 5 million tons of matériel.

2. Forty, 1995: 1. That meant that everything had to be taken, including £20 million in cash carried by members of the Royal Army Pay Corps (RAPC). The amount of food consumed was also enormous. For example the 53rd (Welsh) Division consumed 6 million rations (14,363 tons of food) in the European campaign of 1944–45 – the equivalent of each soldier eating fourteen times his own bodyweight (Forty, 1998: 134–8).

3. A division – an organizational form first pioneered by the French revolutionary army in 1792 (Parker, 1995: 198) – was the smallest unit capable of operating independently. Each infantry division in the US army (66 of the 89 US divisions existing in 1945 were infantry divisions) comprised – on average – over 15,000 troops plus vehicles and artillery (though the assault divisions on D-Day were much larger). Each division comprised three or perhaps four regiments and each regiment comprised three or sometimes four battalions and various assorted companies (HQ, anti-tank, cannon and service). Each battalion was made up of three or four rifle companies and a heavy weapons company (carrying heavy machine guns and mortars) and totalled around 870 troops in all. A rifle company had three rifle platoons and one weapons platoon (the latter carried the light machine guns and light mortars) and each rifle platoon had three squads, the smallest unit, of twelve soldiers. Squads were divided into a squad leader, a two soldier scouting section, a four-soldier fire section and a five-soldier manoeuvre and assault section (Forty, 1995: 70–1/174). In 1942 a US Airborne division comprised one paratroop and two glider regiments, around 8,500 troops in all. By 1944 the makeup had changed to three paratroop and one glider regiment, around 7,500 troops in all (Ramsey, 1995: 263).

4. Kier, 1997: 22.

5. Balkoski, 1999: 18–21.

6. Eiler, 1997: 100–3.

7. Eiler, 1997.

8. Wright, 1998: 64–6. The typical British Army structure was as follows (though each army and each element therein was somewhat idiosyncratic):

10 soldiers = 1 Squad
30 soldiers = 1 Platoon (3 Squads)
90–120 soldiers = 1 Company (3 or 4 Platoons)
360–800 soldiers = 1 Battalion (4, 5 or 6 Companies + HQ + armour + artillery)
1,080–2,880 soldiers = 1 Brigade (3 or 4 Battalions + HQ + armour + artillery)
10–20,000 soldiers = 1 Division (3 Brigades + HQ +armour + artillery)
Division = 3 brigades = 4,320 soldiers + 3 machine gun battalions (900) + 13,280 service troops. To make total 18,500 troops.

By comparison the 'tail' of Waffen SS units tended to be much smaller, closer to half the size of the British equivalent division (Blandford, 1999: 120–2) Thus a typical British infantry division in 1944 comprised about 18,000 soldiers in total: 8,482 infantry, 6,289 from other combat arms, and 3,576 HQ and services. The division would have three brigades of three battalions, three field artillery regiments, one anti-tank regiment with 17lb guns, a light anti-aircraft regiment with 40mm Bofors guns, an armoured reconnaissance regiment, a machine gun battalion which included 4.2 inch mortars, an engineer regiment, a signals regiment, service corps personnel. Ordnance and electrical engineers (Graham, 1999: 134). Two divisions would typically make up a 'Corps' and two 'Corps' comprised an army. An Army Group combined two armies.

In the US forces a conventional infantry division comprised 15,000 troops in three regiments, each of which had three battalion and each battalion was made up of about six companies with four platoons per company. A company was usually led by a captain and a platoon led by a lieutenant. Each platoon had four squads of a dozen soldiers including a sergeant and a corporal. A typical US armoured division did not comprise just tanks but, normally, three tank battalions (with four platoons in each battalion and four tanks to a platoon, i.e., 48 tanks to a division); three battalions of armoured infantry (infantry carried in half-tracks); three battalions of armoured artillery (self-propelled guns); an armoured cavalry reconnaissance battalion; a tank destroyer battalion; and an armoured engineers' battalion. But the vast majority of divisions in the US army during the Second World War (68 of 91) were infantry. Four of the others were airborne and one was a cavalry division, all of which operated as infantry divisions. In effect 73 of the 91 divisions were infantry (McManus, 1998: 6–7).

9. Eiler, 1997: 297–8.
10. Wilson, 1997: 284–5.
11. The numbers avoiding military service may have been critical in extending the war. For example, Eisenhower claimed that if he had an additional ten divisions in late 1944 he could have ended the war by the end of that year (Eiler, 1997: 404).
12. Eiler, 1997: 397. There were 13 draft classifications:

IA Fit for general military service
IB Fit for limited military service
IC Member of the Armed Forces
ID Student fit for general military service
IE Student fit for limited military service
IIA Deferred for critical civilian work
IIIA Deferred due to dependants
IVA Already served in the armed services
IVB Deferred by law (such as draft officials)
IVC Alien
IVD Minister
IVE Conscientious Objector (there were 42,793 registered; only 5,000 men were imprisoned for failing to register, most of these were Jehovah's Witnesses)
IVF Physically, Mentally or Morally unfit for service (Wright, 1998: 8, 265).

13. Forty, 1995: 188; Wright, 1998: 41.
14. Eiler, 1997: 423; Linderman, 1997: 1.

15. Forty, 1995: 8–11.
16. Cooper, 1998: 243.
17. Linderman, 1997: 44–6. In early 1941 American Divisions had comprised four regiments – as they had done in the First World War – but the 'square division' of 22,000 troops was generally regarded as too immobile for modern warfare and the regular US Army changed to a 'triangular division' of 15,500 troops in three regimental formations in late 1941. Each regiment had three battalions and each battalion had three or four companies composed of three platoons that themselves had three squads. Normally, A,B,C, and D Companies were allotted to the 1st battalion; E,F, G, and H Companies were the 2nd battalion's responsibility; and I, K, L and M Companies were with the 3rd Battalion (no one seems to know why J Company was always omitted) (Balkoski, 1999: 95). In March 1942 the 29th Division also moved to a triangular formation when the 176th Infantry departed (Balkoski, 1999: 24–38).
18. Mets, 1997: 242–3.
19. Linderman, 1997: 187.
20. Quoted in Eiler, 1997: 111.
21. Keegan, 1992: 106.
22. Hastings, 1993a: 60.
23. Ellis, 1990: 228.
24. Eisenhower, 1995a: 19.
25. Ellis, 1990: 229.
26. McManus, 1998: 206.
27. Quoted in McManus, 1998: 207.
28. Quoted in Linderman, 1997: 55.
29. Bruce, 1999: 117.
30. US officers in Europe received a monthly allowance of alcohol that makes my consumption levels seemed positively pathetic: two pints of scotch, one pint of gin, one or two bottles of Cognac, one bottle of Cointreau and one bottle of Champagne. Several young lieutenants assumed the ration was for their entire platoon until put straight by letters in the *Stars and Stripes* (Linderman, 1997: 200). British sailors were allocated one tot of rum per day – that was composed of one third of a gill of rum mixed with two parts water. The drink was known as grog after Admiral Vernon whose nickname was Grogram after his coat. Being drunk on board ship was still a serious offence however, so that, for example, on 24 April 1944 a drunken stoker was arrested and sentenced to six months in jail the following day. Two days later the stoker was back on board because the jail was full and his sentence was commuted to six months loss of leave (Maher, 1996: 22, 99–100). Being drunk was also an offence for British soldiers under the Army Act, as was catching VD and incurring a self-inflicted wound (which is what VD was considered to be) (Lewin, 1998: 39).
31. Masters, 1997: 142.
32. Wright, 1998: 152.
33. Quoted in Linderman, 1997: 195.
34. Quoted in Linderman, 1997: 197.
35. Lindeman, 1997: 198/206.
36. Linderman, 1997: 211.

37. Quoted in Linderman, 1997: 208.
38. Quoted in Eiler, 1997: 459.
39. Freeman, 1998: 166.
40. Quoted in Wright, 1998: 262.
41. Quoted in Eiler, 1997: 133.
42. Quoted in Wright, 1998: 261.
43. Eiler, 1997: 132–7.
44. Quoted in Eiler, 1997: 141.
45. Eiler, 1997: 140–53.
46. Named after 'Roger's Rangers', an irregular unit of raiders in the French and Indian wars, and formed in May 1942 and based on the British Commandos.
47. Quoted in Eiler, 1997: 11.
48. O'Neill, 1994: 582.
49. Wright, 1998: 3.
50. Drez, 1996: 17.
51. Frank Sinatra, perhaps the most famous 4-F, was also one of the most unpopular individuals as far as many combat soldiers were concerned, though their sisters would probably have disagreed. However, Sinatra quickly learned that any continuing popularity required him not to play the hero to the troops and just to sing songs (Linderman, 1997: 317).
52. Wilson 1997: 294.
53. Forty, 1995: 11. American paratroops used black face cream made by Elizabeth Arden (Wright, 1998: 292).
54. Cooper, 1998: 78.
55. French, 2000: 70–1.
56. Drez, 1996: 30.
57. Quoted in Neillands and de Normann, 1993: 45. American rations were divided into five kinds:

    'A' Rations comprised 70 per cent fresh food.
    'B' Rations added canned single items, such as tomatoes and powdered eggs. (By the end of 1941, the dried egg factory in Denison, Texas, was cracking 1.5 million eggs a day. Eisenhower was, coincidentally, born in Denison).
    'C' Rations were canned 'meals' in ten combinations plus crackers, sugar, coffee, jam and the ubiquitous 'SPAM'. In addition C Rations included toilet paper and cigarettes. The cigarettes were often the Lucky Strike with the red bull's eye. The original packet had been green but the green dye was all used for munitions.
    'D' Rations were the emergency bars of 600-calorie chocolate, so hard that you really did need your own teeth to eat them.
    'K' Rations were also complete meals but, unlike 'C' Rations did not need to be heated (Wright, 1998: 26–7).

58. McManus, 1998: 8–13.
59. Eiler, 1997: 104.
60. Cooper, 1998: 56.
61. Whitehouse and Bennett, 1995: 15.
62. Wright, 1998: 20, 25.

63. Goldstein et al, 1994: 50.
64. Quoted in D'Este, 1995: 457.
65. Collier, 1999: 24.
66. Legg, 1994: 5. When a black American soldier was sentenced to death for an 'offence' against a local West Country woman, 10,000 locals petitioned the government for a stay of execution (Blandford, 1999: 53).
67. 250,000 women served in the Auxiliary Territorial Service (ATS) – the replacement for the First World War's Women's Army Auxiliary Corps (WAACs) – primarily in the anti-aircraft units or as drivers, office workers and telephonists and so on. Additionally, another quarter of a million women enrolled in the Civil Defence, the Royal Observer Corps, the Women's Land Army, and the First Aid Nursing Yeomanry. Women were barred from engaging in combat – except for those recruited to the SOE who sent 50 women agents to France. These women circumvented the combat prohibition by enrolling in the First Aid Nursing Yeomanry (FANY) (Forty, 1998: 318–19). In 1999 women were not allowed to serve in combat in the British Army but they were allowed in 'supporting roles'. In today's US forces women are not allowed to serve in tanks but they are allowed to be air force pilots or even join the 'Navy Seals'. The French also women in their air force but not the infantry. The Chinese Army has women generals but they are not allowed to serve in combat. Women are permitted in combat in Canada, the Netherlands, Belgium and Norway. Women in the German Army cannot serve in combat units but can carry arms for self-defence (*Guardian*, 2 July 1999).
68. Balkoski, 1999: 50–2.
69. Lewin, 1998: 169.
70. Quoted in Ambrose, 1995: 131.
71. Quoted in Ambrose, 1995: 136.
72. Ambrose, 1995: 139.
73. Grove, 1994: 48–9.
74. Quoted in Ambrose, 1995: 134. On 25 July 1944, an accidental gas alarm was sounded in the area controlled by the US 3rd Armoured Division in Normandy. That night a vapour was seen escaping from a US decontamination truck and once again the gas alarm was sounded. The result was, to all intents and purposes, pandemonium. General Bradley was horrified at the panic and issued an immediate order forbidding any gas alarms – even if gas was used: 'Any soldier giving the gas alarm, regardless of the circumstances, is to be shot on sight by the closest available soldier' (quoted in Cooper, 1998: 43). In August 1944 Cooper (1998: 85) recalled meeting a German officer who surrendered just before the fall of Paris and revealed the whereabouts of a poison gas depot near Alençon. Anthrax bombs were tested by the British at Porton Down in 1941 and in field tests in 1942 on Gruinard Island in north Scotland and Penclawdd in south Wales (*Guardian*, 21 July 1999). A report in the *Guardian* on 20 August 1999 suggested that at least one British serviceman, RAF mechanic Ronald Maddison, had died in the 1950s after being given 200mg of Sarin at Porton Down.
75. Pitcairn-Jones, 1994: 66.
76. Quoted in Collier, 1999: 124.

77. Hobbes, 1999: 138.
78. The German term was *Schnellboot* (S-Boot) but the Allies called them 'E' for 'Enemy'. They were double the size the British Motor Torpedo Boat or US PT Boat.
79. Including ten officers who were privy to BIGOT secrets. BIGOT was the highest level of secrecy, above 'Top Secret' about Operation Overlord and derived from the reverse letter order of 'To Gib' the imprint placed on all papers provided to people going to Gibraltar in November 1942 to discuss the invasion of North Africa (Breuer, 1995: 172). 'Dead Man's Bay' was the name given to the area in Thomas Hardy's novels on the basis of earlier shipwrecks (Legg, 1994: 40).
80. Small, 1998: 31.
81. Quoted in Kilvert-Jones, 1999: 41.
82. This was not just to protect the Overlord operation – photos of American dead were only allowed to be published after September 1943 and even the first photo of three dead Marines at Tarawa lying in the sand with no sign of their faces or their injuries was regarded by some as 'making a mockery of sacrifice' (quoted in Linderman, 1997: 328).
83. Small, 1999: 14. *Secret History: D-Day Disaster*, Channel 4, 27 July 1998.
84. Hastings, 1993a: 60.
85. Quoted in Eiler, 1997: 107.
86. Wright, 1998: 147–9.
87. Mitchell, 1997: 313.
88. The lifespan of a lieutenant was probably even shorter than that of a rifle-man. In the ETO it was estimated at around one month in combat (Linderman, 1997: 30). Even that was long compared to the 24 hours life expectancy of a Soviet private during the battle of Stalingrad (Channel 4: 'The War of the Century', 19 October 1999). The response of many similarly despised groups is to increase the issue that generates the contempt, thus animal slaughterers insist on wearing blood stained overalls when drinking after work and adopt bloodspots for hobbies (Ackroyd and Crowdy, 1990: 3–12). Similarly, the 'untouchables' who clean the streets of Benares now Varanasi (Searle-Chatterjee, 1979).
89. Quoted in Collier, 1999: 60.
90. Quoted in Linderman, 1997: 238.
91. See Grint and Case, 1998.
92. Quoted in Ellis, 1990: 335–6.
93. Balkoski, 1999: 225–7.
94. Quoted in Kilvert Jones, 1999: 85.
95. Quoted in Mitchell, 1997: 310.
96. Balkoski, 1999: 223.
97. Man, 1994: 50. In 1942 five Sullivan brothers died after their warship, the *Juneau* was sunk and it became US policy to split family members up to prevent such a recurrence. However, Company A of the 116th Regiment suffered 90 per cent casualties and had 22 deaths from one village, Bedford, Virginia, including three sets of brothers. The closest case to the fictional Private Ryan was that of the Niland family from Buffalo, New York, who had three brothers in Normandy and one in Burma, as well as two cousins, one of whom jumped over St Mère-Eglise. Fritz Niland

(101st Airborne) was asked to identify a dead brother and discovered that it was not the one he expected to find and he had, therefore, lost both brothers (Sergeant Robert Niland, 506th PIR, 82nd Airborne and Lt Preston Niland, 22nd Infantry, 4th Division). The cousin in Burma (who had gone to school with Charles Deglopper, winner of the Medal of Honour at La Fière bridge) was declared missing and Fritz Niland was withdrawn from active service. His cousin was eventually discovered to have been taken prisoner and survived the war (Bremner, 1998: 50–1; Holt and Holt, 1999: 110). There was a 'real' Private Ryan involved in D-Day in the shape of Private Jim Ryan, a tank driver with the Westminster Dragoons who landed on Sword Beach. His story is captured in the video *The True Story of Private Ryan* (Paradox Films). The Niland brothers are buried in the US Military Cemetery overlooking Omaha Beach (plot F, row 15, No. 11 & 12), as are 38 other pairs of brothers and a father and son (the Reeds, plot E, row 20, No. 19 & 20). In total there are 9,286 bodies in the cemetery, 307 are unknown and four are women, killed on active service in the Red Cross and the Woman's Auxiliary Corps (Holt and Holt, 1999: 116).

98. Quoted in Kilvert-Jones, 1999: 47.
99. McManus, 1998: 266.
100. Quoted in Delaforce, 1999: 36.
101. Quoted in Ambrose, 1995: 471.
102. Quoted in McManus, 1998: 124–5.
103. Quoted in Ambrose, 1995: 143.
104. Quoted in Collier, 1999: 128.
105. Ambrose, 1995: 160;Drez, 1996: 28.
106. Quoted in Ambrose, 1995: 49. Freud's assertion about the cause of heroism is similarly developed: 'No instinct we possess is ready for a belief in [our own] death. This is perhaps the secret of heroism' (quoted in Ferguson, 1998: 365).
107. See Grint, 1995.
108. The rituals were many and varied, with bomber crews making a particularly superstitious group, though the rituals were often counterpoised: some groups went out of their way to arrange dates for the evening after a raid, while others openly spoke of their imminent deaths – so as not to court fate. One B-29 crew of 11 in the Pacific theatre insisted that all 11 crew members wore identical hats on each mission (Linderman, 1997: 68). When Brendan Maher joined the British navy as a Royal Naval Volunteer Reserve in 1942 his auntie sent a whole box of assorted crucifixes, rosary beads, medals and so on – enough to equip the whole of Maher's hutmates (Maher, 1996: 17).
109. Quoted in Linderman, 1997: 85.
110. Quoted in Drez, 1996: 187.
111. Quoted in Delaforce, 1999: 108.
112. Linderman, 1997: 87–9.
113. In the summer of 1942 the US Army introduced V-mail, a system for reducing the standard 8.5 x 11 inch letters to a 16mm film for transmission, when they were enlarged to a 4 x 6 inch format. The technique reduced the weight of 2,575lbs of mail to just 45lbs. Between that summer

and September 1944, 790 million V-mails were sent (Linderman, 1997: 390; Wright, 1998: 152).
114. Quoted in Linderman, 1997: 276.
115. Quoted in Linderman, 1997: 289.
116. *Reveille*, 16 March 1942. *Reveille* was a fortnightly services newspaper founded in May 1940. Examples can be seen in *Union Jack* (London: HMSO/ Imperial War Museum).
117. McManus, 1998: 183.
118. Quoted in McManus, 1998: 189.
119. Quoted in Bolkoski, 1999: 65.
120. Quoted in Balkoski, 1999: 218–19.
121. Indeed, Patton was close to Churchill in his assumption that the war against Germany was just the opening act of the next war against the USSR.
122. Quoted in Collier, 1999: 73.
123. Quoted in Balkoski, 1999: 63.
124. Quoted in Linderman, 1997: 49.
125. Quoted in Linderman, 1997: 52.

Chapter 9

1. Three forms of SS unit existed:

   Reichsdeutsche divisions for those born inside the 1938 borders and whose units had the prefix *Jäger* or *Panzer*
   Freiwillige (volunteer) divisions for Germans born outside the borders
   Waffen (weapons) for foreign volunteers (Lucas, 1998: 10–11).

2. Macksey, 1996: 79. On the other hand, the decision to halt the assault upon Dunkirk for 48 hours in May 1940 was taken by von Rundstedt and confirmed by Hitler (Macksey, 1996: 89).
3. Quoted in Macksey, 1996: 132.
4. Badsey, 1994a: 283.
5. Salewski, 1994: 270–2.
6. Kier, 1997: 13–14.
7. Ambrose, 1993: 218.
8. Fraser, 1999: 100.
9. Balkoski, 1999: 80–2, 96.
10. Macksey, 1996: 192.
11. Quoted in Blandford, 1999: 130.
12. Williamson, 1999: 45.
13. Emphasis in original.
14. Quoted in Man, 1994: 95.
15. Church, 2000: 8–10.
16. Hastings, 1993a: 370.
17. Ambrose, 1995: 52–3. One of the (many) reasons why Montgomery incurred the wrath of the Americans was his claim, after the Battle of the Bulge, that he had 'employed the whole power of the British Group of

armies' to successfully counter the German advance. In fact this was a semantic confusion: the group of two American divisions was under Montgomery's control but there were precious few British troops involved, as can be gleaned by a comparison of the casualties from the battle: over 75,500 American and just 1,408 British (Neillands, 1996: 44).

18. Dupuy, 1977: 328–32.
19. Quoted in Blandford, 1999: 49–50.
20. Reynolds, 1997: 1.
21. Reynolds, 1999: 18.
22. Macksey, 1996: 77; Reynolds, 1999: 6.
23. Reynolds, 1999: 1–32.
24. Quoted in Reynolds, 1997: 12.
25. Reynolds, 1997: 16/22.
26. Williamson, 1999: 150.
27. Reynolds, 1999: 14.
28. Reynolds, 1999: 15.
29. Reynolds, 1997: 19.
30. See Santosuosso, 1997.
31. Quoted in Reynolds, 1997: 20.
32. Quoted in Blandford, 1999: 50.
33. Kier, 1997: 30.
34. Reynolds, 1999: 14.
35. Williamson, 1999: 48.
36. Macksey, 1996: 32–3.
37. Quoted in Holborn, 1986: 289.
38. Quoted in Holborn, 1986: 291.
39. Quoted in Kier, 1997: 153.
40. Kier, 1997: 150–1.
41. Lucas, 1998: 25.
42. Murray, 1995: 323.
43. Quoted in Linderman, 1997: 53.
44. Quoted in D'Este, 1983: 281.
45. French, 2000: 58–9.
46. Quoted in Kier, 1997: 150.
47. Quoted in French, 2000: 45. Dill became Chief of the General Staff in 1940.
48. Schweppenburg, 1999: 411.
49. Lucas, 1998: 23–4.
50. Lucas, 1998: 3–4.
51. Ironically, the Israeli Army adopted the training methods that replicated some aspects of the training provided for the SS: minimal square bashing and maximum effort devoted to combat skills and inducing a martial spirit (Luttwak and Horowitz, 1975).
52. Reynolds, 1997: 34.
53. SS atrocities against Jews, Poles, Russians and anyone else regarded as non-Aryan were commonplace but they were also frequent against the troops of the Western Allies. On 7 June 1944, 23 captured Canadians were executed by the 25th SS *Panzergrenadier* Regiment of the 12th SS *HJ* Panzer Division under Kurt Meyer at Buron, north-west of Caen. In

December 1945 the commanding officer of the 25th, Kurt Meyer, was sentenced to death by a Canadian Military Court Martial; the sentence was subsequently commuted to life imprisonment. Meyer was released in 1954 and died in 1961 (Neillands and de Normann, 1993: 303). But atrocities against such troops long pre-dated the Normandy campaign. On 26 May 1940 units of the SS *Totenkopf* executed around 100 POWs from the Royal Norfolk Regiment at Le Paradis near Dunkirk. On 28 May, 80 British POWs were murdered by units from the SS *Leibstandarte* at Wormhoudt. Just over four years later, during the Ardennes Offensive, a number (between 20 and 120) of American POWs were executed by the same SS division at Malmédy (Williamson, 1996: 56–8; 241–2). This one event seems to have hardened many Americans against the Germans in general and the SS in particular. As Harold Leinbaugh commented: 'the Germans had committed their worst mistake of the war on the western front. We had fought by rules ... . In the heat of battle prisoners were sometimes killed. We knew that. But this was mass murder, and the SS was going to have to pay and pay heavily' (quoted in Linderman, 1997: 138).

54. Quoted in Hastings, 1993a: 212.
55. Keegan, 1992: 64.
56. Förster, 1997: 265–6.
57. Schulte, 1997: 282.
58. Wright, 1998: 191.
59. The Soviet attack on Berlin was extremely costly. Zhukov, the Soviet commander, had already experienced 30,000 Soviet dead and 700 tanks in the four day assault upon Seelow, just to the east of Berlin which ended on 18 April. For ten days between 20 and 30 April the Soviet Army forced its way into Berlin. Under fire from between 100,000 and 300,000 defenders, including children as young as seven firing *Panzerfausts*, the Soviet Army lost almost one third of its assault force – 300,000 of 1 million, including 100,000 dead, as well as half of its tanks (2,000 of the 4,000 it started with), in addition to 527 planes. Berlin surrendered formally on May 2 (Grabsky, 1993: 182–4). Thus in the last weeks of the war Zhukov's forces alone suffered, on average, almost 10,000 dead each day.
60. Cooper, 1998: 287–8.
61. Ambrose, 1995: 33. The Luftwaffe did not have an R&R policy in the Battle of Britain – unlike the RAF – and German pilots were expected to fly until they died, got killed, or got promoted. This contributed to *Kanalkrankheit* – Channel Sickness – a complaint of fatigue, cramps and sickness common towards the end of the Battle (Robinson, 2005: 167).
62. Goldstein et al., 1994: 18–19.
63. Schweppenburg, 1999: 412.
64. Masters, 1997: 180.
65. Quoted in Badsey, 1994c: 159.
66. Ryan (1960: 180–1) quotes the account of Edward Ashworth, a British sailor, who on landing his LCT on Juno beach decided to secure a German helmet for a souvenir. He followed six German prisoners being led over the sand dunes by some Canadian troops and when he reached the Germans found them all with their throats slashed. Jean Paul Pallud claims that executions of enemy troops, particularly by American Airborne troops was

common in the early part of the Normandy campaign. For instance, he
claims that 25 German and Georgian POWs were executed by members of
the 502nd PIR at Herguerie on June 6. On 8 June armoured cars from C
squadron the Inns of Court, captured ten officers from the *Panzer Lehr*
artillery regiment and ordered them to walk in front of the vehicles as
human shields. When they refused the senior officer, Luxemburger was
beaten and tied to the front of one of the cars, the rest – except Major
Zeisler who escaped – were executed. When the cars tried to return to their
lines they were shot at by anti-tank guns of the 12th SS Panzer Division
HJ, who freed Luxemburger, though he died ten days later. On the same
day as Luxemburger's capture and release the 12th SS HJ executed 20
Allied prisoners at Audrieu for which Kurt Meyer was convicted. Three
other Canadian prisoners were executed on June 9 at Putot by 26th SS
Panzergrenadier Regiment after another of the 'executed' *Panzer Lehr*
officers managed to escape after the shooting. Two officers of the
Regiment were tried and executed for the murder in January 1949
(Ramsey, 1995: 624–5).

67. Gale, 1995: 240.
68. Ramsey, 1995: 308.
79. Delaforce, 1998: 97.
70. Quoted in Kilvert-Jones, 1999: 133.
71. Messenger, 1994b: 502; Shilleto, 1999: 38. Louis Renault proved himself
    a keen collaborator by retooling his car plant to build tanks for the
    Germans. Renault died in prison in 1946 awaiting trial for treason and
    Renault was nationalized by the French government (Harvey, 1994:
    259–60).
72. Badsey, 1994c: 110. Even the SS had numerous non-German units includ-
    ing at least one each from the Netherlands, Belgium, Denmark, Norway,
    Finland, India, an International Division, Croatia, Bosnia, Ukraine, Latvia,
    Hungary, Estonia, Albania, Italy, Belorussia, Czechoslovakia, France and
    Spain. In addition around 100 Swedes volunteered for the SS as did 60
    British citizens. The latter made up the 'British Free Corps' of ex-POWs
    led by John Amery, the son of a British minister in Churchill's government
    (Williamson, 1996: 107–39).
73. Blandford, 1999: 15.
74. Shilleto, 1999: 38.
75. Carell, 1995: 10.
76. Man, 1994: 47. Bedell Smith, 1995: 30.
77. Keegan, 1992: 131.
78. The photographer Robert Capa of *Life* magazine was attached to this
    company.
79. Neillands and de Normann, 1993: 32.
80. The average age in the naval batteries in Normandy was however, hardly
    youthful, at 45 and there was even one 56-year-old in uniform (Carell,
    1995: 21).
81. Mitcham, 1994a.
82. Holt and Holt, 1999: 193.
83. Marcks was killed by an Allied aircraft on 12 June 1944 near St Lô.
84. Kilvert-Jones, 1999: 67.

85. Quoted in Balkoski, 1999: 67.
86. Ryan, 1960: 153.
87. Balkoski, 1999: 71.
88. Balkoski, 1999: 100.
89. Kilvert-Jones, 1999: 69. The majority of the 2,041 enemy prisoners captured by the Allies on the first day of Operation Dragoon, the invasion of southern France in August 1944, were of Polish origin (Westall, 1994: 38).
90. The two remaining battalions of the *Kampfgruppe* were not deployed from the position where they had halted at 0550 until 0835. Kraisse, assuming that the Omaha landings were repulsed, sent them both to Gold beach, fifteen miles away, to halt the British attacks. By the time they arrived it was afternoon and, once again, too late. Thus even though Cota's troops had taken Vierville at about 1100 Kraisse was not informed until late afternoon. Indeed his penultimate reserves, the 620 troops of the 352nd Engineer Battalion were not deployed towards St Laurent until 1825. The last group, 625 soldiers of the *Feldbataillon* (replacement battalion) reached the coast the following morning. On 7 June only one more battalion of German reinforcements arrived to support Kraisse, from the 30th *Schnelle* (Mobile) Brigade. Balkoski, 1999: 75, 148–9.
91. Lewin, 1998: 197.
92. Quoted in Ambrose, 1995: 357.
93. Whitehouse and Bennett, 1997:104.
94. Drez, 1996: 185.

Chapter 10

1. Doughty, 1994: 79.
2. Fraser, 1999: 321–2.
3. Macksey, 1996: 201.
4. Badsey, 1994c: 255/77.
5. Badsey, 1990: 25.
6. Quoted in Ambrose, 1995: 25.
7. Balkoski, 1999: 227.
8. In the 1920s an American report suggested that the 1914–18 war had generated 23,000 new millionaires. Even amongst ordinary working people the war provided an economic feast: in 1917, when US soldiers earned $1 a day in France, American shipyard workers were earning $18 a day (Eiler, 1997: 306).
9. Eiler, 1997: 468; Wright, 1998: 37.
10. Quoted in Eiler, 1997: 44.
11. Eiler, 1997: 59–60.
12. O'Neill, 1994: 581.
13. Eiler, 1997: 311. Over $7.5 billion was 'renegotiated' back to the Treasury (Eiler, 1997: 325).
14. Wright, 1998: 226.
15. Eiler, 1997: 170, 291.
16. Eiler, 1997: 370.

17. Quoted in Linderman, 1997: 336.
18. Badsey, 1994a: 283.
19. Eiler, 1997: 374/424.
20. Wright, 1998: 37.
21. Eiler, 1997: 198.
22. Eiler, 1997: 188.
23. Eiler, 1997: 334–5.
24. Wright, 1998: 38. There were actually two such Rosies. One was Rosie B. Bonavita, a riveter who built Grumman Avenger aircraft. The other was Rose Will Monroe, a riveter who built B-24 and B-29 aircraft at Ford's Willow Run plant in Michigan. Rose posed with the polka dot bandanna in the 'We Can Do IT!' adverts. She died in 1997 (Wright, 1998: 39).
25. Wright, 1998: 58–62.
26. Wright, 1998: 60.
27. Eiler, 1997: 268, 275.
28. Collier, 1999: 26.
29. Graham, 1999: 137.
30. Ambrose, 1995: 57; Keegan, 1995: 98.
31. Forty, 1995: 22.
32. Doughty, 1994: 19.
33. Quoted in Botting, 1978: 50.
34. Botting, 1978: 66–75.
35. Lewin, 1998: 167; Badsey, 1994c: 28; Ross, 1997: 105.
36. Goldstein at al., 1994: 50.
37. Quoted in Pitcairn-Jones, 1994: 72.
38. Quoted in Collier, 1999: 128.
39. Turkel, 1984: 256; Whitehouse and Bennett, 1995: 15.
40. Harper, 1997: 45.
41. Forty, 1995: 49–50.
42. Ryan, 1960: 82.
43. Bedell Smith, 1995: 31.
44. Much to de Gaulle's disgust; he publicly branded it 'counterfeit' even though it had been printed in 1938 and was outraged when Roosevelt informed him that a military government would control France immediately after the war and introduce a new currency (Montgomery, 1995: 126).
45. Only the 101st Airborne troops, and not those of the 85nd Airborne, were issued with 'crickets'. Bizarrely, the 85th Airborne had used them in Sicily and Italy and suffered from the rather obvious problem: they gave away the holder's position. In consequence the 85th used the password 'Flash' and the countersign 'Thunder' (Ramsey, 1995: 308).
46. Ambrose, 1995: 153/191; Goldstein et al., 1994: 48; Kemp, 1994: 151.
47. Keegan, 1992: 85.
48. Drez, 1996: 129. So cumbersome and novel was the equipment that some paratroopers waited until the D-Day flight across the channel to discover not only that a fully equipped paratrooper could not squeeze through the rear door of the glider to the toilet but that it was impossible to undo one's uniform sufficiently to use the bucket that was passed round when the door problem was discovered (Ridgway, 1995: 263).

49. Doughty, 1994: 34.
50. Doughty, 1994: 54.
51. Doughty, 1994: 51; Ramsay, 1995: 181.
52. Allegedly from combining parts of the names of the original designers: Mr Hammick of the Iraq Petroleum Company and Mr Ellis of the Burmah Oil Company (Holt and Holt, 1999: 143).
53. Legg, 1994: 34.
54. Neillands and de Normann, 1993: 74. British fuel cans were notoriously poor, sometimes leaking up to 30 per cent of their contents in transit. The German 20-litre (4.5-gallon) 'Jerry Can' was much more robust and keenly treasured by the Allied forces (Forty, 1998: 110).
55. Turner, 1994: 35.
56. Leigh-Mallory, 1995: 615.
57. Wootten, 1994: 425.
58. Cooper, 1998: 89.
59. Montgomery was not an admirer of Mountbatten. He was, in Montgomery's eyes, 'a very gallant sailor. Had three ships sunk under him. *Three* ships sunk under him. [Pause]. Doesn't know how to fight a battle' (quoted in D'Este, 1983: 21).
60. Delaforce, 1998: 18.
61. Tracy, 1998: 358–9.
62. Quoted in Ramsey, 1995: 196. Eventually the British Mulberry became known as Port Winston.
63. Collier, 1999: 44.
64. Collier, 1999: 43.
65. Turner, 1994: 30.
66. Hickling, 1995; 582–3.
67. Ramsay, 1995: 197.
68. Quoted in Collier, 1999: 52.
69. Collier, 1999: 45. At one time there was even a plan for an artificial breakwater comprising a wall on air bubbles (Botting, 1978: 47).
70. Ramsey, 1995: 586.
71. Bruce, 1999: 169–72.
72. Ramsey, 1995: 197.
73. One of the popular rumours at the time was that they were giant supports for enormous submarine traps (Doughty, 1994: 41).
74. Quoted in Collier, 1999: 46.
75. Ryan, 1960: 51.
76. Pitcairn-Jones, 1994: 30/68.
77. Ramsey, 1995: 583–4.
78. Bruce, 1999: 176.
79. Hickling, 1995: 581, 593/607.
80. Ramsey, 1995: 602–3.
81. Bruce, 1999: 179.
82. Keegan, 1992: 163.
83. Quoted in Bruce, 1999: 148.
84. Doughty, 1994: 45.
85. Quoted in Collier, 1999: 49.
86. Badsey, 2006: 52–3.

87. Botting, 1978: 48; Neillands and de Normann, 1993: 67.

88. Lewin, 1998: 176.

89. Neillands and de Normann, 1993: 71; Turner, 1994: 54.

90. Doughty, 1994: 97; Pitcairn-Jones, 1994: 51. Kilvert-Jones, 1999: 40, puts the number at 278.

91. Neillands and de Normann, 1993: 69; Turner, 1994: 54/71.

92. Bruce, 1999: 105.

93. Hall, 1994b: 356–7.

94. Ramsey, 1995: 208.

95. Doughty, 1994: 84.

96. Bruce, 1999: 65.

97. Quoted in Ambrose, 1995: 173.

98. Neillands and de Normann, 1993: 232. Some soldiers had the same opinion about what the British call military 'bullshit' and the Americans' 'chickenshit': it was intended to so frustrate a soldier that battle was preferable to parades, marching, drilling and endless cleaning of boots.

99. Quoted in McManus, 1998: 57.

100. Bruce, 1999: 37, 64.

101. Legg, 1994: 28.

102. Bruce, 1999: 151.

103. The term 'Flak' originated in the German word for anti-aircraft gun (*Flugabwehrkanone*) (Bruce, 1999:71).

104. Neillands and de Normann, 1993: 69–70.

105. Legg, 1994: 102.

106. Quoted in Steinberg, 1998: 106.

107. The earliest known amphibious craft was the 'amphibious battle wagon' designed by Agostino Ramelli (1531–1600). Several amphibious military vehicles were tested by the British and American forces in the 1920s, including an amphibious tank, the British 'Johnson Light Infantry Tank' in 1922 and Christie's two US models (*Wheels and Tracks*, No. 24, 1988: 53–4).

108. Bruce, 1999: 200, 273.

109. Steinberg, 1998: 104–19.

110. *Parade* was an illustrated weekly published by British troops for British troops from August 1940 until February 1948. Examples can be seen in *Union Jack* (London: HMSO / Imperial War Museum).

111. Quoted in Campbell, 1988: 35.

112. Parker, 1995: 335.

113. Kilvert-Jones, 1999: 76.

114. Quoted in Balkoski, 1999: 124.

115. *Wheels and Tracks*, No. 24, 1988: 26–7.

116. Bruce, 1999: 185.

117. Pitcairn-Jones, 1994: 81.

118. Pitcairn-Jones, 1994: 80.

119. Maher, 1996: 77–115.

120. Quoted in Maher, 1996: 120. In 1974 when Ken Small (1999: 95) tried to raise a DD Sherman that had sunk off Slapton Sands in 1944, he was informed by the US authorities – the Defence Supply Agency – that even though the tank had been in 60 feet of water for 30 years they did not consider it abandoned!

121. Maher, 1996: 41–3.
122. Turner, 1994: 42/71; 190–1.
123. The captain of the E-boat that sank the *Svenner*, Korvettenkapitän Hoffman, was awarded the Knight's Cross for his action. The USS *Corry* was sunk by an acoustic 'Oyster mine' off Utah Beach.
124. Carell, 1995: 81.
125. Pitcairn-Jones, 1994: 44.
126. Braddon, 1956: 150.
127. Quoted in Pitcairn-Jones, 1994: 129.
128. Lloyd-Owen, 1994: 4–5/10.

Chapter 11

1. Quoted in Delaforce, 1998: 15.
2. 449 Neillands and de Normann, 1993: 156–7; Turner, 1994: 37.
3. Ambrose, 1995: 143; Forty, 1995: 52; Fowle, 1994: 216.
4. Fowle, 1994: 215–16.
5. Neillands and de Normann, 1993: 193.
6. Ramsey, 1995: 353.
7. Pitcairn-Jones, 1994: 107.
8. Harper Group, 1997: 38; Neillands and de Normann, 1993: 33–4.
9. Ramsey, 1995: 527.
10. Delaforce, 1999: 53.
11. Balkoski, 1999: 94–5.
12. Ramsey, 1995: 386.
13. When Hobart was asked to meet Churchill the former first of all refused to go – unless he was reinstated – and then asked whether he should 'come dressed as a civilian, as a Major-General of the British Army or as a Corporal in the Home Guard?' When Churchill did meet Hobart the Prime Minister said to General Dill, 'Remember it isn't only the good boys who help to win wars. It is the sneaks and the stinkers as well!' (quoted in Delaforce, 1998: 54).
14. Quoted in Delaforce, 1998: 57.
15. Botting, 1978: 48, 153.
16. Younger, 1994: 218.
17. Quoted in Delaforce, 1998: 74. The Germans had designed and built a 130-ton mine destroying vehicle that was 50 feet long, 13 feet tall and impervious to the mines its weight detonated as it rolled over them (Russell, 1981: 183).
18. Cooper, 1998: 126.
19. Bruce, 1999: 134.
20. Carell, 1995: 86. In the invasion of southern France, Operation Dragoon, on 15 August 1944, the problem of rocket firing landing craft was partially resolved by the introduction of 'Woofus' craft which fired their rocket in ranks rather than in one total and simultaneous blow (Westall, 1994: 21).
21. Macksey, 1994: 72.
22. Quoted in Delaforce, 1998: 80.
23. Ford, 1999: 78.

24. Delaforce, 1998: 68–9.
25. Gander, 1999: 118. The USSR even developed a tank designed to glide to its destination. A variant of the T-26 had wings and a tail unit (Gander, 1999: 129).
26. Delaforce, 1998: 24.
27. Macksey, 1996: 96.
28. Turner, 1994: 33.
29. Gander, 1999: 196–7.
30. Small, 1999: 128.
31. Neillands and de Normann, 1993: 50.
32. Delaforce, 1998: 67.
33. Holt and Holt, 1999: 190.
34. Quoted in Pitcairn-Jones, 1994: 90.
35. Quoted in Ramsey, 1995: 457.
36. Quoted in Ramsey, 1995: 478.
37. Turner, 1994: 143–5.
38. Balkoski, 1999: 124.
39. Ambrose, 1995: 270–4, 362–3.
40. Compare Ambrose (1995: 511) with Neillands and de Normann, 1993: 193 and Turner, 1994: 121.
41. Ramsey, 1995: 342.
42. Botting, 1978: 134.
43. Quoted in Pitcairn-Jones, 1994: 90.
44. Pitcairn-Jones, 1994: 80.
45. In 1918 the Allies had 800 tanks in the field, the Germans only 20 (Ferguson, 1998: 290).
46. Davidson and Levy, 1996: 70–2.
47. Hastings, 1993a: 226–7. When Germany's tank ace, Michael Wittmann (credited with destroying 138 enemy tanks and 132 anti-tank guns) arrived in Villers-Bocage, 15 miles south-west of Caen on 13 June his Tiger tanks destroyed 27 Allied tanks for the loss of two Tigers in a single day (Badsey, 1994c; 150; Veranov, 1998: 503).
48. Fletcher, 2000.
49. Cf. Buckley, 2006a: 85.
50. Copp, 1997: 153; Reynolds, 1997: 24.
51. Quoted in Linderman, 1997: 25.
52. Cooper, 1998: 176, 198.
53. Quoted in Delaforce, 1999: 37.
54. Ford, 1999: 7.
55. Quoted in Forty, 1998: 3.
56. Forty, 1998: 68.
57. Forty, 1998: 108.
58. French, 2000.
59. Quoted in Graham, 1999: 79.
60. Quoted in Blandford, 1999: 262.
61. Quoted in Blandford, 1999: 262.
62. Forty, 1998: 68–9.
63. Blandford, 1999: 6.
64. Graham, 1999: 82.

65. Graham, 1999: 82.
66. Quoted in the *Crusader: Eighth Army Weekly*, Vol.2, No. 22. *Crusader*, the Eighth Army weekly was founded in May 1942. Examples can be seen in *Union Jack* (London: HMSO/Imperial War Museum).
67. Gudgin, 1997: 75.
68. Fraser, 1999: 88.
69. Quoted in Delaforce, 1998: 29.
70. Quoted in Delaforce, 1998: 32.
71. Quoted in Hastings, 1993a: 225.
72. Delaforce, 1998: 47.
73. Quoted in Reynolds, 1997: 25.
74. Ford, 1999; Hastings, 1993a: 225; Neillands and de Normann, 1993: 54. Forty (1998: 213) suggests the gun was in production in August 1942.
75. Sabot (from the old French word for a shoe made from a single block of wood) ammunition employed a 'soft' dumbbell outer case which shattered on firing but filled the barrel thus adding impetus to the tungsten-carbide core projectile. The Imperial War Museum suggests that the muzzle velocity of Sabot ammunition was approximately 3,950 feet per second, twice that of the conventionally gunned Sherman with almost four times the penetrative power. Even the King Tiger's armoured protection was allegedly inadequate against it (Blackburn, 1998: 213 and Appendix C). Nonetheless, several shots from a firefly failed to penetrate the armoured cupola at 'Hillman' behind Sword beach on D-Day (Ramsey, 1995: 555).
76. D'Este, 1983: 17.
77. Quoted in Blandford, 1999: 263.
78. Forty, 1995: 39/43.
79. Blandford, 1999: 123.
80. Graham, 1999: 5.
81. Gudgin, 1997: 139–40.
82. Cooper, 1998: 20.
83. Christie went on to ever more radical designs, culminating in a flying tank with demountable wings (Ford, 1999: 10).
84. Macksey, 1996: 80.
85. Ford, 1999. M4s had welded upper hulls; M4A1s had cast upper hulls; M42As were the diesel variants, used primarily by the Soviet and British forces (Ford, 1999).
86. Gudgin, 1997.
87. Overy, 1995: 332.
88. Turner, 1994: 33.
89. Forty, 1998.
90. Forty, 1995: 134.
91. The M26 Pershing had 102mm of armour, a 90mm gun and a faster engine – but it was still regarded by many of its users as inferior to the German Tiger (McManus, 1998: 37). However, the M26A1E2 Super Pershing weighing 53 tons and carrying a 90mm gun with a very long barrel, generating a shot velocity of 3,850 feet per second. This was 600 feet per second faster than a King Tiger and meant that the US gun could penetrate 13 inches of armour at 100 yards. The Super Pershing did eventually enter the war, though only two made it to Europe before peace was

declared and even then additional armour was added to protect it from German attack (Cooper, 1988: 198, 267).

92. Quoted in Linderman, 1997: 26.
93. Quoted in McManus, 1998: 36.
94. Ellis, 1993: 154.
95. Quoted in Delaforce, 1999: 38.
96. Cooper (1998: 68) describes how skilled welders could cut the end of the 'offending' shell and weld it back into the hole it had made in the tank.
97. Cooper, 1998: 111.
98. Cooper, 1998: 25; Ford, 1999: 55.
99. Cooper, 1998: 295–6.
100. Gander, 1999: 26.
101. Cooper, 1998: 303.
102. Delaforce, 1999: 78.
103. Ford, 1999: 30.
104. Ford, 1999.
105. Cooper, 1998: 153.
106. Cooper, 1998: 23–5, 90–1.
107. Cooper, 1998: 166.
108. Mitchell, 1997: 307.
109. Quoted in Lofgren, 1994: 4.
110. Cooper, 1998: 28.
111. Quoted in Green, 1955: 285–6.
112. Green, 1955: 287–8.
113. Gander, 1995; Ford, 1999.
114. Cooper, 1998: 229.
115. Quoted in Baily, 1983: 1.
116. Quoted in Lofgren, 1994: 1.
117. Quoted in Hobbes, 1999: 102.
118. Ford, 1999: 91; Gudgin, 1997: 90.
119. Baily, 1983: 3–7.
120. Quoted in Ambrose, 1995: 264. Rodney's 16-inch guns fired a shell weighing over one ton over 20 miles (Ramsey, 1995: 521). German large artillery was also powerful and accurate. During the battle of Aachen in September 1944, Lt Cooper's 3rd (US) Armoured Division found itself under attack from a 210mm railway howitzer, stationed at Eschweiler eight miles away. The gun fired three rounds which left three overlapping 50-foot-wide craters (Cooper, 1998: 133).
121. Ambrose, 1995: 270. In Operation Dragoon, the invasion of the south of France on 15 August 1944, the naval gunfire was better directed and co-ordinated in some areas to produce a walking barrage that preceded and protected the advancing troops. Even then some of the gun emplacements withstood tremendous attack. For example, the St Mandrier forts that guard Toulon were bombarded on 25 August with almost 2,500 heavy naval shells from the ten strong battle group of battleships and cruisers – but to little effect. On the following day a further 2,000 shells were fired in the space of three hours but still the fort refused to surrender. On 27 August the British battleship *Ramillies* fired 48 shells at the fort, 34 landing within 50 yards of the target and the following day the fort surrendered with 2,000 troops. On

inspection it was found that despite over 4,500 shells, one of the two 13.4 inch guns was still operational and that most of the troops had remained perfectly safe deep underground (Westall, 1994: 23/49–50).

122. Quoted in Blandford, 1999: 13.
123. Quoted in Blandford, 1999: 14.
124. Ferguson, 1998: 308.
125. Neillands and de Normann, 1993: 242.
126. Keegan, 1992: 135.
127. Badsey, 1994c: 120; Man, 1994: 65.
128. Ryan, 1960: 182. The DD were not especially successful in Operation Dragoon to invade the south of France either. On Delta Beach, 7 of the 12 used were blown up by mines, even though general losses were extremely light (Westall, 1994: 24).
129. Balkoski, 1999: 104–5. The Germans had relied upon horse drawn equipment in the First World War too: in 1918 the Germans had 30,000 motorised vehicles with wooden or steel 'tyres'; the Allied forces had 100,000 motorised vehicles with rubber tyres (Ferguson, 1998: 290).
130. Copp, 1997: 154.
131. Cooper, 1998: 190–2.
132. Mets, 1997: 251.
133. Dunphie and Johnson, 1999: 130.
134. Carell, 1995: 221. Nebelwerfer was literally 'smoke-thrower' because it was originally designed when all German tanks and anti-tanks weapons were forbidden, not because it was originally designed as a chemical weapon.
135. Quoted in Linderman, 1997: 56.
136. Linderman, 1997: 59–60.
137. Ellis, 1993: 88/9, 177.
138. Badsey, 1994c: 114; Forty, 1995: 124.
139. Delaforce, 1999: 94.
140. Balkoski, 1999: 117.
141. Churchill, 2000: 86–8.
142. French, 2000: 39.
143. McManus, 1998: 45–7.
144. Quoted in Eiler, 1997: 117.
145. Balkoski, 1999: 83.
146. Data reconstructed from Balkoski, 1999: 279–81.
147. McManus, 1998: 99/103; Marshall, 1947.
148. Balkoski, 1999: 90.
149. Linderman, 1997: 59.
150. Cooper, 1998: 176–7.
151. Balkoski, 1999: 98.
152. Quoted in Carell, 1995: 33.
153. Bergen, 1994: 166–7; Fisher, 1994: 518.

Chapter 12

1. Alfred de Vigny [1797–1863] quoted in Schulte, 1997: 283.
2. Keegan, 1997: 3, quoting from an unknown source.

3. Keegan, 1993.
4. Whitehouse and Bennett, 1995: 35.
5. Whitehouse and Bennett, 1995: 39.
6. Quoted in Bartov, 1991: 117.
7. Quoted in Delaforce, 1999: 6.
8. Quoted in Delaforce, 1999: 102.
9. Quoted in Delaforce, 1999: 139.
10. Quoted in Mitchell, 1997: 308.
11. In 1946 at the International Military Tribunal at Nuremberg, the SS (including the Waffen-SS) was indicted as a criminal organization (Williamson, 1999: 150).
12. Grey, 1959.
13. Quoted in Bruce, 1999: 153.
14. Quoted in Whitehouse and Bennett, 1995: 48.
15. For some soldiers, combat seems to have unhinged them and turned them into killing machines. David Rubitsky, for instance, was estimated to have killed around 500 Japanese soldiers single-handedly (Linderman, 1997: 262).
16. Quoted in Bates, 1998: 2.
17. Quoted in Delaforce, 1999: 53.
18. Maher, 1996: 121.
19. Bourke, 1999.
20. Personal communication, 16 September 1999.
21. Quoted in Linderman, 1997: 214.
22. Quoted in Linderman, 1979: 236.
23. Delaforce, 1999: 1.
24. Quoted in Linderman, 1997: 244.
25. Quoted in Delaforce, 1999: 50.
26. Drez, 1996: 7.
27. Men classified as fathers (III-As) were protected from conscription for the first three years of the draft until late 1943. By D-Day half of all the new conscriptees were fathers (Wright, 1998: 48–9).
28. Marlon Brando, Liberace, Gary Cooper and Errol Flynn were categorized as IV-Fs, the first with a knee injury, the second with a bad back, the third with a hip problem, and the fourth with a heart condition. Ronnie Reagan did enlist but his poor eyesight prevented combat duties (Wright, 1998: 81, 93).
29. Quoted in Linderman, 1997: 317.
30. Quoted in Linderman, 1997: 4.
31. Whitehouse and Bennett, 1995: 22.
32. Ellis, 1990: 249.
33. Quoted in Terkel, 1984: 258.
34. Linderman, 1997: 30.
35. Wright, 1998: 206.
36. Some 1.8 million men were rejected by the US medical boards because of psychiatric problems – though one such examiner managed to evaluate 512 people on one day, each one took a minute to assess. One third of a million troops were discharged from the US Army in the Second World War (Wright, 1998: 4).

37. Quoted in Copp, 1975: 51.
38. Quoted in Badsey, 1994c: 175.
39. Whitehouse and Bennett, 1995: 125.
40. Ellis, 1990: 251/296.
41. Fraser, 1999: 105; MacManus, 1998: 7.
42. McManus, 1998: 162.
43. Quoted in Linderman, 1997: 356.
44. Linderman, 1997: 356.
45. Cooper, 1998: 29.
46. Quoted in Delaforce, 1999: 36.
47. Quoted in Copp, 1997: 150.
48. Ellis, 1999: 103–6.
49. Quoted in McManus, 1998: 249.
50. Quoted in McManus, 1998: 258.
51. Quoted in Delaforce, 1999: 35.
52. There was little connection between casualty rates and desertion or mutiny in the First World War. For example, the most mutinous army, the Russian, suffered disproportionately low casualties while the highest casualty rates of the war (as a proportion of those mobilized) – were suffered by the Serbs (37 per cent), the Turks (27 per cent), and the Scots (26 per cent) without major disciplinary problems (Ferguson, 1998: 298–9).
53. The 51st Division did not have a smooth start to their Normandy campaign. A change of CO from Wimberley to Bullen-Smith, accompanied by immediate dispersal of the division in support of other units and some clumsily planned actions, led to high casualty rates and a rapid drop in morale. On 26 July Bullen-Smith was replaced by Rennie and after this the division seems to have recovered its reputation.
54. Ellis, 1990: 255–70.
55. Quoted in Ellis, 1990: 269.
56. Quoted in Man, 1994: 95.
57. Fraser, 1999: 106.
58. Berghahn, 1987: 170.
59. Williamson, 1996: 78.
60. Soviet troops were also executed for desertion in large numbers, especially during 1941 when the 'blocking detachments' of NKVD troops, positioned behind the ordinary troops, shot at least 8,000 for 'cowardice or desertion' (BBC2, 1999).
61. Hastings, 1993a: 290.
62. McManus, 1998: 185.
63. Neillands, 1995: 42.
64. Quoted in Ramsey, 1995: 575. One British officer surrendering to the 10th SS Panzer Division in Normandy refused to hand over his pistol on the grounds that he was a British officer and the pistol was his personal weapon. He was relieved of his weapon and decided not to die as a gentleman (Williamson, 1999: 95–6).
65. Badsey, 1990: 8. Rommel was a deeply unpopular officer with many of the German High Command (Macksey, 1996: 125). See also Hargreaves, 2006: 9.
66. Ellis, 1990: 315.

67. Quoted in Ellis, 1990: 340–1.
68. See Grint, 1997: 92–5.
69. Ellis, 1990: 340.
70. Ellis, 1990: 347/52.
71. Quoted in Ellis, 1990: 369.
72. The solidarity of the small group has historically been exploited most significantly in elite units whose limited size and the tightly defined requirements often generated a military success and influence well beyond their notional 'effects'. The Persian King, Xerxes, for example, deployed his 'Immortals' – so named because entry could only be acquired by the death of an existing 'Immortal' – against the Spartans at Thermopylae in 480 BC, and one could argue that the entire Spartan army was composed of an elite force, even though the king's bodyguard (*Hippeis*) were the elite of the elite. As well shall see, one of the characteristics of elite units is the ability of most to use their initiative and to assume command wherever necessary. In the Spartan army this sometimes led to a refusal to obey orders, especially if the subordinate officers and troops regarded an order as leading to dishonourable action (Warry, 1980: 46–7). In the Theban army 150 years earlier, 150 male couples formed the 300-strong 'Sacred Band' originally formed as an elite guard for the Theban citadel, developed into a unit whose framework of solidarity was rooted in the homosexual relationship between lovers and the assumption that one partner would not desert the other on the battlefield. When the Sacred Band was all but eliminated at the battle of Chaerona in 338 BC Philip II of Macedon, their destroyer, allegedly cried over their massed bodies proclaiming: 'Perish any man who suspects that these men either did or suffered anything that was base'. Quoted in Warry, 1980: 64.
73. Quoted in Linderman, 1997: 264.
74. Linderman, 1997: 294.
75. Levi, 1986: 122.
76. Linderman, 1997: 96–7.

Chapter 13

1. The original school building was demolished in 1970.
2. Quoted in Breuer, 1995: 173.
3. Turner, 1994: 24. The airborne invasion of Nadzab, New Guinea, on 5 September 1943 by 1,700 US paratroopers had been much more successful (Steinberg, 1998: 98).
4. Mrozek, 1994: 205.
5. Lewin, 1998: 154.
6. Bedell Smith, 1995: 30.
7. Ramsey, 1995: 305.
8. Dennis Wheatley quoted in Ramsey, 1995: 223.
9. The bridges over the canal and river were originally code named 'Euston 1' and 'Euston 2' respectively. However, within days of their capture the canal bridge was renamed 'Pegasus Bridge' in honour of the winged insignia of the British Airborne forces. In November 1993 the original

bridge, built in the 1930s, was dismantled and a longer, wider version replaced it in April 1994 (Ramsey, 1995: 229).

10. Botting, 1978: 91.
11. Ambrose, 1995: 196.
12. Man 1994: 37.
13. Ridgeway, 1995: 262.
14. Quoted in Collier, 1999: 56.
15. Ross, 1997: 59. By the time of Operation Dragoon, the invasion of southern France in August 1944, the airdrops had still not been mastered; although the American drops were generally accurate less than half the British airborne troops landed in the correct zones (Westall, 1994: 28).
16. Ridgeway, 1995: 264.
17. Ridgeway, 1995: 270.
18. Lt Colonel Vandervoort (whose character was played by John Wayne in *The Longest Day*) broke his ankle on landing but continued to command the 2nd Battalion of the 505th PIR from an ammunition cart (Ramsey, 1995: 272). Col. George Moseley, CO of the 502nd PIR broke his leg on landing in Normandy and insisted on being pushed around in a wheelbarrow – until Maxwell Taylor ordered him to return to England (Taylor, 1995: 212).
19. Until two days before D-Day Ridgeway had planned to land by glider rather than parachute.
20. Quoted in Kemp, 1994: 60.
21. Ridgeway, 1995: 277.
22. Holt and Holt, 1999: 57.
23. Ridgeway, 1995: 280. Ridgeway suggests there were 1,282 dead and 2,373 seriously wounded when the Division was finally pulled out on July 8.46 per cent of the infantry had either been killed or severely wounded and of the four regimental and 12 battalion commanders, 15 had either been killed, wounded or captured.
24. Quoted in Mrozek, 1994: 206.
25. Neillands and de Normann, 1993: 126.
26. Badsey, 1994c 54.
27. Quoted in Drez, 1996: 72.
28. Collier, 1999: 160.
29. Taylor, 1995: 303.
30. Taylor, 1995: 290.
31. Heifetz (1994)
32. Taylor, 1995: 305.
33. He only just escaped court-martial because of his previous war record. Ramsey, 1995: 313.
34. Lucas, 1994b: 506.
35. Bain, 1994: 409–410; Taylor, 1995: 315.
36. Gale, 1995: 215.
37. The successful attack by ten German DFS 230 gliders on Fort Eben Emael, Belgium's allegedly impregnable fort, on 10 May 1940, had impressed the Allies, especially Hap Arnold. He had suggested raising 6,000 glider pilots on a voluntary basis and 100,000 British troops had put themselves forward initially. Most were rejected, but on 1 June 1942 the first glider

pilots of the new Glider Pilot Regiment (GPR), part of the Army Air Corps, began their training at Tilshead Camp, Salisbury when five officers and 45 other ranks were addressed by their commanding officer, George Chatterton. He impressed upon them all that they were not just pilots but soldiers too. Like his American Airborne colleagues, Chatterton's approach was to *dissuade* people from joining or remaining as the most effective way of selecting the best volunteers (Collier, 1999: 64). Having reduced the numbers to an acceptable level, Chatterton then trained his troops to use their initiative by setting them tasks in pairs, having dropped them off from the back of a lorry with 2 shillings and 6 pence (about 12p) between them. The kind of tasks were extraordinary:

• Obtain 30 minutes dual control on a steamroller
• Secure a reasoned critique of euthanasia from Professor Julian Huxley
• Secure a duck's egg signed by the singer Elizabeth Welch.

But equally extraordinary was the survival rate of these British glider pilots: 600 landed in Normandy on D-Day itself and 580 came back for a second mission (Collier, 1999: 65). Overall, 59 glider pilots (25 American and 34 British) were killed in Normandy and 227 became casualties. A further 53 were made POW (Devlin, 1994: 281).
38. Morrison, 1999: 1–31.
39. Morrison, 1999: 32.
40. Shilleto, 1999: 124.
41. Turner, 1994: 79.
42. *D-Day Heroes*, 1998 DD Video, Rainbow Productions; General Gale suggests 20 yards (Gale, 1995: 227).
43. Drez, 1996: 101.
44. Quoted in Gale, 1995: 228.
45. Quoted in Shilleto, 1999: 48.
46. Lt Brotheridge, in charge of D Company, was killed crossing the bridge and was probably the first Allied officer killed on D-Day itself, though he died about an hour after being shot in the neck and thus after Lance-Corporal Fred Greenhalgh who was thrown from number 3 glider and drowned in the pond (Bowyer, 1995: 133; Gale, 1995: 227). The first Allied soldier killed on D-Day depends, of course, on when D-Day actually began. Lance-Corporal Edward Hull, A Co. 9th Battalion of the Parachute Regiment destined for the Merville battery – and part of the only glider that actually made the link up with Otway's troops – was accidentally shot at Broadwell airfield on the evening of 5 June and died on D-Day. He is buried in North Hinksey cemetery near Oxford. The first American casualties occurred when a gammon grenade exploded as paratroopers of the HQ Co., 1st Battalion, 505th PIR of the 82nd Airborne were emplaning at Spanhoe airfield. Three were killed instantly and one died the following day. Several paratroopers were killed as they descended early on D-Day (Stackpoole, 1995: 256–7). The first senior German officer to die was probably Lt General Falley, commander of the German 91st *Luftlande* Division who was shot by Lt Brannen, 3rd Battalion, 508th PIR, 82nd Airborne when Falley's car was ambushed on D-Day (Ridgeway, 1995: 267); Carell, 1995: 37).

47. Quoted in Shilleto, 1999: 51.
48. The café was originally known as the Buvette du Tramway and was the first building to be liberated in France. Georges Gondrée, the owner, had hidden 99 bottles of champagne in the garden and dug them up to celebrate his liberation. The café then became known as the Café Gondrée or the Pegasus Bridge Café. Georges Gondrée died in 1969 and the café was then run first by his wife and subsequently by his daughters until 1994 (Ramsey, 1995: 231). In June 1999 the restored bridge and a museum were opened. A month before this John Howard – who had visited the bridge every year since the war – died at the age of 86.
49. Quoted in Shilleto, 1999: 60.
50. Quoted in Shilleto, 1999: 64.
51. Morrison, 1999: 37.
52. Drez, 1996: 114.
53. Ramsey, 1995: 245.
54. Quoted in Shilleto, 1999: 71.
55. Carell, 1995: 38.
56. The Allies assumed the guns were 4 six inch fixed coastal guns but they were actually four 10cm Czech (Skoda) field howitzers (Ramsey, 1995: 236).
57. Carell, 1995: 53; Ramsey, 1995: 237.
58. Quoted in Ramsey, 1995: 238.
59. Bowyer, 1995: 103.
60. Quoted in Shilleto, 1999: 96.
61. As usual the figures are disputed. Shilleto (1999: 104) suggests that about 70 of the 150 British attackers walked away but only six of the 130 defenders did so.
62. Botting, 1978: 98; Shilleto, 1999: 100.
63. Compare Turner (1994: 87–9) to Badsey (1994c: 65).
64. Shilleto, 1999: 167.
65. Carrel, 1995: 57.
66. Quoted in Kemp, 1994: 153.
67. Quoted in Kemp, 1994: 153–4.
68. Richter was relieved of command of the 716th Division in September. He ended the war as commander of a static *Luftwaffe* division in Norway (Mitcham, 1994b: 458).
69. Quoted in Hansen, 2006: 45.
70. Quoted in Holt and Holt, 1999: 23.
71. Hargreaves, 2006: 21.
72. Neillands and de Norman, 1993: 102.
73. Carell, 1995: 104.
74. Mitcham, 1994c: 570.
75. Quoted in Ramsey, 1995: 560.
76. Quoted in Blandford, 1999: 42.
77. Veranov, 1998: 500.
78. Badsey, 1994c 112.
79. Blandford, 1999: 56.
80. Botting, 1978: 187.
81. Reynolds, 1997: 68–70.

82. Reynolds, 1997: 80.
83. Ambrose, 1995: 481.
84. Reynolds, 1997: 68–71.
85. Veranov, 1998: 496.
86. Quoted in Hargreaves, 2006: 54.
87. Zimmerman, 1995b: 319.
88. Quoted in Ryan, 1960: 188.
89. Quoted in Ryan, 1960: 189.
90. Ambrose, 1995: 579.
91. Quoted in Collier, 1999: 199.
92. Badsey, 2006: 49.

Chapter 14

1. Quoted in Wright, 1998: 292.
2. Mitchell, 1997: 310.
3. Turner, 1994: 113.
4. Quoted in Ambrose, 1995: 378.
5. Quoted in Ambrose, 1995: 359.
6. Quoted in McManus, 1998: 227. See also pp. 202; 218–21.
7. Dunphie and Johnson, 1999: 31.
8. Self-propelled artillery comprised artillery guns on tank chassis capable of firing on approach to the beaches.
9. Pitcairn-Jones, 1994: 98.
10. Ramsey, 1995: 442.
11. Quoted in Blandford, 1999: 32.
12. Blandford, 1999: 36.
13. Blandford, 1999: 38.
14. Dunphie and Johnson, 1999: 63–72.
15. Neillands and de Normann, 1993: 219.
16. Turner, 1994: 127.
17. Ramsey, 1995: 432.
18. Quoted in Blandford, 1999: 20.
19. Dunphie and Johnson, 1999: 46.
20. Ramsey, 1995: 437.
21. Neillands and de Normann, 1993: 231.
22. Dunphie and Johnson, 1999: 47.
23. Sergeant Hollis had, in his own words, a 'good working relationship' with Major Lofthouse. Just before the invasion Hollis was given a square box by Lofthouse and told to 'give one of these to each of the men Sergeant Major Hollis'. 'So I opened it and it was a box of French letters, and I said, "What's to do? Are we going to fight 'em or fuck 'em?"' (quoted in Holt and Holt, 1999: 158). The condoms were, of course, to protect the muzzle of their rifles and machine guns from sea water.
24. Dunphie and Johnson, 1999: 47; Ramsey, 1995: 440–1.
25. Dunphie and Johnson, 1999: 98. Sergeant Hollis was once again in action on Hill 102 when he managed to throw a grenade at one position – albeit with the pin still in. Fortunately for Hollis the Germans were unaware of

his mistake and by the time they had realized he had rushed their position and killed them (Dunphie and Johnson, 1999: 94–5).

26. Ramsey, 1995; 428.
27. Ironically, a month before D-Day aerial reconnaissance had revealed hitherto unknown 'rocks' off Juno and an extra delay was authorized for landing here to take advantage of a slightly higher tide. Subsequent analysis revealed the new rocks to be seaweed (Ramsey, 1995: 200).
28. Pitcairn-Jones, 1994: 84.
29. Botting, 1978: 157; Delaforce, 1999: 18. This was slightly more than the other eastern beaches, though Gold lost more LCAs (Stacey, 1995: 453).
30. Holt and Holt, 1999: 187–8.
31. Quoted in Ramsey, 1995: 478.
32. Quoted in Delaforce, 1998: 98.
33. Stacey, 1995: 474–5.
34. Stacey, 1995: 480.
35. Ramsey, 1995: 462–4.
36. Ambrose, 1995: 536–8.
37. Unfortunately a passing Typhoon was shot down by one salvo from an LCT Rocket off Juno Beach (Pitcairn-Jones, 1994: 100).
38. Pitcairn-Jones, 1994: 99.
39. Ramsey, 1995: 468.
40. Ramsey, 1995: 479.
41. Sapper Anderson saw many of these in a tarpaulin covered stack of forty bodies at St Aubin on D-Day+2.
42. Stacey, 1995: 490–1.
43. The film was made for SHAEF and first shown in August 1944 (Ramsey, 1995: 504).
44. Ramsey, 1995: 506.
45. Some of the confusion over the casualty figures relates less to the number of casualties and more to the number of troops landed.
46. Neillands and de Normann, 1993: 242/51.
47. Ramsey, 1995: 515.
48. Ryan, 1960: 178/9.
49. Neillands and de Normann, 1993: 250.
50. Neillands and de Normann, 1993: 239.
51. Quoted in Ramsey, 1995: 458.
52. Quoted in Blandford, 1999: 45.
53. Lewin, 1998: 200.
54. Blandford, 1999: 45–9; Ramsey, 1995: 455.
55. The *Panzergrenadiers* were infantry troops trained to operate in conjunction within an armoured division.
56. By the time the 12th SS *HJ* had left France, through the Falaise Gap, only 600 of the original 19,000 were still with it – a casualty rate of around 97 per cent (Williamson, 1996).
57. Ramsey, 1995: 500–1.
58. D'Este, 1983.
59. Messenger, 1994a: 257.
60. In the film, *The Longest Day*, the 200 French Commandos under Philippe Kieffer, CO of No. 10 (Inter-Allied Commando) are prominent in attacking

the Casino at Ouistreham, though the building had, in fact, been demolished
by the Germans in 1942 to improve the line of fire (Ramsey, 1995: 549). No.
10 Commando, never a full sized unit, comprised both French and anti-Nazi
German troops. By D-Day+7 only 70 of the 200 French Commandos
remained alive.

61. Maher, 1996: 222.
62. Ramsay, 1995: 181.
63. Bruce, 1999: 139.
64. Pitcairn-Jones, 1994: 89.
65. Quoted in Pitcairn-Jones, 1994: 102.
66. Pitcairn-Jones, 1994: 103–4; Delaforce, 1998: 95.
67. Quoted in Blandford, 1999: 31–2.
68. Quoted in Blandford, 1999: 32.
69. Ramsey, 1995: 528.
70. Maher, 1996: 116.
71. Quoted in Delaforce, 1999: 10.
72. Quoted in Blandford, 1999: 26.
73. Quoted in Blandford, 1999: 34.
74. Blandford, 1999: 27.
75. Quoted in Blandford, 1999: 35.
76. Quoted in Blandford, 1999: 93.
77. Quoted in Blandford, 1999: 95.
78. Ramsey, 1995: 539.
79. Masters, 1997: 149.
80. Quoted in Delaforce, 1999: 67 (original emphasis).
81. Ramsey, 1995: 556–7.
82. D'Este, 1983: 137.
83. Man, 1994: 69; Belchem, 1995: 550.
84. Von Schweppenburg wrote a pessimistic report to Hitler about the
    Normandy campaign on June 23 – and was promptly relieved of his office
    (Schweppenburg, 1999: 417).
85. Bennett, 1995: 72–5; Dunphie and Johnson, 1999: 81.
86. Stacey, 1995: 461.
87. Pitcairn-Jones, 1994: 145/52.
88. Lloyd-Owen, 1994: 11.
89. Most of the maps of Utah Beach show the actual landings occurring on
    Uncle Red and Tare Green – as planned – but this is because the beaches
    were relabelled after the event to fit the event rather than the plan.
90. Pitcairn-Jones, 1994: 93.
91. Holt and Holt, 1999: 48.
92. Veranov, 1998: 498.
93. Badsey, 1994c: 77–8.
94. Carell, 1995: 45.
95. Carell, 1995: 65.
96. Quoted in Neillands and de Normann, 1993: 164.
97. Neillands and de Normann, 1993: 168.
98. Ramsey, 1995: 383.
99. Kemp, 1994: 69.
100. Quoted in Bradley, 1995: 384.

101. Neillands and de Normann, 1993: 168.
102. Quoted in Bradley, 1995: 329.
103. Quoted in Kilvert-Jones, 1999: 95.
104. Quoted in Bradley, 1995: 329.
105. Ramsey, 1995: 330 (neither Bradley nor the official Rangers' report mentions the late switch in command).
106. Kilvert-Jones, 1999: 71. It was from the top of one of these ladders that Staff Sergeant Stivison fired one of the two Lewis guns, with the ladder apparently swaying 45 degrees each way as the DUKW swung in the water 90 feet below (Ramsey, 1995; 331).
107. Bradley, 1995: 327.
108. Quoted in Pitcairn-Jones, 1994: 97.
109. Quoted in Drez, 1996: 262.
110. Quoted in Kilvert-Jones, 1999: 104.
111. Ramsey, 1995: 331.
112. Rudder, 1954 quoted in Ramsey, 1995: 335.
113. Kilvert-Jones, 1999: 56.
114. Botting, 1978: 153.
115. Quoted in Ambrose, 1995: 534.
116. Ambrose, 1995: 358.
117. Bradley, 1995: 324.
118. Bradley, 1995: 363.
119. Delaforce, 1998: 111.
120. Quoted in Delaforce, 1998: 112–13.
121. Collier, 1999: 180.
122. Quoted in Pitcairn-Jones, 1994: 94.
123. The general staff of SHAEF was divided between G1 (Personnel), G2 (Intelligence), G3 (Battle Planning), and G4 (Supply and Transport).
124. Quoted in Bradley, 1995: 327.
125. Balkoski, 1999: 75–8.
126. Ryan, 1960: 154.
127. Ryan, 1960; 156.
128. Quoted in Drez, 1996: 251.
129. Ramsey, 1995: 176.
130. Quoted in Kilvert-Jones, 1999: 76.
131. Quoted in Ambrose, 1995: 124–5.
132. Bradley, 1995: 328.
133. Ramsey, 1995: 343.
134. Quoted in Pitcairn-Jones, 1994: 96.
135. Ross, 1997: 107.
136. Balkoski, 1999: 128–9.
137. Balkoski, 1999: 141–2.
138. Quoted in Kilvert-Jones, 1999: 112.
139. Quoted in Man, 1994: 47.
140. Quoted in Ellis, 1990: 268.
141. Quoted in Man, 1994: 48.
142. Ramsey, 1995: 361.
143. Bruce, 1999: 82.
144. Quoted in Ramsey, 1995: 344–5.

145. Drez, 1996: 228.
146. Ramsey, 1995: 346.
147. Matthews, 2003.
148. Quoted in Ramsey, 1995; 348–9.
149. Neillands, and de Normann, 1993: 184.
150. Quoted in Pitcairn-Jones, 1994: 90.
151. Collier, 1999: 192.
152. Ambrose, 1995: 127–8.
153. Quoted in Holt and Holt, 1999: 152.
154. Quoted in Ambrose, 1995: 338.
155. Quoted in Ryan, 1960: 128. The 29th Division's 16th RCT was opera-
     tionally, and temporarily, under the command of the 1st Division at the
     time of the assault.
156. Kilvert-Jones, 1999: 126.
157. Quoted in Ambrose, 1995: 339.
158. Quoted in Balkoski, 1999: 133.
159. This point was also reached during Julius Caesar's invasion of Britain
     when, according to legend, the standard bearer of the Xth legion, on
     seeing the immobility of the Roman forces, jumped off his ship declaring:
     'Jump down, comrades, unless you want to surrender our eagle to the
     enemy. I, at any rate, mean to do my duty to my country and my general'
     (Peddie, 1994: 119).
160. Balkoski, 1999: 138–9.
161. Quoted in Badsey, 1994c: 84.
162. Quoted in Ambrose, 1995: 344.
163. Quoted in Ambrose, 1995: 348.
164. Turner, 1994: 107.
165. Quoted in Goldstein et al., 1994: 86.
166. The problem of noise is particularly well portrayed in the movie, *Saving
     Private Ryan*, to the point where it is almost impossible to know who says
     what in the initial beach assault.
167. Quoted in Drez, 1996: 207.
168. Kilvert-Jones, 1999: 120–1.
169. Quoted in Kilvert-Jones, 1999: 121.
170. Quoted in Ambrose, 1995: 342.
171. Quoted in Ambrose, 1995: 344.
172. Quoted in Ambrose, 1995: 345.
173. Sun Tzu, quoted in Grint, 1997: 46.
174. Turner, 1994: 109–11.
175. Kilvert-Jones, 1999: 161.
176. Neillands and Normann, 1993: 189.
177. Quoted in Ambrose 1995: 461.
178. Quoted in Balkoski, 1999: 265.
179. Botting, 1978: 137.
180. Kilvert-Jones, 1999: 143–4.
181. Quoted in Kemp, 1994: 72. See D'Este, 1983: 114 on the possible
     confusion.
182. Kilvert-Jones, 1999: 155.
183. Quoted in Kilvert-Jones, 1999: 155.

184. Quoted in Kilvert-Jones, 1999: 6, 149/52.
185. Quoted in Neillands, and Normann, 1993: 185–6.
186. Quoted in Ambrose, 1995:355/6–7.
187. Turner, 1994: 119.
188. Neillands and Normann, 1993: 192.
189. Quoted in McManus, 1998: 120.
190. Quoted in Ambrose, 1995: 380.
191. Man, 1994: 54.
192. Bradley, 1995: 396–7.
193. Ambrose, 1995: 434–5.
194. Goldstein et al. (1994: 87) suggest he sent major Chester Hansen at 1000.
195. Quoted in Kilvert-Jones, 1999: 127.
196. Quoted in McManus, 1998: 118.
197. Kilvert-Jones, 1999: 127.
198. Quoted in Ramsey, 1995: 351.
199. Kilvert-Jones, 1999: 146.
200. Neillands and de Normann, 1993: 198.
201. Ambrose, 1995: 477; Ramsey, 1995: 364.
202. Ramsey, 1995: 368.
203. Turner, 1994: 153.
204. Quoted in Pitcairn-Jones, 1994: 97.
205. Quoted in Kilvert-Jones, 1999: 168.
206. Beaver, 1994: 496–7.
207. Quoted in Ambrose, 1995: 389.
208. Quoted in Ryan, 1960: 191.
209. Quoted in Ryan, 1960: 99.
210. Hargreaves (2006: 52) suggests it was 8,000 rounds.
211. Carell, 1995: 92.
212. Quoted in Drez, 1996: 221.
213. Quoted in Drez, 1996: 210.
214. Carell, 1995: 91; Ryan, 1960: 191.
215. Quoted in Blandford, 1999: 30.
216. Ryan, 1960: 191.
217. Kilvert-Jones, 1999: 131–2.
218. Carell, 1995: 89.
219. Quoted in Ramsey, 1995: 494.
220. Ramsey, 1995: 373.
221. Quoted in Ramsey, 1995: 496.
222. Quoted in Balkoski, 1999: 148.
223. Balkoski, 1999: 220.
224. Balkoski, 1999: 173–94.
225. Quoted in Bennett, 1995: 65.
226. Quoted in Carell, 1995: 100.
227. Ambrose, 1995: 576–7.
228. Bayeux was liberated on 8 June and became the first free town (Botting, 1978: 184).
229. Quoted in Goldstein et al., 1994: 109.
230. Quoted in Ambrose, 1995: 578. A British version of this, in response to what they saw as a penchant for friendly bombing, was: 'When the RAF

bombed, the Germans ducked; when the Luftwaffe bombed the British ducked; when the Americans bombed, everyone ducked' (Delaforce, 1999: 37).
231. Rundstedt, 1995: 619.

Chapter 15

1. Ferguson, 1998: 295.
2. Fraser, 1999: 108.
3. Wright, 1998: 68, 227–8.
4. Hargreaves, 2006: 13.
5. Hall, 1994: 138.
6. Some estimates suggest 150,000.
7. Ramsey, 1995: 620.
8. Again estimates vary with some as high as 10,000 and some as low as 4,900.
9. Botting, 1978: 161; Man, 1994: 71.
10. Ambrose, 1995: 319.
11. Man, 1994: 86.
12. Neillands and de Normann, 1993: 294.
13. Mrozek, 1994: 206.
14. Kilvert-Jones, 1999: 10; Ambrose, 1994: 43.
15. Balkoski, 1999: ix-x, 228.
16. Ryan, 1960: 171. The invasion of southern France, Operation Dragoon, in August 1944 was far less costly for the Allies. Between 15 August and 25 September 324,069 troops and their supplies and transport were landed from 2,250 ships. Their initial advance covered 400 miles in 27 days, capturing 60,000 enemy soldiers at negligible cost (Westall, 1994: 56–7).
17. Holt and Holt, 1999: 169, 181.
18. Delaforce, 1999: 151.
19. Crookenden, 1994: 521.
20. D'Este, 1983: 167, 263; Ramsey, 1995: 620; Shilleto, 1999: 168.
21. Masters, 1997: 324.
22. Blandford, 1999: 132.
23. Farrar-Hockley, 1994: 11.
24. Delaforce, 1999: 58.
25. Fraser, 1999: 339–41.
26. Sheffield, 1997.
27. US casualties for the entire war were approximately 405,400 dead or missing, 670,800 wounded and 139,700 POWs. Around 300,000 of the 405,400 dead or missing were known to have died in action with 185,400 from the Army or Marine Corps and 91,000 from the Air Force and Navy. Some 89 per cent of the wounded (574,300) were army ground troops with the marines accounting for almost all of the remainder (67,200) (McManus, 1998: 131).
28. Quoted in Eiler, 1997: 410.
29. Eiler, 1997: 423.
30. Capp, 1997: 148–9.

31. Wilson, 1997: 30.
32. Hastings, 1993a: 249.
33. Forty, 1995: 24.
34. Ellis, 1990: 296–7.
35. Mitchell, 1997: 306.
36. Ellis, 1993: 162.
37. Balkoski, 1999: 91.
38. Quoted in McManus, 1998: 136.
39. Delaforce, 1999: 40.
40. Badsey, 1994a: 283; Shilleto, 1999: 195.
41. Ellis, 1993: 232.
42. Hastings, 1993a: 62.
43. Williamson, 1999: 162; Ellis, 1990: 232/44–5.
44. Badsey, 1990: 48, 72/85.
45. Nosowicz, 2,000: 27.
46. Man, 1994: 95.
47. Mitcham, 1994b: 458.
48. Guth, 1994: 141.
49. Heinemann, 1994a: 414.
50. Blandford, 1999: 223.
51. Delaforce, 1999: 91.
52. Blandford, 1999: 254–6.
53. Blandford, 1999: 72, 86.
54. Ramsey, 1995: 487/617.
55. Quoted in Ramsey, 1995: 568.
56. See Evans, 2004, on Operation Sealion.

Bibliography

Ambrose, S. E. (1994), 'Omaha Beach' in Chandler and Collins.

Ambrose, S. E. (1995), *D-Day June 6, 1944* (London: Touchstone).

Ambrose, S. E. (2000), 'D-Day Fails' in Cowley, R. (ed.) *What If? Military Historians Imagine What Might Have Been* (London: Palgrave Macmillan).

Anderson, D. (1994a), 'Australia' in Chandler and Collins.

Anderson, D. (1994b), 'New Zealand' in Chandler and Collins.

Bachrach, P. and Baratz, M. S. (1962), 'The Two Faces of Power', *American Political Science Review*, 56 (4), 942–52.

Badsey, S. (1994a), 'Great Britain' in Chandler and Collins.

Badsey, S. (1994b), 'Resources, Allied and German Compared' in Chandler and Collins.

Badsey, S. (1994c), *D-Day: From the Normandy Beaches to the Liberation of France* (London: Tiger).

Badsey, S. (2006), 'Culture, Controversy, Caen and Cherbourg' in Buckley (2006).

Baily, C. M. (1983), *Faint Praise: American Tanks and Tank Destroyers during World War II* (Hamden, CT: Archon).

Bain, D. E. (1994), '101st Airborne Division' in Chandler and Collins.

Balkoski, J. (1999), *Beyond the Beachhead: the 29th Infantry Division in Normandy* (Mechanicsburg, PA.: Stackpole).

Barabasi, A. L. (2003), *Linked* (London: Penguin).

Barbier, M. K. (2006), 'Deception and Planning of D-Day' in Buckley (2006).

BBC2 (1999), *War of the Century* (12 October).

Beaver, D. R. (1994), '2nd Infantry Division' in Chandler and Collins.

Bedell Smith, W. (1995), 'Supreme Headquarters, Allied Expeditionary Force' in Ramsey.

Beinhocker, E. D. (1999), 'Robust Adaptive Strategies', *Sloan Management Review*, 40 (3), Spring, 95–106.

Belchem, D. (1995), 'Sword Area' in Ramsey.

Bennett, R. (1995), 'Ultra' in Ramsey.

Bergen, J. D. (1994), 'Communication' in Chandler and Collins.

Berghahn, V. R. (1987), *Modern Germany* (Cambridge: Cambridge University Press).

Berlin, I. (1978), *The Hedgehog and the Fox: An Essay on Tolstoy's View of History* (London: Phoenix).

Blackburn, G. G. (1998), *The Guns of Normandy: A Soldier's Eye View, France 1944,* (London: Constable).

Blanford, E. (1999), *Two Sides of the Beach: The Invasion and Defence of Europe in 1944* (Shrewsbury: Airlife).

Bourke, J. (1999), *An Intimate History of Killing: Face to Face Killing in the Twentieth Century* (London: Granta).

Bowyer, M. J. F. (1995), *Aircraft for the Many: A Detailed Survey of the RAF's Aircraft in June 1944* (Sparkford: Patrick Stephens).

Botting, D. (1978), *The D-Day Invasion* (Richmond, VA: Time-Life).

Bradbury, J. (1998), *The Battle of Hastings* (Stroud: Sutton).

Braddon, R. (1956), *Cheshire V.C.: A Story of War and Peace* (London: Companion).

Bradley, O. (1995), 'Omaha and Utah Areas' in Ramsey.

Bratton, J., Grint, K. and Nelson, D. (2005), *Organizational Leadership* (Mason, OH: Thomson/South-Western).

Bremner, I. (1998) 'Saving Private Ryan', *History Today*, 48 (11), 50–1.

Breuer, W. B. (1995), *Feuding Allies: The Private Wars of the High Command* (New York: John Wiley).

Brooke, A. (2001), *War Diaries 1939–1945* (edited by Danchev, V. and Todman, D.) (London: Weidenfeld and Nicholson).

Brown, D. (1994), 'Air Spotting Pool' in Chandler and Collins.

Brown, N. G. (1994), 'Weather' in Chandler and Collins.

Bruce, C. J. (1999), *Invaders: British and American Experience of Seaborne Landings 1939–1945* (London: Chatham).

Buckley, J. (ed.) (2006), *The Normandy Campaign 1944: Sixty Years On* (London: Routledge).

Buckley, J. (2006a), 'British Armoured Operations in Normandy' in Buckley (2006).

Campbell, A. H. (1988), 'WWII Production of LVTs', *Wheels and Tracks*, 24, 30–5.

Carell, P. (1995), *Invasion! They're Coming!* (Atglen, PA: Schiffer).

Caulkin, S. (2003), 'Break Out of the Budget Cycle', *Observer*, Management Section, 20 July.

Chandler, D. G. and Collins, J. L. (eds) (1994), *The D-Day Encyclopedia* (Oxford: Helicon).

Channel 4 (C4a) (1999), *Hidden Love*, 23 August.

Channel 4 (C4b) (1999), *Green and Pleasant Land*, 12 December.

Collier, R. (1999), *D-Day* (London: Seven Dials).

Cooper, B. Y. (1998), *Death Traps: The Survival of an American Armoured Division in World War II* (Novato, CA: Presidio).

Copp, T. (2006), 'The 21st Army Group in Normandy: Towards a New Balance Sheet' in Buckley (2006).

Crang, J. A. (1997), 'The British Soldier on the Home Front' in Addison, P. and Calder, A. (eds) *Time to Kill* (London: Pimlico).

Crookenden, N. (1994), '6th Airborne Division' in Chandler and Collins.

Croucher, R. (1982), *Engineers at War 1939–1945* (London: Merlin).

Dahl, R. A. (1961), *Who Governs?* (New Haven, CT: Yale University Press).

Danchev, A. and Todman, D. (2001), *War Diaries 1939–45* (London: Weidenfeld and Nicolson).

Darlow, S. (2004), *D-Day Bombers: The Veterans' Story* (London: Grub Street).

Davidson, M. and Levy, A. (1996), *Decisive Weapons* (London: BBC).

Davies, N. (1999), 'But We Never Did Stand Quite Alone', *Guardian*, 13 November.

Deighton, L. (1995), *Blood, Tears and Folly: An Objective Look at World War II* (London: Pimlico).

Delaforce, P. (1998), *Churchill's Secret Weapons: The Story of Hobart's Funnies* (London: Robert Hale).

Delaforce, P. (1999), *Marching to the Sound of Gunfire: Northwest Europe 1944–5* (Stroud: Wrens Park).

Darwin, R. T. (1941), *The Oxford Dictionary of Quotations* (London: Book Club Associates).

Doughty, M. (ed.) (1994), *Hampshire and D-Day* (Crediton: Southgate).

D'Este, C. (1983), *Decision in Normandy: The Unwritten Story of Montgomery and the Allied Campaign* (London: Companiam Collins).

Devlin, G. M. (1994), 'Gliders' in Chandler and Collins.

Douglas, W. A. B. (1994), 'Royal Canadian Navy' in Chandler and Collins.

Drez, R. J. (1994), *Voices of D-Day* (Baton Rouge, LA and London: Louisiana State University Press).

Dunphie, C. and Johnson, G. (1999), *Gold Beach: Inland from King – June 1944* (Barnsley: Leo Cooper).

Dupuy, T. N. (1977), *A Genius for War: The German Army and Staff, 1807–1945* (London: McDonald and Jay).

Durkheim, E. (1933), *The Division of Labour and Society* (New York: Free Press).

Durschmied, E. (1999), *The Hinge Factor* (London: Coronet).

Eiler, K. E. (1997), *Mobilizing America: Robert P. Patterson and the War Effort 1940–1945* (Ithaca, NY and London: Cornell University Press).

English, J. A. (1994), 'Canada' in Chandler and Collins.

Eisenhower, D. D. (1995a), 'Operation "Overlord"' in Ramsey.

Eisenhower, D. D. (1995b), 'OK, Let's Go?' in Ramsey.

Etzioni, A. (1964), *Modern Organizations* (Englewoood Cliffs, NJ and London: Prentice-Hall).

Evans, M. M. (2004), *Invasion! Operation Sealion 1940* (Harlow: Pearson Education).

Ezard, J. (2000), 'Glenn Miller "Victim of RAF"', *Guardian*, 12 February.

Farrar-Hockley, A. (1994), 'Airborne Forces' in Chandler and Collins.

Ferguson, N. (1998), *The Pity of War* (London: Penguin).

Fisher, E. F. (1994a), 'Atlantic Wall' in Chandler and Collins.

Fisher, E. F. (1994b), 'Organization Todt' in Chandler and Collins.

Fletcher, D. (ed.) (2000), *Tiger: The Tiger Tank, A British View* (CD-ROM, Bovington: The Tank Museum).

Ford, R. (1999), *The Sherman Tank* (Staplehurst: Spellmount).

Forty, G. (1995), *US Army Handbook 1939–1945* (Stroud: Sutton).

Forty, G. (1998), *British Army Handbook 1939–1945* (Stroud: Sutton).

Fowle, B. W. (1994), 'Engineers' in Chandler and Collins.

Fraser, D. (1999), *And We Shall Shock Them: The British Army in the Second World War* (London: Cassell).

Freeman, R. A. (1998), *The Fight for the Skies: Allied Fighter Action in Europe and North Africa, 1939–45* (London: Arms and Armour).

French, D. (2000), *Raising Churchill's Army* (Oxford: Oxford University Press).

Funk, A. L. (1994a), 'French Casualties' in Chandler and Collins.

Funk, A. L. (1994b) 'French Resistance' in Chandler and Collins.

Furtado, P. (1992), *World War II* (London: Chancellor).

Gale, R. (1995), '6th Airborne Division' in Ramsey.

Gander, T. J. (1999), *Collins Jane's World War Two Tanks* (Glasgow: HarperCollins).

Gates, D. (1994), 'Transformation of the Army' in Chandler, D. and Beckett, I (eds) *The Oxford Illustrated History of the British Army* (Oxford: Oxford University Press).

Gelb, N. (1996), *Ike and Monty: Generals at War* (London: Constable).

Gell-Man, M. (1994) *The Quark and the Jaguar* (London: Abacus).

Gladwell, M. (2002), *The Tipping Point* (London: Abacus).

Gleick, J. (1987) *Chaos: Making a New Science* (London: Abacus).

Grabsky, P. (1993), *The Great Commanders* (London: Boxtree).

Graham, D. (1999), *Against Odds: Reflections on the Experiences of the British Army, 1914–45* (Basingstoke: Macmillan (now Palgrave Macmillan).

Gray, P. (2006), 'Caen – The Martyred City' in Buckley (2006).

Grey, J. G. (1959), *The Warriors: Reflections on Men in Battle* (New York: Harper & Row).

Green, C. M. (1955), *The Ordnance Department: Planning Munitions for War* (Washington, DC. Office of the Chief of Military History, Department of the Army).

Grint, K. (2001), *The Arts of Leadership* (Oxford: Oxford University Press).

Grint, K. (2005a) *Leadership: Limits and Possibilities.* (Basingstoke: Palgrave Macmillan).

Grint, K. (2005b), Problems, Problems, Problems: The Social Construction of Leadership', *Human Relations*, 58 (11), 1467–94.

Grint, Katy (1999), 'Handbags at Ten Paces: Gender and Violence', unpublished Sociology thesis, London School of Economics.

Grove, E. J. (1994), 'Amphibious Assault Training' in Chandler and Collins.

Gudgin, P. (1997), *Armoured Firepower: The Development of Tank Armament 1939–45* (Stroud: Sutton).

Guth, E. P. (1994), German Casualties' in Chandler and Collins.

Hall, D. E. (1994a), 'Casualties: Allied Casualties' in Chandler and Collins.

Hall, D. E. (1994b), 'Medical Support' in Chandler and Collins.

Hansen, M. (2006), 'The German Commanders on D-Day' in Buckley (2006).

Harries, M. and Harries, S. (1991), *Soldiers of the Sun: The Rise and Fall of the Imperial Japanese Army 1868–1945* (London: Heinemann).

Hargreaves, R. (2006), *The Germans in Normandy* (Barnsley: Pen and Sword).

Harvey, D. J. (1994), 'France' in Chandler and Collins.

Hastings, M. (1993a), *Overlord* (London: Macmillan (now Palgrave Macmillan)).

Hastings, M. (1993b), *Bomber Command* (London: Papermac).

Hastings, M. (2005), *Warriors* (London: HarperCollins).

Hayes, J. D. (1999), 'Developments in Naval Warfare' [online]. Available: http://gi.grolier.com/wwii/wwii_12.html

Heifetz, R. (1994), *Leadership Without Easy Answers* (Cambridge, MA: Harvard University Press).

Heinemann, W. (1994a), '*Panzer Lehr* Division' in Chandler and Collins.

Heinemann, W. (1994b), '2nd Panzer Division' in Chandler and Collins.

Herbert, U. (1997), *Hitler's Foreign Workers* (Cambridge: Cambridge University Press).

Hesketh, R. (1999), *Fortitude: The D-Day Deception Campaign* (London: St. Ermin's).

Hickling, H. (1995), 'Gooseberry and Mulberry' in Ramsey.

Hinsley, F. H. (1994), 'Deception' in Chandler and Collins.

Holborn, H. (1986), 'The Prusso-German School' in Paret, P. (ed.) *Makers of Modern Strategy* (Oxford: Oxford University Press).

Holland, J. H. (1995), *Hidden Order* (Reading, MA: Addison-Wesley).

Holland, J. H. (1998), *Emergence: from Chaos to Order* (Oxford: Oxford University Press).

Holt, T, and Holt, V. (1999), *Major and Mrs Holt's Battlefield Guide to the Normandy Landing Beaches* (Barnsley: Leo Cooper).

Howieson, B. and Kahn, H. (2002), 'Leadership, Management and Command: The Officer's Trinity' in Gray, P. W. and Cox, S. (eds) *Air Power Leadership: Theory and Practice* (Norwich: HMSO).

Hughes, T.A. (1995), *Overlord: General Pete Queseda and the Triumph of Tactical Airpower in World War II* (New York: Free Press).

Jackson, A. (2006) *British Empire and the Second World War* (London: Hambledon Continuum).

Kauffman, S. (1993), *The Origins of Order* (Oxford: Oxford University Press).

Kauffman, S. (1995), *At Home in the Universe* (London: Viking).

Keegan, J. (1992), *Six Armies in Normandy* (London: Pimlico).

Keegan, J. (1993), *A History of Warfare* (London: Hutchinson).

Keegan, J. (1995), *The Battle for History: Refighting the Second World War* (London: Hutchinson).

Keegan, J. (ed.) (1999), *The Penguin Book of War* (London: Viking).

Kier, E. (1997), *Imagining War: French and British Military Doctrine Between the Wars* (Princeton, NJ: Princeton University Press).

Kilvert-Jones, J. (1999), *Omaha Beach: V Corps' Battle for the Normandy Beachhead* (Barnsley: Leo Cooper).

Kim, W. C. and Mauborgne, R. (2003), 'Tipping Point Leadership', *Harvard Business Review*, April, 60–6.

Kimball, W. (1997), *Forged in War* (London: HarperCollins).

Kipling, S. H. (1999), 'The Royal Naval Commandos' [online]. Available: http://ourworld.compuserve.com/homepages/Keith_Oakley/rmhist.htm

Kirk, R. (1997), *Panzer* (Sky History, 8 March).

Krulak, C. C. 1999 'The Strategic Corporal: Leadership In The Three Block War', *Marines Magazine*, January, 1–6.

Lee, N. de (2006), 'American Tactical Innovation' in Buckley (2006).

Legg, R. (1994), *D-Day Dorset* (Wincanton: Dorset Publishing).

Leigh-Mallory, T. (1995a), 'Air Operations for D-Day' in Ramsey.

Leigh-Mallory, T. (1995b), 'Airfield Construction' in Ramsey.

Lewin, R. (1998), *Montgomery* (Conshohocken, PA: Combined Publishing).

Linderman, G. F. (1997), *The World Within War: America's Combat Experience in World War II* (Cambridge, MA and London: Harvard University Press).

Lloyd-Owen, J. H. (1994), *The Campaign in North-West Europe June 1944–May 1945* (London: HMSO).

Long, V. A. Cracknell (2000), *From Britain with Love* (Newmarket, VA: Denecroft).

Lucas, J. (1994), '2nd SS Panzer Division *Das Reich*' in Chandler and Collins.

Lucas, J. (1998), *The German Army Handbook* (Stroud: Sutton).

Lukes, S. (1974) *Power: A Radical View* (London: Macmillan (now Palgrave Macmillan).

Luttwak, E. and Horowitz, D. (1975), *The Israeli Army* (New York: Harper and Row).

Macdonald, C. B. (1947), *Company Commander* (Short Hills, NJ: Burford).

McLeod, R. (1995), 'Special Duty Operations' in Ramsey.

McManus, J. C. (1998), *The Deadly Brotherhood: The American Combat Soldier in World War II* (Novato, CA: Presidio).

McPhail, H. (1999), *The Long Silence: Civilian Life Under the German Occupation of Northern France* London: IB Tauris).

Macksey, K. (1994), 'Artillery: Allied' in Chandler and Collins.

Macksey, K. (1996), *Why the Germans Lose at War: The Myth of German Superiority* (London: Greenhill).

Magenheimer, H. (1998), *Hitler's War: Germany's Key Strategic Decisions 1940–1945* (London: Arms and Armour).

Maher, B. A. (1996), *A Passage to Sword Beach* (Annapolis, MA: Naval Institute Press).

Margolis, J. (1999), 'Good Morning, Campers', *Guardian*, 21 April.

Marshall, S. L. A. (1947), *Men Against Fire* (New York: The Infantry Journal and William Morrow).

Masters, P. (1997), *Striking Back: A Jewish Commando's War Against the Nazis* (Novato, CA: Presidio).

Matthews, M. E. (2003), 'Why Does the *NYT* Continue to Cite Historian SLA Marshall after the Paper Discredited Him in a Front Page Story Years Ago?' [online]. Available: http://hnn.us/articles/1356.html

May, E. R. (2000), *Strange Victory: Hitler's Conquest of France* (New York: Hill and Wang).

Melvin, M. (2006), 'The German Perspective' in Buckley (2006).

Merida, P. C. (2003), 'The Strategic Corporal in Kosovo' [online]. Available: www.msiac.dmso.mil/ootw_documents/CplinKosovo.pdf

Messenger, C. (1994a), '4th Special Services Brigade' in Chandler and Collins.

Messenger, C. (1994b), 'Rundstedt' in Chandler and Collins.

Mets, D. R. (1997), *Master of Airpower: General Carl. A. Spaatz* (Novato, CA: Presidio).

Mierzejewski, A. C. (1994), 'Railroads' in Chandler and Collins.

Miller, R. (1998), *The Resistance* (Richmond, VA: Time-Life).

Mitcham, S. W. (1994a), '716th Infantry Division' in Chandler and Collins.

Mitcham, S. W. (1994b), 'Richter, Walter' in Chandler and Collins.

Mitcham, S. W. (1994c), '21st Panzer Division' in Chandler and Collins.

Mitroff, I. I. and Anagnos, G. (2000), *Managing Crises Before They Happen* (New York: Amacon).

Mitroff, I. I. (2004), Grading Bush: The President's Job Performance as the Chief Crisis Manager of the Nation' [online]. Available: www.mitroff.net/documents/Grading_President_Bush.pdf

Montgomery, B. L. (1995), 'Plans and Preparations' in Ramsey.

Morgan, G. (1997), *Images of Organization* (Newbury Park, CA: Sage).

Morrison, A. (1999), *Silent Invader* (Shrewsbury: Airlife).

Mrozek, S. J. (1994), '82nd Airborne' in Chandler and Collins.

Murray, W. (1994), 'Air Strategy: German' in Chandler and Collins.

Murray, W. 1995: 'The World at War 1941–45' in Parker, G. (ed.) *Cambridge Illustrated History of Warfare* (Cambridge: Cambridge University Press).

Neillands, R. (2001), *The Bomber War* (London: John Murray).

Neillands, R. (2002), *The Battle of Normandy 1944* (London: Cassell).

Neillands, R. and de Normann, R. (1994), *D-Day 1944: Voices from Normandy* (London: Orion).

Nosowicz, D. (2000), 'Ten Key Things About Beaches', *Observer*, 6 February.

Nye, J. S. (2004), *Power in the Global Information Age: From Realism to Globalization* (London: Routledge).

Oakley, D. (1994), '1st Special Service Brigade' in Chandler and Collins.

O'Neill, W. L. (1994), 'United States of America' in Chandler and Collins.

Orange, V. (2006), 'Arthur Tedder and the Transportation Plan' in Buckley (2006).

Overy, R. (1995), *Why the Allies Won* (London: Jonathan Cape).

Overy, R. (2000) How Significant *Was* the Battle?' in Addison, P. and Crang, J. A. (eds) *The Burning Blue: A New History Of The Battle Of Britain* (London: Pimlico).

Parker, G. (1995), *The Cambridge Illustrated History of Warfare* (Cambridge: Cambridge University Press).

Peddie, J. (1994), *The Roman War Machine* (Stroud: Sutton).

Pitcairn-Jones, L. J. (1994), *Operation Neptune: The Landings in Normandy 6th June 1944. Battle Summary No. 39* (London: HMSO).

Prefer, N. N. (1998), *Patton's Ghost Corps* (Novato, CA: Presidio).

Price, A. (1994a), 'Electronic Warfare' in Chandler and Collins.

Price, A. (1994b), 'II Air Corps' in Chandler and Collins.

Prigogine, I. (1997), *The End of Certainty* (New York: Free Press).

Pyman, H. (1995), 'Gold Area' in Ramsey.

Ramsay, B. H. (1995), 'Operation "Neptune"' in Ramsey.

Ramsey, W. G. (ed.) (1995), *D-Day Then and Now* (London: After the Battle Publications).

Raugh, H. E. (1994), 'Allied Medals' in Chandler and Collins.

Reynolds, M. (1997), *Steel Inferno: 1st SS Panzer Corps in Normandy* (Staplehurst: Spellmount).

Reynolds, M. (1999) *Men of Steel: 1st SS Panzer Corps in the Ardennes and Eastern Front 1944–45* (Staplehurst: Spellmount).

Ridgway, M. B. (1995), '82nd Airborne Division' in Ramsey.

Rittell, H. and Webber, M. (1973), 'Dilemmas in a General Theory of Planning', *Policy Sciences*, 4, 155–69.

Roberts, A. (2003), *Hitler and Churchill: Secrets of Leadership* (London: BBC).

Robinson, D. (2005), *Invasion, 1940: The Truth about the Battle of Britain and What Stopped Hitler* (London: Constable).

Rodney, W. (1994), 'Royal Canadian Air Force' in Chandler and Collins.

Ross, S. T. (1997), *American War Plans 1941–45* (London: Frank Cass).

Rudder, J. E. (1954), 'I Took My Son to Omaha Beach', *Collier's Magazine*, 11 June.

Rundstedt, G. von (1995), 'An Appreciation' in Ramsey.

Russell, F. (1981), *The Secret War* (Richmond, VA: Time-Life).

Ryan, C. (1960), *The Longest Day: June 6, 1944* (London: Victor Gollancz).

Salewski, M. (1994), 'Germany' in Chandler and Collins.

Santosuosso, A. (1997), *Soldiers, Citizens, and the Symbols of War* (Oxford: Westview).

Schattschneider, E. F. (1960), The *Semi-Sovereign People: A Realist View of Democracy in America* (New York: Reinhart and Winston).

Schulte, T. J. (1997), 'The German Soldier in Occupied Russia' in Addison, P. and Calder, A. (eds) *Time to Kill* (London: Pimlico).

Schurman, D. M. (1994), 'Mynarski, Andrew Charles' in Chandler and Collins.

Schweppenburg, G. von (1999), 'On the Other Side of the Hill' in Keegan (1999).

Shilleto, C. (1999), *Pegasus Bridge and Merville Battery* (Barnsley: Leo Cooper).

Small, K. (1999), *The Forgotten Dead* (London: Bloomsbury).

Signal, E. F. (1994), 'Signal: Allied and German' in Chandler and Collins.

Somerville, C. (1998), *Our War: How the British Commonwealth Fought the Second World War* (London: Weidenfeld and Nicholson).

Sorley, L. (1994), '4th Infantry Division' in Chandler and Collins.

Stacey, C. P. (1995), 'Juno Area' in Ramsey.

Stacey, R. D., Griffin, D. and Shaw, P. (2000), *Complexity and Management: Fad or Radical Challenge to Systems Thinking?* (London: Routledge).

Stackpoole, A. (1995), 'D-Day's First Fatal Casualty' in Ramsey.

Stafford, D. (2003), *Ten Days to D-Day: Countdown to the Liberation of Europe* (New York and London: Little, Brown).

Steinberg, R. (1998), *Island Fighting* (Richmond, VA: Time-Life).

Stenton, F. (1971), *Anglo-Saxon England* (Oxford: Oxford University Press).

Taylor, M. D. (1995), '101st Airborne Division' in Ramsey.

Tedder, A. W. (1995), 'Command Decisions' in Ramsey.

Thomas, C. S. (1994), 'German Medals' in Chandler and Collins.

Toase, F. (1994), '7th Armoured Division' in Chandler and Collins.

Tracy, N. (ed.) (1998), *The Naval Chronicle: The Contemporary Record of the Royal Navy at War, Vol. 1, 1793–1798* (London: Chatham).

Travis, A. (1999), 'Normandy Victory', *Guardian*, 17 September.

Tsouras, P. (1994), *Disaster at D-Day* (London: Greenhill).

Turner, J. F. (1994), *Invasion '44: The Full Story of D-Day* (Shrewsbury: Airlife).

United States War Department (1942), *Over There: Instructions for American Servicemen in Britain, 1942* (reproduced in 1994 by Bodleian Library, Oxford University).

Veranov, M. (1997), *Third Reich at War* (London: Robinson).

Votaw, J. F. (1994), '1st Infantry Division' in Chandler and Collins.

Warry, J. (1980), *Warfare in the Classical World* (London: Salamander).

Watters, B. (2004), 'Mission Command: *Auftragstaktik*', paper presented to the Leadership Symposium, RAF Cranwell, 13 May.

Weick, K. E. (1993), 'The Collapse of Sense-Making in Organizations: The Mann Gulch Disaster', *Administrative Science Quarterly*, 38, 628–52.

Weick, K. E. (1995), *Sensemaking in Organizations* (Newbury Park, CA: Sage).

Westall, W. E. H. (1994), *Invasion of the South of France: Operation 'Dragoon', 15th August 1944* (London: HMSO).

Wheatley, M. (1992) *Leadership and the New Science* (New York: Berrett-Koehler).

Wheeler, J. S. (1999), *The Making of a World Power* (Stroud: Sutton).

Williamson, G. (1994), *The SS: Hitler's Instrument of Terror* (London: Sidgwick and Jackson).

Williamson, G. (1999), *Loyalty Is My Honour: Personal Accounts from the Waffen-SS* (London: Brown Packaging Goods).

Wootten, G. (1994), 'PLUTO' in Chandler and Collins.

Wright, M. (1998), *What They Didn't Teach You About World War II* (Novato, CA: Presidio).

Younger, A. E. (1994), 'British Engineers' in Chandler and Collins.

Zaleznik, A. (1977), 'Managers and Leaders: Are They Different?', *Harvard Business Review*, 55 (5), 67–80.

Zimmerman, O. B. (1995a), 'German Defences' in Ramsey.

Zimmerman, O. B. (1995b), '*Die Invasion hat begonnen!*' in Ramsey.

Zimmerman, P. (forthcoming), *The First "Gung Ho" Marine: Evans F. Carlson of the Raiders* (Novato, CA: Presidio).

Index

Printed in the United States
By Bookmasters